INTRODUCTION TO FINANCIAL ACCOUNTING

INTRODUCTION TO FINANCIAL ACCOUNTING

fifth edition

Andrew Thomas
with contributions from
Sandra Brosnan

The **McGraw·Hill** *Companies*

London · Boston · Burr Ridge, IL · Dubuque, IA · Madison, WI · New York · San Francisco · St. Louis
Bangkok · Bogotá · Caracas · Kuala Lumpur · Lisbon · Madrid · Mexico City · Milan · Montreal · New Delhi
Santiago · Seoul · Singapore · Sydney · Taipei · Toronto

Introduction to Financial Accounting, fifth edition
Andrew Thomas
ISBN 10: 0-07-710808-6
ISBN 13: 9780077108083

Published by McGraw-Hill Education
Shoppenhangers Road
Maidenhead
Berkshire
SL6 2QL
Telephone: 44 (0) 1628 502 500
Fax: 44 (0) 1628 770 224
Website: www.mcgraw-hill.co.uk

British Library Cataloguing in Publication Data
A catalogue record for this book is available from the British Library

Library of Congress Cataloguing in Publication Data
The Library of Congress data for this book has been applied for from the Library of Congress

Acquisitions Editor: Mark Kavanagh
Development Editor: Rachel Crookes
Senior Marketing Manager: Marca Wosoba
Senior Production Editor: Eleanor Hayes

Text Design by Claire Brodmann
Cover design by Ego Creative Ltd
Typeset by Mathematical Composition Setters Ltd, Salisbury, Wiltshire
Printed and bound in Singapore by Markono Print Media Pte Ltd

ISBN 10: 0-07-710808-6
ISBN 13: 9780077108083

Brief Table of Contents

Detailed Table of Contents

Preface

This book is primarily intended to be an introductory text for students taking a degree in accounting or business studies with a substantial element of accounting. However, it also covers the financial accounting syllabus for Part One of the Association of Chartered Certified Accountants, the Foundation stage of the Chartered Institute of Management Accountants and the Introductory, Intermediate and Advanced Levels of the Certified Accounting Technicians. Furthermore, the book provides a more than adequate coverage of the financial accounting content of the accounting syllabuses for the General Certificate of Education at Advanced level.

The author is a senior lecturer in accounting at the University of Birmingham and a Certified Accountant, and has been a member of the panel of examiners of one of the major professional accountancy bodies for over 15 years.

The main aim of this book is to provide an in-depth detailed introduction to financial accounting with the greatest possible clarity of exposition and academic rigour. Another major aim is the provision of an appropriate balance between theory and the application of accounting methods. Each element in this balance is important. A proper understanding of accounting requires underpinning by an appreciation of its theoretical foundations. Although this may be readily recognized in the case of degree students, it is no less true of other students. Theory is often presented in textbooks in isolation, but this book integrates theory into understanding of accounting methods. The other side of this balance, represented by the application of accounting, depends upon a thorough grasp of the mechanics of financial accounting. The book therefore examines in depth many of what are normally regarded as the basic aspects of accounting, particularly where this involves applications of important points of principle.

The structure of the book follows a proven pattern based on the author's not inconsiderable experience of teaching at this level. Each chapter deals with a specific aspect of accounting, irrespective of how brief or lengthy this might be. This is intended to permit lecturers to choose that combination of chapters which fits their syllabus. However, it is important to appreciate that the order in which the chapters are presented is significant. There are also particular groupings of chapters, for example: Chapters 6 to 8 deal with books of prime entry; Chapters 16 to 18 examine aspects of internal control and accuracy; and Chapters 19 and 20 involve a consideration of incomplete records.

The structure within each chapter also follows a deliberate pattern. These usually start by examining the purpose, theoretical foundation and practical relevance of the topic. This is followed by a description of the accounting methods and then comprehensive examples. A further unique feature of the book is that after most examples there is a series of notes. These are intended to explain the unfamiliar and more difficult aspects of the example in order that the reader is able to follow the example. The notes also provide guidance on further aspects of the topic that may be encountered in examination questions, such as alternative forms of wording.

Each chapter also contains a set of written review questions and numerical exercises designed by the author to test whether the student has fulfilled the learning objectives set out in the chapter, as well as past questions from various examining bodies. ACCA students should note that not all of the latter fall within the current syllabus. The review questions and exercises are presented in a coherent progressive sequence designed to test understanding of terminology, legal requirements, theoretical foundations, etc. The exercises are presented in order of difficulty. The later examples are therefore often quite demanding. However, students should be able to answer these from reading the chapter. Moreover, the questions are not repetitive but have been selected because each tests some aspect of the topic not covered in a previous question. In addition, the exercises have been graded according to their level of difficulty. This is rather subjective for a book that focuses on the introductory level, but it is hoped that the following classification may be useful to students and lecturers:

> *Level I* questions of a standard lower than those commonly found in the first year of an undergraduate degree in accounting or the professional accountancy bodies examinations and which can usually be completed in a relatively short time (i.e. less than about 35 minutes).
>
> *Level II* questions of a standard commonly found in the first year of an undergraduate degree in accounting or the professional accountancy bodies examinations and which can usually be completed in about 35 minutes.
>
> *Level III* questions of a standard slightly higher than those commonly found in the first year of an undergraduate degree in accounting or the professional accountancy bodies examinations, and/or more advanced in the depth of knowledge required to answer them, and which can usually be completed in about 45 minutes.

All users, especially lecturers, should also be aware that some exercises are extensions of other exercises in previous chapters. This is intended to provide a more comprehensive understanding of the relationship between different topics in accounting, such as day books and cash books, and provisions for depreciation and bad debts. There are suggested solutions to about one-third of the numerical exercises in Appendix 2 to this textbook. The answers to the rest of the numerical exercises are contained in a *Teachers' Solutions Manual* that is on the website for this book (see below).

Each chapter also includes learning objectives, learning activities, a summary, and a list of key terms and concepts. The learning objectives at the start of each chapter set out the abilities and skills that the student should be able to demonstrate after reading the chapter. Students should also refer back to these after reading each chapter. Similarly, students should satisfy themselves that they can explain the meaning of the key terms and concepts listed at the end of each chapter. The summaries provide a comprehensive but concise review of the contents of each chapter that students should find useful for revision purposes. The learning activities differ from those found in most other textbooks, which often take the form of mini-questions with model answers similar to the exercises provided here for each chapter. In contrast, the learning activities in this book are mostly real-life activities of a project/case study type which require students to apply their knowledge to practical situations. They frequently necessitate students collecting publicly available data from actual companies, or their own financial affairs.

There is an Online Learning Centre for this book which can be fond at *www.mcgraw-hill.co.uk/textbooks/thomas*. This contains additional material that is available free of charge. For more details and a full list of available supplements, please see page xx.

The fifth edition has required the author to make a number of difficult decisions. Most of these arise from the proposal, at the time of writing, that as from 2005 all listed/quoted companies in the EU (i.e. including the UK) prepare their consolidated financial statements in accordance with International Accounting Standards (IASs). Consolidated financial statements are not commonly examined at the introductory level, and thus may seem irrelevant.

However, in anticipation of compliance with IASs being extended to all other companies' financial statements, it seems likely that these companies will be allowed to adopt voluntarily IASs in the preparation of their published accounts, and some will probably do so.

Since virtually all of this book relates to organizations that do not need to prepare consolidated financial statements, the author has decided to retain its current focus on UK accounting standards for the time being. However, in order to accommodate examination syllabuses that now include IASs, the author has added a separate new chapter on IASs near the end of the book. Subsequent convergence/harmonization of UK and IASs will be included on the web site for the book as updates.

The other main theme of the fifth edition is simplification. The most obvious form that this takes is the deletion of whole and parts of chapters on topics that are no longer commonly examined at the introductory level. This includes hire purchase, investment accounts, branch accounts and funds flow statements. Some later chapters have been moved forward to replace these. Furthermore, numerous clarifications have been added to the remaining material.

Chapter 22 on the use of computers in accounting has also been extensively revised and updated. The aim is to explain the possibilities that are opened up by the new technology, and to identify some of the changes in working practice that are required. The author is indebted to Dr Andrew Hawker for writing this chapter. Dr Hawker, a lecturer in computing in the Department of Accounting and Finance at the University of Birmingham, has spent most of his working life in large industrial computer companies dealing with applications of computers to accounting.

The author gratefully acknowledges the permission of the following bodies to reproduce copies of their past examination questions: The Association of Chartered Certified Accountants (ACCA), The Association of Accounting Technicians (AAT), The Associated Examining Board (AEB) and The Joint Matriculation Board (JMB).

Finally, the author thanks Judith Sutcliffe for her patience and accuracy in the preparation of the original manuscript.

Summary of accounting standards covered by the fifth edition

Statement of Standard Accounting Practice 9—Stocks and Long-term Contracts (1988).
Statement of Standard Accounting Practice 13—Accounting for Research and Development (1989).
Statement of Standard Accounting Practice 17—Accounting for Post Balance Sheet Events (1980).
Financial Reporting Standard 1—Cash Flow Statements (1996).
Financial Reporting Standard 2—Accounting for Subsidiary Undertakings (1992).
Financial Reporting Standard 3—Reporting Financial Performance (1999).
Financial Reporting Standard 10—Goodwill and Intangible Assets (1997).
Financial Reporting Standard 12—Provisions, Contingent Liabilities and Contingent Assets (1998).
Financial Reporting Standard 15—Tangible Fixed Assets (1999).
Financial Reporting Standard 18—Accounting Policies (2000).
Statement of Principles for Financial Reporting (1999).

Andrew Thomas

Acknowledgements

Our thanks go to the following reviewers for their comments at various stages in the text's development:

Barry Smith
Falconer Mitchell
Nick Rowbottom
Zulfiqar Shah
Iris Bosa

And for reviewing the text and contributing a case study, we'd like to thank Robert Jupe.

The publishers would also like to thank Sandra Brosnan, not only for her valuable case studies, but also for her contribution during the production process.

Guided Tour

chapter

1

The nature and objectives of financial accounting

Learning objectives

Learning Objectives

Each chapter opens with a set of learning objectives, summarizing what readers should learn from each chapter.

Key Terms and Concepts

These are highlighted throughout the chapter, with page number references at the end of each chapter so they can be found quickly and easily.

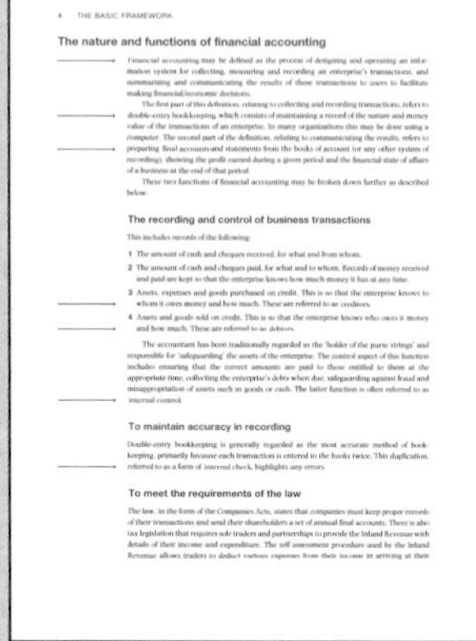
The nature and functions of financial accounting

The recording and control of business transactions

To maintain accuracy in recording

To meet the requirements of the law

Figures and Tables

Figures and tables help you to visualize the various economic models, and to illustrate and summarize important concepts.

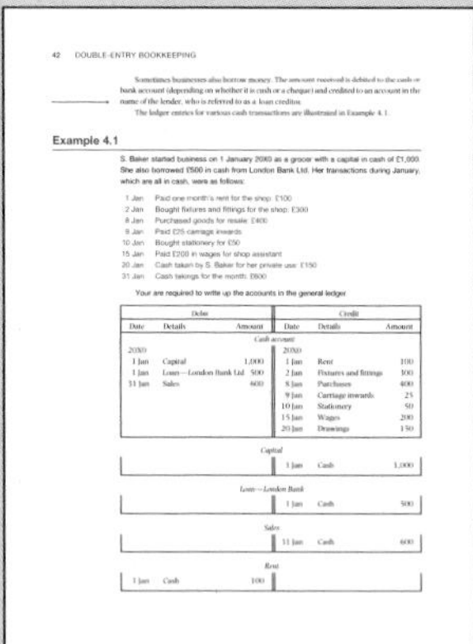
Example 4.1

Learning Activity

These quick activities give opportunities to test your learning and practise accountancy methods throughout the book.

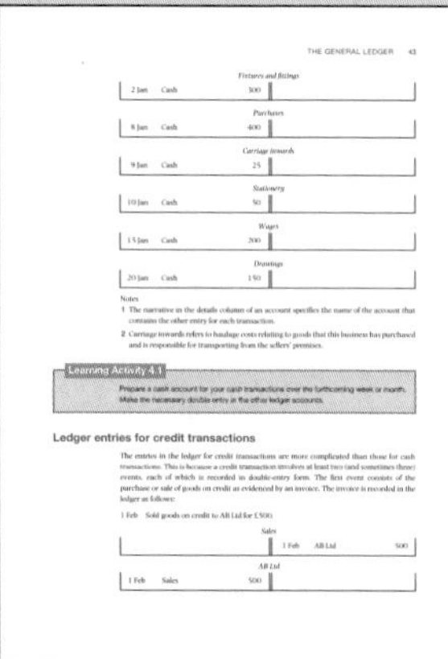
Learning Activity 4.1

Ledger entries for credit transactions

Chapter Summary

This briefly reviews and reinforces the main topics covered in each chapter to ensure you have acquired a solid understanding of the key topics.

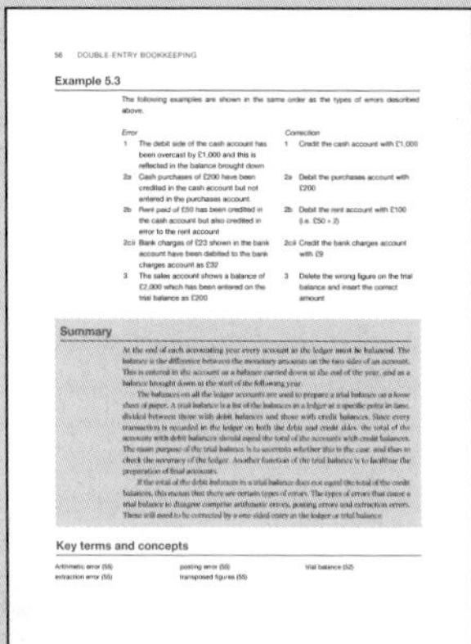
Example 5.3

Summary

Key terms and concepts

Review Questions

These questions help you review and apply the knowledge you have acquired from each chapter. They are pitched at different levels to ensure all readers have questions appropriate to their stage of learning.

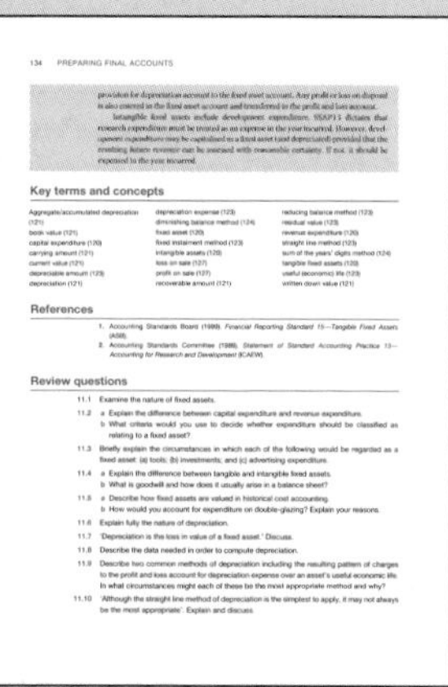
Key terms and concepts

References

Review questions

Exercises

This end-of-chapter feature is the perfect way to practice the techniques you have been taught and apply the methodology to real-world situations.

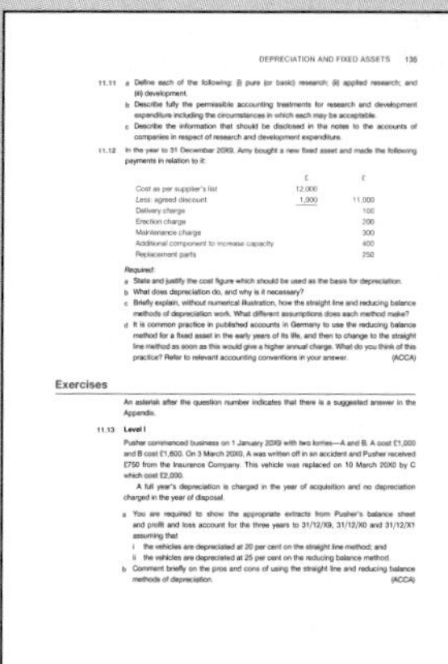

Exercises

Case Studies Appendix

Appendix 1 includes 4 brand new case studies designed to test how well you can apply the main techniques learned. Each case study has its own set of questions and answers can be found on the Online Learning Centre.

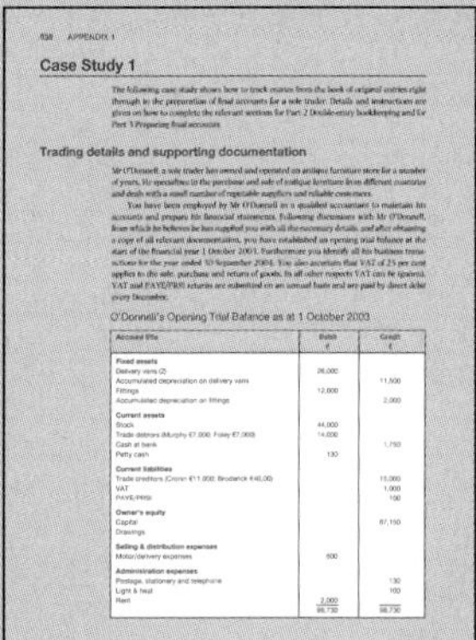

Case Study 1

Trading details and supporting documentation

O'Donnell's Opening Trial Balance as at 1 October 2003

Solutions Appendix

Appendix 2 at the end of the book provides the answers to the questions and exercises set in the book. Use it to check your workings.

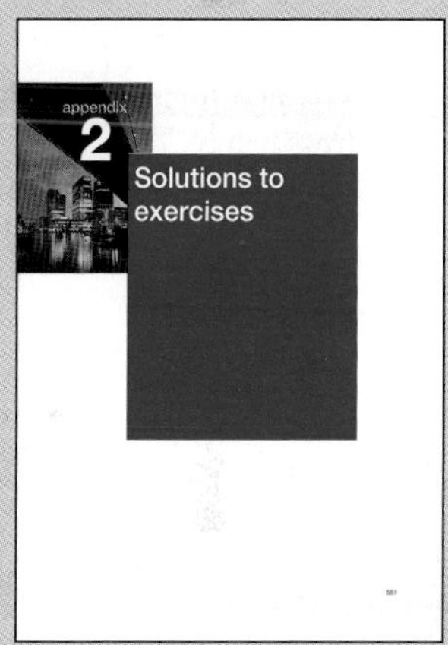

appendix 2

Solutions to exercises

Online Learning Centre (OLC)

Visit www.mcgraw-hill.co.uk/textbooks/thomas today!

Technology to enhance learning and teaching

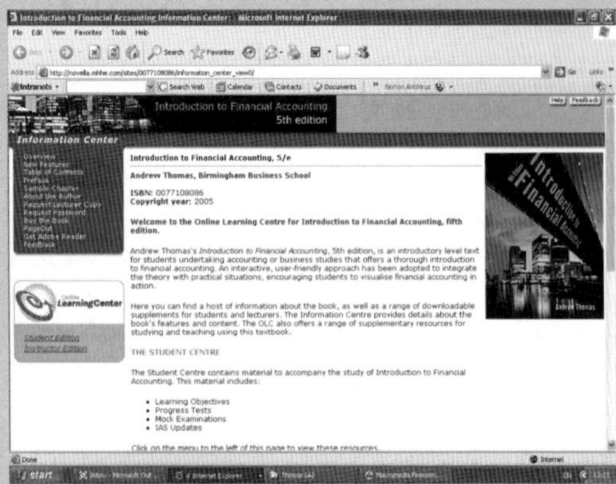

After completing each chapter, log on to the supporting Online Learning Centre website. Take advantage of the study tools offered to reinforce the material you have read in the text.

Resources for students include:

- Progress tests
- International Accounting Standards updates
- Learning objectives

Also available for lecturers:

- Tutorial exercises
- PowerPoint slides
- Case Study Solutions
- Answers to Exercises
- Mock exams

For lecturers: Primis Customised Content Centre

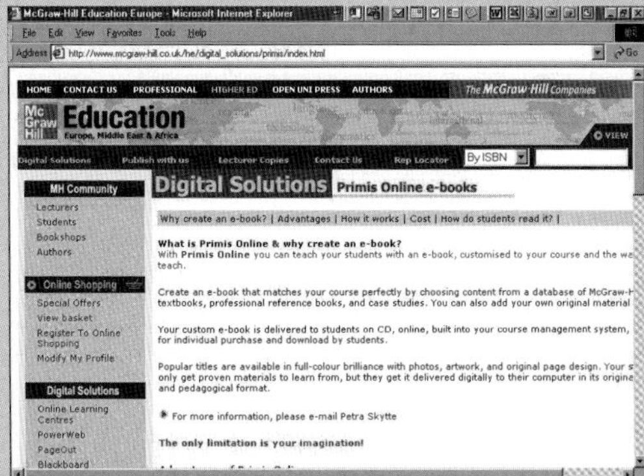

If you need to supplement your course with additional cases or content or wish to create a customised e-Book or print book to suit your course, visit www.primiscontentcenter.com or e-mail primis_euro@mcgraw-hill.com for more information.

Study Skills

We publish guides to help you study, research, pass exams and write essays, all the way through your university studies.

Visit **www.openup.co.uk/sg/** to see the full selection and get £2 discount by entering promotional code **study** when buying online!

Computing Skills

If you'd like to brush up on your Computing skills, we have a range of titles covering MS Office applications such as Word, Excel, PowerPoint, Access and more.

Get a £2 discount off these titles by entering the promotional code **app** when ordering online at www.mcgraw-hill.co.uk/app

part 1

THE BASIC FRAMEWORK

The nature and objectives of financial accounting

Learning objectives

After reading this chapter you should be able to:

1 explain the meaning of the key terms and concepts listed at the end of the chapter;

2 describe the nature and functions of double-entry bookkeeping and financial accounting;

3 discuss the objectives and limitations of company annual accounts;

4 identify the users of annual reports and describe their information needs;

5 describe the legislation and other rules governing the contents of company annual reports;

6 describe the current institutional framework relating to the setting and enforcement of accounting standards.

The nature and functions of financial accounting

Financial accounting may be defined as the process of designing and operating an information system for collecting, measuring and recording an enterprise's transactions, and summarizing and communicating the results of these transactions to users to facilitate making financial/economic decisions.

The first part of this definition, relating to collecting and recording transactions, refers to **double-entry bookkeeping**, which consists of maintaining a record of the nature and money value of the transactions of an enterprise. In many organizations this may be done using a computer. The second part of the definition, relating to communicating the results, refers to preparing **final accounts** and statements from the books of account (or any other system of recording), showing the profit earned during a given period and the financial state of affairs of a business at the end of that period.

These two functions of financial accounting may be broken down further as described below.

The recording and control of business transactions

This includes records of the following:

1. The amount of cash and cheques received, for what and from whom.
2. The amount of cash and cheques paid, for what and to whom. Records of money received and paid are kept so that the enterprise knows how much money it has at any time.
3. Assets, expenses and goods purchased on credit. This is so that the enterprise knows to whom it owes money and how much. These are referred to as **creditors**.
4. Assets and goods sold on credit. This is so that the enterprise knows who owes it money and how much. These are referred to as **debtors**.

The accountant has been traditionally regarded as the 'holder of the purse strings' and responsible for 'safeguarding' the assets of the enterprise. The control aspect of this function includes ensuring that the correct amounts are paid to those entitled to them at the appropriate time, collecting the enterprise's debts when due, safeguarding against fraud and misappropriation of assets such as goods or cash. The latter function is often referred to as **internal control**.

To maintain accuracy in recording

Double-entry bookkeeping is generally regarded as the most accurate method of bookkeeping, primarily because each transaction is entered in the books twice. This duplication, referred to as a form of **internal check**, highlights any errors.

To meet the requirements of the law

The law, in the form of the Companies Acts, states that companies must keep proper records of their transactions and send their shareholders a set of annual final accounts. There is also tax legislation that requires sole traders and partnerships to provide the Inland Revenue with details of their income and expenditure. The self assessment procedure used by the Inland Revenue allows traders to deduct various expenses from their income in arriving at their taxable profit. There is thus a financial incentive for all businesses to maintain records of their transactions.

To present final accounts to the owners of the business

These comprise a profit and loss account showing the amount of profit and thus the **financial performance** of a business for a given period, and a balance sheet showing its **financial position** at the end of that period. The latter will include the following items:

1 The amount of cash and money at the bank.
2 Other assets that the business owns, such as goods for resale, vehicles and machinery.
3 Debtors and creditors.
4 The amount of capital that has been invested in the business by its owner(s).
5 Any money that has been borrowed by the business.

In the case of a sole trader, these final accounts show the owner his or her 'earnings' for the period and may be used to evaluate the profitability of the business. However, they are often primarily used to determine the owner's tax liability. Final accounts perform similar functions in the case of companies. However, company final accounts are also designed to give information to third parties to enable them to evaluate the profitability and financial stability of the company. These include prospective shareholders, trade unions and employees, creditors and those who have lent the company money, government departments and social pressure groups. This is discussed further later.

This function of financial accounting is often referred to as **stewardship**, which may be defined as the accountability of an enterprise's management for the resources entrusted to them. **Accountability** refers to the management's responsibility to provide an account/report on the way in which the resources entrusted to them have been used.

To present other financial reports and analyses

This includes the use of ratios to evaluate the following matters:

1 The profitability of the business.
2 The level of activity and productivity.
3 The solvency and liquidity position (i.e. whether the business will be able to pay its debts).
4 The efficiency of credit control procedures.
5 The efficiency of stock control procedures.
6 The effect of any loans on the business's profitability and financial stability.

To facilitate the efficient allocation of resources

Viewing the function of financial accounting at a more general, abstract level, its ultimate *raison d'être* is usually described as being to facilitate the efficient and effective allocation of resources. This is generally given a macroeconomic interpretation as providing information to investors so that capital is directed towards more efficient firms. A less common but similar interpretation would be to extend this to providing information to prospective employees so that labour is directed towards more efficient firms. The same interpretation could also be extended to other potential users of final accounts and providers of resources in a broad sense that embraces quality of life and environmental considerations, etc. This would include others such as bank lenders, creditors/suppliers, the government and the public in general.

This function of financial accounting can also be viewed at a microeconomic or individual firm level. One of the main purposes of financial accounting may be said to be to enable an organization's management to operate the enterprise efficiently and effectively. This embraces at least three of the functions referred to above, namely, the recording and control of business transactions, accuracy in recording and the preparation of final accounts (for management use). However, this function of accounting is more commonly attributed to management accounting, particularly in larger organizations.

Management accounting can be defined as the provision of information to an organization's management for the purposes of planning, control and decision making. The latter includes production, marketing, investment and financing decisions.

Learning Activity 1.1

Imagine that you are in business in a small general store or as a plumber. Prepare a list of the financial information about the business that you would expect to be able to obtain from your records. Compare this with the above and consider any differences.

The objectives of company final accounts

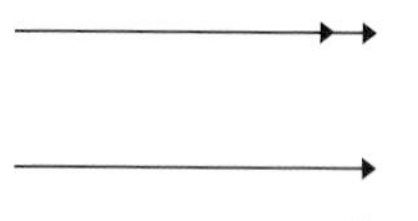

As explained above, one of the main functions of financial accounting is the preparation of **final accounts**, also commonly referred to as **financial statements**. These consist of a profit and loss account and a balance sheet. In the case of companies, the final accounts are often referred to as **published accounts**. These are sent to shareholders in the form of a pamphlet known as the **annual or corporate report**. It is therefore usual to discuss the objectives of company final accounts in terms of the functions of annual reports.

The function of annual reports is related to beliefs about the role of business organizations in society and their objectives. Up until about the mid-1970s the accountancy profession took the view that the primary objective of a business enterprise was to maximize its profit and the wealth of its shareholders. This was reinforced by disciplines such as economics that gave prominence to the classical theory of the firm. The function of annual reports was thus regarded as being to provide information about the profitability and financial position of a company to those with whom it has a capital contractual relationship, namely shareholders and loan creditors.

However, during the 1970s there was a swing in society's beliefs towards the idea that business enterprises exist for the benefit of the community as a whole. Similarly, developments in disciplines such as economics and modern organization theory cast doubt on whether profit maximization was a meaningful description of business objectives. For example, Herbert Simon argues that business enterprises are 'satisficers', that is, they seek to earn a satisfactory level of profit. Also, a survey of large UK companies undertaken by the accountancy profession found that 'the majority view of those replying to the survey seems to be that their primary objective is to make a profit for the benefit of a number of groups. It is not the majority view that the maximization of shareholder's profit is the primary objective.'

Other respondents to this survey described their primary objective as being survival, or in terms of the service that they provide.

It follows from this that enterprises are accountable to a number of different groups (employees, the public, etc.), and that the function of annual reports is to provide each of them with information. This is the view taken by *The Corporate Report*,[1] which is the UK accountancy bodies' most detailed statement on the function/objective of annual reports, their users and the information that they need. It is not mandatory, but represents one of the most comprehensive pieces of published work in this area, and has probably led to a number of new developments in accounting practices as well as more recent UK statements on these matters that are described later in this chapter.

The basic philosophy of *The Corporate Report* is reflected in the need for what is called **public accountability** which is described as follows: 'there is an implicit responsibility to report publicly ... incumbent on every entity whose size or format renders it significant; ... we consider the responsibility to report publicly (referred to ... as public accountability) is separate from and broader than the legal obligation to report and arises from the custodial role played in the community by economic entities; ... they are involved in the maintenance of standards of life and the creation of wealth for and on behalf of the community.'

The 'custodial role' of business enterprises refers to their responsibility to use the assets with which they have been entrusted to create wealth and maintain the standard of living, and other considerations such as the quality of the environment. It follows from this notion of public accountability that the objective or function of annual reports is: 'to communicate economic measurements of and information about the resources and performance of the reporting entity useful to those having reasonable rights to such information.' 'Reasonable rights' is defined as follows: 'A reasonable right to information exists where the activities of an organisation impinge or may impinge on the interest of a user group.'

A similar study of the function of annual reports was undertaken in 1973 by the American Institute of Certified Public Accountants (AICPA); this is known as *The Objectives of Financial Statements*.[2] This document emphasizes the use to which the information is put: 'The basic objective of financial statements is to provide information useful for making economic decisions.' It also regards annual reports as principally intended for those groups who only have access to limited information about the enterprise: 'An objective of financial statements is to serve primarily those users who have limited authority, ability, or resources to obtain information and who rely on financial statements as their principal source of information about an enterprise's economic activities.'

The most recent pronouncement by the UK accountancy profession on the objective of financial statements is in the *Statement of Principles for Financial Reporting* prepared by the Accounting Standards Board (ASB) in 1999.[3] It is similar to the material in *The Corporate Report*[1] but contains some significant developments. The main parts of this document are reproduced below.

The objective of financial statements is to provide information about the reporting entity's financial performance and financial position that is useful to a wide range of users for assessing the stewardship of the entity's management and for making economic decisions.

That objective can usually be met by focusing exclusively on the information needs of present and potential investors, the defining class of user. Present and potential investors need information about the reporting entity's financial performance and financial position that is useful to them in evaluating the entity's ability to generate cash (including the timing and certainty of its generation) and in assessing the entity's financial adaptability.

The financial performance of an entity comprises the return it obtains on the resources it controls, the components of that return and the characteristics of those components.

An entity's **financial position** encompasses the economic resources it controls, its financial structure, its liquidity and solvency, its risk profile and risk management approach, and its capacity to adapt to changes in the environment in which it operates.

Information about the ways in which an entity generates and uses cash in its operations, its investment activities and its financing activities provides an additional perspective on its financial performance—one that is largely free from allocation and valuation issues.

An entity's **financial adaptability** is its ability to take effective action to alter the amount and timing of its cash flows so that it can respond to unexpected needs or opportunities.

The users of annual reports and their information needs

The users of annual reports identified in *The Corporate Report* are[1] as follows:

1 *The equity investor group*, including existing and potential shareholders.
2 *The loan creditor group*, including existing and potential holders of debentures and loan stock, and providers of short-term secured and unsecured loans and finance.
3 *The employee group*, including existing, potential and past employees.
4 *The analyst–adviser group*, including financial analysts and journalists, economists, statisticians, researchers, trade unions, stockbrokers and other providers of advisory services such as credit rating agencies.
5 *The business contact group*, including customers, trade creditors and suppliers and, in a different sense, competitors, business rivals and those interested in mergers, amalgamations and takeovers.
6 *The government*, including tax authorities, departments and agencies concerned with the supervision of commerce and industry, and local authorities.
7 *The public*, including taxpayers, ratepayers, consumers and other community and special interest groups such as political parties, consumer and environmental protection societies and regional pressure groups.

Each of the above groups is said by *The Corporate Report* to have certain 'information needs'. These are described below with respect to each group of users.

The equity investor group

A basic premise in *The Corporate Report* is that 'investors require information to assist in reaching share trading decisions ... and in reaching voting decisions at general meetings. ... In particular investors will wish to make judgments concerning likely movements in share prices [and] likely levels of future dividend payments.' Similarly, the US *Objectives of Financial Statements* says that 'An objective of financial statements is to provide information useful to investors ... for predicting potential cash flows to them'. Thus, according to *The Corporate Report* investors require information for the following purposes:

1 To evaluate the performance of the entity and its management, and assess the effectiveness of the entity in achieving its objectives.

2 To assess the economic stability and vulnerability of the reporting entity including its liquidity (i.e. whether it will have enough money to pay its debts), its present or future requirements for additional capital, and its ability to raise long- and short-term finance.

3 To estimate the value of users' own or other users' present or prospective interests in or claims on the entity.

4 To ascertain the ownership and control of the entity.

5 To estimate the future prospects of the entity, including its capacity to pay dividends and to predict future levels of investment.

Accountants have traditionally regarded published accounts as fulfilling two main functions: (1) stewardship; and (2) facilitating share trading and lending decisions. The concept of stewardship roughly corresponds with everyday usage of the word and refers to the directors' responsibility to account for the uses to which they have put the shareholders' investment. This is the one function of published accounts on which most accountants agree. *The Corporate Report* does not discuss this as such but rather emphasizes the share-trading and decision-making function of annual reports. However, it is debatable whether past data are likely to be useful in predicting future profits, dividends or share prices. The literature on efficient market theory suggests that the content of annual reports has little, if any, predictive value. Published accounts may therefore only perform a stewardship and feedback function.

The loan creditor group

According to *The Corporate Report*, 'the information needs of loan creditors are similar in many respects to the needs of equity investors. If their securities are listed on a stock exchange they will have to make trading decisions.' However, certain information will be of particular relevance, such as that relating to:

1 The present and likely future cash position, since this will determine whether the company will be able to pay the annual interest on loans and repay the moneys borrowed as and when they become due.

2 The economic stability and vulnerability of the company in so far as this reflects the risk of possible default in repayment of moneys borrowed by the company.

3 Prior claims on the company's assets in the event of its going into liquidation.

The employee group

The Corporate Report states that the right of the employee group to information arises because 'the reporting entity has a responsibility for the future livelihood and prospects of its employees'. Employees will require information to enable them to assess the security of employment and the prospects for promotion. They may also require information for the purpose of wage bargaining. Such information may relate to 'the ability of the employer to meet wage demands, management's intentions regarding employment levels, locations and working conditions, the pay, conditions and terms of employment of various groups of employees and the contributions made by employees in different divisions. In addition, employees are likely to be interested in indications of the position, progress and prospects of the employing enterprise as a whole and about individual establishments and bargaining units.' Some companies produce employee reports that usually contain a summary of the year's trading results in a simplified form.

The analyst–adviser group

According to *The Corporate Report*, 'the information needs of the analyst–adviser group are likely to be similar to the needs of the users who are being advised. For example, the information needs of stockbrokers are likely to be similar to the needs of investors and those of trade unions are likely to be similar to the needs of employees.' *The Corporate Report* also makes the point that this group, because of their expertise, will tend to demand more elaborate information than other groups.

The business contact group

This consists of the following groups:

1 *Customers*. These may be concerned about the reporting entity's continued existence because of its importance as a source of supply, particularly where long-term contracts for the supply of goods have been entered into. Similarly, if the reporting entity is engaged in construction work, customers will wish to assess the likelihood of its being able to complete long-term contracts. In the case of manufactured goods, such as computers and vehicles, customers will be concerned about the reporting entity's continued existence because of its warranty obligations and the need for spare parts. Annual reports may thus be useful to customers in assessing the likelihood of the reporting entity's continued existence.
2 *Suppliers*. Trade creditors will require information relating to the reporting entity's ability to pay its debts. In addition, they would be concerned about the reporting entity's continued existence if it is a major customer. A supplier may also have to decide whether to increase its production capacity in order to meet the reporting entity's future demands.
3 *Competitors and takeover bidders*. The rationale for competitors having a right to information is a little vague but seems to rest on the premise that interfirm comparisons of performance and costs can facilitate improvements in efficiency. Similarly, given that mergers and takeovers of less efficient firms are in the public interest, a case can be made for the disclosure of information to potential bidders.

The government

The Corporate Report states that 'central and local government departments and agencies have a right to information as representatives of the public and other user groups'. The Inland Revenue and HM Customs & Excise have a statutory right to information about the reporting entity for the purpose of assessing its liability to taxation. Furthermore, the 'government needs information to estimate the effects of existing and proposed levies and other financial and economic measures, to estimate economic trends including balance of payments figures [and] to promote economic efficiency'.[1] In the UK most of this information is collected through special government returns. However, in some other countries corporate reports perform this function.

The public

According to *The Corporate Report* the public has a right to information because of the custodial role that economic entities play in society and the impact that they can have on the community and the environment: 'Such organisations, which exist with the general consent of the community, are afforded special legal and operational privileges, they compete for resources of manpower, materials and energy and they make use of community-owned assets such as roads and harbours.'

Some members of the public may be concerned about the employment policies of the reporting entity and therefore want information relating to local employment levels or discrimination in employment, for example. Other members of the public may be interested in any plans that the reporting entity has that affect the environment, including issues relating to conservation and pollution. Other matters of a political or moral nature may also be of particular concern to some sections of the community, such as contributions to political organizations, pressure groups or charities, and whether the reporting entity is trading with countries having repressive political regimes. Some of this information must be disclosed under the Companies Acts (i.e. donations to political parties and charities), but *The Corporate Report* implies that the reporting entity also has a responsibility to make public any matters that might be regarded by the community as of general concern.

Users and their information needs

The most recent pronouncement by the UK accountancy profession on the users of financial statements and their information needs is in the *Statement of Principles for Financial Reporting* prepared by the ASB in 1999.[3] It is similar to the material in *The Corporate Report* but contains some slight differences, and provides a useful summary of the users and their information needs. The main parts of this document are reproduced below.

a *Present and potential investors (hereafter generally referred to simply as 'investors').* In its stewardship role, management is accountable for the safekeeping of the entity's resources and for their proper, efficient and profitable use. Providers of risk capital are interested in information that helps them to assess how effectively management has fulfilled this role. They are also interested in information that is useful in making decisions about their investment or potential investment in the entity. They are, as a result, concerned with the risk inherent in, and return provided by, their investments, and need information on the entity's financial performance and financial position that helps them to assess its cash-generation abilities and its financial adaptability.

b *Lenders.* Lenders are interested in information that helps them to assess whether their loans will be repaid, and related interest will be paid, when due. Similarly, potential lenders are interested in information that helps them to decide whether to lend to the entity and on what terms.

c *Suppliers and other trade creditors.* Suppliers and other trade creditors are interested in information that helps them to decide whether to sell to the entity and to assess the likelihood that amounts owing to them will be paid when due.

d *Employees.* Employees are interested in information on their employer's stability and profitability, with particular reference to that part (for example, the subsidiary or branch) of the entity in which they work. They are also interested in information that enables them to assess their employer's ability to provide remuneration, employment opportunities, and retirement and other benefits.

e *Customers.* Customers are interested in information about the entity's continued existence. That is especially so when they have a long-term involvement with, or are dependent on, the entity, as will generally be the case if product warranties are involved or if specialized replacement parts may be needed.

f *Governments and their agencies.* Governments and their agencies are interested in the allocation of resources and, therefore, the activities of entities. They also require information that assists them in regulating the activities of entities, assessing taxation and providing a basis for national statistics. Although much of this information is obtained through special purpose financial reports, its consistency with published general-purpose financial reports such as financial statements often needs to be demonstrated.

g *The public.* Entities affect members of the public in a variety of ways. For example, they may make a substantial contribution to a local economy by providing employment and using local suppliers. The public, including the local community, may therefore be interested in information that is useful in assessing the trends and recent developments in the entity's prosperity and the range of its activities.

The limitations of financial statements

This section provides a summary of the debate relating to whether financial statements achieve the objective given in the *Statement of Principles for Financial Reporting.*[3] The debate involves a broad range of issues, and thus will be confined to those addressed in the *Statement of Principles for Financial Reporting.*[3] There are four main themes. The first is often referred to as the adequacy of financial statements in meeting users' information needs, and includes a debate about general-purpose versus specific-purpose financial reports. The second relates to problems of classification, aggregation and allocation. The third involves the lack of non-financial information in financial statements. The fourth theme in the debate concerns the use of largely historical information. This includes the use of historical cost accounting, which refers to recording transactions at the price that has been agreed in an arm's-length transaction. The limitations of historical cost accounting are discussed in depth in Chapters 2 and 23, and problems of classification, aggregation and allocation embrace a wide range of issues discussed throughout the book. This section will thus focus on the first of the above themes.

Some companies voluntarily publish specific-purpose financial reports, each of which is aimed at a particular class or classes of users of financial statements. These include a statement of value added, employment report, employee report, environmental report and simplified financial statements. Some of these are included in the annual report with the financial statements, and others are published as separate documents. However, there is a fundamental presumption underlying most of the authoritative pronouncements on financial reporting that financial statements should be general-purpose documents. This is based on the premise that the main information needs of users other than investors are the same as those of investors. That is, they all need information about the financial performance and financial position of the reporting entity in order to assess its ability to provide rewards (dividends, wages, etc.) and the likelihood of its continued existence, respectively. This is explained in the *Statement of Principles for Financial Reporting*[3] as follows: 'That objective (of financial statements) can usually be met by focusing exclusively on the information needs of present and potential investors, the defining class of user ...: all potential users are interested, to varying degrees, in the financial performance and financial position of the entity as a whole .... Therefore, in preparing financial statements, the rebuttable assumption is made that financial statements that focus on the interest that investors have in the reporting entity's financial performance and financial position will, in effect, also be focusing on the common interest that all users have in that entity's financial performance and financial position.'

The Corporate Report[1] also acknowledges the common information needs of users, but further recognizes the role of specific-purpose reports, such as some of those mentioned above, in meeting the information needs of users other than investors. This has not been pursued by the ASB in its *Statement of Principles for Financial Reporting.*[3]

The other three main themes in the debate about the limitations of financial statements, introduced above, are described in the *Statement of Principles for Financial Reporting*[3] as follows: 'financial statements have various inherent limitations that make them an imperfect vehicle for reflecting the full effects of transactions and other events on a reporting entity's financial performance and financial position. For example:

a they are a conventionalised representation of transactions and other events that involves a substantial degree of classification and aggregation and the allocation of the effects of continuous operations to discrete reporting periods.

b they focus on the financial effects of transactions and other events and do not focus to any significant extent on their non-financial effects or on non-financial information in general.

c they provide information that is largely historical and therefore do not reflect future events or transactions that may enhance or impair the entity's operations, nor do they anticipate the impact of potential changes in the economic environment.

These inherent limitations mean that some information on the financial performance and financial position of the reporting entity can be provided only by general purpose financial reports other than financial statements—or in some cases is better provided by such reports.'

Learning Activity 1.2

Visit the website of a large public limited company and find their latest annual report and accounts. Read through it and make a note of whatever information you find that is likely to be useful to a potential investor. Then draw up a list of any other information that you think would be useful to a potential investor.

The regulatory framework of accounting

The **regulatory framework of accounting** is a general term used to describe the legislation and other rules that govern the content and format of company final accounts. There is no legislation or other regulations covering the final accounts of sole traders and partnerships. However, it is generally accepted that their accounts should closely follow the rules and regulations relating to companies since these are regarded as 'best practice'. There are three sources of rules and regulations governing the content and format of company final accounts:

1. The Companies Acts 1985 and 1989, with which all companies are required to comply.
2. The International Stock Exchange, London Admission of Securities to Listing regulations (commonly known as the **Yellow Book**), with which all companies whose shares are listed on the London Stock Exchange are expected to comply.
3. The accounting standards produced by the Accounting Standards Committee (ASC) and Accounting Standards Board (ASB) with which most (but not all) companies are expected to comply. These are discussed further later.

The UK accountancy profession comprises six major professional accountancy bodies:

1 The Institute of Chartered Accountants in England and Wales (ICAEW).
2 The Institute of Chartered Accountants in Scotland (ICAS).
3 The Institute of Chartered Accountants in Ireland (ICAI).
4 The Association of Chartered Certified Accountants (ACCA).
5 The Chartered Institute of Management Accountants (CIMA).
6 The Chartered Institute of Public Finance and Accountancy (CIPFA).

In 1970 the ICAEW set up the Accounting Standards Steering Committee (ASSC). Subsequently, all the other above professional bodies became members of this committee. Its name was changed in 1975 to the Accounting Standards Committee (ASC). In 1990 the ASC was replaced by the Accounting Standards Board (ASB).

The ASC represented the six major professional accountancy bodies on matters relating to the form and content of company final accounts. It issued accounting standards known as **Statements of Standard Accounting Practice (SSAP)** with which most company final accounts are still expected to comply. Each of these SSAPs specifies how particular items or transactions are to be treated in the final accounts of companies.

The ASB continues to perform the same function as the ASC, but is more independent of the professional accountancy bodies and has greater power to enforce accounting standards. Before the ASC could issue an SSAP, it required the approval of each of the six professional accountancy bodies. In contrast, the ASB can issue a **Financial Reporting Standard (FRS)** without approval from any other body.

A more detailed description of the UK institutional framework concerned with the setting of accounting standards is shown diagrammatically in Figure 1.1. It comprises the following bodies.

The Financial Reporting Council (FRC)

The FRC is a company limited by guarantee that is financed in approximately equal proportions by its members, which comprise the government, City institutions (such as the London Stock Exchange, and the clearing banks) and the six major professional accountancy bodies. Its chairperson is appointed jointly by the Secretary of State for Trade and Industry and the Governor of the Bank of England.

FIGURE 1.1 Institutional framework for setting accounting standards.

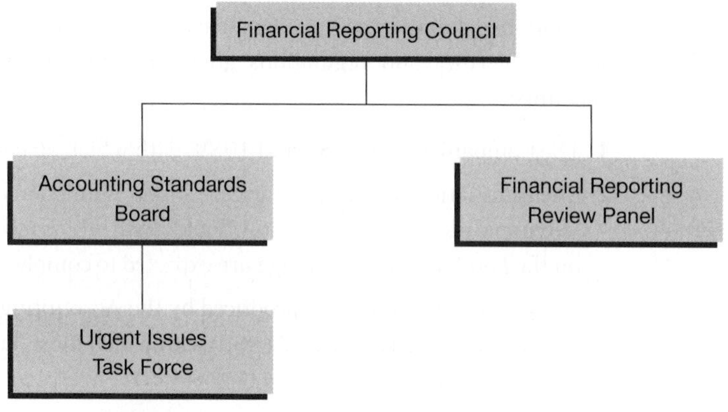

The FRC has overall responsibility for standard setting in the UK. Its main roles are: (1) to guide the ASB on work programmes, broad policy matters and issues of public concern; (2) to ensure that the work of the standard setting bodies is properly financed and carried out efficiently and effectively; and (3) to act as a proactive voice in public debate and to make representations to government and the accountancy profession to improve the quality of relevant legislation and accounting practice.

The Accounting Standards Board (ASB)

The ASB is also a limited company established as a subsidiary of the FRC with a full-time chairperson and technical director. A subsidiary is a company that is owned and/or controlled by another company. In short, its main role is to develop, issue, revise and withdraw accounting standards. These are referred to as **Financial Reporting Standards (FRS)**. The published accounts of most companies are expected to comply with SSAPs and FRSs.

Before the ASB issues a FRS it publishes a **Discussion Draft (DD)**, which later becomes a **Financial Reporting Exposure Draft (FRED)**. These are essentially proposed standards which are open to public debate and representations to the ASB. After examining public representations on a FRED it is often amended by the ASB before being issued as an FRS.

The ASB has published a *Statement of Aims*[4] which sets out its aims and how it intends to achieve these aims. The more important parts of this are reproduced below:

> 'Aims
> The aims of the Accounting Standards Board (the Board) are to establish and improve standards of financial accounting and reporting, for the benefit of users, preparers, and auditors of financial information.
> *The Board intends to achieve its aims by:*
>
> **1** Developing principles to guide it in establishing standards and to provide a framework within which others can exercise judgement in resolving accounting issues.
>
> **2** Issuing new accounting standards, or amending existing ones, in response to evolving business practices, new economic developments and deficiencies being identified in current practice.
>
> **3** Addressing urgent issues promptly.'

This may be contrasted with the aims of SSAPs formulated by the ASC in their *Explanatory Foreword to SSAPs*,[5] which states that 'their primary aim is to narrow the areas of difference and variety in the accounting treatment of the matters with which they deal'.

The Financial Reporting Review Panel (FRRP)

The FRRP is also a subsidiary of the FRC. Its function is to investigate complaints about any company's published accounts where these contain an apparent material departure from an accounting standard and/or the Companies Acts, including in particular the requirement to show 'a true and fair view'. If the FRRP decides that the departure results in failure to give a true and fair view, it will in the first instance request the company to revise its accounts. Where a company's directors decline the request, the FRRP is empowered by the Companies Acts to apply to the court for a declaration that the accounts do not comply with the requirements of the Companies Acts and an order requiring the directors of the company to prepare revised accounts.

The Urgent Issues Task Force (UITF)

The UITF is a committee of the ASB whose members are people of major standing with expertise in financial reporting. It produces what are referred to as consensus pronouncements under the title of **Abstracts**. The following description of the role of the UITF is taken from the *Foreword to UITF Abstracts*:[6]

> The UITF's main role is to assist the ASB with important or significant accounting issues where there exists an accounting standard or a provision of companies legislation (including the requirement to give a true and fair view) and where unsatisfactory or conflicting interpretations have developed or seem likely to develop. In such circumstances it operates by seeking a consensus as to the accounting treatment that should be adopted. Such a consensus is reached against the background of the ASB's declared aim of relying on principles rather than detailed prescription.

The published accounts of companies are expected to comply with the Abstracts issued by the UITF. Abstracts consequently may be taken into consideration by the FRRP in deciding whether financial statements call for review.

Summary

Financial accounting is the process of designing and operating an information system for collecting, measuring and recording business transactions, and summarizing and communicating the results of these transactions to users to facilitate the making of financial/economic decisions. The first part of this definition, relating to collecting and recording business transactions, is called double-entry bookkeeping. The purposes of financial accounting are to record and control the business transactions, maintain accuracy in recording, meet the requirements of the law, present final accounts and other financial reports to the owners of the enterprise, and facilitate the efficient allocation of resources.

The final accounts of companies are often referred to as the published accounts or financial statements, and include a profit and loss account and balance sheet. These are contained in a document called the annual report and accounts. The functions of annual reports are related to society's beliefs about the objective(s) of business enterprises. The basic philosophy of the accountancy bodies is that of public accountability. This underlies their view of the objective of financial statements as being to provide information about the reporting entity's financial performance and financial position that is useful to a wide range of users for assessing the stewardship of management and for making economic decisions. These users include investors, employees, lenders, suppliers and other trade creditors, customers, governments and their agencies, and the public. Each of these will have particular information needs.

The contents of company financial statements are governed by the regulatory framework. This comprises the Companies Acts, London Stock Exchange regulations, and accounting standards. The latter includes Statements of Standard Accounting Practice (SSAP) issued by the now defunct Accounting Standards Committee (ASC), and Financial Reporting Standards (FRS) issued by the Accounting Standards Board (ASB). The standard-setting process is currently under the control of the Financial Reporting Council (FRC) and also includes a Financial Reporting Review Panel (FRRP) and the Urgent Issues Task Force (UITF).

Key terms and concepts

Abstracts (16)
accountability (5)
Accounting Standards Board (ASB) (15)
annual/corporate report (6)
creditors (4)
debtors (4)
Discussion Draft (DD) (15)
double-entry bookkeeping (4)
final accounts (4)
financial accounting (4)
financial adaptability (8)
financial performance (5)
financial position (5)
Financial Reporting Council (FRC) (14)
Financial Reporting Exposure Draft (FRED) (15)
Financial Reporting Review Panel (FRRP) (15)
Financial Reporting Standard (FRS) (14)
financial statements (6)
internal check (4)
internal control (4)
management accounting (6)
public accountability (7)
published accounts (6)
regulatory framework of accounting (13)
Statement of Standard Accounting Practice (SSAP) (14)
stewardship (5)
Urgent Issues Task Force (UITF) (16)
Yellow Book (13)

References

1. Accounting Standards Steering Committee (1975). *The Corporate Report* (ICAEW).
2. American Institute of Certified Public Accountants (1973). *The Objectives of Financial Statements* (AICPA).
3. Accounting Standards Board (1999). *Statement of Principles for Financial Reporting* (ASB).
4. Accounting Standards Board (1991). *Statement of Aims* (ASB).
5. Accounting Standards Committee (1986). *Explanatory Foreword to SSAPs* (ICAEW).
6. Accounting Standards Board (1994). *Foreword to UITF Abstracts* (ASB).

Review questions

An asterisk after the question number indicates that there is a suggested answer in the Appendix.

1.1 Explain the nature and functions of financial accounting.

1.2 Explain briefly each of the following: internal control; internal check; stewardship; and accountability.

1.3 **a** Describe the recording and control function of financial accounting.
b Explain the role of financial accounting with regard to the presentation of final accounts.

1.4 **a** Outline the objective of financial statements as set out in the ASB *Statement of Principles for Financial Reporting* (1999).
b Identify the users of financial statements and briefly describe their information needs as set out in the ASB *Statement of Principles for Financial Reporting* (1999).

1.5* **a** Describe the sources of the rules and regulations that govern the content and format of company final accounts.
b Outline the institutional framework by which the accountancy profession has influenced the content and format of company final accounts during the last two decades.

1.6 Describe the current institutional framework concerned with the setting and enforcement of accounting standards.

1.7 Explain the aims of the Accounting Standards Board and the means by which it intends to achieve these aims.

1.8 The objective of financial statements is to provide information about the reporting entity's financial performance and financial position that is useful to a wide range of users for assessing the stewardship of the entity's management and for making economic decisions (*Statement of Principles for Financial Reporting*).

Required:

a State five potential users of company published financial statements, briefly explaining for each one their likely information needs from those statements.

b Briefly discuss whether you think that UK company published financial statements achieve the objective stated above, giving your reasons. Include in your answer two ways in which you think the quality of the information disclosed in financial statements could be improved.

(ACCA)

1.9 The existing procedures for setting accounting standards in the UK were established in 1990.

Required:

a Explain the roles of the following in relation to accounting standards:

i Financial Reporting Council (FRC)

ii Accounting Standards Board (ASB)

iii Financial Reporting Review Panel (FRRP)

iv Urgent Issues Task Force (UITF).

b Explain how the standard setting authority approaches the task of producing a standard, with particular reference to the ways in which comment or feedback from interested parties is obtained.

c It is possible that there could be a difference between the requirements of Financial Reporting Standards and those of the Companies Acts in preparing financial statements? How may such a difference be resolved?

(ACCA)

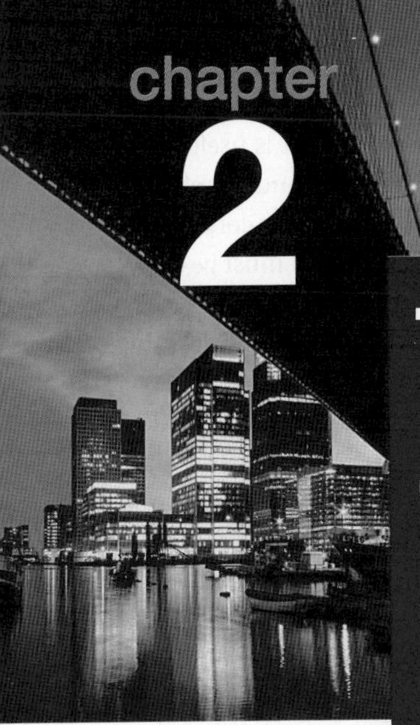

The accounting equation and its components

Learning objectives

After reading this chapter you should be able to:

1. explain the meaning of the key terms and concepts listed at the end of the chapter;
2. explain the relevance of the accounting entity concept in financial accounting;
3. describe the accounting equation, including how it is reflected in balance sheets;
4. explain the nature of assets, liabilities and capital;
5. prepare simple balance sheets and compute the profit from these;
6. explain the nature of profit and capital maintenance, including their interrelationship;
7. explain the relevance of the accounting period concept in financial accounting;
8. distinguish between revenue expenditure and capital expenditure, including their effects on a balance sheet;
9. discuss the relevance and limitations of the historical cost concept in financial accounting.

The accounting entity

The fundamental objective of financial statements as defined by the Accounting Standards Board (ASB) in its *Statement of Principles for Financial Reporting*[1] is 'to provide information about the reporting entity's financial performance and financial position that is useful to a wide range of users for assessing the stewardship of the entity's management and for making economic decisions.' This statement includes a reference to a critically important concept for accounting: 'the reporting entity'. Before going any further this entity concept must be clarified. The idea is so basic that it might have passed the casual observer unnoticed. However, explicit recognition will help to avoid many sources of potential confusion and lay the foundation for the subsequent development of a structure for accounting processes.

At its simplest, the reporting or **accounting entity** is just the organizational unit that is the object of focus of the particular accounting process. It may be a particular company, club or business partnership that forms the entity, for example. We are used to hearing that a financial report relates to a specific organization, but now the organization is being called an entity. The use of the word entity emphasizes the properties of being separate and discrete. Greater precision is demanded by accounting in deciding what is, and is not, part of the entity. Boundaries are being created to separate out the accounting entity. Realizing that these boundaries are necessary, even though they may be artificial, is the key to the entity concept. It becomes possible to accept that a business may be separate from its sole proprietor.

By defining the boundaries of the organizational unit, the accounting entity concept determines the transactions that will be recorded in the accounts. For example, when a local plumber buys tools to carry out his work, that action can be regarded as a purchase by the business, while when the same man buys a cinema ticket this would be seen as a personal purchase. In the same way, the salary paid to a company director is treated not as some internal transfer within a company but as a payment to an officer as a separate individual. In general, accounting sets up 'the business', 'the company' and 'the club' as entities which are artificial constructs, separate from their owners and employees as individuals.

At times this approach is shared with that of the law. In the UK, a company is a legal entity regarded, in law, as a separate body and, correspondingly, the company is an accounting entity. By contrast, there may be no legal demarcation between an unincorporated business and its sole proprietor. The artificial nature of accounting entities has implications of its own, which are most obvious in the case of the single-owner, unincorporated business. The accountant might set up the business as an accounting entity, but this does not and cannot give it a legal existence which enables it, in the eyes of the law, separately to own property or other possessions, make contractual agreements or carry out transactions. What the accountant has created as separate is, in fact, just a part of the proprietor's domain so that anything that can be treated as being owned by the business actually belongs to the proprietor. The 'business' is simply a useful connector.

One accounting entity can be a part of another accounting entity. For example, a branch of a retail chain store (such as Marks & Spencer plc) may be treated as a separate accounting entity for internal reporting purposes. However, the branch will also be a part of the business as a whole, which would be treated as another accounting entity for external reporting purposes. Similarly, one company may be a subsidiary of (i.e. owned by) another (holding) company. In this case the subsidiary will be one accounting entity, and its final accounts must also be consolidated with those of the holding (owner) company into group final accounts, representing another accounting entity.

In sum, an accounting entity can be a legal entity, part of a legal entity, a combination of several legal entities, part of another accounting entity, or a combination of accounting entities.

The accounting/reporting entity concept is also sometimes referred to as the **business entity** or simply the **entity** concept. However, an accounting entity will not necessarily be a business.

The balance sheet as an accounting equation

An accounting entity may also be viewed as a set of assets and liabilities. Perhaps the most familiar form this takes is the **balance sheet**. As an equation this would appear as follows:

Proprietor's **ownership interest** in the business = net resources of the business

The ownership interest or claims are called owner's **equity** or owner's **capital**. The net resources or net assets are analysed into assets and liabilities.

In relatively simple terms, an **asset** can be defined as a tangible or intangible resource that is owned or controlled by an accounting entity, and which is expected to generate future economic benefits. Examples of assets include land and buildings, motor vehicles, plant and machinery, tools, office furniture, fixtures and fittings, office equipment, goods for resale (known as stock/inventory), amounts owed to the accounting entity by its customers (i.e. debtors), money in a bank cheque account, and cash in hand.

The use of the word 'net' to describe the resources or assets possessed by the business recognizes that there are some amounts set against or to be deducted from the assets. There are two major types of such deductions: liabilities and provisions. In relatively simple terms, a **liability** can be defined as a legal obligation to transfer assets or provide services to another entity which arises from some past transaction or event. Liabilities represent claims by outsiders (compared to the owners, whose claims are equity or capital) and may include such items as loans made to the business and amounts owed for goods supplied (i.e. creditors). As the name suggests, **provisions** are amounts provided to allow for liabilities which may be anticipated but not yet quantified precisely, or for reductions in asset values. However, although there are some important matters to consider in relation to provisions, it will be entirely appropriate for present purposes to think of provisions as simply a special category of liability, and to postpone detailed attention until later. Chapters 11 and 12 are both particularly concerned with provisions.

Given that liabilities can be regarded as being negative in sign in relation to assets, the **accounting equation** can now be stated in the form:

Assets – Liabilities = Capital

or alternatively

Assets = Capital + Liabilities

This equation is based on what is sometimes referred to as the **duality** or **dual aspect concept**. Every transaction has two aspects, one represented by an asset and the other a liability, or two changes in either the assets or the liabilities. For example, the purchase of an asset on credit will increase the assets and the liabilities by the same amount. The purchase of a vehicle for cash will increase the value of the vehicle assets but decrease the amount of the asset of cash. These two aspects of each transaction are also reflected in the duality of double-entry bookkeeping, as explained in later chapters.

The accounting equation is a fundamental equation and is a valuable basis from which to begin understanding the whole process of accounting. It sets out the balance sheet relationship which will hold at any point in time, although in practice a complete and detailed balance sheet may only be produced once at the end of a period of a month or even a year. It is worth pointing out, then, that most accounting activity is concerned with individual transactions; nevertheless, the balance sheet equation remains a focus towards which the activity is directed.

However, for now we will examine accounting simply in terms of balance sheets. Let us trace how this approach reflects the setting up of the plumbing business mentioned earlier.

Suppose Adam Bridgewater decided to start his business by opening a bank account for business transactions and depositing £2,000 into it on 1 July 20X1. The balance sheet equation would show owner's capital as being equal to the asset cash at bank, both being £2,000. There are several ways of presenting this: in practice companies usually adopt a vertical approach, placing capital vertically below the net assets in the form:

Bridgewater (Plumber)
Balance sheet as at 1 July 20X1

Assets	£
Cash at bank	2,000
Capital	2,000

However, a side-by-side or horizontal presentation may illustrate more clearly the equation format. A question arises: on which side should assets be included? There is considerable variation and it is a matter of convention. The most useful convention at this stage is to put assets on the left-hand side, as shown below. However, there is a long, well-established tradition in accounting of putting assets on the right-hand side, and liabilities and capital on the left-hand side. This convention is used in subsequent chapters because it is common in examination questions. The lack of consistency may seem unnecessarily confusing, but students need to be prepared to encounter either convention.

Bridgewater (Plumber)
Balance sheet as at 1 July 20X1

Assets	£		£
Cash at bank	2,000	*Capital*	2,000

If on 2 July 20X1 he draws out £800 cash and spends it all purchasing tools, then cash at bank will be decreased and a new asset, the tools, is introduced on the balance sheet.

Bridgewater (Plumber)
Balance sheet as at 2 July 20X1

Assets	£		£
Tools	800	*Capital*	2,000
Cash at bank	1,200		
	2,000		2,000

In this case one asset is increased by exactly the same amount as another is decreased, so that the accounting equation, Assets equals Capital plus Liabilities, continues to exist.

On 3 July he buys a range of plumbing accessories for resale for £300 from the local storekeeper, but arranges to pay in the next few days. The arrangement is described as 'on credit'. The storekeeper becomes a creditor since he is now owed a debt of £300. There is no problem in maintaining the balance of the equation when including the effects of this transaction in the business balance sheet, since the new liability of £300 owed to the store exactly complements the £300 increase in assets represented by the stock of accessories:

Bridgewater (Plumber)
Balance sheet as at 3 July 20X1

Assets	£		£
Tools	800	*Liability*—creditor	300
Stock	300	*Capital*	2,000
Cash at bank	1,200		
	2,300		2,300

The manner in which the two components of the change in the balance sheet are complementary, so that the equality of the two sides remains intact, is worthy of note since it underlies the principles of double-entry bookkeeping developed in Chapter 4. Another event in the life of this business offers further illustration. If, on the next day, Bridgewater pays the store the £300 to clear the outstanding debt, this will decrease both the cash and the creditor—an asset and a liability—by the same amount, giving:

Bridgewater (Plumber)
Balance sheet as at 4 July 20X1

Assets	£		£
Tools	800	*Capital*	2,000
Stock	300		
Cash at bank	900		
	2,000		2,000

Learning Activity 2.1

Prepare a balance sheet listing your assets and liabilities, or those of your family. Use the original purchase price of the assets.

The accounting equation and profit reporting

Drawing up a balance sheet after each of the enormous number of transactions carried out every day or week in large corporations would be very time consuming and inefficient, and a business cannot be expected to do so. However, it is normal for even small businesses to produce a balance sheet once a year. Annual reporting has taken on a significance of its own for many reasons. A year's activity encompasses all the seasons, and many statistics of economic and business performance are produced on this basis. Examples include annual inflation rates, annual interest rates, annual salaries, annual tax allowances and, not surprisingly, annual profits.

Bridgewater may be interested to see how his business has progressed in its first year. For him to be able to draw up a balance sheet he needs to know the amounts to include for assets and liabilities at that date. Suppose he has the following amounts relating to the position at the end of the day's trading on 30 June 20X2:

Assets of business: Building £5,000; tools £1,100; stock of accessories £500; debtors £350; cash at bank £200.
Liabilities: Bank loan £3,500; creditors £450.

Many changes and transactions are likely to have taken place during the year to reach this position, but these have not been tracked from balance sheet to balance sheet. The absence of a figure for capital will not prevent the balance sheet being drawn up, given that it is the only missing figure in the accounting equation. So the balance sheet becomes:

Bridgewater (Plumber)
Balance sheet as at 30 June 20X2

Assets	£	*Liabilities*	£
Building	5,000	Bank loan	3,500
Tools	1,100	Creditors	450
Stock	500		3,950
Debtors	350	*Capital* (to balance)	3,200
Cash	200		
	7,150		7,150

Capital has been made to be the balancing item, and by this means all balance sheets would inevitably balance. This inevitability is consistent with recognizing that the business is an entity which is an artificial creation. It cannot have any net ownership of its own. However, the capital figure at the end of the year is different to that at the beginning, and analysis and explanation of that change is needed to provide a more complete picture. In this case we see that the increase in the year by the difference between opening and closing capital is £3,200 – £2,000 = £1,200. How could this have arisen?

One possible explanation is that Bridgewater paid some more money into the business. In this case let us decide that we know that he paid in a further £1,000. Of course, the opposite to paying would be taking money out, so let us say that he took out £750 for personal use. The net effect will produce an increase of £1,000 – £750 = £250. The rest of the increase in capital (i.e. £1,200 – £250 = £950) would be profit, i.e. increased capital generated by the business itself.

A simple example will illustrate how profit is able to generate increases in capital. A trader is able to start a small venture with £30 in cash, equivalent to £30 capital. She uses the money to buy a bath. When she sells the bath for £40 she now has £40 cash and has increased capital by £10.

To provide a more useful definition of profit as increased capital, accounting has made use of explanations given by the economist Hicks,[2] to define **profit** as the maximum amount that could be withdrawn in a period from the business while leaving the capital intact. In the case of Bridgewater's business, the capital which is kept intact is the £2,000 figure at the start of the period. Measuring profit in relation to capital which is kept intact is commonly described as a **capital maintenance** approach, which forms one of the major pillars of profit measurement theory. It is implicit in all profit measurement approaches that will be drawn upon in this book.

The accounting period and profit reporting

The accounting period concept is a means of dividing up the life of an accounting entity into discrete periods for the purpose of reporting performance and showing its financial position

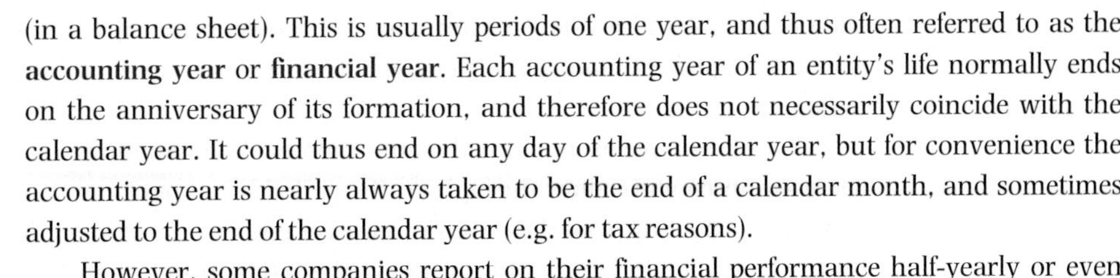

(in a balance sheet). This is usually periods of one year, and thus often referred to as the **accounting year** or **financial year**. Each accounting year of an entity's life normally ends on the anniversary of its formation, and therefore does not necessarily coincide with the calendar year. It could thus end on any day of the calendar year, but for convenience the accounting year is nearly always taken to be the end of a calendar month, and sometimes adjusted to the end of the calendar year (e.g. for tax reasons).

However, some companies report on their financial performance half-yearly or even quarterly. Thus, the accounting period can be less than one year.

The accounting period concept is also sometimes referred to as the **time interval** or **time period** concept.

The previous section commenced by recognizing the significance of annual reporting in assessing business performance. Profit is defined in terms of potential consumption 'in a period'. Although the use of a period of a year is no more than a convention—albeit a very useful one—the idea of periodic reporting is fundamental to present-day accounting. In relation to maintenance of capital, the second year of the plumbing business's performance will be measured in profit terms in relation to that year's opening capital, i.e. the £3,200 closing capital from year one. The approach adopted in accounting is an extension of the use of the entity concept. For accounting purposes, each complete period, usually of a year, is treated as a separate entity. It inherits as its opening balance sheet the closing balance sheet of the previous period.

One response which follows from the needs of periodic reporting is to classify items into two types: those that will be included in the closing balance sheet to be properly carried forward as part of the opening position of the new entity commencing next period, and those that are properly attributable to the period just finished. An aspect of this has already been seen in the simple illustration of buying and selling a bath to make a profit. The transactions involved are all treated as being complete by the time the profit figure for the year is calculated. Details of the buying and selling transactions are not part of the next year's position except to the extent that they form an element contained within the total capital figure.

The approach adopted here will be only briefly described now, as it is taken up more fully in Chapter 10. It is known as the matching process. Sales associated with a particular period are recognized as the revenue of that period. The expenditures used up in that period in creating those sales are matched against them. The aggregate sales less the aggregate expenditures matched against them gives the profit for the year.

Expenditure of the type which is to be matched against the period's revenue and is used up in the period is identified as **revenue expenditure**, and this is distinguished from **capital expenditure**—that which represents amounts which it is appropriate to carry forward as part of the next year's opening balance sheet. Expenditure on tools, which represent the long-term equipment of the business, is capital expenditure and is carried forward from balance sheet to balance sheet. Rental expenditure on a building used during the year will be revenue expenditure—what it provides is used up in the period; the purchase of the building, however, would be capital expenditure, as it is entirely appropriate to represent ownership being carried forward from period to period.

Static and dynamic approaches to profit determination

The previous two sections described two approaches to measuring profit in the accounts of business. The first can be identified as a comparative static approach. It computes profit through a comparison of the opening and closing capital positions, adjusting these for additions and withdrawals of capital made by the owners during the year. Each balance sheet is a static representation of the elements of the accounting equation at a particular point in time.

The alternative is a more dynamic approach attempting to record increases and decreases in capital values throughout the period by recognizing the increases as revenue items and deducting from these the decreases or costs incurred in producing those revenues. By tracking the changes within a period the latter 'transaction based or net production method' indicates the sources of profit.

Elements of the use and limitations of historical cost in accounting measurement

For accounting statements to represent the various values of assets and liabilities and to be able to aggregate these, it is necessary for a **measurement unit** to be established and a **valuation model** to be adopted. We have already been using a measurement unit, the £ sterling. Providing this represents a stable unit for expressing economic values, money measurement will be appropriate to accounting statements intended to reflect the performance and financial position of business entities. Money provides a common denominator for measuring, aggregating and reporting the performance of an accounting entity and the attributes of transactions and items. Examples of other less plausible alternatives might include the amount of energy (e.g. electrical) or labour hours consumed in creating an asset. A measurement unit that takes the form of money is frequently referred to as the **money measurement concept**.

As regards a valuation model, the price that is agreed in an arm's-length transaction when an asset or liability is originally acquired provides readily available objective valuations expressed in terms of monetary units of measurement. This is the major source of valuation used by **historical cost accounting**. Sales are recorded at the contracted sales value and purchases at the agreed purchase price. This approach has many strengths. It permits accounts to be produced by collecting information about the business transactions—clearly a process which is commercially useful in tracking down what amounts have to be paid and collected and what cash balances remain after making payments and collections. Amounts are determined 'automatically' by the transactions themselves rather than being left to the judgement and possible abuse of individuals. For these and other reasons historical cost continues to be the predominant basis for accounting record keeping and reporting.

However, it is not without disadvantages. These arise largely because there is change over time in prices (both of individual items and as a result of inflation). As a result, accounting reports based on historical costs may become unrealistic. Balance sheets will contain values for assets which are out of date, being based on prices when they were originally purchased, which may be several years ago; capital which is being maintained in the profit measurement process represents a value which is also out of date, in terms of both its value to the owners, and the capacity of the facilities that it could provide for the business. The matching process becomes debased to the extent that sales may be made at prices which, although above the original purchase price of the items being sold, are below the current replacement price. This would mean that a business might be reporting a profit on a sale even though this put it in the position where it was no longer able to buy the goods it owned prior to the sale.

These limitations must be borne in mind when the appraisal of accounts is considered in Chapter 30. Attempts to address these drawbacks produce considerable complexity. As a result these will not be considered in any depth until Chapter 23.

Learning Activity 2.2

Repeat Learning activity 2.1 in about one month's time, or better still for about a year ago, if possible. Calculate the change in the value of capital over this period and list the main reasons for the change. What do these tell you about the nature of the profit, capital maintenance and the effect of valuing assets at their historical cost?

Summary

The accounting entity concept defines the boundaries of the organizational unit which is the focus of the accounting process, and thus the transactions that will be recorded. An accounting entity may also be viewed as a set of assets and liabilities, the difference between the money values of these being the capital. This is referred to as the accounting equation, and can be presented in the form of a balance sheet in which the assets and liabilities are valued at their historical cost.

The accounting period concept divides up the life of an entity into discrete periods (usually of one year) for the purpose of reporting profit and its financial state of affairs. The profit for an accounting year can be measured either in terms of the change in the value of the capital over this period, or by a process of matching sales revenue with the expenditure incurred in generating that revenue. This involves distinguishing between revenue expenditure and capital expenditure.

Key terms and concepts

Accounting/reporting entity (20)
accounting equation (21)
accounting period and year (25)
asset (21)
balance sheet (21)
business entity (21)
capital (21)
capital expenditure (25)
capital maintenance (24)
duality (21)
equity (21)
financial year (25)
historical cost accounting (26)
liability (21)
measurement unit (26)
money measurement concept (26)
ownership interest (21)
profit (24)
provision (21)
revenue expenditure (25)
time interval/period (25)
valuation model (26)

References

1. Accounting Standards Board (1999). *Statement of Principles for Financial Reporting* (ASB).
2. Hicks, J. R. (1946). *Value and Capital* (2nd edn), Clarendon Press, Oxford.

Review questions

2.1 Explain the relevance of the entity concept in accounting.

2.2 Define and distinguish between the following:

a assets and liabilities;

b capital and revenue expenditure.

2.3 **a** State the accounting equation and explain its components.

b The financial position of a business at any time is represented in the balance sheet. Why is it that every business entity's position should 'balance'?

2.4 Explain briefly what is meant by the following terms: profit; capital; capital maintenance.

2.5 Explain the relevance of the accounting period concept in accounting.

2.6 Discuss the relevance and limitations of the historical cost concept in accounting.

Exercise

An asterisk after the question number indicates that there is a suggested answer in the Appendix.

2.7* **Level I**

J. Frank commenced business on 1 January 20X9. His position was:

Assets: land and buildings, £7,500; fixtures, £560; balance at bank, £1,740.
Liabilities: mortgage on land and buildings £4,000.
He traded for a year, withdrawing £500 for his personal use and paying in no additional capital. His position on 31 December 20X9 was:

Assets: land and buildings, £7,500; fixtures, £560; delivery van, £650; sundry debtors, £470; stock, £940; balance at bank, £1,050; cash in hand, £80.
Liabilities: mortgage on land and buildings, £5,000; sundry creditors, £800.
Calculate Frank's profit or loss for 20X9.

part

2

DOUBLE-ENTRY BOOKKEEPING

chapter 3

Basic documentation and books of account

Learning objectives

After reading this chapter you should be able to:

1. explain the meaning of the key terms and concepts listed at the end of the chapter;
2. distinguish between cash transactions and credit transactions;
3. describe the nature of trade discount and cash discount;
4. list the documents and describe the procedure relating to a credit transaction;
5. describe the contents of those documents which are entered in the books of account;
6. explain the purpose of books of prime entry;
7. list the books of prime entry and state what each is used to record.

Basic documentation for cash and credit transactions

In accounting, a **cash transaction** is one where goods or services are paid for in cash or by cheque when they are received or delivered. A **credit transaction** is one where payment is made or received some time after delivery (normally in one instalment). This should not be confused with hire purchase or credit card transactions. Credit transactions are extremely common in many industries. The credit terms of most UK businesses are that goods which are delivered at any time during a given calendar month should be paid for by the end of the following calendar month.

FIGURE 3.1 Interfirm documentation for a credit transaction.

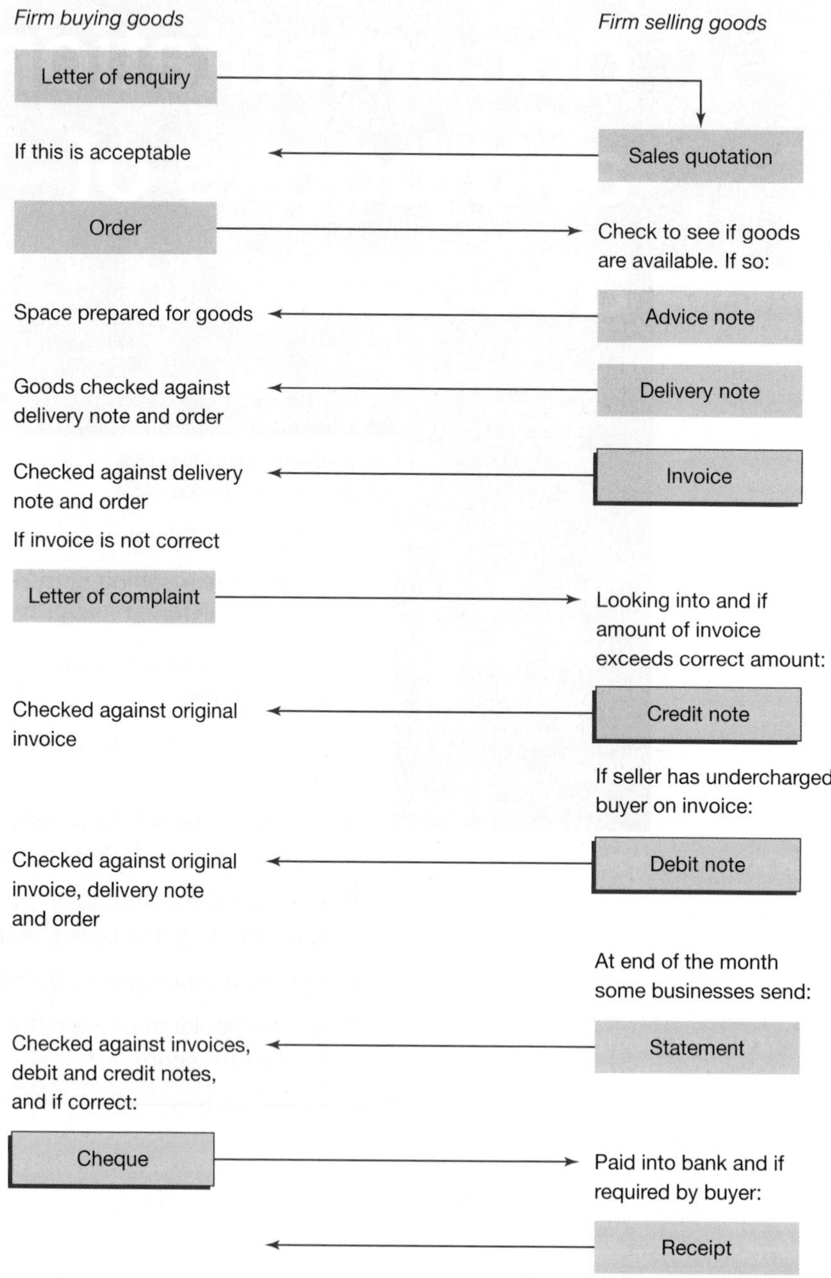

Credit transactions often involve **trade discount**. This is a discount given by one trader to another. It is usually expressed as a percentage reduction of the recommended retail price of the goods, and is deducted in arriving at the amount the buyer is charged for the goods.

A large number of businesses also allow their customers **cash discount**. This is a reduction in the amount that the customer has to pay provided payment is made within a given period stipulated by the seller at the time of sale (e.g. 5 per cent if paid within 10 days).

A cash transaction is recorded in the books of account from the receipt received if paid in cash, or from the cheque book stub if paid by cheque. A credit transaction, in contrast, involves a number of documents, not all of which are recorded in the books of account. Figure 3.1 shows, in chronological order, the documents and procedures relating to a business transaction on credit, including who originates each document. Note that only the invoice, debit note, credit note and cheque are recorded in the books of account.

The main documents involved in a credit transaction are discussed below.

The invoice

The purpose of the **invoice**, which is sent by the seller, is primarily to inform the buyer how much is owed for the goods supplied. It is *not* a demand for payment. A specimen invoice is shown in Figure 3.2. The information shown on an invoice consists of the following items:

- the name and address of the seller
- the name and address of the buyer
- the invoice and delivery note number of the seller (usually the same)

FIGURE 3.2 An invoice.

FROM: Trendy Gear Ltd
High Street
London

TO: Catalogue Times Ltd
Middlesex Street
London

INVOICE NO: 38167
Date: 30 January 20X5

Delivered to: 23 Oxford Road, London

No. of units	Details	Unit price	Total price
100	Dresses size 14, pattern No, 385	£6.50	£650
50	Leather bags, pattern No, 650	£3.00	£150
			£800
	Less: 25 per cent trade discount		£200
			£600
	Add: VAT AT $17\frac{1}{2}$ per cent		£105
			£705
	Tights unavailable – to follow later		

Date of Delivery: 30 January 20X5
Mode of Delivery: Our transport
Cash Discount Terms: 5 per cent monthly account
Your Order No: 6382

- the date of the invoice
- the address to which the goods were delivered
- the buyer's order number
- the quantity of goods supplied
- details of the goods supplied
- the price per unit of each of the goods
- the total value of the invoice before value added tax (VAT)*
- the trade and cash discount
- VAT payable and the total value of the invoice including VAT
- when payment should be made
- the seller's terms of trade.

The buyer checks the invoice against his or her order and the delivery note (or usually with a goods received note prepared by his or her receiving department). If correct, the invoice is then entered in the buyer's books. Similarly, a copy of the invoice would have been entered in the seller's books.

The debit note

A **debit note** is sent by the seller if she or he has undercharged the buyer on the invoice. It has basically the same layout and information as the invoice except that instead of details of the goods it shows details of the undercharge. It is recorded in the books of the seller and buyer in the same way as an invoice.

The credit note

A **credit note** may be sent by the seller for a number of reasons. These include:

- The buyer has returned goods because they were not ordered, or they were the wrong type, quantity or quality, or are defective.
- The seller has overcharged the buyer on the invoice. This may be due to an error in the unit price or calculations.

A credit note has basically the same layout and information as an invoice, except that instead of the details of the goods it will show the reason why it has been issued.

A credit note will be recorded in the books of the seller and buyer in a similar way to the invoice, except that the entries are the reverse. It is perhaps worth mentioning here the reason why this document is called a credit note. This is because it informs the buyer that his account in the books of the seller is being credited. Conversely, a debit note informs the buyer that his account in the seller's books is being debited. This is discussed in more depth in on the next chapter.

* Value added tax affects a large number of sales and purchase transactions which in turn must be incorporated in the recording of those transactions. Including VAT introduces little in the way of principles but some additional detail. In order to concentrate on the subject matter developed in this book, VAT is recognized here but its treatment is postponed to a later chapter.

The statement

As explained above, the most common terms of credit in the UK are that a buyer should pay for all the goods invoiced to him or her by the seller during a particular calendar month at the end of the following calendar month. The statement is a list of the invoices, debit notes and credit notes that the seller has sent to the buyer during a given calendar month, and thus shows how much the buyer owes the seller and when it should be paid. The statement is often a copy of the buyer's account in the seller's books. This is illustrated in Figure 3.3. The layout shown is a computerized system of bookkeeping.

The statement may be kept by the buyer for reference purposes or returned to the seller with the buyer's cheque. In either case neither the buyer nor the seller records the statement in the books. Not all businesses use statements.

The cheque

This is the most common form of payment in business because of its convenience and safety. Most cheques are crossed and therefore have to be paid into a bank account. This makes it possible to trace the **cheque** if it is stolen and fraudulently passed on to someone else. A crossed cheque may be paid into anyone's bank account if the payee endorses (i.e. signs) the back of the cheque. However, if the words 'account payee only' are written between the crossings it must be paid into the account of the person named on the cheque.

The information that must be shown on a cheque consists of the following items:

- the date
- the signature of the drawer (i.e. payer)
- the name of the drawee (i.e. the bank at which the drawer has his or her account)
- the name of the payee (i.e. who is to receive the money)
- the words 'Pay ...' or 'Order the sum of ... '
- the amount of money in figures and in words.

FIGURE 3.3 A statement.

Seller's name and address

Buyer's name and address — Month: January 20X5

Date of invoice	Invoice/Credit note no.	Debits (amount of invoices and debit notes)	Credits (amount of credit notes and payments)	Balance
2 Jan	426	£23.12		£23.12
9 Jan	489	£16.24		£39.36
16 Jan	563	£52.91		£92.27
22 Jan	Cheque		£25.14	£67.13
25 Jan	1326		£6.00	£61.13

Amount due on 28 February: £61.13

Cash discount terms: 5 per cent monthly

The bank account number of the drawer, and the cheque and bank number are also shown on preprinted cheques.

Since there is only one copy of a cheque it is essential to write on the cheque stub or counterfoil to whom the cheque was paid (i.e. the payee), the amount and what the payment was for. Without this information the books of account cannot be written up.

The bank paying-in book

The paying-in book provides a record of the cash and cheques received that have been paid into the business's bank account. The information shown on the **bank paying-in book** stub consists of:

- the date
- the amounts paid in, from whom they were received, and to what they relate.

Cash and cheques received paid into the business's bank account are recorded in the books of account from the information on the bank paying in book stub or counterfoil, which must therefore be accurate and complete.

The receipt

The law requires the seller to give the buyer a **receipt** for goods or services that have been paid for in cash. However, there is no legal requirement to do so in the case of payments by cheque. A receipt must contain the following information:

- the name of the payer
- the signature of the recipient
- the amount of money in figures and in words
- the date.

A receipt is only recorded in the books of accounts when it relates to cash receipts and payments.

Books of account

The main book of account in which all transactions are recorded is called the **ledger**. However, before a transaction is recorded in the ledger it must first be entered in a **book of prime entry**. These books are designed to show more detail relating to each transaction than appears in the ledger. They also facilitate making entries in the ledger, in that transactions of the same type can be posted periodically in total rather than one at a time. Sometimes there are analysis columns in each book of prime entry in which are collected all those transactions relating to the same type of expenditure or income. A business may use up to nine books of prime entry, which consist of the following.

1 The **sales day book**, in which is recorded the sale on credit of those goods bought specifically for resale. It is written up from copies of sales invoices and debit notes retained by the seller. The amount entered in the sales day book is after deducting trade discount (but before deducting cash discount).

2 The **purchases day book**, in which is recorded the purchase on credit of goods intended for resale. It is written up from the invoices and debit notes received from suppliers. The amount entered in the purchases day book is after deducting trade discount (but before deducting cash discount).

3 The **sales returns day book**, in which is recorded the goods sold on credit that are returned by customers. It is written up from copies of credit notes retained by the seller.

4 The **purchases returns day book**, in which is recorded the goods purchased on credit that are returned to suppliers. It is written up from the credit notes received from suppliers.

5 The **petty cash book**, in which is recorded cash received and cash paid. This is written up from receipts (or petty cash vouchers where employees are reimbursed expenses).

6 The **cash book**, in which are recorded cheques received (and cash paid into the bank) and payments made by cheque (and cash withdrawn from the bank). This is written up from the bank paying-in book and cheque book stubs.

7 The **bills receivable book**, in which are recorded bills of exchange received by the business from debtors. A **bill of exchange** can best be described as being similar to a post-dated cheque, except that instead of being written out by the person paying the money, it is prepared by the business to whom the money is owed and then signed by the debtor. When the period of credit given by the bill of exchange has expired, which is usually 30, 60 or 90 days, the creditor presents the bill to the debtor's bank and receives payment.

FIGURE 3.4 Books of account and related documents.

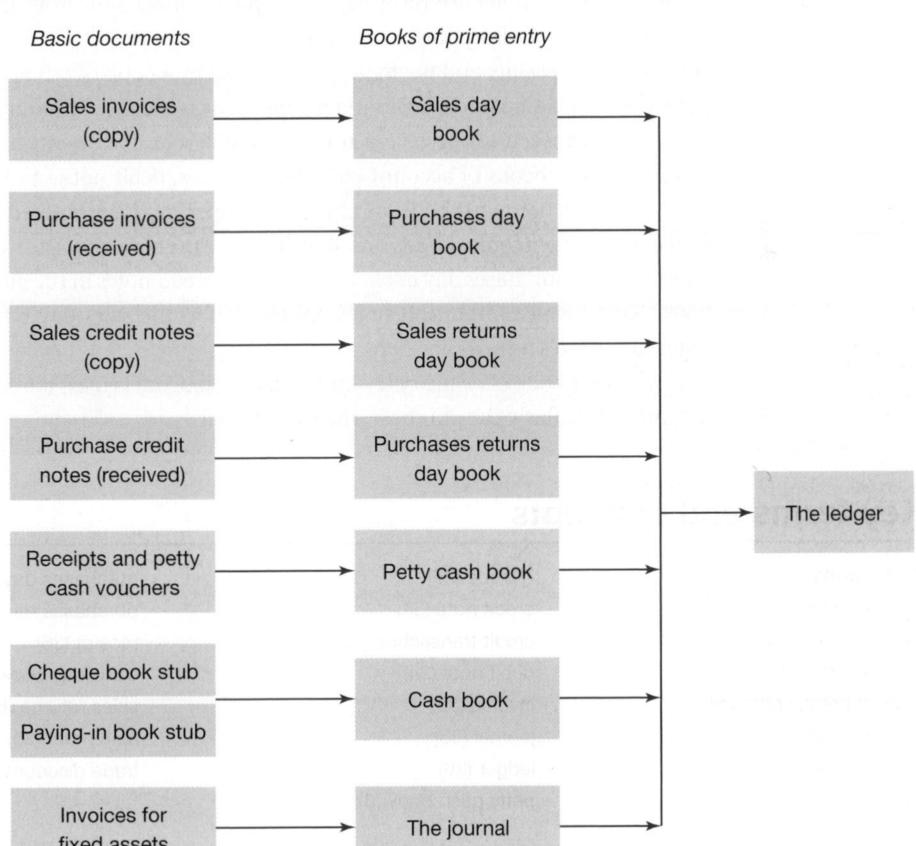

8 The **bills payable book**, in which are recorded bills of exchange given to creditors as payment.

9 The **journal**, in which are recorded any transactions that are not included in any of the other books of prime entry. At one time all entries were passed through the journal, but now it is primarily used to record the purchase and sale of fixed assets on credit, the correction of errors, opening entries in a new set of books and any remaining transfers. Fixed assets are items not bought specifically for resale, such as land and buildings, machinery or vehicles. The journal is written up from copies of the invoice.

Figure 3.4 provides a summary of the main seven books of prime entry, including the documents from which each is written up. Each of these books of prime entry is discussed in depth in later chapters.

Summary

In accounting a distinction is made between cash and credit transactions. A cash transaction is one where goods or services are paid for in cash or by cheque when they are received or delivered. A credit transaction is one where payment is made or received some time after delivery. Credit transactions often involve trade discount and cash discount. Trade discount is a discount given by one trader to another in arriving at the price of the goods. Cash discount is a reduction in the amount that the customer has to pay provided payment is made within a given period stipulated by the seller.

Cash transactions are recorded in the books of account from the receipt if paid or received in cash, or from the cheque book and bank paying-in book if paid or received by cheque. Cash receipts and payments are entered in a book of prime entry known as the petty cash book. Cheque receipts and payments are entered in the cash book.

Credit transactions involve a number of different documents, but those which are recorded in the books of account comprise invoices, debit notes and credit notes. These arise in connection with both purchases and sales, and are entered in a set of books of prime entry commonly known as day books. Purchase invoices and debit notes are entered in the purchases day book, and purchase credit notes in the purchases returns day book. Sales invoices and debit notes are entered in the sales day book, and sales credit notes in the sales returns day book.

A further book of prime entry known as the journal is used to record all other transactions, particularly the purchase and sale of fixed assets on credit.

Key terms and concepts

Bank paying-in book (36)
bill of exchange (37)
bills payable book (38)
bills receivable book (37)
book of prime entry (36)
cash book (37)
cash discount (33)
cash transaction (32)
cheque (35)
credit note (34)
credit transaction (32)
debit note (34)
invoice (33)
journal (38)
ledger (36)
petty cash book (37)
purchases day book (37)
purchases returns day book (37)
receipt (36)
sales day book (36)
sales returns day book (37)
statement (35)
trade discount (33)

Review questions

An asterisk after the question number indicates that there is a suggested answer in the Appendix.

3.1 Explain the difference between a cash transaction and a credit transaction.

3.2 Explain the difference between trade discount and cash discount.

3.3 Outline the purpose and content of: (a) an invoice; (b) a debit note; and (c) a credit note.

3.4 Explain the difference between an invoice and: (a) a statement; (b) a receipt.

3.5* List the books of prime entry with which you are familiar and briefly describe what each is intended to record, including the documents used to write them up.

3.6 Briefly describe the nature of a bill of exchange.

3.7 Explain the purpose of books of prime entry.

chapter 4

The general ledger

Learning objectives

After reading this chapter you should be able to:

1. explain the meaning of the key terms and concepts listed at the end of the chapter;
2. explain the principles of double-entry bookkeeping, including the purpose of having different ledger accounts;
3. describe the format and contents of the ledger and ledger accounts;
4. distinguish between asset and expense accounts, and between capital, liability and income accounts;
5. enter cash (including cheque) transactions and credit transactions in the ledger.

The principles of double-entry bookkeeping

Double-entry bookkeeping is a systematic method of recording an enterprise's transactions in a book called the **ledger**. Each page of the ledger is split into two halves, the left half called the **debit side** and the right half called the **credit side**. The ledger is divided into sections called **accounts**. In practice, each of these accounts is on a separate page.

The money value of each transaction is entered once on each side of the ledger in different accounts. For example, if we take one transaction such as the sale of goods for cash of £100 on 6 January this would be recorded as follows:

Debit				Credit			
Date	Details	Folio	Amount	Date	Details	Folio	Amount
			Cash account (page 1)				
6 Jan	Sales	p. 2	100				
			Sales account (page 2)				
				6 Jan	Cash	p. 1	100

The main purposes of this system are to provide a means of ascertaining the total amount of each type of income and expenditure, the value of the assets owned by the business (e.g. cash), and how much is owed to and by the business. For example, the cash account shows how much money the business has at any time. Also, when there are several transactions, the sales account will contain all the sales made during a period and thus it is possible to see at a glance the total sales for that period. Similarly, other accounts, such as wages and postage, will show the total amount spent on each of these types of expenses. These are referred to as **expense** or **nominal accounts**. The information is used to ascertain the profit or loss for a given period.

When the total amount of money on the debit side of an account is greater than that on the credit side, the account is said to have a **debit balance**. When the reverse is the case, the account is said to have a **credit balance**. An account which contains a debit balance represents either an asset (such as cash) or an expense or loss. An account with a credit balance represents capital, a liability, income (such as sales) or a gain.

Ledger entries for cash transactions

When cash is received it is entered on the debit side of the **cash account** and credited to the account to which the transaction relates. When cash is paid out it is entered on the credit side of the cash account and on the debit side of the account to which the transaction relates. The same occurs with cheques received and paid, except that they are entered in an account called the **bank account** instead of the cash account.

When someone starts a business they usually put money into the business. This is debited to the cash or bank account (depending on whether it is cash or a cheque) and credited to a **capital account**. Money introduced at a later date by the proprietor as additional capital is treated in the same way. Any money withdrawn by the proprietor is credited in the cash or bank account (depending on whether it is cash or a cheque) and debited to a **drawings account**.

Sometimes businesses also borrow money. The amount received is debited to the cash or bank account (depending on whether it is cash or a cheque) and credited to an account in the name of the lender, who is referred to as a **loan creditor.**

The ledger entries for various cash transactions are illustrated in Example 4.1.

Example 4.1

S. Baker started business on 1 January 20X0 as a grocer with a capital in cash of £1,000. She also borrowed £500 in cash from London Bank Ltd. Her transactions during January, which are all in cash, were as follows:

1 Jan	Paid one month's rent for the shop: £100
2 Jan	Bought fixtures and fittings for the shop: £300
8 Jan	Purchased goods for resale: £400
9 Jan	Paid £25 carriage inwards
10 Jan	Bought stationery for £50
15 Jan	Paid £200 in wages for shop assistant
20 Jan	Cash taken by S. Baker for her private use: £150
31 Jan	Cash takings for the month: £600

Your are required to write up the accounts in the general ledger.

Debit			Credit		
Date	Details	Amount	Date	Details	Amount
			Cash account		
20X0			20X0		
1 Jan	Capital	1,000	1 Jan	Rent	100
1 Jan	Loan—London Bank Ltd	500	2 Jan	Fixtures and fittings	300
31 Jan	Sales	600	8 Jan	Purchases	400
			9 Jan	Carriage inwards	25
			10 Jan	Stationery	50
			15 Jan	Wages	200
			20 Jan	Drawings	150

Capital

			1 Jan	Cash	1,000

Loan—London Bank

			1 Jan	Cash	500

Sales

			31 Jan	Cash	600

Rent

1 Jan	Cash	100			

Fixtures and fittings

2 Jan	Cash	300			

Purchases

8 Jan	Cash	400			

Carriage inwards

9 Jan	Cash	25			

Stationery

10 Jan	Cash	50			

Wages

15 Jan	Cash	200			

Drawings

20 Jan	Cash	150			

Notes

1 The narrative in the details column of an account specifies the name of the account that contains the other entry for each transaction.

2 Carriage inwards refers to haulage costs relating to goods that this business has purchased and is responsible for transporting from the sellers' premises.

Learning Activity 4.1

Prepare a cash account for your cash transactions over the forthcoming week or month. Make the necessary double entry in the other ledger accounts.

Ledger entries for credit transactions

The entries in the ledger for credit transactions are more complicated than those for cash transactions. This is because a credit transaction involves at least two (and sometimes three) events, each of which is recorded in double-entry form. The first event consists of the purchase or sale of goods on credit as evidenced by an invoice. The invoice is recorded in the ledger as follows:

1 Feb Sold goods on credit to AB Ltd for £500.

Sales

			1 Feb	AB Ltd	500

AB Ltd

1 Feb	Sales	500			

2 Feb Purchased goods on credit from CD Ltd for £250.

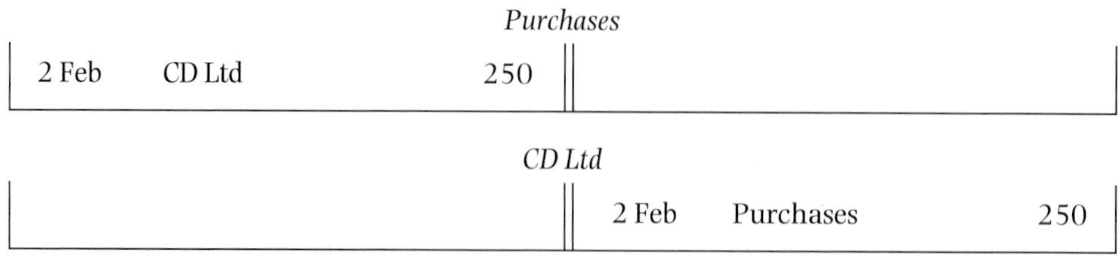

Purchases

2 Feb	CD Ltd	250			

CD Ltd

			2 Feb	Purchases	250

The business or person to whom goods are sold on credit is referred to as a **trade debtor**. In the above example, AB Ltd is a debtor of the business whose books are being prepared. The term 'debtor' arises from the existence of an account in the seller's books which contains more on the debit side than on the credit side.

The business or person from whom goods are purchased on credit is referred to as a **trade creditor**. In the above example, CD Ltd is a creditor of the business whose books are being prepared. The term 'creditor' arises from the existence of an account in the purchaser's books which contains more on the credit side than on the debit side.

A second event which may occur when goods are bought and sold on credit is the return of goods. This can arise because some of the goods delivered were not ordered, or are defective, etc. When goods are returned the seller sends the buyer a credit note. This is recorded in the ledger as follows:

3 Feb AB Ltd returned goods invoiced for £100.

Sales return (inwards)

3 Feb	AB Ltd	100			

AB Ltd

1 Feb	Sales	500	3 Feb	Sales returns	100

4 Feb Returned goods to CD Ltd invoiced for £50.

Purchases return (outwards)

			4 Feb	CD Ltd	50

CD Ltd

4 Feb	Purchases returns	50	2 Feb	Purchases	250

The debtor's and creditor's accounts thus show the amounts of money owed at any point in time.

The third event which occurs when goods are bought and sold on credit is the transfer of money in settlement of the debt. This is recorded in the ledger as follows:

5 Feb Received from AB Ltd cash of £400.

Cash

5 Feb	AB Ltd	400			

AB Ltd

1 Feb	Sales	500	3 Feb	Sales returns	100
			5 Feb	Cash	400

6 Feb Paid CD Ltd £200 in cash.

Cash

			6 Feb	CD Ltd	200

CD Ltd

4 Feb	Purchases returns	50	2 Feb	Purchases	250
6 Feb	Cash	200			

An illustration of both credit and cheque transactions is shown in Example 4.2.

Example 4.2

E. Blue commenced business in 1 July 20X0 as a wholesale greengrocer with capital in the bank of £2,000. His transactions during July were as follows:

1 July	Bought a second-hand van by cheque for £800
3 July	Paid insurance on the van by cheque for £150
7 July	Purchased goods costing £250 on credit from A. Brown
11 July	Sold goods on credit to B. Green amounting to £450
14 July	Paid carriage outwards by cheque amounting to £20
16 July	Returned goods to A. Brown of £50
18 July	Repairs to van paid by cheque: £30
20 July	B. Green returned goods of £75
23 July	Sent A. Brown a cheque for £140
26 July	Received a cheque from B. Green for £240
31 July	Paid telephone bill by cheque: £65
31 July	Paid electric bill by cheque: £45

You are required to write up the accounts in the general ledger.

Debit			Credit		
Date	Details	Amount	Date	Details	Amount
		Bank account			
20X0			20X0		
1 July	Capital	2,000	1 July	Vehicles	800
26 July	B. Green	240	3 July	Motor expenses	150
			14 July	Carriage outwards	20
			18 July	Motor expenses	30
			23 July	A. Brown	140
			31 July	Telephone and postage	65
			31 July	Light and heat	45

Capital

			1 July	Bank	2,000

Vehicles

1 July	Bank	800			

Motor expenses

3 July	Bank	150			
18 July	Bank	30			

Purchases

7 July	A. Brown	250			

A. Brown

16 July	Returns	50	7 July	Purchases	250
23 July	Bank	140			

Sales

			11 July	B. Green	450

B. Green

11 July	Sales	450	20 July	Returns	75
			26 July	Bank	240

Purchases returns (outwards)

			16 July	A. Brown	50

Sales returns (inwards)

20 July	B. Green	75			

Carriage outwards

14 July	Bank	20			

Telephone and postage

31 July	Bank	65			

Light and heat

31 July	Bank	45			

Notes

1 The narrative in the details column of the expense accounts is 'bank' because the double entry is in the bank account.

2 Where there is more than one transaction relating to the same type of expenditure these are all entered in the same account (e.g. motor expenses). However, the purchase of a vehicle is shown in a different account from the running costs, referred to as an **asset account**.

3 Lighting and heating expenses, such as coal, electricity, gas and heating oil, are usually all entered in an account called light and heat. The same principle is applied in the case of the telephone and postage account, the rent and rates account and the printing and stationery account.

4 Carriage outwards refers to haulage costs relating to goods that this business has sold and is responsible for delivering.

5 A business sometimes pays cash into its bank account and at other times withdraws cash from its bank account. The ledger entries for these transactions are as follows:

a Paying cash into the bank:
Debit bank account
Credit cash account

b Withdrawing cash from a bank account:
Debit cash account
Credit bank account.

A further related complication occurs where a business pays cash sales into its bank account. This can be treated as two transactions. The first transaction is cash sales which are recorded as a debit in the cash account and a credit in the sales account. The second is the payment of this money into the bank which is recorded as in (a) above. Alternatively, where cash sales are banked on a regular basis, such as daily, the more common method of recording this is simply to debit the bank account and credit the sales account. There are thus no entries in the cash account.

Learning Activity 4.2

Prepare a bank account for your cheque transactions over the forthcoming week or month. Make the necessary double entry in the other ledger accounts.

Summary

After being recorded in a book of prime entry all business transactions are entered in another book called the ledger. This is based on the double-entry principle and comprises various accounts. Each account is divided into two halves, the left half called the debit side and the right half called the credit side. The money value of every transaction is recorded once on each side of the ledger in different accounts. The main purposes of this system are to provide a means of ascertaining the total amount of each type of income and expenditure, and the value of the assets and liabilities at any point in time. When the total amount on the debit side of an account is greater than that on the credit side, the account is said to have a debit balance. When the reverse is the case, the account is said to have a credit balance. An account which contains a debit balance represents either an asset, an expense or a loss. An account with a credit balance represents capital, a liability, income or a gain.

The ledger entries for cash transactions are made in a cash account (if in cash) or a bank account (if by cheque). These are then posted to the opposite side of another account representing the nature of the transaction. The ledger entries for credit transactions are more complicated because these are treated in accounting as comprising at least two separate transactions: the purchase (or sale) of goods on credit; and the settlement of the debt. The purchase of goods is debited to the purchases account and credited to a creditors' account. The sale of goods is credited to the sales account and debited to a debtors' account. When the creditor is paid this is credited to the cash (or bank) account and debited to the creditors' account. When money is received from a debtor this is debited to the cash (or bank) account and credited to the debtor's account.

Key terms and concepts

Accounts (41)
asset account (47)
bank account (41)
capital account (41)
cash account (41)
credit balance (41)
credit side (41)
debit balance (41)
debit side (41)
double-entry bookkeeping (41)
drawings account (41)
expense account (41)
ledger (41)
loan creditor (42)
nominal account (41)
trade creditor (44)
trade debtor (44)

Exercises

An asterisk after the question number indicates that there is a suggested answer in the Appendix.

4.1* **Level I**

H. George commenced business as a butcher on 1 October 20X6 with a capital in cash of £5,000. Her transactions during October 20X6, which were all in cash, are as follows:

1 Oct	Rent of shop: £200
2 Oct	Purchases of goods: £970
4 Oct	Bought fixtures and fittings: £1,250
6 Oct	Borrowed £3,500 from S. Ring
9 Oct	Purchased delivery van: £2,650
12 Oct	Sold goods for £1,810
15 Oct	Paid wages of £150
18 Oct	Purchases: £630
19 Oct	Drawings: £350
21 Oct	Petrol for van: £25
22 Oct	Printing costs: £65
24 Oct	Sales: £1,320
25 Oct	Repairs to van: £45
27 Oct	Wages: £250
28 Oct	Purchased stationery costing £35
30 Oct	Rates on shop: £400
31 Oct	Drawings: £175

You are required to record the above transactions in the ledger.

4.2* **Level I**

L. Johnson started business on 1 March 20X8 with a capital of £10,000 in a bank current/cheque account. During March 20X8 he made the following transactions:

1 Mar	Paid £5,000 by cheque for a 10-year lease on a shop
2 Mar	Bought office equipment by cheque at a cost of £1,400
4 Mar	Bought goods costing £630 from E. Lamb on credit
6 Mar	Paid postage of £35 by cheque
9 Mar	Purchases by cheque: £420
11 Mar	Sold goods on credit to G. Lion for £880
13 Mar	Drawings by cheque: £250
16 Mar	Returned goods costing £180 to E. Lamb
18 Mar	Sold goods and received a cheque for £540 in payment
20 Mar	Paid telephone bill by cheque: £120
22 Mar	G. Lion returned goods invoiced at £310
24 Mar	Paid gas bill by cheque: £65
26 Mar	Sent E. Lamb a cheque for £230
28 Mar	Received a cheque for £280 from G. Lion
30 Mar	Paid electricity bill of £85 by cheque
31 Mar	Paid bank charges of £45

You are required to enter the above transactions in the ledger.

4.3 **Level I**

N. Moss commenced business on 1 May 20X4 with a capital of £5,000 of which £1,000 was in cash and £4,000 in a bank current/cheque account. Her transactions during May were as follows:

1 May	Borrowed £2,000 from Birmingham Bank Ltd in the form of a cheque
2 May	Paid rent of £750 by cheque
5 May	Paid wages of £120 in cash
8 May	Purchased goods for £1,380 by cheque
10 May	Sold goods for £650 cash
12 May	Drawings in cash: £200
15 May	Bought goods on credit for £830 from S. Oak
18 May	Sold goods on credit for £1,250 to K. Heath
20 May	Bought shop fittings of £2,500 by cheque
23 May	Paid water rates of £325 in cash
25 May	Paid gas bill of £230 by cheque
27 May	Returned goods costing £310 to S. Oak
28 May	K. Heath returned goods with an invoice value of £480
29 May	N. Moss introduced further capital of a £3,000 cheque
30 May	Bought stationery of £90 in cash
31 May	Sent S. Oak a cheque for £300
31 May	Received a cheque for £500 from K. Heath.

You are required to show the above transactions in the general ledger.

The balancing of accounts and the trial balance

Learning objectives

After reading this chapter you should be able to:

1. explain the meaning of the key terms and concepts listed at the end of the chapter;
2. balance and close ledger accounts;
3. describe the nature and purposes of a trial balance;
4. prepare a trial balance from the ledger or a list of ledger account balances;
5. describe the types of error that cause a trial balance to disagree;
6. make the ledger entries necessary to correct errors that cause a trial balance to disagree.

The balancing of accounts

At the end of every accounting period it is necessary to balance each account in the ledger. This has to be done at least annually, and more likely monthly.

The procedure for balancing an account is as follows:

1 Leave one line under the last entry in the ledger account and draw parallel lines on the top and bottom of the next line in the amounts column on each side.

2 Add up each side of the ledger account and calculate the difference using a separate piece of paper.

3 If the amount of the debit side exceeds that on the credit side, enter the difference on the credit side immediately after the last entry on that side. Where the amount on the credit side exceeds that on the debit side, the difference should be entered on the debit side immediately after the last entry on that side. This should be described as the 'balance carried down' (c/d) and appear above the parallel lines. Enter the same figure on the opposite side below the parallel lines. This should be described as the 'balance brought down' (b/d).

4 Enter the total of each side of the ledger account between the parallel lines. These two figures should now be the same.

This is illustrated below using three accounts from the answer to Example 4.2.

Bank account

20X0			20X0		
1 July	Capital	2,000	1 July	Vehicles	800
26 July	B. Green	240	3 July	Motor expenses	150
			14 July	Carriage outwards	20
			18 July	Motor expenses	30
			23 July	A. Brown	140
			31 July	Telephone	65
			31 July	Light and heat	45
			31 July	Balance c/d	990
		2,240			2,240
1 Aug	Balance b/d	990			

A. Brown

16 July	Returns	50	7 July	Purchases	250
23 July	Bank	140			
31 July	Balance c/d	60			
		250			250
			1 Aug	Balance b/d	60

B. Green

11 July	Sales	450	20 July	Returns	75
			26 July	Bank	240
			31 July	Balance c/d	135
		450			450
1 Aug	Balance c/d	135			

If an account contains only one entry it is not necessary to calculate the balance. Where an account contains several entries all on the same side the balance may be entered as described above. However, in practice it is common just to enter a subtotal as follows:

Motor expenses

3 July	Bank	150
18 July	Bank	30
		180

If the total of each side of an account is the same there will be no balance and thus the total amount is simply entered between the parallel lines.

The purposes and preparation of a trial balance

The **trial balance** is neither a part of the ledger nor a book of prime entry (although it is often prepared on paper with the same ruling as the journal). It is a list of the balances in the ledger at the end of an accounting period, divided between those accounts with debit balances and those with credit balances. Since every transaction recorded in the ledger consists of both a debit and a credit entry, the total of the balances on each side should be the same. This is checked by entering on the trial balance the balance of each account in the ledger, and adding up each side.

The purposes of the trial balance may be summarized as follows:

1 To ascertain whether the total of the accounts with debit balances equals the total of the accounts with credit balances. If so, this proves that the same money value of each transaction has been entered on both sides of the ledger. It also proves the arithmetic accuracy of the ledger accounts. However, a trial balance can agree but there may still be errors in the ledger. For example, an amount may have been entered on the correct side but in the wrong account, or a transaction could have been completely omitted.

2 The trial balance is also used for the preparation of final accounts which show the profit or loss for the period and the assets and liabilities at the end of that period. In practice this is done in the form of an extended trial balance. This is discussed further in Chapter 14.

An illustration of the preparation of a trial balance is given in Example 5.1. The amounts are taken from the ledger in Example 4.2.

Example 5.1

E. Blue

Trial balance as at 31 July 20X0

Name of account	*Debit*	*Credit*
Bank	990	
Capital		2,000
Vehicles	800	
Motor expenses	180	
Purchases	250	
A. Brown		60
Sales		450

continued

Name of account (continued)	*Debit*	*Credit*
B. Green	135	
Purchases returns		50
Sales returns	75	
Carriage outwards	20	
Telephone and postage	65	
Light and heat	45	
	2,560	2,560

If a trial balance does not agree, students often fail to take a systematic approach to ascertaining the reason. It is therefore suggested that the following procedure be adopted, which will minimize effort and time spent looking for the errors.

1 Recast the trial balance.
2 Check that no account has been omitted from the trial balance. This sometimes happens with the cash and bank balances as they are usually in separate books.
3 Check that each amount entered in the trial balance is on the correct side. This is quick to do once you become familiar with the nature of different ledger accounts.
4 Check to see that the amounts entered in the trial balance are the same as those shown in the ledger accounts.
5 If the error has still not been found it will then be necessary to check all the entries in the ledger.

It is also worth noting that often in examinations no marks are given for correct trial balance totals. The student will therefore only lose marks for the error that caused it to disagree. Thus do not spend more than a few minutes trying to make a trial balance agree.

A further illustration of the preparation of a trial balance is given in Example 5.2. The data in the question would not be presented in this manner in practice, but the question is a useful way of testing your knowledge of which ledger accounts contain debit balances and which contain credit balances.

Example 5.2

The following is a list of the balances appearing in the general ledger of T. Wall at 30 September 20X0:

	£
Capital	32,890
Drawings	5,200
Loan from M. Head	10,000
Cash	510
Bank overdraft	1,720
Sales	45,600
Purchases	29,300
Returns inwards	3,800
Returns outwards	2,700
Carriage inwards	960
Carriage outwards	820

continued

	£
Trade debtors	7,390
Trade creditors	4,620
Land and buildings	26,000
Plant and machinery	13,500
Listed investments	4,800
Interest paid	1,200
Interest received	450
Rent received	630
Salaries	3,720
Repairs to buildings	810
Plant hire charges	360
Bank charges	240

You are required to prepare a trial balance.

T. Wall

Trial balance as at 30 September 20X0

Name of account	*Debit*	*Credit*
Capital		32,890
Drawings	5,200	
Loan from M. Head		10,000
Cash	510	
Bank overdraft		1,720
Sales		45,600
Purchases	29,300	
Returns inwards	3,800	
Returns outwards		2,700
Carriage inwards	960	
Carriage outwards	820	
Trade debtors	7,390	
Trade creditors		4,620
Land and buildings	26,000	
Plant and machinery	13,500	
Listed investments	4,800	
Interest paid	1,200	
Interest received		450
Rent received		630
Salaries	3,720	
Repairs to buildings	810	
Plant hire charges	360	
Bank charges	240	
	98,610	98,610

Notes

1 The cash account can only have a debit balance. However, the bank account may contain either a debit or a credit balance. A credit balance occurs where the business is overdrawn at the bank.

2 The items 'Trade debtors' and 'Trade creditors' are common in trial balances. These are the totals of the individual personal accounts of credit customers and suppliers, respectively.

3 The item 'Listed investments' refers to money invested in stocks and shares that are listed/quoted on the International Stock Exchange, London.

Learning Activity 5.1

Prepare a trial balance for the ledger relating to Learning activities 4.1 and 4.2.

Types of error that cause a trial balance to disagree

As explained above, one of the purposes of a trial balance is to ascertain whether the total of the debit balances in the ledger is the same as the total of the credit balances. The reason why this may not be the case is because of the existence of one or more of the following errors:

1 **Arithmetic errors**, such as the incorrect addition of the amounts on one side of an account, and/or in the calculation of a balance.

2 **Posting errors**. These may take three forms: (a) where a transaction has been entered on one side of the ledger but not on the other side; (b) where a transaction has been entered twice on the same side; or (c) where the correct amount of a transaction has been entered on one side of the ledger but the wrong amount has been entered on the other side. The most common errors of the latter type are of two forms: (i) where a zero is omitted from the end of an amount (for example, a transaction for £33,000 entered on one side of the ledger as £3300), and (ii) **transposed figures**, where the correct amount of a transaction has been entered on one side of the ledger but two or more of the figures have been reversed when the entry was made on the other side (for example, an amount of £323 entered on one side as £332). A difference of 9, 90, or another number divisible by 9 on the trial balance may indicate that there is a transposition error.

3 **Extraction error**, where the correct balance is shown in the ledger account but the wrong amount is entered on the trial balance, or the correct amount is put on the wrong side.

The first two types of error above have to be corrected by a one-sided ledger entry. The correction could be done by changing the figure to the correct amount. However, it should not be done this way. The correction should take the form of another entry so that some record exists of the correction of the error. Furthermore, in practice it is frequently impractical to correct errors by simply changing a figure to the correct amount, since this usually also necessitates numerous other changes to subsequent totals and balances (e.g. an error in the bank account which occurred several months previously). Where an error is corrected by means of another entry it is essential that the details of the correction indicate where the original error is located.

An illustration of the types of error described above and their correction is given in Example 5.3.

Example 5.3

The following examples are shown in the same order as the types of errors described above.

	Error		*Correction*
1	The debit side of the cash account has been overcast by £1,000 and this is reflected in the balance brought down	1	Credit the cash account with £1,000
2a	Cash purchases of £200 have been credited in the cash account but not entered in the purchases account.	2a	Debit the purchases account with £200
2b	Rent paid of £50 has been credited in the cash account but also credited in error to the rent account	2b	Debit the rent account with £100 (i.e. £50 × 2)
2cii	Bank charges of £23 shown in the bank account have been debited to the bank charges account as £32	2cii	Credit the bank charges account with £9
3	The sales account shows a balance of £2,000 which has been entered on the trial balance as £200	3	Delete the wrong figure on the trial balance and insert the correct amount

Summary

At the end of each accounting year every account in the ledger must be balanced. The balance is the difference between the monetary amounts on the two sides of an account. This is entered in the account as a balance carried down at the end of the year, and as a balance brought down at the start of the following year.

The balances on all the ledger accounts are used to prepare a trial balance on a loose sheet of paper. A trial balance is a list of the balances in a ledger at a specific point in time, divided between those with debit balances and those with credit balances. Since every transaction is recorded in the ledger on both the debit and credit sides, the total of the accounts with debit balances should equal the total of the accounts with credit balances. The main purpose of the trial balance is to ascertain whether this is the case, and thus to check the accuracy of the ledger. Another function of the trial balance is to facilitate the preparation of final accounts.

If the total of the debit balances in a trial balance does not equal the total of the credit balances, this means that there are certain types of errors. The types of errors that cause a trial balance to disagree comprise arithmetic errors, posting errors and extraction errors. These will need to be corrected by a one-sided entry in the ledger or trial balance.

Key terms and concepts

Arithmetic error (55)
extraction error (55)
posting error (55)
transposed figures (55)
trial balance (52)

Review questions

5.1 Explain the main purposes of a trial balance.

5.2 Describe the types of errors that cause a trial balance to disagree.

Exercises

An asterisk after the question number indicates that there is a suggested answer in the Appendix.

5.3* **Level I**

Prepare a trial balance for Example 4.1.

5.4* **Level I**

Prepare a trial balance from your answer to Question 4.1 in Chapter 4.

5.5* **Level I**

Prepare a trial balance from your answer to Question 4.2 in Chapter 4.

5.6 **Level I**

Prepare a trial balance from your answer to Question 4.3 in Chapter 4.

5.7* **Level I**

The following is a list of balances in the ledger of C. Rick at 31 May 20X3:

	£
Cash at bank	2,368
Purchases	12,389
Sales	18,922
Wages and salaries	3,862
Rent and rates	504
Insurance	78
Motor expenses	664
Printing and stationery	216
Light and heat	166
General expenses	314
Premises	10,000
Motor vehicles	3,800
Fixtures and fittings	1,350
Debtors	3,896
Creditors	1,731
Cash in hand	482
Drawings	1,200
Capital	12,636
Bank loan	8,000

Prepare a trial balance.

5.8* **Level I**

The following is a list of balances in the general ledger of R. Keith at 30 June 20X2:

	£
Capital	39,980
Drawings	14,760
Loan—Bromsgrove Bank	20,000
Leasehold premises	52,500
Motor vehicles	13,650
Investment	4,980
Trade debtors	2,630
Trade creditors	1,910
Cash	460
Bank overdraft	3,620
Sales	81,640
Purchases	49,870
Returns outwards	960
Returns inwards	840
Carriage	390
Wages and salaries	5,610
Rent and rates	1,420
Light and heat	710
Telephone and postage	540
Printing and stationery	230
Bank interest	140
Interest received	620

Prepare a trial balance.

5.9* **Level I**

A trial balance failed to agree. On investigation the following errors were found:

- **a** Wages of £250 have been credited in the cash account but no other entry has been made.
- **b** The credit side of the sales account has been undercast by £100 and this is reflected in the balance brought down.
- **c** Purchases of £198 shown in the purchases account have been entered in the creditors' account as £189.
- **d** The drawings account contains a balance of £300, but this has been entered on the trial balance as £3,000.
- **e** Bank interest received of £86 has been credited in the bank account and the interest received account.

Describe the entries needed to correct the above errors.

Day books and the journal

Learning objectives

After reading this chapter you should be able to:

1 explain the meaning of the key terms and concepts listed at the end of the chapter;

2 describe the transactions and documents that are recorded in each of the day books and the journal;

3 enter credit transactions in the appropriate day books or journal and post these to the relevant ledger accounts;

4 prepare opening journal entries to record capital introduced other than cash, and the takeover of another sole trader.

The contents of the day books and the journal

Before a transaction is recorded in the ledger, it must first be entered in a book of prime entry. These are intended to facilitate the posting of the ledger, in that transactions of the same type are entered in the same book of prime entry which is periodically posted to the ledger in total (rather than one transaction at a time).

There are several books of prime entry. This chapter examines only those which are used to record credit transactions. These consist of: (1) the sales day book; (2) the purchases day book; (3) the sales returns day book; (4) the purchases returns day book; and (5) the journal. The transactions recorded in these books are as follows.

The sales day book

This is used to record the sale on credit of those goods bought specifically for resale. It is written up from copies of the sales invoices and debit notes retained by the seller. The amount entered in the sales day book is after deducting **trade discount**. At the end of each calendar month the total of the sales day book is credited to the sales account in the ledger and the amount of each invoice and debit note is debited to the individual debtors' accounts.

The purchases day book

This is used to record the purchase on credit of those goods bought specifically for resale. It is written up from the invoices and debit notes received from suppliers. The amount entered in the purchases day book is after deducting trade discount. At the end of each calendar month the total of the purchases day book is debited to the purchases account in the ledger and the amount of each invoice and debit note received is credited to the individual creditors' accounts.

The sales returns day book

This is used to record the credit notes sent to customers relating to goods they have returned or where they have been overcharged on the invoice. Note that the entry is made when a credit note has been issued, and not when the goods are returned or the amount of the invoice is queried. The sales returns day book is written up from copies of the credit notes retained by the seller. The amount shown in the sales returns day book is after deducting trade discount. At the end of each calendar month the total of the sales returns day book is debited to the sales returns account in the ledger and the amount of each credit note credited to the individual debtors' accounts.

The purchases returns day book

This is used to record the credit notes received from suppliers relating to goods returned or where there has been an overcharge on the invoice. Note that the entry is made when a credit note is received and not when the goods are returned or the amount of the invoice is queried. The purchases returns day book is written up from the credit notes received from suppliers. The amount entered in the purchases returns day book is after deducting trade discount. At the end of each calendar month the total of the purchases returns day book is credited to the purchases returns account in the ledger and the amount of each credit note received is debited to the individual creditors' accounts.

The journal

The journal is used to record a variety of things, most of which consist of accounting adjustments, such as the correction of errors, rather than transactions. However, the journal is also used to record transactions which are not appropriate to any other book of prime entry, the most common being the purchase and sale of **fixed assets** on credit. These are items not specifically bought for resale but to be used in the production and distribution of those goods normally sold by the business. Fixed assets are durable goods that usually last for several years and are normally kept by the business for more than one year. Examples include land and buildings, plant and machinery, motor vehicles, furniture, fixtures and fittings, and office equipment.

Unlike the sales, purchases and returns day books, the journal has debit and credit columns. These are not a part of the double entry in the ledger. They are used to indicate what entries are going to be made in the ledger in respect to a given transaction or adjustment. Each entry in the journal consists of the name of the account that is to be debited (and the amount) and the name of the account that is to be credited (and the amount). The nature of the entry must also be explained in a narrative which commonly starts with the word 'being'. This is of particular importance because of the variety of entries that are made in the journal.

An illustration of the entries in the above five books of prime entry is given in Example 6.1.

Another use of the journal is referred to as **opening entries**. An opening entry is an entry to record the capital introduced into the business by the owner when it consists of assets in addition to cash and, possibly, liabilities. As the name implies, this entry usually occurs when the business is formed and the books are being opened. However, it is also used to record the takeover of another business. This is illustrated in Example 6.2.

Example 6.1

Bright Spark is an electrical goods wholesaler. The transactions during June 20X0, which are all on credit, were as follows:

1 June	Bought on credit from Lights Ltd various bulbs with a retail price of £1,000 and received 20 per cent trade discount
4 June	Sold goods on credit to Electrical Retailers Ltd for £500 and allowed them 10 per cent trade discount on this amount
8 June	Sent Electrical Retailers Ltd a credit note for goods returned that had a retail value of £300
10 June	Sold goods on credit to Smith Retailers Ltd for £600 after deducting 40 per cent trade discount
12 June	Purchased goods with a retail value of £1,000 from Switches Ltd who allowed us 30 per cent trade discount
15 June	Purchases on credit from Cables Ltd goods costing £550
16 June	Sent Smith Retailers Ltd a credit note for goods returned which had a retail value of £100
18 June	Switches Ltd sent us a credit note for £300 in respect of goods returned
19 June	Received a credit note for goods returned to Lights Ltd that had a retail value of £250
25 June	Sold goods to General Retailers Ltd on credit for £250

continued

27 June Sent General Retailers Ltd a credit note for £50 to rectify an overcharge on their invoice

28 June Sold goods on credit to Electrical Retailers Ltd at a price of £560

29 June Purchased on credit a motor van from Brown Ltd which cost £800

30 June Sold on credit to London Trading Co. some fixtures and fittings no longer required in the shop for £350. (Prior to this the business owned fixtures costing £1,000.)

You are required to make the necessary entries in the books of prime entry and general ledger.

Sales day book

Date	Name of debtor	Our invoice number	Folio	Amount £
20X0				
4 June	Electrical Retailers Ltd			450
10 June	Smith Retailers Ltd			600
25 June	General Retailers Ltd			250
28 June	Electrical Retailers Ltd			560
				£1,860

Sales returns day book

Date	Name of debtor	Our credit note number	Folio	Amount £
20X0				
8 June	Electrical Retailers Ltd			270
16 June	Smith Retailers Ltd			60
27 June	General Retailers Ltd			50
				£380

Purchases day book

Date	Name of creditor	Our ref. no. for supplier's invoice	Folio	Amount £
20X0				
1 June	Lights Ltd			800
12 June	Switches Ltd			700
15 June	Cables Ltd			550
				£2,050

Purchases returns day book

Date	Name of creditor	Our ref. no. for supplier's credit note	Folio	Amount £
20X0				
18 June	Switches Ltd			300
19 June	Lights Ltd			200
				£500

The ledger

Debit			Credit		
Date	Details	Amount	Date	Details	Amount
			Sales		
			20X0		
			30 June	Total per sales day book	1,860
			Electrical Retailers Ltd		
20X0					
4 June	Sales	450	8 June	Returns	270
28 June	Sales	560			
			Smith Retailers Ltd		
10 June	Sales	600	16 June	Returns	60
			General Retailers Ltd		
25 June	Sales	250	27 June	Returns	50
			Sales returns		
30 June	Total per sales returns day book	380			
			Purchases		
30 June	Total per purchases day book	2,050			
			Lights Ltd		
19 June	Returns	200	1 June	Purchases	800
			Switches Ltd		
18 June	Returns	300	12 June	Purchases	700
			Cables Ltd		
			15 June	Purchases	550
			Purchases returns		
			30 June	Total per purchases returns day book	500

Notes

1 The amount posted to the sales account is the total credit sales for the month as shown in the sales day book; the amounts entered in the debtors' accounts are the amount of each invoice as shown in the sales day book.

2 The amount posted to the purchases account is the total credit purchases for the month as shown in the purchases day book; the amounts posted to the creditors' accounts are the amount of each invoice as shown in the purchases day book.

3 The entries for returns are made in the same way. That is, the totals of the returns day books are entered in the returns accounts and the amount of each credit note is posted to the appropriate debtor's or creditor's account.

The journal

Date	Details (account in which the ledger entry is to be made)		Folio	Debit amount	Credit amount
20X0					
29 June	Motor vehicles	Dr		800	
	To Brown Ltd.				800
	Being purchase on credit of motor van reg. no. ABC123				
30 June	London Trading Co.	Dr		350	
	To fixtures and fittings				350
	Being sale on credit of shop fittings				

The ledger

Motor vehicles

20X0					
29 June	Brown Ltd	800			

Brown Ltd

			20X0		
			29 June	Motor vehicles	800

Fixtures and fittings

1 June	Balance b/d	1,000	30 June	London Trading Co.	350
			30 June	Balance c/d	650
		1,000			1,000
1 July	Balance b/d	650			

London Trading Co.

30 June	Fixtures and fittings	350			

Notes

1 The fixtures and fittings that were sold must obviously have already been owned by the business. Their cost is therefore included in the balance brought down on the debit side of the fixtures and fittings account along with the cost of other fixtures and fittings owned at that date.

2 The London Trading Co. is referred to as a sundry debtor and Brown Ltd as a sundry creditor.

Example 6.2

A. King went into business on 1 March 20X6 by taking over a firm owned by B. Wright. The purchase consideration was £47,500 which had been computed by valuing the assets and liabilities that were taken over as follows:

	£
Shop	30,000
Fixtures and fittings	12,500
Stock	4,600
Trade debtors	3,100
Trade creditors	2,700

You are required to show the opening entries in the journal of A. King.

The journal

Date	Details/account		Debit	Credit
20X6				
1 Mar	Land and buildings	Dr	30,000	
	Fixtures and fittings	Dr	12,500	
	Stock	Dr	4,600	
	Trade debtors	Dr	3,100	
	To trade creditors			2,700
	To capital			47,500
			50,200	50,200
	Being assets and liabilities introduced into business by owner from takeover of an existing business			

Notes

1 The ledger entries will consist of debiting and crediting the accounts shown above in the details column. In the case of debtors and creditors the amounts will be entered in the personal accounts of the individuals/firms concerned.

2 The capital of £47,500 is the difference between the total assets and liabilities brought into the business. This will be credited to the capital account.

Summary

Before a transaction is recorded in the ledger, it must first be entered in a book of prime entry. These are intended to facilitate the posting of the ledger, in that transactions of the same type are entered in the same book of prime entry which is periodically posted to the ledger in total rather than one transaction at a time.

Credit transactions are recorded in a set of books of prime entry known as day books. The sales day book is used to record the sale of goods on credit of those goods specifically bought for resale, and is written up from copies of the sales invoices. The purchases day book is used to record the purchase on credit of those goods intended for resale, and is written up from the invoices received from suppliers. The sales returns and purchases returns day books are used to record returns, and are written up from the credit notes.

The posting of day books to the ledger follows a common principle. The total of the day book is entered in the relevant nominal account (i.e. sales, purchases, sales returns or purchases returns), and the individual invoices or credit notes shown in the day book are posted to the debtors' or creditors' personal accounts.

Credit transactions not relating to goods for resale (or services), such as the purchase and sale of fixed assets, are recorded in another book of prime entry known as the journal.

This is also used to record transactions which are not appropriate to any other book of prime entry, and various accounting adjustments that are not the subject of a transaction such as the correction of errors. The format of the journal includes a details column and two money columns labelled debit and credit. The narrative in the details column and amounts in the money columns indicate the entries that will be made in the ledger in respect of a given transaction or item.

Key terms and concepts

Fixed assets (61)
journal (61)
opening entries (61)
purchases day book (60)
purchases returns day book (60)
sales day book (60)
sales returns day book (60)
trade discount (60)

Review questions

6.1 **a** Outline the purposes of those books of prime entry referred to as day books.

b Describe the contents, and state which documents are used to write up each of the following:

i The sales day book;
ii The purchases day book;
iii The sales returns day book;
iv The purchases returns day book.

6.2 **a** State two fundamentally different types of transactions/items that are recorded in the journal.

b Describe how these two transactions are recorded in the journal.

Exercises

An asterisk after the question number indicates that there is a suggested answer in the Appendix.

6.3 **Level I**

B. Jones is in business as a builders' merchants. The following credit transactions took place during April 20X5:

1 Apr	Bought goods on credit from Brick Ltd for £725
2 Apr	Sold goods on credit to Oak Ltd for £410
4 Apr	Bought goods costing £315 from Stone Ltd on credit
7 Apr	Sold goods on credit to Pine Ltd for £870
11 Apr	Bought goods costing £250 from Slate Ltd on credit
15 Apr	Sold goods to Lime Ltd for £630 on credit
17 Apr	Bought goods on credit from Brick Ltd for £290
19 Apr	Received a credit note for £120 from Brick Ltd
22 Apr	Sent Oak Ltd a credit note for £220
24 Apr	Stone Ltd sent us a credit note for £75 in respect of goods returned
27 Apr	Sent Pine Ltd a credit note for £360

You are required to make the necessary entries in the books of prime entry and the general ledger.

6.4* **Level I**

B. Player buys and sells soft furnishings and office equipment. During August 20X7 she had the following credit transactions:

1 Aug	Bought goods on credit from Desks Ltd which had a retail price of £1,000 and trade discount of 25 per cent
3 Aug	Purchased goods with a retail price of £500 from Chairs Ltd who allowed 30 per cent trade discount
6 Aug	Sold goods on credit to British Cars Ltd for £700 less 10 per cent trade discount
10 Aug	Received a credit note from Desks Ltd in respect of goods returned which had a retail price of £300 and trade discount of 25 per cent
13 Aug	Sold goods to London Beds Ltd on credit. These had a retail value of £800 and trade discount of 15 per cent
16 Aug	Sent British Cars Ltd a credit note in respect of goods returned that were invoiced at a retail price of £300 less 10 per cent trade discount
18 Aug	Purchased goods on credit from Cabinets Ltd that had a retail value of £900 and trade discount of 20 per cent
21 Aug	Received a credit note from Chairs Ltd for goods returned that had a retail price of £200 and 30 per cent trade discount
23 Aug	Sold goods on credit to English Carpets Ltd for £1,300 less 10 per cent trade discount
25 Aug	Sent London Beds Ltd a credit note relating to an overcharge of £100 in the retail value of those goods delivered on 13 August which carried trade discount of 15 per cent

You are required to make the necessary entries in the books of prime entry and the ledger.

6.5* **Level I**

Show the journal and ledger entries in respect of the following:

a On 20 April 20X5 purchased on credit a machine not for resale from Black Ltd at a cost of £5,300.

b On 23 April 20X5 sold on credit a motor vehicle for £3,600 to White Ltd. This had previously been used to deliver goods sold.

c On 26 April 20X5 purchased some shop fittings for £480 on credit from Grey Ltd. These were not for resale.

d On 28 April 20X5 sold on credit to Yellow Ltd for £270 a typewriter that had previously been used in the sales office.

6.6* **Level I**

W. Green decided to go into business on 1 August 20X8 by purchasing a firm owned by L. House. The purchase consideration was £96,000 which had been computed by valuing the assets and liabilities that were taken over as follows:

	£
Premises	55,000
Plant and machinery	23,000
Goods for resale	14,600
Trade debtors	6,300
Trade creditors	2,900

You are required to show the opening entries in the journal and ledger of W. Green.

The cash book

Learning objectives

After reading this chapter you should be able to:

1. explain the meaning of the key terms and concepts listed at the end of the chapter;
2. describe the format of two-column and three-column cash books;
3. explain the relationship between a cash book and the cash and bank accounts in the ledger, including the implications of its being a book of prime entry as well as a part of the double-entry system;
4. explain the function of the cash discount columns in cash books;
5. enter transactions in a two-column or three-column cash book and post these to the appropriate ledger accounts.

Introduction

The pages of the **cash book**, like the ledger, are divided into two halves, the debit on the left and the credit on the right. A cash book can take one of three forms:

1 A **two-column cash book** in which are recorded cash received and paid in one column on each side, and cheques received and paid in the other column on each side. This essentially combines and replaces the ledger accounts for cash and bank.

2 A **two-column cash book** in which are recorded cheques received and paid in one column on each side, and cash discount in the other column on each side (discussed further below).

3 A **three-column cash book** in which are recorded: (a) cash received and paid in one column on each side; (b) cheques received and paid in one column on each side; and (c) cash discount in the remaining column on each side (discussed further below).

In practice, cash received and paid is usually recorded in a separate petty cash book. Thus, the cash book normally consists of a two-column cash book of type 2 above.

The two-column cash book

The two-column cash book is used to record receipts and payments by cheque. It is written up from the bank paying-in book and cheque book stubs. The cash book is used instead of a bank account in the ledger. This is because there are usually a large number of transactions involving the receipt and payment of cheques, and if these were recorded in a bank account in the ledger it would become cumbersome. Moreover, it permits a division of labour in that one person can write up the cash book while another is working on the ledger. This also reduces the possibility of errors and provides a check on the work of the person who writes up the cash book where it is posted to the ledger by someone else.

In addition to being a book of prime entry, the cash book is part of the double-entry system. Thus, debits in this book are credited to an account in the ledger and no further entries are necessary. Similarly, credits in this book are debited to an account in the ledger and no further entries are necessary.

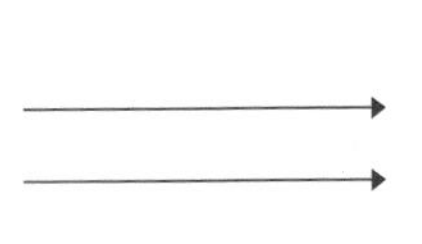

The two-column cash book gets its name from the existence of two money columns on the debit side and two on the credit side. The additional column on the debit side is used to record the cash **discount allowed** to debtors and the extra column on the credit side is used to record the cash **discount received** from creditors. Both of these additional columns are, like the day books, memorandum columns in that each item entered in these columns requires both a debit and a credit in the ledger.

Cash discount is a reduction given (in addition to trade discount) by the supplier of goods to a buyer if the latter pays for them within a period stipulated by the seller at the time of sale. Often in practice all goods supplied during a particular calendar month must be paid for by the end of the following calendar month if cash discount is to be obtained. Note that cash discount is not deducted on the invoice but is calculated from the amount shown on the invoice, and deducted at the time of payment.

Apart from the entries in these two additional columns, the cash book is written up in the same way as the bank account. A debit balance on the cash book represents the amount of money the business has in the bank. Unlike the cash account, the cash book may have a credit balance which means that the business has an overdraft at the bank.

An illustration of the entries in the two-column cash book is given in Example 7.1. The question and that part of the answer relating to the entries in the cash book, shown on a separate page, should be read now.

Example 7.1

Using the answer to Example 6.1, enter the following transactions in a two-column cash book and write up the accounts in the general ledger.

Capital at 1 July 20X0 £5,750
Bank balance at 1 July 20X0 £4,750

Bright Spark has the following cheque receipts and payments during July 20X0.

1 July	Cash sales paid into the bank: £625
3 July	Received a cheque for £70 for goods sold
4 July	Paid rent by cheque: £200
6 July	Received a cheque from the London Trading Co. for £350
8 July	Paid an electricity bill by cheque: £50
11 July	Sent Brown Ltd a cheque for £800
13 July	Bought a car which cost £1,000 and paid by cheque
16 July	The owner of Bright Spark paid into the business a cheque for £900 as additional capital
20 July	Paid wages of £150 by cheque
23 July	Purchases paid for by cheque: £670
24 July	The proprietor withdrew a cheque for £100
31 July	Paid Lights Ltd a cheque for their June account of £600 and they allowed us 5 per cent cash discount
31 July	Sent Switches Ltd a cheque for their June account of £400 and deducted $2\frac{1}{2}$ per cent cash discount
31 July	Paid Cables Ltd a cheque for £300 on account
31 July	Received from Smith Retailers Ltd a cheque for £525 after allowing them £15 cash discount
31 July	Received a cheque for £720 from Electrical Retailers Ltd in full settlement of their account, which amounted to £740
31 July	General Retailers Ltd paid £190 by cheque after deducting cash discount of £10 which was not allowed by us

As explained above, the cheques received and paid shown in the debit and credit amount columns respectively are posted to the relevant ledger accounts in the normal manner. However, the amounts shown in the memorandum columns relating to the discount allowed and received require both a debit and a credit entry in the ledger. In simple terms, the entry for discount allowed is:

Debit Discount allowed account
Credit Debtor's personal account

Similarly, the entry for discount received is:

Debit Creditor's personal account
Credit Discount received account

This can be illustrated using just two of the personal accounts in Examples 6.1 and 7.1 as follows:

Smith Retailers Ltd

20X0			20X0		
10 June	Sales	600	16 June	Returns	60
			31 July	Bank	525
			31 July	Discount allowed	15
		600			600

Discount allowed

31 July	Smith Retailers	15			

Lights Ltd

19 June	Returns	200	1 June	Purchases	800
31 July	Bank	570			
31 July	Discount received	30			
		800			800

Discount received

			31 July	Lights Ltd	30

However, entering each item of discount in the discount allowed and discount received accounts individually is inefficient, and defeats the main objective of the two-column cash book. The memorandum columns in the two-column cash book are intended to provide a means of ascertaining the total discount allowed and discount received for the period. The total of the memorandum discount allowed column is debited to the discount allowed account and the amount of each item of discount allowed is credited to the individual debtors' accounts. Similarly, the total of the memorandum discount received column is credited to the discount received account and the amount of each item of discount received is debited to the individual creditors' accounts.

It can thus be seen that the memorandum discount columns in the cash book operate on the same principle, and perform the same function, as day books. That is, they facilitate the bulk posting of transactions to the ledger by aggregating items of the same type. However, since they are not a part of the double-entry system, each item requires both a debit and a credit entry in the ledger.

The proper ledger entries for discount allowed and discount received can now be illustrated by completing Example 7.1 using the answer to Example 6.1 as follows on page 73:

Cash book

Date	Details	Folio	Memo: Discount allowed	Debit amount	Date	Details	Folio	Cheque number	Memo: Discount received	Credit amount
20X0					20X0					
1 July	Balance	b/d		4,750	4 July	Rent and rates		54301		200
1 July	Sales			625	8 July	Light and heat		2		50
3 July	Sales			70	11 July	Brown Ltd		3		800
6 July	London Trading Co.			350	13 July	Motor vehicles		4		1,000
16 July	Capital			900	20 July	Wages		5		150
31 July	Smith Retailers Ltd		15	525	23 July	Purchases		6		670
31 July	Electrical Retailers		20	720	24 July	Drawings		7		100
31 July	General Retailers Ltd			190	31 July	Lights Ltd		8	30	570
					31 July	Switches Ltd		9	10	390
					31 July	Cables Ltd		10		300
					31 July	Balance	c/d			3,900
			35	8,130					40	8,130
1 Aug	Balance	b/d		3,900						

The ledger

Sales

20X0			20X0		
30 June	Total per sales returns day book	380	30 June	Total per sales day book	1,860
			1 July	Bank	625
			3 July	Bank	70

London Trading Co.

30 June	Fixtures and fittings	350	6 July	Bank	350

Fixtures and fittings

1 June	Balance b/d	1,000	30 June	London Trading Co.	350
			31 July	Balance c/d	650
		1,000			1,000
1 Aug	Balance b/d	650			

Capital

24 July	Bank—drawings	100	1 July	Balance b/d	5,750
31 July	Balance c/d	6,550	16 July	Bank—capital introduced	900
		6,650			6,650
			1 Aug	Balance b/d	6,550

Discount allowed

31 July	Total per cash book	35			

Smith Retailers Ltd

10 June	Sales	600	16 June	Returns	60
			31 July	Bank	525
			31 July	Discount allowed	15
		600			600

Electrical Retailers Ltd

4 June	Sales	450	8 June	Returns	270
28 June	Sales	560	31 July	Bank	720
			31 July	Discount allowed	20
		1,010			1,010

General Retailers Ltd

25 June	Sales	250	27 June	Returns	50
			31 July	Bank	190
			31 July	Balance c/d	10
		250			250
1 Aug	Balance c/d	10			

Rent and Rates

4 July	Bank	200			

Light and Heat

8 July	Bank	50			

Brown Ltd

11 July	Bank	800	29 June	Motor vehicles	800

Motor vehicles

29 June	Brown Ltd	800	31 July	Balance c/d	1,800
13 July	Bank	1,000			
		1,800			1,800
1 Aug	Balance b/d	1,800			

Wages

20 July	Bank	150			

Purchases

30 June	Total per purchases day book	2,050	30 June	Total per purchases returns day book	500
23 July	Bank	670			

Discount received

			31 July	Total per cash book	40

Lights Ltd

19 June	Returns	200	1 June	Purchases	800
31 July	Bank	570			
31 July	Discount received	30			
		800			800

Switches Ltd

18 June	Returns	300	12 June	Purchases	700
31 July	Bank	390			
31 July	Discount received	10			
		700			700

Cables Ltd

31 July	Bank	300	15 June	Purchases	550
31 July	Balance c/d	250			
		550			550
			1 Aug	Balance b/d	250

Notes

1 The personal accounts are usually balanced at the end of each month.

2 The entries in the purchases and sales accounts in respect of returns are an inferior alternative to having purchases returns and sales returns accounts.

3 The entry in the capital account in respect of drawings is an inferior alternative to having a drawings account.

The three-column cash book

The three-column cash book is not common in practice, but is sometimes required in examination questions. It can be seen as an extension of the two-column cash book described above. The additional column on each side is used to record cash received (debit side) and cash payments (credit side). These columns are intended to replace the cash account in the ledger. Thus, the three-column cash book is used instead of the cash account and bank account in the ledger.

In addition to being a book of prime entry, the three-column cash book is part of the double-entry system. Thus, entries in either the cash or bank columns require only one further entry in another ledger account on the opposite side.

The only additional complication that arises in the case of the three-column cash book concerns cash paid into the bank and cash withdrawn from the bank. At this point the reader may find it useful to refer back to Note 5 of Example 4.2, which explains the double entry for these items. The form which this takes in the three-column cash book is as follows:

a Paying cash into the bank:
Debit Bank account column
Credit Cash account column

b Withdrawing cash from the bank:
Debit Cash account column
Credit Bank account column

The three-column cash book is not common in practice because in most businesses cash received and paid is usually recorded in a separate petty cash book instead of a cash account. This is discussed further in the next chapter.

An illustration of the three-column cash book is given in Example 7.2.

Example 7.2

B. Andrews is in business as a motor factor and parts agent. The balances shown in her cash book at 1 December 20X2 were: bank, £1,630 and cash, £820. The following receipts and payments occurred during December 20X2:

2 Dec	Received a cheque for £1,000 from J. Sutcliffe as a loan repayable in five years
3 Dec	Purchased a personal computer for £1,210 and paid by cheque
4 Dec	Purchased in cash goods for resale costing £340
5 Dec	Paid wages of £150 in cash
6 Dec	Cash sales paid into bank: £480
8 Dec	Purchases by cheque: £370
9 Dec	Cash sales of £160
11 Dec	Cheque sales: £280
12 Dec	Paid telephone bill of £320 by cheque
15 Dec	Paid cash of £200 into bank
17 Dec	Drawings by cheque: £250
18 Dec	Bought stationery of £80 in cash
20 Dec	Introduced additional capital in the form of a cheque for £500
21 Dec	Paid water rates of £430 by cheque

continued

Cash book

Date	Details	Memo: Discount allowed	Bank	Cash	Date	Details	Memo: Discount received	Bank	Cash
20X2					20X2				
1 Dec	Balance b/d	—	1,630	820	3 Dec	Office equipment		1,210	
2 Dec	J. Sutcliffe—loan		1,000		4 Dec	Purchases			340
6 Dec	Sales		480		5 Dec	Wages			150
9 Dec	Sales			160	8 Dec	Purchases		370	
11 Dec	Sales		280		12 Dec	Telephone		320	
15 Dec	Cash		200		15 Dec	Bank			200
20 Dec	Capital		500		17 Dec	Drawings		250	
23 Dec	Bank			100	18 Dec	Stationery			80
24 Dec	A. Green	35	640		21 Dec	Rates		430	
28 Dec	J. Evans	45	860		23 Dec	Cash		100	
29 Dec	B. Court		920		24 Dec	K. Vale	40	530	
					27 Dec	M. Fenton	25	720	
					31 Dec	Balance c/d		2,580	310
		80	6,510	1,080			65	6,510	1,080
1 Jan	Balance b/d	—	2,580	310					

23 Dec	Withdrew cash of £100 from the bank
24 Dec	Sent K. Vale a cheque for £530 after deducting cash discount of £40
24 Dec	Received a cheque for £640 from A. Green who deducted £35 cash discount
27 Dec	Paid M. Fenton £720 by cheque after deducting £25 cash discount
28 Dec	J. Evans sent us a cheque for £860 after deducting £45 cash discount
29 Dec	Received a cheque from B. Court for £920 who deducted £50 cash discount which we did not allow

You are required to enter the above transactions in a three-column cash book.

Learning Activity 7.1

Prepare a two-column cash book with cash and bank columns to record your cash and cheque transactions over the forthcoming week or month. Make the necessary double entry in the other ledger accounts.

Summary

The cash book is both a book of prime entry and part of the double-entry system in the ledger, and thus has the same format as a ledger account. It usually takes one of two forms: a two-column cash book or a three-column cash book. The two-column cash book has two money columns on each side. One column on each side is used to record cheques received and paid. The other column on each side is used to record cash discount allowed and cash discount received. The two-column cash book replaces the bank account in the ledger, and is written up from the bank paying-in book and cheque book stubs. The three-column cash book has three money columns on each side. Two of these are the same as the two-column cash book. The third is used to record cash receipts and payments, and is written up from copies of the receipts. The three-column cash book replaces the bank and cash accounts in the ledger.

Because the cash book is a part of the double-entry system, entries in the cash book in respect of cash and cheque transactions need only to be posted to the opposite side of the relevant ledger account. However, this is not the case with regard to the entries in the cash discount columns. These columns are memoranda, and essentially intended to serve the same purpose as day books: namely to facilitate the periodic bulk posting of items of the same type. Thus, the total of the memo discount allowed column is debited to the discount allowed account in the ledger, and the individual amounts are credited to the relevant debtors' personal accounts. Similarly, the total of the memo discount received column of the cash book is credited to the discount received account, and the individual amounts are debited to the relevant creditors' personal accounts.

Key terms and concepts

Cash book (69)
cash discount (69)
discount allowed (69)
discount received (69)
three-column cash book (69)
two-column cash book (69)

Review questions

7.1 Describe the different forms of two- and three-column cash books with which you are familiar.

7.2 Describe the entries in the cash book and ledger in respect of discount allowed and discount received.

Exercises

An asterisk after the question number indicates that there is a suggested answer in the Appendix.

7.3 Level I

B. Jones is in business as builders' merchants. The following receipts and payments by cheque took place during May 20X5:

1 May	Bank balance per cash book: £3,680
3 May	Introduced additional capital: £2,000
4 May	Sales by cheque: £840
7 May	Purchases by cheque: £510
10 May	Paid wages by cheque: £200
13 May	Paid rent by cheque: £360
15 May	Cash sales paid into bank: £490
18 May	Purchased shopfittings for £2,450
20 May	Paid gas bill of £180
23 May	Bought stationery by cheque: £70
26 May	Drawings by cheque: £250
31 May	Sent Brick Ltd a cheque for £850 after deducting £45 cash discount
31 May	Received a cheque from Oak Ltd for £160 after deducting £30 cash discount
31 May	Paid Stone Ltd £220 after deducting cash discount of £20
31 May	Pine Ltd sent us a cheque for £485 after deducting £25 cash discount
31 May	Sent Slate Ltd a cheque for £480 after deducting cash discount of £40. However, Slate Ltd did not allow the discount
31 May	Lime Ltd sent us a cheque for £575

Show the entries in respect of the above in a two-column cash book.

7.4 Level I

Using your answers to Question 6.3 in Chapter 6 and Question 7.3 above:

a make the necessary entries in the general ledger given a balance on the capital account at 1 May 20X5 of £3,680; and

b prepare a trial balance at 31 May 20X5.

7.5* Level I

B. Player buys and sells soft furnishings and office equipment. During September 20X7 the following receipts and payments occurred:

1 Sep	Bank balance per cash book: £1,950
1 Sep	Cash balance per cash book: £860
3 Sep	Cash sales paid into bank: £470

4 Sep	Cash purchases: £230
6 Sep	Paid electricity bill of £510 by cheque
9 Sep	Sales by cheque: £380
10 Sep	Drew a cheque for £250 in respect of wages
12 Sep	Cash sales: £290
15 Sep	Paid £40 in cash for travelling expenses
16 Sep	Paid water rates by cheque: £410
19 Sep	Drawings in cash: £150
20 Sep	Purchases by cheque: £320
21 Sep	Paid postage of £30 in cash
22 Sep	Paid cash of £350 into bank
24 Sep	Introduced further capital of £500 by cheque
25 Sep	Purchased a delivery vehicle for £2,500 and paid by cheque
26 Sep	Received a cheque for £1,000 from B. Jones as a three-year loan
27 Sep	Returned goods costing £170 and received a cash refund
28 Sep	Paid tax and insurance on delivery vehicle of £280 in cash
29 Sep	Withdrew cash of £180 from bank
30 Sep	Received a cheque from British Cars Ltd for £350 after deducting £10 cash discount
30 Sep	Received a cheque from London Beds Ltd for £580 after deducting £15 cash discount
30 Sep	Paid Desks Ltd a cheque for £500 after deducting £25 cash discount
30 Sep	Paid Chairs Ltd a cheque for £190 after deducting £20 cash discount
30 Sep	Received a cheque from English Carpets Ltd for £1,100 after deducting £70 cash discount. However, this cash discount was not allowed
30 Sep	Paid Cabinets Ltd a cheque for £500 on account

Enter the above in a three-column cash book.

7.6* **Level I**

Using your answers to Question 6.4 in Chapter 6 and Question 7.5 above:

a make the necessary entries in the ledger given a balance on the capital account at 1 September 20X7 of £2,810; and

b prepare a trial balance at 30 September 20X7.

chapter

8

The petty cash book

Learning objectives

After reading this chapter you should be able to:

1. explain the meaning of the key terms and concepts listed at the end of the chapter;
2. explain the relationship between a petty cash book and the cash account in the ledger, including the implications of the petty cash book being a book of prime entry as well as a part of the double-entry system;
3. describe the format of a columnar petty cash book;
4. explain the function of the analysis columns in a columnar petty cash book;
5. describe the petty cash imprest system and its advantages;
6. enter transactions in a columnar petty cash book using the imprest system, and post these to the appropriate ledger accounts.

Introduction

The **petty cash book** is used to record the receipt and payment of small amounts of cash. Any large amounts of cash received and cash takings are usually paid into the bank and thus recorded in the cash book. The petty cash book is written up from receipts and petty cash vouchers (where employees are reimbursed expenses).

The petty cash book is used instead of a cash account in the ledger. This is because there is usually a large number of transactions in cash, and if these were recorded in a cash account in the ledger it would become cumbersome. Like the cash book, it also permits a division of labour and facilitates improved control. In addition to being a book of prime entry, the petty cash book is part of the double-entry system. Thus, debits in this book are credited to an account in the ledger and no further entries are necessary. Similarly, credits in this book are debited to an account in the ledger and no further entries are necessary.

The columnar petty cash book

It is usual for a **(columnar) petty cash book** to have analysis columns on the credit side. Each column relates to a particular type of expenditure, such as postage, stationery or travelling expenses. These are intended to facilitate the posting of entries to the ledger. Every item of expenditure is entered in both the credit column and an appropriate analysis column. At the end of each calendar week or month the total of each analysis column is debited to the relevant account in the ledger. Thus, instead of posting each transaction to the ledger separately, expenditure of the same type is collected together in each analysis column and the total for the period posted to the relevant ledger account.

The imprest system

Many firms also operate their petty cash on an **imprest system**. At the beginning of each period (week or month) the petty cashier has a fixed amount of cash referred to as a 'float'. At the end of each period (or the start of the next) the petty cashier is reimbursed the exact amount spent during the period, thus making the float up to its original amount. The reimbursement usually takes the form of a cheque drawn for cash. The amount of the petty cash float is determined by reference to the normal level of petty cash expenditure in each period.

The advantages of the imprest system are as follows:

1 It facilitates control of the total petty cash expenditure in each period as the petty cashier cannot spend more than the amount of the float except by applying to the management for an increase.

2 It deters theft of cash by the petty cashier since a large cash balance cannot be accumulated by drawing cash from the bank at irregular intervals.

3 The entries in the petty cash book are kept up to date because the cash expenditure is not reimbursed until the petty cash book is written up and the total amount of expenditure for the period is known.

4 It discourages the practice of loans and subs from petty cash since these would have to be accounted for at the end of the period, and in addition may result in insufficient cash to meet the necessary expenditure.

An illustration of a columnar petty cash book and the imprest system is shown in Example 8.1.

Example 8.1

A. Stone uses a columnar petty cash book to record his cash payments. He also operates an imprest system with a float of £150. During August 20X6 the cash transactions were as follows:

1 Aug	Postage stamps: £5
2 Aug	Cleaning materials: £13
4 Aug	Telegram: £2
5 Aug	Gratuity to delivery man: £4
7 Aug	Tea, milk, etc.: £1
9 Aug	Rail fare: £11
10 Aug	Paper clips and pens: £6
13 Aug	Window cleaner: £10
18 Aug	Travelling expenses: £7
21 Aug	Envelopes: £3
22 Aug	Postage stamps: £9
24 Aug	Stationery: £14
27 Aug	Taxi fare: £12
28 Aug	Office cleaning: £8
31 Aug	Received reimbursement to make float up to £150

You are required to make the necessary entries in the petty cash book using appropriate analysis columns, and show the relevant ledger accounts.

The petty cash book

Debit	Credit								
Amount £	Date	Details	Amount £	Telephone and postage £	Cleaning £	Printing and stationery £	Travelling expenses £	Miscellaneous expenses £
	20X6							
b/d 150	1 Aug	Stamps	5	5				
	2 Aug	Materials	13		13			
	4 Aug	Telegram	2	2				
	5 Aug	Gratuity	4					4
	7 Aug	Tea and milk	1					1
	9 Aug	Rail fare	11				11	
	10 Aug	Clips and pens	6			6		
	13 Aug	Windows	10		10			
	18 Aug	Travelling	7				7	
	21 Aug	Envelopes	3			3		
	22 Aug	Stamps	9	9				
	24 Aug	Stationery	14			14		
	27 Aug	Taxi	12				12	
	28 Aug	Office	8		8			
105	31 Aug	Reimbursement	105	16	31	23	30	5
	31 Aug	Balance c/d	150					
255			255					
b/d 150	1 Sep							

In some firms the cash reimbursement is made at the beginning of the next period, in which case the entries are as follows:

	31 Aug	Totals	105	16	31	23	30	5
	31 Aug	Balance c/d	45					
150			150					
b/d 45								
105	1 Sep	Reimbursement						
150								

The ledger

Telephone and postage

31 Aug Total per PCB 16

Cleaning

31 Aug Total per PCB 31

Printing and stationery

31 Aug Total per PCB 23

Travelling expenses

31 Aug Total per PCB 30

Miscellaneous expenses

31 Aug Total per PCB 5

Cash book

31 Aug Cash 105

Notes

1 When designing a columnar petty cash book it is necessary first to decide on the appropriate number of analysis columns. This is done by identifying the number of different types of expenditure for which there is more than one transaction. In Example 8.1 there are four different types, namely postage, cleaning, stationery and travelling expenses. These four plus a column for miscellaneous expenses give five columns. The headings for each of these columns should be the same as the name of the ledger account to which the total of the column will be posted.

2 The details column of the petty cash book is used to describe the nature of each transaction rather than the name of the ledger account containing the double entry, since this is given at the head of the analysis column in which the item is entered.

3 The items entered in the miscellaneous expenses column sometimes have to be posted to several different ledger accounts according to the nature of each transaction.

4 When cash is withdrawn from the bank to restore the float to its original amount the ledger entry consists of:
Debit petty cash book
Credit cash book (bank account)

5 When answering examination questions which contain cash and cheque items but do not specifically require a petty cash book, it is advisable to use a three-column cash book.

Learning Activity 8.1

Prepare a columnar petty cash book for your cash transactions over the forthcoming week or month. Make the necessary double entry in the other ledger accounts.

Summary

The petty cash book is both a book of prime entry and a part of the double-entry system in the ledger, and thus has the same format as a ledger account. It is used to record cash receipts and payments, and is written up from copies of the receipts and petty cash vouchers. The petty cash book replaces the cash account in the ledger, and thus entries in this book need only to be posted to the opposite side of the relevant ledger accounts.

The most common form of petty cash book is a columnar petty cash book. This has several analysis columns on the credit side, each relating to a particular type of expenditure. These columns are memoranda, and essentially intended to serve the same purpose as day books, namely to facilitate the periodic bulk posting of transactions of the same type.

Many organizations also operate their petty cash on an imprest system. This essentially comprises a fixed cash float which is replenished at the end of each period by an amount equal to that period's cash expenditure. The imprest system has several very important advantages including facilitating control of the total cash expenditure for a period, deterring the theft of cash, discouraging cash loans/subs, and ensuring that the entries in the petty cash book are kept up to date.

Key terms and concepts

Columnar petty cash book (81) imprest system (81) petty cash book (81)

Review questions

8.1 **a** Describe the purpose and format of a columnar petty cash book.
b Explain how you would determine the appropriate number of analysis columns.

8.2 **a** Describe how a petty cash imprest system operates.
b Explain how such a system facilitates control.

Exercises

An asterisk after the question number indicates that there is a suggested answer in the Appendix.

8.3* **Level I**

C. Harlow has a petty cash book which is used to record his cash receipts and payments. This also incorporates an imprest system which has a float of £400. During February 20X2 the following cash transactions took place:

1 Feb	Purchases: £31
3 Feb	Wages: £28
6 Feb	Petrol for delivery van: £9
8 Feb	Bus fares: £3
11 Feb	Pens and pencils: £8
12 Feb	Payments for casual labour: £25
14 Feb	Repairs to delivery van: £17
16 Feb	Copying paper: £15
19 Feb	Goods for resale: £22
20 Feb	Train fares: £12
21 Feb	Repairs to premises: £35
22 Feb	Postage stamps: £6
23 Feb	Drawings: £20
24 Feb	Taxi fares: £7
25 Feb	Envelopes: £4
26 Feb	Purchases: £18
27 Feb	Wages: £30
28 Feb	Petrol for delivery van: £14

On 28 February 20X2 the cash float was restored to £400.

Record the above in the petty cash book using appropriate analysis columns and make the necessary entries in the ledger.

8.4 Level I

The Oakhill Printing Co. Ltd operates its petty cash account on the imprest system. It is maintained at a figure of £80 on the first day of each month. At 30 April 20X7 the petty cash box held £19.37 in cash. During May 20X7, the following petty cash transactions arose:

		£
1 May	Cash received to restore imprest	to be derived
1 May	Bus fares	0.41
2 May	Stationery	2.35
4 May	Bus fares	0.30
7 May	Postage stamps	1.70
7 May	Trade journal	0.95
8 May	Bus fares	0.64
11 May	Correcting fluid	1.29
12 May	Typewriter ribbons	5.42
14 May	Parcel postage	3.45
15 May	Paper clips	0.42
15 May	Newspapers	2.00
16 May	Photocopier repair	16.80
19 May	Postage stamps	1.50
20 May	Drawing pins	0.38
21 May	Train fare	5.40
22 May	Photocopier paper	5.63
23 May	Display decorations	3.07
23 May	Correcting fluid	1.14

continued

		£
25 May	Wrapping paper	0.78
27 May	String	0.61
27 May	Sellotape	0.75
27 May	Biro pens	0.46
28 May	Typewriter repair	13.66
30 May	Bus fares	2.09
1 June	Cash received to restore imprest	to be derived

Required:

Open and post the company's petty cash account for the period 1 May to 1 June 20X7 inclusive and balance the account at 30 May 20X7.

In order to facilitate the subsequent double-entry postings, all items of expense appearing in the 'payments' column should then be analysed individually into suitably labelled expense columns.

(ACCA)

part

3

PREPARING FINAL ACCOUNTS

The final accounts of sole traders

Learning objectives

After reading this chapter you should be able to:

1 explain the meaning of the key terms and concepts listed at the end of the chapter;

2 explain the purpose and structure of profit and loss accounts, including the subtotals for gross profit and net profit;

3 explain the purpose and structure of balance sheets, including the subtotals for net current assets, total assets less current liabilities and net assets;

4 describe the nature of administrative expenses, selling and distribution expenses, fixed assets, current assets, current liabilities long-term liabilities and capital;

5 explain the relevance of stock and the cost of sales in the determination of the gross profit;

6 prepare a simple trading and profit and loss account and balance sheet from a trial balance using either an account/horizontal format or a vertical format;

7 make all the necessary ledger account and journal entries relating to the preparation of trading and profit and loss accounts.

Introduction

Final accounts consist of a profit and loss account and balance sheet. These are prepared at the end of the business's accounting year after the trial balance has been completed. Some businesses also produce final accounts half yearly, quarterly or even monthly. The purpose, structure and preparation of the profit and loss account and balance sheet are discussed below.

The purpose and structure of profit and loss accounts

The **profit and loss account** provides a summary of the results of a business's trading activities during a given accounting year. It shows the profit or loss for the year. The purpose of a profit and loss account is to enable users of accounts, such as the owner, to evaluate the financial performance of a business for a given accounting year. It may be used to determine the amount of taxation on the profit.

Chapter 2 explained that **profit** can be defined as the amount which could be taken out of a business as drawings in the case of a sole trader or partnership, or is available for distribution as dividends to shareholders in the case of a company, after maintaining the value of the capital of a business. Profit is not the same as an increase in the amount of money the business possesses. It is the result of applying certain accounting principles to the transactions of the business. These will be described in detail in the next chapter.

The basic format of a profit and loss account is as follows:

ABC
Profit and loss account for the year ended ...

	£	£
Sales		X
Less: cost of sales		X
Gross profit		X
Less: other costs and expenses:		
Selling and distribution costs	X	
Administrative expenses	X	
Interest payable on loans	X	
		X
Net profit		X

In the accounts of sole traders and partnerships the actual composition of each of the above groupings of costs would be shown. Selling and distribution costs include advertising expenditure, the wages of delivery-van drivers, motor expenses including petrol and repairs, etc. Administrative expenses usually comprise the salaries of office staff, rent and rates, light and heat, printing and stationery, telephone and postage, etc. The published final accounts of companies contain a classification of costs similar to that shown above.

The purpose and structure of balance sheets

The **balance sheet** is a list of the assets and liabilities, and capital, of a business at the end of a given accounting year. It therefore provides information about the resources and debts of the reporting entity. This enables users of accounts to evaluate its financial position, in particular whether the business is likely to be unable to pay its debts. The balance sheet is like a photograph of the financial state of affairs of a business at a specific point in time.

Balance sheets contain five groups of items, as follows.

1 **Fixed assets**
These are items not specifically bought for resale but to be used in the production or distribution of those goods normally sold by the business. Fixed assets are durable goods that usually last for several years, and are normally kept by a business for more than one accounting year. Examples of fixed assets include land and buildings, plant and machinery, motor vehicles, office equipment, furniture, fixtures and fittings.

2 **Current assets**
These are items that are normally kept by a business for less than one accounting year. Indeed, the composition of each type of current asset is usually continually changing. Examples include stocks, trade debtors, short-term investments, money in a bank cheque account and cash.

3 **Current liabilities**
These are debts owed by a business that are payable within one year (often considerably less) of the date of the balance sheet. Examples include trade creditors and bank overdrafts.

4 **Long-term liabilities**
These are debts owed by a business that are not due until after one year (often much longer) from the date of the balance sheet. Examples include loans and mortgages.

5 **Capital**
This refers to the amount of money invested in the business by the owner(s).

The structure of a balance sheet is shown in the diagram below. Note that the items shown in colour are subtotals or totals which should be shown on the balance sheet:

ABC
Balance sheet as at ...

Fixed assets
\+
(Current assets
– Current liabilities
= **Net current assets**)
=
Total assets less current liabilities
–
Long-term liabilities
=
Net assets
=
Capital

Learning Activity 9.1

Prepare a balance sheet listing your assets and liabilities, or those of your family. Use an appropriate method of classifying the assets and liabilities and show the relevant totals and subtotals.

The gross profit: stock and the cost of sales

The first stage in the determination of the profit for the year involves calculating the gross profit. It is usually carried out in the profit and loss account. However, this part of the profit and loss account is sometimes presented as a separate account referred to as the trading account.

The **gross profit** for a given period is computed by subtracting the cost of goods sold/cost of sales from the sales revenue. It is important to appreciate that the cost of goods sold is not usually the same as the amount of purchases. This is because most businesses will have purchased goods that are unsold at the end of the accounting period. This is referred to as **stock** or **inventory**.

A manufacturing business will have a number of different types of stocks. However, for simplicity the following exposition is confined to non-manufacturing businesses whose stock consists of goods purchased for resale that have not undergone any further processing by the entity.

The **cost of sales** is determined by taking the cost of goods in stock at the start of the period, adding to this the cost of goods purchased during the period, and subtracting the cost of goods unsold at the end of the period. The cost of sales is then deducted from the sales revenue to give the gross profit. This is illustrated in Example 9.1.

Example 9.1

S. Mann, whose accounting year ends on 30 April, buys and sells one type of product. On 1 May 20X8 there were 50 units in stock which had cost £100 each. During the subsequent accounting year he purchased a further 500 units at a cost of £100 each and sold 450 units at a price of £150 each. There were 100 units which cost £100 each that had not been sold at 30 April 20X9. You are required to compute the gross profit for the year.

S. Mann
Trading account for the year ended 30 April 20X9

Units		£	£
450	Sales revenue		67,500
	Less: Cost of goods sold:		
50	Stock of goods at 1 May 20X8	5,000	
500	*Add*: Goods purchased during the year	50,000	
550	Cost of goods available for sale	55,000	
100	*Less*: Stock of goods at 30 April 20X9	10,000	
450	Cost of sales		45,000
	Gross profit for the year		22,500

Note

1 The number of units is not usually shown in a trading account. They have been included in the above to demonstrate that the cost of sales relates to the number of units that were sold.

The preparation of final accounts

The trading account

The **trading account** is an account in the ledger and is thus a part of the double-entry system. It is used to ascertain the gross profit and is prepared by transferring the balances on the sales, purchases and returns accounts to the trading account. In addition, certain entries are required in respect of stock. These are as follows:

1 Stock at the start of the period:
   Debit trading account
   Credit stock account

2 Stock at the end of the period:
   Debit stock account
   Credit trading account

Note that the stock at the start of the period will be the stock at the end of the previous period. The ledger entries in respect of stocks are illustrated below using the data in Example 9.1. Prior to the preparation of the trading account the ledger will appear as follows:

Sales

			20X9		
			30 Apr	balance b/d	67,500

Purchases

20X9					
30 Apr	Balance b/d	50,000			

Stock

20X8					
30 Apr	Balance b/d	5,000			

The trading account will then be prepared as follows:

Sales

20X9			20X9		
30 Apr	Trading a/c	67,500	30 Apr	Balance b/d	67,500

Purchases

20X9			20X9		
30 Apr	Balance b/d	50,000	30 Apr	Trading a/c	50,000

Stock

20X8			20X9		
30 Apr	Balance b/d	5,000	30 Apr	Trading a/c	5,000
20X9					
30 Apr	Trading a/c	10,000			

S. Mann

Trading account for year ending 30 April 20X9

	£		£
Stock at 1 May 20X8	5,000	Sales	67,500
Purchases	50,000	Stock at 30 April 20X9	10,000
Gross profit c/d	22,500		
	77,500		77,500
		Gross profit b/d	22,500

Notes

1 The gross profit is the difference between the two sides of the trading account and must be brought down to the opposite side of the account.

2 No date columns are shown in the trading account since the date appears as part of the heading of the account.

3 When the trading account is prepared in account form the stock at the end of the year may be shown as either a credit entry or deducted on the debit side as shown below. This has the advantage of showing the cost of sales.

S. Mann

Trading account for the year ended 30 April 20X9

Opening stock	5,000	Sales	67,500
Add: Purchases	50,000		
	55,000		
Less: Closing stock	10,000		
Cost of sales	45,000		
Gross profit c/d	22,500		
	67,500		67,500
		Gross profit b/d	22,500

4 The trading account is an account in the ledger and thus part of the double-entry system. However, when it is prepared for submission to the management, the owner(s) of a business or the Inland Revenue, it is often presented vertically as shown at the start of Example 9.1.

5 No entries other than those shown above (and the correction of errors) should be made in a stock account. It is not a continuous record of the value of stock.

6 The debit balance in the stock account on 30 April 20X8 was the result of an entry identical to that on 30 April 20X9.

7 The stock shown in a trial balance will always be that at the end of the previous year (and thus the opening stock of the year to which the trial balance relates).

The profit and loss account

The profit and loss account is an account in the ledger and thus a part of the double-entry system. It is used to ascertain the **net profit** (or **loss**) for the year and is prepared in the same way as the trading account. That is, the balances on the income and expense accounts in the ledger are transferred to the profit and loss account by means of a double entry.

The balance sheet

The balance sheet is a list of the balances remaining in the ledger after the trading and profit and loss accounts have been prepared. In effect it is like a trial balance except that the balance sheet is presented using a different format. Note that the balances are not transferred to the balance sheet by means of a double entry.

In practice, and in examinations, it is usual to prepare final accounts from the information given in the trial balance. However, it is important to appreciate that the ledger entries described above also have to be done, although students are not normally expected to show them in their answer to examination questions.

An illustration of the preparation of final accounts, including the required ledger entries, is shown in Example 9.2.

Example 9.2

The following is the trial balance of A. Dillon at 31 March 20X0.

	Debit	*Credit*
	£	£
Capital		42,140
Drawings	13,600	
Loan from S. Rodd		10,000
Bank	5,800	
Cash	460	
Sales		88,400
Purchases	46,300	
Sales returns	5,700	
Purchases returns		3,100
Stock at 1 Apr 19X9	8,500	
Carriage inwards	2,400	
Carriage outwards	1,600	
Trade debtors	15,300	
Trade creditors		7,200
Motor vehicles	23,100	
Fixtures and fittings	12,400	
Wages and salaries	6,800	
Rent	4,100	
Light and heat	3,200	
Telephone and postage	1,700	
Discount allowed	830	
Discount received		950
	151,790	151,790

The stock at 31 March 20X0 was valued at £9,800. The loan from S. Rodd is repayable on 1 January 20X4.

You are required to prepare the trading and profit and loss accounts and a balance sheet.

Sales

Trading a/c	88,400	Balance b/d	88,400

Sales returns

Balance b/d	5,700	Trading a/c	5,700

Purchases

Balance b/d	46,300	Trading a/c	46,300

Purchases returns

Trading a/c	3,100	Balance b/d	3,100

Stock

Balance b/d	8,500	Trading a/c	8,500
Trading a/c	9,800		

Carriage inwards

Balance b/d	2,400	Trading a/c	2,400

Carriage outwards

Balance b/d	1,600	Profit and loss a/c	1,600

Wages and salaries

Balance b/d	6,800	Profit and loss a/c	6,800

Rent

Balance b/d	4,100	Profit and loss a/c	4,100

Light and heat

Balance b/d	3,200	Profit and loss a/c	3,200

Telephone and postage

Balance b/d	1,700	Profit and loss a/c	1,700

Discount allowed

Balance b/d	830	Profit and loss a/c	830

Discount received

Profit and loss a/c	950	Balance b/d	950

Drawings

Balance b/d	13,600	Capital	13,600

Capital

Drawings	13,600	Balance b/d	42,140
Balance c/d	49,660	Profit for year	21,120
	63,260		63,260
		Balance b/d	49,660

All other accounts contain only the balances shown in the trial balance.

A. Dillon
Trading and profit and loss accounts for the year ended 31 March 20X0

	£	£		£
Stock at 1 Apr 20X9		8,500	Sales	88,400
Purchases	46,300		*Less*: returns	5,700
Less: Returns	3,100			82,700
	43,200			
Add: Carriage inwards	2,400	45,600		
		54,100		
Less: Stock at 31 Mar 20X0		9,800		
Cost of sales		44,300		
Gross profit c/d		38,400		
		82,700		82,700
Carriage outwards		1,600	Gross profit b/d	38,400
Wages and salaries		6,800	Discount received	950
Rent		4,100		
Light and heat		3,200		
Telephone and postage		1,700		
Discount allowed		830		
Net profit c/d		21,120		
		39,350		39,350
Capital a/c		21,120	Net profit b/d	21,120

A. Dillon
Balance sheet as at 31 March 20X0

Credit	£	*Debit*	£	£
Capital		*Fixed assets*		
Balance at 1 Apr 20X9	42,140	Motor vehicles		23,100
Add: Profit for year	21,120	Fixtures and fittings		12,400
	63,260			35,500
Less: Drawings	13,600	*Current assets*		
Balance at 31 Mar 20X0	49,660	Stock	9,800	
Long-term liabilities		Debtors	15,300	
Loan from S. Rodd	10,000	Bank	5,800	
Current liabilities		Cash	460	
Creditors	7,200			31,360
	66,860			66,860

Notes

1 The gross profit is the difference between the two sides of the trading account and must be brought down to the opposite side of the profit and loss account.

2 The net profit is the difference between the two sides of the profit and loss account. This is brought down to the credit side of the profit and loss account and then transferred to the capital account by debiting the profit and loss account and crediting the capital account. The reason for this transfer is because the profit belongs to the owner and it increases the amount of capital he or she has invested in the business.

3 If the debit side of the profit and loss account exceeds the credit side this is shown as a net loss (carried down) on the credit side and debited to the capital account.

4 The balance on the drawings account at the end of the period must be transferred to the capital account.

5 Each of the transfers from the ledger accounts to the trading and profit and loss accounts should also be entered in the journal.

6 Notice that the debit balances remaining in the ledger after the profit and loss account has been prepared are shown on the right-hand side of the balance sheet and the credit balances on the left-hand side. This may seem inconsistent with the debit and credit sides of the ledger being on the left and right, respectively. However, it is a common form of presentation in accounting.

7 Like the trial balance, the total of each side of the balance sheet should be the same. That is, the total of the ledger accounts with debit balances should equal the total of the ledger accounts with credit balances. If this is not the case it indicates that an error has occurred in the preparation of the trading and profit and loss account (or the balance sheet).

8 The current assets in the balance sheet are shown in what is called their reverse order of liquidity. The latter refers to how easily assets can be turned into cash.

9 The current liabilities are sometimes shown on the balance sheet as a deduction from current assets.

10 The entries on the balance sheet in respect of capital are a summary of the capital account in the ledger.

11 Carriage inwards is added to the cost of purchases because it relates to the haulage costs of goods purchased. Carriage outwards is shown in the profit and loss account because it relates to the haulage costs of goods sold and is thus a selling and distribution expense.

When the trading and profit and loss account and balance sheet are presented to the owner(s) of a business and the Inland Revenue it is common to use a vertical format. This is illustrated next using the data in Example 9.2.

A. Dillon

Trading and profit and loss accounts for the year ending 31 March 20X0

	£	£	£
Sales			88,400
Less: Returns			5,700
			82,700
Less: Cost of sales:			
Stock at 1 Apr 20X9		8,500	
Add: Purchases	46,300		
Less: Returns	3,100		

	43,200	
Add: Carriage inwards	2,400	
	54,100	
Less: Stock at 31 Mar 20X0	9,800	
		44,300
Gross profit		38,400
Add: Discount received		950
		39,350
Less: Expenditure:		
Carriage outwards	1,600	
Wages and salaries	6,800	
Rent	4,100	
Light and heat	3,200	
Telephone and postage	1,700	
Discount allowed	830	18,230
Net profit for the year		21,120

Balance sheet as at 31 March 20X0

	£	£
Fixed assets		
Motor vehicles		23,100
Fixtures and fittings		12,400
		35,500
Current assets		
Stock	9,800	
Debtors	15,300	
Bank	5,800	
Cash	460	
	31,360	
Less: Current liabilities		
Creditors	7,200	
Net current assets		24,160
Total assets less current liabilities		59,660
Less: Long-term liabilities		
Loan from S. Rodd		10,000
Net assets		49,660
Capital		
Balance at 1 Apr 20X9		42,140
Add: Profit for year		21,120
		63,260
Less: Drawings		13,600
Balance at 31 Mar 20X0		49,660

Summary

Final accounts comprise a trading and profit and loss account, and balance sheet. These are prepared at the end of the accounting year after the trial balance has been completed. The trading and profit and loss accounts provide a summary of the results of a business's trading activities during a given accounting year. They show the gross and net profit or loss for the year, and enable users to evaluate the performance of the enterprise. The balance sheet is a list of the assets and liabilities (and capital) of a business at the end of a given accounting year. It enables users to evaluate the financial position of the enterprise, including whether it is likely to be able to pay its debts. In the balance sheet assets are classified as either fixed or current, and liabilities as either current or long term. The balance sheet also contains several useful subtotals comprising net current assets, total assets less current liabilities, and net assets.

The gross profit is the difference between the sales revenue and the cost of sales. The cost of sales is the amount of purchases as adjusted for the opening and closing stocks. The stock at the end of an accounting year has to be entered in the ledger by debiting a stock account and crediting the trading account. The trading and profit and loss accounts are then prepared by transferring the balances on the nominal accounts in the ledger to these accounts.

The balance sheet is a list of the balances remaining in the ledger after the trading and profit and loss accounts have been prepared. It is extracted in essentially the same way as a trial balance, but presented using a more formal layout to show the two groups of both assets and liabilities, and pertinent subtotals.

Key terms and concepts

Balance sheet (90)
capital (91)
cost of sales (92)
current assets (91)
current liabilities (91)
final accounts (90)
fixed assets (91)
gross profit (92)
inventory (92)
long-term liabilities (91)
loss (95)
net assets (91)
net current assets (91)
net profit (95)
profit (90)
profit and loss account (90)
stock (92)
total assets less current liabilities (91)
trading account (93)

Review questions

9.1 **a** Explain the purposes of a profit and loss account and a balance sheet.
b Describe the structure of each.

9.2 Explain the relevance of stocks of goods for resale in the determination of the gross profit.

9.3 Explain each of the entries in the following stock account:

Stock

Trading account	4,600	Trading account	4,600
Trading account	6300		

Exercises

An asterisk after the question number indicates that there is a suggested answer in the Appendix.

9.4* **Level I**

The following is the trial balance of R. Woods as at 30 September 20X6:

	Debit	*Credit*
	£	£
Stock 1 Oct 20X5	2,368	
Purchases	12,389	
Sales		18,922
Salaries and wages	3,862	
Rent and rates	504	
Insurance	78	
Motor expenses	664	
Printing and stationery	216	
Light and heat	166	
General expenses	314	
Premises	5,000	
Motor vehicles	1,800	
Fixtures and fittings	350	
Debtors	3,896	
Creditors		1,731
Cash at bank	482	
Drawings	1,200	
Capital		12,636
	33,289	33,289

The stock at 30 September 20X6 is valued at £2,946.

You are required to prepare a trading and profit and loss account for the year ended 30 September 20X6 and a balance sheet at that date.

9.5* **Level I**

On 31 December 20X3, the trial balance of Joytoys showed the following accounts and balances:

	Debit	*Credit*
	£	£
Bank	500	
Capital		75,000
Bank loan		22,000
Inventory	12,000	
Purchases	108,000	
Sales		167,000
Rent, rates and insurance	15,000	
Plant and machinery at cost	70,000	
Office furniture and fittings at cost	24,000	

continued

	Debit	*Credit*
	£	£
Discount allowed	1,600	
Bank interest	400	
Discount received		3,000
Wages and salaries	13,000	
Light and heat	9,000	
Drawings	10,000	
Returns outwards		4,000
Returns inwards	1,000	
Creditors		16,000
Debtors	22,500	
	287,000	287,000

You are given the following information:

1 The inventory at 31 December 20X3 was valued at £19,500.
2 The bank loan is repayable in 5 years' time.

You are required to prepare a trading and profit and loss account for the year ended 31 December 20X3, and a balance sheet at that date.

9.6* **Level I**

The following is the trial balance of A. Evans as at 30 June 20X2:

	Debit	*Credit*
	£	£
Capital		39,980
Drawings	14,760	
Loan—Solihull Bank		20,000
Leasehold premises	52,500	
Motor vehicles	13,650	
Investments	4,980	
Trade debtors	2,630	
Trade creditors		1,910
Cash	460	
Bank overdraft		3,620
Sales		81,640
Purchases	49,870	
Returns outwards		960
Returns inwards	840	
Carriage outwards	390	
Stock	5,610	
Rent and rates	1,420	
Light and heat	710	
Telephone and postage	540	
Printing and stationery	230	
Bank interest	140	
Interest received		620
	148,730	148,730

You are given the following additional information:

1 The stock at 30 June 20X2 has been valued at £4,920.
2 The bank loan is repayable on 1 June 20X5.

You are required to prepare a trading and profit and loss account for the year ended 30 June 20X2 and a balance sheet as at that date.

9.7 Level I

The following is the trial balance of J. Peters as at 30 September 20X0:

	Debit	*Credit*
	£	£
Capital		32,890
Drawings	5,200	
Loan from A. Drew		10,000
Cash	510	
Bank overdraft		1,720
Sales		45,600
Purchases	29,300	
Returns inwards	3,800	
Returns outwards		2,700
Carriage inwards	960	
Carriage outwards	820	
Trade debtors	7,390	
Trade creditors		4,620
Land and buildings	26,000	
Plant and machinery	13,500	
Listed investments	4,800	
Interest paid	1,200	
Interest received		450
Rent received		630
Stock	3,720	
Repairs to buildings	810	
Plant hire charges	360	
Bank charges	240	
	98,610	98,610

Further information:

1 The stock at 30 September 20X0 was valued at £4,580.
2 The loan from A. Drew is repayable on 1 January 20X7.

You are required to prepare a trading and profit and loss account for the year ended 30 September 20X0 and a balance sheet as at that date.

chapter 10

Accounting principles, concepts and policies

Learning objectives

After reading this chapter you should be able to:

1. explain the meaning of the key terms and concepts listed at the end of this chapter;
2. explain the nature of accounting principles, accounting concepts, measurement bases, accounting policies and estimation techniques;
3. explain the nature of the going concern assumption, the accruals concept and the matching principle, including their implications for the preparation of financial statements;
4. describe the objectives against which an entity should judge the appropriateness of accounting policies, i.e. relevance, reliability, comparability and understandability;
5. describe the constraints that an entity should take into account in judging the appropriateness of accounting policies;
6. describe the requirements of FRS18 with regard to the selection, review, changing and disclosure of accounting policies and estimation techniques.

Introduction

An appreciation of the conceptual and theoretical foundations of financial accounting is fundamental to the preparation, understanding and interpretation of final accounts/ financial statements. This can be described as a set of rules, principles, postulates, conventions and methods. In order to clarify these matters, in 1971 the Accounting Standards Steering Committee (ASSC or ASC) issued *Statement of Standard Accounting Practice 2—Disclosure of Accounting Policies* (SSAP2),[1] which described the conceptual foundations of accounting as comprising accounting concepts, accounting bases and accounting policies. In 1999 this was superseded by the *Statement of Principles for Financial Reporting* published by the Accounting Standards Board (ASB).[2] SSAP2 was then replaced by the ASB *Financial Reporting Standard 18—Accounting Policies* (FRS18)[3] in 2000.

One of the main aims of this chapter is to provide a summary of the relevant parts of FRS18. The more detailed *Statement of Principles for Financial Reporting* is dealt with in Chapter 31. This chapter also draws on parts of SSAP2 which, although it has now been officially withdrawn, provides some very precise, concise and thus more easily remembered definitions.

The nature of accounting principles

The most useful way of describing the nature of **accounting principles** is probably in terms of the contents of the *Statement of Principles for Financial Reporting.*[2] This comprises the following:

1. The objective of financial statements, as explained in Chapter 1.
2. The reporting entity, as explained in Chapter 2.
3. The qualitative characteristics of financial information, comprising relevance, reliability, comparability and understandability. These are explained below.
4. The elements of financial statements such as the nature of assets, liabilities, ownership interest, gains and losses. **Assets** are defined as 'rights or other access to future economic benefits controlled by an entity as a result of past transactions or events'. **Liabilities** are defined as 'obligations of an entity to transfer economic benefits as a result of past transactions or events'. **Ownership interest** is defined as 'the residual amount found by deducting all of the entity's liabilities from all of the entity's assets'. **Gains** are defined as 'increases in ownership interest not resulting from contributions from owners'. **Losses** are defined as 'decreases in ownership interest not resulting from distributions to owners'.
5. Recognition in financial statements which refers to 'depicting an item both in words and by a monetary amount'. This includes the accruals concept which is explained below.
6. Measurement in financial statements of the elements such as in terms of their historical cost. This includes the going concern assumption. Measurement bases and the going concern assumption are explained below.
7. Presentation of financial information such as in the form of a profit and loss account and balance sheet.
8. Accounting for interests in other entities, which is dealt with in Chapter 33.

Accounting principles and the *Statement of Principles for Financial Reporting* are explained in more detail in terms of a conceptual framework of accounting in Chapter 31.

Accounting concepts

Accounting concepts were defined in SSAP2 as 'broad basic assumptions which underlie the periodic financial accounts of business enterprises'.[1] FRS18 identifies two accounting concepts that it describes as being 'part of the bedrock of accounting' and playing 'a pervasive role in financial statements'. These comprise the going concern assumption and the accruals concept.

Going concern

The **going concern** assumption or hypothesis is described in FRS18 as follows: 'The information provided by financial statements is usually most relevant if prepared on the hypothesis that the entity is to continue in operational existence for the foreseeable future'.[3]

The implication of this is that assets will normally be valued, and shown in the balance sheet, at their historical cost. It is assumed that the entity will continue to operate over the remaining useful life of the fixed assets. Similarly, monetary assets and liabilities, such as debtors and creditors, are shown in the balance sheet at the amounts that will be received and paid in the ordinary course of business. However, if there is reason to believe that the entity will not be able to continue in business, the assets should be valued on a cessation basis; that is, at their net realizable value.

According to FRS18, 'financial statements are usually prepared on the basis that the reporting entity is a going concern because measures based on break-up values tend not to be relevant to users seeking to assess the entity's cash-generation ability and financial adaptability.'

FRS18 requires that 'an entity should prepare its financial statements on a going concern basis, unless

a the entity is being liquidated or has ceased trading, or

b the directors have no realistic alternative but to liquidate the entity or to cease trading,

in which circumstances the entity may, if appropriate, prepare its financial statements on a basis other than that of a going concern.'

Furthermore, FRS18 requires that 'when preparing financial statements, directors should assess whether there are significant doubts about an entity's ability to continue as a going concern.'

Accruals concept

According to FRS18, 'an entity should prepare its financial statements, except for cash flow information, on the accrual basis of accounting.'

The **accruals concept** is described in FRS18 as follows: 'The accrual basis of accounting requires the non-cash effects of transactions and other events to be reflected, as far as is possible, in the financial statements for the accounting period in which they occur, and not, for example, in the period in which any cash involved is received or paid.'[3]

This description of the accruals concept broadly corresponds with the first part of the definition given in SSAP2 which states that 'revenue and costs are accrued (that is, recognised as they are earned or incurred, not as money is received or paid)'.[1] The so-called 'non-cash effects of transactions and other events' being reflected in 'the accounting period in which they occur' essentially corresponds to revenue and costs being 'recognised as they are earned or incurred'. In most instances this refers to the accounting period in which the goods or services physically pass from the seller to the buyer.

In the case of sales revenue, this notion has traditionally been referred to as the **revenue recognition/realization concept**. It relates to the assumption that a sale is deemed to have taken place at that point in time at which the goods are delivered or services provided, and not when the proceeds of sale are received. In practice this is normally also the date of the invoice. However, where the invoice is rendered some time after the date of delivery, the sale is deemed to have taken place on the date of delivery and not the date of the invoice. This is referred to in the above SSAP2 definition of the accruals concept as being the point in time at which revenue is '*earned*'.

FRS18 contains a slightly different approach to realization which refers to the realization of profits rather than just sales revenue. It states that 'in preparing financial statements, an entity will have regard to requirements in companies legislation that only profits realised at the balance sheet date should be included in the profit and loss account .... It is generally accepted that profits shall be treated as realised, for these purposes, only when realised in the form either of cash or of other assets the ultimate cash realisation of which can be assessed with reasonable certainty.'

The accruals concept also relates to the assumption that costs should be recognized as arising when they occur, and not as money is paid. That is, goods for resale are deemed to have been purchased on the date they are received. This is referred to in the above SSAP2 definition of the accruals concept as being the point in time at which costs are '*incurred*'. Similarly services consumed for which no invoice has been received at the end of an accounting year (e.g. electricity, gas, telephone) are treated as a cost for that year, and the amount due is treated as a liability. These are referred to as accrued expenses. In contrast, services paid for in advance (e.g. rent, insurance, road tax, local government taxes) that have not been received at the end of an accounting year are treated as a cost of the following accounting year, and thus carried forward as an asset at the end of the current year. These are referred to as prepaid expenses or prepayments. Accrued and prepaid expenses are dealt with in more depth in a later chapter.

The accruals concept has traditionally been taken also to include the matching principle (alternatively, concept or process). This is reflected in that part of the definition of the accruals concept in SSAP2 not discussed thus far. According to SSAP2, under the accruals concept, 'revenue and costs are accrued (that is, recognised as they are earned or incurred, not as money is received or paid), matched with one another so far as their relationship can be established or justifiably assumed, and dealt with in the profit and loss account of the period to which they relate.'[1]

As can be seen in the above definition, FRS18 takes a slightly different approach to the accruals concept which does not focus on when a relationship can be established or justifiably assumed. Moreover, the *Statement of Principles for Financial Reporting*[2] does not use the notion of matching as the main driver of the recognition process which focuses on the recognition of assets and liabilities and gains and losses, rather than the matching of revenues and costs. However, matching is both implicit and explicit in legislation and a number of accounting standards such as SSAP9 which is described below.

The **matching** principle refers to the assumption that in the measurement of profit, costs should be set against the revenue which they generate at the point in time when this arises. A classic example of the application of the matching principle is stock. Where goods are bought in one accounting year but sold in the next, their cost is carried forward as stock at the end of the year and set against the proceeds of sale in the accounting year in which it occurs.

This is expounded in *SSAP9—Stocks and Long Term Contracts*,[4] as follows: 'The determination of profit for an accounting year requires the matching of costs with related revenues. (Where costs) have been incurred in the expectation of future revenue, and when this will not arise until a later year it is appropriate to carry forward this cost to be matched with the revenue when it arises; the applicable concept is the matching of cost and revenue in the year in which the revenue arises rather than in the year in which the cost is incurred.'

In terms of the calculation of the gross profit in the trading account, this process of carrying forward costs takes the form of the computation of the cost of sales. The cost is carried forward by being deducted from purchases in the form of the stock at the end of the year. It is brought forward to the following year in the form of the opening stock which is matched against the proceeds of sale by virtue of its being included in the cost of sales.

A more theoretical view of the matching principle is that it refers to ascertaining profit on the basis of a cause and effect relationship. Costs cause or give rise to certain effects which take the form of revenue. Matching is thus the determination of profit by attributing specific causes to particular effects at the point in time at which the effects occur.

The accruals concept and matching principle can be illustrated vividly by a simplified example. Suppose a business only had the following transactions:

15 Jan	purchased goods costing £100 on credit
15 Feb	paid for the goods purchased on 15 January
15 Mar	sold on credit for £150 the goods purchased on 15 January
15 Apr	received payment for the goods sold on 15 March

The accruals (and matching) concept dictates that:

1 The cost of the goods was *incurred* in January.

2 The sales revenue was *earned* in March.

3 There was no profit or loss in January, February or April. The profit of £50 arose in March, the cost of the goods being carried forward as stock at the end of January and February.

Unfortunately the application of the accruals concept in general, and the revenue recognition concept and matching principle in particular, is not always as simple as implied above. Although the contents of this section thus far would usually be sufficient to answer most examination questions at this level, students might be expected to demonstrate an awareness of its relevance to current issues. There have recently been several high profile cases of large companies throughout the world where abuses of the revenue recognition and matching principles has resulted in the overstating of profits, and in some cases, corporate bankruptcy. Moreover, standard-setting bodies have been reviewing revenue recognition rules for some years.

Many of the issues concerning revenue recognition arise where the revenue received in one accounting year relates to goods or services that the business will provide in the next, or future, accounting year(s). Examples include revenue from the installation of security and IT systems, different forms of prepayments associated with various mobile phone and other telecommunication services including television, extended warranties and maintenance agreements, etc. The latter provides a good illustration of the general issues and underlying principles.

When consumers purchase electrical goods they are often encouraged to buy an extended warranty. The consumer pays a one-off premium at the time of purchase, and the seller undertakes to maintain and/or repair the item for some fixed future period of often three or five years. The customer is invoiced at the time of sale. Thus applying the revenue recognition concept, as described above, might suggest that the premium would be treated as earned/realized in the profit and loss account in the year of sale, which is a practice that some companies have sought to adopt in their accounts.

However, this does not accord with the matching principle. The costs of the repairs that the seller is obliged to make under the extended warranty will be incurred over several future accounting years, and thus the matching principle dictates that the premium received should be spread over this period. This is referred to as **deferred income**, and is discussed further in the chapter on the accounts of clubs.

This is not the end of the problem. The issue now arises as to how much of the premium should be recognized as revenue in each of the future accounting years. The repairs to the item in question are likely to be more common and more costly as the item becomes older. A proper matching would thus require a higher proportion of the premium to be recognized in each of the later years. The precise proportion to be recognized in each year will thus be highly subjective/arbitrary, which is where the further possibility of abuse arises.

Furthermore, the extended warranty illustration does not highlight another very subjective decision. Extended warranties cover a fixed number of years, whereas other goods and services of a similar nature often do not relate to a given period of time. In applying the matching principle it will thus be necessary to determine over how many years the income should be recognized. This again gives scope for revenue manipulation.

Similar issues arise in deciding whether expenditure should be treated as capital (i.e. on fixed assets) or revenue (i.e. expenses), and in the case of capital expenditure, over what period to write off the asset and how much should be charged to each year. This is discussed further in the next chapter.

The nature of measurement bases

Measurement bases are defined in FRS18 as: 'those monetary attributes of the elements of financial statements—assets, liabilities, gains, losses and changes to shareholders' funds—that are reflected in financial statements.

Where a business holds an asset that was purchased, the asset will have a number of qualities that may be expressed in terms of 'values'. As well as the amount for which it was acquired, it will have a current net realisable value and, if it is capable of being replaced, it will have a current replacement cost. These are examples of monetary attributes of the asset. Other examples arise when different monetary attributes are combined in a formula. For example, in a historical cost system stocks are stated at the lower of historical cost and net realisable value. Similarly, in a current value measurement system, the current value of an asset, using the value to the business rule, is the lower of replacement cost and recoverable amount (which is itself the higher of value in use and net realisable value).

Monetary attributes fall into two broad categories—those that reflect current values and those that reflect historical values. Some monetary attributes will be suitable for use in financial statements only in conjunction with others. A monetary attribute, or combination of attributes, that may be reflected in financial statements is called a measurement basis.'[3]

The nature of accounting policies

Accounting policies are defined in FRS18 as: 'those principles, bases, conventions, rules and practices applied by an entity that specify how the effects of transactions and other events are to be reflected in its financial statements through

1 recognising,

2 selecting measurement bases for, and

3 presenting

assets, liabilities, gains, losses and changes to shareholders' funds. Accounting policies do not include estimation techniques.

Accounting policies define the process whereby transactions and other events are reflected in financial statements. For example, an accounting policy for a particular type of expenditure may specify whether an asset or a loss is to be recognised; the basis on which it is to be measured; and where in the profit and loss account or balance sheet it is to be presented.'[3]

SSAP2 provided a more concise definition of accounting policies as being: 'the specific accounting bases judged by business enterprises to be the most appropriate to their circumstances and adopted by them for the purpose of preparing their financial accounts.'[1]

Some simple examples of accounting policies are the choice between treating expenditure on items such as tools and equipment, and development expenditure, as expenses in the profit and loss account or as fixed assets in the balance sheet. Another example given in FRS18 is whether to include certain expenditure as a part of the cost of sales or alternatively under the heading of administrative expenses in the profit and loss account. A similar example is whether to show investments in the balance sheet as either a fixed asset or a current asset.

Accounting policies are dealt with in more detail later. The most important part of this topic at this stage comprises the objectives and constraints in selecting accounting policies discussed below.

The nature of estimation techniques

Estimation techniques are defined in FRS18 as: 'the methods adopted by an entity to arrive at estimated monetary amounts, corresponding to the measurement bases selected, for assets, liabilities, gains, losses and changes to shareholders' funds.

Estimation techniques implement the measurement aspects of accounting policies. An accounting policy will specify the basis on which an item is to be measured; where there is uncertainty over the monetary amount corresponding to that basis, the amount will be arrived at by using an estimation technique.

Estimation techniques include, for example:

a methods of depreciation, such as straight-line and reducing balance, applied in the context of a particular measurement basis, used to estimate the proportion of the economic benefits of a tangible fixed asset consumed in a period;

b different methods used to estimate the proportion of trade debts that will not be recovered, particularly where such methods consider a population as a whole rather than individual balances.'[3]

These methods used to arrive at estimates, including the above examples, are dealt with in detail in subsequent chapters, particularly the next two chapters.

Objectives and constraints in selecting accounting policies

According to FRS18, 'the objectives against which an entity should judge the appropriateness of accounting policies to its particular circumstances are:

a relevance;

b reliability;

c comparability; and

d understandability.

The constraints that an entity should take into account in judging the appropriateness of accounting policies to its particular circumstances are:

a the need to balance the different objectives set out above; and

b the need to balance the cost of providing information with the likely benefit of such information to users of the entity's financial statements.'[3]

These are described below.

Relevance

Relevance is explained in FRS18 as follows: 'Financial information is relevant if it has the ability to influence the economic decisions of users and is provided in time to influence those decisions. Relevant information possesses either predictive or confirmatory value or both.'[3]

Reliability

Reliability is explained in FRS18 as follows: 'Financial information is reliable if:

a it can be depended upon by users to represent faithfully what it either purports to represent or could reasonably be expected to represent, and therefore reflects the substance of the transactions and other events that have taken place;

b it is free from deliberate or systematic bias (i.e. it is neutral);

c it is free from material error;

d it is complete within the bounds of materiality; and

e under conditions of uncertainty, it has been prudently prepared (i.e. a degree of caution has been applied in exercising judgement and making the necessary estimates).

Appropriate accounting policies will result in financial information being presented that is reliable. They will present transactions and other events in a way that reflects their substance. A transaction or other event is faithfully represented in financial statements if the way in which it is recognised, measured and presented in those statements corresponds closely to the effect of that transaction or event.

Often there is uncertainty, either about the existence of assets, liabilities, gains, losses and changes to shareholders' funds, or about the amount at which they should be measured. Prudence requires that accounting policies take account of such uncertainty in recognising and measuring those assets, liabilities, gains, losses and changes to shareholders' funds. In conditions of uncertainty, appropriate accounting policies will require more confirmatory evidence about the existence of an asset or gain than about the existence of a liability or loss, and a greater reliability of measurement for assets and gains than for liabilities and losses.'[3]

Comparability

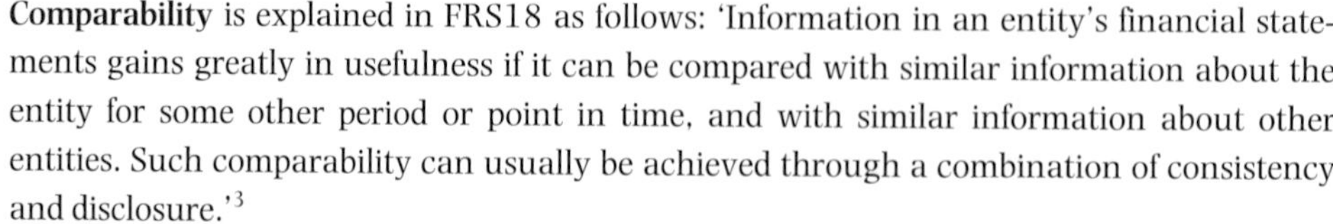

Comparability is explained in FRS18 as follows: 'Information in an entity's financial statements gains greatly in usefulness if it can be compared with similar information about the entity for some other period or point in time, and with similar information about other entities. Such comparability can usually be achieved through a combination of consistency and disclosure.'[3]

SSAP2 provided a very precise definition of **consistency** as referring to the 'consistency of accounting treatment of like items within each accounting period and from one period to the next.'[1] For example, if the purchase of a certain type of tool or item of equipment is treated as a fixed asset (rather than an expense), then similar tools and equipment bought in the same period should be treated in the same way, i.e. as a fixed asset. Furthermore, these tools and equipment should also be treated as fixed assets in subsequent years.

Understandability

Understandability is explained in FRS18 as follows: 'Information provided by financial statements needs to be capable of being understood by users having a reasonable knowledge of business and economic activities and accounting and a willingness to study with reasonable diligence the information provided.'[3]

Balancing the different objectives

According to FRS18, 'there can be tensions between the different objectives set out above. In particular, sometimes the accounting policy that is most relevant to a particular entity's circumstances is not the most reliable, and vice versa. In such circumstances, the most appropriate accounting policy will usually be that which is the most relevant of those that are reliable.

There can also be tension between two aspects of reliability—neutrality and prudence. Whilst neutrality involves freedom from deliberate or systematic bias, prudence is a potentially biased concept that seeks to ensure that, under conditions of uncertainty, gains and assets are not overstated and losses and liabilities are not understated. This tension exists only where there is uncertainty, because it is only then that prudence needs to be exercised. In the selection of accounting policies, the competing demands of neutrality and prudence are reconciled by finding a balance that ensures that the deliberate and systematic understatement of assets and gains and overstatement of liabilities and losses do not occur.'[3]

The disclosure of accounting policies and estimation techniques

The following are extracts from FRS18 relating to the selection, review, changing and disclosure of accounting policies and estimation techniques.[3]

'An entity should adopt accounting policies that enable its financial statements to give a true and fair view. Those accounting policies should be consistent with the requirements of accounting standards, Urgent Issues Task Force (UITF) Abstracts and companies legislation.

Where it is necessary to choose between accounting policies that satisfy the conditions above, an entity should select whichever of those accounting policies is judged by the entity to be most appropriate to its particular circumstances for the purpose of give a true and fair view.

If in exceptional circumstances compliance with the requirements of an accounting standard or UITF Abstract is inconsistent with the requirement to give a true and fair view, the requirements of the accounting standard or UITF Abstract should be departed from to the extent necessary to give a true and fair view. In such circumstances, the disclosures set out later below should be provided.

An entity's accounting policies should be reviewed regularly to ensure that they remain the most appropriate to its particular circumstances for the purpose of giving a true and fair view. However, in judging whether a new policy is more appropriate than the existing policy, an entity will give due weight to the impact on comparability.

Where estimation techniques are required to enable the accounting policies adopted to be applied, an entity should select estimation techniques that enable its financial statements to give a true and fair view and are consistent with the requirements of accounting standards, UITF Abstracts and companies legislation.

Where it is necessary to choose between estimation techniques that satisfy the conditions above, an entity should select whichever of those estimation techniques is judged by the entity to be most appropriate to its particular circumstances for the purpose of giving a true and fair view.

The following information should be disclosed in the financial statements:

a a description of each of the accounting policies that is material in the context of the entity's financial statements

b a description of those estimation techniques adopted that are significant

c details of any changes to the accounting policies that were followed in preparing financial statements for the preceding period, including:
 i a brief explanation of why each new accounting policy is thought more appropriate;
 ii where practicable, the effect of a prior period adjustment on the results for the preceding period, in accordance with FRS 3 'Reporting Financial Performance'; and
 iii where practicable, an indication of the effect of a change in accounting policy on the results for the current period.

Where it is not practicable to make the disclosures described in ii or iii above, that fact, together with the reasons, should be stated

d where the effect of a change to an estimation technique is material, a description of the change and, where practicable, the effect on the results for the current period.

For any material departure from the requirements of an accounting standard, a UITF Abstract or companies legislation, particulars of the departure, the reasons for it and its effect should be disclosed. The information disclosed should include:

a a clear and unambiguous statement that there has been a departure from the requirements of an accounting standard, a UITF Abstract or companies legislation, as the case may be, and that the departure is necessary to give a true and fair view

b a statement of the treatment that the accounting standard, UITF Abstract or companies legislation would normally require in the circumstances and a description of the treatment actually adopted

c a statement of why the treatment prescribed would not give a true and fair view

d a description of how the position shown in the financial statements is different as a result of the departure, normally with quantification, except where

i quantification is already evident in the financial statements themselves; or

ii the effect cannot reasonably be quantified, in which case the directors should explain the circumstances.

Where a departure continues in subsequent financial statements, the disclosures should be made in all such subsequent statements, and should include corresponding amounts for the previous year. Where a departure affects only the corresponding amounts, the disclosures should be given for those corresponding amounts.'[3]

Summary

The conceptual/theoretical framework of accounting may be described as essentially being a set of accounting principles. These are said to comprise the objective of financial statements, the reporting entity, the qualitative characteristics of financial information, the elements of financial statements, recognition in financial statements, measurement in financial statements, presentation of financial information and accounting for interests in other entities.

Recognition and measurement in financial statements include two accounting concepts that have been described as 'part of the bedrock of accounting', namely the accruals concept and going concern assumption, respectively. Accounting concepts can be defined as broad basic assumptions which underlie the periodic financial accounts of business enterprises.

The going concern assumption is described as follows: the information provided by financial statements is usually most relevant if prepared on the hypothesis that the entity is to continue in operational existence for the foreseeable future. The implication of this is that assets will normally be valued, and shown in the balance sheet, at their historical cost.

The accruals concept is described as follows: the non-cash effects of transactions and other events should be reflected, as far as is possible, in the financial statements for the accounting period in which they occur, and not, for example, in the period in which any cash involved is received or paid. It has also been defined as referring to the notion that revenue and costs are accrued (that is, recognized as they are earned or incurred, not as money is received or paid). In most instances this refers to the accounting period in which the goods or services physically pass from the seller to the buyer. The accruals concept has traditionally been taken to also include the matching principle. This refers to the assumption that in the measurement of profit, costs should be set against the revenue which they generate at the point in time when this arises. A classic example of the application of the matching principle is stock.

The preparation of financial statements also involves selecting a measurement basis, accounting policies and estimation techniques. Measurement bases are defined as those monetary attributes of the elements of financial statements—assets, liabilities, gains, losses and changes to shareholders' funds—that are reflected in financial statements. Accounting policies are defined as those principles, bases, conventions, rules and practices applied by an entity that specify how the effects of transactions and other events are to be reflected in its financial statements through recognizing, selecting measurement bases for, and presenting assets, liabilities, gains, losses and changes to shareholders' funds. Estimation techniques are defined as the methods adopted by an entity to arrive at estimated monetary amounts, corresponding to the measurement bases selected, for assets, liabilities, gains, losses and changes to shareholders' funds.

The objectives against which an entity should judge the appropriateness of accounting policies to its particular circumstances are relevance, reliability, comparability and understandability. Financial information is relevant if it has the ability to influence the economic decisions of users and is provided in time to influence those decisions. Relevant information possesses either predictive or confirmatory value or both. Financial information is reliable if: it can be depended upon by users to represent faithfully what it either purports to represent or could reasonably be expected to represent, and therefore reflects the substance of the transactions and other events that have taken place; it is free from deliberate or systematic bias (i.e. it is neutral); it is free from material error; it is complete within the bounds of materiality; and under conditions of uncertainty, it has been prudently prepared (i.e. a degree of caution has been applied in exercising judgement and making the necessary estimates).

Comparability is described as follows: information in an entity's financial statements gains greatly in usefulness if it can be compared with similar information about the entity for some other period or point in time, and with similar information about other entities. Such comparability can usually be achieved through a combination of consistency and disclosure. Understandability is described as follows: information provided by financial statements needs to be capable of being understood by users having a reasonable knowledge of business and economic activities and accounting and a willingness to study with reasonable diligence the information provided.

There are also two constraints that an entity should take into account in judging the appropriateness of accounting policies to its particular circumstances, which are the need to balance the different objectives set out above, and the need to balance the cost of providing information with the likely benefit of such information to users of the entity's financial statements.

There are detailed regulations relating to the selection, review, changing and disclosure of accounting policies and estimation techniques, particularly where there has been a material departure from the requirements of an accounting standard, UITF Abstract or companies legislation.

Key terms and concepts

Accounting concepts (106)
accounting policies (109)
accounting principles (105)
accruals concept (106)
assets (105)
comparability (112)
consistency (112)
deferred income (109)
estimation techniques (110)
gains (105)
going concern (106)
liabilities (105)
losses (105)
matching (107)
measurement bases (109)
ownership interest (105)
relevance (111)
reliability (111)
revenue recognition or realization concept (107)
understandability (112)

References

1. Accounting Standards Steering Committee (1971). *Statement of Standard Accounting Practice 2—Disclosure of Accounting Policies* (ICAEW).
2. Accounting Standards Board (1999). *Statement of Principles for Financial Reporting* (ASB).
3. Accounting Standards Board (2000). *Financial Reporting Standard 18—Accounting Policies* (ASB).
4. Accounting Standards Committee (1988). *Statement of Standard Accounting Practice 9—Stocks and Long Term Contracts* (ICAEW).

Review questions

An asterisk after the question number indicates that there is a suggested answer in the Appendix.

10.1 Describe the nature of accounting principles.

10.2 Define each of the following:

a assets
b liabilities
c ownership interest
d gains
e losses.

10.3 **a** Describe the nature of accounting concepts.
b Explain the nature of the going concern assumption and its implications for the preparation of financial statements.

10.4 Explain the nature of the accruals concept and the matching principle. Give an example of the application of each.

10.5 Describe the nature of each of the following:

a measurement bases
b accounting policies
c estimation techniques.

Give one example of each.

10.6* Explain the nature of 'the objectives against which an entity should judge the appropriateness of accounting policies' given in *FRS18—Accounting Policies*.

10.7 Explain the relevance of prudence to the appropriateness of accounting policies.

10.8 According to *FRS18—Accounting Policies*, there can be tensions between the objectives against which an entity should judge the appropriateness of accounting policies. Explain the nature of these 'tensions' and how they can be balanced or reconciled.

10.9 Describe the information that should be disclosed in financial statements relating to an entity's accounting policies and estimation techniques.

10.10 Describe the information that should be disclosed where an entity's financial statements contain a material departure from the requirements of an accounting standard, UITF Abstract or companies legislation.

10.11 An acquaintance of yours, H. Gee, has recently set up in business for the first time as a general dealer. The majority of his sales will be on credit to trade buyers but he will sell some goods to the public for cash. He is not sure at which point of the business cycle he can regard his cash and credit sales to have taken place.

After seeking guidance on this matter from his friends, he is thoroughly confused by the conflicting advice he has received. Samples of the advice he has been given include:

The sale takes place when:

1 You have bought goods which you know you should be able to sell easily.
2 The customer places the order.
3 You deliver the goods to the customer.
4 You invoice the goods to the customer.
5 The customer pays for the goods.
6 The customer's cheque has been cleared by the bank.

He now asks you to clarify the position for him.

Required:

a Write notes for Gee, setting out, in as easily understood a manner as possible, the accounting conventions and principles which should generally be followed when recognizing sales revenue.

b Examine each of the statements 1–6 above and advise Gee (stating your reasons) whether the method advocated is appropriate to the particular circumstances of his business. (ACCA)

10.12 On 20 December 20X7 your client paid £10,000 for an advertising campaign. The advertisements will be heard on local radio stations between 1 January and 31 January 20X8. Your client believes that as a result sales will increase by 60 per cent in 20X8 (over 20X7 levels) and by 40 per cent in 20X9 (over 20X7 levels). There will be no further benefits.

Required:

Write a memorandum to your client explaining your views on how this item should be treated in the accounts for the three years 20X7 to 20X9. Your answer should include explicit reference to at least *three* relevant traditional accounting conventions, and to the requirements of *two* classes of user of published financial accounts. (ACCA)

10.13 'If a business invests in shares, and the market value of the shares increases above cost then, until and unless the business sells them, no profit is made. If the business invests in stock for resale, and the market value of the stock falls below cost then the loss is recognized even though no sale has taken place.'

'If a business undertakes an intensive advertising campaign which will probably result in increased sales (and profit) in succeeding years it will nevertheless usually write off the cost of the campaign in the year in which it is incurred.'

Required:

Explain the reasoning behind the application of accounting principles in situations such as these and discuss the effect on the usefulness of accounting information in relation to users' needs. (ACCA)

10.14 Classify each of the following as either a measurement basis, accounting policy or estimation technique, and explain your reasons:

a Advertising expenditure that has been treated as a fixed asset rather than an expense;

b The use of the straight line method of depreciation;

c The valuation of an asset at the lower of cost or net realizable value;

d A provision for bad debts of 5 per cent of the amount of trade debtors at the end of the accounting period;

e Land and buildings have been shown on the balance sheet at their current replacement cost;

f Listed investments have been shown on the balance sheet as a current asset;

g The historical cost of stocks has been ascertained by taking a weighted average of the prices paid during the accounting period.

10.15 One of your clients is a beef farmer. She informs you that the price of beef has fallen dramatically over the past few months and that she expects it to fall even further over the next three months. She therefore argues that the prudence principle should be applied to the valuation of her beef herd at the lower of cost or net realizable value; in this case at the latter value. She further asserts that this treatment is reasonable on the grounds that it will reduce her profit for tax purposes by the loss in value of her herd.

One of your colleagues has advised you that this may be a misinterpretation of the prudence principle and could contravene the neutrality principle. Discuss.

10.16 Nesales plc, a large food manufacturer, has purchased the brand name of a chocolate bar from one of its competitors for £5 million. It proposes to include this on its balance sheet as a fixed asset.

Cadberry plc, another large food and soft drinks manufacturer, has spent £5 million this year on promoting a new brand of chocolate bar. It proposes to include this on its balance sheet as a fixed asset.

You are required to discuss whether the proposed accounting treatment of these two items is likely to achieve 'the objectives against which an entity should judge the appropriateness of accounting policies to its particular circumstances' given in *FRS18—Accounting Policies*.

10.17 Minisoft plc, a manufacturer of computer software, has spent £10 million in the current accounting year on staff recruitment, training and development. It proposes to include this on its balance sheet as a fixed asset. Discuss.

Depreciation and fixed assets

Learning objectives

After reading this chapter you should be able to:

1. explain the meaning of the key terms and concepts listed at the end of this chapter;
2. distinguish between capital expenditure and revenue expenditure;
3. describe the nature, recognition and valuation of fixed assets including intangible fixed assets such as goodwill and development expenditure;
4. apply the criteria relating to the nature of fixed assets to specific transactions and items to determine the most appropriate accounting treatment;
5. discuss the nature of depreciation;
6. describe the straight line, reducing balance and sum of the years' digits methods of depreciation including the resulting pattern of charges to the profit and loss account over an asset's useful life, and the circumstances in which each might be the most appropriate;
7. compute the amount of depreciation using the methods in item 6, and show the relevant entries in the journal, ledger, profit and loss account and balance sheet;
8. compute the depreciation on an asset in the years of acquisition and disposal, and the profit or loss on disposal; and show the relevant entries in the journal, ledger, profit and loss account, and balance sheet;
9. describe the permissible accounting treatments for research and development expenditure including the circumstances in which each may be acceptable;
10. show the accounting entries for research and development expenditure in financial statements including the information that must be disclosed in the notes to the accounts.

The nature and types of fixed assets

Fixed assets are items not specifically bought for resale but to be used in the production or distribution of those goods normally sold by the business. They are durable goods that usually last for several years, and are normally kept by a business for more than one accounting year. However, expenditure on such items is only regarded as a fixed asset if it is of a material amount. The Accounting Standards Committee (ASC) defines a **fixed asset** as 'an asset that: (a) is held by an enterprise for use in the production or supply of goods and services, for rental to others, or for administrative purposes and may include items held for the maintenance or repair of such assets; (b) has been acquired or constructed with the intention of being used on a continuing basis; and (c) is not intended for sale in the ordinary course of a business'. A slightly different way of expressing the criteria for what constitutes a fixed asset is that the expenditure must be expected to generate revenue over a number of future years. This is arguably the most important criterion in determining whether expenditure is to be classified as a fixed asset.

Money spent on fixed assets is referred to as **capital expenditure**. All other costs and expenses are referred to as **revenue expenditure**. The latter are entered in the profit and loss account of the year in which the costs are incurred.

Fixed assets are classified as either tangible or intangible. *Financial Reporting Standard 15—Tangible Fixed Assets*[1] defines **tangible fixed assets** as 'assets that have physical substance and are held for use in the production or supply of goods or services, for rental to others, or for administrative purposes on a continuing basis in the reporting entity's activities.' Examples of tangible fixed assets include land and buildings; plant and machinery; motor vehicles; furniture, fixtures and fittings; office equipment (such as computers); and loose tools. Tools that are only expected to last for less than one year are referred to as consumable tools, and treated as revenue expenditure.

Intangible assets are defined by the Accounting Standards Board (ASB) as 'non-financial fixed assets that do not have physical substance but are identifiable and are controlled by the entity through custody or legal rights'. Examples include goodwill, patents, trade marks and development expenditure. Non-financial, also called non-monetary, assets are assets other than cash, money in a bank cheque or deposit account, investments, and amounts receivable such as debtors.

Goodwill usually arises in the balance sheet because at some time in the past the business has taken over, or been formed from, another business. The figure shown in the balance sheet for goodwill is the difference between the amount paid for that business and the value of its net assets. Goodwill is sometimes said to represent the potential future profits or sales arising from a business's reputation and the continuing patronage of existing customers. However, it is much more than this, in that it represents the advantages which are gained from taking over an existing business rather than building up a new business from scratch (e.g. not having to recruit staff, find premises or identify suppliers). Goodwill is discussed in depth in Chapter 25.

Investments are also frequently included under the heading of fixed assets. These may consist of shares and/or debentures that are listed (quoted) on a stock exchange and unlisted securities. Investments should only be classified as a fixed asset where they are held on a long-term basis for the purpose of generating income. If this is not the case, investments should be treated as a current asset.

The recognition and valuation of fixed assets

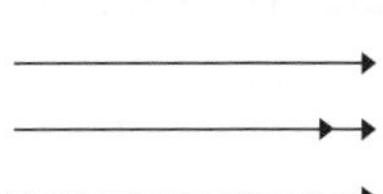

The term 'valuation' refers to the amount at which assets are shown in the balance sheet. In historical cost accounting fixed assets are valued at their historical cost less the **aggregate/accumulated depreciation** from the date of acquisition to the date of the balance sheet. The resulting figure is known as the **written down value** (WDV), net **book value** or net **carrying amount**. Depreciation is discussed below.

Historical cost refers to the purchase price excluding value added tax. The historical cost of a fixed asset may also include a number of additional costs. The cost of land and buildings, for example, may include legal expenses, and the cost of any subsequent extensions and improvements (but not repairs and renewals). Similarly, the cost of machinery is taken to include delivery charges and installation expenses. However, the costs of any extended warranty, maintenance agreement and replacement/spare parts (for future use) that have been included in the purchase price must be removed. Similarly, the cost of vehicles must exclude the first year's road tax and fuel where these have been included in the purchase price.

The Companies Acts and FRS15 allow companies to revalue their tangible fixed assets and show them in the balance sheet at current values rather than historical cost. This is most common in the case of land and buildings that were acquired several years ago, and thus their current market value greatly exceeds the historical cost. According to FRS15, 'the **current value** of a tangible fixed asset to the business is the lower of replacement cost and recoverable amount.' The **recoverable amount** is 'the higher of net realizable value and value in use. Where a tangible fixed asset is revalued all tangible fixed assets of the same class should be revalued.'[1] If a company revalues one or more classes of tangible fixed assets it should continue to adopt the same policy in future years. That is, FRS15 does not allow one-off revaluations. There must be regular revaluations. In the case of land and buildings, FRS15 requires 'a full valuation at least every five years and an interim valuation in year 3. Interim valuations in years 1, 2 and 4 should be carried out where it is likely that there has been a material change in value.'[1]

For the sake of simplicity the remainder of this chapter assumes that fixed assets are valued at historical cost. Revaluations are discussed further in Chapter 25 on changes in partnerships and Chapter 27 on company accounts.

The nature of depreciation

The purchase of a fixed asset occurs in one year but the revenue generated from its use normally arises over a number of years. This is referred to as its useful economic life. If the cost of fixed assets were treated as an expense in the profit and loss account in the year of purchase this would probably result in an excessive loss in that year, and excessive profits in the years in which the revenue arose. This gives a misleading view of the profits and losses of each year and distorts comparisons over time. Thus, the cost of a fixed asset is not treated as an expense in the year of purchase but rather carried forward and written off to the profit and loss account over the useful economic life of the asset in the form of depreciation. The part of the cost of an asset which is 'used up' or 'consumed' in each year of the asset's useful economic life must be set against the revenue which this generates (in conjunction with other factors of production). That part of the cost of a fixed asset which is 'used up' or 'consumed' during an accounting period is referred to as depreciation. Thus, **depreciation** may be defined as the allocation of the cost of a fixed asset over the accounting periods that comprise its useful economic life to the business according to some criterion regarding the amount which is 'used up' or 'consumed' in each of these periods.

Financial Reporting Standard 15—Tangible Fixed Assets[1] defines **depreciation** as 'the measure of the cost or revalued amount of the economic benefits of the tangible fixed asset that have been consumed during the period. Consumption includes the wearing out, using up or other reduction in the useful economic life of a tangible fixed asset whether arising from use, effluxion of time or obsolescence through either changes in technology or demand for the goods and services produced by the asset.'

Obsolescence through technological change refers to the situation where a new model of the asset which is significantly more efficient or performs additional functions comes on to the market. Obsolescence through demand changes occurs when there is a substantial reduction in demand for the firm's product because of, for example, technological advances in competitors' products. Both of these causes of obsolescence usually result in a sudden, relatively large decrease in value of the asset, particularly where it cannot be used for any other purpose.

Another common way of defining depreciation is that it refers to the permanent decrease or loss in value of a fixed asset during a given accounting period. The Companies Act states that 'provisions for diminution in value shall be made in respect to any fixed asset which has diminished in value if the reduction in its value is expected to be permanent'. This conceptualization of depreciation leaves unanswered the question of what is meant by 'value'. Furthermore, many accountants would probably deny that the amount of depreciation shown in final accounts is a reflection of the loss in value of a fixed asset. They argue that accountants are not valuers, and that depreciation is simply the allocation of the cost of a fixed asset over its useful economic life to the business. There is no simple reconciliation of this schizophrenia, which is said to arise from the dual purpose of depreciation as a means of measuring profit and valuing assets.

Depreciation can also be viewed as a provision for the replacement of fixed assets. The annual charge for depreciation in the profit and loss account represents a setting aside of some of the income so that over the useful life of the asset sufficient 'funds' are retained in the business to replace the asset. However, it must be emphasized that no money is usually specifically set aside. Thus, when the time comes to replace the asset, the money needed to do so will not automatically be available. Furthermore, where depreciation is based on the historical cost of the asset the amount of funds set aside will be insufficient to provide for any increase in the replacement cost of the asset. This is discussed further in Chapter 23.

Finally, it should be noted that FRS15 requires all tangible fixed assets except land and investment properties to be depreciated. This includes depreciating buildings. The reason is that although the market value of buildings at any point in time may exceed their historical cost, they nevertheless have a finite life and thus should be depreciated over their useful economic life. However, some businesses do not depreciate their buildings on the grounds that the market value at the end of the year, and/or the estimated residual value at the end of their expected useful life, is not less than the original cost. It is also sometimes argued that since repairs and maintenance costs on buildings are charged to the profit and loss account, to also charge depreciation on an asset, the useful life of which is being effectively maintained into perpetuity, would amount to a double charge and the creation of secret reserves. However, these arguments ignore that depreciation is not a method of valuation of assets but rather a process of allocation of the cost over the asset's useful life which, however long, must still be finite. Buildings, for example, can be entered in the balance sheet at a revalued amount in excess of their cost, but this revalued amount should still be depreciated. Revaluations are discussed further in Chapters 25 and 27.

Methods of depreciation

A number of different methods have been developed for measuring depreciation, each of which will give a different annual charge to the profit and loss account. There is no one method of depreciation that is superior to all others in all circumstances. The most appropriate method will depend on the type of asset and the extent to which it is used in each period. The method of depreciation that is chosen is referred to as one of the business's estimation techniques.

Whichever method is used to calculate depreciation, at least three pieces of data relating to the asset in question are needed: (1) the historical cost; (2) the length of the asset's expected useful economic life to the business; and (3) the estimated residual value of the asset at the end of its useful economic life. The **useful life** of an asset refers to the period which the business regards as being the most economical length of time to keep the particular asset. This will depend on a number of factors, such as the pattern of repair costs. The useful life of an asset may well be considerably shorter than its total life. **Residual value** refers to the estimated proceeds of sale at the end of the asset's useful life to the business. This is usually considerably more than its scrap value. It should be noted that both the useful life and the residual value have to be estimated when the asset is purchased.

The difference between the historical cost of a tangible fixed asset and its residual value is referred to in FRS15 as the **depreciable amount**. According to FRS15, 'the depreciable amount of a tangible fixed asset should be allocated on a systematic basis over its useful economic life. The depreciation method used should reflect as fairly as possible the pattern in which the asset's economic benefits are consumed by the entity.' The two most common methods of depreciation in the UK are the **straight line method** and **reducing balance method**. Another method more common in the US is the sum of the years' digits method. These are described below.

The straight line/fixed instalment method

Under this method the annual amount of depreciation which will be charged to the profit and loss account, referred to as the **depreciation expense**, is computed as follows:

$$\frac{\text{Cost} - \text{Estimated residual value}}{\text{Estimated useful life in years}}$$

However, in practice, and in examination questions, the annual rate of depreciation is usually expressed as a percentage. The annual amount of depreciation is then calculated by applying this percentage to the cost of the asset.

This method gives the same charge for depreciation in each year of the asset's useful life. It is therefore most appropriate for assets which are depleted as a result of the passage of time (e.g. buildings, leases, pipelines, storage tanks, patents and trade marks). The method may also be suitable where the utilization of an asset is the same in each year.

The main advantages of the straight line method are that it is easy to understand and the computations are simple. The main disadvantage is that it may not give an accurate measure of the loss in value or reduction in the useful life of an asset.

The diminishing/reducing balance method

Under this method it is necessary first to compute the annual rate of depreciation as a percentage, as follows:

$$100 - \left(\sqrt[ul]{\frac{\text{Residual value}}{\text{Cost}}} \times 100\right)$$

where ul refers to the estimated useful life.

The annual amount of depreciation which will be charged to the profit and loss account is then computed thus:

Rate of depreciation × WDV of asset (at start of year)

The WDV of the asset refers to its cost less the aggregate depreciation of the asset since the date of acquisition. This method thus gives a decreasing annual charge for depreciation over the useful life of the asset. It is therefore most appropriate for fixed assets that deteriorate primarily as a result of usage where this is greater in the earlier years of their life (e.g. plant and machinery, motor vehicles, furniture and fittings, office equipment). However, this method may also be suitable even if the utilization is the same in each year. The logic behind this apparently contradictory assertion involves taking into consideration the pattern of repair costs. These will be low in the earlier years of the asset's life and high in later years. Thus, the decreasing annual amount of depreciation combined with the increasing repair costs will give a relatively constant combined annual charge in each year of the asset's useful life which is said to reflect the constant annual usage.

The reducing balance method is also said to be a more realistic measure of the reduction in the market value of fixed assets, since this is likely to be greater in the earlier years of the asset's life than later years. However, it is highly questionable whether the WDV of a fixed asset is intended to be a reflection of its market value.

The main criticisms of this method relate to its complexity, and there is an arbitrary assumption about the rate of decline built into the formula.

The sum of the years' digits method

Under this method the annual amount of depreciation which will be charged to the profit and loss account as the depreciation expense is computed by multiplying the depreciable amount by a fraction. The denominator in this fraction is the same each year, and is the sum of a decreasing arithmetic progression, the first number of which is the useful life of the asset and the last is one (e.g. 3 + 2 + 1 = 6). The numerator in the fraction is the number of years of the asset's remaining useful life at the start of the accounting year in question (e.g. 3 years, 2 years, 1 year).

This method gives a decreasing annual charge for depreciation over the useful life of the asset that is similar to but not the same amount as the reducing balance method. The arguments for and against the sum of the years' digits method are thus the same as those relating to the reducing balance method except that the former is simpler. Moreover, the difference in the annual depreciation expense highlights the arbitrary nature of the different assumptions about the rates of decline that are built into the two methods.

A numerical example of the above methods of depreciation is given in Example 11.1 which follows after explaining the accounting entries for depreciation.

Accounting for depreciation

The accounting entries in respect of the annual charge for depreciation are made after the trial balance has been extracted when the profit and loss account is being prepared. These consist of the following:

Debit	Depreciation expense account
Credit	Provision for depreciation account

The depreciation expense account is transferred to the profit and loss account thus:

Debit	Profit and loss account
Credit	Depreciation expense account

The effect is to accumulate the provision while making a charge in the profit and loss account each year.

Example 11.1

D. McDonald has an accounting year ending on 31 December. On 1 January 20X1 he purchased a machine for £1,000 which has an expected useful life of three years and an estimated residual value of £343.

You are required to:

a Calculate the amount of depreciation in each year of the asset's useful life using: (i) the straight line method; (ii) the reducing balance method; and (iii) the sum of the years' digits method.

b Show the journal and ledger entries relating to the purchase and the provision for depreciation in each year (using the amounts calculated from the straight line method).

c Show the relevant entries on the balance sheet for 20X2 (using the amounts calculated from the straight line method).

a. ***The calculation of depreciation***

i The straight line method:

$$\text{Annual depreciation} = \frac{£1{,}000 - £343}{3} = £219 \text{ per annum}$$

ii The reducing balance method:

$$\text{Rate} = 100 - \left(\sqrt[3]{\frac{343}{1{,}000}} \times 100\right) = 100 - (\tfrac{7}{10} \times 100) = 30 \text{ per cent}$$

The annual amount of depreciation is calculated by applying this rate to the cost of the asset minus the aggregate depreciation of previous years (i.e. the WDV at the start of each year) as follows:

For 20X1: 30 per cent of £1,000 = £300
For 20X2: 30 per cent of (£1,000 – 300) = £210
For 19X3: 30 per cent of [£1,000 – (£300 + £210)] = £147

iii The sum of the years' digits method:
Depreciable amount = £(1,000 – 343) = £657
Sum of the years' digits = 3 + 2 + 1 = 6

Annual depreciation:

For 20X1: 3/6 × £657 = £329
For 19X2: 2/6 × £657 = £219
For 19X3: 1/6 × £657 = £109

b. ***The ledger entries***

Plant and machinery

20X1					
1 Jan	Bank	1,000			

Provision for depreciation on plant and machinery

20X1			20X1		
31 Dec	Balance c/d	219	31 Dec	Depreciation expense account	219
20X2			20X2		
31 Dec	Balance c/d	438	1 Jan	Balance b/d	219
			31 Dec	Depreciation expense account	219
		438			438
20X3			20X3		
31 Dec	Balance c/d	657	1 Jan	Balance b/d	438
			31 Dec	Depreciation expense account	219
		657			657
			20X4		
			1 Jan	Balance b/d	657

Depreciation expense account

20X1 31 Dec	Depreciation on plant	219	20X1 31 Dec	Profit and loss account	219
20X2 31 Dec	Depreciation on plant	219	20X2 31 Dec	Profit and loss account	219
20X3 31 Dec	Depreciation on plant	219	20X3 31 Dec	Profit and loss account	219

The journal

20X1 31 Dec	Depreciation expense To provision for depreciation Being the charge for depreciation on plant for 20X1	Dr Cr	219	 219
31 Dec	Profit and loss account To depreciation expense Being the entry to close the depreciation expense account at the year end	Dr Cr	219	 219

The entries for 20X2 and 20X3 would be exactly the same.

c. ***The balance sheet*** at 31 December 20X2 would appear as follows:

Fixed assets	£
Plant and machinery at cost	1,000
Less: aggregate depreciation	438
Written down value	562

Alternatively, where there are several types of fixed assets, it is easier to present the fixed assets in columnar form as follows:

Fixed assets	*Cost*	*Aggregate depreciation*	*WDV*
	£	£	£
Plant and machinery	1,000	438	562

Notes

1 The entries on the balance sheet comprise the balance on the fixed asset account at the end of the year and the balance on the provision for depreciation account at the end of the year. The latter is referred to as the **aggregate or accumulated depreciation** and is deducted from the historical cost to give the WDV, which is the only one of these three figures that enters into the computation of the total of the balance sheet.

2 Because the entries in the depreciation expense account only ever consist of a single debit and credit of the same amount, most people do not use this account. Instead, the annual charge is credited to the provision for depreciation account and debited directly to the profit and loss account. This practice will be adopted in future examples and answers to exercises.

Profits and losses on the disposal of fixed assets

Almost without exception, when an asset is sold at the end of (or during) its useful life the proceeds of sale differ from the estimated residual value (or written down book value if sold during its useful life). Where the proceeds are less than the WDV, this is referred to as a **loss on sale**. Where the proceeds are greater than the WDV this is referred to as a **profit on sale**. This can be illustrated using Example 11.1. Suppose the asset was sold on 31 December 20X3 for £400. The WDV is the difference between the cost of the asset and the aggregate depreciation up to the date of disposal; that is, £1,000 – £657 = £343. The profit (or loss) on sale is the difference between the proceeds of sale and the WDV of the asset. There is thus a profit on sale of £400 – £343 = £57.

The disposal of fixed assets and the resulting profit or loss on sale must be recorded in the ledger. The procedure is as follows.

1 Credit the proceeds of sale to the fixed asset account.

2 Transfer the aggregate depreciation up to the date of disposal from the provision for depreciation account to the fixed asset account.

3 A loss on sale should then be credited to the fixed asset account and debited to the profit and loss account. A profit on sale would be debited to the asset account and credited to the profit and loss account.

The effect of these entries is to eliminate the original cost of the asset from the fixed asset account. This is illustrated below using Example 11.1 and the additional data above.

The ledger entries

Provision for depreciation

20X3			20X3		
31 Dec	Plant and machinery	657	31 Dec	Balance b/d	657

Plant and machinery

20X1			20X3		
1 Jan	Bank—purchase	1,000	31 Dec	Bank—proceeds of sale	400
20X3			31 Dec	Provision for depreciation	657
31 Dec	Profit and loss a/c —profit on sale	57	31 Dec	Profit and loss a/c (any loss on sale)	—
		1,057			1,057

Profit and loss account

Loss on sale of fixed assets	—	Profit on sale of plant and machinery	57

Before the above entries are made in the ledger the following journal entries are necessary.

The journal

20X3 31 Dec	Provision for depreciation To plant and machinery Being the aggregate depreciation at the date of sale of the asset	Dr	657	657
31 Dec	Plant and machinery To profit and loss account Being the profit on sale of plant	Dr	57	57

The depreciation charge on an asset in the years of acquisition and disposal: partial year depreciation

The previous example dealt with the highly unlikely situation of an asset being purchased and sold on the first day and last day of an accounting year, respectively. In practice, these transactions could occur on any day of the year. The way in which depreciation would then be computed depends on the usual practice of the business, or in examinations on what you are explicitly or implicitly instructed to do. Unless the question states otherwise, the depreciation must be calculated on a strict time basis for the period the asset is owned. In examination questions, assets tend to be purchased and sold on the first or last day of a calendar month for simplicity of calculation. It can be argued that in practice one should also calculate depreciation on a strict time basis. The charge for depreciation in the year of purchase would be as follows:

$$\text{Rate of depreciation} \times \text{Cost of asset} \times \frac{\text{Number of months (or days) between the date of purchase and the end of the accounting year in which the asset is purchased}}{12 \text{ (or } 365)}$$

The charge for depreciation in the year of sale would be as follows:

$$\text{Rate of depreciation} \times \text{Cost of asset (or WDV)} \times \frac{\text{Number of months (or days) between the start of the accounting year in which the asset is sold and the date of sale}}{12 \text{ (or 365)}}$$

In practice, to avoid these tedious calculations, some firms have a policy of charging a full year's depreciation in the year of purchase and none in the year of sale. There is little theoretical justification for this. Also, in examination questions, where the date of purchase or sale is not given, this is usually an indication to adopt this policy.

The accounting entries in respect of depreciation on acquisitions and disposals are illustrated in Example 11.2.

Example 11.2

P. Smith has an accounting year ending on 31 December. On 31 December 20X5 her ledger contained the following accounts:

	£
Motor vehicles	50,000
Provision for depreciation on vehicles	23,000

Vehicles are depreciated using the straight line method at a rate of 20 per cent per annum on a strict time basis.

The following transactions occurred during 20X6:

1 Apr	Purchased a van for £5,000
31 Aug	Sold a vehicle for £4,700. This cost £7,500 when it was bought on 31 July 20X4.
30 Sep	Put one car in part exchange for another. The part exchange allowance on the old car was £4,100 and the balance of £3,900 was paid by cheque. The old car cost £10,000 when it was bought on 1 January 20X4.

You are required to show the entries in the motor vehicles and provision for depreciation accounts in respect of the above for 20X6.

Date of acquisitions and disposals	*Details*	*Total depreciation on disposals*	*Depreciation charge for year ending 31 Dec 20X6*
		£	£
	Depreciation on disposals		
31 July 20X4	For year ending 31/12/X4:		
	20 per cent × 7,500 × 5/12	625	
	For year ending 31/12/X5:		
	20 per cent × 7,500	1,500	
31 Aug 20X6	For year ending 31/12/X6:		
	20 per cent × 7,500 × 8/12	1,000	1,000
		3,125	
	Book value at 31/8/X6:		
	7,500 – 3,125 = 4,375		
	Profit on sale		
	4,700 – 4,375 = 325		

1 Jan 20X4	For year ending 31/12/X4:		
	20 per cent × 10,000	2,000	
	For year ending 31/12/X5:		
	20 per cent × 10,000	2,000	
30 Sept 20X6	For year ending 31/12/X6:		
	20 per cent × 10,000 × 9/12	1,500	1,500
		5,500	

Book value at 30/9/X6:
10,000 – 5,500 = 4,500

Loss on sale
4,500 – 4,100 = 400

	Depreciation on acquisitions	
1 Apr 20X6	20 per cent × 5,000 × 9/12	750
30 Sept 20X6	20 per cent × (3,900 + 4,100) × 3/12	400
	Depreciation on remainder	
	20 per cent × (50,000 – 7,500 – 10,000)	6,500
		10,150

Note

1 The 'depreciation on the remainder' of the vehicles is calculated on the vehicles owned at the end of the previous year that was not disposed of during the current year. Those items that were bought and sold during the year have already been depreciated in the previous calculations.

The ledger

Motor vehicles

20X6			20X6		
1 Jan	Balance b/d	50,000	31 Aug	Bank	4,700
1 Apr	Bank	5,000	31 Aug	Provision for depn	3,125
31 Aug	Profit and loss a/c		30 Sep	Part exchange contra	4,100
	—profit on sale	325	30 Sep	Provision for depn	5,500
30 Sep	Bank	3,900	30 Sep	Profit and loss a/c	
30 Sep	Part exchange			—loss on sale	400
	contra	4,100	31 Dec	Balance c/d	45,500
		63,325			63,325
20X7					
1 Jan	Balance b/d	45,500			

Provision for depreciation

20X6			20X6		
31 Aug	Vehicles	3,125	1 Jan	Balance b/d	23,000
30 Sept	Vehicles	5,500	31 Dec	Profit and loss a/c	10,150
31 Dec	Balance c/d	24,525			
		33,150			33,150
			20X7		
			1 Jan	Balance b/d	24,525

Notes

1 When one asset is put in part exchange for another, the part exchange allowance is both debited and credited to the asset account and referred to as a contra. The credit entry represents the proceeds of sale of the old asset, and the debit entry represents a part payment for the new asset. The balance which has to be paid for the new asset in cash is debited to the asset account in the normal way. This together with the debit contra represents the total cost of the new asset.

2 The transfer from the provision for depreciation account to the fixed asset account relating to the aggregate depreciation on disposals must include the depreciation on disposals in respect of the current year. This therefore cannot be done until the total depreciation for the current year has been ascertained. Thus, all the entries in the provision for depreciation account are usually made at the end of the year after the trial balance has been prepared. It is important to note that this also means that any balance on a provision for depreciation account shown in a trial balance must relate to the balance at the end of the previous year.

3 There is another method of accounting for disposals which involves the use of a disposals account. Some examination questions explicitly require the use of a disposals account. Under this method, when a fixed asset is sold the cost of the asset is transferred from the fixed asset account to a fixed asset disposals account. The aggregate depreciation on the asset that has been sold, the proceeds of sale, and the profit or loss on sale are all entered in the disposals account instead of the fixed asset account. The provision for depreciation account contains the same entries whether a disposals account is used or not. The use of a disposals account is illustrated below, taking the information from Example 11.2.

Motor vehicles

20X6			20X6		
1 Jan	Balance b/d	50,000	31 Aug	Disposals account	7,500
1 Apr	Bank	5,000	30 Sep	Disposals account	10,000
30 Sep	Bank	3,900	31 Dec	Balance c/d	45,500
30 Sep	Disposals account —part exchange	4,100			
		63,000			63,000
20X7					
1 Jan	Balance b/d	45,500			

Motor vehicles disposals

20X6			20X6		
31 Aug	Motor vehicles	7,500	31 Aug	Bank	4,700
31 Aug	Profit and loss a/c —profit on sale	325	31 Aug	Provision for depn	3,125
30 Sep	Motor vehicles	10,000	30 Sep	Motor vehicles —part exchange	4,100
			30 Sep	Provision for depn	5,500
			30 Sep	Profit and loss a/c —loss on sale	400
		17,825			17,825

There should never be a balance on the disposals account at the end of the year after the profit and loss account has been prepared.

Accounting for research and development expenditure

SSAP13—Accounting for Research and Development[2] divides research and development into three categories: (1) pure (or basic) research; (2) applied research; and (3) development. These are defined as follows:

1 *Pure (or basic) research*: experimental or theoretical work undertaken primarily to acquire new scientific or technical knowledge for its own sake rather than directed towards any specific aim or application.

2 *Applied research*: original or critical investigation undertaken in order to gain new scientific or technical knowledge and directed towards a specific practical aim or objective.

3 *Development*: use of scientific or technical knowledge in order to produce new or substantially improved materials, devices, products or services, to install new processes or systems prior to the commencement of commercial production or commercial applications, or to improve substantially those already produced or installed.[2]

The accounting treatment of expenditure on pure and applied research may differ from that for development expenditure. SSAP13, like the Companies Act, dictates that expenditure on pure and applied research must be treated as an expense in the year incurred. However, SSAP13 and the Companies Act allow development expenditure to be either expensed in the year incurred or alternatively treated as an intangible fixed asset (and depreciated/amortized). If development expenditure is expected to generate revenue in future years (which is often the case), this may be capitalized. However, if the resulting future revenue cannot be assessed with reasonable certainty (which is also often the case), development expenditure should be expensed. The most appropriate accounting treatment for development expenditure thus hinges on whether the resulting future revenue can be assessed with reasonable certainty, which is why SSAP13 contains the following set of detailed requirements relating to the accounting treatment of development costs:

'Development expenditure should be written off in the year of expenditure except in the following circumstances when it may be deferred to future periods:

a there is a clearly defined project, and

b the related expenditure is separately identifiable, and

c the outcome of such a project has been assessed with reasonable certainty as to:
   i its technical feasibility, and
   ii its ultimate commercial viability considered in the light of factors such as likely market conditions (including competing products), public opinion, consumer and environmental legislation, and

d the aggregate of the deferred development costs, any further development costs, and related production, selling and administration costs is reasonably expected to be exceeded by related future sales or other revenues, and

e adequate resources exist, or are reasonably expected to be available, to enable the project to be completed and to provide any consequential increases in working capital.'[2]

There is also certain information relating to research and development expenditure that should be disclosed in the notes to published company accounts. The requirements of SSAP13 are reproduced below. Notice that the reference to 'deferred expenditure' relates to development expenditure that has been treated as an intangible fixed asset.

a The accounting policy on research and development expenditure should be stated and explained.

b The total amount of research and development expenditure charged in the profit and loss account should be disclosed, analysed between the current year's expenditure and amounts amortised from deferred expenditure.

c Movements on deferred expenditure and the amount carried forward at the beginning and the end of the period should be disclosed. Deferred development expenditure should be disclosed under intangible fixed assets in the balance sheet.[2]

A numerical illustration of accounting for research and development expenditure is given in Exercise 11.18.

Summary

A fixed asset is an asset that is held by an enterprise for use in the production or supply of goods and services, has been acquired with the intention of being used on a continuing basis, and is not intended for sale in the ordinary course of business. It is also usually expected to generate revenue over more than one accounting year. Fixed assets are classified as either tangible or intangible (such as goodwill). Money spent on fixed assets is referred to as capital expenditure. All other costs are referred to as revenue expenditure. Fixed assets are normally valued in the balance sheet at historical cost, which refers to their purchase price.

All fixed assets except for land and investment properties must be depreciated in the final accounts. Depreciation is the measure of the consumption, wearing out, using up or other reduction in the useful economic life of a fixed asset whether arising from use, effluxion of time or obsolescence.

There is a range of acceptable depreciation methods. Management should select the method regarded as most appropriate to the type of asset and its use in the business so as to allocate depreciation as fairly as possible to the periods expected to benefit from the asset's use. The two most common methods are the straight line/fixed instalment method and diminishing/reducing balance method. The former gives the same charge for depreciation in each year of the asset's useful life. The latter results in a decreasing annual charge over the useful life of the asset.

Where an asset is acquired or disposed of during the accounting year, it is normal to compute the depreciation for that year according to the period over which the asset was owned. When an asset is disposed of during the accounting year this usually also gives rise to profit or loss on sale. This is the difference between the proceeds of sale and the written down or book value of the asset. The WDV is the difference between the historical cost and the accumulated/aggregate depreciation from the date of acquisition to the date of disposal.

The ledger entries for depreciation are to credit a provision for depreciation account and debit a depreciation expense account with the annual amount of depreciation. The balance on the depreciation expense account is transferred to the profit and loss account representing the charge for the year. The balance on the provision for depreciation account is shown on the balance sheet as a deduction from the cost of the fixed asset to give the WDV, which enters into the total of the balance sheet. However, the aggregate depreciation on fixed assets disposed of during the year must first be transferred from the provision for depreciation account to the fixed asset account. Any profit or loss on disposal is also entered in the fixed asset account and transferred to the profit and loss account.

Intangible fixed assets include development expenditure. SSAP13 dictates that research expenditure must be treated as an expense in the year incurred. However, development expenditure may be capitalized as a fixed asset (and depreciated) provided that the resulting future revenue can be assessed with reasonable certainty. If not, it should be expensed in the year incurred.

Key terms and concepts

Aggregate/accumulated depreciation (121)
book value (121)
capital expenditure (120)
carrying amount (121)
current value (121)
depreciable amount (123)
depreciation (121)
depreciation expense (123)
diminishing balance method (124)
fixed asset (120)
fixed instalment method (123)
intangible assets (120)
loss on sale (127)
profit on sale (127)
recoverable amount (121)
reducing balance method (123)
residual value (123)
revenue expenditure (120)
straight line method (123)
sum of the years' digits method (124)
tangible fixed assets (120)
useful (economic) life (123)
written down value (121)

References

1. Accounting Standards Board (1999). *Financial Reporting Standard 15—Tangible Fixed Assets* (ASB).
2. Accounting Standards Committee (1989). *Statement of Standard Accounting Practice 13—Accounting for Research and Development* (ICAEW).

Review questions

11.1 Examine the nature of fixed assets.

11.2 **a** Explain the difference between capital expenditure and revenue expenditure.
b What criteria would you use to decide whether expenditure should be classified as relating to a fixed asset?

11.3 Briefly explain the circumstances in which each of the following would be regarded as a fixed asset: (a) tools; (b) investments; and (c) advertising expenditure.

11.4 **a** Explain the difference between tangible and intangible fixed assets.
b What is goodwill and how does it usually arise in a balance sheet?

11.5 **a** Describe how fixed assets are valued in historical cost accounting.
b How would you account for expenditure on double-glazing? Explain your reasons.

11.6 Explain fully the nature of depreciation.

11.7 'Depreciation is the loss in value of a fixed asset.' Discuss.

11.8 Describe the data needed in order to compute depreciation.

11.9 Describe two common methods of depreciation including the resulting pattern of charges to the profit and loss account for depreciation expense over an asset's useful economic life. In what circumstances might each of these be the most appropriate method and why?

11.10 'Although the straight line method of depreciation is the simplest to apply, it may not always be the most appropriate'. Explain and discuss.

11.11 **a** Define each of the following: (i) pure (or basic) research; (ii) applied research; and (iii) development.

b Describe fully the permissible accounting treatments for research and development expenditure including the circumstances in which each may be acceptable.

c Describe the information that should be disclosed in the notes to the accounts of companies in respect of research and development expenditure.

11.12 In the year to 31 December 20X9, Amy bought a new fixed asset and made the following payments in relation to it:

	£	£
Cost as per supplier's list	12,000	
Less: agreed discount	1,000	11,000
Delivery charge		100
Erection charge		200
Maintenance charge		300
Additional component to increase capacity		400
Replacement parts		250

Required:

a State and justify the cost figure which should be used as the basis for depreciation.

b What does depreciation do, and why is it necessary?

c Briefly explain, without numerical illustration, how the straight line and reducing balance methods of depreciation work. What different assumptions does each method make?

d It is common practice in published accounts in Germany to use the reducing balance method for a fixed asset in the early years of its life, and then to change to the straight line method as soon as this would give a higher annual charge. What do you think of this practice? Refer to relevant accounting conventions in your answer. (ACCA)

Exercises

An asterisk after the question number indicates that there is a suggested answer in the Appendix.

11.13 **Level I**

Pusher commenced business on 1 January 20X9 with two lorries—A and B. A cost £1,000 and B cost £1,600. On 3 March 20X0, A was written off in an accident and Pusher received £750 from the Insurance Company. This vehicle was replaced on 10 March 20X0 by C which cost £2,000.

A full year's depreciation is charged in the year of acquisition and no depreciation charged in the year of disposal.

a You are required to show the appropriate extracts from Pusher's balance sheet and profit and loss account for the three years to 31/12/X9, 31/12/X0 and 31/12/X1 assuming that

i the vehicles are depreciated at 20 per cent on the straight line method; and

ii the vehicles are depreciated at 25 per cent on the reducing balance method.

b Comment briefly on the pros and cons of using the straight line and reducing balance methods of depreciation. (ACCA)

11.14* **Level II**

A. Black & Co. Ltd owned two machines which had been purchased on 1 October 20X0, at a combined cost of £3,100 ex works. They were identical as regards size and capacity and had been erected and brought into use on 1 April 20X1. The cost of transporting the two machines to the factory of A. Black & Co. Ltd was £130 and further expenditure for the installation of the two machines had been incurred totalling £590 for the foundations, and £180 for erection.

Provision for depreciation using the straight line method has been calculated from the date on which the machines started work, assuming a life of ten years for the machines. The first charge against profits was made at the end of the financial year, 30 September 20X1.

One of the machines was sold on 31 March 20X9 for £800 ex factory to H. Johnson. The work of dismantling the machine was undertaken by the staff of Black & Co. Ltd at a labour cost of £100. This machine was replaced on 1 May 20X9, by one exactly similar in every way, which was purchased from R. Adams at a cost of £2,800, which covered delivery, erection on the site of the old machine, and the provision of adequate foundations. This new machine was brought into general operation on 1 July 20X9.

You are required to show:

a the journal entries which should be made on 31 March and 1 May 20X9; and

b how you would arrive at the amount of the provision for depreciation as regards the three machines for the year ended 30 September 20X9.

NB. It is the practice of the company to charge depreciation on a *pro rata* time basis each year, and to operate a machinery disposal account where necessary. (ACCA)

11.15 **Level II**

Makers and Co. is a partnership with a small factory on the outskirts of London. They decide to erect an extension to their factory.

The following items appear in the trial balance of the firm, as at 31 December 20X9:

	Debit	*Credit*
	£	£
Purchases	12,800	
Wages	16,400	
Hire of machinery	520	
Plant and machinery at cost to 31 December 20X8	5,900	
Plant and machinery purchased during the year	2,540	
Plant and machinery sold during the year (cost in 20X0 £900; depreciation to 31 December 20X8 £540)		160
Freehold premises at cost to 31 December 20X8 (Land £3,000; Buildings £4,000)	7,000	
Freehold land purchased during the year for a factory extension	2,800	
Provision for depreciation of plant and machinery at 31 December 20X8		2,400
Legal charges	280	

In the course of your examination of the books you ascertain that:

1. Building materials used in building the extension and costing £1,800 had been charged to the purchases account.
2. Wages paid to men engaged in building the extension amounted to £1,500 and had been charged to the wages account.
3. The hire charge was in respect of machinery used exclusively in the construction of the extension.
4. The legal charges, apart from £50 relating to debt collecting, were incurred in the purchase of the land.

It is decided that depreciation on plant and machinery is to be provided at $12\frac{1}{2}$ per cent on the closing book value.

You are required to:

a write up the following ledger accounts:
Factory extensions, Freehold premises, Plant and machinery, and Provision for depreciation of plant and machinery; and

b show therefrom the particulars that should appear on the firm's balance sheet at 31 December 20X9. (ACCA)

11.16* **Level II**

Wexford Ltd, who prepare their accounts on 31 December each year, provide for depreciation of their vehicles by a reducing balance method, calculated as 25 per cent on the balance at the end of the year. Depreciation of plant is calculated on a straight line basis at 10 per cent per annum on cost; a full year's depreciation is charged in the year in which plant is acquired and none in the year of sale.

The balance sheet for 31 December 20X5 showed:

	Vehicles	*Plant*
	£	£
Original cost	25,060	96,920
Accumulated depreciation	14,560	50,120
Net book value	10,500	46,800

During the year ended 31 December 20X6 the following transactions took place:

Purchase of vehicles	£4,750
Purchases of plant	£33,080

	Year of purchase	*Original cost*	*Proceeds of sale*
		£	£
Sale of vehicle 1	20X3	3,200	1,300
Sale of vehicle 2	20X4	4,800	2,960
Sale of plant	20X0	40,000	15,000

You are required to:

a present the ledger accounts relating to the purchases and sales of vehicles and plant for the year ended 31 December 20X6; and

b show the journal entries for depreciation for the year.

11.17 Level II

The balance sheet of Beta Ltd as at 30 June 20X9 shows motor vehicles as follows:

	£
Motor vehicles at cost	61,850
Less: Depreciation	32,426
Net Book Value	29,424

Vehicles are depreciated on the straight line basis over a five year life. Depreciation is charged *pro rata* to time in the year of acquisition but no charge is made in the year of disposal. The disposal account is written up on the last day of each year.

During 20X9–X0 the following vehicle transactions took place:

30 Sep	Purchased delivery van: £8,600
31 Oct	Purchased sales manager's car: £10,700
28 Feb	Purchased lorry: £4,000

The lorry was second-hand and originally cost £9,600.

Sales of vehicles:

31 Oct	Car	£300 originally cost £2,800
31 Dec	Tractor	£540 originally cost £2,400
31 Mar	Van	£420 originally cost £1,900

The car was originally purchased on 1 July 20X5, the tractor on 30 November 20X6 and the van on 1 April 20X7.

You are required to write up the accounts for vehicles, vehicle depreciation and vehicle disposals. (ACCA)

11.18* Level II

Rubens plc is a company in the pharmaceuticals industry which spends heavily on research and development each year. The company's policy is to capitalize development expenditure meeting the conditions in *SSAP13—Research and Development* and to amortize it over five years on the straight line basis beginning when sales revenue is first generated from the developed product. Amortization is apportioned on a time basis in the first year of amortization.

The company's finance director has asked you to compute the amounts for research and development to be included in the financial statements for the year ended 30 September 20X8 in accordance with the company's accounting policy. The company's profit is expected to be about £8m.

The company's ledger accounts for development expenditure and research expenditure, before amortization and other adjustments for the year ended 30 September 20X8, showed the following details:

Project	*Balance at 30.9.X7*	*Expenditure year ended 30.9.X8*	*Balance at 30.9.X8*
	£000	£000	£000
A	600		
B	2,400		
C	3,600	400	4,000
D	1,200	300	1,500
E		800	800
F		400	400

Notes on the projects

A Project A was completed in 20X5 at a total cost of £1m and is being amortized in accordance with the company's policy.

B Project B was completed in June 20X7. Sales revenue began on 1 November 20X7.

C Project C is not yet complete and development is proceeding. It continues to meet the criteria for capitalization in SSAP13.

D Project D was abandoned during the year ended 30 September 20X8 when a competitor launched a superior product.

E Project E is a new development project commenced in 20X7/X8. It meets the criteria for capitalization in SSAP13.

F Project F was commenced and completed during 20X7/X8. Sales revenue is expected to begin in 20X9.

Research expenditure

The balance on the research expenditure account was £1,800,000, representing payments made during the year ended 30 September 20X8.

Required:

a State the criteria which must be met under *SSAP13—Research and Development* if development expenditure is to be capitalized.

b Compute the amounts to be included in the profit and loss account for research and development expenditure and in the balance sheet for deferred development expenditure, and state the heading under which they should be included or disclosed.

c Prepare notes to the financial statements of Rubins plc giving the supporting information required by *SSAP13—Research and Development*. (ACCA)

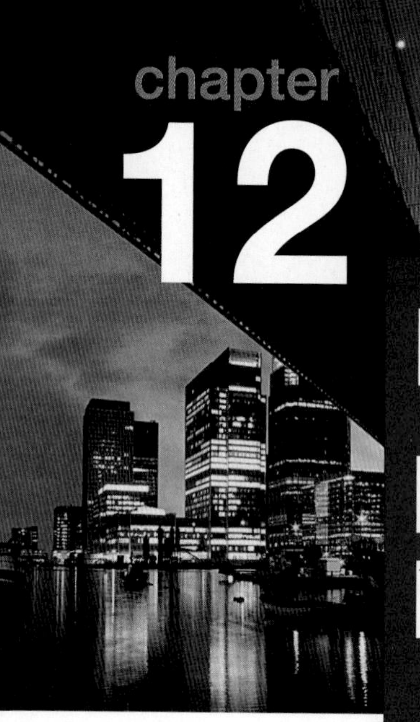

chapter 12

Bad debts and provisions for bad debts

Learning objectives

After reading this chapter you should be able to:

1. explain the meaning of the key terms and concepts listed at the end of the chapter;
2. explain the nature of bad debts, provisions, and provisions for doubtful debts;
3. distinguish between specific and general provisions for doubtful debts;
4. show the entries for bad debts and provisions for doubtful debts in the journal, ledger, profit and loss account, and balance sheet.

The nature of, and ledger entries for, bad debts

When goods are sold on credit it sometimes transpires that the debtor is unwilling or unable to pay the amount owed. This is referred to as a **bad** or **irrecoverable debt**. The decision to treat a debt as bad is a matter of judgement. A debt may be regarded as irrecoverable for a number of reasons, such as being unable to trace the debtor, it not being worth taking the debtor to court, or the debtor being bankrupt. However, if a debtor is bankrupt this does not necessarily mean that the whole of the debt is irrecoverable. When a person is bankrupt his or her possessions are seized and sold in order to pay the creditors. Such payments are often made in instalments known as dividends. Frequently, the dividends do not consist of the repayment of the whole of the debt. Thus, when the 'final dividend' is received the remainder of the debt is irrecoverable.

When a debt is regarded as irrecoverable the entries is the ledger are as follows:

Debit: Bad debts account
Credit: Debtors' account

Occasionally, debts previously written off as bad are subsequently paid. When this happens the ledger entries are the reverse of the above, and the debtors' account is credited with the money received in the normal way.

At the end of the accounting year the balance on the bad debts account is transferred to the profit and loss account.

The nature of, and ledger entries for, provisions for bad debts

A **provision** is the setting aside of income to meet a known or highly probable future liability or loss, the amount and/or timing of which cannot be ascertained exactly, and is thus an estimate. An example would be a provision for damages payable resulting from a legal action where the verdict had gone against the business but the amount of the damages had not been fixed by the court at the end of the accounting year. If the damages had been fixed these would be treated not as a provision but as a liability. Another example of a provision is depreciation.

It should be noted that when accountants talk of setting aside income what they mean is that 'funds' are being retained in the business but not put into a separate bank account. The funds are automatically retained in the business by designating part of the income as a provision, since this reduces the profit that is available for withdrawal by the owner(s) of the business.

The need for a **provision for bad/doubtful debts** essentially arises because goods sold and recognized as sales revenue in one accounting year may not become known to be a bad debt until the following accounting year. Thus, the profit of the year in which the goods are sold would be overstated by the amount of the bad debt. In order to adjust for this, a provision in respect of probable bad debts is created in the year of sale.

A provision for bad debts may consist of either a **specific provision** or a **general provision**, or both. A specific provision involves ascertaining which particular debtors at the year end are unlikely to pay their debts. A general provision is an estimate of the total amount of bad debts computed using a percentage (based on previous years' figures) of the debtors at the end of the current year. Where both specific and general provisions are made, the two amounts are added together and the total is entered in the ledger.

The accounting entries in respect of a provision for bad debts are made after the trial balance has been extracted when the profit and loss account is being prepared. It is important to appreciate that any balance on a provision for bad debts account shown in a trial balance must therefore relate to the balance at the end of the previous year. A charge (or credit) is made to the profit and loss account in each year which consists of an amount necessary to increase (or decrease) the provision at the end of the previous year to the amount required at the end of the current year.

An increase in a provision always consists of:

Debit: Profit and loss account
Credit: Provision for bad debts account

A decrease in a provision is entered:

Debit: Provision for bad debts account
Credit: Profit and loss account

The balance on the provision for bad debts account at the end of the year is deducted from trade debtors in the balance sheet to give the net amount that is expected to be received from debtors; that is, their net realizable value. The principle is similar to that applied in the case of a provision for depreciation where the accumulated depreciation at the end of the year, as shown by the balance on the provision for depreciation account, is deducted from the cost of the fixed asset in the balance sheet. All other provisions such as for legal costs, damages or fines are shown in the balance sheet as a current liability or long-term liability, depending on whether they are payable within one year or more from the date of the balance sheet. The treatment of bad debts and provisions for bad debts is illustrated in Examples 12.1 and 12.2.

Example 12.1

A. Jones has an accounting year ending on 30 November. At 30 November 20X7 his ledger contained the following accounts:

	£
Trade debtors	20,000
Provision for bad debts	1,000

The trade debtors at 30 November 20X8 were £18,900. This includes an amount of £300 owed by F. Simons which was thought to be irrecoverable. It also includes amounts of £240 owed by C. Steven, £150, owed by M. Evans and £210 owed by A. Mitchell, all of which are regarded as doubtful debts.

You have been instructed to make a provision for bad debts at 30 November 20X8. This should include a specific provision for debts regarded as doubtful and a general provision of 5 per cent of trade debtors.

Show the ledger entries in respect of the above and the relevant balance sheet extract.

Provision for bad debts at 30 November 20X8	£
Specific provision—C. Steven	240
M. Evans	150
A. Mitchell	210
	600

General provision—5 per cent × (£18,900 – £300 – £600)	900
	1,500

The ledger

F. Simons

20X8			20X8		
30 Nov	Balance b/d	300	30 Nov	Bad debts	300

Bad debts

20X8			20X8		
30 Nov	F. Simons	300	30 Nov	Profit and loss a/c	300

Provision for bad debts

20X8			20X7		
30 Nov	Balance c/d	1,500	1 Dec	Balance b/d	1,000
			20X8		
			30 Nov	Profit and loss a/c	500
		1,500			1,500
			20X8		
			1 Dec	Balance b/d	1,500

Profit and loss account

Bad debts	300
Provision for bad debts	500

Balance sheet

Current assets	
Debtors (18,900 – 300)	18,600
Less: Provision for bad debts	1,500
	17,100

Notes

1 No entries are made in the accounts of those debtors which comprise the specific provision since these are only doubtful debts and thus not yet regarded as irrecoverable.

2 The balance carried down on the provision for bad debts account at the end of the year is always the amount of the new provision. The amount charged to the profit and loss account is the difference between the provision at the end of the current year and that at the end of the previous year. In this example the provision is increased from £1,000 to £1,500 by a means of credit to the provision for bad debts account of £500 and a corresponding debit to the profit and loss account.

3 In computing the amount of the general provision any bad debts and specific provisions must be deducted from the debtors. Otherwise the specific provision would be duplicated and a provision would be made for debts already written off as bad, which is clearly nonsense.

4 The bad debts written off must also be removed from debtors in preparing the balance sheet.

5 There is another method of accounting for bad debts and provisions for bad debts which essentially involves combining these two accounts. This is shown below.

(Provision for) bad debts

20X8			20X7		
30 Nov	F. Simons	300	1 Dec	Balance b/d	1,000
30 Nov	Balance c/d	1,500	20X8		
			30 Nov	Profit and loss a/c	800
		1,800			1,800
			20X8		
			1 Dec	Balance b/d	1,500

Profit and loss account

Bad debts	800

The combined charge to the profit and loss account for the year in respect of bad debts and the provision for bad debts is the difference between the two sides of the (provision for) bad debts account after inserting the amount of the provision at 30 November 20X8 as a balance carried down. The charge to the profit and loss account under both methods is always the same in total.

Example 12.2

This is a continuation of Exercise 12.1.

During the year ended 30 November 20X9 C. Steven was declared bankrupt and a first dividend of £140 was received from the trustee. M. Evans was also declared bankrupt and a first and final dividend of £30 was received from the trustee. A. Mitchell paid his debt in full. A further debt of £350 owed by R. Jackson that is included in the debtors at 30 November 20X8 proved to be bad.

The trade debtors at 30 November 20X9 were £24,570. This figure is after recording all money received but does not take into account bad debts.

You have been instructed to make a provision for bad debts at 30 November 20X9. This should include a specific provision for doubtful debts and a general provision of 5 per cent of trade debtors.

Show the ledger entries in respect of the above and the relevant balance sheet extract.

Provision for bad debts at 30 November 20X9

	£
Specific provision—C. Steven (£240 – £140)	100
General provision—5 per cent × (£24,570 – £120 – £350 – £100)	1,200
	1,300

The ledger

C. Steven

20X8			20X9		
1 Dec	Balance b/d	240	30 Nov	Bank	140
			30 Nov	Balance c/d	100
		240			240
20X9					
1 Dec	Balance b/d	100			

M. Evans

20X8			20X9		
1 Dec	Balance b/d	150	30 Nov	Bank	30
			30 Nov	Bad debts	120
		150			150

R. Jackson

20X8			20X9		
1 Dec	Balance b/d	350	30 Nov	Bad debts	350

Bad debts

20X9			20X9		
30 Nov	M. Evans	120	30 Nov	Profit and loss a/c	470
30 Nov	R. Jackson	350			
		470			470

Provision for bad debts

20X9			20X8		
30 Nov	Profit and loss a/c	200	1 Dec	Balance b/d	1,500
30 Nov	Balance c/d	1,300			
		1,500			1,500
			20X9		
			1 Dec	Balance b/d	1,300

Profit and loss account

Bad debts	470	Provision for bad debts	200

Balance sheet	£
Current assets	
Debtors (£24,570 – £120 – £350)	24,100
Less: Provision for bad debts	1,300
	22,800

Alternative method

(Provision for) bad debts

20X9			20X8		
30 Nov	M. Evans	120	1 Dec	Balance b/d	1,500
30 Nov	R. Jackson	350	20X9		
30 Nov	Balance c/d	1,300	30 Nov	Profit and loss a/c	270
		1,770			1,770
			20X9		
			1 Dec	Balance b/d	1,300

Notes

1 The amount due from M. Evans is written off as a bad debt because the final dividend in bankruptcy was declared, which means that no more money will be received in respect of this debt. However, the amount due from C. Steven is not written off as a bad debt, despite the fact that he was declared bankrupt, because further dividends are expected. Thus, this debt is the subject of a specific provision in respect of the amount still outstanding.

2 No entries are required where a debt that was previously treated as a specific provision is subsequently paid, as in the case of A. Mitchell.

3 The main method shown above which has separate bad debts and provision for bad debts accounts is the most common in practice. However, this tends to obscure the logic behind provisions for bad debts, because it accounts for the provision separately from the bad debts. The 'alternative method' shown above allows the logic to be demonstrated as follows. The bad debts for the year (£120 + £350 = £470) are set against the provision at the end of the previous year (£1,500). Any under- or overprovision (£1,500 – £470 = overprovision of £1,030) is written back to the profit and loss account. The amount of the provision required at the end of the current year (£1,300) is then created in full by debiting the profit and loss account with this amount. This can be illustrated as follows.

(Provision for) bad debts

20X9			20X8		
30 Nov	M. Evans	120	1 Dec	Balance b/d	1,500
30 Nov	R. Jackson	350	20X9		
30 Nov	Profit and loss a/c		30 Nov	Profit and loss a/c	1,300
	over-provision	1,030			
30 Nov	Balance c/d	1,300			
		2,800			2,800
			20X9		
			1 Dec	Balance b/d	1,300

The debit entry of £1,030 is the reversal of the over-provision. The credit entry of £1,300 is the creation of the new provision. The net effect is the same as in the previous answer—a debit to the profit and loss account of £270 and a balance on the (provision for) bad debts account of £1,300. However, it should be observed that the overprovision of £1,030 as calculated above is an oversimplification. This is not usually readily identifiable since the bad debts normally comprise not only those relating to sales in the previous year for which a provision was created, but also bad debts arising from sales in the current year. The charge to the profit and loss account shown in the 'alternative method' therefore usually comprises: (a) a reversal of the under- or overprovision; (b) the bad debts arising from sales in the current year; and (c) the amount of the new provision at the end of the current year. Furthermore, it should be stressed that nobody would prepare a (provision) for bad debts account in the manner shown immediately above since it involves the unnecessary calculation of the under- or overprovision. However, the illustration serves to demonstrate that: (a) the underlying logic behind the provision for bad debts is essentially to shift the bad debts back into the year in which the goods were sold; (b) this requires an estimate of the provision; and (c) the estimate usually gives rise to an under- or overprovision that has to be reversed. However, this can be done without identifying the under- or overprovision separately by means of a single charge to the profit and loss account when the new provision for bad debts at the end of the current year has been created.

Summary

A debt is treated as irrecoverable if a debtor is unwilling or unable to pay, and the enterprise decides it is uneconomical to pursue the matter further. The ledger entry for irrecoverable debts is to credit the debtors' personal account and debit a bad debts account. The balance on the bad debts account is transferred to the profit and loss account at the end of the accounting year.

A provision is the setting aside of income to meet a known or highly probable future liability or loss, the amount and/or timing of which cannot be ascertained exactly, and is thus an estimate. The most common examples are provisions for depreciation and doubtful/bad debts.

A provision for bad debts may consist of a specific provision and/or a general provision. The accounting entries in respect of a provision for bad debts are made after the trial balance has been extracted when the profit and loss account and balance sheet are being prepared. A charge (or credit) is made to the profit and loss account which consists of an amount necessary to increase (or decrease) the provision at the end of the previous year to the amount required at the end of the current year. The ledger entries are to debit (or credit) the profit and loss account and credit (or debit) a provision for bad debts account. The latter is shown on the balance sheet as a deduction from trade debtors to give a net figure representing the amount that the enterprise expects to receive from these debtors during the forthcoming accounting year.

Key terms and concepts

Bad debts (141)
general provision for bad debts (141)
irrecoverable debt (141)
provision (141)
provision for bad/doubtful debts (141)
specific provision for bad debts (141)

Review questions

12.1 What do you understand by the term 'bad debts'? In what circumstances might a debt be treated as irrecoverable?

12.2 **a** Explain the nature of a provision, including how this differs from a liability.
b Give one example of a provision other than provisions for bad debts and depreciation.

12.3 **a** Explain the nature of a provision for bad debts.
b Explain the difference between a specific and general provision for bad debts.

12.4 Examine the purpose and logic behind a provision for bad debts, with particular reference to the timing of profits and losses arising from credit sales.

Exercises

An asterisk after the question number indicates that there is a suggested answer in the Appendix.

12.5* **Level I**

A business has an accounting year ending on 31 July. It sells goods on credit and on 31 July 20X1 had trade debtors of £15,680. This includes debts of £410 due from A. Wall and £270 from B. Wood, both of which were regarded as irrecoverable.

The business has decided to create a provision for bad debts at 31 July 20X1 of 4 per cent of trade debtors. Previously there was no provision for bad debts.

You are required to show the ledger entries in respect of the above bad debts and provision for bad debts.

12.6* **Level I**

B. Summers has an accounting year ending on 30 April. At 30 April 20X4 his ledger contained the following accounts:

	£
Trade debtors	25,000
Provision for doubtful debts	750

The trade debtors at 30 April 20X5 were £19,500. This includes £620 due from A. Winters and £880 from D. Spring, both of which are thought to be irrecoverable.

You have been instructed to make a provision for bad debts at 30 April 20X5 of 3 per cent of trade debtors.

Show the ledger entries in respect of the bad debts and provision for bad debts.

12.7 **Level I**

The accounts for the year ended 30 November 20X7 of Springboard Ltd included a provision for doubtful debts at that date of £900.

During the year ended 30 November 20X8, the company received £500 from Peter Lyon towards the settlement of a debt of £700 which had been written off as irrecoverable by the company in 20X5. There is no evidence that Peter Lyon will be able to make any further payments to the company.

Trade debtors at 30 November 20X8 amounted to £22,000, which includes the following debts it has now been decided to write off as bad:

	£
Mary Leaf	800
Angus Way	300

In its accounts for the year ended 30 November 20X8, the company is to continue its policy of maintaining a provision for doubtful debts of 5 per cent of debtors at the year end. *Note*: Bad debts written off or recovered are not to be recorded in the provision for doubtful debts account.

Required:

a Prepare the journal entry (or entries) in the books of the company necessitated by the receipt from Peter Lyon.

Notes: 1 Journal entries should include narratives.

2 For the purposes of this question, assume that cash receipts are journalized.

b Prepare the provision for doubtful debts account in the books of the company for the year ended 30 November 20X8.

c Show the entry for debtors which will be included in the balance sheet as at 30 November 20X8 of the company. (AAT)

12.8 **Level I**

The following transactions are to be recorded. At the beginning of year 1 a provision for doubtful debts account is to be opened. It should show a provision of 2 per cent against debtors of £50,000. During the year bad debts of £2,345 are to be charged to the provision account. At the end of year 1 the bad debts provision is required to be 2 per cent against debtors of £60,000.

In year 2 bad debts of £37 are to be charged against the account. At the end of year 2 a provision of 1 per cent against debtors of £70,000 is required.

Required:
Prepare provision for doubtful debts account for the two years. Show in the account the double entry for each item, and carry down the balance at the end of each year.

(ACCA adapted)

12.9 Level II

The balance sheet as at 31 December 20X5 of Zoom Products Ltd included:

Trade debtors	£85,360

The accounts for the year ended 31 December 20X5 included a provision for doubtful debts at 31 December 20X5 of 3 per cent of the balance outstanding from debtors. During 20X6, the company's sales totalled £568,000, of which 90 per cent, in value, was on credit and £510,150 was received from credit customers in settlement of debts totalling £515,000. In addition, £3,000 was received from J. Dodds in a settlement of a debt which had been written off as bad in 20X5; this receipt has been credited to J. Dodds account in the debtors' ledger.

On 30 December 20X6, the following outstanding debts were written off as bad:

J. White	£600
K. Black	£2,000

Entries relating to bad debts are passed through the provision for doubtful debts account, whose balance at 31 December 20X6 is to be 3 per cent of the amount due to the company from debtors at that date.

Required:

a Write up the provision for doubtful debts account for the year ended 31 December 20X6, bringing down the balance at 1 January 20X7.

b Prepare a computation of the amount to be shown as trade debtors in the company's balance sheet at 31 December 20X6. (AAT)

12.10 Level II

Because of the doubtful nature of some debts, P. Rudent instructed his accountants to make a specific provision in the accounts for the year ended 30 June 20X5 against the following debts:

	£
J. Black	28
C. Green	6
B. Grey	24
Fawn Ltd	204

He also instructed that a general provision of 5 per cent for doubtful debts should be created on the other debtors, which at 30 June 20X5 amounted to £8,000.

No further business transactions were entered into with any of these debtors during the year ended 30 June 20X6, but an amount of £9 was received from J. Black's trustee in bankruptcy by way of a first dividend; a first and final dividend of £70 was received from the liquidator of Fawn Ltd and B. Grey paid his debt in full. A further debt of £95 due from S. White proved to be bad.

On 30 June 20X6 P. Rudent instructed his accountants to maintain the provision existing against C. Green's debt and to provide for the balance owing by J. Black, and to make further provision for debts owing by J. Blue £19 and R. Brown £15. The other debtors amounted to £7,500 and the accountants were instructed to make the provision for doubtful debts equal to 5 per cent of these debts.

Show what entries should be made in P. Rudent's nominal ledger to record these facts.

(ACCA)

12.11* **Level II**

M. Shaft has an accounting year ending on 31 December. At 31 December 20X6 the ledger contained the following balances:

	£
Plant and machinery	30,000
Provision for depreciation on plant and machinery	12,500
Trade debtors	10,760
Provision for bad debts	1,260

The provision for bad debts consisted of a general provision of £500 and specific provisions comprising: A. Bee £320; C. Dee £180; and F. Gee £260.

The following transactions occurred during 20X7:

31 Mar	Part exchanged one piece of plant for another. The part exchange allowance on the old plant was £4,000 and the balance of £1,000 was paid by cheque. The old plant cost £8,000 when it was purchased on 1 July 20X5.
30 Apr	A. Bee was declared bankrupt and a first dividend of £70 was received from the trustee.
15 June	A debt of £210 owed by J. Kay that is included in the debtors at 31 December 20X6 was found to be bad.
3 Aug	C. Dee paid his debt in full.
7 Oct	F. Gee was declared bankrupt and a first and final dividend at £110 was received from the trustee.

Plant and machinery is depreciated using the reducing balance method at a rate of 25 per cent per annum on a strict time basis. The trade debtors at 31 December 20X7 were £12,610. This figure is after recording all money received but does not take into account any of the above bad debts. The relevant specific provisions and a general provision for bad debts of 5 per cent should be maintained at 31 December 20X7.

You are required to:

a Show the ledger entries in respect of the above, including the charges to the profit and loss account and the balances at 31 December 20X7. Show your workings clearly and take all calculations to the nearest £.

b Briefly discuss the similarities between provisions for bad debts and depreciation.

chapter

13 Accruals and prepayments

Learning objectives

After reading this chapter you should be able to:

1. explain the meaning of the key terms and concepts listed at the end of the chapter;
2. explain the conceptual foundation of accruals and prepayments, including the nature of the resulting charge to the profit and loss account;
3. describe the nature of accruals and prepayments and how the amounts can be ascertained in practice;
4. show the entries for accruals and prepayments in the journal, ledger, profit and loss account, and balance sheet;
5. prepare simple final accounts from a trial balance making the required adjustments for accruals and prepayments.

The nature of, and ledger entries for, accrued expenses

As discussed in Chapter 10, the accruals concept dictates that costs are recognized as they are incurred, not when money is paid. That is, goods and services are deemed to have been purchased on the date they are received. This gives rise to **accrued expenses/accruals**. These are 'creditors' in respect of services received which have not been paid for at the end of the accounting year. Accrued expenses can obviously only occur where services are paid for in arrears, such as electricity or gas.

An accrual may comprise either or both of the following:

1 Invoices received (for expenses) that have not been paid at the end of the accounting year.
2 The value of services received for which an invoice has not been rendered at the end of the accounting year.

In the case of the latter, this requires an estimate to be made of the amount of the services consumed during the period between the date of the last invoice and the end of the accounting year. This may be based on any one of the following:

1 A meter reading taken at the end of the accounting year.
2 The amount consumed over a corresponding period during the current year.
3 The amount consumed during the same period of the previous year as adjusted for any change in the unit price.

However, in practice final accounts are often not prepared until some time after the end of the accounting year. By that time the invoice covering the period in question is likely to have been received and can thus be used to ascertain the value of the services consumed during the relevant period.

Although accrued expenses are essentially creditors, rather than have a separate creditors' account it is usual to enter accruals in the relevant expense account. This consists of debiting the amount owing at the end of the year to the expense account as a balance *carried down* and crediting the same account as a balance *brought down*. Thus, the amount that will be transferred to the profit and loss account consists of the amount paid during the year plus the accrual at the end of the year (less the accrual at the start of the year). This will reflect the total value of the services that have been received during the current accounting year. The balance brought down is entered on the balance sheet as a current liability. This is illustrated in Example 13.1.

Example 13.1

D. Spring has an accounting year ending on 31 December. The following amounts have been paid for electricity:

Date paid	*Quarter ended*	£
29 Mar 20X6	28 Feb 20X6	96
7 July 20X6	31 May 20X6	68
2 Oct 20X6	31 Aug 20X6	73
5 Jan 20X7	30 Nov 20X6	82
3 Apr 20X7	28 Feb 20X7	105

You are required to show the entries in the light and heat account for the year ended 31 December 20X6 and the relevant balance sheet extract.

Workings

Accrual at 1 Jan 20X6 = $\frac{1}{3} \times £96 = £32$

Accrual at 31 Dec 20X6 = $£82 + (\frac{1}{3} \times £105) = £117$

Light and heat

20X6			20X6		
29 Mar	Bank	96	1 Jan	Accrual b/d	32
7 July	Bank	68	31 Dec	Profit and loss a/c	322
2 Oct	Bank	73			
31 Dec	Accrual c/d	117			
		354			354
			20X7		
			1 Jan	Accrual b/d	117

Balance sheet as at 31 December 20X6

	£
Current liabilities	
Creditors and accrued expenses	117

Note

1 The amount transferred to the profit and loss account is the difference between the two sides of the light and heat account after entering the accrual at the end of the year.

The nature of, and ledger entries for, prepaid expenses

The accruals concept also gives rise to **prepaid expenses/prepayments.** These can be described as debtors in respect of services that have been paid for but not received at the end of the accounting year. Prepayments can obviously only occur where services are paid for in advance, such as rent, local government taxes, road tax and insurance.

The amount of the prepayment is ascertained by determining on a time basis how much of the last payment made during the accounting year relates to the services that will be received in the following accounting year.

Although prepaid expenses are essentially debtors, rather than have a separate debtors' account it is usual to enter the prepayment in the relevant expense account. This consists of crediting the amount of the prepayment to the expense account as a balance *carried down* and debiting the same account as a balance *brought down*. Thus, the amount that will be transferred to the profit and loss account consists of the amount paid during the year minus the prepayment at the end of the year (plus the prepayment at the start of the year). This will reflect the total value of the services that have been received during the current accounting year. The balance brought down is entered on the balance sheet as a current asset. This is illustrated in Example 13.2.

Example 13.2

M. Waters has an accounting year ending on 30 June. The following amounts have been paid as rent:

Date paid	*Quarter ended*	£
2 June 20X5	31 Aug 20X5	600
1 Sep 20X5	30 Nov 20X5	600
3 Dec 20X5	28 Feb 20X6	660
5 Mar 20X6	31 May 20X6	660
4 June 20X6	31 Aug 20X6	720

You are required to show the entries in the rent account for the year ended 30 June 20X6 and the relevant balance sheet extract.

Workings

Prepaid at 1 July 20X5 = $\frac{2}{3}$ × £600 = £400
Prepaid at 30 June 20X6 = $\frac{2}{3}$ × £720 = £480

Rent

20X5			20X6		
1 July	Prepayment b/d	400	30 June	Profit and loss	2,560
1 Sep	Bank	600	30 June	Prepayment c/d	480
3 Dec	Bank	660			
20X6					
5 Mar	Bank	660			
4 June	Bank	720			
		3,040			3,040
20X6					
1 July	Prepayment b/d 480				

Balance sheet as at 30 June 20X6

	£
Current assets	
Debtors and prepayments	480

Note

1 The amount transferred to the profit and loss account is the difference between the two sides of the rent account after entering the prepayment at the end of the year.

Accruals and prepayments and the preparation of final accounts from the trial balance

The profit and loss account is usually prepared from the trial balance. This involves adjusting the amounts shown in the latter for any accruals and prepayments at the end of the accounting year. It is important to appreciate that because the trial balance is taken out at the end of the accounting year, the amounts shown in it include any accruals and prepayments at the start of the year. Thus, when preparing a profit and loss account from the trial balance, it is only necessary to add to the amount shown in the trial balance any accrual at the end of the accounting year and to subtract any prepayment.

Learning Activity 13.1

Obtain copies of the electricity bills for the house in which you live. From these prepare a light and heat account relating to the last complete calendar year. Repeat this exercise for insurance.

Summary

The accruals concept dictates that costs are recognized as they are incurred, not as money is paid. That is, goods and services are deemed to have been purchased on the date they are received. This gives rise to accrued and prepaid expenses. Accrued expenses are creditors in respect of services received which have not been paid for at the end of an accounting year. Prepaid expenses are debtors in respect of services that have been paid for but not received at the end of an accounting year.

After a trial balance has been extracted, the final accounts are prepared, which necessitates adjustments relating to accrued and prepaid expenses. These adjustments are made in the relevant expense accounts in the form of a balance at the end of the year. The remaining difference between the two sides of the expense account is transferred to the profit and loss account, and represents the cost of services received during the year. The balance on the expense account is shown on the balance sheet as a current liability in the case of accruals, or as a current asset in the case of prepayments.

Key terms and concepts

Accruals (152)
accrued expenses (152)
prepaid expenses (153)
prepayments (153)

Review questions

13.1 **a** Explain the nature of accrued and prepaid expenses.
b Describe how the amount of each may be ascertained.

Exercises

An asterisk after the question number indicates that there is a suggested answer in the Appendix.

13.2* **Level I**

K. Wills has an accounting year ending on 31 December. The following amounts were paid in respect of rent and gas:

Expense	*Date paid*	*Quarter ended*	£
Rent	1 Nov 20X1	31 Jan 20X2	900
Rent	29 Jan 20X2	30 April 20X2	930
Gas	6 Mar 20X2	28 Feb 20X2	420
Rent	2 May 20X2	31 July 20X2	930

continued

Expense	*Date paid*	*Quarter ended*	£
Gas	4 June 20X2	31 May 20X2	360
Rent	30 July 20X2	31 Oct 20X2	930
Gas	3 Sep 20X2	31 Aug 20X2	270
Rent	5 Nov 20X2	31 Jan 20X3	960
Gas	7 Dec 20X2	30 Nov 20X2	390
Gas	8 Mar 20X3	28 Feb 20X3	450

You are required to show the ledger entries in the rent and light and heat accounts for the year ended 31 December 20X2.

13.3 Level I

Oriel Ltd, whose financial year runs from 1 June to the following 31 May, maintains a combined rent and rates account in its ledger.

Rent is fixed on a calendar year basis and is payable quarterly in advance. Rent was £2400 for the year ended 31 December 20X8 and is £3,000 for the year ending 31 December 20X9.

Oriel Ltd has made the following payments of rent by cheque:

Date	*Amount*	*Details*
20X8	£	
3 Jan	600	Quarter to 31 Mar 20X8
1 Apr	600	Quarter to 30 June 20X8
1 July	600	Quarter to 30 Sep 20X8
1 Oct	600	Quarter to 31 Dec 20X8
20X9		
3 Jan	750	Quarter to 31 Mar 20X9
1 Apr	750	Quarter to 30 June 20X9

Rates are assessed annually for the year from 1 April to the following 31 March and are payable in one lump sum by 30 September. The rates assessment was £2,040 for the year ended 31 March 20X9 and £2,280 for the year ending 31 March 20X0.

Oriel Ltd paid the rates for the year ended 31 March 20X9 by cheque on 30 September 20X8 and intends to pay the rates for the year ended 31 March 20X0 on 30 September 20X9.

Required:

a Prepare the rent and rates account for the year ended 31 May 20X9 only as it would appear in the ledger of Oriel Ltd.

b Explain with particular reference to your answer to (a) the meaning of the term 'matching'. (AAT)

13.4 Level I

Munch Catering Ltd, whose financial year runs from 1 December to the following 30 November, maintains a 'Building occupancy costs' account in its general ledger. This account is used to record all payments in respect of rent, insurance and property taxes on the company's business premises.

Rent is fixed on a calendar year basis and is payable quarterly in advance. Rent was £1,800 for the year ended 31 December 20X9 and is £2,100 for the year ended 31 December 20X0.

Munch Catering Ltd has made the following payments of rent by cheque:

Date	*Amount*	*Details*
20X9	£	
29 Sep	450	Quarter to 31 Dec 20X9
29 Dec	525	Quarter to 31 Mar 20X0
20X0		
30 Mar	525	Quarter to 30 June 20X0
29 June	525	Quarter to 30 Sep 20X0
28 Sep	525	Quarter to 31 Dec 20X0

Munch Catering Ltd paid its building contents insurance premium of £547 for the year to 30 November 20X0 on 17 November 20X9. This policy was cancelled as from 31 May 20X0 and Munch Catering Ltd received a cheque for £150 as a rebate of premium on 21 June 20X0. A new buildings contents insurance policy was taken out with a different insurance company with effect from 1 June 20X0. The premium on this policy was £400 and this was paid in full by cheque by Munch Catering Ltd on 18 May 20X0.

Property taxes are assessed annually for the year from 1 April to the following 31 March and are payable in one lump sum by 30 September. Munch Catering Ltd's assessment was £840 for the year to 31 March 20X0 and £1,680 for the year to 31 March 20X1. Munch Catering Ltd paid the assessment for the year ended 31 March 20X0 by cheque on 2 October 20X9 and the assessment for the year ended 31 March 20X1 by cheque on 26 September 20X0.

Required:
Prepare the 'Building occupancy costs' account for the year ended 30 November 20X0 only as it would appear in the general ledger of Munch Catering Ltd. (AAT)

13.5* **Level I**

The ledger of RBD & Co. included the following account balances:

	At 1 June 20X4	*At 31 May 20X5*
	£	£
Rents receivable: prepayments	463	517
Rent and rates payable		
prepayments	1,246	1,509
accruals	315	382
Creditors	5,258	4,720

During the year ended 31 May 20X5, the following transactions had arisen:

	£
Rents received by cheque	4,058
Rent paid by cheque	7,491
Rates paid by cheque	2,805
Creditors paid by cheque	75,181
Discounts received from creditors	1,043
Purchases on credit	to be derived

Required:
Post and balance the appropriate accounts for the year ended 31 May 20X5, deriving the transfer entries to profit and loss account, where applicable. (ACCA adapted)

13.6 Level II

The balances on certain accounts of Foster Hardware Co. as at 1 April 20X1 were:

	£
Rent and rates payable—accruals	2,200
—prepayments	1,940
Rent receivable—prepayments	625
Vehicles (at cost)	10,540
Provision for depreciation of vehicles	4,720
During the financial year the business	
paid rent by cheque	5,200
paid rates by cheque	3,050
received cheque for rent of sublet premises	960
traded in vehicle—original cost	4,710
—accumulated depreciation	3,080
—part exchange allowance	1,100
paid balance of price of new vehicle by cheque	5,280
Closing balances as at 31 March 20X2 were:	
Rent and rates payable—accruals	2,370
—prepayments	1,880
Rent receivable—prepayments	680
Vehicles (at cost)	to be derived
Provision for depreciation of vehicles	3,890

Required:

Post and balance the appropriate accounts for the year ended 31 March 20X2, deriving the transfer entries to the profit and loss account where applicable. (ACCA)

13.7 Level II

The trial balance of Snodgrass, a sole trader, at 1 January 20X8 is as follows:

	Debit	*Credit*
	£000	£000
Capital		600
Fixed assets (net)	350	
Trade debtors	200	
Prepayments—rent	8	
—insurance	12	
Trade creditors		180
Accruals—electricity		9
—telephone		1
Stock	200	
Bank	20	
	790	790

The following information is given for the year:

	£000
Receipts from customers	1,000
Payments to suppliers	700
Payments for: rent	30
insurance	20
electricity	25
telephone	10
wages	100
Proprietor's personal expenses	50
Discounts allowed	8
Bad debts written off	3
Depreciation	50

At 31 December 20X8 the following balances are given:

	£000
Trade debtors	250
Prepayments—rent	10
—telephone	2
Trade creditors	160
Accruals—electricity	7
—insurance	6
Stock	230

Required:

Prepare a trading and profit and loss account for the year, and a balance sheet as at 31 December 20X8. (ACCA)

The preparation of final accounts from the trial balance

Learning objectives

After reading this chapter you should be able to:

1. explain the meaning of the key terms and concepts listed at the end of the chapter;
2. show the journal and ledger entries relating to the treatment of stocks of tools, stationery, fuel, containers, packing materials, livestock, growing crops, etc.
3. show the journal and ledger entries relating to drawings and capital introduced other than in the form of cash or cheques;
4. describe the accounting treatment of goods on sale or return and show the ledger entries needed to reverse any incorrect treatment;
5. prepare an extended trial balance taking into account adjustments for stocks, depreciation, provisions for bad debts, accruals, prepayments, etc.
6. prepare trading and profit and loss accounts and a balance sheet from an extended trial balance.

Introduction

As explained in Chapter 9, final accounts are prepared after the trial balance has been produced and this involves transferring the balances on various income and expense accounts to the profit and loss account. In addition, the process of preparing final accounts involves a number of **adjustments**, some of which have been described in Chapters 11–13.
These may be summarized as follows:

1 accounting for stocks and work in progress
2 provisions for depreciation
3 provision for bad debts
4 accruals and prepayments
5 the correction of omissions and errors such as bad debts not written off during the year.

Some further adjustments not addressed in the previous chapters are discussed below.

Stocks of tools, stationery and fuels

As explained in Chapter 11, **loose tools** are regarded as fixed assets, whereas **consumable tools** are designated as revenue expenditure. Thus, any stocks of consumable tools, like stocks of stationery and fuel, are treated as current assets. However, irrespective of their classification, the accounting adjustments in respect of these items are essentially the same. That is, the value of the items in stock at the end of the accounting year is entered in the relevant ledger account as a balance *carried down* on the credit side and as a balance *brought down* on the debit side (in exactly the same way as with prepaid expenses). The difference between the two sides of the ledger account is then transferred to the profit and loss account. In the case of loose tools this is described as depreciation, which is referred to as having been computed using the revaluation method.

The principle which is applied to each of these items is as follows:

Stock at end of previous year at valuation
Add: Purchases during the year
Less: Stock at end of current year at valuation
= Charge to profit and loss account

The charge to the profit and loss account represents the value of stationery, fuel or tools that has been consumed during the year. The same principle is also applied in the accounts of farming businesses with respect to livestock and growing crops, and in retailing businesses when accounting for containers and packing materials.

Adjustments for drawings and capital introduced

Drawings may take a number of forms in addition to cash. For example, it is common for the owner to take goods out of the business for his or her personal consumption. This requires an adjustment which may be done by either of two entries: (1) debit drawings and credit purchases with the *cost* of the goods to the business; or (2) debit drawings and credit sales where the goods are deemed to be taken at some other value such as the normal selling price.

Another form of drawings occurs where the business pays the owner's personal debts. A common example of this is taxation on the business profits. Sole traders and partnerships are not liable to taxation as such. It is the owner's personal liability and not that of the business. Therefore, if taxation is paid by the business it must be treated as drawings. The ledger entry is to debit drawings and credit the cash book.

A similar form of drawings occurs when the business has paid expenses, some of which relate to the owner's private activities. The most common example is where the business has paid motor expenses, some of which relate to the owner's private vehicle or the use of a business asset for domestic or social purposes. The ledger entry in this case is to debit drawings and credit the relevant expense account. The principle is exactly the same where the owner takes a fixed asset out of the business for his or her permanent private use.

Some other examples of drawings occasionally found in examination questions include where the owner buys a private asset (e.g. a car, holiday, groceries) for him or herself, or for a friend or relative (e.g. spouse), and pays for it from the business cash or bank account. The ledger entry is to debit drawings and credit the cash book. A similar but more complicated example is where a debtor of the business pays the debt to the owner (who pays the money into his or her private bank account), or alternatively the owner accepts some private service (repairs to his or her private assets, a holiday, etc.) in lieu of payment. In this case the ledger entry is to debit drawings and credit the debtors' account.

After all the drawings for the accounting year have been entered in the drawings account, this account must be closed by transferring the balance to the capital account. The entry is to credit the drawings account and debit the capital account.

→ **Capital introduced** after the start of a business usually takes the form of either cash/cheques or other assets (e.g. a vehicle). The ledger entry is to credit the capital account and debit the appropriate asset account (e.g. cash book, motor vehicles). A slight variation on this occurs when the owner buys a business asset (e.g. vehicle or goods for resale) or pays a business expense or liability from his or her private cash/bank account. In this case the ledger entry is to credit the capital account and debit the relevant asset (e.g. motor vehicles), liability, expense or purchases account. A more complicated version of the same principle is where the owner privately provides some service to a creditor of the business in lieu of payment. The ledger entry for this will be to credit the capital account and debit the creditors' account.

Some of these examples of drawings and capital introduced are quite common in small businesses, and particularly important in the context of partnerships, as will be seen in Chapter 24.

Goods on sale or return

Goods which have been sent to potential customers on sale or return or on approval must not → be recorded as sales until actually sold. In the ledger, **goods on sale or return** at the end of an accounting year are included in stock at cost.

Sometimes, in examination questions, goods on sale or return are recorded as sales. This is an error and must be reversed by means of the following entries:

Debit sales account Credit trade debtors	with the selling price of the goods
Debit stock account Credit trading account	with the cost price of the goods

Note that the entries in the stock account and trading account take the form of increasing the amount of the closing stock.

The extended trial balance

As explained above, the preparation of final accounts involves various adjustments. In the preceding three chapters these were described mainly in terms of the necessary ledger entries. However, in practice and in examinations final accounts are usually prepared from the trial balance, the ledger entries being done at some later date when the final accounts are completed.

Because the preparation of final accounts from the trial balance involves a large number of adjustments, in practice it is usual to make these adjustments using an **extended trial balance**. This may take a number of forms, but a useful approach is to set it up to comprise eight columns made up of four pairs as follows:

1 The trial balance debit side
2 The trial balance credit side
3 Adjustments to the debit side
4 Adjustments to the credit side
5 The profit and loss account debit side
6 The profit and loss account credit side
7 The balance sheet debit side
8 The balance sheet credit side

The first two columns are the normal trial balance. Columns 3 and 4 are used to make adjustments to the figures in the trial balance in respect of provisions for depreciation and bad debts, accruals and prepayments, etc. Columns 5 and 6 are used to compute the amounts that will be entered in the profit and loss account. Columns 7 and 8 are used to ascertain the amounts that will be shown in the balance sheet.

Columns 3 and 4 relating to the adjustments are used like the journal in that items entered in these columns are intended to represent entries that will be made in the ledger. For example, one simple adjustment is the transfer of drawings to the capital account. This takes the form of an entry in the credit adjustment column on the line containing the balance on the drawings account, with a corresponding entry in the debit adjustment column on the line containing the balance on the capital account, in the trial balance.

Furthermore, adjustments may take the form of an entry in one of the adjustments columns and one of the profit and loss account columns. This is because the adjustment columns and the profit and loss account columns relate to entries that will be made in the ledger. However, no adjustments must be entered in the balance sheet columns because the balance sheet does not involve entries in the ledger.

The most common adjustments found in the extended trial balance are as follows:

1 *Provisions for depreciation.* Debit the profit and loss account column and credit the adjustment column on the line containing the balance on the provision for depreciation account in the trial balance.

2 *Provision for bad debts.* Debit the profit and loss account column and credit the adjustment column on the line containing the balance on the provision for bad debts account with any increase in the provision (opposite for any decrease).

3 *Accruals and prepayments.* Debit and credit the adjustment columns on the line relating to the expense in question.

4 *Stock at the end of the year*. Debit the adjustment column and credit the profit and loss account column. To avoid confusion this may be done on a new line separate from the stock at the start of the year, as in Example 14.1.

After all the necessary adjustments have been made in the adjustment and profit and loss account columns, the amounts that will be entered in the profit and loss account and balance sheet columns can be ascertained. These are found by cross casting the amounts relating to each ledger account shown in the original trial balance. For example, if the original trial balance contained a rent account with a debit balance, any prepayment shown in the credit adjustment column would be deducted from this and the difference entered in the profit and loss account debit column. The prepayment shown in the debit adjustment column would also be extended across and entered in the balance sheet debit column. Expenses with accrued charges are treated in a similar way.

When all the amounts have been entered in the profit and loss account and balance sheet columns, the profit (or loss) can be computed in the normal manner as the difference between the two profit and loss account columns. The profit is entered in the profit and loss account debit column and the credit adjustment column. The latter is then extended into the balance sheet credit column and eventually added to the capital account balance.

When all the items in the trial balance have been extended across into the profit and loss account and balance sheet columns and the profit has been ascertained, the amounts in these columns are entered in the final version of the profit and loss account and balance sheet. An illustration of the use of the extended trial balance is given in Example 14.1.

Finally, it should be observed that although the extended trial balance is very common in practice, the time allocated to answering examination questions is unlikely to allow for full presentation of the extended trial balance, and this is rarely a requirement. Without the extended trial balance it becomes difficult to answer final accounts questions in a logical and accurate manner. Some students therefore find it helpful to make use of the trial balance printed on the question paper. Adjustment columns can be drawn on the right-hand side of the trial balance on the question paper, and the necessary adjustments made in rough form to permit the final accounts to be prepared in the examination answer book.

Example 14.1

T. King has an accounting year ending on 30 April. The following trial balance was prepared for the year ended 30 April 20X6:

	Debit £	*Credit* £
Capital		59,640
Drawings	7,600	
Bank overdraft		1,540
Cash	1,170	
Plant and machinery	87,000	
Provision for depreciation on plant		27,000
Sales		68,200
Purchases	42,160	
Debtors	15,200	
Creditors		12,700
Provision for bad debts		890

Bad debts	610	
Rent	4,200	
Light and heat	3,700	
Stationery	2,430	
Stock	5,900	
	169,970	169,970

You have been given the following additional information:

1 Plant and machinery is depreciated using the reducing balance method at a rate of 10 per cent per annum.
2 The provision for bad debts at 30 April 20X6 should be 5 per cent of debtors.
3 There is an accrual at 30 April 20X6 in respect of gas amounting to £580, and rent prepaid of £600.
4 Stock at 30 April 20X6 was £7,220.

You are required to prepare an extended trial balance at 30 April 20X6 and final accounts in vertical form.

Workings

1. Depreciation = 10 per cent × (£87,000 – £27,000) = £6,000
2. Provision for bad debts = (5 per cent × £15,200) – £890 = £130 decrease

The extended trial balance is shown on the next page.

T. King

Trading and profit and loss account for the year ended 30 April 20X6

	£	£
Sales		68,200
Less: Cost of sales:		
Stock at 1 May 20X5	5,900	
Add: Purchases	42,160	
	48,060	
Less: Stock at 30 April 20X6	7,220	40,840
Gross profit		27,360
Add: Provision for bad debts		130
		27,490
Less: Expenditure		
Rent	3,600	
Light and heat	4,280	
Stationery	2,430	
Bad debts	610	
Depreciation on plant	6,000	16,920
Net profit		10,570

T. King
Extended trial balance as at 30 April 20X6

	Trial balance		Adjustments		Profit and loss a/c		Balance sheet	
	Dr £	Cr £	Dr £	Cr £	Dr £	Cr £	Dr £	Cr £
Capital		59,640	7,600					52,040
Drawings	7,600			7,600				
Bank overdraft		1,540						1,540
Cash	1,170						1,170	
Plant and machinery	87,000						87,000	
Provision for depreciation on plant		27,000		6,000	6,000			33,000
Sales		68,200				68,200		
Purchases	42,160				42,160			
Debtors	15,200						15,200	
Creditors		12,700						12,700
Provision for bad debts		890	130			130		760
Bad debts	610				610			
Rent	4,200		600	600	3,600		600	
Light and heat	3,700		580	580	4,280			580
Stationery	2,430				2,430			
Stock at 1 May 20X5	5,900				5,900			
Stock at 30 April 20X6			7,220			7,220	7,220	
Profit				10,570	10,570			10,570
	169,970	169,970			75,550	75,550	111,190	111,190

Balance sheet as at 30 April 20X6

	£	£	£
Fixed assets	*Cost*	*Acc. Depn*	*WDV*
Plant and machinery	87,000	33,000	54,000
Current assets			
Stock of goods		7,220	
Debtors	15,200		
Less: Provision for bad debts	760	14,440	
Prepayments		600	
Cash		1,170	
		23,430	
Less: Current liabilities			
Bank overdraft	1,540		
Creditors	12,700		
Accruals	580	14,820	
Net current assets			8,610
Net assets			62,610
Capital			
Balance at 1 May 20X5			59,640
Add: Net profit			10,570
			70,210
Less: Drawings			7,600
Balance at 30 April 20X6			62,610

Summary

The process of preparing final accounts from a trial balance involves a number of adjustments relating to accounting for stocks, provisions for depreciation, provisions for bad debts, and accruals and prepayments. In addition, it will be necessary to make further adjustments in respect of any stocks of tools, stationery, fuel, etc. These are treated as a debit balance on the relevant expense account, and shown on the balance sheet as a current asset. The remaining difference between the two sides of the expense account is transferred to the profit and loss account, and represents the value of goods consumed during the year.

In practice it is common to prepare final accounts using an extended trial balance. This comprises the usual trial balance money columns but with additional money columns to the right. The first pair of these comprises adjustment columns which are used to make the adjustments referred to above. The second pair represents the entries in the profit and loss account; and the third pair represents the amounts shown in the balance sheet. The amounts which are entered in the profit and loss account and balance sheet columns are ascertained by cross casting the figures relating to each ledger account shown in the original trial balance and the adjustment columns.

Key terms and concepts

Exercises

An asterisk after the question number indicates that there is a suggested answer in the Appendix.

14.1* **Level II**

The following is the trial balance of C. Jones as at 31 December 20X9:

	Debit	*Credit*
	£	£
Capital		45,214
Drawings	9,502	
Purchases	389,072	
Sales		527,350
Wages and salaries	33,440	
Rent and rates	9,860	
Light and heat	4,142	
Bad debts	1,884	
Provision for doubtful debts		3,702
Debtors	72,300	
Creditors		34,308
Cash at bank	2,816	
Cash in hand	334	
Stock	82,124	
Motor car—cost	7,200	
—depreciation		2,100
	£612,674	£612,674

You are provided with the following additional information:

1 Stock at 31 December 20X9 has been valued at £99,356.
2 The rent of the premises is £6,400 p.a., payable half-yearly in advance on 31 March and 30 September.
3 Rates for the year ending 31 March 20X0 amounting to £1,488 were paid on 10 April 20X9.
4 Wages and salaries to be accrued amount to £3,012.
5 Depreciation on the car is to be provided using the straight line method at a rate of 20 per cent per annum.
6 It has been agreed that further debts amounting to £1,420 are to be written off against specific customers, and the closing provision is to be adjusted to 5 per cent of the revised debtors' figure.

You are required to prepare the trading profit and loss account for the year ended 31 December 20X9, and a balance sheet at that date. This should be done using an extended trial balance.

14.2* **Level II**

The following is the trial balance of J. Clark at 31 March 20X6:

	Debit	*Credit*
	£	£
Capital		60,000
Drawings	5,600	
Purchases/sales	34,260	58,640
Returns inwards/outwards	3,260	2,140
Carriage inwards	730	
Carriage outwards	420	
Discount allowed/received	1,480	1,970
Plant and machinery at cost	11,350	
Provision for depreciation on plant		4,150
Motor vehicles	13,290	
Provision for depreciation on vehicles		2,790
Goodwill	5,000	
Quoted investments	6,470	
Freehold premises at cost	32,000	
Mortgage on premises		10,000
Interest paid/received	1,000	460
Stock	4,670	
Bank and cash	2,850	
Wages	7,180	
Rent and rates	4,300	
Provision for bad debts		530
Debtors/creditors	8,070	4,340
Light and heat	2,640	
Stationery	450	
	145,020	145,020

You are given the following additional information:

1 Goods on sale or return have been treated as sales. These cost £300 and were invoiced to the customer for £400.
2 The provision for bad debts is to be adjusted to 10 per cent of debtors.
3 At 31 March 20X6 there is electricity accrued of £130 and rates prepaid amounting to £210.
4 Stock at 31 March 20X6 was valued at £3,690.
5 During the year the proprietor has taken goods costing £350 from the business for his own use.
6 Depreciation on plant is 25 per cent on the reducing balance method and on vehicles 20 per cent by the same method.
7 Unrecorded in the ledger is the sale on credit on 1 July 20X5 for £458 of a motor vehicle bought on 1 January 20X4 for £1,000.
8 There are bad debts of £370 that have not been entered in the ledger.
9 There was a stock of stationery at 31 March 20X6 which cost £230.

You are required to prepare a trading and profit and loss account for the year and a balance sheet at the end of the year.

14.3 Level II

The following trial balance has been extracted from the ledger of Andrea Howell, a sole trader, as at 31 May 20X9, the end of her most recent financial year.

	Debit	*Credit*
	£	£
Property, at cost	90,000	
Equipment, at cost	57,500	
Provision for depreciation (as at 1 June 20X8)		
—property		12,500
—equipment		32,500
Stock, as at 1 June 20X8	27,400	
Purchases	259,600	
Sales		405,000
Discounts allowed	3,370	
Discounts received		4,420
Wages and salaries	52,360	
Bad debts	1,720	
Loan interest	1,560	
Carriage out	5,310	
Other operating expenses	38,800	
Trade debtors	46,200	
Trade creditors		33,600
Provision for bad debts		280
Cash on hand	151	
Bank overdraft		14,500
Drawings	28,930	
13 per cent loan		12,000
Capital, as at 1 June 20X8		98,101
	612,901	612,901

The following additional information as at 31 May 20X9 is available:

1 Stock as at the close of business was valued at £25,900.

2. Depreciation for the year ended 31 May 20X9 has yet to be provided as follows:

   Property: 1 per cent using the straight line method.
   Equipment: 15 per cent using the straight line method.

3 Wages and salaries are accrued by £140.

4 'Other operating expenses' include certain expenses prepaid by £500. Other expenses included under this heading are accrued by £200.

5 The provision for bad debts is to be adjusted so that it is 0.5 per cent of trade debtors as at 31 May 20X9.

6 'Purchases' include goods valued at £1,040 which were withdrawn by Mrs Howell for her own personal use.

Required:

Prepare Mrs Howell's trading and profit and loss account for the year ended 31 May 20X9 and her balance sheet as at 31 May 20X9. (AAT)

14.4 Level II

S. Trader carries on a merchanting business. The following balances have been extracted from his books on 30 September 20X1:

	£
Capital—S. Trader, at 1 Oct 20X0	24,239
Office furniture and equipment	1,440
Cash drawings—S. Trader	4,888
Stock on hand—1 Oct 20X0	14,972
Purchases	167,760
Sales	203,845
Rent	1,350
Light and heat	475
Insurance	304
Salaries	6,352
Stationery and printing	737
Telephone and postage	517
General expenses	2,044
Travellers' commission and expenses	9,925
Discounts allowed	517
Discounts received	955
Bad debts written off	331
Debtors	19,100
Creditors	8,162
Balance at bank to S. Trader's credit	6,603
Petty cash in hand	29
Provision for doubtful debts	143

The following further information is to be taken into account:

1 Stock on hand on 30 September 20X1 was valued at £12,972.
2 Provision is to be made for the following liabilities and accrued expenses as at 30 September 20X1: rent £450; lighting and heating £136; travellers' commission and expenses £806; accountancy charges £252.
3 Provision for doubtful debts is to be raised to 3 per cent of the closing debtor balances.
4 Office furniture and equipment is to be depreciated by 10 per cent on book value.
5 Mr Trader had removed stock costing £112 for his own use during the year.

You are required to prepare:

a Trading and profit and loss accounts for the year ended 30 September 20X1 grouping the various expenses under suitable headings; and
b a balance sheet as at that date. (ACCA)

14.5 Level II

F. Harrison is in business as a trader. A trial balance taken out as at 31 January 20X6 was as follows:

	Debit	*Credit*
	£	£
Purchases	42,400	
Sales		50,240
Returns inwards and outwards	136	348
Salaries and wages	4,100	
Rent, rates and insurance	860	
Sundry expenses	750	
Bad debts	134	
Provision for doubtful debts at 1 Feb 20X5		280
Stock on hand at 1 Feb 20X5	13,630	
Fixture and fittings:		
At 1 Feb 20X5	1,400	
Additions on 30 Sep 20X5	240	
Motor vehicles:		
At 1 Feb 20X5	920	
Sale of vehicle (book value at 1 Feb 20X5 £80)		120
Sundry debtors and creditors	4,610	3,852
Cash at bank and in hand	3,820	
F. Harrison Capital a/c—Balance at 1 February 20X5		20,760
F. Harrison Drawings a/c	2,600	
	£75,600	£75,600

You are required to prepare trading and profit and loss accounts for the year ended 31 January 20X6, and draw up a balance sheet as on that date.

The following information is to be taken into account:

1 Included in sales are goods on sale or return which cost £240 and which have been charged out with profit added at 20 per cent of sale price.
2 Outstanding amounts not entered in the books were: rent £36, sundry expenses £90.
3 Prepayments were: rates £60, insurance £10.
4 Stock on hand on 31 January 20X6 was valued at £15,450.
5 Provision for doubtful debts is to be £340.
6 Depreciation is to be provided for as follows: fixtures and fittings 10 per cent per annum, motor vehicles 25 per cent per annum. (ACCA)

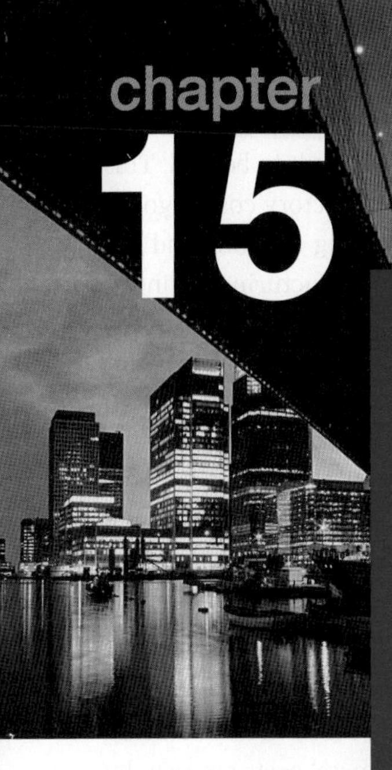

Manufacturing accounts and the valuation of stock

Learning objectives

After reading this chapter you should be able to:

1. explain the meaning of the key terms and concepts listed at the end of the chapter;
2. describe the main differences between the final accounts of a commercial enterprise and those of a manufacturing business;
3. explain the classification of costs into direct and indirect costs;
4. describe the different categories of stocks found in a manufacturing business and show how these are treated in the ledger and final accounts;
5. explain the purpose of a manufacturing account and the various subtotals normally found in this account;
6. prepare a manufacturing account, trading and profit and loss account, and balance sheet for a manufacturing business in account form or vertical format;
7. explain the nature of manufacturing profits and show the entries in the final accounts;
8. describe the methods of valuation of work in progress (WIP) and explain the relationship between these and the treatment of WIP in the manufacturing account;
9. discuss the method of valuation of finished goods stock including its impact on the gross profit;
10. describe the perpetual inventory system;
11. describe the main methods of identifying the cost of fungible stocks and demonstrate their application in the valuation of stocks and the cost of sales;
12. discuss the circumstances in which each of the main methods of identifying the cost of fungible stocks may be justifiable, and describe their impact on the gross profit.

Introduction

The main differences between the accounts of commercial and manufacturing businesses stem from the former buying goods for resale without further processing, whereas the latter buy raw materials and components which are processed into finished goods to be sold. This makes it necessary for a manufacturing business to calculate the total factory cost of goods produced. The amount is computed in what is termed a manufacturing account and the result shown in place of 'purchases' in the trading account of a non-manufacturing business. Furthermore, the stocks in the trading account are the stock of finished goods unsold at the start and end of the accounting year. Apart from these differences the profit and loss account of a manufacturing business is the same as that of a commercial business, in that they both contain selling and distribution costs/overheads, administrative expenses/overheads and financial charges (such as interest). The balance sheet is also the same, except that of a manufacturing business will also include a number of different categories of stock, which will be described later.

The classification of costs

One of the major differences between the accounts of a commercial and manufacturing business concerns the classification of costs. In a manufacturing business, costs are usually classified as either direct costs or indirect costs/overheads.

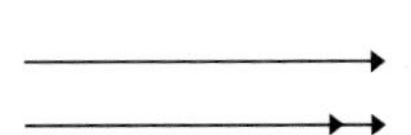

Direct costs are those which can be traced, attributed to or identified with a particular product, and comprise direct materials, direct labour/wages and **direct expenses. Direct materials** consist of any goods that form a part of the final product. These are composed of the raw materials and components which a manufacturing business turns into its finished product. In the case of, for example, a car manufacturer, one of its raw materials may be iron ore used to produce engines. However, the material inputs do not just consist of raw materials. For example, some of the materials purchased by a car manufacturer may include steel, which is the finished product of another industry. Similarly, many companies find it cheaper to buy rather than manufacture parts of their finished product. For example, car manufacturers buy components such as tyres and lighting equipment from outside suppliers. Thus, direct materials consist of raw materials and various types of components that make up the final product.

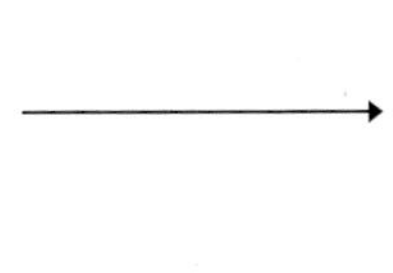

Direct labour typically comprises the wages of those employees who physically work on the products or operate the machines that are used to produce the finished products. Wages paid to foremen, supervisors, cleaners, maintenance staff, etc., are not direct wages.

Direct expenses are any expenses that are directly attributable to a specific product. The most common direct expenses are royalties paid for the right to produce the finished product, the cost of any special drawings and subcontracted work.

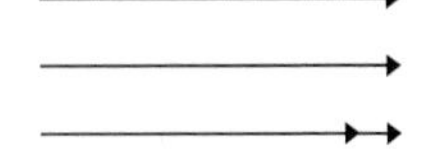

Indirect costs/overheads are those costs that cannot be traced, attributed to or identified with a particular product, and comprise **factory/production/manufacturing overheads, selling and distribution overheads**, and **administrative overheads.** Examples of factory overheads include the wages of supervisors, foremen, maintenance and cleaning staff, power, consumable tools, repairs to plant and depreciation of plant.

Categories of stocks

A manufacturing business also differs from a commercial business in that it has a number of different categories of stocks as follows.

Direct materials

This category is composed of raw materials and components that have been purchased but not put into production at the end of the accounting year.

Work in progress (WIP)

This refers to goods that are not complete at the end of the accounting year.

Finished goods

This category consists of goods that have been produced but which are unsold at the end of the accounting year.

Purposes and preparation of a manufacturing account

As has already been mentioned, the main purpose of a **manufacturing account** is to calculate the **factory cost of completed production**. This replaces the purchases in the trading account and thus must be done before the trading account can be prepared (after the trial balance has been completed). In calculating the cost of the products that have been completed during the accounting year it is usual to show the following in the manufacturing account in the order shown below.

1. *The direct material cost* of goods that have been put into production during the year. To calculate this it will be necessary to adjust the cost of purchases of direct materials for the opening and closing stocks thus:

   Direct materials in stock at start of year
   add: Purchases of direct materials during year
   less: Direct materials in stock at end of year
   = Cost of direct materials put into production during year

   It is also common to add any carriage inwards to the cost of purchases.

2. *The direct labour costs*
3. *The direct expenses*
4. *The **prime cost** of production*
   This is the sum of the direct materials, direct labour and direct expenses.
5. *The factory overheads*
6. *The total factory costs*
   This is the sum of the prime costs and the factory overheads.
7. *The **factory cost of completed production***
   The total factory costs relate to both those products that have been completed during the year and those which are only partially completed at the end of the year. To arrive at the

factory cost of completed production it is therefore necessary to make an adjustment for the opening and closing work in progress (WIP) thus:

WIP at start of year
add: Total factory costs
less: WIP at end of year
= Factory cost of completed production

The factory cost of completed production is transferred to the trading account in place of 'purchases' in a non-manufacturing business. The cost of sales is computed by adjusting the factory cost of completed production for the opening and closing stocks of finished goods thus:

Stock of finished goods at start of year
add: Factory costs of completed production
less: Stock of finished goods at end of year
= Cost of goods sold

Note that all the above adjustments in respect of direct materials stocks, WIP and finished goods are applications of the matching principle. An illustration of the preparation of a manufacturing account is shown in Example 15.1.

Example 15.1

The following information relating to the year ended 30 April 20X7 has been extracted from the books of A. Bush, a motor vehicle component manufacturer.

	£
Sales	298,000
Stocks of direct materials at 1 May 20X6	7,900
Stocks of direct materials at 30 Apr 20X7	6,200
Work in progress at 1 May 20X6	8,400
Work in progress at 30 Apr 20X7	9,600
Stocks of finished goods at 1 May 20X6	5,400
Stocks of finished goods at 30 Apr 20X7	6,800
Purchase of direct materials	68,400
Direct wages	52,600
Production supervisors' salaries	34,800
Sales staff salaries	41,700
Accounting staff salaries	38,200
Royalties paid for products produced under licence	17,500
Cost of power for machinery	9,200
Repairs to plant	6,700
Bad debts	5,100
Interest on bank loan	7,400
Depreciation on plant	18,600
Depreciation on delivery vehicles	13,200
Depreciation on accounting office equipment	11,500

Prepare manufacturing, trading, and profit and loss accounts for the year ended 30 April 20X7, showing clearly the total direct/prime costs, manufacturing/factory costs, cost of completed production and cost of sales.

A. Bush
Manufacturing, trading and profit and loss accounts for the year ended 30 April 20X7

	£		£
Direct materials:		*Cost of completed*	
Stock at 1/5/X6	7,900	*production c/d*	208,300
Add: Purchases	68,400		
	76,300		
Less: Stock at 30/4/X7	6,200		
	70,100		
Direct wages	52,600		
Royalties	17,500		
Prime costs	140,200		
Factory overheads:			
Supervisors' salaries	34,800		
Power	9,200		
Repairs to plant	6,700		
Depreciation on plant	18,600		
Manufacturing costs	209,500		
Add: WIP at 1/5/X6	8,400		
	217,900		
Less: WIP at 30/4/X7	9,600		
	208,300		208,300
Finished goods:		Sales	298,000
Stock at 1/5/X6	5,400		
Add: Cost of completed production b/d	208,300		
	213,700		
Less: Stock at 30/4/X7	6,800		
Cost of sales	206,900		
Gross profit c/d	91,100		
	298,000		298,000
Selling and distribution costs		*Gross profit b/d*	91,100
Sales staff salaries	41,700		
Depreciation on delivery vehicles	13,200		
Bad debts	5,100		
Administrative costs:			
Accounting staff salaries	38,200		
Depreciation on office equipment	11,500		
Interest on loan	7,400	*Net loss c/d*	26,000
	117,100		117,100
Net loss b/d	26,000		

Notes

1 The above has been shown in account form to emphasize the double entry. However, a vertical presentation is usually preferable as illustrated in most of the solutions to the exercises.

2 Any proceeds from the sale of scrap direct materials are normally credited to the manufacturing account, thus reducing the cost of completed production.

Manufacturing profits

In some businesses, manufactured goods are transferred from the factory to the warehouse at market prices, or an approximation thereof in the form of cost plus a given percentage for profit. This is intended to represent the price that the warehouse would have to pay if it bought the goods from an external supplier, or the price that the factory would receive if it sold the goods to an external customer. This is commonly referred to as the **transfer price**. The purpose of having internal transfer prices is said to be to make the managers in the factory and warehouse more aware of the impact of market forces, increase motivation and facilitate the evaluation of their performance.

The accounting entries are relatively straightforward. The figure for completed production carried down from the manufacturing account to the trading account will simply be at some transfer price or valuation other than cost. This gives rise to a **manufacturing profit** (or loss) which will be the difference between the two sides of the manufacturing account. The double entry for this profit (or loss) is to credit (or debit) the profit and loss account. While this accounting treatment of the manufacturing profit (or loss) may be adopted in the final accounts prepared for internal management purposes, it would not be acceptable for external reporting because it contravenes SSAP9, which requires that finished goods stocks are valued at factory cost (discussed in detail below). The finished goods stocks will have been valued at the transfer price, which means that the manufacturing profit includes unrealized profit contained in any increase in finished goods stocks over the year. Any such unrealized profit should be transferred to a provision for unrealized (manufacturing) profit account by crediting this account and debiting the profit and loss account. Where there is a decrease in finished goods stocks over the year the entries are the opposite. After these entries have been made there should be a balance on the provision for unrealized profit account equal to the manufacturing profit contained in the finished goods stock at the end of the year. This is deducted from the value of finished goods stocks (at transfer price) in the balance sheet, thus reducing it to factory cost.

The valuation of finished goods and work in progress

The work in progress (WIP) shown in the manufacturing account is usually valued at production/factory cost; that is, prime costs plus factory overheads. This is why the adjustment for the opening and closing WIP is made after the total factory costs have been computed. Similarly, the finished goods stock shown in the trading account is normally valued at factory cost. This is consistent with the valuation of the completed production, which is also included in the trading account at factory cost. Thus, neither the WIP nor finished goods stock includes other overheads such as selling and distribution costs, administrative expenses and interest. Sometimes WIP is valued at prime cost: that is, excluding factory overheads. In this case the adjustment for WIP must be made before the factory overheads in the manufacturing account.

The above assertions relating to the valuation of WIP and finished goods stock can be explained further by reference to *SSAP9—Stocks and Long Term Contracts.*[1] This states that 'in order to match costs and revenue, costs of stocks should comprise that expenditure which has been incurred in the normal course of business in bringing the product or service to its present location and condition. This expenditure should include, in addition to cost of purchase (of direct materials), such costs of conversion as are appropriate to the location and condition. **Costs of conversion** comprise: (a) costs which are specifically attributable to units of production, i.e. direct labour, direct expenses and sub-contracted work; (b) production overheads.' Note that this specifically excludes selling, distribution and administrative overheads.

Finally, it is important to consider that sometimes goods in stock may have to be sold at a price which is below their cost. If there are goods in stock at the end of a given accounting year which are expected to result in a loss, those goods should be valued and entered in the accounts at their expected proceeds of sale and not their cost. This is because SSAP9 dictates that 'stocks normally need to be stated at cost, or, if lower, at net realizable value. The comparison of cost and net realizable value needs to be made in respect of each item of stock separately. **Net realizable value** [NRV] is the estimated proceeds from the sale of items of stock (and WIP) less all further costs to completion and less all costs to be incurred in marketing, selling and distributing directly related to the items in question.'[1]

The identification of the cost of stock

In the case of both manufacturing and non-manufacturing businesses the determination of the cost/purchase price of goods in stock often presents a major problem. It is frequently not possible to identify the particular batch(es) of goods that were purchased which are in stock at the end of the year. This is referred to as **fungible stock**, which means substantially indistinguishable goods. In these circumstances it is necessary to make an *assumption* about the cost of goods in stock. There are a number of possible assumptions, but the most reasonable assumption will depend on the type of goods involved, the procedure for handling the receipt and sale of stocks, prices, etc. According to SSAP9, the most appropriate assumption is one which 'provides a fair approximation to the expenditure actually incurred'.[1] This is discussed further below.

Most large businesses operate what is called a **perpetual inventory system**, which is a continuous record of the quantity and value of stock. It includes a stores ledger containing an account for each type of good that is purchased. The **stores ledger** accounts are used to record the quantities and prices of goods purchased, the quantities and cost of goods sold (or issued to production in the case of direct materials), and thus the balance and cost of goods in stock after each receipt and sale. However, this system also requires an assumption or decision about the cost of goods in stock, and thus the cost of goods that were sold.

As explained above, there are a number of possible assumptions, or what are referred to as bases/methods of identifying/pricing the cost of stock. The bases make assumptions about the flow of items in stock. These flow assumptions are not selected as a result of the actual way in which stock is used but in order to reflect a particular view of the economic effects of stock usage in accounts. Three common approaches are: (1) 'first in, first out' (FIFO); (2) 'last in, first out' (LIFO); and (3) weighted average. These assume, respectively, that: (1) the oldest stock is sold first; (2) the most recently purchased stock is sold first; and (3) the cost of sales comprises the average cost of all the purchases in stock. Each of these methods is described below using Example 15.2.

Example 15.2

P. Easton commenced business on 1 January 20X1 as a dealer in scrap iron. The following purchases and sales were made during the first six months of 20X1:

Jan	Purchased 40 tonnes at £5 per tonne
Feb	Purchased 50 tonnes at £6 per tonne
Mar	Sold 30 tonnes at £10 per tonne
Apr	Purchased 70 tonnes at £7 per tonne
May	Sold 80 tonnes at £15 per tonne

You are required to prepare:

a a perpetual inventory record of the quantities and values of goods purchased, sold and stock; and

b a trading account showing the gross profit for the six months to 30 June 20X1 given that the above are the only purchases and sales.

State any assumptions that you make.

Learning Activity 15.1

Attempt part (b) of the above example before proceeding further. An answer which claims it cannot be done is not acceptable. It must be done! Justify any assumptions and then compare them with the following.

1. First in, first out (FIFO)

The FIFO assumption is that the goods sold are those which have been in stock for the longest time. The stock is therefore composed of the most recent purchases that make up the quantity in stock, and the cost of stock is the price paid for these. Given the FIFO assumption, the answer to Example 15.2 will be as follows.

Stores ledger account

Date	Purchases			Cost of sales			Balance in stock		
	Units	Price	Value	Units	Price	Value	Units	Price	Value
Jan	40	5	200				40	5	200
Feb	50	6	300				40	5	200
							50	6	300
							90		500
Mar				30	5	150	10	5	50
							50	6	300
							60		350
Apr	70	7	490				10	5	50
							50	6	300
							70	7	490
							130		840
May				10	5	50			
				50	6	300			
				20	7	140	50	7	350
				80		490			
Totals			990			640			

P. Easton
Trading account for the six months ended 30 June 20X1

	£	£
Sales: 30 tonnes @ £10	300	
80 tonnes @ £15	1,200	1,500
Less: Cost of sales—		
Purchases	990	
Less: Stock at 30 June 20X1	350	640
Gross profit		860

The FIFO method is based on the premise that the physical movement of goods over time will have this sequence of events, particularly where the goods are perishable. The use of the FIFO method is favoured by SSAP9 and the Inland Revenue.

2. Last in, first out (LIFO)

The LIFO assumption is that the goods sold are those which have been in stock for the shortest time. The stock is therefore composed of those goods which have been held for the longest time, and the cost of stock is the price paid for these. Given the LIFO assumption, the answer to Example 15.2 will be as follows.

Stores ledger account

Date	Purchases			Cost of sales			Balance in stock		
	Units	Price	Value	Units	Price	Value	Units	Price	Value
Jan	40	5	200				40	5	200
Feb	50	6	300				50	6	300
							40	5	200
							90		500
Mar				30	6	180	20	6	120
							40	5	200
							60		320
Apr	70	7	490				70	7	490
							20	6	120
							40	5	200
							130		810
May				70	7	490			
				10	6	60	10	6	60
				80		550	40	5	200
							50		260
Totals			990			730			

P. Easton
Trading account for the six months ended 30 June 20X1

	£	£
Sales		1,500
Less: Cost of sales—		
Purchases	990	
Less: Stock at 30 June 20X1	260	730
Gross profit		770

The LIFO method may be in accordance with the physical movement of goods in some circumstances. For example, purchases of coal, iron ore, sand and gravel are likely to be piled one on top of the other, and thus goods taken from the top of the heap will probably consist of the most recent purchases. In most other instances it is an unrealistic assumption. However, even where this is the case the LIFO method may be justified in times of rising prices on the grounds that the cost of sales will reflect the most recent prices. This is said to give a more realistic figure of profit since the most recent price is an approximation of the current cost of the goods sold (i.e. their replacement cost). Thus, one argument for the LIFO method is that where historical cost accounting is used it gives a 'true and fair view' of the profit in times of changing prices.

The LIFO method is discouraged by SSAP9 and the Inland Revenue. The arguments put forward against its use are that LIFO 'results in stocks being stated in the balance sheet at amounts that bear little relationship to recent cost levels',[1] and it is a poor substitute for a proper system of accounting for changing prices.

3. Weighted average method

The weighted average method is based on the assumption that the goods sold and the stock, comprise a mixture of each batch of purchases. The cost of sales and stock is therefore taken to be a weighted average of the cost of purchases. Given the weighted average assumption, the answer to Example 15.2 will be as follows. Notice that a new weighted average is computed after each purchase.

Stores ledger account

Date	Purchases			Cost of sales			Balance in stock		
	Units	Price	Value	Units	Price	Value	Units	Price	Value
Jan	40	5	200				40	5	200
Feb	50	6	300				90	5.556	500
Mar				30	5.556	167	60	5.556	333
Apr	70	7	490				130	6.331	823
May				80	6.331	506	50	6.331	317
Totals			990			673			

Workings for weighted average cost:
February = £500 ÷ 90 units = £5.556
April = £823 ÷ 130 units £6.331
All calculations to 3 decimal places.

P. Easton
Trading account for the six months ended 30 June 20X1

	£	£
Sales		1,500
Less: Cost of sales—		
Purchases	990	
Less: Stock at 30 June 20X1	317	673
Gross profit		827

Where purchases are mixed together the weighted average method can be justified on the grounds that it is in accordance with the physical events. This often occurs when goods are stored in a single container that is rarely completely emptied, such as in the case of nuts and bolts, liquids and granular substances, etc. Another justification is that when prices are fluctuating it gives a more representative normal price and thus more comparable cost of sales figures.

The weighted average method is approved by SSAP9 and acceptable to the Inland Revenue.

FIFO and LIFO compared

Clearly each of these methods of calculating the cost of stock results in different values for stock and profit. In times of constantly rising prices, FIFO will give a higher figure of profits and value of stock than LIFO because it matches older, lower costs against revenues. A business should choose whichever method is appropriate to its particular circumstances and apply this consistently in order that meaningful comparisons can be made. FIFO is by far the most common method used in practice in the UK because it is favoured by SSAP9 and the Inland Revenue. The valuation of stocks is a controversial issue in accounting, and is one of the areas most open to deliberate manipulation.

Summary

Manufacturing businesses usually classify all their costs as either direct or indirect/ overheads. Direct costs comprise direct materials, direct labour and direct expenses. Overheads are classified as either factory overheads, selling and distribution costs, or administrative expenses. Manufacturing businesses also normally have a number of different types of stocks which comprise stocks of direct materials, work in progress (WIP) and finished goods.

The main difference between the final accounts of manufacturing businesses and those of commercial undertakings is that the former includes a manufacturing account. This is used to ascertain the cost of completed production which is entered in the trading account in place of the purchases of a non-manufacturing business. The computation of the cost of completed production necessitates certain adjustments in respect of stocks of direct materials and WIP which are similar to those relating to the calculation of the cost of sales.

WIP and finished goods stocks are usually valued at their factory cost. Direct materials stocks are normally valued at cost. However, SSAP9 dictates that if the net realizable value (NRV) of any of these stocks is lower than their cost, they must be included in the final accounts at their NRV. Furthermore, it is frequently not possible to identify the cost of goods in stock. This is referred to as fungible stock, which means that the goods are substantially indistinguishable from each other. In these circumstances it is necessary to make an assumption about the cost of goods in stock and thus the cost of goods sold (or issued to production in the case of direct materials). The most common assumptions are first in, first out (FIFO), last in, first out (LIFO), and a weighted average cost. In times of changing prices each will give a different value of stocks, the cost of sales and thus the profit.

Key terms and concepts

Administrative overheads (174)
costs of conversion (178)
direct costs (174)
direct expenses (174)
direct labour (174)
direct materials (174)
factory cost of completed production (175)
factory/production/manufacturing overheads (174)
finished goods (175)
first in first out (180)
fungible stock (179)
indirect costs (174)
last in first out (181)
manufacturing account (175)
manufacturing profits (178)
net realizable value (179)
overheads (174)
perpetual inventory system (179)
prime cost (175)
selling and distribution overheads (174)
stores ledger (179)
transfer price (178)
weighted average method (182)
work in progress (175)

Reference

1. Accounting Standards Committee (1988). *Statement of Standard Accounting Practice 9—Stocks and Long Term Contracts* (ICAEW).

Review questions

15.1 a Explain the difference between direct costs and overheads.
b Describe the different types of direct costs and overheads found in a manufacturing business.

15.2 Describe the different categories of stocks normally held by a manufacturing business.

15.3 a Explain the main purpose of a manufacturing account.
b Describe the structure and main groups of costs found in a manufacturing account.

15.4 a Explain the difference between the total factory cost of production and the factory cost of completed production.
b What is the justification for adjusting the total factory cost for work in progress rather than, say, the total prime/direct cost?

15.5 Work in progress and finished goods stocks should be valued at the cost of purchase and conversion. Explain.

15.6 Explain how the matching principle is applied to the valuation of stocks.

15.7 Explain the circumstances in which stocks might be shown in the accounts at a value different from their historical cost.

15.8 Explain fully the basis on which finished goods stock and work in progress should be valued in final accounts.

15.9 a What is a perpetual inventory system?
b Describe three methods of calculating the cost of fungible stocks.
c Explain the circumstances in which each of these methods may be justifiable.

15.10 'In selecting a method of calculating the cost of stock, management should ensure that the method chosen bears a reasonable relationship to actual costs. Methods such as ... LIFO do not usually bear such a relationship' (ASC, SSAP9). Discuss.

Exercises

An asterisk after the question number indicates that there is a suggested answer in the Appendix.

15.11* **Level I**

The trial balance extracted at 30 April 20X4 from the books of Upton Upholstery, a furniture manufacturer, is given below.

	Debit	*Credit*
	£	£
Factory machinery at cost	28,000	
Factory machinery depreciation 1/5/X3		5,000
Office equipment	2,000	
Office equipment depreciation 1/5/X3		800
Trade debtors and creditors	15,000	16,000
Cash and bank	2,300	
Bank loan		11,000
Stocks 1/5/X3—Raw materials	4,000	
Incomplete production	16,400	
Finished goods	9,000	
Carriage inwards	1,200	
Carriage outwards	700	
Purchases—Raw materials	84,000	
Light and heat	3,000	
Rent and rates	6,600	
Direct factory wages	19,900	
Office wages	5,200	
Sales commission to selling agents	1,400	
Sales of finished goods		140,000
Capital account		35,000
Drawings	9,100	
	£207,800	£207,800

Notes

1 At 30 April 20X4, accrued direct factory wages amounted to £600 and office wages £100; rent paid included £600 paid on 20 January 20X4, for the period 1 January to 30 June 20X4.
2 Records showed that, at the year end, stock values were as follows; raw materials £5,400; incomplete production £17,000; finished goods £8,000.
3 Depreciation should be allowed for factory machinery on the straight line method over seven years, and office equipment on the reducing balance method at 25 per cent p.a.
4 A provision of £1,000 should be made for doubtful debts.
5 Light and heat should be apportioned between the factory and office in the ratio 4 : 1, respectively; rent and rates in the ratio 3 : 1, respectively.

You are required to prepare manufacturing, trading, and profit and loss accounts for the year ended 30 April 20X4 and a balance sheet at that date.

15.12* **Level II**

From the following information prepare manufacturing, trading, and profit and loss accounts for the year ended 31 December 20X9. Show clearly the prime cost, factory cost of completed production, cost of sales, gross profit, selling and distribution overheads, administrative overheads, and net profit.

	£
Stock of raw materials at 1 January 20X9	2,453
Work in progress valued at factory cost at 1 January 20X9	1,617
Stock of finished goods at 1 January 20X9	3,968
Purchases of raw materials	47,693
Purchases of finished goods	367
Raw materials returned to suppliers	4,921
Carriage outwards	487
Carriage inwards	683
Direct wages	23,649
Administrative salaries	10,889
Supervisors' wages	5,617
Royalties payable	7,500
Electricity used in factory	2,334
Light and heat for administrative offices	998
Sales staff salaries and commission	8,600
Bad debts	726
Discount received	2,310
Discount allowed	1,515
Depreciation—plant	13,400
—delivery vehicles	3,700
—office fixtures and furniture	1,900
Rent and rates (factory $\frac{3}{4}$, office $\frac{1}{2}$)	4,800
Delivery expenses	593
Postage and telephone	714
Printing and stationery	363
Proceeds from the sale of scrap metal	199
Interest payable on loan	3,000
Bank charges	100
Insurance on plant	1,750
Advertising	625
Repairs to plant	917
Sales	145,433

Purchases of raw materials include £2,093, and direct wages £549, for materials and work done in constructing an extension to the factory.

Stock of raw materials at 31 December 20X9	3,987
Work in progress valued at factory cost at 31 December 20X9	2,700
Stock of finished goods at 31 December 20X9	5,666

15.13 Level II

W. Wagner, a manufacturer, provided the following information for the year ended 31 August 20X0:

	£
Stocks at 1 Sep 20X9	
Raw materials	25,000
Work in progress	15,900
Finished goods	26,600
Raw materials purchased	176,600
Factory general expenses	14,800
Direct wages	86,900
Repairs to plant and machinery	9,900
Factory lighting and heating	20,010
Carriage inwards	1,910
Carriage outwards	2,500
Sales	320,000
Raw materials returned	7,800
Factory maintenance wages	19,000
Administrative expenses	30,000
Selling and distribution expenses	15,100
Plant and machinery at cost	178,000
Freehold land and buildings at cost	160,000
Provision for depreciation on plant and machinery (at 1 Sep 20X9)	80,000

Additional information:

1 Amounts owing at 31 August 20X0:

	£
Direct wages	4,800
Factory heating and lighting	1,500

2 Depreciation on plant and machinery is to be provided at 10 per cent per annum on cost. There were no sales or purchases of plant and machinery during the year.

3 All manufactured goods are transferred to the warehouse at factory cost plus 10 per cent.

4 Stocks at 31 August 20X0:

	£
Raw materials	30,000
Work in progress	17,800
Finished goods	35,090

The raw materials are valued at cost, the work in progress at factory cost, while the stock of finished goods is valued at the factory transfer price.

Required:

a A manufacturing account for the year ended 31 August 20X0.

b A trading and profit and loss account for the year ended 31 August 20X0.

(AEB adapted)

15.14 Level II

Zacotex Ltd, a manufacturer, produced the following financial information for the year ended 31 March 20X9.

	£
Raw material purchases	250,000
Direct labour	100,000
Direct expenses	80,900
Indirect factory labour	16,000
Factory maintenance costs	9,700
Machine repairs	11,500
Sales of finished goods during the year	788,100
Stocks at 1 April 20X8:	
Raw materials	65,000
Finished goods	48,000
Work in progress	52,500
Other factory overhead	14,500
Factory heating and lighting	19,000
Factory rates	11,500
Administration expenses	22,000
Selling and distribution expenses	36,800

Additional information:

1 The stocks held at 31 March 20X9 were:

Raw materials	£51,400
Finished goods	£53,800
Work in progress	£41,000

NB: Raw materials are valued at cost; finished goods at factory cost; work in progress at factory cost.

Of the raw materials held in stock at 31 March 20X9, £15,000 had suffered flood damage and it was estimated that they could only be sold for £2,500. The remaining raw material stock could only be sold on the open market at cost less 10 per cent.

2 One-quarter of the administration expenses are to be allocated to the factory.

3 The raw materials purchases figure for the year includes a charge for carriage inwards. On 31 March 20X9 a credit note for £1,550 was received in respect of a carriage inwards overcharge. No adjustment had been made for this amount.

4 Expenses in arrear at 31 March 20X9 were:

	£
Direct labour	6,600
Machine repairs	1,700
Selling and distribution expenses	4,900

5 Plant and machinery at 1 April 20X8:

	£
At cost	250,000
Aggregate depreciation	75,000

During the year an obsolete machine (cost £30,000, depreciation to date £8,000) was sold as scrap for £5,000. On 1 October 20X8 new machinery was purchased for £70,000 with an installation charge of £8,000.

The company depreciates its plant and machinery at 10 per cent per annum on cost on all items in company ownership at the end of the accounting year.

6 An analysis of the sales of finished goods revealed the following:

	£
Goods sold for cash	105,000
Goods sold on credit	623,100
Goods sold on sale or return: returned	25,000
Goods sold on sale or return: retained and invoice confirmed	35,000
	788,100

7 On 1 April 20X8 the company arranged a long-term loan of £250,000 at a fixed rate of interest of 11 per cent per annum. No provision had been made for the payment of the interest.

Required:

For the year ended 31 March 20X9:

a A manufacturing account showing prime cost and factory cost of goods produced.

b A trading and profit and loss account.(AEB adapted)

15.15 Level II

On 1 April 20X5, Modern Dwellings Ltd commenced business as builders and contractors. It expended £14,000 on the purchase of six acres of land with the intention of dividing the land into plots and building 72 houses thereon.

During the year ended 31 March 20X6 roads and drains were constructed for the project at a total cost of £8,320. Building was commenced, and on 31 March 20X6, 30 houses had been completed and eight were in the course of construction.

During the year the outlay on houses was as follows:

	£
Materials, etc.	36,000
Labour and subcontracting	45,000

The value of the work in progress on the uncompleted houses at 31 March 20X6 amounted to £8500, being calculated on the actual cost of materials, labour and subcontracting to date.

During the year, 24 houses had been sold, realizing £80,000.

Prepare a trading account for the year ended 31 March 20X6. It can be assumed that the plots on which the 72 houses are to be built are all of equal size and value. (ACCA)

15.16 Level II

After stocktaking for the year ended 31 May 20X5 had taken place, the closing stock of Cobden Ltd was aggregated to a figure of £87,612.

During the course of the audit which followed, the undernoted facts were discovered:

1 Some goods stored outside had been included at their normal cost price of £570. They had, however, deteriorated and would require an estimated £120 to be spent to restore them to their original condition, after which they could be sold for £800.

2 Some goods had been damaged and were now unsaleable. They could, however, be sold for £110 as spares after repairs estimated at £40 had been carried out. They had originally cost £200.
3 One stock sheet had been over-added by £126 and another under-added by £72.
4 Cobden Ltd had received goods costing £2,010 during the last week of May 20X5 but because the invoices did not arrive until June 20X5, they have not been included in stock.
5 A stock sheet total of £1,234 had been transferred to the summary sheet as £1,243.
6 Invoices totalling £638 arrived during the last week of May 20X5 (and were included in purchases and in creditors) but, because of transport delays, the goods did not arrive until late June 20X5 and were not included in closing stock.
7 Portable generators on hire from another company at a charge of £347 were included, at this figure, in stock.
8 Free samples sent to Cobden Ltd by various suppliers had been included in stock at the catalogue price of £63.
9 Goods costing £418 sent to customers on a sale or return basis had been included in stock by Cobden Ltd at their selling price, £602.
10 Goods sent on a sale or return basis to Cobden Ltd had been included in stock at the amount payable (£267) if retained. No decision to retain had been made.

Required:
Using such of the above information as is relevant, prepare a schedule amending the stock figure as at 31 May 20X5. State your reason for each amendment or for not making an amendment. (ACCA)

15.17 Level II

Your company sells, for £275 each unit, a product which it purchases from several different manufacturers, all charging different prices. The manufacturers deliver at the beginning of each week throughout each month. The following details relate to the month of February.

		Quantity	*Cost each*	*Sales (units)*
Opening stock		10	£145	
Deliveries:	Week 1	20	£150	15
	Week 2	34	£165	33
	Week 3	50	£145	35
	Week 4	30	£175	39

From the above data you are required to:

a Prepare stock records detailing quantities and values using the following pricing techniques:
  i last in, first out (LIFO);
  ii first in, first out (FIFO);
  iii weighted average cost (calculated monthly to the nearest £).

b Prepare trading accounts using each of the stock pricing methods in (a) above and showing the gross profit for each method.

c Compare the results of your calculations and state the advantages and disadvantages of FIFO and LIFO pricing methods in times of inflation. (JMB)

15.18* **Level II**

A businessman started trading with a capital in cash of £6,000 which he placed in the business bank account at the outset.

His transactions, none of which were on credit, were as follows (in date sequence) for the first accounting period. All takings were banked immediately and all suppliers were paid by cheque. He traded in only one line of merchandise.

Purchases		*Sales*	
Quantity	*Price per unit*	*Quantity*	*Price per unit*
No.	£	No.	£
1,200	1.00		
1,000	1.05	800	1.70
600	1.10	600	1.90
900	1.20	1,100	2.00
800	1.25	1,300	2.00
700	1.30	400	2.05

In addition he incurred expenses amounting to £1,740, of which he still owed £570 at the end of the period.

Required:

Prepare separately using the FIFO (first in, first out), the LIFO (last in, first out) and weighted average (calculated for the period to the nearest penny) methods of stock valuation:

a a statement of cost of sales for the period; and

b a balance sheet at the end of the period.

Note: Workings are an integral part of the answer and must be shown. (ACCA adapted)

15.19 **Level II**

S. Bullock, a farmer, makes up his accounts to 31 March each year. The trial balance extracted from his books as at 31 March 20X6 was as follows:

	Debit	*Credit*
	£	£
Purchases—Livestock, seeds, fertilizers, fodder, etc.	19,016	
Wages and National Insurance	2,883	
Rent, rates, telephone and insurance	1,018	
Farrier and veterinary charges	34	
Carriage	1,011	
Motor and tractor running expenses	490	
Repairs—Farm buildings	673	
Implements	427	
Contracting for ploughing, spraying and combine work	308	
General expenses	527	
Bank charges	191	
Professional charges	44	
Sales		29,162
Motor vehicles and tractors—As at 1 April 20X5	1,383	
Additions	605	
Implements—As at 1 April 20X5	2,518	
Additions	514	

Valuation as at 1 April 20X5:		
Livestock, seeds, fertilizers, fodder, etc.	14,232	
Tillages and growing crops	952	
Loan from wife		1,922
Minister Bank		4,072
S. Bullock—Capital at 1 April 20X5		6,440
Current account at 1 April 20X5		6,510
Drawings during the year	1,280	
	£48,106	£48,106

	£	£
On 31 March 20X6:		
Debtors and prepayments were:		
Livestock sales	1,365	
Motor licences	68	
Liabilities were: Seeds and fertilizers		180
Rent, rates and telephone		50
Motor and tractor running expenses		40
Professional charges		127
Contracting		179
General expenses		54

Included in the above-mentioned figure of £50 is £15 for rent and this is payable for the March 20X6 quarter. In arriving at this figure the landlord has allowed a deduction of £235 for materials purchased for repairs to the farm buildings, which were carried out by S. Bullock, and is included in the 'Repairs to farm buildings' shown in the trial balance. In executing these repairs it was estimated that £125 labour costs were incurred and these were included in 'Wages and National Insurance'. This cost was to be borne by S. Bullock.

The valuation as at 31 March 20X6 was:

	£
Livestock, seeds, fertilizers, fodder, etc.	12,336
Tillages and growing crops	898

Depreciation, calculated on the book value as at 31 March 20X6, is to be written off as follows:

Motor vehicles and tractors 25 per cent per annum
Implements 12 per cent annum

You are requested to prepare:

a the profit and loss account for the year ended 31 March 20X6; and
b the balance sheet as at that date. (ACCA)

INTERNAL CONTROL AND CHECK

chapter

16

The bank reconciliation statement

Learning objectives

After reading this chapter you should be able to:

1 explain the meaning of the key terms and concepts listed at the end of the chapter;

2 explain the purpose and nature of bank reconciliations;

3 identify and correct errors and omissions in a cash book;

4 prepare a bank reconciliation statement.

The purpose and preparation of bank reconciliations

The purpose of preparing a **bank reconciliation statement** is to ascertain whether or not the balance shown in the cash book at the end of a given accounting period is correct by comparing it with that shown on the bank statement/passbook supplied by the bank. In practice, these two figures are rarely the same because of errors, omissions and the timing of bank deposits and cheque payments.

The bank reconciliation is not done in a book of account and thus is not a part of the double-entry system. It must be prepared at least yearly before the final accounts are compiled. Because most businesses usually have a large number of cheque transactions they often prepare a bank reconciliation statement either monthly or at least quarterly.

The first step in the preparation of a bank reconciliation involves identifying payments, and sometimes receipts, that are on the bank statement but which have not been entered in the cash book. Such payments may include dishonoured cheques, bank charges and interest, standing orders for hire purchase instalments, insurance premiums and loan interest. Occasionally, receipts such as interest and dividends received by credit transfer are also found to be on the bank statement but not in the cash book. When these omissions of receipts and payments occur the remedy is obviously to enter them in the cash book and compute a new balance. However, in examination questions the student is sometimes required to build them into the bank reconciliation statement instead.

In addition to the above omissions there are nearly always receipts and payments in the cash book which at the date of the reconciliation have not yet been entered by the bank on the bank statement. These consist of:

1. Cheques and cash received that have been paid into the bank and entered in the cash book but which have not yet been credited on the bank statement at the end of the accounting period when the bank reconciliation the bank reconciliation statement is being prepared. These are referred to as **amounts not yet credited.**
2. Cheques drawn that have been sent to the payee and entered in the cash book but which have not yet been presented to our bank for payment or which have not yet passed through the bank clearing system and thus do not appear on the bank statement at the end of the accounting period when the bank reconciliation statement is being prepared. These are referred to as **cheques not yet presented.**

Example 16.1 shows the procedure involved in preparing a bank reconciliation statement.

Example 16.1

The following is the cash book of J. Alton for the month of June 20X5

Cash book

20X5		£		20X5		£	
1 June	Balance b/d	1,000		2 June	D. Cat	240	✓
11 June	A. Hand	370	✓	13 June	E. Dog	490	✓
16 June	B. Leg	510	✓	22 June	F. Bird	750	
24 June	C. Arm	620		30 June	Balance c/d	1,200	
30 June	Cash	180					
		2,680				2,680	

The following is the statement of J. Alton received from his bank:

Bank statement

Date	Details	Debit £	Credit £	Balance £
19X5				
1 June	Balance			1,000
5 June	D. Cat	240 ✓		760
15 June	A. Hand		370 ✓	1,130
18 June	E. Dog	490 ✓		640
20 June	Dividend received		160	800
21 June	B. Leg		510 ✓	1,310
30 June	Bank charges	75		1,235

In practice, bank statements do not usually show the names of the people from whom cheques were received and paid. It is therefore necessary to identify the payments by means of the cheque number. However, the use of names simplifies the example for ease of understanding. The procedure is essentially the same.

The first step is to tick all those items which appear in both the cash book and on the bank statement during the month of June. A note is made of the items which are unticked:

1 Cheques and cash paid into the bank and entered in the cash book but not credited on the bank statement by 30 June 20X5 = C. Arm £620 + Cash £180 = £800.

2 Cheques drawn and entered in the cash book not presented for payment by 30 June 20X5 = F. Bird £750.

3 Amounts received by credit transfer shown on the bank statement not entered in the cash book = Dividends £160.

4 Standing orders and other payments shown on the bank statement not entered in the cash book = Bank charges £75.

Clearly, items 1 and 2 above will eventually appear on the bank statement in a later month. Items 3 and 4 must be entered in the cash book. However, the purpose of the bank reconciliation statement is to ascertain whether the difference between the balance in the cash book at 30 June 20X5 of £1,200 and that shown on the bank statement at the same date of £1,235 is explained by the above list of unticked items. Alternatively, are there other errors or omissions that need to be investigated?

The bank reconciliation statement will appear as follows:

J. Alton
Bank reconciliation statement as at 30 June 20X5

	£	£
Balance per cash book		1,200
Add: Dividends received not entered in cash book	160	
Cheques not yet presented	750	910
		2,110
Less: Bank charges not entered in cash book	75	
Amounts not yet credited	800	875
Balance per bank statement		1,235

It can thus be seen that since the above statement reconciles the difference between the balances in the cash book and on the bank statement, there are unlikely to be any further errors or omissions.

Notes

1 The dividends received are added to the cash book balance because it is lower than the bank statement balance as a result of this omission. In addition, it will increase by this amount when the dividends are entered in the cash book.

2 The bank charges are deducted from the cash book balance because the bank statement balance has been reduced by this amount but the cash book balance has not. In addition, the cash book balance will decrease by this amount when the bank charges are entered in the cash book.

3 The cheques not yet presented are added to the cash book balance because it has been reduced by this amount whereas the bank statement balance has not.

4 The amounts not yet credited are deducted from the cash book balance because it has been increased by this amount whereas the bank statement balance has not.

Sometimes in examination questions the student is not given the cash book balance. In this case the bank reconciliation statement is prepared in reverse order as follows:

	£	£
Balance per bank statement		1,235
Add: Amounts not yet credited	800	
Payments on bank statement not in the cash book	75	875
		2,110
Less: Cheques not yet presented	750	
Receipts on bank statement not in the cash book	160	910
= Balance per cash book		1,200

An alternative method of dealing with bank reconciliation is to amend the cash book for any errors and omissions, and only include in the bank reconciliation statement those items which constitute timing differences. This is illustrated in Example 16.2, along with some other items frequently found in examination questions.

Example 16.2

The following is a summary from the cash book of Home Shopping Ltd for March 20X8;

Cash book	£		£
Opening balance b/d	5,610	Payments	41,890
Receipts	37,480	Closing balance c/d	1,200
	43,090		43,090

When checking the cash book against the bank statement the following discrepancies were found:

1 Bank charges of £80 shown in the bank statement have not been entered in the cash book.
2 The bank has debited a cheque for £370 in error to the company's account.
3 Cheques totalling £960 have not yet been presented to the bank for payment.

4 Dividends received of £420 have been credited on the bank statement but not recorded in the cash book.
5 There are cheques received of £4,840 which are entered in the cash book but not yet credited to the company's account by the bank.
6 A cheque for £170 has been returned by the bank marked 'refer to drawer' but no entry relating to this has been made in the books.
7 The opening balance in the cash book should have been £6,510 and not £5,610.
8 The bank statement shows that there is an overdraft at 31 March 20X8 of £1,980.

You are required to:

a make the entries necessary to correct the cash book; and

b. prepare a bank reconciliation statement as at 31 March 20X8.

Cash book	£		£
Balance b/d	1,200	Bank charges	80
Dividends	420	Refer to drawer	170
Error in balance	900	Balance c/d	2,270
	2,520		2,520
Balance b/d	2,270		

Home Shopping Ltd
Bank reconciliation statement as at 31 March 20X8

	£	£
Balance per cash book		2,270
Add: Cheques not yet presented		960
		3,230
Less: Amounts not yet credited	4,840	
Cheque debited in error	370	5,210
Balance per bank statement (overdrawn)		1,980

Notes

1 The cheque debited in error is shown in the bank reconciliation statement rather than the cash book because it will presumably be corrected on the bank statement in due course and thus not affect the cash book.

2 Sometimes in examination questions the cash book contains a credit (i.e. overdrawn) balance. In this case, the bank reconciliation statement is prepared by reversing the additions and subtractions which are made when there is a favourable cash book balance. The bank reconciliation statement will thus appear as follows:

Balance per cash book (credit/overdrawn)
Add: Amounts not yet credited
Less: Cheques not yet presented
= Balance per bank statement

Alternatively, if the cash book balance is not given in the question and the bank statement contains an overdrawn balance, the bank reconciliation statement would be prepared as follows:

Balance per bank statement (debit/overdrawn)
Add: Cheques not yet presented
Less: Amounts not yet credited
= Balance per cash book

Learning Activity 16.1

Find your most recent bank statement and your cheque book. Prepare a reconciliation of the balance shown on your bank statement with that shown on your record of cheques received and drawn. If you do not keep a continuous record of your cheque receipts and payments, and thus the current balance, do so in future and repeat the exercise when you receive your next bank statement.

Summary

After extracting a trial balance but before preparing final accounts at the end of each accounting year, the first thing that needs to be done is to check the accuracy of the cash book (or bank account in the ledger). This takes the form of a bank reconciliation, which involves reconciling the balance in the cash book at the end of the year with that shown on the statement received from the bank. These will probably be different for two main reasons. First, there may be errors or omissions where amounts shown on the bank statement have not been entered properly in the cash book. These should be corrected in the cash book. Second, there are likely to be timing differences. These consist of cheques paid into the bank and cheques drawn entered in the cash book, but not shown on the bank statement at the end of the year. These timing differences are entered on the bank reconciliation statement as explanations for the difference between the balance in the cash book and that on the bank statement. If the timing differences provide a reconciliation of the two balances, the cash book balance is deemed to be correct. Otherwise, the reasons for any remaining difference will need to be investigated.

Key terms and concepts

Amounts not yet credited (196) bank reconciliation statement (196) cheques not yet presented (196)

Review questions

16.1 Explain the purpose of a bank reconciliation statement.

16.2 Describe the procedures involved in the collection of the data needed to prepare a bank reconciliation statement.

Exercises

An asterisk after the question number indicates that there is a suggested answer in the Appendix.

16.3 **Level II**

The following is a summary from the cash book of the Hozy Co. Ltd for October 20X7.

	£		£
Opening balance b/f	1,407	Payments	15,520
Receipts	15,073	Closing balance c/f	960
	£16,480		£16,480

On investigation you discover that:

1 Bank charges of £35 shown on the bank statement have not been entered in the cash book.
2. A cheque drawn for £47 has been entered in error as a receipt.
3. A cheque for £18 has been returned by the bank marked 'refer to drawer', but it has not been written back in the cash book.
4. An error of transposition has occurred in that the opening balance in the cash book should have been carried down as £1,470.
5. Three cheques paid to suppliers for £214, £370 and £30 have not yet been presented to the bank.
6. The last page of the paying-in book shows a deposit of £1,542 which has not yet been credited to the account by the bank.
7. The bank has debited a cheque for £72 in error to the company's account.
8. The bank statement shows an overdrawn balance of £124.

You are required to:

a show what adjustments you would make in the cash book; and
b prepare a bank reconciliation statement as at 31 October 20X7. (ACCA)

16.4* **Level II**

The following is a summary of the cash book of Grow Ltd for March 20X9:

	£		£
Opening balance b/d	4,120	Payments	46,560
Receipts	45,320	Closing balance c/d	2,880
	49,440		49,440

On investigation you discover that at 31 March 20X9:

1 The last page of the paying-in book shows a deposit of £1,904 which has not yet been credited by the bank.
2 Two cheques paid to suppliers for £642 and £1,200 have not yet been presented to the bank.
3 Dividends received of £189 are shown on the bank statement but not entered in the cash book.
4 Bank charges of £105 shown on the bank statement have not been entered in the cash book.
5 A cheque for £54 has been returned by the bank marked 'refer to drawer', but it has not been written back in the cash book.
6 A cheque drawn for £141 has been entered in error as a receipt in the cash book.
7 The bank has debited a cheque for £216 in error to the company's account.

You are required to:

a show the adjustments that should be made in the cash book; and
b prepare a bank reconciliation statement at 31 March 20X9.

16.5* **Level II**

On 15 May 20X8, Mrs Lake received her monthly bank statement for the month ended 30 April 20X8. The bank statement contained the following details:

Date	Particulars	Payments	Receipts	Balance
		£	£	£
1 Apr	Balance			1,053.29
2 Apr	236127	210.70		842.59
3 Apr	Bank Giro Credit		192.35	1,034.94
6 Apr	236126	15.21		1,019.73
6 Apr	Charges	12.80		1,006.93
9 Apr	236129	43.82		963.11
10 Apr	427519	19.47		943.64
12 Apr	236128	111.70		831.94
17 Apr	Standing Order	32.52		799.42
20 Apr	Sundry Credit		249.50	1,048.92
23 Apr	236130	77.87		971.05
23 Apr	236132	59.09		911.96
25 Apr	Bank Giro Credit		21.47	933.43
27 Apr	Sundry Credit		304.20	1,237.63
30 Apr	236133	71.18		1,166.45

For the corresponding period, Mrs Lake's own records contained the following bank account:

Date	Details	£	Date	Details	Cheque No.	£
1 Apr	Balance	827.38	5 Apr	Purchases	128	111.70
2 Apr	Sales	192.35	10 Apr	Electricity	129	43.82
18 Apr	Sales	249.50	16 Apr	Purchases	130	87.77
24 Apr	Sales	304.20	18 Apr	Rent	131	30.00
30 Apr	Sales	192.80	20 Apr	Purchases	132	59.09
			25 Apr	Purchases	133	71.18
			30 Apr	Wages	134	52.27
			30 Apr	Balance		1,310.40
		£1,766.23				£1,766.23

Required:

a Prepare a statement reconciling the balance at 30 April as given by the bank statement to the balance at 30 April as stated in the bank account.

b Explain briefly which items in your bank reconciliation statement would require further investigation. (ACCA)

16.6 Level II

A young and inexperienced bookkeeper is having great difficulty in producing a bank reconciliation statement at 31 December. He gives you his attempt to produce a summarized cash book, and also the bank statement received for the month of December. These are shown below. You may assume that the bank statement is correct. You may also assume that the trial balance at 1 January did indeed show a bank overdraft of £7,000.12.

Cash book summary—draft

	£	£	£	
1 Jan			35,000.34	Payments Jan–Nov
Opening overdraft		7,000.12		
Jan–Nov receipts	39,500.54			
Add: Discounts	500.02			
		40,000.56	12,000.34	Balance 30 Nov
		47,000.68	47,000.68	
1 Dec		12,000.34		Payments Dec
				Cheque No.
Dec receipts	178.19		37.14	7654
	121.27		192.79	7655
	14.92		5,000.00	7656
	16.88		123.45	7657
		329.26	678.90	7658
			1.47	7659
Dec Receipts	3,100.00		19.84	7660
	171.23		10.66	7661
	1,198.17	4,469.40	10,734.75	Balance c/d
		16,799.00	16,799.00	
31 Dec Balance		10,734.75		

Bank statement—31 December

Withdrawals		Deposits	Balance		
	£	£			£
			1 Dec	O/D	800.00
7650	300.00	178.19			
7653	191.91	121.27			
7654	37.14	14.92			
7651	1,111.11	16.88			
7656	5,000.00	3,100.00			
7655	129.79	171.23			
7658	678.90	1,198.17			
Standing order	50.00	117.98			
7659	1.47				
7661	10.66				
Bank charges	80.00		31 Dec	O/D	3,472.34

Required:

a A corrected cash book summary and a reconciliation of the balance on this revised summary with the bank statement balance as at 31 December, as far as you are able.

b A brief note as to the likely cause of any remaining difference. (ACCA)

16.7 Level II

The balance sheet and profit and loss account of Faults Ltd show the following two items:

Bank balance—Overdrawn	£3,620
Profit and loss account—Trading profit for year	£23,175

However, the balance as shown on the bank statement does not agree with the balance as shown in the cash book. Your investigation of this matter reveals the following differences, and additional information:

1. Cheque payments entered in the cash book but not presented to the bank until after the year end—£3,138.
2. Bankings entered in the cash book but not credited by the bank until after the year end—£425.
3. Cheques for £35 and £140 received from customers were returned by the bank as dishonoured, but no entries concerning these events have been made in the cash book.
4. Items shown on bank statements but not entered in the cash book:

   Bank charges, £425.
   Standing order—Hire purchase repayments on purchase of motor car, 12 @ £36.
   Standing order—Being quarterly rent of warehouse, £125, due on each quarter day.
   Dividend received on investment, £90.

5. The cheques were returned by the bank for the following reasons: the £35 cheque requires an additional signature and should be honoured in due course; the £140 cheque was unpaid due to the bankruptcy of the drawer and should be treated as a bad debt.
6. The hire purchase repayments of £36 represent £30 capital and £6 interest.
7. A cheque for £45 received from a customer in settlement of his account had been entered in the cash book as £450 on the payments side, analysed to the purchases ledger column and later posted.

You are required to prepare:

a a statement reconciling the cash book balance with the bank statement; and

b a statement showing the effect of the alterations on the trading profit. (ACCA adapted)

chapter

17

Control accounts

Learning objectives

After reading this chapter you should be able to:

1. explain the meaning of the key terms and concepts listed at the end of the chapter;
2. describe the division of the general ledger into several different ledgers;
3. explain the nature of control accounts, including the sources of the entries;
4. prepare sales/debtors' ledger control and purchases/creditors' ledger control accounts;
5. explain the purposes of control accounts;
6. identify and correct errors and omissions relating to the different personal ledgers and control accounts.

The nature and preparation of control accounts

Up until this point it has been assumed that the books of account include a single general ledger. However, in practice it is usual for this to be split into at least three different ledgers, consisting of the following:

1. A **sales/debtors' ledger**, which contains all the personal accounts of debtors.
2. A **purchases/creditors' ledger**, which contains all the personal accounts of creditors.
3. An **impersonal ledger**, which contains all other accounts. These comprise the nominal (i.e. sales, purchases, wages and expense) accounts, capital, and assets and liabilities other than debtors and creditors.

The main reasons for dividing the general ledger into three ledgers in a manual accounting system are:

1. Where there is a large number of transactions a single ledger becomes physically too heavy to handle.
2. It allows more than one person to work on the ledgers at the same time.
3. It provides a means of **internal control** for checking the accuracy of the ledgers, facilitates the location of errors, and can deter fraud and the misappropriation of cash. This is achieved through the use of control accounts which are described below.

The above also serves to highlight that the advantages of dividing the general ledger, and having control accounts, where the accounting system is computerized are largely confined to security matters such as restricting access to minimize the possibility of fraud.

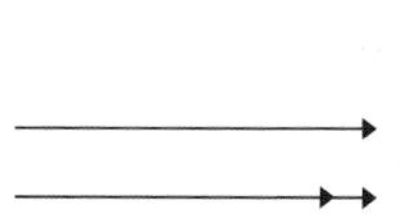

In a manual accounting system with the above three ledgers, it is usual for the impersonal ledger to contain a **control account** for each of the other ledgers. These will comprise a **sales/debtors' ledger control account** and a **purchases/creditors' ledger control account** (sometimes also referred to as **total accounts**). These control accounts contain *in total* the entries that are made in the personal ledgers, and are normally written up monthly from the totals of the relevant books of prime entry. For example, in the case of credit sales, the individual invoices shown in the sales day book are entered in each of the debtor's personal accounts in the sales ledger, and the total sales for the month as per the sales day book is debited to the debtors' control account in the impersonal ledger and credited to the sales account.

Where an impersonal ledger contains debtors' and creditors' control accounts these constitute part of the double entry and therefore enter into the trial balance which would be prepared for the impersonal ledger alone. In these circumstances the balances on the sales and purchases ledgers are outside the double-entry system and are thus not entered in the trial balance.

A simple illustration of the preparation of control accounts is shown in Example 17.1.

Example 17.1

The books of Copper Tree Ltd include three ledgers comprising an impersonal ledger, debtors' ledger and creditors' ledger. The impersonal ledger contains debtors' ledger and creditors' ledger control accounts as part of the double entry.

The following information relates to the accounting year ended 30 June 20X8:

	£
Debtors' ledger control account balance on 1 July 20X7 (debit)	5,740
Creditors' ledger control account balance on 1 July 20X7 (credit)	6,830
Sales	42,910
Purchases	38,620
Cheques received from debtors	21,760
Cheques paid to creditors	19,340
Returns outwards	8,670
Returns inwards	7,840
Carriage outwards	1,920
Carriage inwards	2,130
Discount received	4,560
Discount allowed	3,980
Bills of exchange payable	5,130
Bills of exchange receivable	9,720
Bad debts	1,640
Provision for bad debts	2,380
Amounts due from customers as shown by debtors' ledger, transferred to creditors' ledger	950
Cash received in respect of a debit balance on a creditors' ledger account	810

You are required to prepare the debtors' ledger and creditors' ledger control accounts.

Debtors' ledger control

Balance b/d	5,740	Bank	21,760
Sales	42,910	Returns inwards	7,840
		Discount allowed	3,980
		Bills receivable	9,720
		Bad debts	1,640
		Transfer to creditors	950
		Balance c/d	2,760
	48,650		48,650
Balance b/d	2,760		

Creditors' ledger control

Bank	19,340	Balance b/d	6,830
Returns outwards	8,670	Purchases	38,620
Discount received	4,560	Cash	810
Bills payable	5,130		
Transfer from debtors	950		
Balance c/d	7,610		
	46,260		46,260
		Balance b/d	7,610

Notes

1 The carriage inwards, carriage outwards and provision for bad debts are not entered in the control accounts since they do not appear in the individual debtors' or creditors' accounts in the personal ledgers.

2 The transfer of £950 between the debtors' and creditors' control accounts is intended to reflect the total of the transfers between the debtors' and creditors' ledgers during the year. These usually occur where the business buys and sells goods to the same firm. Thus, instead of exchanging cheques, the amount due as shown in the debtors' ledger is set against the amount owed as shown in the creditors' ledger (or vice versa depending on which is the smaller).

3 The cash received of £810 in respect of a debit balance on a creditors' ledger account is credited to the creditors' account and the creditors' control account. A debit balance in the creditors' ledger usually arises because a supplier has been overpaid as a result of either duplicating a payment or paying for goods that are the subject of a credit note. The cash received is a refund to correct the previous overpayment.

4 Bills of exchange were explained briefly at the end of Chapter 3. The most relevant characteristics are that bills of exchange are a method of payment where the business which owes the money signs a document undertaking to make payment after the expiry of a specified period (usually 30, 60 or 90 days). This document is referred to as a **bill of exchange receivable** in the case of a debtor and a **bill of exchange payable** in the case of a creditor. The essential point is that in the debtors' and creditors' personal accounts the debt is treated as paid on the date the bill of exchange is signed (and not when the money is actually received or paid, which is at a later date). The same therefore applies in the control accounts.

5 The balances carried down on the control accounts at the end of the period are the difference between the two sides of the accounts.

6 Some examination questions contain amounts described as a *credit* balance on the debtors' control account and/or a *debit* balance on the creditors' control account (at the beginning and/or end of the period). Although individual debtors' and creditors' personal accounts can have credit or debit balances, respectively (for the reasons outlined in note 3 above), it is unclear how the control accounts can have such balances. Each control account can only throw up one balance, which is the difference between the two sides of the account. However, if these perverse balances are encountered in an examination question, the following procedure should be adopted: a credit balance on the debtors' control account should be entered as a credit balance brought down (and debit balance carried down), and the closing debit balance calculated as the difference between the two sides of the control account in the normal way. Similarly, a debit balance on the creditors' control account should be entered as a debit balance brought down (and credit balance carried down), and the closing credit balance calculated as the difference between the two sides of the control account in the normal way.

7 The entries for any bad debts recovered are the reverse of those for bad debts. Allowances given and allowances received should be treated in the same way as returns inwards and outwards, respectively. Any interest charged on overdue (debtors') accounts should be debited to the debtors' control account and credited to an interest receivable account.

Purposes of control accounts

The main purpose of a control account is to provide a check on the accuracy of the ledger to which it relates. Since the entries in the control account are the same (in total) as those in the ledger to which it relates, the balance on the control account should equal the total of a list of balances of the individual personal accounts contained in the ledger. If the balance on the control account is the same as the list of balances, this proves that the ledger is arithmetically accurate and that all the items in the books of prime entry have been entered in the ledger on the correct side.

The main function of control accounts is therefore to facilitate the location of errors highlighted in the trial balance by pinpointing the personal ledger in which these errors are likely to be found. Furthermore, the existence of control accounts is likely to deter fraud and the misappropriation of funds since it is usually prepared by the accountant as a check on the clerk who is responsible for the personal ledger. Finally, control accounts facilitate the preparation of (monthly or quarterly) final accounts since the total values of debtors and creditors are immediately available.

The use of control accounts in the location of errors is illustrated in Example 17.2.

Example 17.2

The books of C. Hand Ltd include three ledgers comprising an impersonal ledger, a debtors' ledger and a creditors' ledger. The impersonal ledger contains debtors' ledger and creditors' ledger control accounts as part of the double entry.

The following information relates to the accounting year ended 30 April 20X8:

	£
Debtors' ledger control account balance on 1 May 20X7 (debit)	8,460
Cheques received from debtors	27,690
Sales	47,320
Returns outwards	12,860
Returns inwards	7,170
Carriage inwards	3,940
Bills receivable	8,650
Bills payable	4,560
Discount received	5,710
Discount allowed	2,830
Provision for bad debts	1,420
Bad debts	970
Proceeds of bills receivable	6,150
Amounts due from customers as shown by debtors' ledger transferred to creditors' ledger	830
Total of balances in debtors' ledger on 30 April 20X8	9,460

a You are required to prepare the debtors' ledger control account for the year ended 30 April 20X8.

b After the preparation of the control account the following errors were identified:

  i The total of the sales returns day book has been overcast by £360.

  ii A cheque received for £225 has been entered on the wrong side of a debtors' personal account.

iii The total of the discount allowed column in the cash book is shown as £2,830 when it should be £3,820.

iv A sales invoice for £2,000 has been entered in the sales day book as £200 in error.

Prepare a statement showing the amended balances on the debtors' ledger and the debtors' ledger control account. Compute the amount of any remaining undetected error.

(a)

Debtors' ledger control

Balance b/d	8,460	Bank	27,690
Sales	47,320	Returns inwards	7,170
		Bills receivable	8,650
		Discount allowed	2,830
		Bad debts	970
		Transfer to creditors	830
		Balance c/d	7,640
	55,780		55,780
Balance b/d	7,640		

(b) *Debtors' ledger*

	£
Original balances	9,460
Add: Sales day book error (£2,000 – £200)	1,800
	11,260
Less: Cheque received posted to wrong side of debtors' account (£225 × 2)	450
Amended balance	10,810

Debtors' ledger control account

		£
Original balance		7,640
Add: Sales returns day book overcast	360	
Sales day book error (£2,000 – £200)	1,800	2,160
		9,800
Less: Discount allowed undercast		990
Amended balance		8,810

Undetected error = £10,810 – £8,810 = £2,000

Notes

1 The returns outwards, carriage inwards, bills payable, discount received and provision for bad debts are not entered in the debtors' ledger control account. The proceeds of bills of exchange receivable should also not be entered in the debtors' ledger control account. As explained above, the entry in the control account in respect of bills receivable of £8,650 is made when the bills were signed as accepted by the debtor and not when the proceeds are received. This is dealt with in a separate account, shown below.

Bills receivable

Debtors' control	8,650	Bank	6,150
		Balance c/d	2,500
	8,650		8,650
Balance b/d	2,500		

2 The difference of £2,000 between the amended balances on the debtors' ledger and the debtors' ledger control account indicates that there are still one or more errors in the debtors' ledger and/or the debtors' ledger control account.

3 Instead of computing the amended balance on the debtors' ledger control account in vertical/statement form above, some examination questions require this to be done in the debtors' ledger control account. This method can take two forms. One way is to prepare a control account containing the correct amounts for all the items. The other method is to prepare a control account with the original (uncorrected) amounts and, after computing the closing balance, show the entries necessary to correct the errors. Notice that this is essentially the same procedure as that shown in Example 16.2 relating to bank reconciliations. The first method is usually expected where an examination question describes the errors before stating the requirement to prepare a control account. The second method is usually expected where an examination question states the requirement to prepare a control account before describing the errors, such as in Example 17.2 above, but unlike the example above, does not explicitly require a statement showing the amended balance on the control account. In this case the items shown in the answer to Example 17.2 that have been added to the 'original' debtors' ledger control account balance would be simply debited to the control account, and those that have been deducted would be credited to the control account. In practice, errors are not normally identified until after the control accounts have been prepared and thus these would usually be corrected as separate entries in the control accounts.

Alternative systems

Sometimes, in practice, control accounts are not part of the double entry in the impersonal ledger. Instead, they are prepared on a loose sheet of paper and are thus purely memoranda. The entries still consist of totals from the relevant day books and other books of prime entry. However, in this case the impersonal and personal ledgers must be taken together to produce a trial balance. The values of debtors and creditors in such a trial balance are therefore a list of the balances in the personal ledgers.

Summary

It is common for medium and large enterprises to divide their general ledger into three ledgers: an impersonal ledger, a sales/debtors' ledger, and a purchases/creditors' ledger. The impersonal ledger usually contains a control account for each of the other two personal ledgers. These constitute a part of the double entry and are thus included in the trial balance that would be prepared for the impersonal ledger alone. Thus, sales and purchases ledgers are maintained on a single-entry memorandum basis and are not included in the trial balance.

The purchases and sales ledger control accounts are written up from the totals of the relevant books of prime entry. The main purpose of a control account is to provide a check on the accuracy of the ledger to which it relates, and facilitate the location of errors. The balance on a control account should equal the total of a list of balances in the ledger to which it relates. If this is not the case the reasons for the difference will need to be investigated.

Key terms and concepts

Bill (of exchange) payable (208)
bill (of exchange) receivable (208)
control account (206)
impersonal ledger (206)
internal control (206)
purchases/creditors' ledger (206)
purchases/creditors' ledger control account (206)
sales/debtors' ledger (206)
sales/debtors' ledger control account (206)
total account (206)

Review question

17.1 Explain the main purposes of control accounts.

Exercises

An asterisk after the question number indicates that there is a suggested answer in the Appendix.

17.2* **Level I**

The following information has been extracted from the books of a trader at 1 July 20X6:

	£
Amount owing by debtors	40,000
Amount owing by creditors	31,200

The transactions during the year ended 30 June 20X7 were as follows:

Returns inwards	15,750
Returns outwards	8,660
Discount received	3,187
Discount allowed	5,443
Sales	386,829
Purchases	222,954
Bad debts written off	3,400
Cheques received from customers	230,040
Cheques paid to suppliers	108,999

You are required to write up the sales ledger control account and the purchase ledger control account for the year ended 30 June 20X7.

17.3 **Level I**

The following particulars relating to the year ended 31 March 20X9 have been extracted from the books of a trader:

	£
Debtors' ledger control account balance on 1 April 20X8 (debit)	7,182
Sales	69,104
Cash received from debtors	59,129
Discounts allowed	1,846
Discounts received	1,461
Returns inwards	983
Returns outwards	627
Bills receivable accepted by debtors	3,243

Bad debts written off	593
Cash paid in respect of a credit balance on a debtors' ledger account	66
Amounts due from customers as shown by debtors' ledger transferred to creditors' ledger	303
Interest charged on debtors' overdue account	10
Credit balance on debtors' ledger control account on 31 March 20X9	42

Prepare the debtors' ledger control account for the year ended 31 March 20X9, using relevant figures selected from the data shown above. (ACCA)

17.4* **Level II**

The books of Trader Ltd include three ledgers comprising an impersonal ledger, debtors' ledger and creditors' ledger. The impersonal ledger contains debtors' ledger and creditors' ledger control accounts as part of the double entry.

The following information relates to the month of January 20X1:

	£	
Debtors' control account balance on 1 January 20X1	4,200	debit
Debtors' control account balance on 1 January 20X1	300	credit
Creditors' control account balance on 1 January 20X1	250	debit
Creditors' control account balance on 1 January 20X1	6,150	credit
Credit sales for the month	23,000	
Credit purchases for the month	21,500	
Returns inward	750	
Returns outward	450	
Carriage inwards	25	
Carriage outwards	15	
Cheques received from debtors	16,250	
Cheques paid to creditors	19,800	
Discount allowed	525	
Discount received	325	
Irrecoverable debts	670	
Provision for bad debts	400	
Cheques received from debtors, dishonoured	1,850	
Bills of exchange payable, accepted by us	4,500	
Bills of exchange receivable, accepted by debtors	5,300	
Bad debts recovered	230	
Cash received from bills receivable	4,850	
Debtors' balances set against accounts in the creditors' ledger	930	
Cash paid on bills payable	3,700	
Interest charged on debtors' overdue accounts	120	
Allowances received	280	
Allowances given	340	
Debtors' control account balance on 31 January 20X1	240	credit
Creditors' control account balance on 31 January 20X1	420	debit

You are required to prepare the debtors' ledger and creditors' ledger control accounts for January 20X1.

17.5* **Level II**

The following particulars relating to the year ended 31 March 20X7 have been extracted from the books of Ball and Chain Ltd. All sales have been recorded in personal accounts in the debtors' ledger, and the debtors' ledger control account is part of the double entry in the impersonal ledger.

	£
Debtors' ledger control account balance on 1 April 20X6 (debit)	14,364
Sales	138,208
Cheques received from debtors including bad debts recovered of £84	118,258
Discounts allowed	3,692
Discounts received	2,922
Returns inwards	1,966
Returns outwards	1,254
Bills receivable	6,486
Bad debts written off	1,186
Provision for bad debts	1,800
Cash paid in respect of a credit balance on a debtors' ledger account	132
Amounts due from customers as shown by debtors' ledger transferred to creditors' ledger	606
Interest charged on debtors' overdue account	20
Total of balances in debtors' ledger on 31 March 20X7 (debit)	20,914

a Prepare the debtors' ledger control account for the year ended 31 March 20X7 using relevant figures selected from the data shown above.

b Subsequently, the following errors have been discovered:

i The total of the sales day book has been undercast by £1,000.

ii An entry of £125 in the returns inward book has been entered on the wrong side of the debtor's personal account.

iii Discount allowed of £50 had been entered correctly in a debtor's personal account but no other entries have been made in the books.

iv A cheque for £3,400 from a debtor has been entered correctly in the cash book but has been posted to the debtor's personal account as £4,300.

Prepare a statement showing the amended balances on the debtors' ledger and the debtors' ledger control account.

17.6* **Level II**

The books of K. Wills include three ledgers comprising the impersonal ledger, debtors' ledger and creditors' ledger. The impersonal ledger contains debtors' ledger and creditors' ledger control accounts as part of the double entry.

The following information relates to the accounting year ended 30 June 20X9:

	£
Debtors' ledger control account balance on 1 July 20X8 (debit)	17,220
Creditors' ledger control account balance on 1 July 20X8 (credit)	20,490
Cheques received from debtors	45,280
Cheques paid to creditors	38,020
Sales	98,730

Purchases	85,860
Returns outwards	16,010
Returns inwards	18,520
Bills of exchange payable	21,390
Bills of exchange receivable	29,160
Discount received	7,680
Discount allowed	6,940
Bad debts	4,920
Cash received in respect of a debit balance on a creditors' ledger account	2,430
Amount due from customers as shown by debtors' ledger, transferred to creditors' ledger	2,850
Total balances in creditors' ledger on 30 June 20X9 (credit)	20,700

a You are required to prepare the debtors' ledger and creditors' ledger control accounts.

b After the preparation of the above control accounts the following errors were discovered:

i The total of the purchases day book has been overcast by £500.

ii Returns outwards of £180 have been entered on the wrong side of the personal account concerned.

iii Discount received of £120 has been entered correctly in the appropriate personal account but is shown in the cash book as £210.

iv A cheque paid for £340 has been entered correctly in the cash book but has been posted to the creditors' personal account as £3,400.

You are required to prepare a statement showing the amended balances on the creditors' ledger and the creditors' ledger control account. Compute the amount of any remaining undetected error.

17.7 Level II

The following figures relating to the year ended 31 March 20X8 have been extracted from the books of a manufacturer:

	£
Total of sales ledger balances as per list	8,300
Total of bought ledger balances as per list	1,270
Balance on sales ledger control account	8,160
Balance on bought ledger control account	1,302

The balances on the control accounts, as shown above, have been included in the trial balance and in this trial balance the total of the credit balances exceeded the total of the debit balances by £58.

Subsequently, the following errors have been discovered:

1 Goods returned by a customer to the value of £10 have been entered on the wrong side of his personal account.

2 The total of the sales day book for the month of March has been undercast by £80.

3 The total of the purchases for the month of March had been correctly shown as £653 in the bought day book and control account, but incorrectly posted to the purchases account as £635.

4 An allowance of £10 made by a supplier because of a slight defect in the goods supplied had been correctly entered in the personal account concerned, but no other entries had been made in the books.

5 A credit balance of £22 on a supplier's personal account had been overlooked and therefore did not appear in the list of bought ledger balances.

An undetected error still remained in the books after the discovery of the above-mentioned errors.

You are required to:

a prepare a statement showing the amended totals of the balances on the sales and bought ledgers and the amended balances on each of the control accounts assuming that the errors discovered have been corrected;

b calculate the amount of undetected error and to state where in the books you consider such error is to be found. (ACCA)

17.8 Level II

Fox & Co. maintain control accounts, in respect of both the sales ledger and purchase ledger, within their nominal ledger. On 31 December 20X1 the net total of the balances extracted from the sales ledger amounted to £9,870, which figure did not agree with the balance shown on the sales ledger control account. An examination of the books disclosed the following errors and omissions, which when rectified resulted in the corrected net total of the sales ledger balances agreeing with the amended balance of the control account.

1 £240 standing to the credit of Rice's account in the purchase ledger had been transferred to his account in the sales ledger, but no entries had been made in the control accounts in respect of this transfer.

2 Debit balances of £42 in the sales ledger had been extracted as credit balances when the balances were listed at 31 December 20X1.

3 £8,675, a month's total in the sales day book, had been posted to the control account as £8,765 although posted correctly to the sales account.

4 A balance of £428 owing by Stone had been written off to bad debts as irrecoverable, but no entry had been made in the control account.

5 Entries on the debit side of Hay's account in the sales ledger had been undercast by £100.

6 The following sales ledger balances had been omitted from the list of balances at 31 December 20X1—debits £536, credits £37.

7 The sale of goods to Croft amounting to £60 had been dealt with correctly and debited to his account. Croft had returned such goods as not being up to standard and the only treatment accorded thereto was the crossing out of the original entry in Croft's account.

8 £22 allowed to Field as discount had been correctly recorded and posted. Subsequently, this discount had been disallowed and a like amount had been entered in the discounts received column in the cash book and posted to Field's account in the purchase ledger and included in the total of discounts received.

You are required to:

a give the journal entries, where necessary, to rectify these errors and omissions, and, if no journal entry is necessary, to state how they should be rectified; and

b prepare the sales ledger control account showing the balance before and after rectification has been made, and reconcile the balance carried forward on this account with the total of balances extracted from the sales ledger. (ACCA)

chapter

18

Errors and suspense accounts

Learning objectives

After reading this chapter you should be able to:

1. explain the meaning of the key terms and concepts listed at the end of the chapter;
2. describe the types of error that do not cause a trial balance to disagree;
3. explain the purposes of a suspense account;
4. show journal and ledger entries for the correction of both errors that do and do not cause a trial balance to disagree, including those relating to suspense accounts;
5. prepare a revised profit and loss account and balance sheet after the correction of errors.

Introduction

As explained in Chapter 5, one of the main purposes of the trial balance is to check the accuracy of a ledger. If a trial balance agrees this indicates the following:

1 There are no arithmetic errors in the ledger accounts.

2 Every transaction recorded in the ledger has been entered once on each side.

However, there can still be errors in the ledger that do not cause a trial balance to disagree. These are explained below.

Types of error that do not cause a trial balance to disagree

Error of principle

This refers to when a transaction has been entered on both sides of the ledger but one of the entries is in the wrong *class/type* of account. For example, an expense has been debited to an asset account in error (or vice versa), or income credited to a liability account in error (or vice versa). Another common example is where the proceeds of sale of a fixed asset have been credited to the sales account in error.

Error of commission

This refers to when a transaction has been entered on both sides of the ledger and in the correct *class/type* of account but one of the entries is in the wrong account. For example, stationery has been entered in the purchases account in error, or cheques posted to the wrong personal account.

Error of omission

This refers to where a transaction has not been recorded anywhere in the books of account. The classic example is bank charges omitted from the cash book.

Error of original/prime entry

This refers to when an incorrect amount has been entered in a book of prime entry. That is, the amount entered in the book of prime entry is different from that shown on the original document. This will mean that the wrong amount has been entered on both sides of the ledger. For example, a sales invoice for £980 entered in the sales day book as £890 will result in both the sales and debtors' (control) accounts containing a figure of £890 instead of £980.

Compensating errors

A compensating error is two separate errors which are totally unrelated to each other except that they are both of the same amount. Neither of these two errors is of the four types above but rather would individually cause a trial balance to disagree.

Double posting error

This refers to where the correct amount has been entered in a day book (of prime entry) but the wrong amount is shown on both sides of the ledger. Another type of double posting error can be said to have occurred when the correct amount of a transaction has been entered on the wrong side of both of the accounts to which it has been posted. A slightly different example is rent received recorded as rent paid.

Illustrations of these errors and their correction are shown in Example 18.1. The errors are presented in the same order as the above list.

Example 18.1

State the title of each of the following errors and show the journal entries needed for their correction.

1. Plant that was acquired at a cost of £5,000 has been credited in the cash book but debited to the purchases account in error.
2. The purchase of consumable tools for £80 has been debited to the repairs account in error.
3. Bank charges of £27 shown on the bank statement have not been entered in the cash book.
4. A purchase invoice received from A. Creditor for £1,000 has been entered in the purchases day book as £100.
5. Wages paid of £40 have not been posted to the wages account, and the debit side of the purchases account has been overcast by £40.
6. Rent received of £400 has been entered in both the cash book and the ledger as rent paid.

The journal		*Debit*	*Credit*
		£	£
1 Plant and machinery	Dr	5,000	
To purchases account			5,000
Being correction of error of principle			
2 Consumable tools	Dr	80	
To repairs account			80
Being correction of error of omission			
3 Bank charges	Dr	27	
To cash book			27
Being correction of error of omission			
4 Purchases account	Dr	900	
To A. Creditor/creditors' control			900
Being correction of error of prime entry			
(no correction of purchases day book is necessary)			
5 Wages account	Dr	40	
To purchases account			40
Being correction of compensating error			
—wages not posted and purchases account overcast			
6 Cash book	Dr	800	
To rent payable account			400
To rent receivable account			400
Being correction of rent receivable of £400 entered as rent payable			

Suspense accounts

Suspense accounts are used for two purposes:

1. Recording undefined transactions. That is, where money is received or paid but there is no record of what it relates to, the amount would be entered in the cash book and posted to a suspense account. When the nature of the transaction is known, the amount is transferred from the suspense account to the appropriate account.
2. To record in the ledger any difference on a trial balance and thus make it agree. If a trial balance fails to agree by a relatively small amount and the error(s) cannot be found quickly, the difference is inserted in the trial balance (to make it agree) and in a suspense account. The entry in the suspense account must be on the same side of the ledger as the entry in the trial balance. At a later date when the error(s) are located they are corrected by means of an entry in the suspense account and the other in the account containing the error. This correction through the suspense account is necessary because the original entry in the suspense account (which made the trial balance agree) in effect corrected all the errors in total. Thus, the correction must effectively be moved from the suspense account to the account that contains the error.

An illustration of the use of suspense accounts is given in Example 18.2.

Example 18.2

A trial balance failed to agree because the debit side exceeds the credit side by £2,509. A suspense account has been opened into which the difference is entered. Subsequently, the following errors were identified:

1 The debit side of the cash book has been overcast by £1,000.
2 Goods bought by cheque for £200 have been credited in the cash book but not entered in the purchases account.
3 Rent paid of £50 has been credited in the cash book but also credited in error to the rent account.
4 Car repairs of £23 shown in the cash book have been debited to the motor expenses account as £32 in error.
5. The sales account contains a balance of £2,000 but this has been entered in the trial balance as £200.

You are required to prepare the journal entries needed to correct the above errors and show the entries in the suspense account.

The journal		*Debit*	*Credit*
		£	£
1 Suspense account	Dr	1,000	
Cash book			1,000
Being correction of arithmetic error			
2 Purchases account	Dr	200	
Suspense account			200
Being correction of posting error			
3 Rent account	Dr	100	
Suspense account			100
Being correction of posting error (£50 × 2)			

		Dr	Cr
4	Suspense account	Dr 9	
	Motor expenses		9
	Being correction of transposed figures		
5	Suspense account	Dr 1,800	
	Trial balance (no ledger entry)		1,800
	Being correction of extraction error		

Suspense account

Cash book	1,000	Difference on trial balance	2,509
Motor expenses	9	Purchases	200
Extraction error on sales	1,800	Rent	100
	2,809		2,809

Notes

1 It should be noted that only errors of the type which cause a trial balance to disagree are corrected by means of an entry in the suspense account; that is, arithmetic and posting errors described in Chapter 5. This is clearly because errors that cause a trial balance to disagree give rise to the original entry in the suspense account.

2 The correction of errors via a suspense account always involves a double entry in the ledger, with one exception. This relates to the correction of extraction errors, such as item 5 above, where the only ledger entry is in the suspense account. A useful way of working out whether the entry in the suspense account is a debit or credit is to imagine what entry is needed to correct the trial balance; the entry in the suspense account will be on the opposite side of the ledger.

3 Sometimes in examination questions and in practice the errors that have been identified are not the only errors. In this case there will still be a balance on the suspense account after the known errors have been corrected. This shows the amount of the remaining errors.

4 Occasionally in examination questions and in practice the final accounts are prepared before the errors in the suspense account have been found and corrected. In this instance the suspense account will be shown on the balance sheet. In practice, it will disappear when the errors in the suspense account are corrected along with the necessary changes to the items in the final accounts that are wrong. However, instead of correcting the final accounts, some examination questions require students to prepare a statement amending the original/draft (i.e. wrong) figure of profit. In this case it will be necessary also to show the effect of correcting each error on the original profit, as an addition to or subtraction from this figure, thus arriving at a revised amount of profit.

Summary

There are two main types of errors that will cause a trial balance to disagree. These consist of arithmetic and posting errors. There are six types of error that do not cause a trial balance to disagree. These consist of errors of principle, errors of commission, errors of omission, errors of original/prime entry, compensating errors, and double posting errors. Errors that cause a trial balance to disagree are normally corrected by means of a one-sided ledger (and journal) entry. Errors that do not cause a trial balance to disagree are always corrected by means of a two-sided ledger (and journal) entry.

Suspense accounts are used for two purposes. One is to record transactions, the nature of which is unknown. The other is to record in the ledger any difference on a trial balance, and thus make it agree. When the error(s) that gave rise to the difference are located, they are corrected by means of one entry in the suspense account and a corresponding entry in the account containing the error. Only errors that cause a trial balance to disagree are corrected by means of an entry in the suspense account.

Errors giving rise to the creation of a suspense account should be located and corrected before final accounts are prepared. However, if errors are discovered after the preparation of the final accounts, the effect of their correction on the profit and loss account and balance sheet should be taken into consideration. This may involve preparing revised final accounts.

Key terms and concepts

Compensating errors (218)
double posting error (219)
error of commission (218)
error of omission (218)
error of original/prime entry (218)
error of principle (218)
suspense account (220)

Review questions

18.1 Describe the types of errors that:

a cause a trial balance to disagree;

b do not cause a trial balance to disagree.

18.2 Describe the two main uses of a suspense account.

Exercises

An asterisk after the question number indicates that there is a suggested answer in the Appendix.

18.3 **Level I**

The draft trial balance of Regent Ltd as at 31 May 20X8 agreed. The business proceeded with the preparation of the draft final accounts and these showed a profit of £305,660. However, a subsequent audit revealed the following errors:

1 Bank charges of £56 had been omitted from the cash book.
2 The purchases journal had been overcast by £400.
3 The sales journal had been undercast by £100.
4 An invoice for £127 received from Alpha Ltd had been entered into the purchases journal as £217. (This is quite independent of the error made in the purchases journal referred to above.)
5 It is now considered prudent to write off the balance of £88 on P. Shadey's account as bad.
6 An invoice from Caring Garages Ltd for £550 in respect of servicing Regent Ltd's motor vehicles had been posted to the debit of motor vehicles account.
7 Depreciation of 10 per cent per annum has been provided for on motor vehicles inclusive of the £550 invoice referred to in point 6 above.

Regent Ltd maintains control accounts for debtors and creditors in its general ledger. Individual accounts for debtors and creditors are maintained on a memorandum basis only.

Required:

a Prepare journal entries to show how the above errors would be corrected. (Note: dates and narratives not required.)

b What is the profit for the year after correcting the above errors? (AAT)

18.4* **Level I**

When preparing a trial balance the bookkeeper found it disagreed by £600, the credit side being that much greater than the debit side. The difference was entered in a suspense account. The following errors were subsequently found:

1 A cheque for £32 for electricity was entered in the cash book but not posted to the ledger.
2 The debit side of the wages account is overcast by £28.
3 There is a debit in the rent account of £198 which should be £918.
4 The purchase of a van for £3,000 has been posted to the debit side of the purchases account in error.
5 A cheque received from A. Watt for £80 has been credited to A. Watson's account in error.
6 The sale of some old loose tools for £100 had been credited to sales account in error.
7 An amount of £17 paid for postage stamps has been entered in the carriage outwards account in error.
8 Bank charges of £41 shown on the bank statement have not been entered in the books.
9 An amount of £9 for stationery has been entered in the cash book but not posted to the stationery account. Cash sales of £43 are entered correctly in the cash book but posted to the sales account as £34.
10 A credit sale to J. Bloggs of £120 was entered in the sales day book as £12.
11 A credit balance of £62 shown in the discount received account has been entered on the debit side of the trial balance.

You are required to prepare the journal entries necessary to correct the above errors and show the suspense account.

18.5 **Level II**

At the end of January 20X0 a trial balance extracted from the ledger of Gerald Ltd did not balance and a suspense account was opened for the amount of the difference. Subsequently, the following matters came to light:

1 £234 had been received during January from a debtor who owed £240. No entry has been made for the £6 outstanding but it is now decided to treat it as a cash discount.
2 Returns to suppliers during January were correctly posted individually to personal accounts but were incorrectly totalled. The total, overstated by £100, was posted to the returns account.
3 A bank statement drawn up to 31 January 20X0 showed a credit balance of £120 while the balance of the bank account in the trial balance was an overdraft of £87. The difference was found on reconciliation to comprise:
   i a direct debit for the annual subscription to a trade association, £70, for which no entry had been made in the books of account;

ii an entry in the bank account for payment to a supplier shown as £230 instead of £320;

iii unpresented cheques on 31 January totalled £327;

iv the remainder of the difference was due to an addition error in the bank account.

4 A cheque for £163 was received during January in full settlement of a debt which was written off in the previous financial year. It was correctly entered in the bank account but not posted elsewhere, pending instructions.

5 A debtor's account with a balance of £180 had been taken out of the looseleaf ledger when a query was investigated and not replaced at the time the trial balance was extracted.

6 A credit note for £5 sent to a customer in respect of an allowance had been posted to the wrong side of the customer's personal account.

Required:

Show what correcting entries need to be made in the ledger accounts in respect of these matters. Set out your answer as follows:

Item	Account(s) to be debited £	Account(s) to be credited £

(ACCA adapted)

18.6 Level II

Chi Knitwear Ltd is an old-fashioned firm with a handwritten set of books. A trial balance is extracted at the end of each month, and a profit and loss account and balance sheet are computed. This month, however, the trial balance will not balance, the credits exceeding debits by £1,536.

You are asked to help and after inspection of the ledgers discover the following errors.

1 A balance of £87 on a debtor's account has been omitted from the schedule of debtors, the total of which was entered as debtors in the trial balance.

2 A small piece of machinery purchased for £1,200 had been written off to repairs.

3 The receipts side of the cash book had been undercast by £720.

4 The total of one page of the sales day book had been carried forward as £8,154, whereas the correct amount was £8,514.

5 A credit note for £179 received from a supplier had been posted to the wrong side of his account.

6 An electricity bill in the sum of £152, not yet accrued for, is discovered in a filing tray.

7 Mr Smith, whose past debts to the company had been the subject of a provision, at last paid £731 to clear his account. His personal account has been credited but the cheque has not yet passed through the cash book.

You are required to:

a write up the suspense account to clear the difference; and

b state the effect on the accounts of correcting each error. (ACCA)

18.7 Level II

The draft final accounts of RST Ltd for the year ended 30 April 20X5 showed a net profit for the year of £78,263.

During the subsequent audit, the following errors and omissions were discovered. At the draft stage a suspense account had been opened to record the net difference.

1. Trade debtors were shown as £55,210. However:
   - i bad debts of £610 had not been written off;
   - ii the existing provision for doubtful debtors, £1,300, should have been adjusted to 2 per cent of debtors;
   - iii a provision of 2 per cent for discounts on debtors should have been raised.
2. Rates of £491 which had been prepaid at 30 April 20X4 had not been brought down on the rates account as an opening balance.
3. A vehicle held as a fixed asset, which had originally cost £8,100 and for which £5,280 had been provided as depreciation, had been sold for £1,350. The proceeds had been correctly debited to bank but had been credited to sales. No transfers had been made to a disposals account.
4. Credit purchases of £1,762 had been correctly debited to purchases account but had been credited to the supplier's account as £1,672.
5. A piece of equipment costing £9,800 and acquired on 1 May 20X4 for use in the business had been debited to purchases account. (The company depreciates equipment at 20 per cent per annum on cost.)
6. Items valued at £2,171 had been completely omitted from the closing stock figure.
7. At 30 April 20X5 an accrual of £543 for electricity charges and an insurance prepayment of £162 had been omitted.
8. The credit side of the wages account had been underadded by £100 before the balance on the account had been determined.

Required:

Using relevant information from that given above:

a prepare a statement correcting the draft net profit;

b post and balance the suspense account. (Note: The opening balance of this account has not been given and must be derived.) (ACCA)

18.8* Level II

Miscup showed a difference on their trial balance of £14,650. This was posted to a suspense account so that the accounts for the year ended 31 March 20X9 could be prepared. The following balance sheet was produced:

Miscup

Balance sheet as at 31 March 20X9

	£	£		£	£	£
			Fixed assets	*Cost*	*Depreciation*	*Net*
Capital		125,000	Freehold premises	60,000	—	60,000
Profit for the year		33,500	Motor vehicles	25,000	11,935	13,065
		158,500	Fixtures and fittings	1,500	750	750
				86,500	12,685	73,815

Current liabilities			*Current assets*		
Trade creditors and			Stocks	75,410	
accrued charges	41,360		Debtors	37,140	
Bank overdraft	1,230		Cash in hand	75	
		42,590			112,625
					186,440
			Suspense account		14,650
		£201,090			£201,090

On checking the books to eliminate the suspense account you find the following errors:

1 The debit side of the cash book is undercast by £10,000.
2 A credit item of £5,000 in the cash book on account of a new building has not been posted to the nominal ledger.
3 The purchase day book has been summarized for posting to the nominal ledger but an item of purchases of £100 has been entered in the summary as £1,000 and a further transport charge of £450 has been entered as £45.
4 An item of rent received, £45, was posted twice to the nominal ledger from the cash book.
5 The debit side of the debtors' control account was undercast by £100.
6 On reconciling the bank statement with the cash book it was discovered that bank charges of £3,250 had not been entered in the cash book.
7 Depreciation of motor vehicles was undercharged by £500.
8 Stocks were undervalued by £1,250.
9 Suppliers' invoices totalling £2,110 for goods included in stock had been omitted from the books.

You are required to show:

a the journal entries necessary to eliminate the balance on the suspense account; and
b the balance sheet of Miscup as at 31 March 20X9, after correcting all the above errors.

(ACCA)

SPECIAL ITEMS, CASES AND ENTITIES

Single entry and incomplete records

Learning objectives

After reading this chapter you should be able to:

1 explain the meaning of the key terms and concepts listed at the end of the chapter;

2 describe the different forms of incomplete records;

3 prepare final accounts from incomplete records and single entry.

Introduction

Incomplete records is a general term given to a situation where the transactions of an organization have not been recorded in double-entry form (or using a computer system), and thus there is not a full set of records of the enterprise's transactions. This is quite common in practice in the case of sole traders. It is often too expensive for small businesses to maintain a complete system of double-entry bookkeeping. In addition, many sole traders often claim to have little practical use for any records other than how much money they have, and the amounts of debtors and creditors. Many sole traders are usually able to remember, without records, what fixed assets they own, and any long-term liabilities they owe. In the case of small businesses the accountant is therefore usually engaged not to write up the books, but to ascertain the profit of the business for tax purposes. Often, but not always, a balance sheet is also prepared.

In practice, there are three different forms of incomplete records:

1 *Incomplete records of revenue income and expenditure.* That is, there are no basic documents or records of revenue income and expenditure, or the records are inadequate. This situation usually arises where the books and documents have been accidentally destroyed (e.g. in a fire) or the owner failed to keep proper records. In these circumstances it is not possible to construct a trading and profit and loss account. However, it may still be possible to ascertain the profit for the period provided there is information available relating to the assets and liabilities of the business at the start and end of the relevant period.
2 *Single entry.* This term is used to describe a situation where the business transactions have only been entered in a book of prime entry, usually a cash book, and not in the ledger. However, one would also expect to be able to obtain documents or information relating to the value of fixed assets, stocks, debtors, creditors, accruals, prepayments and any long-term liabilities. Given that this is available, it would be possible to prepare a trading and profit and loss account and balance sheet.
3 *Incomplete single entry.* This term may be used to describe a variation on point 2 where there are no books of account (or these are incomplete) but the receipts and payments can be ascertained from the bank statements and/or supporting documents. In this case it would be necessary to produce a cash book summary from the information given on the bank statements, paying in book and cheque book stubs. The final accounts will then be prepared from the cash book summary together with the supporting documents and information referred to in point 2.

The procedure for preparing final accounts from these three different forms of incomplete records is described below.

Incomplete records of revenue income and expenditure

As explained in the Introduction to this chapter, in these circumstances it is not possible to construct a trading and profit and loss account. However, it may still be possible to ascertain the profit for the relevant period provided that the information to prepare a balance sheet at the start and end of the period is available.

This involves the application of the comparative static approach to profit measurement described in Chapter 2. The profit (or loss) is found by calculating the difference between the net asset value of the business at the start and end of the period as shown by the two balance sheets. The logic behind this computation is that an increase in net assets can only come from two sources, either additional capital introduced by the owner or profits generated from the sale of goods and/or other assets. This is illustrated below.

Balance sheet as at 1 January 20X1

Capital	20,000	Assets	25,000
		Less: Liabilities	5,000
	20,000	Net assets	20,000

Balance sheet as at 31 December 20X1

Capital	30,000	Assets	38,000
		Less: Liabilities	8,000
	30,000	Net assets	30,000

Ignoring the possibility of additional capital introduced during the year, this business has a profit for the year of £30,000 − £20,000 = £10,000. This is computed by ascertaining the increase in either the net assets or the capital. Both must give the same answer. Any decrease in net assets or capital will mean there has been a loss for the year.

However, part of the increase in net assets and capital may be due to additional capital being introduced during the year of, say, £3,000. In this case the profit for the year is that part of the increase in net assets and capital which is not the result of additional capital introduced during the year, thus:

	£
Net assets/capital at end of year	30,000
Less: Net assets/capital at start of year	20,000
Increase in capital	10,000
Less: Capital introduced	3,000
Profit for the year	7,000

In addition, the owner of the business may have made drawings during the year of, say, £4,000. These will reduce the capital and net assets at the end of the year. In this case the profit for the year is the increase in net assets/capital less the capital introduced, plus the drawings for the year, i.e. £10,000 − £3,000 + £4,000 = £11,000.

In sum, profits (or losses) are reflected in an increase (or decrease) in the net asset value of a business over a given period. The net asset value corresponds to the capital. The profit or loss can thus be ascertained by computing the change in capital over the year and adjusting this for any capital introduced and/or drawings during the year. This is presented in the form of a statement, as shown below. Notice that this statement is simply a reordering of the entries normally shown in the capital account of a sole trader as presented in the balance sheet.

Statement of profit or loss for the year ended 31 December 20X1

	£
Capital at end of current year	30,000
Less: Capital at end of previous year	20,000
Increase in capital	10,000
Add: Drawings during the year including any goods taken by the proprietor for his or her own use	4,000
	14,000
Less: Capital introduced during the year either in the form of cash or any other asset	3,000
Profit for the year	11,000

Before this statement can be prepared it is necessary to calculate the capital at the end of the current year and at the end of the previous year. This is done by preparing a balance sheet at each of these dates. These are referred to as a **statement of affairs**. This is illustrated in Example 19.1.

Example 19.1

A. Ferry has been in business for the last 10 years as an electrical retailer, and has asked you to compute her profit for the year ended 31 December 20X8.

She has no business bank account and kept no records of her income and expenditure apart from the purchase and sale of fixed assets, stock, debtors and creditors, and a running cash balance. She has been able to give you the following information relating to her affairs:

1 At 31 December 20X8 the business owns freehold land and buildings used as a shop and workshop. This cost £10,000 on 1 July 20X2.

2 During the year ended 31 December 20X8 the business owned the following vehicles:

Date of purchase	*Cost*	*Date of sale*	*Proceeds*
31 Mar 20X5	£1,000	31 Oct 20X8	£625
1 May 20X6	£1,200	unsold at 31 Dec 20X8	
1 July 20X8	£2,000	unsold at 31 Dec 20X8	

You estimate that the above vehicles have a useful working life of five years and no residual value. In previous years these have been depreciated using the straight line method.

3 During the year ended 31 December 20X8 the owner has put £5,280 in cash into the business and taken out £15,900 as drawings.

4 Amounts outstanding at:

	31 Dec 20X7	31 Dec 20X8
	£	£
Debtors	865	645
Creditors	390	480
Accruals	35	20
Prepayments	40	25

Included in debtors at 31 December 20X8 are doubtful debts of £85.

5 Stocks have been valued at £565 on 31 December 20X7, and £760 on 31 December 20X8. The latter amount includes a television which cost £60 and was worthless at that date due to it having been accidentally damaged beyond repair.

6 The cash balances at 31 December 20X7 and 20X8 were £285 and £165, respectively.

You are required to calculate the profit for the year ended 31 December 20X8, showing clearly your workings.

Workings

	£	£
Motor vehicles owned at 31 December 20X7		
Purchased 31/3/X5		1,000
Purchased 1/5/X6		1,200
Total cost		2,200

Depreciation using the fixed instalment method		
20 per cent × £1,000 × 2 years 9 months	550	
20 per cent × £1,200 × 1 year 8 months	400	
		950
Written down value at 31 December 20X7		1,250

	£	£
Motor vehicles owned at 31 December 20X8		
Purchased 1/5/X6		1,200
Purchased 1/7/X8		2,000
Total cost		3,200
Depreciation using the fixed instalment method		
20 per cent × £1,200 × 2 years 8 months	640	
20 per cent × £2,000 × 6 months	200	
		840
Written down value at 31 December 20X8		2,360

Balance sheet as at 1 January 20X1

A. Ferry

Statement of affairs as at 31 December 20X7

	£		£
Capital	12,580	Freehold land and buildings	10,000
Accruals	35	Motor vehicles	1,250
Creditors	390	Stock	565
		Debtors	865
		Prepayments	40
		Cash	285
	13,005		13,005

A. Ferry

Statement of affairs as at 31 December 20X8

	£	£			£	£
Capital		13,310	*Fixed assets*			
			Freehold land & buildings			
			at cost			10,000
Current liabilities			Motor vehicles at cost		3,200	
Accruals	20		*Less*: Aggregate			
Creditors	480	500	depreciation		840	2,360
						12,360
			Current assets			
			Prepayments		25	
			Stock (760 – 60)		700	
			Debtors	645		
			Less: Provision: for			
			doubtful debts	85	560	
			Cash		165	
						1,450
		13,810				13,810

A. Ferry
Statement of profit for the year ended 31 December 20X8

	£
Capital at 31 December 20X8	13,310
Less: Capital at 31 December 20X7	12,580
	730
Add: Drawings	15,900
	16,630
Less: Capital introduced	5,280
Net profit for the year	11,350

Notes

1 There is no need to compute the profit or loss on disposals of fixed assets since this will automatically be reflected in the increase in net assets/capital. However, it is necessary to compute the written down value (or possibly market value) of fixed assets at the end of each year as shown in the workings in order to prepare the statement of affairs.

2 The stock at 31 December 20X8 excludes the cost of the television that was damaged beyond repair of £60.

3 Doubtful debts have been provided for by reducing the amount of debtors at 31 December 20X8.

4 The amounts for capital in the statement of affairs are the difference between the two sides of these balance sheets.

5 It is usual to treat the statement of affairs at the end of the previous year as workings not requiring any formal presentation. However, the statement of affairs at the end of the current year should contain the usual headings and subtotals and be in a form presentable to the owner and other interested parties such as the Inland Revenue. A vertical presentation may therefore be preferable.

Single entry

As explained in the introduction, **single entry** refers to the situation where a business has some record of its receipts and payments, fixed assets, stocks, debtors, creditors, accruals, prepayments and long-term liabilities. However, these records are not in double-entry form and usually consist of just a cash book.

One possibility is for the accountant to complete the records by posting the receipts and payments to the appropriate accounts in the ledger either in full or summarized form. The final accounts are then prepared from the trial balance in the normal way. This is common in practice. However, in very small businesses this may be too expensive and/or impractical. In this case the final accounts are prepared directly from the cash book or a summary thereof, and the appropriate adjustments made for debtors, creditors, provisions, accruals, prepayments, etc. Examination questions on this topic also usually take the same form. An illustration of this treatment of single-entry records is given in Example 19.2. Because of the importance and length of the workings, the procedure for answering the question is presented as a series of steps. These are well worth memorizing as a model for answering such questions.

Example 19.2

The following is the balance sheet of L. Cook at 31 December 20X5.

	£		£
Capital	19,240	Freehold land and buildings	
Trade creditors	2,610	at cost	12,500
Electricity accrued	30	Motor vehicles (cost £5,000)	2,900
		Rates prepaid	60
		Stock of goods for resale	1,650
		Trade debtors	3,270
		Bank	1,500
	21,880		21,880

The only book kept by Cook is a cash book, a summary of which for the year ended 31 December 20X6 has been prepared as follows:

	£		£
Balance b/d	1,500	Rates	140
Cash takings banked	4,460	Salaries	2,820
Cheques from debtors	15,930	Electricity	185
Additional capital	500	Bank charges	10
		Motor expenses	655
		Payments to creditors	16,680
		Stationery	230
		Sundry expenses	40
		Balance c/d	1,630
	22,390		22,390

From the supporting documents it has been ascertained that:

1 The following amounts have been paid from the cash takings before they were banked:

Drawings	£22,000
Purchases	£560
Petrol	£85
Repairs to buildings	£490

2 Cook has taken goods out of the business for his own use that cost £265.
3 Motor vehicles have been depreciated in past years at 20 per cent per annum by the reducing balance method.
4 Stock at 31 December 20X6 was valued at £1,960.
5 The trade debtors and trade creditors outstanding at the end of the year are £2,920 and £2,860, respectively.
6 At 31 December 20X6 there are rates prepaid of £70 and electricity accrued of £45. You expect to charge Cook £100 for your services.

Prepare a trading and profit and loss account for the year ended 31 December 20X6 and a balance sheet at that date. Present your answer in vertical form and show all your workings clearly.

Workings/procedure

1 If necessary, prepare a statement of affairs as at the end of the previous year to ascertain the capital at that date.

2 If necessary, prepare a summarized cash book from the bank statements, etc., to ascertain the balance at the end of the year and the total amounts received and spent on each type of income and expenditure, and assets.

3 a Compute the net credit purchases by preparing a creditors' control account as follows:

Creditors' control

20X6			20X6		
31 Dec	Bank	16,680	1 Jan	Balance b/d	2,610
31 Dec	Balance c/d	2,860	31 Dec	Net purchases	16,930
		19,540			19,540

The net purchases figure is the difference between the two sides.

b Compute the cash and cheque purchases and then the total purchases:
Total purchases = £560 + £16,930 = £17,490

4 a Compute the net credit sales by preparing a debtors' control account as follows:

Debtors' control

20X6			20X6		
1 Jan	Balance b/d	3,270	31 Dec	Bank	15,930
31 Dec	Net sales	15,580	31 Dec	Balance c/d	2,920
		18,850			18,850

The net sales figure is the difference between the two sides.

b Compute the cash and cheque sales and then the total sales:

Cash sales = £4,460 + £22,000 + £560 + £85 + £490 = £27,595
Total sales = £27,595 + £15,580 = £43,175

Note that sometimes the computations in (a) and (b) have to be combined. This is necessary when the cash and/or cheque sales are not given separately from the cheques received from debtors. In this case the total cash and cheques received in respect of sales are credited to the control account. The same principle would also have to be used in the case of purchases when cash and/or cheque purchases are not given separately from cheques paid to creditors.

5 Compute the charges to the profit and loss account for those expenses with accruals or prepayments by preparing the relevant ledger accounts. Alternatively, in examinations this may be shown as workings in the profit and loss account.

Light and heat

20X6			20X6		
31 Dec	Bank	185	1 Jan	Accrual b/d	30
31 Dec	Accrual c/d	45	31 Dec	Profit and loss a/c	200
		230			230

Rates

20X6			20X6		
1 Jan	Prepayment b/d	60	31 Dec	Profit and loss a/c	130
31 Dec	Bank	140	31 Dec	Prepayment c/d	70
		200			200

6 Compute the charges and/or credits to the profit and loss account in respect of any provision for bad debts, depreciation, sales of fixed assets, etc. Alternatively, if these are relatively simple, in examinations, they may be shown as workings in the profit and loss account.

Motor vehicles

Depreciation expense = 20% × £2,900 = £580

Aggregate depreciation = (£5,000 – £2,900) + £580 = £2,680

7 Prepare the final accounts, remembering to add together any cheque and cash expenditure of the same type (e.g. motor expenses in this example), and include any fixed assets acquired, drawings (e.g. goods taken by the proprietor), capital introduced, etc.

L. Cook

Trading and profit and loss account for the year ended 31 December 20X6

	£	£
Sales		43,175
Less: Cost of sales—		
Stock at 1 Jan 20X6	1,650	
Add: Purchases (17,490 – 265)	17,225	
	18,875	
Less: Stock at 31 Dec 20X6	1,960	16,915
Gross profit		26,260
Less: Expenditure—		
Rates (60 + 140 – 70)	130	
Salaries	2,820	
Light and heat (185 + 45 – 30)	200	
Bank charges	10	
Motor expenses (655 + 85)	740	
Stationery	230	
Sundry expenses	40	
Repairs to buildings	490	
Depreciation on vehicles (20 per cent × 2,900)	580	
Accountancy fees	100	5,340
Net profit		20,920

Balance sheet as at 31 December 20X6

	£	£	£
Fixed assets	*Cost*	*Agg. depn.*	*WDV*
Freehold land and buildings	12,500	—	12,500
Motor vehicles	5,000	2,680	2,320
	17,500	2,680	14,820
Current assets			
Stock		1,960	
Trade debtors		2,920	
Prepayments		70	
Bank		1,630	
		6,580	

Current liabilities			
Trade creditors	2,860		
Accruals (45 + 100)	145	3,005	
Net current assets			3,575
Net assets			18,395
Capital			
Balance at 1 Jan 20X6			19,240
Add: Capital introduced			500
Net profit			20,920
			40,660
Less: Drawings (22,000 + 265)			22,265
Balance at 31 Dec 20X6			18,395

Notes

1 The goods taken by the proprietor for his own use of £265 have been added to drawings and deducted from purchases (rather than added to sales) because the question gives their cost.

2 In the workings for the debtors' control account, the term net sales is used to emphasize that this is after deducting returns, the amount of which is unknown and cannot be ascertained. However, if the returns were known, these would be entered in the debtors' control account and the profit and loss account in the normal manner. More importantly, if the value of any bad debts, discount allowed, etc., were known, these would have to be entered in the debtors' control account and profit and loss account in the normal way. The same principles apply to the creditors' control account where there are returns, discount received, etc.

3 In some single-entry questions there are petty cash balances at the start and end of the accounting year. Where the balance in cash at the end of the year is greater than at the start, the increase must be added to the cash takings that were banked in order to ascertain the cash sales (in Workings 4(b) above). The reason is simply because the increase in the cash float must have come from cash sales. Put another way, the cash takings banked are after deducting/excluding the increase in the cash balance. To ascertain the cash sales therefore necessitates adding back any increase in the cash float, or deducting any decrease from the cash takings that were banked. Where there are cash balances/floats at the start and end of the year, an alternative to the one-line computation of cash sales shown in Workings 4(b) above is to prepare a petty cash account. The cash sales will be the difference between the two sides of the account after entering the opening and closing cash balances, the amounts paid from the cash takings, and the takings that were banked. This may have the added advantage of reminding students to include the various items of petty cash expenditure in the final accounts.

4 Many businesses accept credit cards such as Visa or Mastercard in payment for goods that they sell to the public. This gives rise to special problems where there are incomplete records in the form of single entry. Most credit card companies charge a commission of up to 5 per cent of the value of goods sold. Thus, if a business sells goods with a selling price of, say, £200 the amount it receives will be £190 (i.e. 95 per cent of £200). The normal ledger entries for this sale will be to credit the sales account with £200 and debit a credit card debtors' account with the amount it expects to receive of £190. The difference of £10

commission should be debited to a commission account that will be transferred to the profit and loss account at the end of the year.

Where there is only single entry, the accounting records in respect of **credit card sales** will consist of a debit in the cash book of the amounts received from the credit card company during the year. It is therefore necessary to compute the value of sales before deducting the commission. This is done in two stages. The first stage is to calculate the total credit card sales for the year after deducting commission by means of a credit card debtors' account in which the amount received is adjusted to take into account the opening and closing amounts owing. The second stage is to gross up the total credit card sales after deducting commission to ascertain the total credit card sales before deducting commission. Using the example above, this would be $100/95 \times £190 = £200$. The £200 is then included in sales in the trading account, and the difference of $£200 - £190 = £10$ commission is shown as a separate item of expense in the profit and loss account.

Summary

There are three different forms of incomplete records. The first is incomplete records of revenue income and expenditure. This refers to where there are no documents or records of revenue income and expenditure. It is therefore not possible to prepare a profit and loss account. However, the profit may be ascertained by calculating the difference between the capital/net asset value of the business at the start and end of the year by preparing balance sheets at each of these dates. The profit is found by adjusting the change in capital over the year for any capital introduced and/or drawings.

The second form of incomplete records is known as single entry. This refers to where the business transactions have been entered in a cash book but not posted to a ledger. The third form of incomplete records is incomplete single entry. This refers to where there are no books of account but a cash book summary can be prepared from the bank statements and/or supporting documents.

In this case of incomplete single entry and single entry it is therefore possible to prepare a profit and loss account and balance sheet. This can be done by posting the amounts shown in the summarized cash book to the ledger, extracting a trial balance and preparing final accounts in the normal way. Alternatively, students are normally required in examinations to prepare final accounts from the summarized cash book by means of workings. These usually take the form of creditors' and debtors' control accounts, in order to ascertain the purchases and sales, respectively, together with those expense accounts which have accruals and/or prepayments at the start and end of the year.

Key terms and concepts

Credit card sales (239)
incomplete records (230)
single entry (234)
statement of affairs (230)

Review questions

19.1 Describe the different forms of incomplete records with which you are familiar.

Exercises

An asterisk after the question number indicates that there is a suggested answer in the Appendix.

19.2* **Level II**

The following is the balance sheet of Round Music as at 30 June 20X4:

	£		£
Capital	42,770	Plant	31,000
Creditors	5,640	Stock	9,720
Accruals	90	Debtors	6,810
		Prepayments	150
		Bank	820
	48,500		48,500

During the year ended 30 June 20X5 there was a fire which destroyed the books of account and supporting documents. However, from questioning the proprietor you have been able to obtain the following information:

1 The plant at 30 June 20X4 cost £50,000 and has been depreciated at 10 per cent per annum by the fixed instalment method on a strict time basis. Additional plant was purchased on the 1 April 20X5 at a cost of £20,000. Plant costing £10,000 on 1 January 20X2 was sold on 1 October 20X4 for £4,450.
2 Stock at 30 June 20X5 was valued at £8,630. This includes goods costing £1,120 that are worthless because of fire damage.
3 Debtors and creditors at 30 June 20X5 were £6,120 and £3,480, respectively. Debtors include doubtful debts of £310.
4 Accruals and prepayments at 30 June 20X5 were £130 and £80, respectively.
5 There was a bank overdraft at 30 June 20X5 of £1,430.
6 During the year the business had borrowed £7,000 from Lickey Bank which was repayable on 1 January 20X8.
7 During the year the owner introduced additional capital of £5,000 and made drawings of £18,500 by cheque. The proprietor also took goods costing £750 from the business for his own use.

You are required to compute the profit for the year ended 30 June 20X5 and prepare a balance sheet at that date. Present your answer in vertical form showing clearly the cost of fixed assets and the aggregate depreciation.

19.3 **Level II**

Jane Grimes, retail fruit and vegetable merchant, does not keep a full set of accounting records. However, the following information has been produced from the business's records:

1 Summary of the bank account for the year ended 31 August 20X8:

	£		£
1 Sep 20X7 balance brought forward	1,970	Payments to suppliers	72,000
Receipts from trade debtors	96,000	Purchase of motor van (E471 KBR)	13,000
		Rent and rates	2,600

	£		£
Sale of private yacht	20,000	Wages	15,100
Sale of motor van		Motor vehicle expenses	3,350
(A123 BWA)	2,100	Postage and stationery	1,360
		Drawings	9,200
		Repairs and renewals	650
		Insurances	800
		31 Aug 20X8 balance carried forward	2,010
	£120,070		£120,070

2 Assets and liabilities, other than balance at bank:

As at	1 Sept 20X7	31 Aug 20X8
	£	£
Trade creditors	4,700	2,590
Trade debtors	7,320	9,500
Rent and rates accruals	200	260
Motor vans:		
A123 BWA—At cost	10,000	—
Provision for depn	8,000	—
E471 KBR—At cost	—	13,000
Provision for depn	—	To be determined
Stock in trade	4,900	5,900
Insurances prepaid	160	200

3 All receipts are banked and all payments are made from the business bank account.

4 A trade debt of £300 owing by Peter Blunt and included in the trade debtors at 31 August 20X8 (see point 2 above) is to be written off as a bad debt.

5 It is Jane Grime's policy to provide depreciation at the rate of 20 per cent on the cost of motor vans held at the end of each financial year; no depreciation is provided in the year of sale or disposal of a motor van.

6 Discounts received during the year ended 31 August 20X8 from trade creditors amounted to £1,000.

Required:

a Prepare Jane Grime's trading and profit and loss account for the year ended 31 August 20X8.

b Prepare Jane Grime's balance sheet as at 31 August 20X8. (AAT)

19.4* **Level II**

The following is the balance sheet of A. Fox at 31 July 20X8.

	£		£
Capital	48,480	Freehold land and buildings (at cost)	35,000
Creditors	5,220	Fixtures and fittings (cost £10,000)	5,800
Electricity accrued	60	Stock	3,300
		Debtors	6,540
		Bank	3,000
		Telephone prepaid	120
	53,760		53,760

The only book kept by A. Fox is a cash book in which all transactions passed through the bank account are recorded. A summary of the cash book for the year ended 31 July 20X9 has been prepared as follows:

	£		£
Balance b/d	3,000	Wages	5,640
Cash takings banked	18,920	Telephone	280
Cheques from debtors	31,860	Electricity	370
Additional capital	1,000	Motor expenses	1,810
		Payments to creditors	33,360
		Printing	560
		Purchases	4,500
		Balance c/d	8,260
	54,780		54,780

From the supporting documents it has been ascertained that:

i The following amounts have been paid from the cash takings before they were banked:

	£
Drawings	4,000
Purchases	1,120
Car repairs	980
Window cleaning	170

ii Stock at 31 July 20X9 was valued at £3,920.

iii At 31 July 20X9 there are telephone charges prepaid of £140 and electricity accrued of £290.

iv The trade debtors and trade creditors outstanding at the end of the year are £5,840 and £5,720, respectively.

v Fox has taken goods out of the business for his own use that cost £530.

vi Fixtures and fittings have been depreciated in past years at 20 per cent per annum by the reducing balance method.

You are required to prepare a trading and profit and loss account for the year ended 31 July 20X9 and a balance sheet at that date. Present your answer in vertical form.

19.5 Level II

Miss Fitt owns a retail shop. The trading and profit and loss account and balance sheet are prepared annually by you from records consisting of a bank statement and a file of unpaid suppliers and outstanding debtors.

The following balances were shown on her balance sheet at 1 January 20X8:

	£
Shop creditors	245
Shop fittings (cost £250) at written down value	200
Stock in hand	475
Debtors	50
Cash at bank	110
Cash float in till	10

The following is a summary of her bank statement for the year ended 31 December 20X8:

	£
Takings banked	6,983
Payments to suppliers	6,290
Rent of premises to 31 December 20X8	400
A. Smith—shopfitters	85
Advertising in local newspaper	50
Sundry expenses	38

You obtain the following additional information:

1 Takings are banked daily and all suppliers are paid by cheque, but Miss Fitt keeps £15 per week for herself, and pays her assistant £11 per week out of the takings.
2 The work done by A. Smith was for new shelving and repairs to existing fittings. The cost of new shelves was estimated at £50.
3 The cash float in the till was considered insufficient and raised to £15.
4 Miss Fitt took £75 worth of goods for her own use without payment.
5 Your charges will be £25 for preparing the accounts.
6 The outstanding accounts file shows £230 due to suppliers, £10 due in respect of sundry expenses, and £85 outstanding debtors.
7 Depreciation on shop fittings is provided at 10 per cent on cost, a full year's charge being made in year of purchase.
8 Stock in hand at 31 December 20X8 was £710.

You are required to prepare Miss Fitt's trading and profit and loss account for the year ended 31 December 20X8, and her balance sheet as at that date. (ACCA)

19.6 Level II

A year ago, you prepared accounts for A. Wilson, a retailer. His closing position was then:

Balance sheet at 31 March 20X0

	£	£
Delivery van (cost £4,800 in May 20X8)		2,880
Stock		6,410
Debtors (£1,196 *less* provision £72)		1,124
Owing from Askard Ltd		196
		10,610
Bank balance	70	
Trade creditors	2,094	
Accountant's fee	120	
Provision for legal claim	600	2,884
Wilson's capital		£7,726

Mr Wilson does not keep full records (despite your advice) and once again you have to use what information is available to prepare his accounts to 31 March 20X1. The most reliable evidence is a summary of the bank statements for the year. It shows:

	£	£
Balance at 1 Apr 20X0 (overdraft)		(70)
Cash and cheques from customers		33,100
Cheques from Askard Ltd		7,840
		40,870

Less cheques drawn for:		
Wilson's personal expenses	7,400	
Van—tax, insurance, repairs	440	
Rent, rates and general expenses	2,940	
Cash register	400	
Accountant's fee	120	
Trade creditors	28,284	
Legal claim settled	460	40,044
Balance at 31 Mar 20X1		826

For some of the sales Askard credit cards are accepted. Askard Ltd charges 2 per cent commission. At the end of the year the amount outstanding from Askard Ltd was £294.

Some other sales are on credit terms. Wilson keeps copies of the sales invoices in a box until they are settled. Those still in the 'unpaid' box at 31 March 20X1 totalled £1,652, which included one for £136 outstanding for 4 months—otherwise they were all less than 2 months old. Wilson thinks he allowed cash discounts of about £150 during the year. The debt of £72 outstanding at the beginning of the year for which a provision was made was never paid.

The amount of cash and cheques received from credit customers and from cash sales was all paid into the bank except that some cash payments were made first. There were estimated as:

	£
Part-time assistance	840
Petrol for van	800
Miscellaneous expenses	200
Wilson's drawings	2,000

Invoices from suppliers of goods outstanding at the year end totalled £2,420. Closing stock was estimated at £7,090 (cost price) and your fee has been agreed at £200. It has been agreed with the Inspector of Taxes that £440 of the van expenses should be treated as Wilson's private expenses.

Required:
Prepare the profit and loss account for Wilson's business for the year to 31 March 20X1 and a balance sheet at that date. (ACCA)

19.7 Level II

David Denton set up in business as a plumber a year ago, and he has asked you to act as his accountant. His instructions to you are in the form of the following letter.

Dear Henry
I was pleased when you agreed to act as my accountant and look forward to your first visit to check my records. The proposed fee of £250 p.a. is acceptable. I regret that the paperwork for the work done during the year is incomplete. I started my business on 1 January last, and put £6,500 into a business bank account on that date. I brought my van into the firm at that time, and reckon that it was worth £3,600 then. I think it will last another three years after the end of the first year of my business use.

I have drawn £90 per week from the business bank account during the year. In my trade it is difficult to take a holiday, but my wife managed to get away for a while. The travel agent's bill for £280 was paid out of the business account. I bought the lease of the yard and office for £6,500. The lease has 10 years to run, and the rent is only £300 a year payable in advance on the anniversary of the date of purchase, which was 1 April. I borrowed £4,000 on that day from Aunt Jane to help pay for the lease. I have agreed to pay her 10 per cent interest per annum, but have been too busy to do anything about this yet.

I was lucky enough to meet Miss Prism shortly before I set up on my own, and she has worked for me as an office organizer right from the start. She is paid a salary of £3,000 per annum. All the bills for the year have been carefully preserved in a tool box, and we analysed them last week. The materials I have bought cost me £9,600, but I reckon there was £580-worth left in the yard on 31 December. I have not paid for them all yet; I think we owed £714 to the suppliers on 31 December. I was surprised to see that I had spent £4,800 on plumbing equipment, but it should last me five years or so. Electricity bills received up to 30 September came to £1,122; but motor expenses were £912, and general expenses £1,349 for the year. The insurance premium for the year to 31 March next was £800. All these have been paid by cheque but Miss Prism has lost the rate demand. I expect the Local Authority will send a reminder soon since I have not yet paid. I seem to remember that the rates came to £180 for the year to 31 March next.

Miss Prism sent out bills to my customers for work done, but some of them are very slow to pay. Altogether the charges made were £29,863, but only £25,613 had been received by 31 December. Miss Prism thinks that 10 per cent of the remaining bills are not likely to be paid. Other customers for jobs too small to bill have paid £3,418 in cash for work done, but I only managed to bank £2,600 of this money. I used £400 of the difference to pay the family's grocery bills, and Miss Prism used the rest for general expenses, except for £123 which was left over in a drawer in the office on 31 December.

Kind regards,
Yours sincerely,
David.

You are required to draw up a profit and loss account for the year ended 31 December, and a balance sheet as at that date. (ACCA)

For further questions on incomplete records see Chapter 24 on the final accounts of partnerships.

chapter

20

The final accounts of clubs

Learning objectives

After reading this chapter you should be able to:

1. explain the meaning of the key terms and concepts listed at the end of the chapter;
2. describe the main differences between the final accounts of a business enterprise and those of a club, with particular reference to its capital;
3. show the accounting entries in respect of annual subscriptions and explain their conceptual foundation;
4. prepare the final accounts of clubs, including from incomplete records, comprising a receipts and payments account, bar trading account, income and expenditure account, and statement of affairs;
5. show the accounting entries in respect of various items usually only arising in the accounts of clubs, and explain their conceptual foundation;
6. apply the principles in point 5 above to other transactions, items and organizations such as charities.

Introduction

A club is an organization whose primary aim is to provide a service to its members (e.g. sports and social clubs) and/or some section of the community (e.g. senior citizens). One of its main financial objectives is therefore not to earn a profit but often simply to break even. Thus, in the final accounts of clubs the profit and loss account is replaced with an **income and expenditure account**. Any difference between the income and expenditure for the year is referred to as an excess of income over expenditure, or vice versa (i.e. not a profit or loss). The income and expenditure account is prepared using the same principles as the profit and loss account, namely the matching and accrual of revenue income and expenditure. However, the contents differ in that income will take the form of subscriptions, entrance fees from sports activities, surpluses on a bar, dances, raffles, gaming machines, annual dinners, etc.

Another major difference between clubs and business enterprises is that clubs are usually managed by voluntary officers. Members of the club therefore frequently expect them to provide an account of the money that has been received and the way in which it has been spent. Thus, final accounts of clubs often include a **receipts and payments account**. This is simply a summary of the cash book showing the opening and closing cash and bank balances and the total amounts received and spent on each type of income and expenditure, assets, etc.

Many clubs are quite small and may have few, if any, assets and liabilities other than cash. It therefore serves little purpose to prepare a balance sheet, particularly if a receipts and payments account has been produced. However, some clubs are relatively large. In this case the final accounts should include a balance sheet which is also sometimes called a **statement of affairs**. It will take the same form as for business enterprises with one major difference, which is that the capital account is replaced by an **Accumulated/general fund**. This is an accumulation of previous years' surpluses (less deficits) of income over expenditure, and represents the net worth of the club. Unlike the capital account of business enterprises, there cannot be capital introduced or drawings against the accumulated fund. The only other significant difference between the balance sheet of a business enterprise and that of a club is that the latter also contains subscriptions in arrear and subscriptions in advance. These are examined further later.

Although clubs are not primarily trading organizations they frequently engage in certain activities that are intended to make a profit/surplus as a way of raising additional funds or subsidizing other functions, for example, the sale of drinks and snacks, gaming machines, raffles and dances. Where these involve material amounts of money it is usual to compute the profit or loss on the activity in a separate account such as a **bar trading account**. Where the amounts are less significant the income, expenditure and resulting surplus (or deficit) should be shown in the income and expenditure account, e.g. annual dinner or dance.

Annual subscriptions

Many clubs require their members to pay an annual subscription. These are usually accounted for on an accruals basis, that is, applying the accruals concept. This means that the amount which is credited to the income and expenditure account in respect of subscriptions is the amount due for the year, irrespective of whether this has all been received.

The application of the accruals concept gives rise to subscriptions in arrear and subscriptions in advance in the final accounts. Where some members have not paid their subscriptions at the end of a given accounting year these are referred to as **subscriptions**

in arrear, and treated as debtors. Where some members have paid their subscriptions for the following accounting year these are referred to as **subscriptions in advance**, and treated as creditors.

However, as in the case of accrued and prepaid expenses, debtors and creditors in respect of subscriptions are not entered in separate personal accounts. Instead, these are recorded in the subscriptions account. Subscriptions in arrear are entered in the subscriptions account as a balance carried down on the credit side and a balance brought down on the debit side. Subscriptions in advance are entered in the subscriptions account as a balance carried down on the debit side and a balance brought down on the credit side. Thus, subscriptions in arrear are shown on the balance sheet as a current asset and subscriptions in advance are shown as a current liability.

Sometimes subscriptions are recorded in the income and expenditure account on a strict cash received basis and not an accruals basis. In this case there will not be any subscriptions in arrear or advance in the final accounts. It is sometimes justified on the grounds that members, unlike other debtors, are more likely to fail to pay subscriptions in arrear, and clubs are unlikely to take legal or other action to force payment. However, the use of the cash received basis is not common in examination questions and should only be applied where specifically required.

The preparation of final accounts of clubs

It is common to find that the books of accounts of a club have been kept on a **Single-entry** basis. This means that the procedure to be followed in the preparation of the final account will be as described in Chapter 19. This is illustrated in Example 20.1.

Example 20.1

City Football Club has the following assets and liabilities at 1 July 20X7: freehold land and buildings at cost £50,000; equipment at written down value (WDV) £12,200; grass mower at cost £135; bar creditors £1,380; subscriptions in advance £190; subscriptions in arrear £105; bar stocks £2,340; rates in advance £240; electricity accrued £85.

A summary of the receipts and payments during the year ended 30 June 20X8 is as follows:

	£		£
Bank balance at 1 July 20X7	695	Rates	490
Bar takings banked	5,430	Electricity	255
Subscriptions received	3,610	Purchase of new grass mower	520
Sale of dance tickets	685	Bar steward's wages	2,200
Gate money received	8,490	Bar creditors	4,980
		Band for dance	490
		Postage and telephone	310
		Printing and stationery	175
		Bank balance at 30 June 20X8	9,490
	18,910		18,910

You are given the following additional information:

1 Bar stocks at 30 June 20X8 £2,560.
2 Bar creditors at 30 June 20X8 £980.
3 Rates paid include £400 for the 6 months to 30 September 20X8.
4 Electricity in arrear at 30 June 20X8 £70.
5 Subscriptions in arrear at 30 June 20X8 £95.
6 Subscriptions in advance at 30 June 20X8 £115.
7 The following amounts have been paid from bar takings before they were banked: sundry expenses £25, bar purchases £235, office salaries £1,200, stationery £45, and travelling expenses £140.
8 The new grass mower was purchased by putting in part exchange the old one, for which the trade in value was £180.
9 Depreciation on the equipment is 20 per cent p.a. using the reducing balance method. No depreciation is charged on the grass mower.

You are required to prepare:

a a bar trading account for the year ended 30 June 20X8;
b an income and expenditure account for the year ended 30 June 20X8;
c a balance sheet as at 30 June 20X8.

Show clearly all your workings.

Workings/procedure

1 If necessary, prepare a statement of affairs as at the end of the previous year in order to ascertain the accumulated/general fund.

City Football Club
Statement of affairs as at 30 June 20X7

Fixed assets	£	£	£
Freehold land and buildings at cost			50,000
Equipment at WDV			12,200
Grass mower at cost			135
			62,335
Current assets			
Subscriptions in arrear		105	
Stock		2,340	
Prepaid expenses		240	
Bank		695	
		3,380	
Less: Current liabilities			
Accrued expenses	85		
Creditors	1,380		
Subscriptions in advance	190	1,655	
			1,725
Accumulated fund at 30 June 20X7			64,060

2 If necessary, prepare a receipts and payments account for the year in order to ascertain the bank and cash balance at the end of the year and the total amounts received and spent on each type of income and expenditure, and on assets.

3 a Compute the net credit bar purchases by preparing a creditors' control account:

Creditors' control

20X8			20X7		
30 June Bank	4,980	1 July	Balance b/d		1,380
30 June Balance c/d	980	20X8			
		30 June	Net purchases		4,580
	5,960				5,960

The figure for net credit purchases is the difference between the two sides.

b Compute the cash and cheque bar purchases and then the total bar purchases:

Total purchases = £235 + £4,580 = £4,815

4 a Compute the net credit bar sales, if any, by preparing a debtors' control account.

b Compute the cash and cheque bar sales and then the total bar sales:

Cash and total sales = £5,430 + £25 + £235 + £1,200 + £45 + £140 = £7,075

5 Ascertain the income for the year in respect of subscriptions by preparing the ledger account. Alternatively, in examinations this may be shown as workings in the income and expenditure account.

Subscriptions

20X7			20X7		
1 July	Subs in arrear b/d	105	1 July	Subs in advance b/d	190
20X8			20X8		
30 June	Subs for year	3,675	30 June	Bank	3,610
30 June	Subs in advance c/d	115	30 June	Subs in arrear c/d	95
		3,895			3,895

The figure for subs for the year of £3,675 is the difference between the two sides. It is credited to the income and expenditure account.

6 Compute the expenditure for the year in respect of those expenses with accruals and prepayments by preparing the relevant ledger accounts. Alternatively, in examinations this may be shown as workings in the income and expenditure account:

Rates

20X7			20X8	
1 July	Prepayment b/d	240	30 June Income and expenditure a/c	530
20X8			30 June Prepayment c/d (3/6 × 400)	200
30 June	Bank	490		
		730		730

Light and heat

20X8			20X7		
30 June	Bank	255	1 July	Accrual b/d	85
30 June	Accrual c/d	70	20X8		
			30 June	Income and expenditure a/c	240
		325			325

7 Ascertain the depreciation charges for the year and any profit or loss on the sale of fixed assets:

Depreciation on equipment = 20 per cent × £12,200 = £2,440
Profit on sale of grass mower = £180 − £135 = £45

8 Prepare the bar trading account, income and expenditure account, and balance sheet, remembering to add together any cheque and cash expenditure of the same type (e.g. stationery) and make any other necessary adjustments, such as the purchase of fixed assets.

City Football Club
Bar trading account for the year ended 30 June 20X8

	£	£
Sales		7,075
Less: Cost of sales—		
Stock at 1 July 20X7	2,340	
Add: Purchases	4,815	
	7,155	
Less: Stock at 30 June 20X8	2,560	
	4,595	
Other bar costs—		
Steward's wages	2,200	6,795
Profit on bar		280

City Football Club
Income and expenditure account for the year ended 30 June 20X8

	£	£
Income		
Gate receipts		8,490
Subscriptions		3,675
Profit on bar		280
Income from dance	685	
Cost of dance	(490)	
Surplus on dance		195
Profit on sale of fixed asset		45
		12,685

Less: Expenditure			
Rates (490 + 240 – 200)			530
Light and heat (255 + 70 – 85)			240
Postage and telephone			310
Printing and stationery (175 + 45)			220
Sundry expenses		25	
Office salaries		1,200	
Travelling expenses		140	
Depreciation on equipment		2,440	5,105
Excess of income over expenditure			7,580

City Football Club
Balance sheet as at 30 June 20X8

	£	£	£
Fixed assets			
Freehold land and buildings at cost			50,000
Equipment at WDV		12,200	
Less: Depreciation		2,440	9,760
Grass mower (520 + 180)			700
			60,460
Current assets			
Subscriptions in arrear		95	
Stock		2,560	
Prepayments		200	
Bank		9,490	
		12,345	
Less: Current liabilities			
Subscriptions in advance	115		
Creditors	980		
Accruals	70	1,165	
Net current assets			11,180
Net assets			71,640
Accumulated fund			
Balance at 30 June 20X7			64,060
Add: Excess of income over expenditure for the year			7,580
Balance at 30 June 20X8			71,640

Special items

As seen above, clubs have a variety of different forms of income, many of which are not found in business enterprises. Some of these are not common in practice but provide examples that examiners can use to test important principles. Those most frequently encountered in examinations are discussed below.

Donations, bequests and gifts

Small donations, bequests and gifts in the form of money are credited to the income and expenditure account. Donations and gifts in the form of domestic goods (such as furniture for the clubhouse or old clothes for resale) with a relatively small value are not usually recorded in the income and expenditure account (until they are sold, when just the sale proceeds are recorded).

However, where donations of money or other assets are of a material amount (i.e. large in relation to the size of the club's normal income), the generally accepted best practice is to credit such items direct to the accumulated fund instead of the income and expenditure account. This is because it would probably be misleading to credit the income and expenditure account with large amounts of income which is of a non-recurring nature. Members might be misled into thinking that the resulting surplus for the year was likely to be repeated in future years and thus could be used to cover additional recurring expenditure or reduced bar prices! The corresponding debit entry would be in the receipts and payments account in the case of money, or to the relevant asset account where the donation or bequest takes some other form, such as land, buildings or paintings. In the latter case the amount entered in the accounts would be a valuation.

Membership/entrance fees

Clubs which have valuable assets that are in great demand, such as golf and other sports facilities, often require new members to pay an entry or joining fee (in addition to the annual subscription). To treat this as income for the year in which it was received by crediting the income and expenditure account would be a breach of the matching principle, the reason being that this fee is in the nature of a prepayment by the member for services which the club is obliged to provide over his or her period of membership, which is usually several years.

Such fees are referred to as **deferred income**, and the matching principle dictates that these should be credited to the income and expenditure account over the number of years which the club expects to have to provide the member with its services. Clearly, the decision relating to the length of this period is highly subjective. One possibility is the average number of years that people remain members of the club. However, in practice a more arbitrary period may be selected depending on the nature of the club's services and the size of the membership fee.

The accounting entries in respect of joining fees are thus to credit these to a deferred income account, and each year to transfer a given proportion (e.g. 10 per cent if to be spread over 10 years) to the income and expenditure account. The balance on the deferred income account is shown on the balance sheet after (and separate from) the accumulated fund.

Life membership subscriptions

Instead of paying an annual subscription some clubs permit their members to make a once-only payment which entitles them to membership for life. These are referred to as life membership subscriptions and, like entrance fees above, are in the nature of a prepayment by the member for services that the club is obliged to provide over the remainder of his or her life. They must therefore not be credited to the income and expenditure account as income of the year they are received.

Life membership subscriptions are a form of deferred income, and the matching principle dictates that they be spread over the number of years which the club expects to have to provide the life member with its services. Clearly, the decision relating to the length of this period is highly subjective. One possibility is the average number of years between people becoming life members and their death. However, in practice a more arbitrary period may be selected depending on the nature of the club's services. For example, the period may be considerably longer for a golf club or social club than an athletics club or senior citizens club, since the period of life membership of the latter is restricted by physical and age constraints.

The accounting entries in respect of life membership subscriptions are thus to credit these to a deferred income account, and each year to transfer a given proportion (e.g. 5 per cent if to be spread over 20 years) to the income and expenditure account. The balance on the deferred income account is shown on the balance sheet after (and separate from) the accumulated fund.

There is, however, an alternative treatment of life membership subscriptions which is based on the argument that because the period of membership cannot be predicted with reasonable certainty, the income should not be recognized until the member dies. Thus, all the life membership subscriptions are credited to a fund account, and when a member dies his or her subscription is transferred to the accumulated fund (or possibly the income and expenditure account). The life membership subscription fund account is shown in the balance sheet just below the accumulated fund and separate from any items that have been treated as deferred income, such as membership/entrance fees. This method of treating life membership subscriptions would be adopted in examination questions that do not give any indication of the length of time over which these should be credited to income, and which give details of how many life members died during the accounting year.

Prize funds

Some clubs give prizes or other monetary awards to their members and/or other people that they wish to honour or assist for educational reasons. These are frequently financed from a separate fund, which may have been created by the club or from money that was donated for the express purpose of making the award. When the fund is set up the money donated for this purpose is invested in securities which provide some sort of income. This often takes the form of government stocks carrying a fixed rate of interest. The prizes or awards are usually paid out of the interest received and not the original donation, which remains invested.

The accounting entries for prize funds can be confusing, partly because they involve two related accounts. The first is a prize fund account which appears on the balance sheet along with other funds such as the accumulated fund and any life membership subscription fund. The other is a prize fund investment account which is usually treated as a fixed asset. When the fund is set up, the money set aside or donated for this purpose is debited to the prize fund investment account and credited to the prize fund account.

When income is received from the prize fund investments this is debited in the receipts and payments account and credited to the prize fund account. When the prizes are awarded the amounts are credited in the receipts and payments account and debited to the prize fund account. This is illustrated in Example 20.2.

Example 20.2

Parkview plc donated £10,000 to the City Club on 31 December 20X0. It was agreed that the annual income from this is to be used to make a grant to members' children for educational purposes. The donation was invested in 10 per cent Government Stock on 1 January 20X1. The annual income of £1,000 was received on 31 December 20X1 and this was given to J. Smith as a grant on 1 January 20X2.

Show how this would be recorded in the ledger of City Club.

Receipts and payments (R & P)

20X0			20X1		
31 Dec	Grant fund— Parkview donation	10,000	1 Jan	Grant fund investments	10,000
20X1			20X2		
31 Dec	Grant fund—interest	1,000	1 Jan	Grant fund—J. Smith	1,000

Grant fund investments

20X1					
1 Jan	R & P	10,000			

Parkview grant fund

20X2			20X0		
1 Jan	R & P—J. Smith	1,000	31 Dec	R & P	10,000
			20X1		
			31 Dec	R & P—interest	1,000

Note

1 The balance on the grant fund at the end of each accounting year is normally the same as that on the grant fund investment account. However, as in the above example, these may differ because of time lags between the receipt of investment income and the payment of the grant.

Learning Activity 20.1

Visit the website of a large charity and find a copy of their latest annual report and accounts. Prepare a list of the main differences between this document and the annual report of the public limited company that you obtained for Learning activity 1.2. Alternatively, perform the same task using the annual report of a football club. However, this is likely to be less relevant since professional football clubs are not clubs as such, but rather, like some charities, limited companies, a few of whom, such as Tottenham and Manchester United, have their shares listed/quoted on the London Stock Exchange.

Summary

The final accounts of clubs differ from those of business enterprises in a number of ways. Because clubs are non-profit-seeking organizations the profit and loss account is replaced by an income and expenditure account. However, this is prepared using the same principles, such as the accruals concept. Clubs are also usually managed by voluntary officers whom the members expect to provide a summarized cash book known as a receipts and payments account. The balance sheet of clubs is much the same as that of a business except that the capital is replaced by a general/accumulated fund which is an accumulation of previous years' excesses of income over expenditure. Some clubs engage in trading activities such as a bar, in which case it is necessary to include in the final accounts a bar trading account.

Another major difference between clubs and businesses is that the former often have a variety of different forms of income not normally associated with the latter—in particular annual subscriptions. These are usually accounted for in the income and expenditure account on an accrual basis. This gives rise to subscriptions in advance and arrear which are shown on the balance sheet as a current liability or current asset, respectively. However, sometimes subscriptions are accounted for on a strict cash received basis.

The books of account of clubs are often kept on a single-entry basis. In this case the final accounts will be prepared using the same procedure as described in the previous chapter, with the addition of workings relating to the subscriptions account.

The final accounts of clubs also sometimes contain a number of special items not normally found in the accounts of businesses, but which involve the application of certain common principles. Two of these are entrance/joining fees and life membership subscriptions. The matching principle dictates that these be treated as deferred income. Furthermore, donations, bequests and gifts of a material amount should be credited direct to the club's accumulated fund rather than the income and expenditure account where it is of a non-recurring nature. Finally, a club may operate a prize or grant fund. This must be accounted for by means of a fund separate from the general/accumulated fund, and a separate prize fund investment account.

Key terms and concepts

Accumulated/general fund (247)
bar trading account (247)
bequests (253)
deferred income (253)
donations (253)
gifts (253)
income and expenditure account (247)
life membership subscriptions (253)
membership/entrance fees (253)
prize funds (254)
receipts and payments account (247)
single entry (248)
statement of affairs (247)
subscriptions in advance (248)
subscriptions in arrear (247)

Review questions

20.1 Explain the difference between a receipts and payments account and an income and expenditure account.

20.2 Explain the nature of an accumulated fund in the balance sheet of a club.

20.3 Describe the entries in the accounts of a club for each of the following and explain the justification for each treatment:

a Donation of second-hand clothing for resale.

b A gift of a large amount of cash.

c A bequest of premises to be used as a clubhouse.

20.4 Describe two possible methods of accounting for each of the following in the accounts of clubs and explain the theoretical/conceptual justification for each method:

a Membership/entrance fees.

b Life membership subscriptions.

20.5 Explain the nature and accounting entries in respect of prize funds in the accounts of clubs.

Exercises

An asterisk after the question number indicates that there is a suggested answer in the Appendix.

20.6 Level II

The secretary of the Woodland Hockey Club gives you the following summary of his cash book for the year ended 31 May 20X9:

	£		£
Balances at commencement of year:		Rent	234
At bank	63	Printing and stationery	18
In hand	10	Affiliation fees	12
Subscriptions:		Captain's and secretary's expenses	37
Supporters	150	Refreshments for visiting teams	61
Supporters 20X9–20X0 season	20	Annual social	102
Fees per game	170	Equipment purchased	26
Annual social	134	Balance at close of year:	
		At bank	49
		In hand	8
	£547		£547

The secretary also gives you the following information:

	31 May 20X8	*31 May 20X9*
	£	£
Amounts due to the club:		
Supporters' subscriptions	14	12
Fees per game	78	53
Re annual social	6	—
Amounts owing by the club:		
Rent	72	54
Printing	—	3
Secretary's expenses	4	8
Refreshments	13	12

On 31 May 20X8 the club's equipment appeared in the books at £150. It is desired that $12\frac{1}{2}$ per cent be written off the book value of the equipment as it appears on 31 May 20X9.

You are required to:

a Show your computation of the club's accumulated fund as on 31 May 20X8.

b Prepare the income and expenditure account showing the result for the year ended 31 May 20X9, and the balance sheet as on that date. (ACCA)

20.7 Level II

The treasurer of the Senior Social Club has prepared the following summary of the club's receipts and payments for the year ended 30 November 20X0.

Senior Social Club

Receipts and payments account for the year ended 30 November 20X0

	£		£
Cash and bank balances b/f	810	Secretarial expenses	685
Members' subscriptions	4,250	Rent	2,500
Donations	1,480	Visiting speakers' expenses	1,466
Sales of competition tickets	1,126	Donations to charities	380
		Prizes for competitions	550
		Purchase of equipment	1,220
		Stationery and printing	469
		Balance c/f	396
	7,666		7,666

On 1 December 20X9 the club owned equipment which had cost £3,650 and which was valued at £2,190. The club's equipment as at 30 November 20X0 (inclusive of any purchases during the year) was valued at £1,947.

The following information is available:

As at	*1 Dec 20X9*	*30 Nov 20X0*
	£	£
Stocks of prizes	86	108
Owing to suppliers of prizes	314	507
Subscriptions in arrears	240	580
Subscriptions in advance	65	105

Required:

a Calculate the value of the accumulated fund of the club as at 1 December 20X9.

b Prepare a subscriptions account for the year ended 30 November 20X0 showing clearly the amount to be transferred to the club's income and expenditure account for the year.

c Prepare a statement showing the surplus or deficit made by the club on competitions for the year ended 30 November 20X0.

d Prepare an income and expenditure account for the year ended 30 November 20X0.

e Prepare the club's balance sheet as at 30 November 20X0. (AAT)

20.8* **Level II**

The Elite Bowling and Social Club prepares its annual accounts to 31 October. The following receipts and payments account has been prepared by the treasurer:

	£		£
Cash in hand, 31 Oct 20X7	10	Bar purchases	1,885
Balances at bank, 31 Oct 20X7		Wages	306
Current account	263	Rent and rates	184
Deposit account	585	Lighting and heating	143
Spectators' entrance fees	54	New mower (less allowance	
Subscriptions: to 31/10/X7	30	for old one £40)	120
to 31/10/X8	574	General expenses	132
to 31/10/X9	44	Catering purchases	80
Bar takings	2,285	Additional furniture	460
Deposit account interest	26	Cash in hand at 31/10/X8	8
Catering receipts	120	Balances at bank 31/10/X8	
		Current account	176
		Deposit account	497
	£3,991		£3,991

The following information is also supplied:

1 The book values of the fixed assets on 31 October 20X7 were: furniture, fixtures and fittings £396 (cost £440), and mower £20 (cost £120).

2 The current assets and liabilities were as follows:

	31 Oct 20X7	*31 Oct 20X8*
	£	£
Bar stock at cost	209	178
Amount owed to the brewery for bar purchases	186	248
Due for rent and rates	12	26
Due for lighting and heating	9	11
Subscriptions in arrear	30	50

3 During the year the steward commenced to provide light refreshments at the bar and it has been agreed that in the annual accounts provision should be made for the payment to him of a bonus of 40 per cent of the gross profit arising from this catering venture.

4 Depreciation to furniture, fixtures and fittings is to be provided at a rate of 10 per cent on cost. No depreciation is to be provided on the new mower, but a full year on the new furniture.

You are required to prepare:

a a statement showing the general fund of the club as on 31 October 20X7;

b an income and expenditure account for the year ended 31 October 20X8 (showing separately gross profit on bar sales and catering); and

c a balance sheet as at 31 October 20X8. (ACCA)

20.9* **Level III**

The treasurer of a club has given you the following account of its activities during the year ended 30 June 20X8.

Receipts		*Payments*	
	£		£
Bank balance at 1/7/X7 (including £75 received during the year ended 30/6/X7 on the prize fund investments)	390	Additional billiard table with accessories bought 1/7/X7	300
Annual subscriptions (including £20 relating to previous year)	340	Repairs to billiard tables	50
Life membership subscriptions (5 @ £16)	80	Purchases for bar	3,680
Sundry lettings	180	Steward's wages and expenses	400
Bar receipts	4,590	Rates	140
Receipts for billiards	275	Lighting and heating	72
Gifts from members	3,500	Cleaning and laundry	138
Income from £1,500 5 per cent defence bonds allocated specifically for a prize fund	75	Sundry expenses	80
		Prizes awarded for previous year from income available at 1/7/X7	75
		Repayment of 5 per cent mortgage on 30/6/X8 with interest for two years	4,400
		Bank balance at 30/6/X8	95
	£9,430		£9,430

You are also given the following information:

1 The freehold building, owned and occupied by the club, was purchased for £6,000 many years ago.
2 On 1 July 20X2, the club acquired six billiard tables for which they paid £1,200, and it is considered that the tables have a life of 12 years.
3 The bar stock at 1 July 20X7 was £150 and at 30 June 20X8 £180.
4 Annual subscriptions outstanding from members at 30 June 20X8 amounted to £10.
5 On 1 July 20X7 there were 25 life members who had paid subscriptions of £16 each. During the year ended 30 June 20X8 three of these members had died.

You are required to prepare an income and expenditure account and balance sheet showing clearly how you have treated the subscriptions of life members and the prize fund. (ACCA)

20.10 **Level III**

You have agreed to take over the role of bookkeeper for the AB sports and social club. The summarized balance sheet on 31.12.X4 as prepared by the previous bookkeeper contained the following items. All figures are in £s.

Assets	£	£
Heating oil for clubhouse		1,000
Bar and cafe stocks		7,000
New sportsware, for sale, at cost		3,000
Used sportsware, for hire, at valuation		750

Equipment for groundsperson—cost	5,000	
—depr.	3,500	1,500
Subscriptions due		200
Bank—current account		1,000
—deposit account		10,000
Claims		
Accumulated fund		23,150
Creditors—bar and cafe stocks		1,000
—sportsware		300

The bank account summary for the year to 31.12.X5 contained the following items.

	£
Receipts	
Subscriptions	11,000
Bankings—bar and cafe	20,000
—sale of sportsware	5,000
—hire of sportsware	3,000
Interest on deposit account	800
Payments	
Rent and repairs of clubhouse	6,000
Heating oil	4,000
Sportsware	4,500
Groundsperson	10,000
Bar and cafe purchases	9,000
Transfer to deposit account	6,000

You discover that the subscriptions due figure as at 31.12.X4 was arrived at as follows.

	£
Subscriptions unpaid for 20X3	10
Subscriptions unpaid for 20X4	230
Subscriptions paid for 20X5	40
Corresponding figures at 31.12.X5 are:	
Subscriptions unpaid for 20X3	10
Subscriptions unpaid for 20X4	20
Subscriptions unpaid for 20X5	90
Subscriptions paid for 20X6	200

Subscriptions due for more than 12 months should be written off with effect from 1.1.X5.

Asset balances at 31.12.X5 include:	£
Heating oil for club house	700
Bar and cafe stocks	5,000
New sportsware, for sale, at cost	4,000
Used sportsware, for hire, at valuation	1,000

Closing creditors at 31.12.X5 are:	£
For bar and cafe stocks	800
For sportsware	450
For heating oil for clubhouse	200

Two-thirds of the sportsware purchases made in 20X5 had been added to stock of new sportsware in the figures given in the list of assets above, and one-third had been added directly to the stock of used sportsware for hire.

Half of the resulting 'new sportsware for sale at cost' at 31.12.X5 is actually over two years old. You decide, with effect from 31.12.X5, to transfer these older items into the stock of used sportsware, at a valuation of 25 per cent of their original cost.

No cash balances are held at 31.12.X4 or 31.12.X5. The equipment for the grounds-person is to be depreciated at 10 per cent per annum, on cost.

Required:

Prepare income and expenditure account and balance sheet for the AB sports club for 20X5, in a form suitable for circulation to members. The information given should be as complete and informative as possible within the limits of the information given to you. All workings must be submitted. (ACCA)

chapter

21

Value added tax, columnar books of prime entry and the payroll

Learning objectives

After reading this chapter you should be able to:

1 explain the meaning of the key terms and concepts listed at the end of the chapter;

2 outline the system of value added tax (VAT) found in the UK;

3 show the entries in the books of prime entry and ledger in respect of VAT;

4 explain the purpose of columnar books of prime entry;

5 show the entries in columnar day books and the cash book, and the posting of these entries to the ledger;

6 outline the PAYE system found in the UK, prepare a simple payroll and explain its contents;

7 show the journal and ledger entries relating to the items usually contained in a payroll.

Value added tax

Value added tax (VAT) is a **sales tax** that is ultimately borne by the consumer. Most businesses charge their customer with (output) VAT and buy goods and services which are subject to (input) VAT. However, these businesses do not usually suffer VAT as a cost of inputs, in that the input VAT is set off against the output VAT and periodically the difference is paid to HM Customs & Excise or a refund obtained. Consequently, none of the items shown in the final accounts normally includes VAT. The only exceptions to this are debtors and creditors. Furthermore, there may be a current liability for VAT at the end of an accounting year that represents the difference between output and input VAT which has not been paid to HM Customs & Excise at that date.

Various rates of VAT have existed at various times. The current standard rate is 17.5 per cent. Some products are zero rated, i.e. bear no VAT; some businesses are exempt so that they do not charge VAT on their outputs but do have to pay VAT on their inputs.

The accounting entries for VAT are relatively straightforward in principle. When goods which are subject to VAT are purchased for cash, the price including VAT is credited in the cash book. The corresponding debit consists of two entries: the cost excluding VAT is debited to the purchases account, and the amount of VAT is debited to a VAT account. Similarly, when goods that are subject to VAT are purchased on credit, the price including VAT is credited to the creditors' account. The corresponding debit consists of two entries: the cost excluding VAT is debited to the purchases account, and the amount of VAT is debited to a VAT or HM Customs & Excise account, which is essentially a personal account. Conversely, when goods which are subject to VAT are sold on credit, the price including VAT is debited to the debtors' account. The corresponding credit consists of two entries: the price excluding VAT is credited to the sales account, and the amount of VAT is credited to the VAT account. A simple illustration is given in Example 21.1.

Example 21.1

A. Ltd buys goods on credit from B. Ltd at a price of £200 plus 17.5 per cent VAT. A. Ltd then sells these goods to C. Ltd for £320 plus 17.5 per cent VAT. Show the ledger entries in the book of A. Ltd.

B. Ltd

		Purchases + VAT	235

Purchases

B. Ltd	200		

VAT

B. Ltd	35	C. Ltd	56

C. Ltd

Sales + VAT	376		

Sales

		C. Ltd	320

Periodically, the VAT account is balanced and the difference between the two sides paid to HM Customs & Excise where this is a credit balance, or a refund obtained where there is a debit balance.

A further complication with VAT is that some businesses are classed as either **zero rated** or **exempt**. This means that they do not have to charge their customers with VAT. In the case of zero-rated businesses, they obtain a refund of the VAT that they have paid on goods and services purchased. Thus, input VAT is debited to the VAT account, and the only credit entry in this account is a cheque received from HM Customs & Excise as a refund. However, businesses that are classed as exempt do not get a refund. In this case there is no VAT account in the ledger because the cost of goods and services purchased including VAT is simply debited to the relevant nominal account.

Columnar books of prime entry

A **columnar book of prime entry** is one which contains analysis columns. The use of analysis columns in a petty cash book was described in Chapter 8. In practice, most of the other books of prime entry, namely the day books and cash book, also frequently contain analysis columns. Each is described below.

The simplest are the sales day book and sales returns day book. These often contain analysis columns relating to the different departments or types of product that the business sells. This makes it possible to compute the gross profit of each department in departmental trading account. The sales and sales returns day books also usually contain an analysis column in respect of VAT.

The purchases day book and purchases returns day book also often contain analysis columns. These may relate to the different departments or types of products. However, a more common form of columnar purchases day book contains not just credit purchases of goods for resale, but also expenses incurred on credit (e.g. the purchase of stationery) and the purchase of fixed assets on credit. Indeed, any invoice received in respect of goods or services purchased on credit is often recorded in the columnar purchases day book. The purchases and purchases returns day books also usually contain an analysis column relating to VAT.

Lastly, the cash book frequently also contains memorandum analysis columns on both the debit and credit sides. Those on the credit side are much the same as in the petty cash book. The columns on the debit side are used in the same way but obviously relate to different types of receipts. The cash book also usually contains an analysis column on each side relating to VAT.

As explained in the context of columnar petty cash books, the purpose of having analysis columns in books of prime entry is to facilitate the posting of the ledger. Each column relates to a particular type of income or expenditure such as stationery or motor expenses. Every transaction is entered in the total column and an appropriate analysis column. At the end of each calendar month the total of each analysis column is posted to the relevant account in the ledger. Thus, instead of posting each transaction to the ledger separately, income and expenditure of the same type is collected together in analysis columns and the total for the period posted to the relevant account.

Illustrations of the use of columnar day books and cash books are given in Examples 21.2 and 21.3, respectively. The latter is a continuation of the former.

Example 21.2

A. Singh is in business as a builders' merchant. The following credit transactions took place during August 20X5:

2 Aug Purchased goods for resale from AB Ltd for £560 plus 17.5 per cent VAT.
5 Aug Bought stationery from CD Ltd for £120 plus 17.5 per cent VAT.
10 Aug Purchased fixtures and fittings for the shop from EF Ltd for £2,000 plus 17.5 per cent VAT.
18 Aug Sold goods to YZ Ltd for £1,000 plus 17.5 per cent VAT.
23 Aug Sold some old loose tools previously used in the shop to WX Ltd for £1,600 plus 17.5 per cent VAT.
25 Aug Returned goods costing £200 + VAT to AB Ltd and received a credit note.
29 Aug Returned stationery costing £40 + VAT to CD Ltd and received a credit note.

You are required to make the necessary entries in the relevant columnar books of prime entry and the ledger.

Purchases day book (PDB)

Date	*Name of creditor*	*Total*	*VAT*	*Purchases*	*Stationery*	*Misc.*
20X5		£	£	£	£	£
2 Aug	AB Ltd	658	98	560		
5 Aug	CD Ltd	141	21		120	
10 Aug	EF Ltd	2,350	350			2,000
		3,149	469	560	120	2,000

Sales day book (SDB)

Date	*Name of debtor*	*Total*	*VAT*	*Sales*	*Misc.*
20X5		£	£	£	£
18 Aug	YZ Ltd	1,175	175	1,000	
23 Aug	WX Ltd	1,880	280		1,600
		3,055	455	1,000	1,600

Purchases returns day book (PRDB)

Date	*Name of creditor*	*Total*	*VAT*	*Purchases*	*Stationery*	*Misc.*
20X5	£	£	£	£	£	£
25 Aug	AB Ltd	235	35	200		
29 Aug	CD Ltd	47	7		40	
		282	42	200	40	—

The ledger

Purchases

20X5					
31 Aug	Total per PDB	560			

Stationery

31 Aug	Total per PDB	120	31 Aug	Total per PRDB	40

Fixtures and fittings

10 Aug	EF Ltd	2,000			

VAT

31 Aug	Total per PDB	469	31 Aug	Total per SDB	455
			31 Aug	Total per PRDB	42

AB Ltd

25 Aug	Returns + VAT	235	2 Aug	Purchases + VAT	658

CD Ltd

29 Aug	Stationery + VAT	47	5 Aug	Stationery + VAT	141

EF Ltd

			10 Aug	Fixtures + VAT	2,350

Purchases returns

			31 Aug	Total per PRDB	200

Sales

			31 Aug	Total per SDB	1,000

Loose tools

			23 Aug	WX Ltd	1,600

YZ Ltd

18 Aug	Sales + VAT	1,175			

WX Ltd

23 Aug	Loose tools + VAT	1,880			

Note

1 The amount of each invoice (including VAT) shown in the total columns of the day books is posted individually to the debtors' and creditors' personal accounts in the normal way. The total of the VAT columns in each day book is posted to the VAT account. Similarly, the total of each of the other analysis columns in the day books is posted to the relevant ledger account. The only exception to this is the miscellaneous column, where each entry would often have to be posted separately because they normally involve more than one ledger account.

Example 21.3

A. Singh had the following cheque receipts and payments during September 20X5:

1 Sep	Balance at bank £8,000.
3 Sep	Introduced additional capital of £900.
7 Sep	Sold goods for £400 plus 17.5 per cent VAT.
12 Sep	Received a cheque from YZ Ltd for £1,140 after deducting £35 cash discount.
20 Sep	Drawings £250.
22 Sep	Purchased goods for resale costing £320 plus 17.5 per cent VAT.
23 Sep	Bought stationery costing £200 plus 17.5 per cent VAT.
25 Sep	Purchased a motor vehicle for £5,000 plus 17.5 per cent VAT.
27 Sep	Paid AB Ltd £398 after deducting £25 cash discount.
29 Sep	Paid HM Customs & Excise the VAT outstanding at the end of August 20X5 of £28.

You are required to make the necessary entries in a columnar cash book and the ledger.

The columnar cash book (debit side) (CB)

Date	*Details*	*Total*	*VAT*	*Debtors*	*Discount allowed*	*Sales*	*Misc.*
20X5		£	£	£	£	£	£
1 Sep	Balance b/d	8,000					8,000
3 Sep	Capital	900					900
7 Sep	Sales	470	70			400	
12 Sep	Y Ltd	1,140		1,140	35		
		10,510	70	1,140	35	400	8,900

The columnar cash book (credit side) (CB)

Date	*Details*	*Total*	*VAT*	*Creditors*	*Discount received*	*Purchases*	*Stationery*	*Misc.*
20X5		£	£	£	£	£	£	£
20 Sep	Drawings	250						250
22 Sep	Purchases	376	56			320		
23 Sep	Stationery	235	35				200	
25 Sep	Motor vehicles	5,875	875					5,000
27 Sep	AB Ltd	398		398	25			
29 Sep	HM Customs & Excise	28	28					
	Totals	7,162	994	398	25	320	200	5,250
30 Sep	Balance c/d	3,348						
		10,510						

The ledger

Capital

			20X5		
			3 Sep	Bank	900

Sales

			31 Aug	Total per SDB	1,000
			30 Sep	Total per CB	400

YZ Ltd

18 Aug	Sales + VAT	1,175	12 Sep	Bank	1,140
			12 Sep	Discount allowed	35
		1,175			1,175

Discount allowed

30 Sep	Total per CD	35			

Drawings

20 Sep	Bank	250			

Purchases

31 Aug	Total per PDB	560			
30 Sep	Total per CD	320			

Stationery

31 Aug	Total per PDB	120	31 Aug	Total per PRDB	40
30 Sep	Total per CB	200			

Motor vehicles

25 Sep	Bank	5,000			

AB Ltd

25 Aug	Returns + VAT	235	2 Aug	Purchases + VAT	658
27 Sep	Bank	398			
27 Sep	Discount received	25			
		658			658

Discount received

			30 Sep	Total per CB	25

VAT

31 Aug	Total per PDB	469	31 Aug	Total per SDB	455
31 Aug	Balance c/d	28	31 Aug	Total per PRDB	42
		497			497
30 Sep	Total per CB (credit)	994	1 Sep	Balance b/d	28
			30 Sep	Total per CB (debit)	70
			30 Sep	Balance c/d	896
		994			994
1 Oct	Balance b/d	896			

Notes

1 The total of all the analysis columns on the debit side of the cash book except the discount allowed column should equal the total of the total column. Similarly, the total of all the analysis columns on the credit side of the cash book except the discount received column should equal the total of the total column.

2 The total of each analysis column in the cash book is posted to the relevant ledger account. The exceptions to this are miscellaneous, debtors' and creditors' columns, where each item has to be posted to the ledger individually.

3 Where cheques are received from debtors and paid to creditors, the VAT included in these amounts is not shown in the VAT column of the cash book. This would result in double counting because the VAT has already been entered in the VAT account in the ledger via the VAT columns of the day books when the goods were purchased/sold. The total amount of the cheque is therefore entered in the debtors' and creditors' columns and posted to the personal accounts.

Accounting for wages

The main purpose of this section is to explain the ledger entries relating to wages and salaries, including the source of the data.

The term wages is usually taken to refer to payments to employees that are made weekly and/or computed using an hourly rate. The term salaries is usually taken to refer to payments that are made monthly and/or computed by reference to an annual remuneration. However, the distinction is not critical in that both are often entered in a wages and salaries account.

What is referred to as an employee's **gross pay** is usually computed in one of three ways:

1 The employee's annual salary divided by 12 if paid monthly, or by 52 if paid weekly.

2 On an hourly basis comprising the basic pay plus any overtime. The basic pay is the number of hours worked by an employee in a given week (excluding any overtime) multiplied by his or her hourly rate (e.g. 40 hours @ £6 per hour = £240). The overtime pay is the number of hours worked by an employee in excess of the basic hours multiplied by the hourly overtime rate, which is often something like one and a half times the basic hourly rate [e.g. 5 hours @ ($1\frac{1}{2} \times$ £6) = £45].

3 On a piecework basis, whereby the number of units of output produced by an employee in a given week is multiplied by his or her piecework rate per unit of output (e.g. 200 units @ £1 per unit = £200).

The gross pay may also include any bonus based on some measure of performance. Bonus schemes vary considerably between businesses but a performance measure may take the form of time saved, cost reductions, profit increases, etc.

The amount of money that an employee actually receives is referred to as the **net pay**. This is the gross pay less various deductions, which in the UK include the following:

1 Income tax under the **Pay As You Earn (PAYE)** system. The amount, which is said to be 'deducted at source', is determined from tax tables using the employee's tax code number, both of which are supplied to the employer by the Inland Revenue.

2 National Insurance contributions (NIC). The amount of these is also determined from information supplied to the employer by the Inland Revenue, and usually takes the form of a given percentage of the employee's gross pay.

There may be other deductions from an employee's gross pay such as superannuation contributions to a pension fund set up by the employer.

In the UK the employer is also required to pay NIC in respect of each employee. Similarly, an employer often makes superannuation contributions on behalf of each of its employees. Neither of these is deducted from the employee's gross pay. From the employer's point of view they represent wage costs that are additional to the gross pay.

Employees' wages are computed using a document known as the **payroll**. An illustration of a payroll is given in Figure 21.1.

Some people regard the payroll as a book of prime entry rather than a basic document. Others argue that the ledger entries relating to wages and salaries should first be recorded in the journal.

Before examining the ledger entries it is important to understand some basic principles. The wages and salaries account (or accounts) is used to determine the total wages costs to the employer which will be charged to the profit and loss account. This consists of the total gross pay plus the employer's NIC and any superannuation contributions it has to make. This is not

FIGURE 21.1 Payroll.

Payroll No.	Employee's name	Gross pay	Deductions			Net pay	Employer's NIC
			PAYE tax	NIC	Total		
1002	J. Lennon	360	47	36	83	277	54
1003	R. Starr	240	29	24	53	187	36
1005	G. Harrson	320	38	32	70	250	48
1008	P. McCartney	380	55	38	93	287	57
		1,300	169	130	299	1,001	195

immediately obvious from the ledger entries because the entries representing the gross pay take the form of the net pay and the various deductions from the employees' gross pay.

The reason why the deductions are shown separately arises from the need for a double entry to a liability account representing the employer's responsibility to pass on the deductions from the employees' pay to the appropriate authority. In the case of the PAYE income tax and NIC this is the Inland Revenue.

An illustration of the ledger entries for wages and salaries is given in Example 21.4, which uses the data in Figure 21.1.

Example 21.4

Wages and salaries

Bank/cash—net pay	1,001
Inland revenue—	
PAYE tax	169
Employees' NIC	130
Gross pay	1,300
Employer's NIC	195

Bank/cash

Wages and salaries	1,001

Inland Revenue

Wages and salaries—	
PAYE tax	169
employees' NIC	130
employer's NIC	195

The balance on the wages and salaries account at the end of the accounting year (i.e. £1,495) will be transferred to the profit and loss account.

Summary

Most businesses charge their customers with (output) VAT and buy goods and services that are subject to (input) VAT. Periodically, the input VAT is set off against the output VAT, and the difference paid to HM Customs & Excise. Most businesses therefore neither benefit from output VAT, nor suffer input VAT. Thus, VAT is not included in any of the income, expense or asset accounts (other than debtors and cash) in the ledger or final accounts. VAT is only entered in the cash/bank accounts, and personal accounts of debtors and creditors, with a corresponding entry in a VAT account. However, the accounting treatment of VAT in businesses that are either zero rated or exempt is slightly different.

In practice, it is common for all books of prime entry (other than the journal) to be kept in columnar form. The sales and sales returns day books may have analysis columns that relate to departments or products. So may the purchases and purchases returns day books, although it is more common for these to include columns representing the different expenses incurred on credit, and purchases of fixed assets on credit. The cash book also usually has analysis columns on each side. Those on the debit side normally relate to sales and cheques received from debtors. Those on the credit side normally relate to cheques paid to creditors, purchases and various expenses. The cash book and all the day books also usually have an analysis column for VAT. The purpose of columnar day books and cash books is to facilitate the periodic bulk posting of transactions of the same type to the ledger.

Employee wages are computed using a document known as a payroll. This shows each employee's gross pay, deductions in a respect of PAYE income tax and NIC, and the resulting amount of net pay. It also shows the employer's NIC. The net pay, PAYE tax and NIC of both the employee and employer are all debited to the wages and salaries account in the ledger. The PAYE tax and NIC are credited to a liability account since these have to be paid to the Inland Revenue.

Key terms and concepts

Columnar book of prime entry (265)
exempt (265)
gross pay (270)
net pay (270)
payroll (270)
Pay As You Earn (PAYE) (270)
sales tax (264)
value added tax (264)
zero rated (265)

Review questions

21.1 **a** Briefly explain the nature of value added tax (VAT) and its associated cash flows.
b Describe how this affects the items shown in the final accounts of businesses.
c What does it mean when a business is classified as: (i) zero rated; and (ii) exempt for VAT purposes?

21.2 **a** Explain the main purpose of columnar day books.
b Describe the possible format of: (i) a columnar purchases day book; and (ii) a columnar cash book. Your answer should include reference to VAT.

21.3 **a** Briefly describe how each of the following is computed: (i) employee's gross pay; (ii) employee's net pay.
b Outline the nature of those items that are required by UK law to be deducted from employees' wages and salaries.

Exercises

An asterisk after the question number indicates that there is a suggested answer in the Appendix.

21.4* **Level I**

The following are extracts from the payroll of J. Sutcliffe Ltd for the week ending 24 January 20X9.

	£
Gross wages	6,800
National insurance contributions—	
employees	680
employers	1,020
PAYE tax	950

There were no other deductions from the employees' pay.

You are required to prepare journal entries to record the relevant items shown in the weekly payroll (including any cash payments).

21.5 **Level I**

Mudgee Ltd issued the following invoices to customers in respect of credit sales made during the last week of May 20X7. The amounts stated are all net of value added tax. All sales made by Mudgee Ltd are subject to VAT at 15 per cent.

Invoice no.	*Date*	*Customer*	*Amount*
			£
3045	25 May	Laira Brand	1,060.00
3046	27 May	Brown Bros	2,200.00
3047	28 May	Penfold's	170.00
3048	29 May	T. Tyrell	460.00
3049	30 May	Laira Brand	1,450.00
			5,340.00

On 29 May Laira Brand returned half the goods (in value) purchased on 25 May. An allowance was made the same day to this customer for the appropriate amount.

On 1 May 20X7 Laira Brand owed Mudgee Ltd £2,100.47. Other than the purchases detailed above, Laira Brand made credit purchases of £680.23 from Mudgee Ltd on 15 May. On 21 May Mudgee Ltd received a cheque for £2,500 from Laira Brand.

Required:

a Show how the above transactions would be recorded in Mudgee Ltd's sales book for the week ended 30 May 20X7.

b Describe how the information in the sales book would be incorporated into Mudgee Ltd's double-entry system.

c Reconstruct the personal account of Laira Brand as it would appear in Mudgee Ltd's ledger for May 20X7. (AAT)

21.6 Level I

Kwella Ltd received the following invoices from suppliers during the week commencing 23 November 20X7. All purchases made by Kwella Ltd are subject to value added tax at 15 per cent. The following list gives the *gross* value of each invoice received.

Date received	*Invoice no.*	*Date of invoice*	*Supplier*	*Gross amount* £
23 Nov	GL 788	19 Nov	Glixit plc	506.00
24 Nov	899330	19 Nov	Moblin Ltd	115.00
25 Nov	G 1101	17 Nov	S & G Gates	724.50
26 Nov	AX 1256	23 Nov	Goldrins Glues	1,115.50
27 Nov	CS 772	25 Nov	Wixit Wires Ltd	1,794.00

On 25 November Kwella Ltd rejected all the goods invoiced on 19 November by Moblin Ltd (invoice no. 899330) because they were not what had been ordered. The goods were returned to Moblin Ltd along with Kwella Ltd's debit note (D 56) for the full invoice amount.

On 26 November Kwella Ltd had to return some of the goods purchased on 17 November from S & G Gates (invoice no. G1101) because they were substandard. A debit note (D 57) for a gross value of £241.50 was returned with the goods.

Required:

- **a** Write up Kwella Ltd's purchases book and purchases returns book for the week commencing 23 November 20X7, totalling the columns off as at 28 November 20X7.
- **b** Describe how the information in the purchases book and purchases returns book would be incorporated into Kwella Ltd's ledger.
- **c** The balance brought forward on S & G Gates' account at 1 November 20X7 was £920.00, which Kwella Ltd settled in full by cheque on 13 November after deducting 5 per cent discount. There were no transactions with S & G Gates during the month of November other than those detailed above.

  Reconstruct Kwella Ltd's ledger account for S & G Gates for the month of November 20X7, balancing off the account as at 30 November 20X7. (AAT)

21.7 Level I

A business commenced trading for the week commencing 28 May 20X0 with £79 in cash and a bank overdraft of £515.

The following receipts and payments occurred during the week ending 3 June 20X0.

28 May	Paid travelling expenses of £37 in cash.
29 May	Paid a telephone bill of £115 (including £15 value added tax) by cheque.
29 May	Grant Degan, a credit customer, settled an invoice for £90 paying £81 in cash and receiving £9 discount for prompt settlement.
30 May	Made cash sales totalling £460 including £60 value added tax. The amount was received by cheque and was immediately banked.
31 May	Paid an invoice for £100 from Gaga Ltd by cheque for £92. £8 discount was received for prompt settlement.
1 June	Made cash purchases totalling £115 including value added tax of £15 paying by cheque.
1 June	Made cash sales of £230 inclusive of value added tax of £30.

2 June Paid staff wages of £300. This was partly paid by cheques totalling £230, the balance being paid in cash.

2 June Paid £200 from the till into the business bank account.

Required:

a Draw up a cash book with separate columns for dates, narrations, folios, discount, VAT, bank and cash. Enter the opening balances and record the transactions for the week commencing 28 May 20X0. Balance the cash book as at 3 June 20X0.

b Describe how the totals for the Discount and VAT columns will be entered into the ledger. (AAT)

21.8* **Level II**

After completing a training course at a technical college, Michael Faraday set up in business as a self-employed electrician on 1 January 20X5.

He was very competent at his job, but had no idea how to maintain proper accounting records. Sometimes during 20X5 one of his friends asked Michael how well his business was doing. He replied 'All right ... I think ... but I'm not quite sure'.

In the ensuing conversation his friend asked whether he had prepared accounts yet, covering his first quarter's trading, to which Michael replied that he had not. His friend then stressed that, for various reasons, it was vital for accounts of businesses to be prepared properly.

Shortly afterwards Michael came to see you to ask for your help in preparing accounts for his first quarter's trading. He brought with him, in a cardboard box, the only records he had, mainly scribbled on scraps of paper.

He explained that he started his business with a car worth £700, and £2,250 in cash, of which £250 was his savings and £2,000 had been borrowed from a relative at an interest rate of 10 per cent per annum. It was his practice to pay his suppliers and expenses in cash, to require his customers to settle their accounts in cash and to bank any surplus in a business bank account. He maintained lists of cash receipts and cash payments, of supplies obtained on credit and of work carried out for customers and of appliances sold, on credit.

The list of credit suppliers comprised:

Date supplied 20X5	*Supplier*	*Amount owed* £	*Date paid* 20X5	*Amount paid* £	*Remarks*
Jan	Dee & Co.	337.74	Mar	330.00	Received discount £7.74
	AB Suppliers	528.20	Mar	528.20	
Feb	Simpson	141.34	Mar	138.00	Received discount £3.34
	Cotton Ltd	427.40	Mar	130.00	Payment on account
			Apr	297.40	Remainder
	Dee & Co.	146.82	Mar	140.00	Received discount £6.82
Mar	AB Supplies	643.43	Apr	643.43	
	Simpson	95.60			Not yet paid

The purchase in January from Dee & Co. was of tools and equipment to enable him to carry out electrical repair work. All the remaining purchases were of repair materials, except for the purchase in February from Cotton Ltd, which consisted entirely of electrical appliances for resale.

In addition to the above credit transactions, he had bought repair materials for cash, as follows:

20X5	£
Jan	195.29
Feb	161.03
Mar	22.06

Other cash payments comprised:

20X5		£
Jan	Rent of premises for Jan to Jun 20X5	400.00
	Rates of premises for Jan to Mar 20X5	150.00
	Stationery	32.70
	Car running expenses	92.26
Feb	Sundries	51.54
	Car running expenses	81.42
Mar	Sundries	24.61
	Car running expenses	104.52
	Transfer to bank	500.00

He had also withdrawn £160.00 in cash at the end of each month for living expenses.

The list of credit customers comprised:

Date of sale 20X5	*Customer*	*Amount owed* £	*Date received* 20X5	*Amount received* £	*Remarks*
Jan	D. Hopkins	362.80	Feb	357.00	Allowed discount £5.80
	P. Bolton	417.10	Mar	417.10	
Feb	G. Leivers	55.00	Mar	55.00	
	M. Whitehead	151.72	Apr	151.72	
	N. John Ltd	49.14	Apr	49.14	
	A. Linnekar	12.53	Mar	12.53	
Mar	E. Horton	462.21	Apr	462.21	
	S. Ward	431.08	Mar	426.00	Allowed discount £5.08
	W. Scothern & Co.	319.12			Not yet received
	N. Annable	85.41			Not yet received

The above amounts relate to charges for repair work which he had carried out, except that the amounts shown in February for G. Leivers, N. John Ltd and A. Linnekar are for sales of electrical appliances.

In addition to the above credit transactions, he had cash takings, as follows:

20X5		£
Jan	Repair work	69.44
Feb	Repair work	256.86
Mar	Repair work	182.90
	Appliances	112.81

He estimated that, at the end of March 20X5, his stock of electrical repair materials was £691.02 and of electrical appliances for resale was £320.58, his tools and equipment were worth £300.00 and his car was worth £600.00.

Apart from loan interest, the only accrual was for heating and lighting, £265.00.

Required:

a Prepare:
  i purchase day book with analysis columns for each type of purchase; and
  ii sales day book with analysis columns for each class of business undertaken.

b Open, post to 31 March 20X5 only, and balance a columnar cash book suitably analysed to facilitate ledger postings.

c Open, post to 31 March 20X5 only, and balance a creditors' ledger control account and a debtors' ledger control account. Use the closing balances in your answer to (g) below. (NB: Individual accounts for creditors and debtors are *not* required.)

d Open, post and balance sales and cost of sales accounts, each with separate columns for 'Repairs' and Appliances'.

e Prepare M. Faraday's trading account for the quarter ended 31 March 20X5, distinguishing between gross profit on repairs and on appliance sales.

f Prepare M. Faraday's general profit and loss account for the quarter ended 31 March 20X5.

g Prepare M. Faraday's balance sheet as at 31 March 20X5. (ACCA)

21.9* Level II

M. Essex is in business as a wholesale coal merchant. The following transactions took place during December 20X7:

1 Dec	Balance at bank £5,000.
3 Dec	Purchased goods on credit from English Coal for £400 plus VAT.
4 Dec	Received an invoice for £240 plus VAT from Solihull Garage in respect of vehicle repairs on credit.
5 Dec	Bought stationery costing £240 plus VAT and paid by cheque.
6 Dec	Sold goods on credit to Black for £600 plus VAT.
7 Dec	Bought goods on credit from Scottish Coal for £320 plus VAT.
8 Dec	Paid wages by cheque of £350.
10 Dec	Sold goods for £520 plus VAT and received a cheque for this amount.
11 Dec	Purchased goods costing £720 plus VAT and paid by cheque.
12 Dec	Sold goods on credit to White for £800 plus VAT.
13 Dec	Received an invoice for £360 plus VAT from Solihull Garage relating to motor expenses incurred on credit.
14 Dec	Bought goods for resale costing £480 plus VAT and paid by cheque.
15 Dec	Purchased a motor vehicle on credit from Solihull Garage costing £4,000 plus VAT.

16 Dec	Received telephone bill from English Telecom for £560 plus VAT.
17 Dec	Sold a motor vehicle on credit to Solihull Garage for £2,000 plus VAT.
18 Dec	Sold goods for £640 plus VAT and received a cheque.
19 Dec	Paid insurance premium on vehicles of £720 by cheque.
20 Dec	Purchased stationery for £160 plus VAT by cheque.
23 Dec	Sold on old motor vehicle for £3,000 plus VAT and received a cheque for this amount.
28 Dec	Received a cheque from Black for £680 after deducting £25 cash discount.
29 Dec	Received a cheque from White for £905 after deducting £35 cash discount.
30 Dec	Paid English Coal £450 by cheque after deducting cash discount of £20.
31 Dec	Paid Scottish Coal £346 by cheque after deducting cash discount of £30.

You are required to:

a Write up the sales and purchases day books and the cash book using appropriate analysis columns where there is more than one transaction of the same type.

b Make the necessary entries in the ledger.
Assume the rate of VAT to be 17.5 per cent.

chapter 22

The role of computers in accounting

Learning objectives

After reading this chapter you should be able to:

1. explain the meaning of the key terms and concepts listed at the end of the chapter;
2. describe the nature of the main basic computer concepts;
3. describe the main advantages of computerized accounting systems;
4. discuss the expanding role of computerized accounting systems;
5. explain the main factors which need to be taken into consideration in the design, operation and management of computerized accounting systems;
6. discuss the limitations of computer systems.

Some basic computer concepts

Today, it is commonplace to keep accounts on a computer. Yet all the basic principles of accounting, as described elsewhere in this book, were devised in an age of paperwork and ledgers. As computers took over, a lot of accounting activity disappeared 'under the covers' of sophisticated electronic boxes. The result was that much of the work of accountants was made a lot easier. At the same time, new questions arose. In particular, it is difficult ascertain exactly what is actually going on inside a computer. How can we be sure that it is carrying out all the accounting procedures correctly?

It follows that today's accountants need to understand computers. Otherwise, their understanding of how the accounts have been put together will be incomplete. They do not need to take a nerdy interest in such things as chips, pixels and megahertz ratings. But they must be able to appreciate just how the accounting information is being acquired, held and manipulated in the computer system. This means looking at questions such as the following.

- *how is information captured?* A lot of information is still entered by being typed in via a keyboard, but increasingly it arrives by other means. For example, **optical character recognition** can be used to lift information directly from printed documents (or even hand-written ones, if the writing is good enough). **Bar codes** can be used to locate and count stock items. **Plastic cards** may hold details of a customer's identity, or store a monetary value. **Speech recognition** means that, in appropriate conditions, we can talk directly to the computer. For routine activities, a **mouse** can provide rapid input by enabling the user to 'point and click' on a specially designed screen lay-out, known as a **Graphical User Interface (GUI)**. Each of these methods of collecting information has different levels of accuracy, and needs to be subject to different kinds of checks and controls.
- *how is information stored?* Most computers have a built-in **disk drive**, capable of storing huge numbers of facts and figures. This raw information is usually referred to as **data**. A variety of disks and memory devices are available for transferring data from one system to another. While data is stored, it is important that no-one can tamper with it. One way of achieving this is to use a **write-once** medium, such as a CD which is designed to 'burn in' the data permanently.

FIGURE 22.1 An example of a Sage financial controller sales order screen.

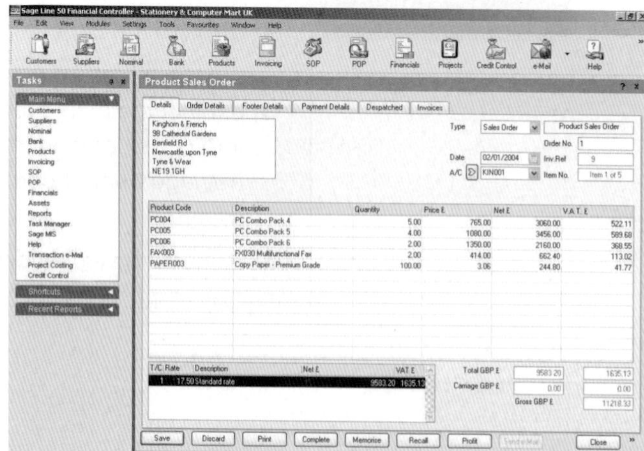

- *how is information processed?* Most businesses buy ready-made **software packages** to run their accounts. There are many thousands of such products on the market. Some are targeted at very specific types of business, such as construction or banking. Packages are now available for even the smallest businesses, such as a local charity or corner shop. At the other end of the scale, larger organization sometimes find that their operations are so complex and specialized that no suitable packages are available. In this case, they may have to commission **bespoke software**. This is an expensive option, and the programs may take many months to design, write and test.

As well as understanding these basic features of the system, the accountant also needs to be sure that the accounts are being protected against unauthorized changes. The widening of access through **networks** of computer systems makes this protection more difficult. Within the office, it is common to connect a number of machines onto a **Local Area Network (LAN)**. For example, this enables people ot share the use of expensive equipment, such as different types of scanners and printers. A larger organization may operate a **Wide Area Network (WAN)**, linking offices many miles apart. Most computers now come with a standard facility for linking to the largest WAN of all, which is the **Internet**. Network technology is constantly improving and becoming more flexible, though the use of **wireless LANs** and the ability to send data across mobile phone networks.

There are many practical benefits for business in networking their systems, particularly in opening up opportunities for electronic commerce (see later in this chapter). Unfortunately, it cannot be assumed that every user of the network has good intentions. Precautions must be taken against malicious attacks, aimed at reading or modifying the company's data, or, in the worst cases, at disabling the computer systems altogether.

Finally, the accountant should always be suspicious of quick and easy solutions. For example, it is easy to set up accounts on **spreadsheet** software. However, as the accounts grow, it will become increasingly difficult to keep track of them; and since spreadsheets are designed to be easily changed and over-written, they are difficult to control and audit. Similarly, an accounting package which can be set up very quickly may prove exasperating in the longer term. If it cannot handle the kind of account codes, periods, and reporting conventions which are used by the business, you may end up with a situation where the business is adapting its procedures to those imposed by the accounting software, rather than the other way round.

Advantages of computerized accounting systems

In the early days of commercial computing, most of the savings made by companies came from reductions in the numbers of clerks needed to process routine transactions. For example, a company with several hundred employees might use the computer to carry out the weekly payroll calculations. Computers would work out all the employees' entitlements and deductions in a fraction of the time required by the clerical teams they displaced. Accounting applications were a popular first choice to be implemented on the computer, because they necessarily involved many such repetitive activities. Often a set of identical tasks, such as calculating the pay for each employee, would be run through the computer in a batch, and this mode of operation became known as **batch processing**.

Batch processes saved labour, but the programs carrying out the processing tended to be very inflexible. The accounting data would be stored in a way which suited the accounting program, making it difficult to access for any other kind of analysis. There was no way in which accounting reports could be created 'on demand'.

All this changed with the arrival of **on-line** or **interactive processing** in the late 1970s. This style of working is taken for granted today, since it is used by everything from a PC package (such as a spreadsheet) to mainframe-based services (for example, as used in Internet-based insurance or banking services). At the time, however, it was regarded as a tremendous innovation for users to be able to interact directly with the computer. As the new interactive techniques developed, so did most of the advantages that can be found in computer systems today. Two particular advantages can be summarized as follows.

Simultaneous access to data

Only a handful of people can study a set of conventional books simultaneously. Through interaction with a computer system, in contrast, large numbers of users can all have access to the same information. Not only can they gain immediate access to the ledger entries of customer X or supplier Y, they can do so without worrying about where the ledgers are held, or whether someone else might be using them at the same time. Similarly, if a change is made to the ledger (for example, customer X finally makes an overdue payment), this information is instantly available to everyone else logged in to the accounting system.

Improved accuracy of data

When data items are being entered interactively (perhaps with an operator filling in an 'electronic form' on the computer screen) the accounting program can carry out a certain amount of checking while the data entry is in progress. It cannot, of course, prevent the operator from making quite fundamental mistakes, such as typing in the wrong amount for a quantity ordered. However, it can do numerous other checks; for example, to prevent a key item of data from being omitted by mistake, or to ensure that the amount received in a payment matches the amount due.

Mistakes can also be avoided by reducing the need for data to be keyed in time and again. For example, a customer's address and other basic details can be typed in during an initial setting-up session. Thereafter, the details are stored in the computer's files, and altered as and when required because of a change in the customer's circumstances (such as a new address or telephone number). All the operator has to do is to type in a customer reference number or surname to initiate a search, and all the relevant detail will be brought up on the screen.

Some systems carry this approach further by providing **default values** for entries where the input is going to be predictable in the great majority of cases. Thus, a default may be set for the price of an item, the size of a discount, or the number of days within which payment is due. In a small minority of cases, the operator may need to change the default to another value. Most of the time, however, the operator merely has to confirm the default value, thus reducing the amount of typing required, and making it less likely that any erroneous values will be entered. A screen which illustrates the use of pre-set details and defaults is shown as Figure 22.2.

Apart from the benefits that result from interactive working, computerized accounting has brought benefits in two other main areas.

Improved detail

Storage in a computer system is not confined in the same way as in the pages of a book. It can handle a more or less indefinite number of rows and columns. Records of transactions do not

FIGURE 22.2 A simplified screen layout for order entry. The operator only needs to enter the shaded values—the computer can generate a new order number, provide today's date, and retrieve details such as the customer's address and the price and description of each product.

Order No. 10025			Thomas Tanks plc 15, Railway Cuttings, Birmingham B15 2TT
Customer code	T009		
Date received	25 09 × 2		
Date required	9 10 × 2		Credit Limit 4000.00
Product code	Quality	Description	Value
PR5544	20	A4 paper	216.20
PR5592	12	markers, black	15.24

therefore have to be confined to very basic information such as the date and amount. A variety of other details can easily be added; for example, when a sale is made, codes can be recorded to show what category of customer this was, the identity of the salesperson, the product type, the sales district, and so on. When details on perhaps hundreds of customers are recorded in this way, they provide a rich source of data for the company to analyse.

Improved reporting

Having recorded accounting transactions in electronic form, the production of reports becomes a matter of running some appropriate software to turn the data into summaries and tables (for management accounting) or standard balance sheet and profit and loss statements (for financial accounting). No longer do staff have to extract information directly from the ledger entries. This saves a lot of staff time, and reduces errors of calculation and transcription. There is, of course, an important proviso: the software used to generate the reports must be free of any errors in its logic. This raises important questions about the role of the accountant. Is he or she to take the computer figures at face value? If so, does this not hand over too much responsibility to the computer programmer? Of course, the accountant cannot check through every line of code appearing in the program, but at the same time he or she should be conscious that no programmer is infallible. Today, a growing proportion of accountants' expertise is centred on checking the reasonableness and consistency of figures generated from computers.

Most accounting software provides facilities for generating period-end and year-end reports as described elsewhere in this book, and will produce a 'trial balance'. This trial balance does not have quite the same role as that described in Chapter 5. For example, most accounting software, while adhering to double-entry conventions in presenting ledger information, does not actually require the user to post the amount on both sides of the ledger—this is usually taken care of automatically by the system. If any errors are apparent in a trial balance the finger of suspicion should fall first and foremost on possible flaws in the software.

Most organizations like to be able to analyse accounting data in other ways, besides the rather formalized summaries provided in the standard financial reports. Reports can generally be produced in one of three ways:

1 The accounting software may allow users to select a certain number of pre-programmed reports. For example, a commonly used report is an analysis of the sales ledger,

to determine which customers are slow payers. An example of an aged debtors' report of this kind is shown in Figure 22.3.

2 The accounting software may contain a general purpose 'report generator'. This permits a more 'do-it-yourself' approach to report generation. The user can design a report from scratch, defining where fields are to appear, what should be shown in each field, and what titles and headings are to be used.

3 The third option is to transfer data from the accounting system into an entirely separate piece of software. The most common choice for this is a spreadsheet. The accounting system will offer an extract or export feature, which allows selected data to be written out to a file in a rows-and-columns format.

The three ways in which reports can be generated are summarized in Figure 22.4. Standard reports are often circulated around the organization on a scheduled basis, for example at the end of each month. 'One-off' reports may be generated on demand, usually with the aid of a more flexible tool such as a spreadsheet. Increasingly, such reports are circulated within the organization via e-mail or other electronic services.

Once accounting software has become firmly established in the organization, a final benefit can be achieved from having data for successive years or periods held in

FIGURE 22.3 Part of a typical computer-generated report. It enables customers with large or long-standing debts to be identified quickly.

SALES LEDGER; ACCOUNT BALANCES (AGED)

Cust. code	*Cust. name*	*Credit limit*	*Balance*	*Current period*	*30 Days*	*Over 30 days*
T009	T. Tanks	4000	1760.15	1203.45	556.70	00.0
T011	B. Timms	5000	4516.25	4020.15	324.10	172.0
T016	N. Todd	1500	1035.65	1035.65	0.00	00.0
T023	M. Tubbs	2500	519.23	380.12	98.56	40.55

FIGURE 22.4 The generation of reports from accounting packages.

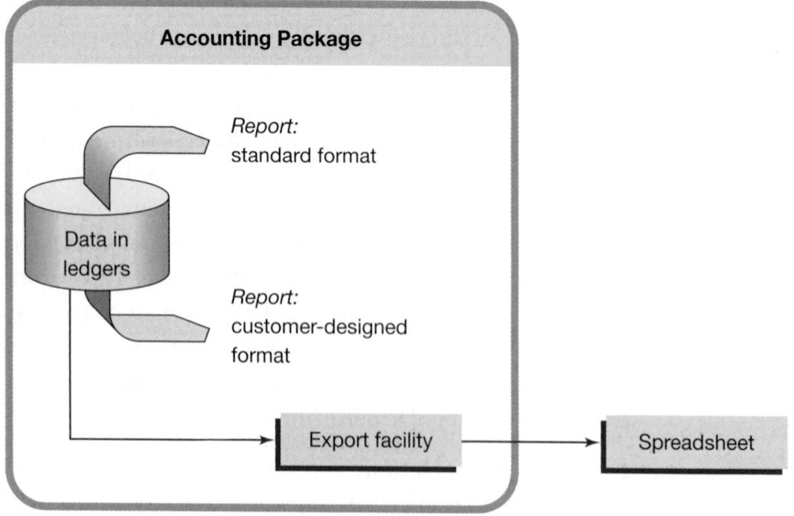

electronic form. This makes it possible to look at how key financial indicators have changed with time, and to predict what will happen if particular trends continue.

Expanding the role of the accounting system

While accountants were often the first people in the organization to use computers, other departments soon followed their example. This led to demands for the various different computer systems to be linked together. Accounting ceased to be a completely separate function, and possibilities opened up for handing information in entirely new ways.

For example, entering up accounting information was no longer restricted to clerks in the accounting department: it could be collected at source from devices such as supermarket check-outs, credit card machines and ticket dispensers. The arrival of the home PC and the Internet meant that customers could be asked to fill in order screens for themselves, rather than having this done for them by a shop assistant or a telephone sales clerk.

Companies began to be much more inventive in their use of computer technology. They no longer used computers to imitate the traditional ways of doing things. Ways were found of speeding up information flows, and helping employees to make decisions more rapidly. This became known as **business process re-engineering (BPR)**. When BPR projects called for changes to accounting systems, as they often did, this sometimes led to intense discussions over possible conflicts with basic accounting principles, particularly in respect of control and audit.

Closer links between systems within the company (as illustrated in Figure 22.5) also led to demands from managers for a better analysis of what was happening in the company as a whole. Integrated software capable of providing this kind of overview began to appear, offering what was termed **enterprise resource planning (ERP)**.

Companies also looked at the outside world, and sought ways of improving the electronic links between themselves and their trading partners. Figure 22.6 shows a typical old-fashioned approach to communications. This is not only involved a delay of a day or two while letters were printed, posted and delivered; all the information printed out by the sender then had to be keyed back into a computer by the recipient. **Electronic data interchange** was the first step in streamlining this process, by defining standard ways of transmitting forms used in common transactions (such as orders, payments, and deliveries) directly

FIGURE 22.5 Extending the range of information available, through integrating the accounting software with software used in other parts of the company.

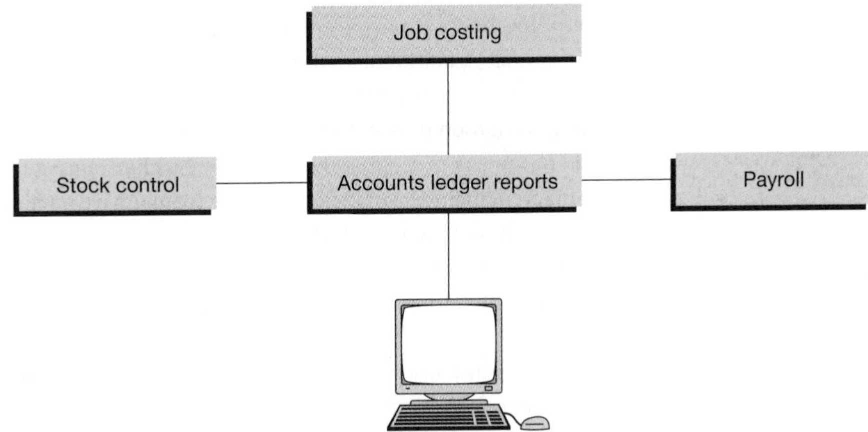

FIGURE 22.6 Intercommunication alternatives.

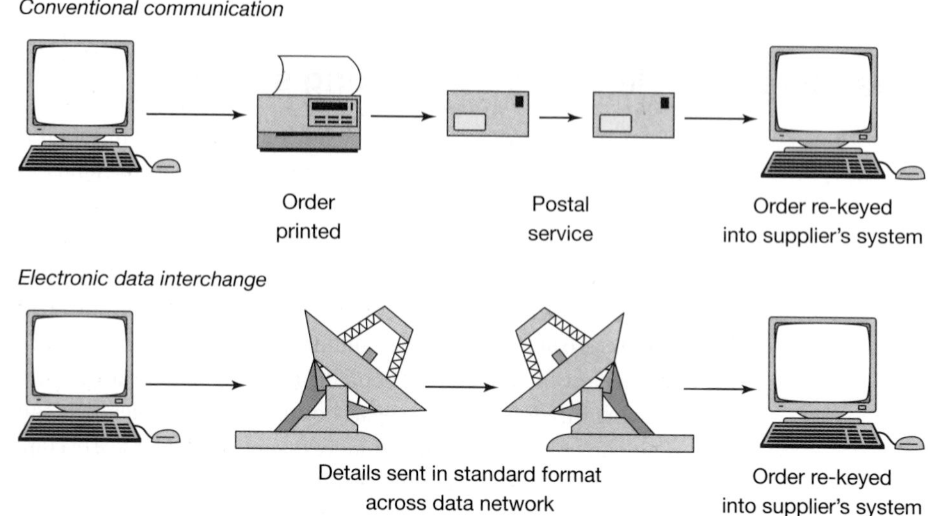

between computers. EDI not only speeded things up, but eliminated the errors which tended to arise when the information was re-keyed (see the lower part of Figure 22.6).

In industries where close collaboration is required (for example, a manufacturer dependent on specialist suppliers, or a travel company booking flights, hotels and car hire), the integration of systems may be taken further than the exchange of EDI messages. With the appropriate restrictions, companies may allow direct access to each other's systems. In this way, the benefits of integration can be spread beyond the boundaries of the individual company.

The design of computerized accounting systems

Even the creation of the most modest accounting package calls for some 're-engineering' of accounting processes as they are transferred to the new technology. Software designers, anxious to make the changeover as easy as possible for users who are familiar with traditional methods, usually retain many of the terms and conventions of bookkeeping. This **user-friendly** approach makes it easier for people to learn how to use the new system, and enables companies to make a more gradual transition, with paper-based functions running alongside computer-based at interim stages of the changeover.

However, the best systems go a good deal further than simply 'putting ledgers on a screen'. For example, traditional methods often centre around day books, which are a convenient place to gather together the records of a series of similar items, such as credit sales. Much of this information may need to be transcribed later into the ledger. Day books are one way of dividing up the process of data capture, so that manageable amounts of work are assigned to different members of the accounting team. As we have seen, the computer system designer does not have to worry about such constraints, as large numbers of people can all be given concurrent access to the same information. In the same way, there is no need to copy data out of one book and into another, since the computer can be programmed to do this automatically.

The designer must also try to anticipate the kind of enquiries that the system users may want to make. For example, suppose that a customer rings up to complain about the non-delivery of goods. Something has clearly gone wrong, but where? The clerk may want to find out when the goods were originally ordered, whether despatch has been requested, what delivery address was specified, and so on. Paper-based methods would call for a lot of hunting through ledgers and filing cabinets at this point. However, a good computer system will allow the clerk to navigate easily through different screens of information while talking to the customer, so that everything can be resolved quickly—if possible, while he or she is still on the line.

The ultimate design challenge arises when the system is to be used directly by the customer, perhaps for ordering goods over the Internet. In this case, the designer cannot assume that the user has any previous knowledge or training. The greatest care must be taken to ensure that all the details of products, prices, and terms and conditions are explained. All these details must be regularly updated, to ensure they are consistent with values held elsewhere in the accounting system. The software must anticipate what will happen in the event of common problems (such as the loss of a connection). Above all, there must be plenty of help and advice screens for the user to turn to, if needed. Paradoxically, if all these rather complicated requirements are met successfully, the customer's impression will be of something which is really easy and straightforward to use.

The management and operation of computerized accounting systems

New methods of carrying out the accounting function call for new approaches to managing them. One of the most important roles is that of the system manager. To some extent, the systems manager makes decisions and carries responsibilities which would previously have belonged to the head or supervisor of a traditional accounts department. However, much of the work is more technical in nature, and has to be carried out using privileged access to the system (protected by a **password** or some other form of security). It requires above all a good understanding of the way the software operates. The system manager will be able to set, and modify, options such as the following:

- the dates and durations of accounting periods;
- the codes to be used for accounts, discounts, sales areas, etc.;
- the default settings to be used, e.g. for credit limits;
- the format of standard reports;
- the routeing of routine output to different printers;
- the kind of access allowed to more junior users of the system;
- the activation of audit and logging facilities.

Because of the complexity of setting up some of these options, it is sometimes assumed that it is best left to technical staff. This is unwise. In assuming that it is 'just a technical matter', the system manager is handing over key areas of control to others, who may not understand the implications of what they are doing, or could use their privileged position to instigate fraud.

System security is one of the biggest challenges facing the system manager. Each user of the system must have access to the facilities needed for the job in hand but no more. As is shown by the example of the clerk dealing with customers over the phone (described earlier), it can be difficult to anticipate exactly what access will be needed, since the clerk may need to search through a different set of screens each time, depending on the nature of the enquiry. Particular care has to be taken in assigning access rights which involve permission for important values to be altered; for example, it may be specified that only a supervisor can change standard prices, or override pre-set credit limits. If the system is linked to other computers across networks, attention will also have to be given to risks arising from malicious intruders (or **hackers**) who may try to gain access to the accounts, or modify the figures in e-mail or EDI messages.

Back-up is another key responsibility. Particularly if the accounting is being done on a central machine, the entire set of accounting records may be held on a single magnetic disk. This is asking for trouble: if the disk malfunctions, all the records will be lost. It is a relatively simple matter to take **back-up copies** regularly. For a small system, it may be feasible to copy all the records on a daily basis. For larger systems, a different approach is sometimes used, where a complete copy is made to start with, but thereafter only the changes are backed up. In either case, the back-up copy needs to be moved to a separate, secure location for storage.

Finally, the system manager should ensure that provision is made for keeping proper **audit trails**. The trail should enable an auditor to check a transaction through every stage of its progress, including any steps handled by the computer. In smaller systems, this may be done by taking regular printouts of key records or documents. More sophisticated systems keep a special log file on disk, which can be used to ascertain when activities were carried out and by whom. As more companies move towards the 'paperless office', and business is done over the Internet or through EDI rather than by post, computer-generated evidence will become an ever more important part of the audit trail.

Some limitations of computer systems

Thus far, it may seem that computers have brought unremitting benefits to accounting. However, they have also thrown up a number of recurring problems for users. The designers of accounting packages, for example, are constantly seeking to include every feature which they think a user might need. However, this can mean that the system manager is presented with a bewildering set of options, and has to devote a lot of time to deciding which features to activate and which to reject. Even then, it is quite likely that some desirable features will be missing, as each business tends to have its own unique requirements. The choice then is between adapting the business's methods to fit in with the way the software works, or seeking special modifications to the software, which is usually an expensive option.

Inflexibility can also appear in a quite different form if accounting operations need to be merged; for example, as a result of one company taking over another. Combining two different computerized systems is rarely straightforward, particularly if they have come from different suppliers. Because each accounting system stores data in its own individual way, moving from one system to another can be a lengthy and cumbersome process.

Finally, the speed and accessibility of computer systems, which make them so attractive to business, also make them particularly vulnerable. This is the main inhibiting factor in the development of **electronic commerce** or e-commerce using the Internet. The technology is already available to enable members of the public to transmit orders directly to vendors' systems and to make payments electronically. However, making systems accessible to the public also makes them more open to attacks by hackers and fraudsters. The development of protective measures against ever more ingenious and sophisticated forms of electronic attack will be a preoccupation of the computer industry for many years to come.

Future directions for computerized accounting

Accounting systems are evolving rapidly. More user-friendly methods are constantly being found of communicating with users, exploiting images and sounds in ways which are far removed from work with traditional ledgers. Greater use of 'intelligent' software will enable systems to offer more guidance to users who get into difficulties, and will also help in detecting and preventing certain kinds of fraud. Improved links between systems will cause some of the traditional barriers between accounting and other functions to disappear. All this will present new challenges for the accountant, in safeguarding the probity and accuracy of accounting information.

Summary

Computerized accounting can be carried out on many different types of hardware, ranging from mainframes to portable PCs. Many options are available for entering data into systems. Keyboards are widely used, while a mouse can be used to make selections via a graphical user interface. Other methods include bar-code readers, optical character recognition and voice recognition.

The most important element of an accounting system is the accounting software which runs on the computer. Early computer systems processed tasks in batches, but modern systems allow interaction directly with users. This gives rise to many of the advantages of computerized working; in particular, through allowing several users to see the same information at once, and in checking data as it is fed in. Computer-based systems can also provide more detail in the accounting records, and can generate a wide range of reports on demand.

Computerized systems have adopted much of the terminology and many of the conventions of traditional bookkeeping, but store and process accounting information in different ways. This in turn means that different approaches need to be taken to their management and control. A systems manager should ensure that staff can gain access only to the facilities they need in their work, and should also ensure that back-up copies of data are made and that audit trails are created.

Computerized accounting systems will continue to become more integrated with other systems, both within and outside the host organization, and this in turn will call for changes in emphasis in the work of the accountant. In particular, accountants will have to devise ways of checking the accuracy of output from the computer, without being able to refer to source documents, day books and ledgers.

Key terms and concepts

Audit trails (288)
back-up copies (288)
bar codes (280)
batch processing (281)
bespoke software (281)
business process re-engineering (BPR) (285)
data (280)
data default values (282)
disc drive (280)
electronic commerce (288)
electronic data interchange (EDI) (285)
enterprise resource planning (ERP) (285)
graphical user interface (GUI) (280)
hackers (288)
interactive processing (282)
Internet (281)
local area network (LAN) (281)
mouse (280)
networks (281)
on-line (282)
optical character recognition (280)
password (287)
plastic cards (280)
software packages (281)
speech recognition (280)
spreadsheet (281)
system security (287)
user-friendly (296)
wide area network (WAN) (281)
wireless LANs (281)
write once (280)

Review questions

An asterisk after the question number indicates that there is a suggested answer in the Appendix.

22.1 Explain the difference between: (a) hardware and software; (b) 'batch' and 'interactive' processing; and (c) a LAN and a WAN.

22.2 A new computerized accounting system is to be introduced into an accounts department that has hitherto used only traditional bookkeeping. Six people work in the department. What advantages might they hope to see from the new system?

22.3 Give an example of *one* way in which a computerized accounting system might:

a reduce errors;

b improve customer service;

c improve the quality of accounting reports.

22.4* 'Good accounting software has the look and feel of traditional bookkeeping methods'. Explain the benefits that might follow from such an approach. Identify *one* accounting function where this approach might not be the best one, and describe how a different approach might be implemented, taking advantage of some of the new possibilities of computing technology.

22.5 A 'system manager' will normally be appointed to take charge of a computerized accounting system. Draw up a brief job description, outlining the duties of such an appointment.

22.6 Explain the main limitations of computer systems.

22.7 Information technology and computerized systems are rapidly increasing in importance in data recording. Do you consider that this trend will eventually remove the need for control accounts to be incorporated in the design of accounting systems? Explain your answer briefly. (ACCA adapted)

22.8 Over the past few decades, routine bookkeeping and accountancy work has been transformed by the extensive use of computers to perform that work.

Required:

a List and briefly explain *two* types of error which could occur in a manual sales ledger system which *could not* occur in a computerized system.

b List and briefly explain *two* types of error which could occur in a manual sales ledger system which *could also* occur in a computerized system.

c Explain the main advantages and disadvantages of computerized accounting systems compared with manual systems. (ACCA)

chapter

23 Accounting for changing price levels

Learning objectives

After reading this chapter you should be able to:

1. explain the meaning of the key terms and concepts listed at the end of the chapter;
2. discuss the limitations of historical cost accounting in times of rising prices, including their impact on the profit and loss account and balance sheet;
3. explain the nature of and difference between forms of price level changes, including how they can be measured;
4. describe different concepts of capital maintenance;
5. explain how assets are valued using historical cost, current cost and current purchasing power accounting;
6. describe the main conceptual differences between current cost accounting and current purchasing power accounting;
7. prepare simple profit and loss accounts and balance sheets using current cost accounting and current purchasing accounting.

Recording transactions at historical cost in the measurement of income

The fundamental ideas of profit introduced in Chapter 2 were based on the accounting definition that profit was the maximum amount that could be withdrawn from a business while leaving the capital intact. This approach as a measure of performance has considerable appeal. As residual beneficiaries, the owners' benefits from the business are entirely dependent on the success of the business. Such success can be readily assessed in terms of what can be taken out of the business while leaving it no worse off than it was at the start of the period. When this is also seen in the more dynamic terms of being the amount by which the revenue earned exceeds the cost of producing those revenues, it is also seen as a measure of operating efficiency—increasing the value of outputs as represented by revenues, while achieving a relative decrease in the inputs measured by the costs matched against that revenue.

It was again in Chapter 2 that the measurement approach utilized by historical cost accounting was described in terms of recording transactions. Subsequent chapters have illustrated this time and again. As an approach to measurement, the transaction basis contributes well to the reliability principle. In the historical cost balance sheet, assets are represented by the capitalized expenditures which have not yet been matched against revenue through depreciation, for example. In the profit and loss account, revenues and costs have all been quantified on the basis of transactions.

However, it would be wrong to deduce that the historical cost basis is entirely objective. Subjectivity has entered into deciding whether an expenditure should be capitalized or not, i.e. whether or not it represented an asset. Choice of methods of depreciation and the determination of provisions both involve substantial judgement. Similar scope exists in the allocation of indirect costs to stock values.

When considered in relation to other measurement attributes, historical cost may stand up less well, particularly when price changes are prevalent either in general, due to inflation, or for specific items arising as a result of changes in technology, tastes or other factors. The asset values will be dependent upon timing so that the same asset may have a different value depending only upon when it is purchased. This promotes neither consistency nor comparability and the likely result is varying mixtures of ages of expenditures both between businesses and between periods for the same business. If prices are generally rising, then although asset values may be regarded as prudent, matching older expenses based on correspondingly lower prices may understate costs relative to revenues and thus overstate profit. Understating asset values and overstating profit cannot be considered free from bias, let alone prudent.

The historical cost convention has adopted particular approaches to the three basic dimensions. The unit of measurement is the currency unit, i.e. the pound sterling in the UK. Even if the purchasing power of the pound changes, there is no response in this dimension by the historical cost convention. As implied above, the valuation model used measures asset values at the original transaction price modified by provisions and write downs due to depreciation, etc. The capital maintained is the money value of the owner's contributed capital plus accumulated profits. This is commonly referred to as **money financial capital maintenance**.

Price change considerations and inflation accounting

Current purchasing power accounting

Price change has two broad impacts on the accounting approaches which have been described. First, **general price change** through **inflation** undermines the stability of the value of the currency unit. Reducing the **purchasing power** of the pound through inflation means that comparison of amounts measured in pounds at different times is distorted.

One response to the problems of price change is to restate the accounts produced on a historical cost basis by adjusting for the change in purchasing power. The procedure is to restate the opening and closing balance sheets by indexing all items in the opening balance sheet and all non-monetary items including owners' capital in the closing balance sheet using **general price level indices**. Monetary items in the closing balance sheet would require no adjustments as they are already stated in current terms. The capital increase shown between the restated balance sheets would be the current purchasing power profit. This approach involves only limited adjustment from historical cost and, since these can be based on publicly available indices such as the **retail price index** (RPI), reliability is not substantially reduced. The unit of measurement that would then be employed would be the pound of current purchasing power at the year end. The purchasing power of the owners' capital would be maintained since it is restated in these terms. This is commonly referred to as **real financial capital maintenance**.

However, the valuation model which adjusts asset values for general changes in prices may result in asset values that are considered to be an entire fiction. Assets do not all change price in line with inflation. In addition, the increase that is being reported would be a combination of realized and unrealized gains, since the upward revaluation of assets by indexing them would be, increasingly, a value without the external evidence that would meet the needs of prudence and realization. A version of this approach, known as **current purchasing power accounting** (CPPA) was put forward in the UK but, given the limitation identified and others, it has been largely rejected.

Current cost accounting

The second major aspect of price change is the **specific price changes** in asset values. The historical cost approach, which recognizes revenues only when they are realized, will produce periodic profits which represent both the results of the current year's operations and gains made in previous periods which are only realized in the current period (although gains which are unrealized in the current period are excluded).

One response to this problem is to recognize unrealized gains in the period to which they relate but to treat these not as part of operating profit. Instead, they can be regarded as **holding gains**, i.e. gains from continuing to own assets during price rises. Measuring profit in relation to opening and closing capital restated to include holding gains of the period produces a concept of **physical/operating capital maintenance**, i.e. identifying the gains that can be withdrawn while permitting a business to own the same physical assets. Profit would be restated by eliminating holding gains. This is aptly described as operating profit, showing the ability of a business to produce revenues over and above the current cost of producing them through operating activities. Any adjustments necessary to eliminate holding gains from profit would be those necessary to restate historical costs, included in the profit and loss account, to current costs.

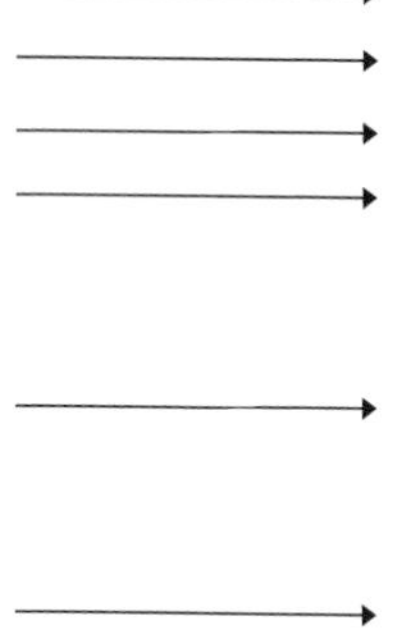

A version of this approach known as **current cost accounting** (CCA) includes such adjustments in three components. These are a **depreciation adjustment**, modifying depreciation to one based on the current cost of assets rather than the historical cost; a **cost of sales adjustment**, adjusting stock values and purchases to current costs; and a **monetary working capital adjustment**, adjusting for the price change of purchases during the creditor period and sales during the debt collection period. There has been much debate about whether there should also be a fourth adjustment, known as a **gearing adjustment**. This is intended to reflect the benefits of having debt capital during periods of increasing prices. The last two adjustments are relatively complicated, and generally regarded as beyond the introductory level.

Considerable subjectivity is involved in identifying suitable **specific price level indices** for each of the possible specific price changes. The resulting reduction in reliability together with the costs of implementing the approach with all its complexities are considered to outweigh the advantages, particularly where the period of holding assets is relatively short and hence the impact of the adjustments is small. Current cost accounting has been widely abandoned as a result.

Realistic examples of accounting for changing price levels are usually very complex and beyond the scope of this book and accounting examinations at this level. However, a relatively simple numerical illustration of CCA and CPPA is shown in Example 23.1.

Example 23.1

A. Solent commenced trading on 1 January 20X5 as a ships' chandler. The capital in cash was £15,000. On that date A. Solent purchased a boathouse for £10,000 and a boat for resale at a price of £5,000. The boathouse is leasehold over a period of 50 years and depreciated using the straight line/fixed instalment method. The replacement cost of the boathouse on 31 December 20X5 was estimated to be £13,000.

The boat was sold on 1 July 20X5 for £8,000 and on the same day an identical boat was purchased for £6,000. This was unsold at 31 December 20X5 and is estimated to have a replacement cost of £7,500.

The RPI at 1 January 20X5 stood at 100, at 1 July 20X5 was 105, and at 31 December 20X5 was 110.

You are required to prepare a profit and loss account for the year and balance sheet at 31 December 20X5 using:

a historical cost accounting (HCA);
b current cost accounting (CCA; using replacement cost);
c current purchasing power accounting (CPPA);
d historical cost accounting with adjustments for current costs (CC).

A. Solent
Profit and loss account for the year ended 31 December 20X5

	HCA	*CCA*	*CPPA*
	£	£	£
Sales	8,000	8,000	8,381
Cost of sales	(5,000)	(6,000)	(5,500)
Gross profit	3,000	2,000	2,881
Depreciation	(200)	(260)	(220)
Operating profit	2,800	1,740	2,661
Loss on holding monetary assets	—	—	(95)
Net profit	2,800	1740	2,566

Workings

$$\text{HCA depreciation} = \frac{£10{,}000}{50\text{ years}} = £200$$

$$\text{CCA depreciation} = \frac{£13{,}000}{50\text{ years}} = £260$$

$$\text{CPPA sales} = £8{,}000 \times \frac{110}{105} = £8{,}381$$

$$\text{CPPA cost of sales} = £5{,}000 \times \frac{110}{100} = £5{,}500$$

$$\text{CPPA depreciation} = \left(£10{,}000 \times \frac{110}{100}\right) \div 50\text{ years} = £220$$

CPPA loss on holding monetary assets: cash of £8,000 – £6,000 = £2,000 from 1 July 20X5 to 31 December 20X5:

$$\frac{110 - 105}{105} \times £2{,}000 = £95$$

A. Solent

Balance sheet as at 31 December 20X5

	HCA	*CCA*	*CPPA*
	£	£	£
Boathouse	10,000	13,000	11,000
Depreciation	(200)	(260)	(220)
	9,800	12,740	10,780
Stock	6,000	7,500	6,286
Cash	2,000	2,000	2,000
	17,800	22,240	19,066
Capital	15,000	15,000	15,000
Capital maintenance reserve	—	5,500	1,500
Profit	2,800	1,740	2,566
	17,800	22,240	19,066

Workings

CCA capital maintenance:

Boathouse Stock

(£13,000 – £10,000) + (£7,500 – £5,000) = £5,500

$$\text{CPPA stock} = £6{,}000 \times \frac{110}{105} = £6{,}286$$

$$\text{CPPA capital maintenance} = £15{,}000 \times \frac{110\text{–}100}{100} = £1{,}500$$

A. Solent

Profit and loss account (HC adjusted for CC) for the year ended 31 December 20X5

	£
Sales	8,000
Cost of sales	(5,000)
Historical cost gross profit	3,000
Depreciation	(200)

Historical cost net profit	2,800
Cost of sales adjustment (£6,000 – £5,000)	(1,000)
Depreciation adjustment (£260 – £200)	(60)
Current cost net profit	1,740

The historical cost balance sheet adjusted for current costs will be as shown for CCA.

Summary

The use of historical cost accounting in times of rising prices is said to overstate the profit because older, lower costs are matched against more recent, higher sales prices. It is also said to distort the values of assets and liabilities in the balance sheet. The assets will have been bought at various points in time when the prevailing levels of prices were different. In addition, the assets are not shown in their current values.

Profit can be conceptualized as the amount that could be withdrawn from a business while leaving the capital intact. This highlights the need for capital maintenance. There are three main concepts of capital maintenance: money financial capital maintenance, real financial capital maintenance and physical/operating capital maintenance.

Changes in price levels take two forms: general price changes associated with inflation which reduce the purchasing power of money, and are measured in the UK by the retail price index (RPI); and specific price changes which refer to the change in price of a specific category of good or asset (e.g. vehicles).

Assets can be valued at either their historical cost, current/replacement cost, or the purchasing power of the money invested in the asset. Current/replacement cost is commonly measured using a specific price index, and purchasing power is measured by means of a general price index such as the RPI. These three methods of asset valuation give rise to three corresponding methods of accounting, known as historical cost accounting (HCA), current cost accounting (CCA) and current purchasing power accounting (CPPA), respectively.

In HCA assets are valued at their historical cost, and profit is measured while ensuring the maintenance of money financial capital. It is argued that in times of changing price levels, CCA or CPPA is more appropriate. In CCA assets are usually valued at replacement cost, and profit is measured while ensuring the maintenance of physical capital or the operating capability of a business. In CPPA assets are valued in terms of current purchasing power, and profit is measured while ensuring the maintenance of real financial capital.

A variation of CCA involves adjusting the profit computed on a historical cost basis to give the current cost profit. This necessitates a cost of sales adjustment, depreciation adjustment, and monetary working capital adjustment. There has been much debate about whether there should also be a gearing adjustment.

Key terms and concepts

Cost of sales adjustment (294)
current cost accounting (294)
current purchasing power accounting (293)
depreciation adjustment (294)
gearing adjustment (294)
general price change (293)
general price level indices (293)
holding gains (293)
inflation (293)
monetary working capital adjustment (294)
money financial capital maintenance (292)
physical/operating capital maintenance (293)
purchasing power (293)
real financial capital maintenance (293)
retail price index (293)
specific price changes (293)
specific price level indices (294)

Review questions

23.1 Explain the limitations of historical cost accounting in times of rising prices.

23.2 Explain fully why there is said to be a need to account for changing prices in final accounts.

23.3 Explain the differences and/or interrelationship between: (a) changes in specific price levels; (b) changes in general price levels; (c) inflation; and (d) the retail price index (RPI).

23.4 a Outline the concept of economic income as defined by Hicks (1946) and explain its relevance in the measurement of profit (see Chapter 2).

b Describe three different concepts of capital maintenance.

23.5 Explain how assets are valued using each of the following measurement methods: (a) historical cost; (b) current cost; and (c) current purchasing power.

23.6 Describe the main conceptual differences between current cost accounting and current purchasing power accounting.

23.7 Explain why the profit computed using historical cost accounting usually differs from that when calculated using replacement cost accounting and current purchasing power accounting.

23.8 Ermine commenced trading on 1 July 20X8 with a capital of £100,000 cash. During the year ended 30 June 20X9, he operated from rented premises and at the end of the year he had sold all his stock. His balance sheet at 30 June 20X9 was:

	£	£
Cash at bank		100,000
		100,000
Capital at 1 July 20X8	100,000	
Profit for year to date	40,000	
	140,000	
Less: drawings	40,000	
		100,000
		100,000

During the year there was inflation of 10 per cent in the country in which he operates.

Required:

a Using this simple example where appropriate, define the terms *financial* capital and *physical* capital, and explain why it may be dangerous for an enterprise if it maintains financial capital but does not maintain physical capital.

b List and briefly explain *three* ways in which the use of historical cost accounting may cause financial statements to be misleading.

c List *three* advantages of historical cost accounting.

Author's note: the term financial capital is used here to refer to money financial capital.

(ACCA)

Exercises

An asterisk after the question number indicates that there is a suggested answer in the Appendix.

23.9* **Level I**

Sally Johnson, while holidaying on a remote island, decides to supplement her holiday money by selling slices of water melon on the beach. She purchases 50 melons for a total of 500 francs and during the week sells them all by slicing each melon into four and selling each slice for 5 francs. At the end of the week she returns to the fruit market and discovers that the price of 50 melons has risen to 650 francs. On her way to the market she had purchased a newspaper in which the headline read 'Island inflation rate now 5 per cent per week'.

a You are required to compute Sally's income for the first week on:
- i a historical cost basis;
- ii a replacement cost basis;
- iii a current purchasing power basis.

b Comment upon the usefulness of the three income figures you have calculated (JMB)

23.10 **Level II**

A. Daley commenced trading on 1 January 20X8 as a second-hand car dealer. His capital in cash was £20,000. On that date Daley acquired a 5-year lease on a lock-up garage at a cost of £5,000.

The following transactions took place during the year, all in cash:

		£
31 Mar 20X8	Purchased a car for resale	10,000
30 Jun 20X8	Sold the car	13,000
30 Sep 20X8	Bought another car for resale	14,000

The relevant indices during the year were:

	RPI	*Garage*	*Vehicles*
1 Jan 20X8	100	100	100
31 Mar 20X8	106	108	105
30 Jun 20X8	112	117	110
30 Sep 20X8	118	125	115
31 Dec 20X8	124	130	120

You are required to prepare a profit and loss account for the year and a balance sheet at 31 December 20X8 using:

- **a** historical cost accounting;
- **b** current cost accounting;
- **c** current purchasing power accounting;
- **d** historical cost accounting with adjustments for current costs.

Make all computations to the nearest £.

part 6

PARTNERSHIPS

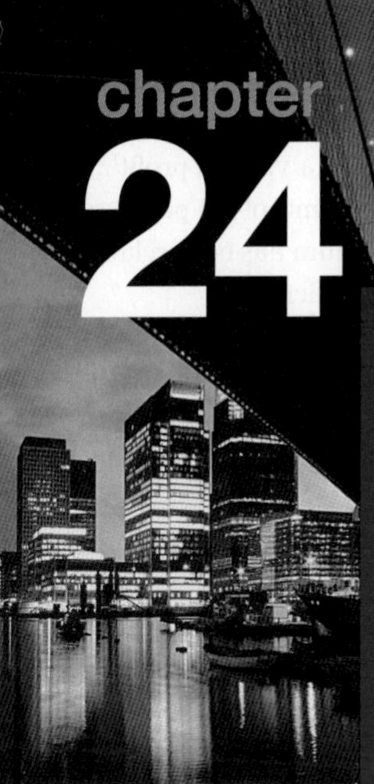

The final accounts of partnerships

Learning objectives

After reading this chapter you should be able to:

1. explain the meaning of the key terms and concepts listed at the end of the chapter;
2. describe the main characteristics of partnerships;
3. explain how profits may be shared between the partners, including the nature and purpose of partners' salaries, interest on capital and interest on drawings;
4. explain the difference between partners' capital, current and drawings accounts;
5. show the journal and ledger entries relating to those items normally found in partners' capital, current and drawings accounts;
6. prepare partnership final accounts, including a profit and loss appropriation account;
7. show the entries in the ledger and final accounts relating to partners' commission and a guaranteed share of profit.

The law and characteristics of partnerships

For a number of commercial reasons, it may be mutually advantageous for two or more people to form a partnership. The Partnership Act 1890 defines a **partnership** as 'the relation which subsists between persons carrying on business in common with a view of profit'. It cannot have fewer than two partners and, at one time, the Act set a limit of 20 partners. However, with the introduction of the Companies Act 1967 this maximum has been relaxed in the case of a number of professional firms, such as accountants and solicitors.

Since partnerships are not able to limit their liability to creditors and other members of the public, there is no need for any special legislation to protect these groups. Thus, partners are largely free to make whatever agreements between themselves that they wish to cover their mutual relationships. The powers and rights of the partners between themselves are

governed by any written agreement they may make. This is referred to as the **articles** or **deed of partnership**. It is important for partners to reach an agreement on matters such as the following:

1 The capital to be introduced by each partner
2 The sharing of profits and losses
3 Partners' drawings
4 The preparation and audit of accounts
5 The dissolution of the partnership
6 The resolution of disputes.

In the absence of any partnership agreement, or if the agreement is silent on any of the items 1–6 above or the following matters, a partnership is subject to the provisions of the Partnership Act 1890, which includes the following:

1 Each partner has **unlimited liability**. That is, if the debts of the partnership cannot be paid because the business has insufficient assets to do so, the creditors have recourse to the private property of the individual partners. The partners are said to be jointly and severally liable for the debts of the firm and therefore a creditor may sue the partnership or any individual partner.
2 Voting powers: in the ordinary day-to-day running of a partnership individual partners often make routine business decisions without consulting the other partners. At the other extreme, certain fundamental decisions, such as to change the type of business in which the partnership is engaged, or the admission of a new partner, require the consent of all the partners. Other major decisions are supposed to be determined by a majority vote. Each partner has one vote. However, a partnership deed may specify some other distribution of voting power.
3 Every partner is entitled to take part in the management of the business. However, some partnership agreements provide for certain partners to be sleeping or limited partners. Neither of these normally takes part in the management of the business.
4 Every partner is entitled to access to the books and papers of the partnership. This includes sleeping and limited partners.
5 Each partner is an agent of the partnership and can thus sign contracts on behalf of the partnership, which will then be legally bound to honour them.

6 A new partner can only be admitted to the partnership if all the existing partners give their consent. However, a partnership deed may specify otherwise.

7 A partnership will be dissolved by:
  a any partner giving notice to the other partner(s) of his or her intention to leave the partnership;
  b the death, insanity or bankruptcy of a partner.

The sharing of profits between the partners

Consider the following situation. A and B enter into partnership; A is to work full-time in the business while B will only spend a few hours each week on partnership business; B is to put into the business £100,000 as capital whereas A is to contribute capital of only £10,000. You are asked by A and B to suggest how the profits might be shared so as to recompense A for working more hours than B in the business, and to compensate B for having put into the business (and therefore put at risk) substantially more capital than A.

The way this is normally done is to give each partner a prior share of the profits as: (1) a salary related to the amount of time each devotes to the business; and (2) **interest on the capital** each invests. The remaining profit, which if often referred to as the **residual profit**, can then be divided between the partners according to whatever they agree is fair. This might be equally, since both have already been compensated for the unequal time and capital they contribute.

Another aspect of sharing partnership profits concerns **interest on drawings**. This is intended to compensate the partner who has annual drawings that are less than those of the other partner. Each partner is charged interest on drawings for the period from the date of the drawings to the end of the accounting year in which the drawings took place.

It is important to appreciate that partners' 'salaries', 'interest on capital' and 'interest on drawings' are not actual payments of money; they are only part of a profit-sharing formula. If any such payments are made to a partner these should be treated as drawings. Indeed, as a general rule *all* payments to partners must be treated as drawings. It should also be observed that salaries, interest on capital and interest on drawings will still arise even if the business makes a loss. In these circumstances they effectively become part of a loss-sharing formula.

If there is no agreement between the partners concerning how profits and losses should be shared, section 24 of the Partnership Act 1890 would be applied as follows:

1 Profits and losses are to be shared equally between the partners.

2 No partner will receive a salary or interest on capital, or be charged interest on drawings.

3 Any loans made by a partner to the business (as distinct from capital introduced) will be entitled to interest at the rate of 5 per cent per annum.

Capital and current accounts

In the accounts of sole traders there would be a capital account and usually a drawings account. In the books of a partnership there will be:

1 A **capital account** for each partner. Unlike the capital account of a sole trader, this will only contain the original capital put into the business plus any further capital introduced at a later date.

2 A **current account** for each partner, in which is entered:
- **a** drawings of money or goods taken by the partner for his or her own use (debit);
- **b** interest charged on drawings (debit);
- **c** interest on loans to the partnership (credit);
- **d** salary (credit);
- **e** interest on capital (credit);
- **f** the partner's share of the residual profit or loss.

There may also be a **drawings account** for each partner in which all goods or money taken by the partners during the year are entered instead of putting them in the partners' current accounts. However, at the end of the year these are transferred to the partners' current accounts. Note also that current accounts are sometimes labelled drawings accounts.

The partners' capital accounts are shown on the balance sheet in the same place as the capital account of a sole trader. Underneath these are entered the balances on the partners' current accounts at the end of the year. If a current account has a debit balance it may be entered after the net current assets but it is more common to deduct (in parentheses) this from the other partners' current accounts.

The profit and loss appropriation account

In partnership final accounts the profit and loss account contains exactly the same entries at that of a sole trader.

After the profit and loss account has been prepared, the profit (or loss) for the year is carried down to a **profit and loss appropriation account** in which is shown the sharing of the profit (or loss) between the partners. The basis for sharing may include partners' salaries, interest on capital and interest on drawings. It will also always contain the division of the remaining amount (the residual profit or loss) in some agreed proportion. The appropriation account is a part of the double entry in the ledger and as a general rule it is worth remembering that the double entry for each item in the appropriation account is on the opposite side of the relevant partner's current account. The contents of the profit and loss appropriation account are illustrated in Example 24.1.

Example 24.1

Bonnie and Clyde are in partnership sharing profits in the ratio 2 : 1. From the following you are required to prepare the profit and loss appropriation account for the year ended 31 December 20X8 and show the relevant items in the balance sheet at that date.

	Bonnie	*Clyde*
	£	£
Capital at 31 Dec 20X7	100,000	80,000
Current account balances at 31 Dec 20X7	16,340	28,290
Drawings—1 Apr 20X8	4,000	8,000
31 Aug 20X8	6,000	9,000
30 Sep 20X8	8,000	—
Salaries	20,000 p.a.	25,000 p.a.
Interest on capital	10 per cent p.a.	10 per cent p.a.
Interest on drawings	5 per cent p.a.	5 per cent p.a.

Clyde introduced additional capital of £10,000 on 1 January 20X8 and Bonnie lent the business £20,000 on 30 June 20X8. The profit for the year ended 31 December 20X8 was £78,700.

Before dividing the profit between the partners, the partners' capital accounts need to be adjusted. These ledger accounts are often prepared in columnar form as follows:

Capital account

Bonnie	*Clyde*			*Bonnie*	*Clyde*
£	£			£	£
		20X8			
		1 Jan	Balance b/d	100,000	80,000
		1 Jan	Bank		10,000
					90,000

The loan from Bonnie is not entered in his capital account but rather in a separate loan account, which constitutes a long-term liability.

Next, it may be useful to prepare a schedule which shows the division of the profits as follows:

	Bonnie	*Clyde*	*Total*
	£	£	£
Profit for 20X8			78,700
Loan interest ($\frac{6}{12}$ × 5 per cent × £20,000)	500	—	(500)
Partners' salaries	20,000	25,000	(45,000)
Interest on capital:			
10 per cent × £100,000	10,000	—	—
10 per cent × £90,000	—	9,000	(19,000)
	30,500	34,000	14,200
Interest on drawings (see note 3)	(350)	(450)	800
	30,150	33,550	15,000
Shares of residual profit (2 : 1)	10,000	5,000	(15,000)
Totals	40,150	38,550	—

Notes

1 The interest on partners' loans is computed using the rate of 5 per cent per annum specified in the Partnership Act 1890, unless you are told that some other rate has been agreed by the partners.

2 The interest on capital is computed using the balances on the partners' capital accounts and not the current accounts, unless you are told the contrary. Note also that in this example the balance on the capital account at the end of the year can be used because the additional capital was introduced at the start of the year. Where additional capital is introduced at some other date it will be necessary to compute the interest on a strict time basis.

3 The interest on drawings is calculated on a monthly basis as follows:

		£
Bonnie	$\frac{9}{12}$ × 5 per cent × £4 000 =	150
	$\frac{4}{12}$ × 5 per cent × £6,000 =	100
	$\frac{3}{12}$ × 5 per cent × £8,000 =	100
		350

Clyde	$\frac{9}{12}$ × 5 per cent × £8,000 =	300
	$\frac{4}{12}$ × 5 per cent × £9,000 =	150
		450

4 The sum of the total of each column in the above schedule should always equal the profit for the year (i.e. £40,150 + £38,550 = £78,700; £30,150 + £33,550 + £15,000 = £78,700, etc.)

The above profit and loss appropriation schedule can be used to make the necessary entries in the profit and loss appropriation account and the partners' current accounts in the ledger. The preparation of a schedule is very efficient because the total of each of the columns, showing each partner's total share of the annual net profit, can be entered in the profit and loss appropriation account and partners' current accounts as single amounts thus:

		£
Debit	Profit and loss appropriation account	78,700
Credit	Current accounts: Bonnie	40,150
	Clyde	38,550

However, for a fuller presentation and to emphasize the double entry, the separate elements are all shown below:

Bonnie and Clyde
Profit and loss appropriation account for the year ended 31 December 20X8

	£	£		£	£
Loan interest—Bonnie			Net profit for year b/d		78,700
($\frac{6}{12}$ × 5 per cent × £20,000)		500	Interest on drawings—		
Salaries—Bonnie	20,000		Bonnie	350	
Clyde	25,000	45,000	Clyde	450	800
Interest on capital—Bonnie					
(10 per cent × £100,000)	10,000				
Clyde					
(10 per cent × £90,000)	9,000	19,000			
Shares of residual profit—					
Bonnie	10,000				
Clyde	5,000	15,000			
		79,500			79,500

The double entry for the items in the appropriation account is in the partners' current accounts, which are usually prepared in columnar form as follows:

Current accounts

	Bonnie	*Clyde*		*Bonnie*	*Clyde*
	£	£		£	£
Drawings	18,000	17,000	Balance b/d	16,340	28,290
Interest on drawings	350	450	Loan interest	500	—
Balance c/d	38,490	49,840	Salaries	20,000	25,000
			Interest on capital	10,000	9,000
			Shares of profit	10,000	5,000
	56,840	67,290		56,840	67,290
			Balance b/d	38,490	49,840

The relevant balances will then be included in the balance sheet thus:

Bonnie and Clyde
Balance sheet as at 31 December 20X8

	£	£
Capital		
Bonnie		100,000
Clyde		90,000
		190,000
Current accounts		
Bonnie	38,490	
Clyde	49,840	88,330
Loan—Bonnie		20,000
		298,330

Alternatively, these can be shown on the balance sheet in columnar form, as follows:

	Bonnie	*Clyde*	*Total*
	£	£	£
Capital	100,000	90,000	190,000
Current accounts	38,490	49,840	88,330
	138,490	139,840	278,330
Loan—Bonnie			20,000
			298,330

In practice and when answering examination questions it is not usual to show final accounts in account form. Thus the profit and loss appropriation account is not normally prepared in account form. Instead this can either be presented as a schedule, as shown above, or in a vertical format as illustrated below. Whichever presentation is adopted, it is advisable to show each of the entries in the partners' current accounts relating to salaries, interest on capital, etc., as above, rather than the totals of each of the partners' columns in the schedule. Moreover, the vertical format shown below is generally preferable to a schedule because the use of an analysis column for each partner serves little purpose when the entries in the partners' current accounts are done individually. This format has thus been used in the solutions to the exercises in the Appendix.

Bonnie and Clyde
Profit and loss appropriation account for the year ended 31 December 20X8

	£	£	£
Net profit for the year			78,700
Add: Interest on drawings—			
Bonnie		350	
Clyde		450	800
			79,500
Less: Loan interest—Bonnie		500	
Salaries—			
Bonnie	20,000		
Clyde	25,000	45,000	

Interest on capital—			
Bonnie	10,000		
Clyde	9,000	19,000	
			64,500
Residual profit			15,000
Shares of residual profit—			
Bonnie			10,000
Clyde			5,000
			15,000

Notes

1 Interest on partners' loans is commonly entered in the appropriation account, particularly in examination questions that do not require the preparation of a profit and loss account. However, this is not strictly an appropriation of profit but rather an expense that should be entered in the profit and loss account as a charge/deduction in arriving at the profit (or loss) for the year.

2 Where money, which is described as salaries, has actually been paid to the partners this must be treated as drawings and not included in the profit and loss account as wages and salaries. However, this may be interpreted as indicating that the partners wish to give themselves a prior share of profits in the form of a salary. In this case the amounts paid must still be treated as drawings but an equivalent amount is also entered in the appropriation account as salaries, as described above.

3 Additional capital introduced during the year may include assets other than cash. This would usually be entitled to interest on capital from the date the assets were introduced until the end of the year in question (and subsequent years).

4 Interest is usually only charged on cash and cheque drawings and not on goods taken by the partners for their own use.

5 Losses would be shared in the same ratio as profit. If, in the case of Example 24.1, the profit for the year had been only £55,000 the schedule of division of profits would be as follows:

	Bonnie	*Clyde*	*Total*
	£	£	£
Profit for year			55,000
Loan interest	500	—	(500)
Salaries	20,000	25,000	(45,000)
Interest on capital	10,000	9,000	(19,000)
	30,500	34,000	(9,500)
Interest on drawings	(350)	(450)	800
	30,150	33,550	(8,700)
Shares of residual loss (2 : 1)	(5,800)	(2,900)	8,700
	24,350	30,650	—

Note that loan interest, salaries, interest on capital and interest on drawings are included even if there is a net loss for the year (i.e. before the appropriation). Salaries, etc., simply increase the amount of the residual loss.

Partners' commission

Some partnership businesses are departmentalized, with each of the selling departments being managed by a different partner. In such circumstances it is common for partners' salaries to take the form of an agreed **partners' commission** expressed as a percentage of the profit of their department. This necessitates the preparation of a trading account for each department which normally takes the form of a columnar trading account containing columns on both the debit and credit sides for each department. Computing the profits of each partner's department is done in the same way as departmental accounts, a short description of which is given in the Appendix to this chapter. Having ascertained the profit of each department the partner's commission can be calculated and then accounted for in exactly the same way as partners' salaries.

A guaranteed share of profit

Some partnership agreements include a clause which states that if a particular partner's share of profit in any year is below some agreed figure, then all or certain other partners will make it up to the agreed amount from their shares of profit. The agreed amount is referred to as a **guaranteed share of profit**. The amount by which the actual share of profit falls short of the guaranteed amount is usually shared (i.e. made up) by the other partners in their profit-sharing ratio. Such a guarantee is fairly common in professional firms as an enticement to an employee to become a partner while at the same time being guaranteed an amount equal to the employee's existing remuneration. The guaranteed amount may include or exclude the partner's interest on capital and/or salary, but in the absence of information to the contrary it is usually taken to be the residual profit share that is guaranteed.

If, in the amended Example 24.1, when profits are only £55,000, Bonnie was guaranteed a share of residual profit of at least £2,000, the profit-sharing schedule would appear as follows:

	Bonnie	*Clyde*	*Total*
	£	£	£
Profit for year	—	—	55,000
Salaries, interest on loan, capital, and drawings	30,150	33,550	(8,700)
Shares of residual loss	2,000	(10,700)	8,700
	32,150	22,850	—

Summary

A partnership exists when between 2 and 20 persons (or more in the case of professional firms) carry on business with a view of profit. One of the main characteristics of partnerships is that the partners have unlimited liability. They are thus jointly and severally liable for the partnership debts. Each partner is also an agent of the partnership, entitled to take part in the management, and has equal voting power.

However, the articles or deed of partnership may contain any form of agreement relating to the rights of partners between themselves. This is particularly important with regard to the sharing of profits and losses. Where partners contribute unequal amounts of capital and/or time, it is common to find a profit-sharing formula that includes giving each partner a prior share of profits as interest on capital and/or a salary. Similarly, where partners have unequal amounts of drawings, they may decide to charge each other interest on drawings as a part of the profit-sharing formula.

The profit and loss accounts of partnerships are the same as those of sole traders. However, the net profit (or loss) is carried down into a profit and loss appropriation account in which is shown the shares of profit appropriated to each partner. The balance sheets of partnerships are also the same as those of sole traders, except that instead of having a single capital account there is a capital and current account for each partner.

Sometimes partners' salaries take the form of a commission which is expressed as a percentage of the gross (or net) profit of a department or branch that is managed by each partner. Some partnership agreements also contain a clause guaranteeing a particular partner a minimum amount as his or her share of the annual profit. In this case, the amount by which the actual share of the annual profit falls short of the minimum is made up from the other partners' share(s) of profit (in their profit-sharing ratio).

Key terms and concepts

Articles/deed of partnership (302)
capital account (303)
current account (304)
drawings account (304)
guaranteed share of profit (309)
interest on capital (303)
interest on drawings (303)
partnership (302)
partners' commission (309)
profit and loss appropriation account (304)
residual profit/loss (303)
salary (303)
unlimited liability (302)

Appendix: Departmental accounts

Where it is decided to produce separate profit and loss results for each trading department within a business, in addition to identifying the sales for each unit and tracking costs which are specifically identifiable to the departments, it is necessary to apportion (i.e. divide up on the basis of ratios) the untraceable overhead costs. No matter how carefully the apportionment ratios are selected, they will depend on the exercise of judgement, and to that extent are arbitrary. The basis should be chosen to attempt to reflect the extra cost likely to be caused by the particular department or, failing that, the benefits the department receives. An illustration of the preparation of departmental accounts is given in Example 24.2.

Example 24.2

Status Stores run three sales departments, clothing, footwear and stationery. For accounting purposes departmental accounts are to be prepared, apportioning building costs (rent, etc.) on the basis of floor space occupied and office administration in proportion to gross profit. The following information has been extracted from the store's accounts for the year ended 31 December 20X1:

	Clothing	*Footwear*	*Stationery*
	£	£	£
Sales	47,000	27,000	26,000
Purchases	23,000	16,000	10,500
Wages	2,500	2,100	1,800

Stocks at 1 Jan 20X1	6,000	1,000	500
Stocks at 31 Dec 20X1	4,000	2,000	1,000
Floor space (in sq. metres)	3,000	2,000	1,000

Rent, rates, lighting, heating and building maintenance (all departments)	£13,800
Administration and office salaries, etc.	£20,000

Status Stores

Departmental trading and profit and loss accounts for the year ended 31 December 20X1

	Clothing		*Footwear*		*Stationery*	
	£	£	£	£	£	£
Sales		47,000		27,000		26,000
Less: Cost of sales:						
Opening stock	6,000		1,000		500	
Add: Purchases	23,000		16,000		10,500	
	29,000		17,000		11,000	
Less: Closing stock	4,000	25,000	2,000	15,000	1,000	10,000
Gross profit		22,000		12,000		16,000
Less: Wages	2,500		2,100		1,800	
Building costs (3 : 2 : 1)	6,900		4,600		2,300	
Administration (22 : 12 : 16)	8,800	18,200	4,800	11,500	6,400	10,500
Net profit		3,800		500		5,500

It is not usual to have separate balance sheets for each department.

Review questions

24.1 **a** Define a partnership.

b What are the legal limits on the number of partners?

c Outline the principal matters normally found in the articles or deed of partnership.

24.2 Describe the main characteristics of a partnership.

24.3 If there is no partnership agreement the provisions of the Partnership Act 1890 apply. List the main provisions of this Act with regard to the rights of partners between themselves, including the sharing of profits or losses.

24.4 Explain each of the following in the context of partnership profit sharing:

a partners' salaries;

b interest on capital;

c interest on drawings;

d residual profit.

24.5 Lane and Hill have decided to form a partnership. Lane is to contribute £150,000 as capital and Hill £20,000. Hill is to work full-time in the business and Lane one day a week. Because Hill has no other income, she anticipates making drawings of £1,000 per month from the partnership. Lane expects to make drawings of about £1,000 per quarter.

You have been asked to advise the partners on how to share profits in such a way as to compensate each of them for their unequal contributions of capital and labour and withdrawals.

24.6 Explain the difference between each of the following ledger accounts in the books of a partnership:

- **a** capital account;
- **b** current account;
- **c** drawings account.

Exercises

An asterisk after the question number indicates that there is a suggested answer in the Appendix.

24.7* **Level I**

Clayton and Hammond are in partnership sharing profits and losses equally. The partnership agreement provides for annual salaries of Clayton: £17,000 and Hammond: £13,000. It also provides for interest on capital of 8 per cent per annum and interest on drawings of 4 per cent per annum.

The following additional information relates to the accounting year ending 30 June 20X6:

	Clayton	*Hammond*
	£	£
Capital at 1 July 20X5	90,000	60,000
Current account at 1 July 20X5	16,850	9,470
Drawings—1 Oct 20X5	3,000	2,000
1 Mar 20X6	5,000	1,000
Capital introduced—1 Nov 20X5	10,000	—
Loan by Hammond—1 Apr 20X6	—	20,000

The net profit shown in the profit and loss account for the year ended 30 June 20X6 was £67,500.

You are required to prepare the profit and loss appropriation account, capital and current accounts. Show all the accounts in account format.

24.8 **Level I**

Light and Dark are in partnership sharing profits and losses in the ratio 7 : 3, respectively. The following information has been taken from the partnership records for the financial year ended 31 May 20X9:

Partners' capital accounts, balances as at 1 June 20X8:

Light	£200,000
Dark	£140,000

Partners' current accounts, balances as at 1 June 20X8:

Light	£15,000Cr
Dark	£13,000Cr

During the year ended 31 May 20X9 the partners made the following drawings from the partnership bank account:

Light	£10,000 on 31 Aug 20X8
	£10,000 on 30 Nov 20X8
	£10,000 on 28 Feb 20X9
	£10,000 on 31 May 20X9
Dark	£7,000 on 31 Aug 20X8
	£7,000 on 30 Nov 20X8
	£7,000 on 28 Feb 20X9
	£7,000 on 31 May 20X9

Interest is to be charged on drawings at the rate of 12 per cent per annum. Interest is allowed on capital accounts and credit balances on current accounts at the rate of 12 per cent per annum. Dark is to be allowed a salary of £15,000 per annum.

The net profit of the partnership for the year ended 31 May 20X9 is £102,940.

Required:

a A computation of the amount of interest chargeable on each partner's drawings for the year ended 31 May 20X9.

b The partnership appropriation account for the year ended 31 May 20X9.

c A computation of the balance on each partner's current account as at 31 May 20X9.

(AAT)

24.9 Level II

The partnership of Sewell, Grange and Jones has just completed its first year in business. The partnership agreement stipulates that profits should be apportioned in the ratio of Sewell 3, Grange 2 and Jones 1 after allowing interest on capital at 12 per cent per annum and crediting Sewell with a salary of £15,000.

The following information relates to their first financial year which ended on 31 October 20X0:

1 The partners introduced the following amounts as capital on 1 November 20X9:

	£
Sewell	50,000
Grange	40,000
Jones	20,000

2 Cash drawings during the year were:

	£
Sewell	3,900
Grange	4,500
Jones	2,400

3 The draft profit and loss account for the year showed a net trading profit of £61,720.

4 Included in the motor expenses account for the year was a bill for £300 which related to Grange's private motoring expenses.

5 No entries had been made in the accounts to record the following:

a As a result of a cash flow problem during April, Grange invested a further £10,000 as capital with effect from 1 May 20X0, and on the same date Jones brought into the business additional items of equipment at an agreed valuation of £6,000. In addition, in order to settle a debt Jones had privately undertaken some work for Foster, a creditor of the partnership. Foster accepted the work as full settlement of the £12,000 the partnership owed her for materials.

b Sewell had accepted a holiday provided by Miller, a debtor of the partnership. The holiday which was valued at £1,000 was accepted in full settlement of a debt of £2,500 that Miller owed to the partnership and that he was unable to pay.

c Each partner had taken goods for his own use during the year at cost as follows:

	£
Sewell	1,400
Grange	2,100
Jones	2,100

Note: It is the policy of the firm to depreciate equipment at the rate of 10 per cent per annum based on the cost of equipment held at the end of each financial year.

Required:

a The profit and loss appropriation account for the year ended 31 October 20X0 showing clearly the corrected net trading profit of the first year's trading.

b The capital and current accounts of Sewell, Grange and Jones for the year ended 31 October 20X0. (AEB)

24.10* **Level II**

The following is the trial balance of Peace and Quiet, grocers, as at 31 December 20X8.

	Debit	*Credit*
	£	£
Capital: Peace		10,000
Capital: Quiet		5,000
Current account: Peace		1,280
Current account: Quiet		3,640
Purchases/sales	45,620	69,830
Debtors/creditors	1,210	4,360
Leasehold shop at cost	18,000	
Equipment at cost	8,500	
Depreciation on equipment		1,200
Shop assistants' salaries	5,320	
Light and heat	1,850	
Stationery	320	
Bank interest and charges	45	
Stock	6,630	
Bank	3,815	
Drawings—Peace 1 May 20X8	2,200	
—Quiet 1 Sep 20X8	1,800	
	95,310	95,310

Additional information:

1 The stock at 31 December 20X8 was valued at £5,970.
2 There is electricity accrued at the end of the year of £60.
3 Stationery unused at 31 December 20X8 was valued at £50.
4 The equipment is depreciated at 10 per cent p.a. on the reducing balance method.

5 There is a partnership deed which says that each partner is to be credited with interest on capital at 10 per cent per annum; salaries of £6,200 per annum for Peace and £4,800 per annum for Quiet; and charged interest on drawings of 8 per cent p.a. The remainder of the profit is to be divided equally between the partners.

6 Included in the capital of Peace is capital introduced of £1,000 on 1 April 20X8 and a loan to the partnership of £2,000 on 1 October 20X8.

You are required to prepare the profit and loss account and appropriation account for the year and a balance sheet at 31 December 20X8. Present your answer in vertical form.

24.11* **Level II**

Peter and Paul, whose year end is 30 June, are in business as food wholesalers. Their partnership deed states that:

a profits and losses are to be shared equally;
b salaries are Peter £20,000 per annum and Paul £18,000 per annum;
c interest on capital of 10 per cent is allowed;
d interest on drawings of 5 per cent is charged;
e interest on loans from partners is given at the rate shown in the Partnership Act 1890.

The trial balance as at 30 June 20X8 is as follows:

	Debit	*Credit*
	£	£
Capital—Peter		100,000
—Paul		80,000
Current accounts—Peter	804	
—Paul		21,080
Loan at 1 July 20X7—Peter		12,000
Freehold premises at cost	115,000	
Plant and machinery at cost	77,000	
Provision for depreciation on plant		22,800
Motor vehicles at cost	36,500	
Provision for depreciation on vehicles		12,480
Loose tools at 1 July 20X7	1,253	
Stock	6,734	
Debtors	4,478	
Creditors		3,954
Bank	7,697	
Electricity accrued at 1 July 20X7		58
Paid for electricity	3,428	
Purchases	19,868	
Sales		56,332
Warehouse wages	23,500	
Rates	5,169	
Postage and telephone	4,257	
Printing and stationery	2,134	
Provision for bad debts		216
Selling expenses	1,098	
	308,920	308,920

You also ascertain the following:

1 Stock at 30 June 20X8 is £8,264.
2 Depreciation by the straight line method is 10 per cent per annum on plant and machinery and 20 per cent per annum on motor vehicles. The latter are used by the administrative staff. The revaluation method of depreciation is used for loose tools. These have a value at 30 June 20X8 of £927.
3 Included in wages are drawings of £6,000 by Peter on 1 March 20X8 and £8,000 by Paul on 1 October 20X7.
4 The provision for bad debts at 30 June 20X8 is to be £180.
5 Debtors include bad debts of £240.
6 Sales include goods which are on sale or return at a price of £200. The cost price of these is £160.
7 Electricity accrued at 30 June 20X8 amounts to £82.
8 Rates prepaid at 30 June 20X8 are £34.

You are required to prepare a profit and loss account and appropriation account for the year ended 30 June 20X8 and a balance sheet at that date. Present your answer in vertical form.

24.12* **Level II**

Simon, Wilson and Dillon are in partnership. The following trial balance has been prepared on 31 December 20X9:

	Debit	*Credit*
	£	£
Capital accounts—Simon		35,000
—Wilson		25,000
—Dillon		10,000
Current accounts—Simon		5,600
—Wilson		4,800
—Dillon	1,800	
Freehold land and buildings	65,000	
Stock	34,900	
Bank	10,100	
Delivery vehicles at cost	30,000	
Provision for depreciation on vehicles		18,000
Goodwill at cost	11,000	
8 per cent mortgage on premises		40,000
Salesmen's salaries	19,480	
Debtors' control account	28,000	
Creditors' control account		25,000
Unquoted investments	6,720	
Loose tools at valuation	1,200	
Sales		130,000
Investment income		800
Returns	400	600
Purchases	64,000	
Rates	12,100	
Motor expenses	2,800	

Provision for bad debts		400
Mortgage interest paid	1,600	
Printing and stationery	1,100	
Extension to premises	5,000	
	295,200	295,200

You are also given the following additional information:

1 The stock at 31 December 20X9 was valued at £31,000.
2 There is investment income accrued at 31 December 20X9 of £320.
3 The stock of stationery at 31 December 20X9 was £170.
4 At the same date there were motor expenses accrued of £240 and rates paid in advance of £160.
5 The provision for bad debts at 31 December 20X9 is to be adjusted to 2 per cent of the trade debtors.
6 Mortgage interest accrued should be provided for at the end of the year.
7 Depreciation on vehicles, on a strict time basis, is 10 per cent per annum using the straight line method.
8 The loose tools in stock at 31 December 20X9 were valued at £960.
9 The following errors have been found:
   a unrecorded in the ledger is the sale of a delivery vehicle on credit on 1 November 20X9 for £1,900—this vehicle cost £2,400 when it was purchased on 1 April 20X7;
   b bad debts for this year of £2,000 have not been written off;
   c bank charges of £130 have been omitted from the books.

Simon and Dillon are to be allocated salaries of £15,000 and £10,000 per annum, respectively. All partners will be entitled to interest on capital of 10 per cent per annum. The remaining profit or loss is shared between Simon, Wilson and Dillon in the ratio of 2 : 2 : 1, respectively.

You are required to prepare in vertical form a profit and loss account and appropriation account for the year ended 31 December 20X9 and a balance sheet at that date.

24.13 Level II

A, B, C and D were partners in a garage business comprising (i) petrol sales, (ii) repairs and servicing, and (iii) second-hand car dealing. A was responsible for petrol sales, B for repairs and servicing and C for second-hand car deals, while D acted purely in an advisory capacity.

The partnership agreement provided the following:

i Interest on fixed capital at 10 per cent per annum.
ii Each working partner to receive commission of 10 per cent of the gross profit of that partner's own department.
iii Profits were shared as follows: A: 2/10, B: 3/10, C: 3/10, D: 2/10.
iv Accounts to be made up annually to 30 September.

A trial balance extracted from the books at 30 September 20X8 showed the following balances:

		Dr	Cr
		£	£
A	Capital account		3,500
	Current account		1,350
	Drawings account	6,000	

B Capital account		7,500
Current account		7,500
Drawings account	13,250	
C Capital account		6,500
Current account		5,500
Drawings account	10,500	
D Capital account		12,500
Current account		2,150
Drawings account	3,500	
Freehold premises at cost	25,000	
Goodwill at cost	10,000	
Servicing tools and equipment at cost	9,000	
Servicing tools and equipment—accumulated depreciation to 1 October 20X7		1,350
Bank balance		10,105
Stocks at 1 October 20X7—Petrol	950	
—Spares	525	
—Second-hand cars	6,350	
Debtors	4,350	
Cash in hand	125	
Creditors		2,350
Sales—Petrol		68,650
—Servicing and repairs		86,750
—Cars		156,000
Purchases—Petrol	58,500	
—Spares	51,650	
—Second-hand cars	118,530	
Wages—Forecourt attendants	5,750	
—Mechanics	31,350	
—Car sales staff	8,550	
—Office personnel	1,850	
Rates	2,500	
Office expenses	1,800	
Heating and lighting	550	
Advertising	775	
Bank interest	350	
	371,705	371,705

The following additional information is obtained:

1 Stock at 30 September 20X8:

	£
Petrol	1,050
Spares	475
Second-hand cars	9,680

2 Depreciation on tools and equipment is to be provided at 5 per cent per annum by the straight line method.

3 Your fees for preparation of the accounts will be £175.
4 The service department did work valued at £11,300 on the second-hand cars.
5 The service department used old cars valued at £550 for spare parts in services and repairs.

You are required to prepare:

a Trading and profit and loss account for the year ended 30 September 20X8.
b Balance sheet at 30 September 20X8.
c Partners' current accounts in columnar form for the year. (ACCA)

24.14 Level II

a When accounting for the relationship of partners *inter se*, the partnership agreement provides the rules which in the first instance are to be applied.

What information would you expect to find in a partnership agreement to provide such rules, and what should you do if the agreement fails to deal with any aspect of the partnership relationship which affects the accounts?

b A, B and C are in partnership, agreeing to share profits in the ratio 4 : 2 : 1. They have also agreed to allow interest on capital at 8 per cent per annum; a salary to C of £5,000 per annum; and to charge interest on drawings made in advance of the year end at a rate of 10 per cent per annum.

A has guaranteed B a minimum annual income of £6,500, gross of interest on drawings. The balance sheet as at 30 June 20X9 disclosed the following:

		£	£
Capitals	A	50,000	
	B	30,000	
	C	10,000	90,000
Current accounts	A	2,630	
	B	521	
	C	(418)	
			2,733
Loan account	A		15,000
Net capital employed			107,733

Drawings during the year were: A £6,400; B £3,100; C £2,000.
Net trading profit for the year to 30 June 20X0 was £24,750.

You are required to prepare the current accounts for the partners as at 30 June 20X0. (ACCA)

24.15 Level II

Brick, Stone and Breeze carry on a manufacturing business in partnership, sharing profits and losses: Brick one-half, Stone one-third and Breeze one-sixth. It is agreed that the minimum annual share of profit to be credited to Breeze is to be £2,200, and any deficiency between this figure and her true share of the profits is to be borne by the other two partners in the ratio that they share profits. No interest is to be allowed or charged on partners' capital or current accounts.

The trial balance of the firm as on 30 June 20X0 was as follows:

	Dr	Cr
	£	£
Stock on 1 July 20X9	7,400	
Purchases	39,100	
Manufacturing wages	8,600	
Salaries	5,670	
Rates, telephone and insurance	1,744	
Incidental trade expenses	710	
Repairs and renewals	1,250	
Cash discounts allowed	280	
Cash discounts received		500
Office expenses	3,586	
Carriage inwards	660	
Carriage outwards	850	
Professional charges	500	
Sales		69, 770
Provision for doubtful debts as at 1 July 20X9		400
Provision for depreciation as at 1 July 20X9:		
Machinery and plant		2,500
Motor vehicles		1,300
Capital accounts:		
Brick		9,000
Stone		5,000
Breeze		4,000
Current accounts as at 1 July 20X9:		
Brick		1,900
Stone	500	
Breeze		400
Freehold buildings, at cost	9,800	
Machinery and plant, at cost	8,200	
Motor vehicles, at cost	2,500	
Bank balance	750	
Sales ledger balances	7,000	
Bought ledger balances		4,330
	99,100	99,100

The following information is given to you:

1 An amount of £3,000, for goods sent out on sale or return, has been included in sales. These goods were charged out to customers at cost plus 25 per cent and they were still in the customers' hands on 30 June 20X0, unsold.
2 Included in the item, repairs and renewals, is an amount of £820 for an extension to the factory.
3 Telephone and insurance paid in advance amounted to £424 and £42 was owing in respect of a trade expense.
4 A debt of £80 has turned out to be bad and is to be written off, and the provision for doubtful debts is to be increased to £520.

5 Provision for depreciation on machinery and plant and on motor vehicles is to be made at the rate of 10 per cent and 20 per cent per annum, respectively, on the cost.
6 The value of the stock on hand on 30 June 20X0 was £7,238.
7 Each month Brick has drawn £55, Stone £45 and Breeze £20, and the amounts have been included in salaries.

You are required:

a to prepare the trading and profit and loss account for the year ended 30 June 20X0;
b to write up the partners' current accounts, in columnar form, for the year; and
c to draw up the balance sheet as on 30 June 20X0. (ACCA)

24.16 Level III

A. Cherry owned a farmhouse and land, the latter being used by him and his sons, Tom and Leo, in carrying on a fruit and poultry business in partnership. The partnership agreement stipulated that the father should take one-sixth of the profits, such to be not less than £1,200 per annum, the sons sharing the remainder equally.

The following are extracts from the trial balance of the business as on 31 December 20X1:

	Dr	Cr
	£	£
Purchases—Poultry	216	
—Feeding stuffs	3,072	
—Sprays and fertilizers	1,451	
—Spraying machine	460	
Wages	2,908	
General expenses (not apportionable)	842	
Sales—Fruit		6,022
—Poultry		558
—Eggs		5,843
—Motor mower (cost £90 written down to £50)		46
Capital accounts—A. Cherry		6,450
—Tom		3,340
—Leo	840	
Drawings—A. Cherry	930	
Equipment at 1 January 20X1 at cost	3,420	
Equipment at 1 January provision for depreciation		1,510

Stocks on hand were as follows:

	31 Dec 20X0	*31 Dec 20X1*
	£	£
Sprays and fertilizers	310	289
Poultry	320	154
Feeding stuffs	363	412

The following additional information is given to you:

1 Drawings by Tom and Leo have been £15 and £14 per week, respectively, which amounts have been included in the wages account. Of the wages, one-quarter is to be charged to the fruit department and three-quarters to the poultry department.

2 The father and son Tom live in the farmhouse and are to be charged jointly per annum £30 for fruit, and £68 for eggs and poultry, such charges being shared equally. Leo is to be charged £38 for fruit and £62 for eggs and poultry.
3 Independent of the partnership, Leo kept some pigs on the farm and in respect of this private venture he is to be charged £140 for feeding stuffs and £40 for wages.
4 A. Cherry is to be credited with £360 for rent of the land (to be charged as to two-thirds to the fruit and one-third to the poultry departments), and Tom is to be credited with £84 by way of salary for packing eggs and dressing poultry.
5 Eggs sold in December 20X1 and paid for in January 20X2 amounted to £243 and this sum was not included in the trial balance.
6 An account to 31 December 20X1 for £24 was received from a veterinary surgeon after the trial balance had been prepared. This account included a sum of £14 in respect of professional work as regards Leo's pigs, which he himself paid.
7 Annual provision was to be made for depreciation on equipment at 10 per cent on cost at the end of the year.

You are required to prepare:

a a trading account (showing separately the trading profit on the fruit and poultry departments) and profit and loss and appropriation accounts for the year ended 31 December 20X1; and

b the partners' capital accounts in columnar form showing the balances as on 31 December 20X1. (ACCA)

24.17 Level III

Field, Green and Lane are in partnership making up accounts annually to 31 March. Owing to staff difficulties proper records were not maintained for the year ended 31 March 20X9, and the partners request your assistance in preparing the accounts for that year.

The balance sheet on 1 April 20X8 was as follows:

	£	£		£	£	£
Capital accounts			*Fixed assets*	*Cost*	*Depn*	*Net*
Field	10,000		Fixed plant	15,000	6,000	9,000
Green	10,000		Motor vehicles	4,000	1,000	3,000
Lane	2,500		Fixtures and fittings	500	250	250
		22,500		19,500	7,250	12,250
Current accounts			*Current assets*			
Field	5,000		Stock in trade		19,450	
Green	2,000		Debtors		10,820	
Lane	500		Prepayments		250	
		7,500	Cash in till		75	
		30,000				30,595
Current liabilities						
Trade creditors	5,350					
Accruals	1,125					
Bank overdraft	6,370					
		12,845				
		42,845				42,845

The accruals in the balance sheet comprised: audit fee £600, heat and light £400, and advertising £125. The prepayment of £250 was in respect of rates.

A summary of the bank statement provides the following information for the year to 31 March 20X9.

	£
Takings banked	141,105
Purchases	111,805
Wages	6,875
Rates and water	6,850
Heat and light	1,720
Delivery and travelling	3,380
Repairs and renewals	1,475
Advertising	375
Printing and stationery	915
Sundry office expenses	215
Bank charges	1,100
Audit fee	600

The following items were paid from the takings before they were banked:

Wages: cleaner £5 per week; van driver's mate £10 per week
Casual labour for the year: £555
Paraffin for shop heating: £445
Advertising: £75
Sundry office expenses: £515
Purchases for resale: £12,635
Hire of delivery vehicle: £20 per week
Partners' drawings per week: Field £40, Green £30, Lane £30.

You ascertain the following additional information:

1 The partners are allowed interest of 5 per cent per annum on their capital accounts.
2 Profits and losses are shared in the ratio Field 5, Green 3, Lane 2; with the proviso that Lane is guaranteed by Field an income of £3,000 per annum, excluding his interest on capital.
3 Certain goods had been appropriated by the partners during the year. The selling price of these goods was £460, allocated as follows: Field £235, Green £110, Lane £115.
4 Depreciation on fixed assets is to be provided at the following rates: fixed plant 5 per cent, motor vehicles 25 per cent and fixtures and fittings 10 per cent, using the straight line method.
5 Accrued charges for heat and light at 31 March 20X9 were £450.
6 Rates of £750 were prepaid at 31 March 20X9.
7 Your charges for the 20X8/X9 audit were estimated at £650.
8 At 31 March 20X9, stocks were £22,345, debtors £11,415, trade creditors £5,920 and cash in till £100.

You are required to prepare:

a the partnership's trading and profit and loss account, and profit and loss appropriation account for the year ended 31 March 20X9; and

b the balance sheet as at 31 March 20X9. (Movements in the partners' current accounts should be shown on the face of the balance sheet.) (ACCA)

chapter

25

Changes in partnerships

Learning objectives

After reading this chapter you should be able to:

1. explain the meaning of the key terms and concepts listed at the end of the chapter;
2. discuss the nature, valuation and accounting treatment of goodwill;
3. compute the value of goodwill;
4. show the journal and ledger entries for the admission of a new partner and/or an outgoing partner, including those relating to goodwill and the effects of a revaluation of assets;
5. show the journal and ledger entries relating to a change in partners' profit-sharing ratio, including the appropriation of profits in the year of the change;
6. prepare the profit and loss appropriation account and balance sheet of a partnership where there is a change in partners or their profit-sharing ratio;
7. show the journal and ledger entries to close the books on a dissolution of partnership.

Introduction

When a partner leaves a partnership owing to, for example, retirement or death, or whenever a new partner is admitted, it has the effect of bringing the old partnership to an end and transferring the business to a new partnership. The retiring partner(s) will want to take out their share of the business assets and any new partner(s) may be expected to introduce capital. Furthermore, a new profit-sharing agreement must be reached. The situation would be relatively simple, in accounting terms, if three conditions could be met:

1 The change occurs at the start or end of an accounting year.
2 The separate assets and liabilities of the business are all included in the accounts at values which the partners agree to be current.
3 No account is taken of 'goodwill'.

The difficulties that arise when these conditions do not apply (which is nearly always) will be discussed later in this chapter. The term goodwill has special significance in accounting and explanation of this is also introduced later.

As explained above, when a partner leaves and/or a new partner is admitted, the law states that the old partnership is dissolved and a new partnership is created. The new partnership frequently takes over the assets and liabilities of the old partnership, normally retains the name of the old partnership (with perhaps a minor amendment to reflect the change of partners), and thus from the perspective of third parties often has the appearance of being a continuing business. For these reasons the partnership usually continues to use the same set of books of account with various adjustments to the capital and current accounts to reflect the change of partners. These are described below.

Retirement of a partner

This can be considered initially using the simplifying assumptions 1, 2 and 3 set out above. The first step in dealing with the retirement of a partner is to ensure that the accounts are complete at the date of retirement, including crediting the partner's current account with the partner's share of profit and debiting the current account with the partner's drawings to this date. The retiring partner's share of the partnership assets is then represented by the sum of the balances on his or her current and capital accounts. As soon as the individual ceases to be a partner, that person no longer has capital invested in the partnership and must thus be treated as a loan creditor. The balances on the former partner's current and capital accounts are, therefore, transferred to a loan account in the individual's name. This loan is eliminated either by one payment, or alternatively there may be a clause in the partnership agreement to make repayment by instalments over time. Since the person is no longer a partner, any interest payable on this loan is an expense of the partnership to be charged in the profit and loss account and not an appropriation of profits as in the case of interest on loans made by partners.

The accounting entries relating to the retirement of a partner are illustrated in Example 25.1.

Example 25.1

Britten, Edwards and Howe are partners sharing profits equally after interest on partners' loans of 5 per cent per annum. Edwards retires on 1 January 20X9 and is to be repaid one year later. Interest on money due to her is to be at 8 per cent per annum.

The balance sheet at 31 December 20X8 was summarized as below, before the appropriation of profit:

	£	£
Capital accounts		
Britten		10,000
Edwards		6,000
Howe		5,000
		21,000
Current accounts		
Britten	1,000	
Edwards	1,500	
Howe	1,100	3,600
Profit and loss account—profit for year		1,000
		25,600
Partners' loan from Edwards		2,000
		27,600
Total assets less current liabilities		27,600

First, the appropriation of profits should be carried out as follows:

	B	*E*	*H*	*Total*
	£	£	£	£
Profit for year				1,000
Interest on loan (5 per cent × £2,000)		100		(100)
				900
Shares of residual profit	300	300	300	(900)
	300	400	300	—

The journal and ledger entries in respect of Edwards' interest on loan and share of profit will be as follows:

		£	£
Profit and loss appropriation account	Dr	400	
Current account—Edwards			400

This produces a balance on Edwards' current account of £1,500 + £400 = £1,900. The balances on the retiring partner's capital, current and loan accounts are then transferred to a new loan account as shown by the following journal entries:

		£	£
Capital account—Edwards	Dr	6,000	
Current account—Edwards	Dr	1,900	
Partners' loan account—Edwards	Dr	2,000	
Loan account—Edwards			9,900
		9,900	9,900

After crediting the other partners' current accounts with their shares of profit the balance sheet on 1 January 20X9 after Edwards' retirement will be as follows:

	£	£
Capital accounts		
Britten		10,000
Howe		5,000
		15,000
Current accounts		
Britten	1,300	
Howe	1,400	
		2,700
		17,700
Total assets less current liabilities		27,600
Less: Loan—Edwards		9,900
Net assets		17,700

Admission of a new partner

When a new partner is admitted to a partnership the value of the assets s/he introduces into the business will be debited to the appropriate asset accounts (e.g. bank) and credited to the new partner's capital account. If the new partner is admitted in the circumstances set out in the introduction to this chapter as three conditions or simplifying assumptions, then these are the only entries that are necessary to account for the admission of a new partner.

However, such circumstances are rarely the case. In particular, the change of partners may not occur at the start or end of an accounting year, but more likely at some time during the accounting year. We will thus now examine the accounting requirements when this condition does not apply, but the other two are still met.

When a new partner is admitted (or an existing partner leaves) part way through an accounting year, it is usual, at least in examination questions, to retain the same accounting year. This means that it will be necessary to ascertain the partners' shares of profit for the period from the start of the accounting year to the date of the change, separately from that for the period from the date of the change until the end of the accounting year.

One possibility is to start by preparing two profit and loss accounts, one for each of these two periods. However, it is more common, at least in examination questions, to assume that the profit has arisen evenly over the accounting year, and thus simply prepare a profit and loss account for the year and divide the profit (or loss) between the two periods on a time basis. Two profit and loss appropriation accounts are then prepared, one for the period from the start of the accounting year to the date of the change, and the other from the date of the change until the end of the accounting year. The reason for this is that the partners' shares of profit will be different for each period, as may be their salaries, rates of interest on capital and interest on drawings. Note that the salaries, interest on capital and interest on drawings for each of the two periods will have to be computed separately, and on a strict time basis.

The two profit and loss appropriation accounts are usually prepared in columnar form since this is quicker and easier. Moreover, it means that each partner's salary, interest on capital, interest on drawings and share of residual profit for each of the two periods can be added together to give the total of each for the year. Obviously this only applies to those partners who were partners before and after the change.

An illustration of the preparation of a profit and loss appropriation account where a new partner is admitted part way through an accounting year is given in Example 25.2 below. Notice that there is no impact on the profit and loss account, and the only effects on the balance sheet relate to the capital introduced by the new partner and the appropriation of profit to the partners' current accounts.

Example 25.2

Brick and Stone are in partnership sharing profits and losses Brick 3/5 and Stone 2/5 after giving each partner 6 per cent pa interest on capital and annual salaries of £28,000 to Brick and £22,000 to Stone.

On 1 July 20X5 Wall was admitted as a partner. From this date profits and losses will be shared equally after giving each partner 10 per cent pa interest on capital and annual salaries of £34,000 to Brick, £26,000 to Stone and £24,000 to Wall.

The accounts are made up to 31 December of each year. The profit for the year ended 31 December 20X5 was £150,000 and this is believed to have arisen evenly over the year. The following is the balance sheet at the 31 December 20X5 before the appropriation of the profit between the partners:

	£000	£000
Fixed assets		675
Current assets	180	
Less: current liabilities	55	125
		800
Capital accounts:		
Brick		300
Stone		200
Wall		100
		600
Current accounts:		
Brick	27	
Stone	23	50
Net profit for the year		150
		800

The above balances on the capital accounts of Brick and Stone have not changed since the 31 December 20X4. The balance on Wall's capital account is the capital she introduced on 1 July 20X5.

You are required to prepare:

a A profit and loss appropriation account for the year ended 31 December 20X5.

b A balance sheet as at 31 December 20X5 showing all the entries in the partners' current accounts after giving effect to the change in partners.

a

Workings

	Brick	*Stone*	*Wall*
	£000	£000	£000
From 1 Jan to 30 June 20X5:			
Salaries			
6/12 × £28k	14		
6/12 × £22k		11	
Interest on capital			
6/12 × 6 per cent × £300k	9		
6/12 × 6 per cent × £200k		6	
From 1 July to 31 Dec 20X5:			
Salaries			
6/12 × £34k	17		
6/12 × £26k		13	
6/12 × £24k			12
Interest on capital			
6/12 × 10 per cent × £300k	15		
6/12 × 10 per cent × £200k		10	
6/12 × 10 per cent × £100k			5

Brick, Stone and Wall

Profit and loss appropriation account for the year ended 31 December 20X5

	Total	*1 Jan to 30 June*		*1 July to 31 Dec*	
	£000	£000	£000	£000	£000
Net profit for the year	150		75		75
Less: salaries					
Brick	31	14		17	
Stone	24	11		13	
Wall	12	—		12	
	67	25		42	
Less: interest on capital					
Brick	24	9		15	
Stone	16	6		10	
Wall	5	—		5	
	45	15		30	
	112		40		72
Residual profit	38		35		3
Shares of residual profit:					
Brick	22		21		1
Stone	15		14		1
Wall	1		—		1
	38		35		3

b

Brick, Stone and Wall

Balance sheet as at 31 December 20X5

	£000	£000	£000	£000
Fixed assets				675
Current assets			180	
Less: current liabilities			55	125
				800
	Brick	*Stone*	*Wall*	*Total*
Capital accounts	300	200	100	600
Current accounts:				
Balance at 1 Jan 20X5	27	23		
Add: salaries	31	24	12	
interest on capital	24	16	5	
shares of residual profit	22	15	1	
Balance at 31 Dec. 20X5	104	78	18	200
	404	278	118	800

Notes

1 In some examination questions the profit does not accrue evenly over the accounting year. These questions usually specify the amounts of profit before and after the change in partners. With this exception the same principles as above would be applied to the preparation of the profit and loss appropriation account. It is unlikely, but students may be required to compute the amounts of profit before and after the change, in which case the necessary information would have to be supplied in the question. This will probably involve apportioning some expenses between the two periods on a time basis. The answer should be presented as columnar profit and loss accounts.

2 When a partner leaves part way through an accounting year, the above principles and procedure would also have to be applied to the appropriation of profits. However, where the outgoing partner leaves the amount due to him/her in the partnership as an interest bearing loan, it will be necessary to prepare the profit and loss appropriation account for the period up to the change in partners before that for the period after the change. This is because the outgoing partner's share of profit, salary, etc. will need to be credited to his current account and then transferred to a loan account at the date of the change in partners. The balance on this account will then be used to ascertain the interest on the loan that needs to be deducted in arriving at the net profit of the period after the change in partners.

Learning Activity 25.1

Imagine you are in business with assets and capital of £100,000. You decide to admit me to your business as a partner. I will bring in capital of £100,000 in cash, and we will share profits and losses equally. The assets of your old business have a market value of £150,000, but we have agreed that they will remain in the books at their historical cost of £100,000 on the grounds of prudence. The day after my admission I give you notice to dissolve our partnership, and the assets of your old business are sold for £150,000. The profit of £150,000 − £100,000 = £50,000 must be shared equally, and thus our capital is now £100,000 + £25,000 = £125,000 each. This is repaid in cash and I therefore walk away with a gain of £25,000 after only having been a partner for two days.

Describe your feelings about the way in which the profit on realization of the assets has been shared, and whether in retrospect you would have done anything differently. The answer is given later in the text.

The revaluation of assets on changes in partners

The values of assets and liabilities shown in the ledger and the balance sheet (i.e. the book values) are not normally the current market values. Therefore, when a new partner is admitted to a business or an existing partner dies or retires it is usually necessary to revalue all the assets and liabilities. The reason for this revaluation is that since assets are normally shown in the accounts at their historical cost there will be **unrealized holding gains and losses** which have not been recorded in the books (e.g. arising from an increase in the market value of property since the date of purchase). These must be taken into account by means of a **revaluation**, and each old partner's capital account credited with their share of the unrealized gains (or debited with their share of any unrealized losses).

Thus, when an existing partner dies or retires, the revaluation ensures that the former partner receives his or her share of any unrealized holding gains. Similarly, when a new partner is admitted the revaluation is necessary to ensure that the old partners receive recognition of their shares of the unrealized holding gains. If this was not done the new partner would be entitled to a share of these gains when they were eventually realized, despite the fact that they arose prior to the partner's admission to the partnership.

Learning Activity 25.1 — Answer

You should not have agreed to the assets remaining in the books at their historical cost. The whole of the difference between their market value and historical cost belongs to you. The principle of prudence does not apply because the assets of your old business were sold to the new partnership, and thus the gain was realized. You should have brought the revaluation of the assets into the books before admitting me as a partner. That way, the whole of the gain would have been credited to your capital account.

An illustration of the ledger entries relating to the revaluation of assets on changes in partners is given in Example 25.3.

Example 25.3

Bill and Harry are in partnership sharing profits equally. On 1 July 20X1 Harry retired and Jane was admitted as a partner who is to contribute cash of £9,000 as capital. Future profits are to be shared, Bill three-fifths and Jane two-fifths.

The balance sheet at 30 June 20X1 was as follows:

	£	£		£	£	£
Capital accounts			*Fixed assets*	*Cost*	*Depn*	*WDV*
Bill		17,000	Plant	13,500	3,300	10,200
Harry		17,500	Fixtures	10,500	2,700	7,800
		34,500		24,000	6,000	18,000
Current accounts			*Current assets*			
Bill	4,800		Stock		13,800	
Harry	2,100	6,900	Debtors		9,450	
			Cash		3,900	27,150
Current liabilities						
Creditors		3,750				
		45,150				45,150

It was decided that stock is to be valued at £12,000 and fixtures are to be valued at £10,350. Of the trade debtors, £1,350 are considered doubtful debts.

The ledger entries relating to the above revaluation and change of partners are required.

It is necessary first to set up a revaluation account in the ledger and enter the increases and decreases in value of all the assets. The resulting profit or loss on revaluation must then be shared between the old partners in their old profit-sharing ratio and entered in their capital accounts. The cash introduced by the new partner is simply credited to her capital account. This is shown below.

Fixtures

Balance b/d	10,500	Provision for depreciation		2,700
Revaluation a/c	2,550	Balance c/d		10,350
	13,050			13,050
Balance b/d	10,350			

Stock

Balance b/d	13,800	Revaluation a/c		1,800
		Balance c/d		12,000
	13,800			13,800
Balance b/d	12,000			

Provision for bad debts

		Revaluation account		1,350

Revaluation account

Write down of stock	1,800	Write up of fixtures		2,550
Provision for bad debts	1,350	Loss on revaluation—		
		Capital Bill	300	
		Capital Harry	300	600
	3,150			3,150

Capital

	Bill	*Harry*	*Jane*		*Bill*	*Harry*	*Jane*
Revaluation a/c	300	300	—	Balance b/d	17,000	17,500	—
Balance c/d	16,700	17,200	9,000	Bank	—	—	9,000
	17,000	17,500	9,000		17,000	17,500	9,000
				Balance b/d	16,700	17,200	9,000

Finally, the transfers in respect of Harry's capital and current accounts must be made, which would involve the following journal entry:

Capital account—Harry	Dr	17,200	
Current account—Harry	Dr	2,100	
Loan account—Harry			19,300
		19,300	19,300

So far, consideration has only been given to situations where any deceased or retiring partners' capital accounts have credit balances and the remaining partners are required to make payments to them. If there is a debit balance on a capital account, a retiring partner will be due to pay this to the partnership. However, if the retiring partner is unable to make this payment, there will be a deficiency to be shared among the remaining partners. The partnership agreement may specify how this sharing is to take place. In the absence of such an agreement, then the precedence of a court ruling in the case of ***Garner v. Murray*** will apply under English law. Under this rule, the deficiency is shared in proportion to the partners' credit balances on their capital accounts at the last balance sheet date before the retirement. Subsequent revaluations are not taken into account in calculating these proportions, nor are profit-sharing ratios.

The nature of goodwill

The precise nature of goodwill is difficult to define in a theoretically sound manner. However, it is generally recognized that goodwill exists, since a value is normally attached to it when a business is purchased. Goodwill usually arises in the accounts where another business has been purchased at some time in the past. Its value frequently takes the form of the excess of the purchase price of the other business over the market value of its net assets. The existence of this excess shows that the purchaser of a business is prepared to pay for something in addition to the net assets. Goodwill is the label given to that something. Thus, in *SSAP22—Accounting for Goodwill,*[1] **goodwill** is defined as 'the difference between the value of a business as a whole and the aggregate of the fair values of its separable net assets'. Goodwill is therefore by definition incapable of realization separately from the business as a whole. Separable/identifiable net assets are the assets and liabilities of an entity that are capable of being disposed of or settled separately, without necessarily disposing of the business as a whole. Fair value is the amount at which an asset or liability could be exchanged in an arm's length transaction.

Where the value of a business as a whole exceeds the total value of its separable net assets this is described as **positive goodwill**. Where the value of a business as a whole is less than the total value of its separable net assets this is referred to as **negative goodwill**. This usually arises where a business is expected to make future losses because of a poor reputation, etc.

Most ongoing businesses are normally worth more as a going concern than is shown by the value of their net tangible assets. Otherwise it would probably be better to shut the business down and sell the separate assets. From this standpoint, goodwill may be said to represent the present value of the future profits accruing from an existing business. Thus, goodwill arises from a number of attributes that an ongoing business possesses, such as the following:

1 The prestige and reputation attaching to the name of a business or its products and thus the likelihood that present customers will continue to buy from the business in future (e.g. Rolls-Royce, Microsoft).
2 Existing contracts for the supply of goods in the future (e.g. construction, aerospace, defence equipment).
3 The location of the business premises (e.g. a newsagent next to a railway station) and other forms of captive customers (e.g. a milk distributor's clientele).
4 The possession of patents, trademarks, brand names and special technical knowledge arising from previous expenditure on advertising and research and development. However, some of these may be accounted for as separate assets.
5 The existence of known sources of supply of goods and services, including the availability of trade credit.
6 The existing staff, including particular management skills. The costs of recruiting and training present employees give rise to an asset that is not recorded in the balance sheet but nevertheless represents a valuable resource to the business. Furthermore, these costs would have to be incurred if a business were started from scratch.
7 Other set-up factors. An existing business has the advantage of having collected together the various items of equipment and other assets necessary for its operations. Obtaining and bringing together these assets usually involves delay and expense, and avoiding this is an advantage of an ongoing business.

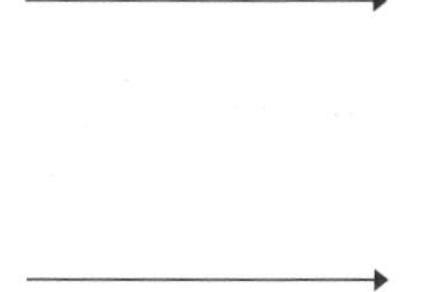

Goodwill is classified as either purchased or non-purchased. **Purchased goodwill** is defined in *FRS 10—Goodwill and Intangible Assets*[2] as 'the difference between the cost of an acquired entity and the aggregate of the fair values of that entity's identifiable assets and liabilities'. It thus essentially refers to the amount paid for goodwill when one business takes over another business. **Non-purchased goodwill** is defined in SSAP22 as 'any goodwill other than purchased goodwill'. It thus essentially refers to what is sometimes described as the inherent or internally generated goodwill of a business that has not been the subject of a takeover.

The recognition of goodwill in accounts

As explained above, all businesses possess either positive or negative goodwill. However, this may or may not be recorded in the books and thus appear on the balance sheet as an intangible fixed asset. FRS10, which superseded SSAP22, states that 'positive purchased goodwill should be capitalized and classified as an asset on the balance sheet'.[2] It specifically prohibits internally generated, i.e. non-purchased goodwill, being recognized as an asset. The main reason for this is that the valuation of non-purchased goodwill is regarded as highly subjective and thus contravenes the principle of reliability.

Although the accounts of sole traders and partnerships do not have to be prepared in accordance with accounting standards, it is nevertheless highly unlikely that these will include goodwill except possibly when another business has been purchased. In the case of a partnership this includes where a new partner is admitted or an existing partner retires or dies. The law states that in each instance the old partnership is dissolved, and thus effectively taken over by the new partnership. The accounts of the new partnership may therefore include goodwill acquired from the purchase of the old partnership. This is examined in detail later in the chapter.

The current established thinking is that the value of goodwill declines with the passage of time and therefore has a finite life. Thus, like most other fixed assets, when purchased goodwill is recorded in the accounts it should be amortized (i.e. depreciated) over its useful economic life. An alternative approach is to write it off immediately against the partners' capital (or reserves in the case of companies) at the time of purchase. This procedure will be described later. However, there is a school of thought that the value of goodwill can be perpetuated by, for example, expenditure on advertising and training, and thus has an infinite life. It is therefore sometimes argued that it is not necessary to amortize goodwill.

SSAP22 allowed companies to write off positive purchased goodwill against reserves. However, this is now prohibited by FRS10, which requires companies to amortize positive purchased goodwill over its useful economic life. FRS10 further states that 'there is a rebuttable presumption that the useful economic lives of purchased goodwill and intangible assets are limited to periods of 20 years or less. This presumption may be rebutted and a useful economic life regarded as a longer period or indefinite only if: (a) the durability of the acquired business or intangible asset can be demonstrated and justifies estimating the useful economic life to exceed 20 years; and (b) the goodwill or intangible asset is capable of continued measurement (so that annual impairment reviews will be feasible)'. In these circumstances positive purchased goodwill may be amortized over a useful economic life greater than 20 years, or if this is indefinite, should not be amortized. However, where this is the case an annual impairment review must be undertaken. In simple terms, this is essentially a revaluation to ensure that the value of goodwill has not been fallen below its book/carrying value.

Finally, FRS10 states that 'no residual value may be assigned to goodwill', and 'a straight-line method should be chosen unless another method can be demonstrated to be more appropriate'.

The valuation of goodwill

As explained previously, the cost of purchased goodwill is deemed to be the excess of the purchase price of a business over the market/fair value of its net assets. In the case of company accounts the value of goodwill is usually computed in precisely this manner. However, in the case of sole traders and partnerships the purchase price of a business is frequently arrived at by valuing the net tangible assets (often at market prices) and, as a separate item, goodwill. This is particularly common where a new partner is admitted or an existing partner leaves.

There are several methods of valuing goodwill. These reflect the customs/conventions of businesses generally and certain trades and professions in particular. It should be emphasized that in practice the amount arrived at using one of these methods is frequently regarded as a starting point in negotiating a final value for goodwill. The most common methods are as follows:

1 A given multiple of the annual turnover. The multiple is intended to represent the number of years' future sales that are likely to result from the goodwill presently attaching to the business. The turnover may be an estimate of future sales, or more likely an average of a given number of past periods. This method is common in the case of retail businesses and professional firms such as accountants and solicitors.

2 A given multiple of the annual profit. Again, the multiple is intended to represent the number of years' future profits that are likely to be generated from the existing goodwill. The annual profit may be either an estimate of the future profit or more likely an average of a given number of past years. The profits used in the computation may be those shown in the audited accounts or alternatively what is termed the **abnormal or super profit**. This refers to the profit shown in the accounts minus a notional charge for interest on capital and proprietors' salaries. It is essentially a hypothetical form of residual profit. The super profit is intended to represent the return from risking money in a business over and above what could be earned by depositing that money elsewhere at a fixed rate of interest and taking employment with a guaranteed salary. This method of valuing goodwill may be particularly appropriate in riskier industries with fluctuating profits, such as engineering and building construction.

3 The excess of the capitalized value of the (past or forecasted) annual (average) profit (or super profit) over the current (market) value of the net tangible assets of the business. The capitalized value is normally computed by multiplying the annual profit by the average price—earnings (P–E) ratio of similar size companies in the same industry whose shares are listed on the stock exchange. The capitalized value is intended to reflect the total value of the business as a going concern. This method may be most appropriate in the case of a large business that is not a company or whose shares are not quoted on a stock exchange.

The admission of a new partner and the treatment of goodwill

When a new partner is admitted to a partnership an adjustment to the old partners' capital accounts is necessary to recognize the value of goodwill which they have created and therefore belongs to them. The principle is exactly the same as with the revaluation of assets except that the goodwill has not previously been recorded in the books. There are three main ways of dealing with this, each of which is described below and illustrated using Example 25.4.

Example 25.4

A and B are in partnership sharing profits in the ratio 3 : 2. The balances on their capital accounts are: A £15,000 and B £20,000.

On 31 December 20X8 they decide to admit C as a partner who is to bring in £42,000 as her capital and receive half of all future profits. The old partners' profit-sharing ratio will continue to be 3 : 2.

Goodwill is to be calculated at twice the average super profits of the last three years. The super profits are after charging interest on capital of 5 per cent per annum and partners' salaries of £12,500 per annum each.

The profits transferred to the profit and loss appropriation account are as follows:

	£
Year ended 31/12/X6	28,560
Year ended 31/12/X7	29,980
Year ended 31/12/X8	32,210

The value to be ascribed to goodwill would first be calculated as follows:

Year ended	Net profits	Salaries	Interest on capital	Super profits
31/12/X6	28,560	25,000	1,750	1,810
X7	29,980	25,000	1,750	3,230
X8	32,210	25,000	1,750	5,460
				10,500

$$\text{Goodwill} = 2 \times \frac{£10{,}500}{3} = £7{,}000$$

Note that the new profit-sharing ratio will be A3 : B2 : C5. This can be explained thus: since C is to receive one-half of all future profits, A's share will be 3 divided by 3 + 2 multiplied by the remaining one-half, i.e. $\frac{3}{5} \times \frac{1}{2} = \frac{3}{10}$. Similarly, B's share will be $\frac{2}{5} \times \frac{1}{2} = \frac{2}{10}$. Thus, the new profit-sharing ratio is A $\frac{3}{10}$, B $\frac{2}{10}$ and C $\frac{5}{10}$, or A3 : B2 : C5.

The different methods of treating goodwill on the admission of a new partner can now be shown as follows.

Method 1

The value of goodwill is debited to a goodwill account and credited to the old partners' capital accounts in their old profit-sharing ratio. This method recognizes the existence of the previously unrecorded asset of goodwill by bringing it into the books. The goodwill is shared between the old partners in their old profit-sharing ratio because it is an asset created by the old partnership which thus belongs to the old partners.

Goodwill

20X8		
31 Dec	Capital A	4,200
31 Dec	Capital B	2,800
		7,000

Capital

		A	B	C
20X8				
31 Dec	Balance b/d	15,000	20,000	—
31 Dec	Bank	—	—	42,000
31 Dec	Goodwill	4,200	2,800	—

Method 2

Earlier in this chapter it was pointed out that goodwill should be amortized over its useful economic life, or alternatively written off against the partners' capital accounts. In Method 1 above the goodwill would be amortized. Method 2 is the alternative treatment. The value of goodwill is first debited to a goodwill account and credited to the old partners' capital accounts in their old profit-sharing ratio (as in Method 1). Then the goodwill is written off by crediting the goodwill account and debiting all the partners in the new partnership in their new profit-sharing ratio. The debit to the partners' capital accounts is in their new profit-sharing ratio because the writing off of goodwill effectively amounts to recognizing a (paper) loss that would otherwise have been charged to future years' profit and loss accounts (as the amortization of goodwill) and thus shared between the new partners in their new profit-sharing ratio.

Goodwill

20X8			20X8		
31 Dec	Capital A	4,200	31 Dec	Capital A	2,100
31 Dec	Capital B	2,800	31 Dec	Capital B	1,400
			31 Dec	Capital C	3,500
		7,000			7,000

Capital

		A	B	C			A	B	C
20X8					20X8				
31 Dec	Goodwill	2,100	1,400	3,500	31 Dec	Balance b/d	15,000	20,000	—
					31 Dec	Bank	—	—	42,000
					31 Dec	Goodwill	4,200	2,800	—

The entries in the goodwill account are a waste of time and paper, and thus Method 2 normally involves only the two sets of entries for goodwill on each side of the partners' capital accounts. Note that this method should be used when you are told that no account for goodwill is to be kept/maintained in the books or that goodwill is not to be recorded in the books.

It should also be observed that this method has the effect of charging the new partner with what is referred to as a premium of £3,500, in that her capital introduced has been reduced by £3,500. This premium represents the purchase by the new partner of her share of goodwill, i.e. $\frac{1}{2}$ of £7,000 = £3,500. She will get this back when the goodwill is eventually realized (if the business is sold) or she leaves.

Method 3

This method is essentially a further shortcutting of Method 2. The net effects of the entries for goodwill in the partners' capital accounts in Method 2 are: C is debited with £3,500; A is credited with £4,200 – £2,100 = £2,100; and B is credited with £2,800 – £1,400 = £1,400. Method 3 consists of simply entering in the partners' capital accounts these net effects, which are referred to as a premium contra. The amount of the premium is debited to the new partners' capital account and credited to the old partners' capital accounts in their old profit-sharing ratio: A $\frac{3}{5} \times$ £3,500 = £2,100 and B $\frac{2}{5} \times$ £3,500 = £1,400.

Capital

		A	B	C			A	B	C
20X8					20X8				
31 Dec	Premium	—	—	3,500	31 Dec	Balance b/d	15,000	20,000	—
					31 Dec	Bank	—	—	42,000
					31 Dec	Premium	2,100	1,400	—

This method should normally only be used where you are told that the new partner is to pay a premium representing the purchase of his or her share of goodwill. The premium is usually given but can be calculated from the goodwill. In this example the premium can be calculated as $\frac{1}{2} \times £7{,}000 = £3{,}500$. The ledger entries would be as shown immediately above. It must be emphasized that this method only gives a correct answer where the old partners share profits (and losses) in the new partnership in the same ratio as the old partnership. If this is not the case, Method 2 must be used instead.

Sometimes it is not possible to compute the premium from the figure of goodwill because the partners have not agreed a method of valuation for goodwill. Instead, you may be told something along the lines that the new partner receives an interest in the new partnership equity/assets which is less than the amount he or she is to invest/pay into the firm. Using the data in Example 25.4 this can be illustrated as follows. C is to be admitted as a partner with a one-half interest in both capital and profits in exchange for £42,000. C's interest in the capital/assets is computed as follows:

	£
Capital/assets/equity of old partnership (£15,000 + £20,000)	35,000
Investment by C	42,000
Capital/assets/equity of new partnership	77,000
C's share of equity of new partnership ($\frac{1}{2} \times £77{,}000$)	38,500

The premium which C is being charged is therefore £42,000 – £38,500 = £3,500. The ledger entries will be similar to those in Method 3. However, these can be shortened to the following:

Journal

		£	£
Bank	Dr	42,000	
Capital—C			38,500
Capital—A			2,100
Capital—B			1,400
		42,000	42,000

Remember that this method only gives the correct answer where the old partners continue to share profits in the same ratio. If this is not the case Method 2 must be used, which will require a notional figure for goodwill to be computed by multiplying the premium by the inverse of the new partner profit-sharing ratio (i.e. $£3{,}500 \times \frac{2}{1} = £7{,}000$).

Finally, it should be mentioned that it is possible for the new partner to receive an interest greater than the amount he or she is to invest. This results in a negative premium, sometimes referred to as a bonus, and negative goodwill.

An outgoing partner and the treatment of goodwill

When a partner leaves, the balances on his or her capital and current accounts are repaid. However, it is necessary first to make an adjustment to the partners' capital accounts in recognition of the value of goodwill that has been created, some of which belongs to the outgoing partner. There are three main ways of dealing with this, which correspond to Methods 1 to 3, respectively, of treating goodwill on the admission of a new partner.

1 The value of goodwill is debited to a goodwill account and credited to the old partners' capital accounts in their old profit-sharing ratio.
2 The value of goodwill is credited to the old partners' capital accounts in their old profit-sharing ratio and debited to the remaining partners' capital accounts in their new profit-sharing ratio. This effectively results in the remaining partners purchasing the outgoing partners' share of goodwill. No goodwill account is maintained in the books.
3 The outgoing partner's share of goodwill is credited to his or her capital account and debited to the remaining partners' capital accounts in their new profit-sharing ratio. Again, no goodwill account is maintained in the books. This method only gives a correct answer where the remaining partners share profits in the new partnership in the same ratio as the old partnership. If this is not the case, Method 2 must be used instead.

Sometimes it is not possible to compute the outgoing partner's share of goodwill from the figure of goodwill, because the partners have not agreed a method of valuation for goodwill. Instead, you may be told something along the lines that the outgoing partner is to receive more than the balance of his or her capital account. This excess is the outgoing partner's share of goodwill. If necessary, a notional figure for goodwill can be computed by multiplying this excess by the inverse of the outgoing partner's profit-sharing ratio.

Incoming and outgoing partners and goodwill

We have thus far dealt with the revaluation of assets on changes in partners and the treatment of goodwill where there is either an incoming or outgoing partner. The final step is to combine all of these and examine the situation where there is both an incoming and outgoing partner. This is a fairly simple step since the treatment of goodwill involves exactly the same principles whether there is an incoming or outgoing partner. An illustration is given in Example 25.5.

Example 25.5

Beech and Oak are in partnership, sharing profits and losses in the ratio 3 : 5, respectively. The balance sheet drawn up on 31 December 20X9 showed the following position:

	£		£	£
Capital accounts		*Fixed assets*		
Beech	11,000	Premises	16,000	
Oak	14,000	Fixtures	6,000	22,000
	25,000	*Current assets*		
Creditors	9,000	Stock	4,000	
		Debtors	3,000	
		Cash	5,000	12,000
	34,000			34,000

Beech retired as from 1 January 20X0 and at the same date Maple was admitted to the partnership. For the purpose of these changes, the premises were revalued at £19,500, fixtures at £4,500, stock at £5,800 and goodwill was agreed at £10,000. A provision for bad debts of £200 is also to be created. The new valuations are to be included in the business books but no account for goodwill is to be maintained. In the new partnership, profits and losses will be divided in the proportions 3 : 2 between Oak and Maple, respectively. Maple, will introduce cash of £15,000 and Beech is to receive payment for his capital in cash, but no other cash is to change hands between partners in implementing the change.

You are required to show the above changes in the revaluation account and the partners' capital accounts.

Revaluation account

Fixtures		1,500	Premises	3,500
Provision for bad debts		200	Stock	1,800
Profit on revaluation—				
Beech	1,350			
Oak	2,250	3,600		
		5,300		5,300

Capital accounts

	Beech	*Oak*	*Maple*		*Beech*	*Oak*	*Maple*
Goodwill contra	—	6,000	4 000	Balance b/d	11,000	14,000	
Cash	16,100	—	—	Profit on			
Balance c/d	—	16,500	11,000	revaluation	1,350	2,250	—
				Goodwill contra	3,750	6,250	—
				Cash	—	—	15,000
	16,100	22,500	15,000		16,100	22,500	15,000

Notes

1 The double entry for the items in the revaluation account will be in the respective asset accounts and the provision for bad debts account.

2 The goodwill is credited to the old partners' capital accounts in their old profit-sharing ratio (Beech $\frac{3}{8} \times$ £10,000 = £3,750; Oak $\frac{5}{8} \times$ £10,000 = £6,250) and debited to the new partners' capital accounts in their new profit-sharing ratio (Oak $\frac{3}{5} \times$ £10,000 = £6,000; Maple $\frac{2}{5} \times$ £10,000 = £4,000).

3 The cash paid to Beech of £16,100 is the balance on his capital account after the revaluation of assets and adjustments for goodwill.

Changes in partners' profit-sharing ratio

Sometimes partners decide to change the proportions in which they share profits and losses. This may occur when the partners agree that one partner is to spend more (or less) time on partnership business, or alternatively one partner's skills have become more (or less) valuable to the partnership.

If a change in the profit-sharing ratio occurs at some time during the accounting year, it will be necessary to divide the profit before appropriations into the periods before and after the change. This is usually done on a time basis. The interest on capital and on drawings, salaries and shares of residual profit are then computed for each period separately. It should be noted that this procedure is the same as when a new partner is admitted and/or a partner leaves during the accounting year.

When there is a change in the profit-sharing ratio it is also necessary to revalue the assets, including goodwill. As in the case of changes in partners, the profit or loss on revaluation is computed in a revaluation account and transferred to the partners' capital accounts. An adjustment must also be made in respect of goodwill, using the principles already described. A simple illustration is given in Example 25.6 and a more complicated version is shown in Example 25.7.

Example 25.6

X and Y are in partnership sharing profits and losses equally. They have decided that as from 1 October 20X5 the profit-sharing ratio is to become X three-fifths and Y two-fifths.

The accounts are made up to 31 December each year. The profit for the year ended 31 December 20X5 was £60,000. The balance sheet at 31 December 20X5 prior to sharing profits is as follows:

	£
Net assets	210,000
Capital X	80,000
Capital Y	70,000
Profit for the year	60,000
	210,000

It was decided that the impact of the change in profit-sharing ratio on each partner's share of the assets would be effected at 31 December 20X5 when the net assets were valued at £250,000. The goodwill was valued at £25,000 but no goodwill account is to be maintained in the books.

You are required to show the entries in the partners' capital accounts and a balance sheet at 31 December 20X5.

Distribution of profit 20X5

	£ *Total*	£ *1 Jan–30 Sep*	£ *1 Oct–31 Dec*
Profit for the year apportioned on a time basis	60,000	45,000	15,000
Shares of profit—X	31,500	22,500	9,000
—Y	28,500	22,500	6,000
	60,000	45,000	15,000

Revaluation account

Profit on revaluation—			Net assets	40,000
Capital X	20,000		(250,000 – 210,000)	
Capital Y	20,000	40,000		
		40,000		40,000

Capital accounts

	X	Y		X	Y
Goodwill contra	15,000	10,000	Balance b/d	80,000	70,000
Balance c/d	129,000	121,000	Shares of profit	31,500	28,500
			Profit on revaluation	20,000	20,000
			Goodwill contra	12,500	12,500
	144,000	131,000		144,000	131,000
			Balance b/d	129,000	121,000

X and Y
Balance sheet as at 31 December 20X5

	£
Net assets	250,000
Capital X	129,000
Capital Y	121,000
	250,000

Example 25.7

Hill and Dale are in partnership sharing profits and losses Hill 3/5 and Dale 2/5 after giving each partner 8 per cent pa interest on capital and annual salaries of £28,000 to Hill and £18,000 to Dale.

They have decided that as from 1 July 20X8 the profits and losses will be shared equally after giving each partner 10 per cent pa interest on capital and annual salaries of £32,000 to Hill and £30,000 to Dale.

The accounts are made up to the 31 December of each year. The profit for the year ended 31 December 20X8 was £150,000 and this is believed to have accrued evenly over the year. The following is the balance sheet at 31 December 20X8 before the appropriation of the profit between the partners and any other entries relating to the change in the partners' profit-sharing ratio:

	£000	£000
Freehold land and buildings at cost		600
Stock		105
Trade debtors		45
Bank		25
		775
Less: trade creditors		35
		740
Capital accounts:		
Hill		300
Dale		250
		550
Current accounts:		
Hill	26	
Dale	14	40
Net profit for the year		150
		740

The above balances on the partners' capital accounts and the land and buildings account are as at 31 December 20X7.

On 1 July 20X8 the freehold land and buildings were revalued at £650,000. The partners have also agreed that the book values of the other assets and liabilities at 1 July 20X8 were their current net realizable values. The goodwill at 1 July 20X8 was valued at £100,000 but no goodwill account is to be maintained in the books.

You are required to prepare:

a The partners' capital accounts as at 1 July 20X8 showing the effects of the change in the partners' profit-sharing ratio on their claims on the partnership assets.
b A profit and loss appropriation account for the year ended 31 December 20X8.
c A balance sheet as at 31 December 20X8 showing all the entries in the partners' current accounts after giving effect to the change in the partners' profit-sharing ratio.

a

Capital accounts

	Hill	Dale		Hill	Dale
	£000	£000		£000	£000
Goodwill	50	50	Balance b/d	300	250
Balance c/d	340	260	Profit on revaluation		
			£(650k – 600k)	30	20
			Goodwill	60	40
	390	310		390	310
			Balance b/d	340	260

b

Workings

	Hill	Dale
	£000	£000
From 1 Jan to 30 June 20X8:		
Salaries		
6/12 × £28k	14	
6/12 × £18k		9
Interest on capital		
6/12 × 8 per cent × £300k	12	
6/12 × 8 per cent × £250k		10
From 1 July to 31 Dec 20X8:		
Salaries		
6/12 × £32k	16	
6/12 × £30k		15
Interest on capital		
6/12 × 10 per cent × £340k	17	
6/12 × 10 per cent × £260k		13

Hill and Dale

Profit and loss appropriation account for the year ended 31 December 20X8

	Total	1 Jan to 30 June		1 July to 31 Dec	
	£000	£000	£000	£000	£000
Net profit for the year	150		75		75
Less: salaries					
Hill	30	14		16	
Dale	24	9		15	
	54	23		31	

Less: interest on capital					
Hill	29	12		17	
Dale	23	10		13	
	52	22		30	
	106		45		61
Residual profit	44		30		14
Shares of residual profit:					
Hill	25		18		7
Dale	19		12		7
	44		30		14

c

Hill and Dale

Balance sheet as at 31 December 20X8

	£000	£000	£000
Fixed assets			
Freehold land and buildings			650
Current assets			
Stock		105	
Trade debtors		45	
Bank		25	
		175	
Less: current liabilities			
Trade creditors		35	
Net current assets			140
Net assets			790
	Hill	*Dale*	*Total*
Capital accounts	340	260	600
Current accounts:			
Balance at 1 Jan 20X8	26	14	
Add: salaries	30	24	
interest on capital	29	23	
shares of residual profit	25	19	
Balance at 31 Dec 20X8	110	80	190
	450	340	790

Notes

1 The requirements in part a of the example, to prepare the partners' capital accounts, are not always explicitly required by examination questions. However, it is always necessary in these circumstances and, where there is interest on capital, will need to be done first.

2 Then the profit and loss appropriation accounts for the periods prior to and after the change in the partners' profit-sharing ratio are prepared. These could be done as two separate accounts but it is quicker and easier to show them in columnar form, as in the above answer. Each partner's salary, interest on capital and share of residual profit for the year shown in the total column of the profit and loss appropriation account is found by simply adding together the respective amounts for each of the periods prior to and after the change in profit sharing ratio.

Dissolution of partnerships

As explained at the start of this chapter, when a partner leaves and/or a new partner is admitted the law states that the old partnership is dissolved and a new partnership is created. However, the phrase '*dissolution* of partnerships' refers to the circumstances where all the partners wish to leave, and thus the activities of the partnership are wound up without a new partnership being created. Partnerships are usually dissolved because either it is unprofitable to carry on trading or the partners no longer wish to be associated with each other for personal reasons.

Accounting for the dissolution of partnerships can be quite complicated when the assets are disposed of over a prolonged period, known as the piecemeal realization of assets, and/or one or more of the partners is insolvent, which may involve the application of the ***Garner v. Murray*** rule described in the previous section on the revaluation of assets. However, these circumstances are not usually examined at the foundation level, and are thus beyond the scope of this book. The basic model of accounting for the dissolution of partnerships is relatively simple, at least after having grasped the previous contents of this chapter.

The chronological sequence of events on the dissolution of partnerships is as follows:

1 Prepare a set of final accounts from the end of the previous accounting year to the date of dissolution, including the usual entries in the partners' current accounts. These will be no different from the usual final accounts apart from relating to a period of less than one year.
2 The assets will be disposed of usually by sale (although some may be taken over by the partners) and the money collected from debtors.
3 The liabilities are repaid in the order trade creditors, loans and then any partners' loans.
4 The balances on the partners' capital (and current) accounts are paid to them.

At the foundation stage examinations the simplifying assumption is usually made that all of the above events occur on the date of dissolution or within a short period thereafter.

The simplest and a perfectly acceptable way of accounting for a dissolution is to transfer *all* of the balances on the asset (except for bank/cash), liability and provision accounts to a realization account. Then, all the money received from the sale of assets (including that collected from debtors) and paid to trade and loan creditors is entered in this account. If any assets (or liabilities) are taken over by the partners, the value placed on these will be entered in the realization account with a double entry to the relevant partners' capital accounts.

However, since liabilities such as trade creditors and loans are technically not realized, some accountants do not enter these in the realization account. Instead, the amounts paid are entered in the relevant liability accounts, and any difference between the book values and amounts paid, such as discount received, are transferred to the realization account.

This highlights an important feature of the realization account concerning its purpose, and brings us to the next stage in the accounting procedure. The realization account performs a similar function to the revaluation account except that instead of being used to determine the profit or loss on revaluation, it is used to ascertain the profit or loss on dissolution. This is then transferred to the partners' capital accounts in their profit-sharing ratio.

Finally, the balances on the partners' current accounts are transferred to their capital accounts, and the resulting balances on the capital accounts are paid to the partners. This will eliminate the balance on the bank and cash accounts, leaving all the ledger accounts now closed. One last complication arises if the resulting balance on any of the partners' capital accounts, before repaying the partners, is a debit balance. At the foundation level students are usually expected to assume that the partner is solvent and thus will pay to the partnership any debit balance on his or her capital account. This should then provide enough money with which to repay the other partners the credit balances on their capital accounts.

An illustration of accounting for the dissolution of partnerships is given in Example 25.8.

Example 25.8

Tom and Jerry, whose accounting year end is 31 December, have been in partnership for several years sharing profits equally. They have decided to dissolve the partnership as on 14 February 20X9. You have already prepared a profit and loss account for the period 1 January 20X9 to 14 February 20X9 and a balance sheet as at the latter date as follows:

	£	£	£
Motor vehicles			20,000
Less: provision for depreciation			6,600
			13,400
Stock		6,700	
Trade debtors	5,900		
Less: provision for bad debts	600	5,300	
Prepaid expenses		500	12,500
			25,900
Less: liabilities			
Trade creditors		3,200	
Bank overdraft		1,600	
Bank loan		2,000	
Loan—Tom		4,000	10,800
			15,100
Capital—Tom			8,000
—Jerry			4,200
			12,200
Current accounts—Tom		4,800	
—Jerry		(1,900)	
			2,900
			15,100

One of the motor vehicles was taken over by Jerry at an agreed valuation of £5,700. The remainder were sold for £6,200. The stock realized £7,100 and £4,900 was received from trade debtors. A refund of the full amount of prepaid expenses was also received.

There were selling expenses in respect of advertising the vehicles and stock for sale of £800. Trade creditors were paid £2,900 in full settlement. The bank loan was repaid, including an interest penalty for early settlement of £400.

The partnership also sold its business name and a list of its customers to a competitor for £1,000.

You are required to show all the ledger entries necessary to close the partnership books.

Motor vehicles

Balance b/d	20,000	Realization	20,000

Provision for depreciation

Realization	6,600	Balance b/d	6,600

Stock

Balance b/d	6,700	Realization	6,700

Trade debtors

Balance b/d	5,900	Realization	5,900

Provision for bad debts

Realization	600	Balance b/d	600

Prepaid expenses

Balance b/d	500	Realization	500

Trade creditors

Bank	2,900	Balance b/d	3,200
Realization	300		
	3,200		3,200

Bank loan

Bank	2,400	Balance b/d	2,000
		Realization	400
	2,400		2,400

Loan—Tom

Bank	4,000	Balance b/d	4,000

Realization account

Vehicles	20,000	Prov. for depn		6,600
Stock	6,700	Prov. for bad debts		600
Trade debtors	5,900	Bank—vehicles		6,200
Prepaid expenses	500	Bank—stock		7,100
Loan interest	400	Bank—debtors		4,900
Bank—expenses	800	Bank—prepayments		500
		Bank—goodwill		1,000
		Trade creditors		300
		Capital—Jerry		5,700
		Loss on realization—		
		Capital Tom	700	
		Capital Jerry	700	1,400
	34,300			34,300

Current accounts

	Tom	*Jerry*		*Tom*	*Jerry*
Balance b/d	—	1,900	Balance b/d	4,800	—
Capital	4,800	—	Capital	—	1,900
	4,800	1,900		4,800	1,900

Capital accounts

	Tom	*Jerry*		*Tom*	*Jerry*
Current a/c	—	1,900	Balance b/d	8,000	4,200
Realization—vehicle	—	5,700	Current a/c	4,800	—
Loss on realization	700	700	Bank	—	4,100
Bank	12,100				
	12,800	8,300		12,800	8,300

Bank

Realization—		Balance b/d	1,600
vehicles	6,200	Trade creditors	2,900
stock	7,100	Bank loan	2,400
debtors	4,900	Realization—	
prepayments	500	expenses	800
goodwill	1,000	Loan—Tom	4,000
Capital—Jerry	4,100	Capital—Tom	12,100
	23,800		23,800

Summary

When a new partner is admitted to a partnership, an existing partner leaves, or there is a change in the profit-sharing ratio, it is usually necessary to revalue all the assets and liabilities. This ensures that the existing/old partners receive their share of the unrealized holding gains (and losses) which arose prior to the change.

When the assets are revalued it is also usually necessary to make certain adjustments to the partners' capital accounts in respect of goodwill. This is defined in SSAP22 as 'the difference between the value of a business as a whole and the aggregate of the fair values of its separable net assets'. In the case of partnerships, goodwill is normally valued as a given multiple of the annual sales or profits. When there is a change of partners, goodwill is brought into the books by debiting a goodwill account and crediting the capital accounts of the existing/old partners in their old profit-sharing ratio. The goodwill must either be amortized over its useful economic life, or alternatively, written off against the new partners' capital accounts in their profit-sharing ratio. This latter treatment can be short-cut by means of adjusting entries on both sides of the partners' capital accounts.

Subsequent to the revaluation of assets and goodwill adjustments, when a new partner is admitted, the capital introduced is credited to his or her capital account. When a partner leaves, the balance on this partner's capital, current and any loan account is transferred to a new loan account, which is repaid in due course.

When a partnership's activities cease there is a dissolution of the partnership. All the assets are realized and the liabilities paid. Any profit or loss on realization is ascertained via a realization account and transferred to the partners' capital accounts. The balances on the partners' capital and current accounts are then repaid.

Key terms and concepts

Abnormal profit (336)
Garner v. Murray (333)
goodwill (333)
negative goodwill (333)
non-purchased goodwill (334)
positive goodwill (334)
purchased goodwill (333)
revaluation (331)
super profit (336)
unrealized holding gains/losses (331)

References

1. Accounting Standards Committee (1989). *Statement of Standard Accounting Practice 22—Accounting for Goodwill* (ICAEW).
2. Accounting Standards Board (1997). *Financial Reporting Standard 10—Goodwill and Intangible Assets* (ASB).

Review questions

25.1 **a** Explain the nature of goodwill.
b Describe the business attributes that are thought to give rise to goodwill.

25.2 **a** What is the difference between positive and negative goodwill?
b What is the difference between purchased goodwill and non-purchased goodwill?

25.3 **a** Explain the circumstances in which goodwill might appear in the books of a partnership.
b Describe how it would be treated in the balance sheet.

25.4 A member of the board of Shoprite Enterprises plc has suggested two accounting policies for consideration by the financial director in preparing the latest set of accounts. These have been summarized as follows:

i The incorporation of goodwill in the accounts as a permanent fixed asset in recognition of the favourable trading situations of several of the business's outlets and also to reflect the quality of management experience in the business.
ii No depreciation to be provided in future on the buildings owned by the company, because their market value is constantly appreciating and, in addition, this will result in an increase in the profit of the company.

Required:

a Briefly explain your understanding of each of the following:
  i goodwill;
  ii depreciation.
b Discuss the acceptability of each of the above suggested accounting policies, highlighting any conflict with accounting concepts and standards. (AEB)

25.5 Describe three different methods of valuing goodwill where the purchase price is unknown.

Exercises

An asterisk after the question number indicates that there is a suggested answer in the Appendix.

25.6 **Level I**

Al and Bert are in partnership, sharing profits equally. At 30 June, they have balances on their capital accounts of £12,000 (Al) and £15,000 (Bert). On that day they agree to bring in their friend Hall as a third partner. All three partners are to share profits equally from now on. Hall is to introduce £20,000 as capital into the business. Goodwill on 30 June is agreed at £18,000.

Required:

a Show the partners' capital accounts for 30 June and 1 July on the assumption that the goodwill, previously unrecorded, is to be included in the accounts.

b Show the additional entries necessary to eliminate goodwill again from the accounts.

c Explain briefly what goodwill is. Why are adjustments necessary when a new partner joins a partnership? (ACCA)

25.7* **Level I**

Brown and Jones are in partnership, sharing profits and losses equally. The balance sheet drawn up on 31 March 20X5 showed the following position:

	£		£	£
Capital accounts		*Fixed assets*		
Brown	110,000	Premises	80,000	
Jones	87,000	Fixtures	60,000	140,000
	197,000	*Current assets*		
Sundry creditors	98,000	Stock	40,000	
		Debtors	30,000	
		Cash	85,000	155,000
	295,000			295,000

Brown retired as from 1 April 20X5 and at the same date Smith was admitted to the partnership. For the purpose of these changes, the premises were revalued at £115,000, fixtures at £68,000, stock at £36,000 and goodwill was agreed at £90,000. A provision for bad debts of £3,000 is also to be created. The new valuations are to be included in the business accounts, but no account for goodwill is to be maintained. In the new partnership, profits and losses will be divided in the proportion 3 : 2 between Jones and Smith, respectively. Smith will introduce cash of £100,000 and Brown is to receive payment for his capital in cash but no other cash is to change hands between partners in implementing the change.

You are required to show the above changes in the revaluation account and partners' capital accounts.

25.8* **Level II**

Blackburn, Percy and Nelson are in partnership sharing profits equally. On 1 January 20X9 Nelson retired and Logan was admitted as a partner. Nelson has agreed to leave the amounts owing to her in the business as a loan until 31 December 20X9. Logan is to contribute £6,000 as capital. Future profits are to be shared, Blackburn one-half and Percy and Logan one-quarter each.

A goodwill account is to be opened and kept in the books. The goodwill should be valued at the difference between the capitalized value of the estimated super profits for the forthcoming year and the net asset value of the partnership at 31 December 20X8 after revaluing the assets. The capitalized value of the expected super profits is to be computed using the price–earnings ratio, which for this type of business is estimated as 8. The super profits are after deducting notional partners' salaries but not interest on capital. The net profit for 20X9 is estimated as £48,750 and it is thought that the partners could each earn £15,000 a year if they were employed elsewhere.

The balance sheet at 31 December 20X8 was as follows:

	£	£		£	£	£
Capital			*Fixed assets*	*Cost*	*Depn*	*WDV*
Blackburn		10,000	Plant	9,000	2,200	6,800
Percy		8,000	Vehicles	7,000	1,800	5,200
Nelson		5,000				
		23,000		16,000	4,000	12,000
Current accounts			*Current assets*			
Blackburn	1,300		Stock		9,200	
Percy	1,900		Debtors		6,300	
Nelson	1,400	4,600	Cash		2,600	18,100
Current liabilities						
Creditors		2,500				
		30,100				30,100

It was decided that stock is to be valued at £8,000 and vehicles at £6,700. Of the trade debtors £900 are considered doubtful debts.

You are required to show the ledger entries relating to the above revaluation and change of partners.

25.9 Level II

Gupta, Richards and Jones are in partnership sharing profits and losses in the ratio 5 : 4 : 3. On 1 January 20X0 Richards retired from the partnership and it was agreed that Singh should join the partnership, paying a sum of £30,000. From this date, profits are to be shared equally between the three partners and, in view of this, Jones agrees to pay a further £10,000 into the partnership as capital.

The balance sheet at 31 December 20X9 showed:

	£	£
Fixed assets		
Property		60,000
Fixtures		30,000
		90,000
Current assets		
Stock	30,000	
Debtors	15,000	
Bank	5,000	
	50,000	
Creditors	10,000	40,000
		130,000
Capital accounts		
Gupta	60,000	
Richards	40,000	
Jones	25,000	
		125,000

Current accounts		
Gupta	1,000	
Richards	2,500	
Jones	1,500	5,000
		130,000

It was agreed that in preparing a revised opening balance sheet of the partnership on 1 January 20X0 the following adjustments should be made:

1 Property is to be revalued at £70,000 and fixtures are to be revalued at £32,000.
2 Stock is considered to be shown at a fair value in the accounts. A provision for doubtful debts of £1,200 is required.
3 Professional fees of £600 relating to the change in partnership structure are to be regarded as an expense of the year to 31 December 20X9, but were not included in the profit and loss account of that year. They are expected to be paid in March 20X0.
4 Goodwill of the partnership as at 31 December 20X9 is estimated at £30,000. No account for goodwill is to be entered in the books, but appropriate adjustments are to be made in the partners' capital accounts.
5 On retirement, Richards is to be paid a sum of £40,000. The balance owing to her will be recorded in a loan account carrying interest of 12 per cent, to be repaid in full after two years.
6 All balances on current accounts are to be transferred to capital accounts. All balances on capital accounts in excess of £20,000 after this transfer are to be transferred to loan accounts carrying interest at 12 per cent.

You are required to:

a compute the balances on the loan accounts of Richards and the new partners on 1 January 20X0, following completion of these arrangements;
b prepare an opening balance sheet for the partnership on 1 January 20X0, following completion of these arrangements;
c explain briefly *three* factors to be taken into account when establishing profit sharing arrangements between partners. (JMB adapted)

25.10 Level II

Street, Rhode and Close carried on business in partnership sharing profits and losses, Street $\frac{5}{12}$, Rhode $\frac{4}{12}$ and Close $\frac{3}{12}$.

Their draft balance sheet as on 31 March 20X9 was as follows:

	£	£		£	£
Capital accounts			*Leasehold premises*	8,000	
Street	8,500		*Less*: Amount written off	800	7,200
Rhode	6,000		Plant and machinery		
Close	4,500		at cost	9,200	
		19,000	*Less*: Provision for depn	2,700	6,500
Current accounts					
Street	850		Stock on hand		5,400
Rhode	1,300		Sundry debtors	4,200	
Close	1,150		*Less*: Provision for		
		3,300	doubtful debts	750	3,450

Loan: Street	4,000	Cash at bank	8,000
Sundry creditors	4,250		
	£30,550		£30,550

Street retired from the partnership on 31 March 20X9 and Rhode and Close decided to carry on the business and to admit Lane as a partner who is to bring in capital of £10,000. Future profits are to be shared equally among Rhode, Close and Lane.

By agreement, the following adjustments were to be incorporated in the books of account as at 31 March 20X9:

1 Plant and machinery to be increased to £6,900, in accordance with a valuer's certificate.
2 Stock to be reduced to £4,860, since some items included therein were regarded as unsaleable.
3 The provision for doubtful debts to be increased to £830.
4 Provision to be made for the valuer's charges, £140.

The partnership deed provided that on the retirement of a partner the value of goodwill was to be taken to be an amount equal to the average annual profit of the three years ending on the date of retirement. The profits of such three years were:

Year ended 31 Mar 20X7 £7,800
Year ended 31 Mar 20X8 £9,400
Year ended 31 Mar 20X9 £11,600

The partners agreed that, in respect of the valuing of goodwill, the profits should be regarded as not being affected by the revaluation. It was decided that an account for goodwill should not be opened in the books, but that the transactions between the partners should be made through their capital accounts.

£3,000 was repaid to Street on 1 April 20X9 and she agreed to leave £12,000 as a loan to the new partnership. Rhode, Close and Lane promised to repay the balance remaining due to Street within six months.

You are required to prepare:

a the revaluation account;
b the partners' capital accounts (in columnar form);
c Street's account showing the balance due to her; and
d the balance sheet of Rhode, Close and Lane as on 1 April 20X9.

(ACCA adapted)

25.11 Level II

Matthew, Mark and Luke were in partnership sharing profits and losses in the ratio 5 : 3 : 2, accounts being made up annually to 30 June. Fixed capitals were to bear interest at the rate of 5 per cent per annum, but no interest was to be allowed or received on current accounts or drawings. Any balance on current accounts was to be paid at each year end.

Luke left the partnership on 30 September 20X6, but agreed to leave his money in the business until a new partner was admitted, provided interest at 5 per cent was paid on all amounts due to him.

John was admitted to the partnership on 1 January 20X7, providing capital of £2,000. It was agreed that the new profit-sharing ratio be Matthew 5, Mark 4, John 1, but Mark was to guarantee John an income of £3,000 per annum in addition to his interest on capital.

At 1 July 20X6 each partner had a fixed capital of £4,000.

Drawings during the year 20X6/20X7 were as follows:

Matthew	£750
Mark	£600
Luke	£220 (to 30 Sep 20X6)
John	£80

The profit for the year to 30 June 20X7 was £20,000, which may be assumed to have accrued evenly over that period.

You are required to show:

a the profit and loss appropriation account; and
b the partners' current accounts for the year ended 30 June 20X7. (ACCA)

25.12 Level II

Hawthorn and Privet have carried on business in partnership for a number of years, sharing profits in the ratio of 4 : 3 after charging interest on capital at 4 per cent per annum. Holly was admitted into the partnership on 1 October 20X4, and the terms of the partnership from then were agreed as follows:

1 Partners' annual salaries to be: Hawthorn £1,800, Privet £1,200, Holly £1,100.
2 Interest on capital to be charged at 4 per cent per annum.
3 Profits to be shared: Hawthorn four-ninths, Privet three-ninths, Holly two-ninths.

On 1 October 20X4, Holly paid £7,000 into the partnership bank and of this amount £2,100 was in respect of the share of goodwill acquired by her. Since the partnership has never created, and does not intend to create, a goodwill account, the full amount of £7,000 was credited for the time being to Holly's capital account at 1 October 20X4.

The trial balance of the partnership at 30 June 20X5 was as follows:

	Dr	Cr
	£	£
Cash at bank	3,500	
Stock at 1 July 20X4	11,320	
Purchases	102,630	
Sales		123,300
Wages and salaries	6,200	
Rates, telephone, lighting and heating	2,100	
Printing, stationery and postage	530	
General expenses	1,600	
Bad debts written off	294	
Capital accounts: Hawthorn		22,000
Privet		11,000
Holly		7,000
Current accounts: Hawthorn	2,200	
Privet	1,100	
Holly	740	
Debtors and creditors	27,480	13,744
Freehold premises	12,000	
Furniture, fixtures and fittings at 1 July 20X4	5,800	
Bad debts reserve		450
	£177,494	£177,494

After taking into account the following information and the adjustment required for goodwill, prepare trading and profit and loss accounts for the year ended 30 June 20X5, and a balance sheet as on that date. On 30 June 20X5:

1 Stock was £15,000.
2 Rates (£110) and wages and salaries (£300) were outstanding.
3 Telephone rental paid in advance was £9.
4 Provision for bad debts is to be adjusted to $2\frac{1}{2}$ per cent of debtors.
5 Depreciation is to be provided on furniture, fixtures and fittings at 10 per cent. Apportionments required are to be made on a time basis. (ACCA)

25.13 Level II

Alpha, Beta and Gamma were in partnership for many years sharing profits and losses in the ratio 5 : 3 : 2 and making up their accounts to 31 December each year. Alpha died on 31 December 20X7, and the partnership was dissolved as from that date.

The partnership balance sheet at 31 December 20X7 was as follows:

Alpha, Beta and Gamma
Balance sheet as at 31 December 20X7

	Cost	*Aggregate depreciation*	*Net book Value*
	£	£	£
Fixed assets			
Freehold land and buildings	350,000	50,000	300,000
Plant and machinery	220,000	104,100	115,900
Motor vehicles	98,500	39,900	58,600
	668,500	194,000	474,500
Current assets			
Stock		110,600	
Trade and sundry debtors		89,400	
Cash at bank		12,600	
		212,600	
Less:			
Current liabilities—trade and sundry creditors		118,400	94,200
			568,700
Less:			
Long-term liability			
Loan—Delta (carrying interest at 10 per cent per annum)			40,000
			528,700
Capital accounts			
Alpha		233,600	
Beta		188,900	
Gamma		106,200	528,700
			528,700

In the period January to March 20X8 the following transactions took place and were dealt with in the partnership records:

1 Fixed assets

	£
Freehold land and buildings—sold for	380,000
Plant and machinery—sold for	88,000
Motor vehicles: Beta and Gamma took over the cars they had been using at the following agreed values:	
Beta	9,000
Gamma	14,000
The remaining vehicles were sold for	38,000

2 Current assets

Stock—taken over by Gamma at agreed value	120,000
Trade and sundry debtors:	
Cash received	68,400
Remainder taken over by Gamma at agreed value	20,000

3 Current liabilities

The trade and sundry creditors were all settled for a total of	115,000

4 Long-term liabilities
   Delta's loan was repaid on 31 March 20X8 with interest accrued since 31 December 20X7
5 Expenses of dissolution £2,400 were paid
6 Capital accounts
   The final amounts due to or from the estate of Alpha, Beta and Gamma were paid/received on 31 March 20X8

Required:
Prepare the following accounts as at 31 March 20X8 showing the dissolution of the partnership:

a Realization account
b Partners' capital accounts
c Cash book (cash account)

Ignore taxation and assume that all partners have substantial resources outside the partnership. (ACCA)

part 7

COMPANIES

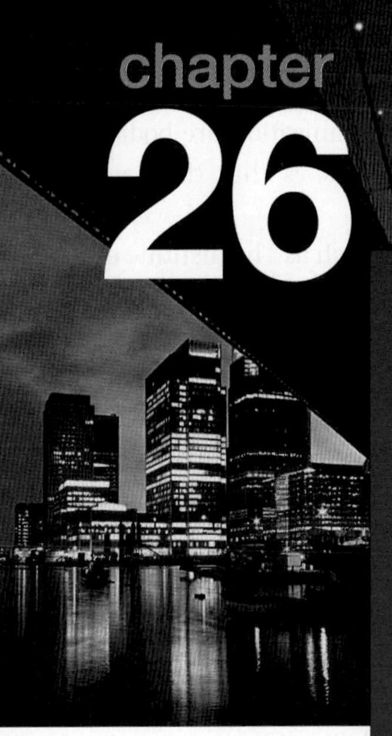

The nature of limited companies and their capital

Learning objectives

After reading this chapter you should be able to:

1. explain the meaning of the key terms and concepts listed at the end of the chapter;
2. describe the main characteristics of limited companies with particular reference to how these differ from partnerships;
3. describe the different classes of companies limited by shares;
4. outline the legal powers and duties of limited companies with reference to their Memorandum and Articles of Association;
5. explain the nature and types of shares and loan capital issued by limited companies;
6. outline the procedure relating to the issue of shares and debentures;
7. explain the nature of a share premium, debenture discount, preliminary expenses, interim and final dividends;
8. discuss the contents and purpose of the auditors' report;
9. describe the contents of a company's statutory books;
10. describe the purpose and proceedings of a company's annual general meeting.

Introduction

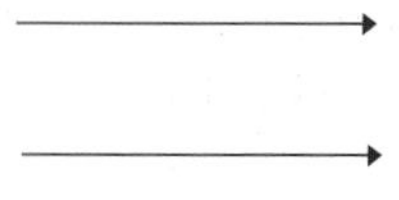

There are several different legal forms of organization. However, these can be all grouped into two categories, known as bodies sole and bodies corporate. **Bodies sole**, or unincorporated bodies, consist of sole traders and partnerships. All other forms of organization are bodies corporate. A key feature of **bodies corporate**, or incorporated bodies, is that they are recognized by law as being a legal entity separate from their members.

A body corporate is one which is created either by Royal Charter, such as The Institute of Chartered Accountants in England and Wales, or by Act of Parliament. The Act of Parliament may either relate to the creation of a specific organization, such as the British Broadcasting Corporation, or alternatively permit the creation of a particular form of legal entity by any group of individuals. The most common forms of legal entity which can be created under such Acts of Parliament include building societies, life assurance and friendly societies, and companies.

A **company** can thus be defined as a legal entity which is formed by registration under the Companies Acts, the main one being the Companies Act 1985 as modified by the Companies Act 1989. There are four types of company: companies whose liability is limited by shares, companies with unlimited liability, companies whose liability is limited by guarantee and companies limited by shares and guarantee. Companies limited by guarantee include organizations such as some professional bodies where the liability of its members is limited to the amount of their annual subscription. The remainder of this chapter deals with companies whose liability is limited by shares. These are commonly known as limited companies.

The characteristics of companies limited by shares

1. A company is a legal entity separate from its shareholders (owners). This means that companies enter into contracts as legal entities in their own right. Thus, creditors and others cannot sue the shareholders of the company but must take legal proceedings against the company. This is referred to as not being able to lift the veil of incorporation.
2. A company has perpetual existence in that the death of one of its shareholders does not result in its dissolution. This may be contrasted with a partnership, where the death of a partner constitutes a dissolution.
3. The liability of a company's shareholders is limited to the nominal value of their shares. **Limited liability** means that if a company's assets are insufficient to pay its debts the shareholders cannot be called upon to contribute more than the nominal value of their shares towards paying those debts.
4. The shareholders of a company do not have the right to take part in its management as such. They appoint directors to manage the company. However, a shareholder may also be a director (or other employee).
5. Each voting share carries one vote at general meetings of the company's shareholders (e.g. in the appointment of directors). There may be different classes of shares, each class having different rights and, possibly, some being non-voting.
6. A limited company must have at least two shareholders but there is no maximum number.

The classes of companies limited by shares

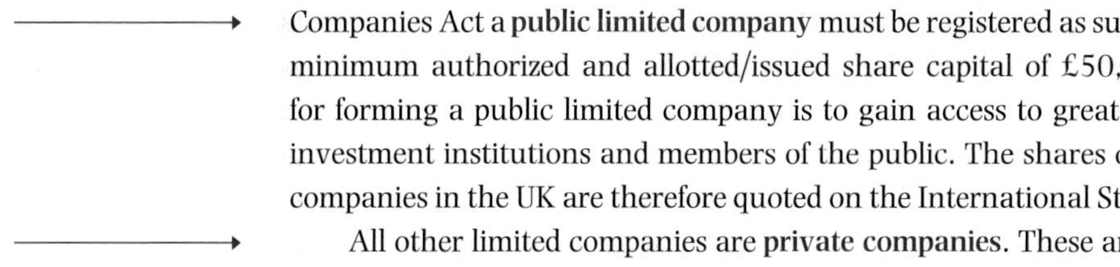

There are two classes of companies limited by shares, namely public and private. Under the Companies Act a **public limited company** must be registered as such and is required to have a minimum authorized and allotted/issued share capital of £50,000. The principal reason for forming a public limited company is to gain access to greater amounts of capital from investment institutions and members of the public. The shares of many, but not all, public companies in the UK are therefore quoted on the International Stock Exchange, London.

All other limited companies are **private companies**. These are not allowed to offer their shares for sale to the general public and thus do not have a stock exchange quotation. One of the main reasons for forming a private rather than a public company is that it enables its owners to keep control of the business, for example, within the family.

The name of a public company must end with the words 'public limited company' or the abbreviation 'PLC'. The name of a private company must end with the word 'limited' or the abbreviation 'Ltd'. A business which does not have either of these descriptions after its name is not a limited company even if its name contains the word company (the only exception being certain companies which have private company status, such as charities, who are permitted under licence to omit the word limited from their name).

The legal powers and duties of limited companies

A company is formed by sending to the Registrar of Companies certain documents and the appropriate fee. The most relevant of these documents are the Memorandum and Articles of Association. These define a company's powers and duties. The **Memorandum of Association** contains:

1 The name of the company, which must end with the words 'public limited company' or 'limited'.

2 The address of the company's registered office.

3 A statement that the ordinary shareholders' liability is limited to the nominal value of their shares.

4 The objects of the company. These refer to the type of trade or industry in which the company will operate and are usually stated in very broad terms. A company must not engage in any trade or business that is not specified in its Memorandum of Association. If it does so the company is said to be trading *ultra vires*, that is beyond its powers, and any such contrast is void.

5 The **authorized/nominal share capital** of the company. That is, the types, nominal value and maximum number of shares the company can offer for sale. This differs from the issued/allotted share capital, which refers to the actual number of shares that have been sold.

6 A statement that the company is either a public limited company or a private limited company.

Any of the above can be subsequently changed by a special resolution passed at a general meeting of the company's shareholders. Such a resolution requires at least 75 per cent of the votes cast.

The **Articles of Association** can best be described as a rule book which sets out the rights of a company's shareholders between themselves. It contains regulations relating to the issue of shares, conduct of meetings, borrowing powers, the appointment of directors, etc. The Companies Acts have provided a model set of articles known as Table A. A company may either make up its own articles or alternatively adopt those in Table A. Furthermore, where there is nothing in a company's articles relating to a particular matter, Table A will apply.

When a company is registered it is issued with what might be described as a birth certificate by the Register of Companies. This is called a **Certificate of Incorporation**. However, before a public limited company can commence trading it must satisfy the Registrar that certain regulations relating to its capital structure have been complied with. When this is done the Registrar issues a **Trading Certificate**, on receipt of which the company can commence trading.

The costs of forming a company, including the above documents, are referred to as **preliminary, promotion or formation expenses.**

The nature and types of shares and loan capital

Companies are financed predominantly by the issue (sale) of shares, loan stock and debentures, and by retaining part of each year's profit. In the UK all shares, loan stock and debentures have a fixed **nominal, par or face value**. This is often £1 or 25 pence in the case of shares and £100 for debentures and loan stock. There are several different types of shares and loan capital, each of which is described below.

Ordinary shares

Possession of an ordinary voting share represents part ownership of a company and it entitles the holder to one vote in general meetings of the company's ordinary shareholders. This gives shareholders the power to appoint and dismiss a company's directors. The holder of an ordinary share is also entitled to a share of the company's annual profit in the form of a **dividend**. The amount of the dividend per share is decided each year by the company's directors and varies according to the amount of profit. In years when the company earns high profits the ordinary shareholders normally receive a large dividend. However, ordinary shareholders run two risks. First, when profits are low they may receive little or no dividend. Second, should the company go bankrupt (into liquidation is the correct legal term) the ordinary shareholders are not entitled to be repaid the value of their shares until after *all* the other debts have been paid. Often, where a company has made substantial losses, there is little or nothing left for ordinary shareholders after the company has paid its other debts.

It should also be noted that a company does not normally repay its ordinary shareholders the money they have invested except in the event of liquidation (or by court order). If an ordinary shareholder wishes to sell his or her shares a buyer must be found. In the case of public companies whose shares are quoted on the International Stock Exchange, London, the seller may use this as a means of disposing of shares. Similarly, a prospective buyer may acquire 'second-hand' shares through the stock exchange.

Preference shares

Unlike ordinary shares, preference shares carry no voting rights. Preference shareholders are entitled to a fixed rate of dividend each year based on the nominal value of the shares. For example, 8 per cent preference shares with a nominal value of £1 each carry an annual dividend of 8 pence per share. A company may make several issues of preference shares at different points in time, each of which can carry a different rate of dividend. Preference shareholders have priority over the ordinary shareholders in that their dividends are a prior claim against profit. The preference dividends are thus deducted before calculating the profit available for distribution to ordinary shareholders as dividends. As in the case of ordinary dividends, the dividend on preference shares is classified as an **appropriation of profit**. The annual dividend on preference shares can be waived (but not varied), but the directors of companies usually try to avoid such drastic action, since it would be an indication of financial weakness.

In the event of a company going into liquidation, the preference shareholders are normally entitled to be repaid the nominal value of their shares before the ordinary shareholders. However, if no money is left after paying the other debts they would receive nothing.

As in the case of ordinary shares, companies do not normally repay preference shareholders the money they have invested except in the event of liquidation. Should a preference shareholder wish to dispose of shares he or she must find a buyer or sell them through the International Stock Exchange, London, if the company has a quotation for the preference shares.

There are two advantages of preference shares from the point of view of a company. One is that, since the rate of dividend is fixed, the company knows in advance what its future annual commitment is in respect of preference dividends. The second advantage is that preference shares are a permanent source of long-term capital which does not have to be repaid. However, since the introduction of the corporation tax system in 1965 it has become unpopular to issue preference shares because the dividend is not an allowable charge against income for tax purposes, while interest on debt is allowable. This makes debt a relatively more attractive source of fixed return finance for most companies. Small companies may be able to take advantage of the tax rules applicable to them to offset this difference.

There are a number of different types of preference shares with rights which vary from those described above. These consist of:

1 **Cumulative preference shares**
As explained above, if there is insufficient profit in any year a preference shareholder may receive no dividend. However, in the case of cumulative preference shares the holders will receive any such arrears of dividends (before any other shareholder receives a dividend) in the first subsequent year that there is sufficient profit to cover the dividend. Most of the preference shares quoted on the International Stock Exchange, London, are cumulative.

2 **Redeemable preference shares**
These differ from other preference shares in that they are repayable by the company on a date fixed when the shares are issued. Because such a reduction in capital may endanger the creditor's interests, the Companies Act states that when a redemption takes place the company must either make a new issue of shares with the same total nominal value, or capitalize an equivalent amount of profits. Capitalization refers to a transfer of retained profits to a capital reserve. This means that the amount transferred cannot be distributed as dividends.

3 **Participating preference shares**
In addition to receiving a fixed rate of dividend, holders of participating preference shares are entitled, along with the ordinary shareholders, to a share of the profit remaining after deducting preference dividends.

Debentures/loan stock

These are often referred to in the press as corporate bonds. Debentures and loan stock are not shares and have no voting rights. They represent a loan to the company and carry a fixed rate of interest per annum based on the nominal value. For example, 10 per cent debentures with a nominal value of £100 each carry annual interest of £10 per debenture. A company may make several issues of debentures or loan stock at different points in time, each of which can have a different rate of interest. Debenture holders are entitled to their interest before the preference and ordinary shareholders receive their dividends, and it must be paid even if there is a loss. The interest on debentures is thus referred to as a charge against profit, whereas dividends constitute an appropriation of profit.

In the event of a company going into liquidation the debenture holders are entitled to be repaid the nominal value of their debentures before the preference and ordinary shareholders. Such debentures are usually referred to as **unsecured**, in that although they rank before the shareholders they are not entitled to be repaid until after all the other creditors. However, some issues of debentures are **secured** on certain of the company's assets by either a **fixed charge** or a **floating charge**. A fixed charge is usually on specified assets such as property, plant or vehicles, and means that the company cannot dispose of those assets. A floating charge is usually on assets such as stock. In this case the company can sell the assets but must replace them with similar assets of an equivalent value.

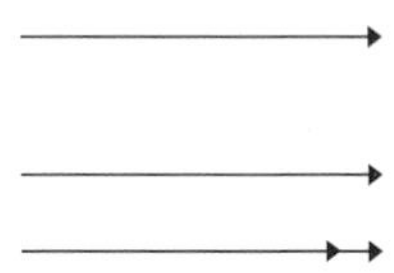

When debentures are secured, an accountant or solicitor may be appointed by the company to act as a trustee for the debenture holders. It is the trustee's responsibility to ensure that the value of the assets is always sufficient to repay the debenture holders. If this is not the case, or if the company may not be able to pay the annual interest on the debentures, the trustee may take legal possession of the assets, sell them and repay the debenture holders. Such drastic action usually results in the company going into liquidation.

Debentures and loan stock are usually repayable at some future date, which is specified when they are issued. This date is often several decades after they are issued. Should debenture holders wish to dispose of their debentures they must find a buyer or sell them through the International Stock Exchange, London, if the company has a quotation for the debentures.

The main advantage of debentures to a company is that the annual interest on debentures is an allowable charge against income for tax purposes.

A comparatively recent variation on debentures that has proved popular is **convertible loan stock/debentures**. These are debentures with a fixed annual rate of interest that also carry the right, at the holder's option, to convert them into a specified number of ordinary shares within a given time period, which is fixed when they are issued. The attraction of convertible loan stock is that the holder hopes to make a capital gain on conversion at some time in the future by virtue of the conversion rate being such that the ordinary shares can be acquired at an effective cost which is lower than the market price at the date of conversion. Suppose, for example, a company issues £100 convertible loan stock at a price of £108, the rate of conversion being 90 ordinary shares for every £100 loan stock. At the date of the issue the ordinary shares are quoted on the stock exchange at a price of £1 each. If at some future date the market price of the shares rises to, say, £1.50 it is beneficial to convert, since the shares would effectively cost £1.20 each (i.e. £108 ÷ 90 shares) compared with a market price of £1.50. These could then be sold for 90 @ £1.50 = £135 to give a capital gain of £135 − £108 = £27. Where the effective cost is more than the current market price it would not be beneficial to convert and so the debentures should be retained.

A summary of the characteristics of shares and loan stock is given in Figure 26.1. A more detailed summary of the different types of preference shares and loan stock is shown in Figure 26.2.

The issue of shares and debentures

Shares can be, and usually are, issued (sold) by the company at a price in excess of their nominal value. The amount by which the issue price exceeds the nominal value is referred to as a **share premium.** In the case of a public limited company whose shares are listed on the stock exchange, the price at which the shares are quoted is usually different from both the nominal value and the issue price. The market price may be either above or below the issue price and the nominal value.

Debentures can be issued by the company at a price that is either greater or less than their nominal value. The latter is referred to as a **debenture discount**.

When shares and debentures are issued the price may be payable by instalments. These consist of amounts payable: (a) on application; (b) on allotment/allocation of the shares by the company; and (c) any number of further instalments, referred to as calls.

FIGURE 26.1 Summary of the characteristics of shares and loan stock.

Ordinary/equity shares	*Preference shares*	*Loan stock/debentures*
1. Owners of the company who are normally entitled to vote at general meetings of the company's shareholders (e.g. to elect directors)	1. No voting rights	1. No voting rights
2. Receive a dividend the rate of which is decided annually by the company's directors. It varies each year depending on the profit and is an appropriation of profit	2. Receive a fixed rate of dividend each year which constitutes an appropriation of profit. Have priority over ordinary dividends	2. Receive a fixed rate of interest which constitutes a charge against income in computing the profit. Have priority over preference dividends
3. Last to be repaid the value of their shares in the event of the company going into liquidation	3. Repaid before the ordinary shareholders in the event of liquidation	3. Repaid before the ordinary and preference shareholders in the event of liquidation
4. Non-repayable except on the liquidation of the company	4. All but one particular type are non-repayable except on liquidation	4. Normally repayable after a fixed period of time
5. Rights specified in Articles of Association	5. Rights specified in Articles of Association	5. Rights specified in the terms of issue
6. Dividends non-deductible for tax purposes	6. Dividends non-deductible for tax purposes	6. Interest deductible for tax purposes

FIGURE 26.2 Summary of the types of preference shares and loan stock.

Types of preference shares

(1) Non-cumulative – do not receive arrears of dividends.

(2) Cumulative – if the dividend on these shares is not paid in any year the holders are entitled to it in the next year that there is sufficient profit before any other shareholder receives a dividend.

(3) Redeemable – the only type of preference share that is repaid by the company after the expiration of a period specified when they were issued

(4) Participating – in addition to receiving a fixed annual rate of dividend they are also entitled to a further dividend which is in the nature of a dividend on ordinary shares.

Advantages: (a) non-repayable (except (3) above); (b) the annual cost/dividend is known, thus facilitating planning; (c) in extreme circumstances the annual dividend can be waived.
Disadvantages: the dividends are not deductible for tax purposes.

Types of loan stock/debentures

(1) Unsecured/naked – in the event of the company going into liquidation these are repaid before the shareholders, but after other creditors.

(2) With a fixed charge – secured on assets that the company cannot dispose of without the trustee for the debenture holders' permission. In the event of the security being in jeopardy, or the company not paying the annual interest, the trustee can take legal possession of the asset(s), sell them and repay the debenture holders.

(3) With a floating charge – the same as debentures with a fixed charge except that the asset(s) on which the debentures are secured can be sold by the company but must be replaced with asset(s) of an equivalent value.

(4) Convertible loan stock – carry the right, at the holder's option, to convert them into ordinary shares within a given time period fixed when they are issued. The rate of conversion is usually such that the holder obtains ordinary shares at a price which is lower than the market price of the shares at the date of conversion.

Advantages: (a) the annual cost/interest is known; (b) the interest is deductible for tax purposes.
Disadvantages: (a) they have to be repaid after the expiration of the period specified when they were issued; (b) the interest must be paid before the shareholders receive any dividend. This can be a burden when the proceeds of the issue have been used to finance expansion that may not result in revenue during the early years. or where there is a reduction in the annual profit or high interest rates.

Public limited companies offer shares, loan stock and debentures for sale to members of the public by means of a document known as a **prospectus**. This usually takes the form of a booklet sent by the company to anyone who expresses an interest in the issue. It may also consist of a full-page advertisement in a national newspaper, such as *The Financial Times*. The contents of a prospectus include: (a) the total number of shares the company wishes to issue and the minimum subscription (i.e. the smallest number for which the applicant can apply); (b) the price of each share, stating the amounts payable on application, allotment and any calls; (c) details of the rights attaching to all classes of shares; and (d) a report by the company's auditors on the profits and dividends of the last five years, and the assets and liabilities at the end of the previous accounting year.

Interim and final dividends

Most large companies pay both interim and final dividends on their ordinary and preference shares. An **interim dividend** is paid halfway through the accounting year, when the profit for the first six months is known. The amount is decided by the directors. The **final dividend** is additional to the interim dividend and, although it relates to the same accounting year, is paid just after the end of the year. This is because the final dividend has to be approved by the ordinary shareholders at the annual general meeting (AGM), and this is always held after the end of the accounting year when the profit for the year is known.

Interest on loan stock and debentures is also often paid in two instalments, one halfway through the accounting year and the other at the end of the year. However, the amount relating to the latter half of the year may be outstanding at the end of the accounting year.

The books of account and published accounts

Companies are required by law to keep proper books of account, and each year to prepare a set of published accounts (i.e. a profit and loss account and balance sheet) which conform with the books of account. The 'books' of account need not necessarily actually be in the form of books, but there must be some set of records of the business transactions (e.g. a computerized system). A copy of the published accounts must be sent to each ordinary shareholder and the Registrar of Companies. The latter are available for inspection by the general public at Companies House.

The auditors' report

Most limited companies are required by law to have their books and annual final accounts audited by an independent qualified accountant. The accounts covered by the audit consist of the profit and loss account and balance sheet.

Although paid by the company, the auditors act on behalf of the ordinary shareholders and are appointed by them at the AGM. The auditors' function is to ascertain, or rather form an opinion of, whether or not *the accounts give a true and fair view of the state of affairs and the profit of the company and have been properly prepared in accordance with the Companies Act*. Their opinion is given in the **auditors' report**, which is attached to the final accounts, and uses wording similar to that in italics in the previous sentence. If the accounts are considered not to give a true and fair view or do not comply with the Companies Acts in some other way, the nature of the departure is usually stated in the auditors' report. This is referred to as a 'qualified' audit report.

It is important to appreciate that the auditor does not guarantee that no fraud or errors have taken place. In the UK, shareholders and loan creditors would be unlikely to receive damages from the auditors if a company subsequently went into liquidation or discrepancies were discovered, unless the auditors are shown to have been negligent. Furthermore, the auditors' report is not intended to be interpreted as passing an opinion on how efficiently and effectively the directors have used the company's assets.

Statutory books

Companies are obliged by law to maintain certain records relating to their capital and directors. These are known as **statutory books** and consist of the following:

1 Register of Members, containing the name, address and number of shares held by each shareholder.

2 Register of Debenture Holders, containing the name, address and number of debentures/loan stock held by each debenture holder.

3 Register of Directors and Company Secretary, stating the name, address and occupation of each.
4 Register of Directors' Shareholdings, showing the number of shares held by each director.
5 Register of Mortgages and Other Charges secured on the company's assets, showing the name and address of the lender and the amount of each loan.
6 Minute Book of General Meetings of the company's ordinary shareholders, containing details of the proceedings and resolutions.
7 Minute Book of Directors' Meetings, containing details of the resolutions.

Companies are also required by law to submit to the Registrar of Companies each year an annual return, showing changes in the entries in the statutory books during that year. This information is available for inspection by the general public at Companies House. The statutory books (except the Minutes of Directors' Meetings) are also required by law to be available for inspection by members of the public at the company's registered office.

The annual general meeting

The law demands that companies hold an **annual general meeting** (AGM). This is a meeting of the ordinary/equity shareholders at which they are entitled to vote on a number of matters. These include the following:

1 To receive and adopt the report of the directors and the published accounts for the year. This provides shareholders with an opportunity to question the directors on the contents of the accounts. The accounts are usually adopted, but if shareholders think that the accounts are inaccurate or misleading they may vote not to accept the accounts. If the shareholders vote not to adopt the accounts this does not mean that another set has to be prepared.
2 To declare and adopt a proposed final dividend for the year on the ordinary shares. The amount of the final dividend is proposed by the directors. The shareholders cannot propose some other figure. Thus, if the shareholders vote not to adopt the proposed dividend they will receive no final dividend for that year.
3 To elect directors. This is a source of the shareholders' power, in that if they are dissatisfied with the accounts, the dividend, or the company's performance they may vote not to re-elect the existing directors. Shareholders also have the right to nominate other people as directors.
4 To appoint auditors and fix their remuneration. The directors normally suggest a specific firm of auditors, and the power to fix their remuneration is often delegated to the directors by the shareholders at the AGM. Large companies usually appoint a reputable national or international firm of accountants to act as auditors.

Summary

A limited company is a separate legal entity that has perpetual existence, and is managed by directors appointed by the members. The liability of its shareholders is limited to the nominal value of their shares. There are two classes of companies limited by shares, known as private limited companies and public limited companies (PLC). A company's powers and the rights of the shareholders are contained in its Memorandum and Articles of Association.

Limited companies are financed predominantly by the issue of ordinary and preference shares, debentures and loan stock. These have a fixed face or nominal value but may be issued at a premium. Ordinary shares usually carry voting rights which give their holders the power to elect directors. They are also entitled to a share of the annual profits as a dividend which can vary each year. Ordinary shares are the last to be repaid in the event of the company going into liquidation. Preference shares are also entitled to an annual dividend but this is at a rate fixed at the time of issue. They may be cumulative, redeemable or participating. Preference shares are repaid before the ordinary shares in the event of liquidation. Most shares are non-repayable except on liquidation. All dividends are an appropriation of profits, and may include both an interim and final dividend. Debentures and loan stock represent a loan to the company for a fixed period of time. These carry a fixed rate of interest which is a charge against income. Debentures and loan stock are repaid before the shares in the event of liquidation, and may be secured by either a fixed or floating charge on the company's assets.

Companies are required by law to keep proper records of their transactions and prepare annual accounts. In most cases these must be audited by independent qualified accountants who prepare a report expressing an opinion on whether the accounts give a true and fair view of the profit and financial state of affairs. A copy of the published accounts and auditors' report must be sent to all the ordinary shareholders. Companies are also required by law to maintain statutory books, and hold an annual general meeting (AGM). At the AGM the ordinary shareholders vote on whether to adopt the published accounts, the dividend proposed by the directors, and the election of directors and auditors.

Key terms and concepts

Annual general meeting (370)
appropriation of profit (365)
Articles of Association (363)
auditors' report (369)
authorized/nominal share capital (363)
bodies corporate (362)
bodies sole (362)
Certificate of Incorporation (364)
company (362)
convertible loan stock/debentures (366)
cumulative preference shares (365)
debenture (366)
debenture discount (367)
dividend (364)
final dividend (369)
fixed charge (366)
floating charge (366)
interim dividend (368)
limited liability (362)
Memorandum of Association (363)
nominal/par/face value (364)
participating preference shares (365)
preliminary/promotion/formation expenses (364)
private company (363)
prospectus (368)
public limited company (363)
redeemable preference shares (365)
secured loan stock/debentures (366)
share premium (367)
statutory books (369)
Trading Certificate (364)
unsecured loan stock/debentures (366)

Review questions

An asterisk after the question number indicates that there is a suggested answer in the Appendix.

26.1 Describe the characteristics of companies limited by shares.

26.2 How does a public limited company differ from a private limited company?

26.3 Describe the contents of the Memorandum and Articles of Association. What are the purposes of these documents?

26.4 What are preliminary expenses?

26.5* Explain the main similarities and differences between ordinary shares, preference shares and debentures/loan stock.

26.6 Explain how each of the following arises:

a a share premium;

b a debenture discount.

26.7 Outline the main contents of a prospectus.

26.8 What is the difference between an interim dividend and a final dividend?

26.9 What is the auditors' report? How useful do you think this is in its present form and with its current legal standing in the UK?

26.10 Describe the contents of the statutory books of companies. What is the purpose of each of these books?

26.11 What is the annual general meeting of a company? Describe the proceedings at such a meeting.

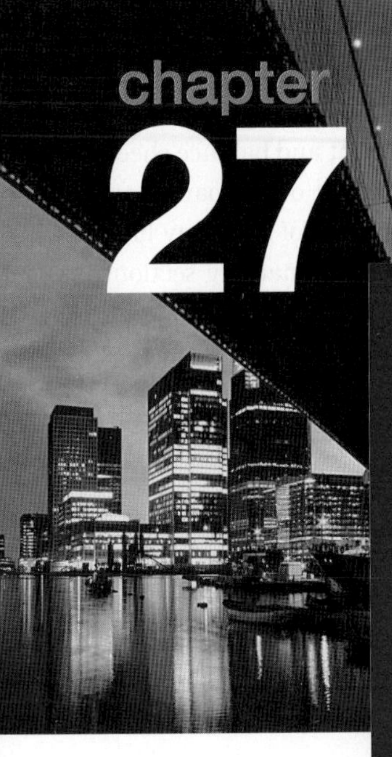

The final accounts of limited companies

Learning objectives

After reading this chapter you should be able to:

1. explain the meaning of the key terms and concepts listed at the end of the chapter;
2. describe the main differences between the final accounts of sole traders and companies, with particular reference to those arising from the latter being a separate legal entity;
3. describe the share capital structure of a company as presented in the balance sheet;
4. explain the nature and types of reserves;
5. show the journal and ledger entries relating to the treatment of preliminary expenses, debenture interest, corporation tax, dividends and transfers to reserves;
6. prepare the final accounts of limited companies prior to putting them in a form suitable for publication;
7. demonstrate a basic understanding of the legal format of published company final accounts and the main provisions of FRS3;
8. prepare a simple set of final accounts in a form suitable for publication and which complies with the Companies Acts, Financial Reporting Standards and Statements of Standard Accounting Practice;
9. explain the nature and accounting treatment of discontinued operations, exceptional items, extraordinary items, prior period adjustments, post balance sheet events and contingencies.

Introduction

The Companies Acts require companies to send their ordinary shareholders a copy of the annual final accounts. These are contained in the annual report, and referred to as financial statements or published accounts. They include a profit and loss account and balance sheet. There are detailed legal requirements relating to the content and format of company final accounts. The first two sections of this chapter deal with the preparation of company final accounts prior to putting them in a form suitable for publication. The remaining sections describe some of the legal requirements relating to their presentation in published form.

As in the case of sole traders and partnerships, it is now common practice for companies to prepare final accounts in vertical form. Furthermore, it is usual to combine the trading and profit and loss accounts into a single profit and loss account. The entries are the same as where there are two accounts.

The differences between the final accounts of companies and those of sole traders are explained below.

The profit and loss account

The contents of the profit and loss account of companies are the same as for sole traders and partnerships, with the following exceptions:

1 In arriving at the net profit, certain items not found in the accounts of sole traders and partnerships are deducted. These consist of directors' emoluments/remuneration (e.g. fees, salaries, pensions, compensation for loss of office), auditors' fees and expenses, interest on debentures, and preliminary/formation/promotion expenses. The latter refers to the costs incurred in forming a company, such as registration fees, and preparation of the Memorandum and Articles of Association. They must not be retained in the accounts as an asset.

2 After the net profit has been computed, various appropriations are made in a section of the profit and loss account, sometimes referred to as the profit and loss appropriation account. These occur in the following order:

   a *Corporation tax* Since a company is a separate legal entity, it is liable for the taxation on its annual profit, which takes the form of corporation tax. Where the profit and loss appropriation account is prepared in vertical form the corporation tax is deducted from the net profit to give the net profit after tax. The double entry for the corporation tax *charge* on the annual profit is to debit the profit and loss appropriation account and credit an account in the name of the Inland Revenue, or more likely, corporation tax.

   b *Preference share dividends* Where the profit and loss appropriation account is prepared in vertical form, these dividends are deducted from the net profit after tax. This is because they are an appropriation of the profit after tax and not a charge against income (like debenture interest). The preference dividends comprise any interim dividend paid plus the final dividend. The interim dividend paid will have been debited to the preference share dividends account in the ledger and thus shown in the trial balance. The final dividend may be outstanding at the end of the accounting year, in which case it is necessary to create an accrual in the preference dividends account and to show the amount owing on the balance sheet as a current liability. The total of the interim and final dividends is then debited to the profit and loss appropriation account, with a corresponding credit in the preference share dividends account.

c *Ordinary share dividends* These are entered in the profit and loss appropriation account after the preference dividends because the latter have a prior claim against profits. The ordinary dividends comprise any interim dividend paid plus the proposed final dividend. The interim dividend paid will have been debited to the ordinary share dividends account and thus shown in the trial balance. The proposed final dividend will always be outstanding at the end of the accounting year and thus it is necessary to create an accrual in the ordinary share dividends account and show the amount owing on the balance sheet as a current liability. The total of the interim and proposed final dividends is then debited to the profit and loss appropriation account and credited to the ordinary share dividends account.

d *Transfer to reserves* The profit remaining after deducting dividends is the undistributed or **retained profit** for the year and is brought down as a credit balance on the profit and loss appropriation account. Note that it is not transferred to the capital account, as in the case of sole traders and partnerships. However, sometimes companies transfer a part of their retained profit to a reserve account. The reason for this is to indicate to shareholders that the directors do not intend to distribute it as dividends but rather have earmarked it for some other use, such as expansion of the business by purchasing additional fixed assets. The entry for a transfer to a reserve is to debit the profit and loss appropriation account and credit the reserve account. There is a difference of opinion in the literature regarding whether the debit entry in the profit and loss appropriation account should appear before or after the preference and ordinary dividends. However, since transfers to reserves are no longer common, the issue is really only academic. Reserves are discussed further below.

The balance sheet

The content of the balance sheet of companies is the same as that of sole traders and partnerships, with the following exceptions:

1. The current liabilities of companies also usually include corporation tax on the annual profit, accrued debenture interest, and the outstanding final dividends on preference and ordinary shares.
2. The long-term liabilities of companies also often include the nominal value of loan stock and debentures.
3. The capital and retained profits of a company are shown separately under two headings comprising the nominal value of the share capital and the reserves. The share capital may take a number of forms. As explained in the previous chapter, when shares are issued the price may be payable by instalments. Thus, at the end of any given accounting year the proceeds of sale may be at a number of possible stages of collection. Each of these is given a particular label in the balance sheet of companies as follows:
   - **a** **Authorized/nominal share capital**. This refers to the types, nominal value and maximum number of shares that the company is permitted by its Memorandum of Association to issue.
   - **b** **Allotted share capital**. This refers to the total nominal value of the number of shares that have actually been issued at the date of the balance sheet. It is sometimes referred to as the issued share capital.
   - **c** **Called-up share capital**. This refers to that part of the allotted share capital which the company has required the shareholders to pay. It will consist of the amounts payable on

application and allotment plus any calls that have been made by the company up to the date of the balance sheet.

The figure for share capital that enters into the total of the balance sheet is the called-up ordinary and preference share capital. This is frequently the same as the allotted share capital. However, if these are different, the allotted capital must be shown as a memorandum figure (i.e. not entering into the total of the balance sheet). The authorized capital must always be disclosed as a memorandum amount. The memorandum authorized and allotted share capital may be shown on the face of the balance sheet or more commonly as a note to the accounts.

Reserves are difficult to define because they take a variety of forms. However, they usually represent some sort of gain or profit, and constitute part of a company's capital. Reserves may be of two types, either distributable or non-distributable. These are also frequently referred to as revenue and capital reserves, respectively. **Revenue/distributable reserves** are those which can be distributed to shareholders as dividends. These include any **general reserve** and the balance on the profit and loss account, both of which consist of retained profits of the current and previous accounting years.

Capital/non-distributable reserves cannot be distributed as dividends. These may take a number of forms. The most common is the balance on a **share premium** account. This arises from shares having been issued at a price in excess of their nominal value. The excess is credited to a share premium account. Another non-distributable reserve is a **revaluation reserve**. This arises if a fixed asset (usually land and buildings) is revalued and shown in the balance sheet at an amount which exceeds its historical cost. The excess is credited to a revaluation reserve account. A third form of non-distributable reserve is a **capital redemption reserve** (CRR). This is a statutory reserve, being identified in the Companies Acts. It arises when shares are redeemed or purchased back from shareholders. Attention is given to the CRR and share repurchase in the next chapter.

The total amount of reserves is added to the called-up share capital and shown on the balance sheet as the **'shareholders' interests'**.

An illustration of the preparation of the final accounts of limited companies is given in Example 27.1.

Example 27.1

The following is the trial balance of XYZ Ltd at 31 March 20X9:

	£	£
Ordinary shares of £1 each, fully paid		100,000
5 per cent preference shares of £1 each, fully paid		20,000
8 per cent debentures		30,000
Share premium		9,500
Revaluation reserve		10,000
General reserve		2,000
Retained profit from previous years		976
Motor vehicles at revaluation	210,000	
Depreciation on vehicles		19,000
Stock	14,167	
Debtors/creditors	11,000	8,012
Provision for doubtful debts		324

Bank balance	9,731	
Purchases/sales	186,000	271,700
Wages and salaries	16,362	
General expenses	3,912	
Directors' remuneration	15,500	
Preliminary expenses	1,640	
Debenture interest	1,200	
Ordinary dividend (interim)	2,000	
	471,512	471,512

You are given the following information:

1 Stock at 31 March 20X9 is valued at £23,487.
2 Depreciation of motor vehicles is to be provided at the rate of 10 per cent per annum on the fixed instalment method.
3 The provision for doubtful debts is to be made equal to 5 per cent of the debtors at 31 March 20X9.
4 Debenture interest of £1,200 and preference share dividends of £1,000 are outstanding at 31 March 20X9.
5 Provision is to be made for taxation on the year's profit amounting to £9,700.
6 There is a proposed final ordinary dividend of 5 pence per share.
7 The directors have decided to increase the general reserve by a further £3,000.
8 The authorized share capital consists of: (a) 200,000 ordinary shares of £1 each; and (b) 50,000 5 per cent preference shares of £1 each. The value of the shares shown in the trial balance is the allotted and called-up capital.

You are required to prepare in vertical form the profit and loss account for the year ended 31 March 20X9 and a balance sheet at that date.

Workings

These could be done arithmetically but are shown below in the form of ledger accounts to help students understand the double entry.

Provision for doubtful debts

Balance c/d	550	Balance b/d	324
(5 per cent × 11,000)		Profit and loss a/c	226
	550		550
		Balance b/d	550

Provision for depreciation

Balance c/d	40,000	Balance b/d	19,000
		Profit and loss a/c	21,000
	40,000		40,000
		Balance b/d	40,000

Debenture interest

Bank	1,200	Profit and loss a/c	2,400
Accrual c/d	1,200		
	2,400		2,400
		Accrual b/d	1,200

Preference dividend

Balance c/d	1,000	Profit and loss a/c	1,000
	1,000		1,000
		Balance b/d	1,000

Ordinary dividends

Bank	2,000	Profit and loss a/c	7,000
Balance c/d (100,000 × 5p)	5,000		
	7,000		7,000
		Balance b/d	5,000

Corporation tax

		Profit and loss a/c	9,700

General reserve

Balance c/d	5,000	Balance b/d	2,000
		Profit and loss a/c	3,000
	5,000		5,000
		Balance b/d	5,000

XYZ Ltd
Profit and loss account for the year ended 31 March 20X9

	£	£
Sales		271,700
Less: Cost of sales		
Stock at 1 Apr 20X8	14,167	
Add: Purchases	186,000	
	200,167	
Less: Stock at 31 Mar 20X9	23,487	
Cost of sales		176,680
Gross profit		95,020
Less: Expenditure		
Wages and salaries	16,362	
General expenses	3,912	
Provision for depreciation	21,000	
Provision for doubtful debts	226	
Directors' remuneration	15,500	
Preliminary expenses	1,640	
Debenture interest	2,400	
		61,040
Profit on ordinary activities before taxation		33,980
Less: Tax on profit on ordinary activities		9,700
Profit on ordinary activities after taxation		24,280
Less: Dividends—		
preference	1,000	
ordinary	7,000	
		8,000
Retained profit for the financial year		16,280
Less: Transfer to general reserve		3,000
		13,280

XYZ Ltd
Balance sheet as at 31 March 20X9

	£	£	£
Fixed assets			
Motor vehicles at revaluation			210,000
Less: Aggregate depreciation			40,000
			170,000
Current assets			
Stock		23,487	
Debtors	11,000		
Less: Provision for doubtful debts	550	10,450	
Bank		9,731	
		43,668	
Less: creditors: amounts falling due within one year			
Creditors	8,012		
Corporation tax	9,700		
Debenture interest	1,200		
Dividends (1,000 + 5,000)	6,000	24,912	
Net current assets			18,756
Total assets less current liabilities			188,756
Less: creditors: amounts falling due after more than one year			
8 per cent debentures			30,000
Net assets			158,756
Authorized share capital			
200,000 ordinary shares of £1 each			200,000
50,000 5 per cent preference shares of £1 each			50,000
			250,000
Allotted and called-up share capital			
100,000 ordinary shares of £1 each			100,000
20,000 5 per cent preference shares of £1 each			20,000
			120,000
Reserves			
Share premium account		9,500	
Revaluation reserve		10,000	
General reserve		5,000	
Profit and loss account (976 + 13,280)		14,256	
			38,756
Shareholders' interests			158,756

Notes

1. The workings for this example are shown in the form of ledger accounts to help students to understand the double entry. In examinations it is usually sufficient to state the necessary additions and subtractions.
2. The amount of the proposed final dividend on ordinary shares is computed by multiplying the dividend per share by the number of shares that have been issued/allotted as shown in

the trial balance, i.e. 5p × (£100,000 ÷ £1) = £5,000. Sometimes the dividend per share is expressed as a percentage. In this case the percentage is applied to the nominal value of the issued/allotted ordinary share capital (e.g. 5 per cent × £100,000 = £5,000). Where additional ordinary shares have been issued during the year, these are usually entitled to the full amount of any dividends that are declared after they have been allotted, such as the proposed final dividend for the year. In answering examination questions students should make this assumption unless told otherwise. Note that the dividend on the new shares is *not* computed on a time basis because it is not a fixed annual rate.

3 It is important to ensure that the amounts entered in the profit and loss account in respect of debenture interest and preference share dividends are the amounts paid plus any which is outstanding at the end of the year. Sometimes in examination questions students are not told how much is outstanding or even that anything is outstanding. In these circumstances the total amount to be entered in the profit and loss account is ascertained using the information given in the question relating to the rates of debenture interest and preference dividends as follows:

8 per cent debentures £30,000
∴ Annual interest = 8 per cent × £30,000 = £2,400.
5 per cent preference shares £20,000
∴ Annual dividend = 5 per cent × £20,000 = £1,000.

The amounts to be entered as current liabilities in the balance sheet can then be found by subtracting the amounts paid as shown in the trial balance as follows:

Debenture interest outstanding = £2,400 – £1,200 = £1,200
Preference dividends outstanding = £1,000 – £0 = £1,000

The reason for adopting this procedure in the case of debenture interest is that the debentures could have been issued at any time during a previous accounting year and thus the interest may be payable on dates other than the end of the accounting year and halfway through the year. This means that the amount of interest outstanding at the end of the accounting year will not necessarily be the total for the year or the last six months. Thus, one cannot assume that the accrual should be 6/12 of the total interest for the year, even though it often is in examination questions. Where debentures or preference shares have been issued during the year, the amount of interest/dividends that is entered in the profit and loss account needs to be calculated on a strict time basis.

4 It is generally accepted practice to prepare the final accounts of companies in vertical form. However, the profit and loss account (and appropriation account) must also be prepared in the ledger by transferring all the balances on the income and expense accounts to this account in the normal manner. Unlike the profit and loss accounts of sole traders and partnerships, the profit and loss account of companies will always contain a balance brought down from the previous year. The retained profit of the current year (after deducting any transfers to reserves) is added to this balance and the resulting figure is carried forward to the next year. This is shown on the above balance sheet under reserves in computational form as £976 + £13,280 = £14,256. It should also be remembered that journal entries are supposed to be made for all the above entries in the ledger.

5 As explained earlier in this chapter, the law allows revenue reserves such as the general reserve and the balance on the profit and loss account at the end of the previous year to be distributed to shareholders as dividends. This is not common in practice or in examination

questions because it is undesirable for economic/commercial reasons. However, a description of the accounting entries may help students to appreciate the nature of reserves. When a dividend is to be distributed from revenue reserves, this will be apparent from the profit and loss appropriation account because the profit after tax will be lower than the amount of the dividends for that year. In this case the retained profit of the previous year (i.e. the balance on the profit and loss account at the end of the previous year shown in the trial balance) should be added to the profit after tax and before dividends. If the profit after tax plus retained profit of the previous year is still less than the dividends, a transfer back from the general reserve must be made of an amount necessary to cover the dividend. The double entry for this transfer is to debit the general reserve and credit the profit and loss appropriation account. In the vertical format this will be an addition to the profit after tax and before dividends.

6 As explained earlier in this chapter, preliminary expenses must not be retained in the accounts as an asset. There are two possible ways of dealing with these. One is to charge them to the profit and loss account, as in the above example. However, this reduces the profit, which many companies wish to avoid if possible. The alternative, and preferred treatment, is to charge preliminary expenses against the balance on the share premium account, the double entry being to credit the preliminary expenses account and debit the share premium account. The amount entered on the balance sheet in respect of the share premium account will then be the difference between the balance shown in the trial balance and the preliminary expenses; that is, the balance on the share premium account after entering the preliminary expenses.

7 In the published accounts of companies current liabilities are referred to as *creditors: amounts falling due within one year*, and long-term liabilities as *creditors: amounts falling due after more than one year*.

8 In the published accounts of companies the net profits (before and after tax) are referred to as the **profit on ordinary activities**. Where a question has no corporation tax the net profit is referred to as the **profit for the financial year**.

Published financial statements

The final accounts of companies that are published and sent to ordinary shareholders in the annual report must be presented in a form that complies with the Companies Acts. The fourth schedule to the Companies Act 1985 contains four permissible formats for the profit and loss account and two permissible formats for the balance sheet. Most companies use what is known as Format 1 for both the profit and loss account and the balance sheet. These are reproduced below in full. They include certain items with which the student will be unfamiliar and go beyond what is required by most of the GCE A level and professional bodies' examinations at this level. In particular, students may need to ignore items that include the phrases 'group undertakings, participating interests, or minority interests'. These only apply to companies that own other companies. With the exception of extraordinary items and deferred taxation the remainder should be understandable at this level. Extraordinary items are explained in the next section of this chapter, and deferred taxation is not usually examined at this level. The formats are reproduced in full for reference purposes. It is not intended that they should be memorized. A precise explanation of what students are expected to know at this level follows immediately afterwards.

Profit and loss account: Format 1

1 Turnover
2 Cost of sales
3 *Gross profit or loss*
4 Distribution costs
5 Administrative expenses
6 Other operating income
7 Income from shares in group undertakings
8 Income from participating interests (excluding group undertakings)
9 Income from other fixed asset investments
10 Other interest receivable and similar income
11 Amounts written off investments
12 Interest payable and similar charges
13 Tax on profit or loss on ordinary activities
14 *Profit or loss on ordinary activities after taxation*
Minority interests
15 Extraordinary income
16 Extraordinary charges
17 Extraordinary profit or loss
18 Tax on extraordinary profit or loss
Minority interests
19 Other taxes not shown under the above items
20 *Profit or loss for the financial year.*

Balance sheet: Format 1

A *Called-up share capital not paid*

B *Fixed assets*

- I Intangible assets
  - 1 Development costs
  - 2 Concessions, patents, licences, trade marks and similar rights and assets
  - 3 Goodwill
  - 4 Payments on account
- II Tangible assets
  - 1 Land and buildings
  - 2 Plant and machinery
  - 3 Fixtures, fittings, tools and equipment
  - 4 Payments on account and assets in course of construction
- III Investments
  - 1 Shares in group undertakings
  - 2 Loans to group undertakings
  - 3 Participating interests (excluding group undertakings)

4 Loans to undertakings in which the company has a participating interest
5 Other investments other than loans
6 Other loans
7 Own shares

C *Current assets*

I Stocks

1 Raw materials and consumables
2 Work in progress
3 Finished goods and goods for resale
4 Payments on account

II Debtors

1 Trade debtors
2 Amounts owed by group undertakings
3 Amounts owed by undertakings in which the company has a participating interest
4 Other debtors
5 Called-up share capital not paid
6 Prepayments and accrued income

III Investments

1 Shares in group undertakings
2 Own shares
3 Other investments

IV Cash at bank and in hand

D *Prepayments and accrued income*

E *Creditors: amounts falling due within one year*

1 Debenture loans
2 Bank loans and overdrafts
3 Payments received on account
4 Trade creditors
5 Bills of exchange payable
6 Amounts owed to group undertakings
7 Amounts owed to undertakings in which the company has a participating interest
8 Other creditors including taxation and social security
9 Accruals and deferred income

F *Net current assets (liabilities)*

G *Total assets less current liabilities*

H *Creditors: amounts falling due after more than one year*

1 Debenture loans
2 Bank loans and overdrafts
3 Payments received on account
4 Trade creditors
5 Bills of exchange payable
6 Amounts owed to group undertakings
7 Amounts owed to undertakings in which the company has a participating interest

8 Other creditors including taxation and social security
9 Accruals and deferred income

I *Provisions for liabilities and charges*
1 Pensions and similar obligations
2 Taxation, including deferred taxation
3 Other provisions

J *Accruals and deferred income*
Minority interests

K *Capital and reserves*
I Called-up share capital
II Share premium account
III Revaluation reserve
IV Other reserves
1 Capital redemption reserve
2 Reserve for own shares
3 Reserves provided for by the articles of association
4 Other reserves
V Profit and loss account
Minority interests

The profit and loss account

The format of published accounts, or what have recently become known as financial statements, must also comply with accounting standards. In particular, *FRS3—Reporting Financial Performance* requires that the profit and loss account includes certain further items, such as dividends, and some additional subtotals. Combining the demands of the Companies Acts and FRS3, the following is a relatively definitive specimen published profit and loss account with which students are usually expected to comply at the introductory level:

Profit and loss account

	£000
Turnover	X
Cost of sales	(X)
Gross profit	X
Distribution costs	(X)
Administrative expenses	(X)
Profit (or loss) on ordinary activities before interest	X
Interest receivable	X
Interest payable	(X)
Profit (or loss) on ordinary activities before taxation	X
Tax on profit on ordinary activities	(X)
Profit (or loss) on ordinary activities after taxation	X
Dividends	(X)
Retained profit (or loss) for the financial year	X

Where an examination question contains no corporation tax, the profit on ordinary activities before and after taxation is referred to as the **profit for the financial year.** The precise distinction between these subtotals is explained later in this chapter.

The key point at this stage is that the separate items which make up the cost of sales, distribution costs, administrative expenses, interest receivable and payable, and dividends should not be shown on the face of the profit and loss account. It is therefore necessary to first ascertain the total of each of these as workings. Note that distribution costs include selling expenses.

Some of the items that are to be classified as either distribution costs or administrative expenses may be obvious from their descriptions (e.g. salespersons' commission, administrative salaries). Others are either less obvious or based on generally accepted conventions. In particular, selling and distribution costs are usually taken to include advertising, carriage outwards, bad debts, changes in the provision for bad debts, discount allowed, motor expenses (including depreciation, profit/losses on disposal) of delivery vehicles, and any costs associated with a warehouse such as wages, repairs to and depreciation of fork-lift trucks and similar 'plant and machinery'. There are few generally accepted conventions regarding the composition of administrative expenses. Examination questions normally need to specify which costs are regarded as administrative expenses, failing which as a last resort these may be taken to include auditors' fees and expenses, discount received, directors' remuneration, office salaries, rent and rates, light and heat, telephone and postage, etc. Frequently, examination questions also require some items (such as those in the previous sentence) to be apportioned between distribution costs and administrative expenses. This is a relatively simple arithmetic exercise in which the amounts are divided between distribution costs and administrative expenses using the basis of apportionment (i.e. percentages for each) given in the question.

The balance sheet

Turning to the format of balance sheets, the Companies Act requires those items shown in Format 1 above that are preceded by a letter or roman numeral to be disclosed on the face of the balance sheet (e.g. B Fixed assets, K III Revaluation reserve), whereas those preceded by arabic numerals may be combined where they are not material (e.g. stocks of raw materials, work in progress and finished goods). The following is thus a specimen published balance sheet containing the minimum requirements that students will need to follow at the introductory level. Further detail is unlikely to be penalized.

Balance sheet

	£000	£000
Fixed assets		
Intangible assets		X
Tangible assets		X
Investments		X
		X
Current assets		
Stocks	X	
Debtors	X	
Investments	X	
Cash at bank and in hand	X	
	X	
Creditors: amounts falling due within one year	(X)	
Net current assets (liabilities)		X
Total assets less current liabilities		X
Creditors: amounts falling due after more than one year		(X)
		X

Capital and reserves	
Called-up share capital	X
Share premium account	X
Revaluation reserve	X
Other reserves	X
Profit and loss account	X
	X

The 'debtors' includes prepayments, and the 'creditors: amounts falling due within one year' includes trade creditors and accruals.

Where this format is followed exactly in answering examination questions, it will be necessary to prepare workings that clearly show how the amounts of, in particular, tangible fixed assets and creditors (both current and long term) have been computed. Alternatively, it is probably advisable, and quicker, to include the items preceded by arabic numerals on the face of the balance sheet where relevant (e.g. trade creditors and accruals).

Notes to the accounts

The Companies Act and accounting standards also require several 'notes' to be attached to the published profit and loss account and balance sheet. Those most commonly examined at the foundation level comprise the following:

1 Changes in fixed assets (and accumulated depreciation)
2 Movements on reserves
3 Statement of total recognized gains and losses
4 Reconciliation of movements in shareholders' funds.

A note on the composition of fixed assets and accumulated depreciation is clearly necessary where only the net written down/book value at the end of the accounting year has been shown on the face of the balance sheet in respect of intangible and tangible fixed assets. In addition, this note must include the cost of acquisitions and disposals, any revaluation, the depreciation charges for the year and the accumulated depreciation on disposals. An illustration is given later in the text.

The note relating to movements on reserves usually includes the share premium account, any revaluation reserve, and the profit and loss account (i.e. retained profits). Movements on these reserves will arise from the issue of shares at a premium, a surplus on the revaluation of fixed assets and the retained profit for the financial year, respectively.

The statement of total recognized gains and losses is relatively simple, at least at the foundation level. It will contain the profit for the financial year plus any unrealized surplus on the revaluation of fixed assets. The purpose of this statement is to show the gains (and losses) accruing to the company's shareholders be they either realized, such as the profit for the year, or unrealized, as in the case of revaluation surpluses.

According to FRS3, 'the profit and loss account and the statement of total recognized gains and losses reflect the performance of a reporting entity in a period. There are, however, other changes in shareholders' funds that can also be important in understanding the change in the financial position of the entity. The purpose of the reconciliation of movements in shareholders' funds is to highlight those other changes.'

An illustration of the preparation of published financial statements including the above four notes is given in Example 27.2.

Example 27.2

The following is the trial balance of Oasis Ltd as at 30 September 20X3.

	£000	£000
Called-up share capital		1,000
Share premium		500
Profit and loss account 1 October 20X2		700
10 per cent debentures (repayable 20X9)		600
Land and buildings at cost	2,500	
Buildings—accumulated depreciation		90
Motor vehicles—at cost	1,400	
—accumulated depreciation		470
Stock	880	
Trade debtors/creditors	420	360
Purchases/sales	3,650	6,540
Warehouse wages	310	
Administrative salaries	190	
Sales staff salaries	70	
Bad debts	20	
Directors' remuneration	280	
Advertising expenditure	60	
Motor expenses	230	
Light and heat	180	
Telephone and postage	80	
Bank overdraft		19
Discount allowed	9	
	10,279	10,279

Further information:

1 The called-up share capital consists of 1 million ordinary shares of £1 each, fully paid.
2 Stock at 30 September 20X3 was £740,000.
3 The auditors' fees and expenses for the year are expected to be £71,000.
4 The estimated corporation tax charge on the profit for the year is £250,000.
5 The directors have proposed a final dividend on the ordinary shares in issue at 30 September 20X3 of 10 pence per share.
6 Depreciation is provided on a straight line basis at 2 per cent per annum for buildings and 20 per cent per annum on vehicles. A full year's charge is made in the year of acquisition and none in the year of disposal.
7 The following items are to be apportioned between distribution costs and administrative expenses as below:

	Distribution	*Administrative*
Directors' remuneration	25%	75%
Light and heat, telephone and postage, buildings depreciation	40%	60%
Motor expenses, vehicle depreciation	50%	50%

8 The following items were unrecorded in the ledger on 30 September 20X3:
   i The issue of 500,000 ordinary shares at £1.50 each fully paid on 31 August 20X3.
   ii The acquisition on credit of a motor vehicle costing £100,000 on 31 August 20X3.
   iii The sale on credit of a motor vehicle for £40,000 on 31 August 20X3. This cost £50,000 when purchased on 1 February 20X1.
9 The land included in the above trial balance cost £1m. The directors have decided to revalue this on 30 September 20X3 at £1.3m.

You are required to prepare the company's profit and loss account for the year and a balance sheet as at 30 September 20X3. This should be in a form suitable for publication, comply with the Companies Acts and accounting standards, and include notes relating to changes in fixed assets, movements on reserves, a statement of total recognized gains and losses, and a reconciliation of movements in shareholders' funds.

Workings

1 *Cost of sales*	£000
Stock at 1 Oct 20X2	880
Purchases	3,650
	4,530
Stock at 30 Sep 20X3	(740)
Cost of sales	3,790

2 *Depreciation*	£000
a Buildings at cost (2,500 – 1,000)	1,500
Depreciation expense (2% × 1,500)	30
Accumulated depreciation at 30 Sep 20X2 (90 + 30)	120
b Motor vehicles at 1 Oct 20X2 at cost	1,400
Acquisition	100
	1,500
Disposal	(50)
Motor vehicles at 30 Sep 20X3 at cost	1,450
Disposal—	
Accumulated depreciation (2 × 20% × 50)	20
Book value (50 – 20)	30
Profit on sale (40 – 30)	10
Depreciation expense (20% × 1,450)	290
Accumulated depreciation at 30 Sep 20X3 (470 – 20 + 290)	740

3 *Distribution costs and administrative expenses*

	Distribution	*Administrative*
	£000	£000
Warehouse wages	310	—
Administrative salaries	—	190
Sales staff salaries	70	—
Bad debts	20	—
Directors' remuneration	70	210
Advertising	60	—
Motor expenses	115	115
Vehicle depreciation	145	145

Profit on sale vehicle	(5)	(5)
Light and heat	72	108
Telephone and postage	32	48
Buildings depreciation	12	18
Discount allowed	9	—
Auditors' fees and expenses	—	71
	910	900

Oasis Ltd

Profit and loss account for the year ended 30 September 20X3

	£000
Turnover	6,540
Cost of sales	(3,790)
Gross profit	2,750
Distribution costs	(910)
Administrative expenses	(900)
Profit on ordinary activities before interest	940
Interest payable (10% × 600)	(60)
Profit on ordinary activities before taxation	880
Tax on profit on ordinary activities	(250)
Profit on ordinary activities after taxation	630
Dividends (1.5m @ 10p)	(150)
Retained profit for the financial year	480

Oasis Ltd

Balance sheet as at 30 September 20X3

	£000	£000	£000
Fixed assets			
Tangible assets (Note 1)			3,390
Current assets			
Stock		740	
Trade debtors		420	
Other debtors		40	
Cash at bank (750 – 19)		731	
		1,931	
Creditors: amounts falling due within one year			
Trade creditors	(360)		
Other creditors (100 + 71)	(171)		
Corporation tax	(250)		
Debenture interest	(60)		
Dividends	(150)	(991)	
Net current assets			940
Total assets less current liabilities			4,330
Creditors: amounts falling due after more than one year			
Debenture loans			(600)
			3,730

Capital and reserves	
Called-up share capital	
1.5m ordinary shares of £1 each	1,500
Share premium account (500 + 250)	750
Revaluation reserve	300
Profit and loss account (700 + 480)	1,180
	3,730

Notes to the accounts

1 *Tangible fixed assets*

	Land £000	*Buildings* £000	*Vehicles* £000	*Total* £000
Cost or valuation				
At 1 Oct 20X2	1,000	1,500	1,400	3,900
Additions	—	—	100	100
Disposals	—	—	(50)	(50)
Revaluation	300	—	—	300
At 30 Sep 20X3	1,300	1,500	1,450	4,250
Accumulated depreciation				
At 1 Oct 20X2	—	90	470	560
Charge for year	—	30	290	320
Disposals	—	—	(20)	(20)
At 30 Sep 20X3	—	120	740	860
Net book value				
At 30 Sep 20X3	1,300	1,380	710	3,390
At 1 Oct 20X2	1,000	1,410	930	3,340

2 *Reserves*

	Share premium £000	*Revaluation reserve* £000	*Profit and loss* £000	*Total* £000
At beginning of year as previously stated	500	—	700	1,200
Premium on issue of shares	250	—	—	250
Transfer from profit and loss account of the year	—	—	480	480
Surplus on land revaluation	—	300	—	300
At end of year	750	300	1,180	2,230

3 *Statement of total recognized gains and losses*

	£000
Profit for the financial year	630
Unrealized surplus on revaluation of land	300
Total recognized gains and losses relating to the year	930

4 *Reconciliation of movements in shareholders' funds*

	£000
Profit for the financial year	630
Dividends	(150)
	480
Other recognized gains and losses relating to the year (net)—revaluation surplus	300
New share capital subscribed	750
Net addition to shareholders' funds	1,530
Opening shareholders' funds £(1,000k + 500k + 700k)	2,200
Closing shareholders' funds	3,730

Reporting financial performance

The Companies Acts, various Statements of Standard Accounting Practice (SSAPs) and Financial Reporting Standards (FRSs) require that certain items be shown separately in published accounts or as notes to the accounts. The most significant of these, which have not been discussed thus far, are explained below. However, it is first necessary to appreciate why these items are required to be shown separately.

As explained in Chapter 1, one of the main objectives of published company accounts is to provide information that is useful in the evaluation of the performance of the reporting entity. One of the principal means of evaluating performance involves making comparisons over time, with other companies and/or forecasts. It may also involve making predictions of future profits, cash flows, etc. Comparisons and predictions of profits are likely to be misleading where the profit includes gains and losses of a non-recurring nature such as relating to operations that have been discontinued or assets destroyed by fire (where uninsured). In order to facilitate comparisons and predictions it is therefore desirable that the following items be disclosed separately in published company accounts.

Acquisitions and discontinued operations

FRS 3—Reporting Financial Performance[1] defines acquisitions and discontinued operations as follows:

Acquisitions. Operations of the reporting entity that are acquired in the period.
Discontinued operations. Operations of the reporting entity that are sold or terminated and that satisfy all of the following conditions:

a The sale or termination is completed either in the period or before the earlier of three months after the commencement of the subsequent period and the date on which the financial statements are approved.

b If a termination, the former activities have ceased permanently.

c The sale or termination has a material effect on the nature and focus of the reporting entity's operations and represents a material reduction in its operating facilities resulting either from its withdrawal from a particular market (whether class of business or geographical) or from a material reduction in turnover in the reporting entity's continuing markets.

d The assets, liabilities, results of operations and activities are clearly distinguishable, physically, operationally and for financial reporting purposes.

Operations not satisfying all these conditions are classified as continuing.

FRS3 requires an analysis of turnover and **operating profit** between continuing operations, acquisitions and discontinued operations. These must be shown separately on the face of the published profit and loss account as follows:

	£million	£million
Turnover:		
Continuing operations		1,000
Acquisitions		500
		1,500
Discontinued operations		400
		1,900
Cost of sales		(800)
Gross profit		1,100
Net operating expenses		(200)
Operating profit:		
Continuing operations	700	
Acquisitions	50	
Discontinued operations	150	900

FRS3 also requires an analysis of the cost of sales and net operating expenses (i.e. distribution costs and administrative expenses) between continuing operations, acquisitions and discontinued operations to be shown as a note to the accounts or included on the face of the profit and loss account.

Exceptional items

Exceptional items used to be accounted for in accordance with *SSAP 6—Extraordinary Items and Prior Year Adjustments.*[2] However, this has been superseded by FRS3, which defines exceptional items as follows:[1]

> Material items which derive from events or transactions that fall within the ordinary activities of the reporting entity and which individually or, if of a similar type, in aggregate, need to be disclosed by virtue of their size or incidence if the financial statements are to give a true and fair view.

Take particular note of the word material and that exceptional items fall within the ordinary activities (i.e. the normal trading activities).

Examples of exceptional items given in FRS3 include: profits or losses on the sale or termination of an operation; costs of a fundamental reorganization or restructuring having a material effect on the nature and focus of the reporting entity's operations; and profits or losses on the disposal of fixed assets. Notice that exceptional items include profits and losses on the termination or disposal of discontinued operations. That is, arising from the sale of fixed assets, as distinct from the operating profit on discontinued operations discussed in the previous section above.

Other examples of exceptional items not given in FRS3 include amounts written off intangible fixed assets (other than amortization); abnormal provisions for bad debts and losses on stock, work in progress and long-term contracts; profits or losses arising on the settlement of insurance claims or the destruction of assets not covered by insurance; and assets that have been nationalized or confiscated by a government.

The treatment of exceptional items in published company accounts depends on the legal requirements relating to the item in question. Where the law requires the item to be shown separately on the face of the profit and loss account in a specific position, then this should be the treatment adopted. Alternatively, where the law requires the item in question to be disclosed as a note to the accounts, then this would be the most appropriate treatment. Similarly, FRS3 requires other exceptional items such as those in the immediately preceding paragraph (e.g. a material abnormal bad debt) to be disclosed as a note to the accounts distinguishing between those arising from continuing operations and those arising from discontinued operations. However, FRS3 requires the examples given in FRS3, listed above, to be shown on the face of the profit and loss account after the operating profit and before the deduction of interest payable. In each case it is also necessary to distinguish between those exceptional items arising from continuing operations and those arising from discontinued operations. The profit and loss account will thus appear as follows, This should be read as a continuation of the previous numerical example.

	£million
Operating profit	900
Profit on sale of properties in continuing operations	300
Loss on disposal of discontinued operations	(100)
Profit on ordinary activities before interest	1,100
Interest payable	(350)
Profit on ordinary activities before taxation	750

Extraordinary items

Extraordinary items also used to be accounted for in accordance with SSAP6 but this has been superseded by FRS3. In order to understand fully the nature of extraordinary items it is necessary to consider also the nature of ordinary items/activities. These are defined in FRS3 as follows:[1]

> *Ordinary activities.* Any activities which are undertaken by a reporting entity as part of its business and such related activities in which the reporting entity engages in furtherance of, incidental to, or arising from, these activities. Ordinary activities include the effects on the reporting entity of any event in the various environments in which it operates, including the political, regulatory, economic and geographical environments, irrespective of the frequency or unusual nature of the events.
>
> *Extraordinary items.* Material items possessing a high degree of abnormality which arise from events or transactions that fall outside the ordinary activities of the reporting entity and which are not expected to recur. They do not include exceptional items nor do they include prior period items merely because they relate to a prior period.

Take particular note of the word 'material' and that extraordinary items 'are not expected to recur'.

FRS3 deliberately provides no examples of extraordinary items because they 'are extremely rare as they relate to highly abnormal events'.

FRS3 requires any extraordinary profit or loss to be shown separately on the face of the profit and loss account (and the associated corporation tax on such items) after the profit on ordinary activities after tax but before dividends. A breakdown of the amount of each extraordinary item must also either be shown on the face of the profit and loss account or in the notes of the accounts together with a description of the nature of each item. The profit and loss account will therefore appear as follows. This should be read as a continuation of the previous numerical example.

	£million	£million
Profit on ordinary activities before taxation		750
Tax on profit on ordinary activities		(250)
Profit on ordinary activities after taxation		500
Extraordinary profit	50	
Tax on extraordinary profit	(20)	
Extraordinary profit after tax		30
Profit for the financial year		530
Dividends		(370)
Retained profit for the financial year		160

Learning Activity 27.1

You should find it useful at this point to combine the three numerical examples given above in respect of acquisitions, discontinued operations, exceptional items and extraordinary items since these provide a fairly comprehensive model of a published profit and loss account. In addition, students may wish to attempt Exercise 27.25 or use the solution as an example of how to answer examination questions on this topic.

Prior period adjustments

These are also defined in FRS3 as 'material adjustments applicable to prior periods arising from changes in accounting policies or from the correction of fundamental errors. They do not include normal recurring adjustments or corrections of accounting estimates made in prior periods.' Take particular note of the word material, and the exclusion of the correction of accounting estimates relating to, for example, the estimated residual value and useful life of fixed assets, and provisions for bad debts.

Examples of prior period adjustments are rare but include a change in the method of stock valuation, and an item previously recorded as a fixed asset that should have been treated as an expense (or vice versa). The most common prior period adjustment arises from the issue of a FRS that would necessitate a company to change one of its accounting policies.

Since prior period adjustments do not relate to the current accounting year they are not entered in the current year's profit and loss account. However, FRS3 requires that the comparative figures for the preceding period should all be restated to take into account the prior period adjustment. Furthermore, FRS3 requires prior period adjustments to be shown in the notes to the accounts relating to movements on reserves and the statement of total recognized gains and losses as follows:

Reserves

	Profit and loss account
	£million
At beginning of year as previously stated	2,450
Prior year adjustment	280
At beginning of year as restated	2,730
Transfer from profit and loss account of the year	160
At end of year	2,890

Statement of total recognized gains and losses

	£million
Profit for the financial year	530
Unrealized surplus on revaluation of properties	40
Total recognized gains and losses relating to the year	570
Prior period adjustment	280
Total gains and losses recognized since last annual report	850

The note to the accounts must also include details of the nature of the prior period adjustment and its associated effect on taxation.

Post balance sheet events

These are defined in *SSAP17—Accounting for Post Balance Sheet Events*[3] as 'those events, both favourable and unfavourable, which occur between the balance sheet date and the date on which the financial statements are approved by the board of directors'. The balance sheet date is of course the end of an accounting year. The date on which the financial statements are approved by the board of directors is usually a month or two after the end of the accounting year, since it takes this amount of time to prepare the financial statements. The statements must then be approved at a meeting of the board of directors.

Post balance sheet events are classified as falling into one of two categories as follows:

1 **Adjusting events** are defined as 'events which provide additional evidence of conditions existing at the balance sheet date. They include events which because of statutory or conventional requirements are reflected in financial statements'.

Examples of adjusting events include any evidence of a permanent diminution in value of fixed assets, investments, stocks and work in progress, the insolvency of a debtor, changes in the rates of taxation, amounts received or receivable in respect of an insurance claim outstanding at the balance sheet date, and errors or frauds which show that the financial statements were incorrect.

SSAP17 requires that a material adjusting event should be included in the financial statements. For example, stocks would be reduced to their net realizable value, a provision created for an insolvent debtor, errors corrected, etc.

2 **Non-adjusting events** are defined as 'post balance sheet events which concern conditions which did not exist at the balance sheet date'. Examples include mergers and acquisitions, reconstructions, issues of shares and debentures, purchases and sales of fixed assets and investments, losses of fixed assets and stocks resulting from a fire or flood, new trading activities and closing existing trading activities, government action (e.g. nationalization), strikes and other labour disputes.

SSAP17 requires that details of material non-adjusting events be disclosed as a note to the financial statements. It is not appropriate to include non-adjusting events in the financial statements since they do not relate to conditions which existed at the balance sheet date. However, it is appropriate to disclose non-adjusting events as a note to ensure that financial statements are not misleading where there is some subsequent material event which affects a company's financial position.

Provisions and contingencies

These are the subject of *FRS 12—Provisions, Contingent Liabilities and Contingent Assets.*[4] This defines a **provision** as 'a liability of uncertain timing or amount'. It further defines **liabilities** as 'obligations of an entity to transfer economic benefits as a result of past transactions or events'.

A **contingency** was defined in *SSAP18—Accounting for Contingencies*[5] as 'a condition which exists at the balance sheet date, where the outcome will be confirmed only on the occurrence or non-occurrence of one or more uncertain future events. A contingent gain or loss is a gain or loss dependent on a contingency'. Note that although the definition does not include the word material, all of the following discussion applies only to contingencies which are material in amount.

Examples of contingent losses include possible liabilities arising from bills of exchange received that have been discounted, corporation tax disputes, failure by another party to pay a debt which the reporting entity has guaranteed, and a substantial legal claim against the company. The latter is the most common example and refers to where a legal action has been brought against the company but the court has not yet pronounced judgment regarding the company's innocence or guilt. This is often simply referred to as a pending legal action. It is regarded as a contingency because whether or not a loss or liability will arise depends on the 'outcome' of the court case (i.e. an 'uncertain future event').

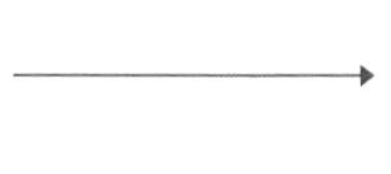

Contingencies comprise contingent assets (or gains) and contingent liabilities (or losses). A **contingent asset** is defined in FRS12 as 'a possible asset that arises from past events and whose existence will be confirmed only by the occurrence of one or more uncertain future events not wholly within the entity's control'. A **contingent liability** is defined in FRS12 as: '(a) a possible obligation that arises from past events and whose existence will be confirmed only by the occurrence of one or more uncertain future events not wholly within the entity's control; or (b) a present obligation that arises from past events but is not recognised because: (i) it is not probable that a transfer of economic benefits will be required to settle the obligation; or (ii) the amount of the obligation cannot be measured with sufficient reliability'.

The accounting treatment of items that may be regarded as either provisions or contingent liabilities hinges on whether the potential obligation has a high or low probability of resulting in a liability. If there is a high probability, or it is very likely, then a provision must be created. If there is a low probability, or it is only a possibility, then it is treated as a contingent liability. In this case details must be given as a note to the financial statements, but no entries are made in the ledger or final accounts (i.e. a provision or liability is not created).

The precise rules about what constitutes a provision are set out in FRS12 as follows:

> A provision should be recognised when: (a) an entity has a present obligation as a result of a past event; (b) it is *probable* that a transfer of economic benefits will be required to settle the obligation; and (c) a reliable estimate can be made of the amount of the obligation.

The notes to the financial statements should disclose for each class of provision: (1) the carrying amount at the start and end of the period; (2) increases and decreases in the provision; (3) amounts charged against the provision; (4) a brief description of the nature of the obligation, and the expected timing of any resulting transfers of economic benefits; and (5) an indication of the uncertainties about the amount or timing of those transfers of economic benefits.

FRS12 states that 'an entity should not recognise a contingent liability'. That is, it should not be recognized as a provision or liability within the ledger or final accounts. A contingent liability is 'a *possible* obligation' that '*probably will not* require a transfer of economic benefits'. This must be shown as a note to the accounts. According to FRS12, 'unless the possibility of any transfer in settlement is remote, an entity should disclose for each class of contingent liability at the balance sheet date a brief description of the nature of the contingent liability and, where practicable: (1) an estimate of its financial effect; (2) an indication of the uncertainties relating to the amount or timing of any outflow; and (3) the possibility of any reimbursement'.

FRS12 also states that 'an entity should not recognise a contingent asset'. That is, it should not be included in the ledger or final accounts. A contingent asset is 'a possible asset' where the 'inflow of economic benefits is *probable* but not virtually certain'. This must be shown as a note to the accounts. According to FRS12, 'where an inflow of economic benefits is probable, an entity should disclose a brief description of the nature of the contingent assets at the balance sheet date and, where practicable, an estimate of their financial effect'.

A possible asset where the inflow of economic benefits is not probable is not recognized in the accounts and no disclosure in the form of a note is required.

Students may be confused by the apparent inconsistency in the definitions and accounting treatment of contingent assets and contingent liabilities which arises from the application of the prudence principle, whereby probable liabilities are recognized (as provisions) but probable assets are not. Similarly, possible (i.e. contingent) liabilities must be disclosed as a note but possible assets are not. Furthermore, the standard starts by defining contingent assets and contingent liabilities as *possible* assets and obligations, and then later implies that a contingent asset is a *probable* (not possible) asset.

It should also be noted that although contingencies are conditions which exist at the balance sheet date, their accounting treatment depends on information available up to the date on which the financial statements are approved by the board of directors.

A useful exercise at this point is to consider the similarities and differences between liabilities, provisions and contingent liabilities. A liability is a debt owed to a known party of a known certain amount. A provision is a known or highly probable future liability or loss, the amount and/or timing of which is uncertain (and thus has to be estimated). A contingent liability is uncertain with regard to its existence, timing and amount, and is thus only a possible liability.

Learning Activity 27.2

Visit the website of a large listed/quoted public limited company and find their latest annual report and accounts. Examine the contents of the profit and loss account, balance sheet and notes to the accounts, paying particular attention to the items discussed in this chapter.

Summary

The profit and loss accounts of companies contain the same items as those of sole traders but in addition includes others such as directors' remuneration, auditors' fees and interest on debentures/loan stock. As in the case of partnerships, the net profit is carried down into another section of the profit and loss account sometimes referred to as the appropriation account. In this are shown the corporation tax, dividends and any transfers to reserves.

The balance sheets of companies are also similar to those of sole traders, except that the capital account is replaced by the called-up share capital and various reserves. These may be of two sorts, either revenue or capital reserves. Revenue reserves such as the retained profits can be distributed as dividends. Capital reserves such as the share premium, revaluation reserve and capital redemption reserve cannot be distributed as dividends. Loan stock and debentures are normally shown on the balance sheet as long-term liabilities at their nominal value.

The final accounts that are published and sent to ordinary shareholders must be presented in a form that complies with the Fourth Schedule to the Companies Act 1985, and various SSAPs and FRSs. One of the main purposes of many accounting standards, particularly FRS3, is to facilitate comparisons and predictions of performance by showing separately in the profit and loss account any items of a non-recurring nature. Thus, FRS3 requires an analysis of turnover and operating profit between continuing operations, acquisitions and discontinued operations. Similarly, FRS3 also states that some exceptional and all extraordinary items should be shown separately in published profit and loss accounts. These both relate to material non-recurring items, the difference being that exceptional items are a part of the ordinary activities whereas extraordinary items fall outside the ordinary activities. Comparisons and predictions may also be distorted where there are material adjustments applicable to prior periods arising from changes in accounting policies or the correction of fundamental errors. These are referred to as prior period adjustments; and FRS3 requires that the comparative figures for the preceding year be restated, and the effect on the retained profits of the previous year shown as a movement on reserves.

In addition to showing certain items separately in final accounts, the Companies Act and various accounting standards require notes to be attached to the profit and loss account and balance sheet. These provide a more detailed breakdown, and in some cases, additional information about conditions prevailing at the balance sheet date, or events that have occurred since. Two examples are contingencies and post balance sheet events, respectively. SSAP17 states that material adjusting events should be provided for in financial statements, and material non-adjusting events be disclosed as a note. Similarly, FRS12 requires that probable material contingent losses be recognized in financial statements as provisions, and possible but not probable material contingent losses be disclosed as a note.

Key terms and concepts

Acquisitions (391)
adjusting events (395)
allotted/issued share capital (375)
authorized/nominal share capital (375)
called-up share capital (375)
capital/non-distributable reserves (376)
capital redemption reserve (376)
contingency (396)
contingent asset (396)
contingent liability (396)
discontinued operations (391)
exceptional items (392)

extraordinary items (393)
general reserve (376)
liabilities (396)
non-adjusting events (395)
operating profit (392)
ordinary activities (393)
post balance sheet events (395)
prior period adjustments (394)
profit for the financial year (381)
profit on ordinary activities (381)
provision (396)
reserves (396)
retained profits (375)
revaluation reserve (376)
revenue/distributable reserves (376)
share premium (376)
shareholders' interests (376)

References

1. Accounting Standards Board (1999). *Financial Reporting Standard 3—Reporting Financial Performance* (ASB).
2. Accounting Standards Committee (1986). *Statement of Standard Accounting Practice 6—Extraordinary Items and Prior Year Adjustments* (ICAEW).
3. Accounting Standards Committee (1980). *Statement of Standard Accounting Practice 17—Accounting for Post Balance Sheet Events* (ICAEW).
4. Accounting Standards Board (1998). *Financial Reporting Standard 12—Provisions, Contingent Liabilities and Contingent Assets* (ASB).
5. Accounting Standards Committee (1980). *Statement of Standard Accounting Practice 18—Accounting for Contingencies* (ICAEW).

Review questions

27.1 Explain the difference between the authorized share capital, allotted share capital and called-up share capital of companies.

27.2 Explain the difference between revenue/distributable reserves and capital/non-distributable reserves, giving three examples of the latter.

27.3 Explain the difference between a reserve and a provision.

27.4 Briefly explain the reason(s) for the separate disclosure of components of financial performance such as discontinued operations, exceptional and extraordinary items in published company accounts.

27.5 **a** Explain the nature of acquisitions and discontinued operations.
b Briefly describe the treatment of each of these items in published company accounts.

27.6 **a** Explain with examples the nature of exceptional items and extraordinary items.
b Briefly describe the treatment of each of these items in published company accounts.

27.7 **a** Explain with examples the nature of prior period adjustments.
b Briefly describe the treatment of prior period adjustments in published company accounts.

27.8 **a** Explain with examples the nature of post balance sheet events.
b Describe the treatment of post balance sheet events in published company accounts.

27.9 **a** Explain with examples the nature of contingent assets and contingent liabilities.
b Describe the treatment of contingent assets and liabilities in published company accounts.

27.10 Explain with an example the difference between current liabilities, provisions and contingent liabilities.

Exercises

An asterisk after the question number indicates that there is a suggested answer in the Appendix.

27.11 Level I

Set out below is the capital section of a company's balance sheet.

	31 Mar 20X8	*31 Mar 20X7*
	£000	£000
Ordinary share capital	140,000	140,000
Preference share capital	—	30,000
Share premium	20,000	20,000
Capital redemption reserve	30,000	—
Revaluation reserve	9,700	7,200
General reserve	27,000	20,000
Profit and loss account	84,900	70,300
	311,600	287,500

You are required to explain the five different reserves that are shown on this company's balance sheet, including in your answer the possible reasons for their existence. (JMB)

27.12 Level I

a The following items usually appear in the final accounts of a limited company:

i interim dividend;
ii authorized capital;
iii general reserve;
iv share premium account.

Required:
An explanation of the meaning of each of the above terms.

b The following information has been obtained from the books of Drayfuss Ltd:

Authorized capital	100,000 8 per cent £1 preference shares
	400,000 50p ordinary shares
Profit and loss account balance 1 Apr 20X8	£355,000
General reserve	£105,000
Issued capital	80,000 8 per cent £1 preference shares (fully paid)
	250,000 50p ordinary shares (fully paid)
Net trading profit for the year to 31 Mar 20X9	£95,000

The preference share interim dividend of 4 per cent had been paid and the final dividend of 4 per cent had been proposed by the directors. No ordinary share interim dividend had been declared, but the directors proposed a final dividend of 15p per share. The directors agreed to transfer to general reserve £150,000.

Required:
The profit and loss appropriation account for the year ended 31 March 20X9. Ignore taxation. (AEB)

27.13 Level II

The following information has been extracted from the balance sheet of Aston Products Ltd as at 30 April 20X5.

	£000
Authorized share capital	
Ordinary shares of 50 pence each	4,000
6 per cent preference share of £1 each	1,500
	5,500
Allotted and called-up share capital	
Ordinary shares of 50 pence each	2,000
6 per cent preference shares of £1 each	1,000
	3,000
Retained profits	950

There were no other reserves in the balance sheet at 30 April 20X5.

You are given the following additional information relating to the year ended 30 April 20X6.

1 The company issued one million ordinary shares at a price of 75 pence each on 1 January 20X6.
2 The management have decided to revalue the land and buildings which cost £400,000 at a value of £600,000.
3 The profit before tax for the year ended 30 April 20X6 was £475,000.
4 The corporation tax on the profit for the year ended 30 April 20X6 was estimated to be £325,000.
5 There are no interim dividends during the year ended 30 April 20X6 but the directors have proposed a final dividend on the preference shares, and a dividend of 10 pence each on the ordinary shares.
6 The directors have agreed to transfer £350,000 to a general reserve at 30 April 20X6.

You are required to prepare in vertical form the profit and loss appropriation account for the year ended 30 April 20X6, and a balance sheet extract at that date showing the composition of the shareholders' interests.

27.14 Level II

Cold Heart plc, which has a turnover of £100 million and pre-tax profit of £10 million, has its accounts drawn up on 30 June each year and at 30 June 20X5 the company's accountant is considering the items specified below.

1 The directors have decided that the change in trading prospects evident during the year means that the goodwill shown at 30 June 20X4 at £200,000 has no value at 30 June 20X5.
2 Research and development expenditure of £7 million has been incurred in the year, and has been written off due to the project being abandoned.
3 Unrealized revaluation surplus of £10 million which arose on the revaluation of the company's buildings during the year.
4 A provision for bad debts of £15 million on the collapse of the company's main customer during the year.
5 A loss of £1 million arising from the closure of the company's retailing activities.

You are required to classify each of the above items into one of the following categories, explaining the reasons for the classification:

- **a** Extraordinary item
- **b** Exceptional (abnormal) item
- **c** Transfer direct to reserves
- **d** Discontinued operations. (JMB adapted)

27.15 Level II

SSAP17 Accounting for post balance sheet events defines the treatment to be given to events arising after the balance sheet date but before the financial statements are approved by the Board of Directors.

Required:

- **a** Define the terms 'adjusting events' and 'non-adjustment events' as they are used in SSAP17.
- **b** Consider each of the following four post balance sheet events.

  If you think the event is an adjusting one, show exactly how items in the accounts should be changed to allow for the event.

  If you think the event is non-adjusting, write a suitable disclosure note, including such details as you think fit.

You may assume that all the amounts are material but that none is large enough to jeopardize the going concern status of the company.

- i The company makes an issue of 100,000 shares which raises £180,000 shortly after the balance sheet date.
- ii A legal action brought against the company for breach of contract is decided, shortly after the balance sheet date, and as a result the company will have to pay costs and damages totalling £50,000. No provision has currently been made for this event. The breach of contract concerned occurred before the balance sheet date.
- iii Stock included in the accounts at cost £28,000 was subsequently sold for £18,000.
- iv A factory in use at the balance sheet date and valued at £250,000 was completely destroyed by fire. Only half of the value was covered by insurance. The insurance company has agreed to pay £125,000 under the company's policy. (ACCA)

27.16 Level II

Your managing director is having a polite disagreement with the auditors on the subject of accounting for contingencies. Since the finance director is absent on sick leave he has come to you for advice.

It appears that your firm is involved in four unrelated legal cases, P, Q, R and S. In case P the firm is suing for £10,000, in case Q the firm is suing for £20,000, in case R the firm is being sued for £30,000 and in case S the firm is being sued for £40,000. The firm has been advised by its expert and expensive lawyers that the chances of the firm winning each case are as follows:

Case	*Percentage likelihood of winning*
P	8
Q	92
R	8
S	92

Required:
Write a memorandum to the managing director which

i explains why FRS12 is relevant to these situations;
ii states the required accounting treatment for each of the four cases in the published accounts;
iii gives journal entries for any necessary adjustments in the double-entry records;
iv suggests the contents of any Notes to the Accounts that are required by the FRS;
v briefly discusses whether FRS12 leads to a satisfactory representation of the position.

(ACCA)

27.17 Level II

The trial balance of Norr Ltd as 31 December 20X9 appeared as follows:

	Dr	Cr
	£	£
Ordinary shares of £1—fully paid		50,000
Purchases	220,000	
Retained profit		30,000
Freehold property—cost	80,000	
Fixtures—cost	15,000	
Fixtures—accumulated depreciation		9,000
Rates	3,000	
Motor vehicles—cost	28,000	
Motor vehicles—accumulated depreciation		14,000
Insurance	2,000	
Stock	40,000	
Debtors	30,000	
Trade creditors		24,000
Sales		310,000
Bank	12,100	
12 per cent debentures		40,000
Debenture interest	2,400	
Wages and salaries	34,000	
Heat and light	4,100	
Professional fees	3,900	
General expenses	1,200	
Motor expenses	2,000	
Provision for bad debts		1,000
Bad debts	300	
	478,000	478,000

Additional information

1 During the year a motor vehicle purchased on 31 March 20X6 for £8,000 was sold for £3,000. The sale proceeds were debited to the bank account and credited to the sales account, and no other entries have been made in the accounts relating to this transaction.

2 Depreciation has not yet been provided for the year. The following rates are applied on the straight line basis, with the assumption of no residual value:

Fixtures and fittings	10 per cent
Motor vehicles	20 per cent

The company's policy is to provide a full year's depreciation in the year of acquisition and no depreciation in the year of disposal.

3 Stock at 31 December 20X9 amounted to £45,000.
4 Rates paid in advance amount to £400. Insurance includes £200 paid in advance. An electricity bill covering the quarter to 31 December 20X9 and amounting to £320 was not received until February 20X0. It is estimated that the audit fee for 20X9 will be £1,500. An accrual also needs to be made in relation to debenture interest.
5 A general provision for bad debt of 4 per cent of debtors is to be carried forward.
6 The directors propose a dividend of £10,000.

You are required to:

a prepare a profit and loss account and balance sheet on the basis of the above information;
b explain the meaning of the terms 'provision' and 'reserve', giving one example of each from the balance sheet you have prepared. (JMB adapted)

27.18 Level II

The Cirrus Co. Ltd has the following balances on its books at 31 December 20X0.

	Dr	Cr
	£	£
50p ordinary shares		20,000
£1 6 per cent preference shares		14,000
Purchases	240,000	
Sales		310,000
Stock at 1 January 20X0	20,000	
Directors' fees	6,000	
Undistributed profit at 1 January 20X0		35,700
10 per cent debentures		20,000
Debenture interest paid	1,000	
Discounts allowed	500	
Administrative expenses	18,400	
Sales staff salaries	18,500	
Selling and distribution expenses	4,000	
Heating and lighting	2,500	
Rent and rates	1,700	
Debtors	14,000	
Provision for doubtful debts at 1 January		300
Creditors		9,700
Land and buildings at cost	65,000	
Vans at cost less depreciation	19,800	
Cash in hand	400	
Bank balance		2,100
	411,800	411,800

The following information is also given:

1 The stock at 31 December 20X0 has been valued at £32,000. Further investigation reveals that this includes some items originally purchased for £3,000 which have been in stock for a long time. They need modification, probably costing about £600, after which it is hoped they will be saleable for between £3,200 and £3,500. Other items, included in the total at their cost price of £5,000, have been sent to an agent and are still at his premises awaiting sale. It cost £200 for transport and insurance to get them to the agent's premises and this amount is included in the selling and distribution expenses.
2 The balance on the vans account (£19,800) is made up as follows:

	£
Vans at cost (as at 1 Jan 20X0)	30,000
Less: Provision for depreciation to 1 Jan 20X0	13,800
	16,200
Additions during 20X0 at cost	3,600
	19,800

Depreciation is provided at 25 per cent per annum on the diminishing balance method. The addition during the year was invoiced as follows:

	£
Recommended retail price	3,000
Signwriting on van	450
Undersealing	62
Petrol	16
Number plates	12
Licence (to 31 Dec 20X0)	60
	3,600

3 The directors, having sought the advice of an independent valuer, wish to revalue the land and buildings at £80,000.
4 The directors wish to make a provision for doubtful debts of $2\frac{1}{2}$ per cent of the balance of debtors at 31 December 20X0.
5 Rates prepaid at 31 December 20X0 amount to £400, and sales staff's salaries owing at that date were £443.
6 The directors have proposed an ordinary dividend of 5p per share and the 6 per cent preference dividend.
7 Ignore VAT.

Required:

a Explain carefully the reason for the adjustments you have made in respect of items 1, 2 and 3 above.

b Prepare a trading and profit and loss account for the year ended 31 December 20X0, and a balance sheet as at that date.

c Briefly distinguish between your treatment of debenture interest and proposed dividends.

(ACCA)

27.19* **Level II**

The following is the trial balance of D. Cooper Ltd as at 30 September 20X9:

	Debit	*Credit*
	£	£
Authorized, allotted and called-up share capital:		
100,000 ordinary shares of £1 each		100,000
50,000 7 per cent preference shares of 50p each		25,000
Leasehold premises at valuation	140,000	
Goodwill	20,000	
Plant and machinery (cost £80,000)	66,900	
Loose tools (cost £13,000)	9,100	
Stock	9,400	
Debtors/creditors	11,200	8,300
Bank overdraft		7,800
Purchases/sales	49,700	135,250
Directors' salaries	22,000	
Rates	4,650	
Light and heat	3,830	
Plant hire	6,600	
Interest on debentures	1,200	
Preliminary expenses	1,270	
10 per cent debentures		24,000
Provision for bad debts		910
Share premium		35,000
Profit and loss account		2,580
Revenue reserve		10,200
Interim dividend on ordinary shares	3,250	
Audit fees	1,750	
Revaluation reserve		9,860
Bad debts	700	
Listed investments	8,000	
Investment income		650
	359,550	359,550

The following additional information is available:

1 Stock at 30 September 20X9 is valued at £13,480.
2 Rates include a payment of £2,300 for the six months from 1 July 20X9.
3 Depreciation on plant is 15 per cent per annum of cost and the loose tools were valued at £7,800 on 30 September 20X9. The company does not amortize goodwill or premises.
4 The provision for bad debts is to be adjusted to 10 per cent of the debtors at the end of the year.
5 The preference share dividends are outstanding at the end of the year and the last half year's interest on the debentures has not been paid.
6 The corporation tax on this year's profit is £6,370.
7 The directors propose to declare a final dividend on the ordinary shares of 13 pence per share and transfer £2,500 to the revenue reserve.

You are required to prepare in vertical form a profit and loss account for the year ended 30 September 20X9 and a balance sheet at that date.

27.20* **Level II**

The following is the trial balance of L. Johnson Ltd as at 31 December 20X8:

	Debit £	*Credit* £
Authorized capital:		
200,000 ordinary shares of £1 each		200,000
90,000 5 per cent preference shares of £1 each		90,000
Issued and called-up capital:		
80,000 ordinary shares		80,000
50,000 5 per cent preference shares		50,000
Freehold buildings (at valuation)	137,000	
Motor vehicle (cost £35,000)	29,400	
Plant and machinery (cost £40,000)	32,950	
Development costs (cost £10,000)	6,600	
Interim dividend on preference shares	1,250	
Provision for bad debts		860
Wages and salaries	5,948	
Bad debts	656	
Discount allowed/received	492	396
Goodwill	10,000	
Listed investments	4,873	
Purchases/sales	78,493	130,846
Capital redemption reserve		9,000
Revaluation reserve		13,500
Formation expenses	250	
Directors' emoluments	13,000	
Returns inwards/outwards	1,629	1,834
Rates	596	
Dividends received		310
Profit and loss account		3,126
Light and heat	1,028	
Audit fee	764	
Revenue reserve		8,400
Share premium		5,600
10 per cent debentures		30,000
Stock	9,436	
Debtors/creditors	11,600	8,450
Bank overdraft		3,643
	345,965	345,965

You are given the following additional information:

1 Corporation tax of £2,544 will be payable on the profit of 20X8.
2 Rates include £200 for the half year ended on 31 March 20X9.
3 Electricity for the quarter to 31 January 20X9 of £330 is not included in the trial balance.
4 The provision for bad debts is to be adjusted to 5 per cent of the debtors at the end of the year.

5 Annual depreciation on the reducing balance method is 25 per cent of vehicles, 20 per cent of plant and 10 per cent of development costs. The company does not amortize goodwill or buildings.
6 Formation expenses are to be written off against the share premium account.
7 Stock at 31 December 20X8 was £12,456.
8 It is proposed to pay a final dividend on the ordinary shares of 6.25 pence per share.
9 The directors have decided to transfer £4,000 to the revenue reserve this year.
10 The debenture interest for the year and the final dividend on the preference shares are outstanding at the end of the year.

You are required to prepare in vertical form a profit and loss account for the year ended 31 December 20X8 and a balance sheet at that date.

27.21* **Level II**

The following is the trial balance of Oakwood Ltd as at 30 June 20X5:

	Debit	*Credit*
	£	£
Authorized capital:		
150,000 ordinary shares of £1 each		150,000
70,000 5 per cent preference shares of £1 each		70,000
Allotted and called-up capital:		
125,000 ordinary shares		125,000
60,000 5 per cent preference shares		60,000
Freehold buildings at cost	165,000	
Development costs (cost £12,000)	5,400	
Goodwill	8,000	
Delivery vehicles (cost £28,000)	18,700	
Plant and machinery (cost £34,000)	31,900	
Listed investments	3,250	
10 per cent debentures		20,000
Share premium		9,000
Revenue reserve		6,100
Interim dividend on ordinary shares	2,000	
Interim dividend on preference shares	1,500	
Provision for bad debts		730
Administrative salaries	6,370	
Bad debts	740	
Discount allowed/received	290	440
Purchases/sales	81,230	120,640
Audit fee	390	
Preliminary expenses	200	
Directors' remuneration	14,100	
Returns inwards/outwards	230	640
Carriage inwards	310	
Rates	600	
Interest received		410
Profit and loss account		7,700
Light and heat	940	

Postage and telephone	870	
Stock	8,760	
Debtors/creditors	10,400	7,890
Bank overdraft		2,630
	361,180	361,180

Additional information:

1 Corporation tax of £1,080 will be payable on the profit of this year.
2 Rates include a prepayment of £150.
3 Gas used in May and June 20X5 of £270 is not included in the trial balance.
4 Stock at 30 June 20X5 was £11,680.
5 The provision for bad debts is to be adjusted to 5 per cent of debtors at 30 June 20X5.
6 Annual depreciation on the reducing balance method is 20 per cent of plant, 10 per cent of vehicles and 25 per cent of development costs. The company does not amortize buildings or goodwill.
7 Sales includes goods on sale or return at 30 June 20X5 which cost £500 and were invoiced to debtors at a price of £1,000.
8 Included in plant and machinery are consumable tools purchased during the year at a cost of £300.
9 The preliminary expenses are to be written off against the share premium account balance.
10 It is proposed to pay a final dividend on the ordinary shares of 3.2 pence per share.
11 The directors have decided to transfer £3,000 to the revenue reserve.

You are required to prepare in vertical form a profit and loss account for the year ended 30 June 20X5 and a balance sheet at that date.

27.22 Level II

The trial balance of Harmonica Ltd at 31 December 20X5 is given below.

	Dr	Cr
	£000	£000
Purchases and sales	18,000	28,600
Stock at 1 Jan 20X5	4,500	
Warehouse wages	850	
Salespersons' salaries and commission	1,850	
Administrative salaries	3,070	
General administrative expenses	580	
General distribution expenses	490	
Directors' remuneration	870	
Debenture interest paid	100	
Dividends—interim dividend paid	40	
Fixed assets—cost	18,000	
—aggregate depreciation, 1 January 20X5		3,900
Trade debtors and creditors	6,900	3,800
Provision for doubtful debts at 1 January20X5		200
Balance at bank		2,080
10 per cent debentures (repayable 20X9)		1,000
Called-up share capital (£1 ordinary shares)		4,000

Share premium account		1,300
Profit and loss account, 1 Jan 20X5		8,720
Suspense account (see Note 3 below)		1,650
	55,250	55,250

The following further information should be allowed for:

1 Closing stock amounted to £5m.
2 A review of the trade debtors total of £6.9m showed that it was necessary to write off debts totalling £0.4m, and that the provision for doubtful debts should be adjusted to 2 per cent of the remaining trade debtors.
3 Two transactions have been entered in the company's cash record and transferred to the suspense account shown in the trial balance. They are:
   a The receipt of £1.5m from the issue of 500,000 £1 ordinary shares at a premium of £2 per share.
   b The sale of some surplus plant. The plant had cost £1m and had a written down value of £100,000. The sale proceeds of £150,000 have been credited to the suspense account but no other entries have been made.
4 Depreciation should be charged at 10 per cent per annum on cost at the end of the year and allocated 70 per cent to distribution costs and 30 per cent to administration.
5 The directors propose a final dividend of 4 pence per share on the shares in issue at the end of the year.
6 Accruals and prepayments still to be accounted for are:

	Prepayments	*Accruals*
	£000	£000
General administrative expenses	70	140
General distribution expenses	40	90
	110	230

7 Directors' remuneration is to be analysed between distribution costs and administrative expenses as follows:

	£000
—distribution	300
—administration	570
	870

8 Ignore taxation.

Required:
Prepare the company's trading and profit and loss account for the year ended 31 December 20X5 and balance sheet as at 31 December 20X5 in a form suitable for publication. Notes to the accounts are not required. (ACCA)

27.23 Level II

Before attempting this question students will need to read the sections of the next chapter relating to rights issues and bonus issues.

The summarized balance sheet of Arbalest Ltd at 30 September 20X6 was as follows:

	Cost	*Aggregate depreciation*	*Net book value*
	£000	£000	£000
Fixed assets			
Land	2,000	nil	2,000
Buildings	1,500	450	1,050
Plant and machinery	2,800	1,000	1,800
	6,300	1,450	4,850
Current assets		3,180	
Less: Current liabilities		2,070	1,110
			5,960
Capital and reserves			
Called-up share capital			
3,000,000 ordinary shares of 50p each			1,500
Share premium account			400
Profit and loss account			4,060
			5,960

During the year ended 30 September 20X7 the company had the following transactions:

1 Nov 20X6	A rights issue of one share for every three held at a price of £1.50 per share. All the rights issue shares were taken up.
1 Dec 20X6	Sale for £70,000 of plant and machinery which had cost £1,000,000 and had a book value of £200,000.
1 Mar 20X7	A bonus (capitalization) issue of one share for every one held at that date using the share premium account as far as possible for the purpose.
1 June 20X7	Purchased a new factory block for £3,000,000 (including land £600,000).
1 July 20X7	Purchased plant and machinery for £1,600,000.
30 Sep 20X7	The company decided to revalue the freehold land held at 30 September 20X6 from £2,000,000 to £2,500,000.

The company depreciation policies are:

Land	No depreciation
Buildings	2 per cent per annum on cost, straight line basis
Plant and machinery	10 per cent per annum on cost, straight line basis

Proportionate depreciation is provided in the year of purchase of an asset, with none in the year of disposal.

The retained profit for the year was £370,000, and the profit for the year was £840,000.

Prepare the following notes required for the company's balance sheet for publication at 30 September 20X7:

a Movements on fixed assets;
b Movements on reserves;
c A statement of total recognized gains and losses;

Ledger accounts for the transactions are not required. (ACCA adapted)

27.24 Level II

The following balances existed in the accounting records of Koppa Ltd at 31 December 20X7:

		£000
Development costs capitalized, 1 Jan 20X7		180
Freehold land as revalued 31 Dec 20X7		2,200
Buildings	—cost	900
	—aggregate depreciation at 1 Jan 20X7	100
Office equipment	—cost	260
	—aggregate depreciation at 1 Jan 20X7	60
Motor vehicles	—cost	200
	—aggregate depreciation at 1 Jan 20X7	90
Trade debtors		1,360
Cash at bank		90
Trade creditors		820
12 per cent debentures (issued 20X0 and redeemable 20X7)		1,000
Called up share capital—ordinary shares of 50p each		1,000
Share premium account		500
Revaluation reserve		200
Profit and loss account 1 Jan 20X7		1,272
Sales		8,650
Purchases		5,010
Research and development expenditure for the year		162
Stock 1 Jan 20X7		990
Distribution costs		460
Administrative expenses		1,560
Debenture interest		120
Interim dividend paid		200

In preparing the company's profit and loss account and balance sheet at 31 December 20X7 the following further information is relevant:

1 Stock at 31 December 20X7 was £880,000.

2 Depreciation is to be provided for as follows:

Land	Nil
Buildings	2 per cent per annum on cost
Office equipment	20 per cent per annum, reducing balance basis
Motor vehicles	25 per cent per annum on cost

Depreciation on buildings and office equipment is all charged to administrative expenses. Depreciation on motor vehicles is to be split equally between distribution costs and administrative expenses.

3 The £180,000 total for development costs as at 1 January 20X7 relates to two projects:

	£000
Project 836: completed project: (balance being amortized over the period expected to benefit from it. Amount to be amortized in 20X7: £20,000)	82
Project 910: in progress:	98
	180

4 The research and development expenditure for the year is made up of:

	£000
Research expenditure	103
Development costs on Project 910 which continues to satisfy the requirements in SSAP13 for capitalization	59
	162

5 The freehold land had originally cost £2,000,000 and was revalued on 31 December 20X7.

6 Prepayments and accruals at 31 December 20X7 were:

	Prepayments	*Accruals*
	£000	£000
Administrative expenses	40	11
Sundry distribution costs		4

7 The share premium account balance arose as a result of the issue during 20X7 of 1,000,000 50p ordinary shares at £1.00 each. All shares qualify for the proposed final dividend to be provided for (see note below).

8 A final dividend of 20p per share is proposed.

Required:
Prepare the company's profit and loss account for the year ended 31 December 20X7 and balance sheet as at that date, in a form suitable for publication as far as the information provided permits. The note detailing reserve movements for the year should be given, but no other notes are required. Ignore taxation. (ACCA)

27.25* **Level II**

Topaz Ltd makes up its accounts regularly to 31 December each year. The company has operated for some years with four divisions, A, B, C and D, but on 30 June 20X6 Division B was sold for £8m, realizing a profit of £2.5m. During 20X6 there was a fundamental reorganization of Division C, the costs of which were £1.8m.

The trial balance of the company at 31 December 20X6 included the following balances:

	Division B		*Divisions A, C and D combined*	
	Dr	Cr	Dr	Cr
	£m	£m	£m	£m
Sales		13		68
Costs of sales	8		41	
Distribution costs (including a bad debt of £1.9m—Division D)	1		6	
Administrative expenses	2		4	
Profit on sale of Division B		2.5		
Reorganization costs, Division C			1.8	
Interest on £10m 10 per cent debenture stock issued in 20X0			1	
Taxation			4.8	
Interim dividend paid			2	
Revaluation reserve				10

A final dividend of £4m is proposed.

The balance on the revaluation reserve relates to the company's freehold property and arose as follows:

	£m
Balance at 1.1.20X6	6
Revaluation during 20X6	4
Balance at 31.12.X6 per trial balance	10

Required:

a i Prepare the profit and loss account of Topaz Ltd for the year ended 31 December 20X6 complying as far as possible with the provisions of the Companies Act 1985 and *FRS3 Reporting Financial Performance*.

ii Prepare the statement of total recognized gains and losses for the year as required by FRS3.

b Explain why the changes to the profit and loss account introduced by FRS3 improve the quality of information available to users of the financial statements. (ACCA)

chapter

28

Changes in share capital

Learning objectives

After reading this chapter you should be able to:

1. explain the meaning of the key terms and concepts listed at the end of the chapter;
2. describe the procedures relating to the issue of shares to the public, forfeited shares, reissued shares, rights issues, bonus issues, and the purchase and redemption of shares;
3. explain the nature and purpose of rights issues and bonus issues;
4. describe the legal restrictions on the purchase and redemption of shares including the reasons for these restrictions;
5. show the journal and ledger entries relating to public issues, forfeited shares, reissued shares, rights issues, bonus issues, and the purchase and redemption of shares;
6. prepare the balance sheet of a limited company immediately after a change in share capital.

Introduction

One feature distinguishing companies from other forms of business organization is the use of finance from the issue of ordinary and preference shares. Chapter 26 drew attention to the characteristics of shares. This chapter focuses on the accounting procedures which are used to record an expansion in the number of shares through issues, and reductions through redemptions.

Share issues to the public

Share issues often involve very large sums of money and, given that a series of actions needs to be taken, are complex matters. Since, in addition, this money is being paid in by members of the public, great care must be taken in the procedures which record the various actions.

It may be useful, before considering the accounting procedures themselves, to review the whole process. A number of methods may be used to issue shares to the public, but the accounting procedures are similar and these can be presented most appropriately by considering an **offer for sale**.

First, an offer is made to the public to apply for shares in the form of a prospectus. At this time the price to be paid for the share is set. This price may be the same as, or above, the par/nominal value of the share. Under the Companies Acts shares may not be issued at below their par value. Where the price is above the nominal value, the additional amount included in the price is the share premium, which must be recorded as one of the capital reserves considered in the previous chapter.

On **application** it is usual for applicants to be required to send money representing part but not all of the price of the shares for which they apply (known as application money). Once the closing date for applications is reached the number of shares applied for must be compared with the number on offer. If applications are lower than the number on offer, the issue is undersubscribed and the company will be required either to cancel the offer and refund the application money or to call upon the underwriters to take up the remaining shares. If the issue is oversubscribed, then a basis for allotting shares must be established. Some applications may be rejected and the application money must be refunded; some may receive a reduced allocation and their excess application money used as further payment towards the price of the shares.

Having established the basis for allocation, shares can then be issued to those who are to get them—an action known as **allotment**. The balance of the price is, typically, payable in instalments, perhaps some on allotment (known as 'allotment money') and some **calls** at a later date (known as 'call money'). There may be more than one instalment, so there would be a first call, second call, etc. Anyone failing to pay a call is liable to *forfeit* their partly paid shares and once forfeited, these may be *reissued* to others on terms agreed for this purpose. These are referred to as **forfeited shares** and **reissued shares**, respectively.

Learning Activity 28.1

Watch the financial press for an issue of shares to the public, such as a government privatization. Obtain a copy of the prospectus and read carefully the terms of the issue with particular reference to the amounts payable on application, allotment and any calls. Note also the relevant dates, dividend entitlement, etc.

The major stages of an issue of shares and the associated cash/bank (i.e. cash book effects) can be summarized as follows:

	Application	Allotment	Call	Forfeit	Reissue
Cash effects on company	Application money received	Allotment money received	Call money received	—	Reissue money received

The double entry to record all of these stages is as follows:

Stage	*Transaction*	*Debit*	*Credit*
1 Application	Money received	Cash	Application and allotment account
2 Allotment	Refund some application money	Application and allotment account	Cash
	Allotment money received	Cash Cash	Application and allotment account
	Issue of shares partly paid	Application and allotment account	Share capital
	Share premium (if any)	Application and allotment account	Share premium
3 Call	Call made	Call account	Share capital
	Call money received	Cash	Call account
4 Forfeit	Called-up value of forfeited shares excluding share premium	Share capital	Forfeited shares account
	Premium included in amount called up (if any)	Share premium	Forfeited shares account
	Amount in the call account relating to arrears on forfeited shares	Forfeited account account	Call account
5 Reissue	Nominal value of shares reissued called up	Reissues account	Share capital
	Money received	Cash	Reissues account
	Amount in forfeited shares account relating to reissue	Forfeited shares account	Reissues account
	Balance on reissues account	Reissues account	Share

Example 28.1 shows how these entries will be reflected in the ledger.

Example 28.1

The issued share capital of Stag plc was £100 million, being 100 million ordinary shares of £1 each fully paid with no share premium account. Since the company wished to expand but had a bank balance of only £1 million it decided to issue more shares. On 2 January 20X1 the company offered 40 million shares to the public at £1.25 each, payable 40p on application, 30p on allotment and 55p on call at 30 June 20X1.

Applications closed on 31 January when applications had been received for 65 million shares. On 4 February, 15 million were rejected and moneys returned, and allotments were made pro rata to the remaining applicants.

Note that since 50 million share applications were not rejected, allotments were on the basis of four shares 50p paid (i.e. 50 million @ 40p ÷ 40 million) for every five shares applied for; a balance of only 30p – (50p – 40p) = 20p per share will be payable on allotment.

The amounts due on allotment were received in full by 28 February.

By 4 July, call money for 32 million shares had been received. The remaining shares (8 million) were forfeited. On 18 July 4 million forfeited shares were reissued at 75p each.

Workings

*Application and allotment*Application money = 65 million @ 0.40 = £26 million
Refunded = 15 million @ £0.40 = £6 million
Allotment money = 40 million @ £0.20 = £8 million
Share premium per share = £1.25 – £1 = £0.25
Total share premium = 40 million @ £0.25 = £10 million
Nominal value of application and allotment = 40 million @ (£0.40 + £0.30 – £0.25) = £18 million.

Call
Nominal value of call = 40 million @ £0.55 = £22 million
Call money received = 32 million @ £0.55 = £17.6 million.

Forfeiture
Called-up value of forfeited shares excluding the share premium = 8 million @ £1 = £8 million
Premium included in the amount called up relating to forfeited shares = 8 million @ £0.25 = £2 million
Amount in call account relating to arrears on forfeited shares = 8 million @ £0.55 = £4.4 million.

Reissue
Reissue money received = 4 million @ £0.75 = £3 million
Nominal value of shares reissued called up = 4 million @ £1 = £4 million
Amount in forfeited shares account relating to reissue = 4 million @ (£0.40 + £0.30) = £2.8 million.

The entries to record the application and allotment will appear in the ledger as shown below (all amounts in £ millions):

Bank

2 Jan	Balance b/d	1	4 Feb	Appln and allotment	6
31 Jan	Appln and allotment	26		Balance c/d	29
28 Feb	Appln and allotment	8			
		35			35
	Balance b/d	29			

Application and allotment

4 Feb	Bank	6	31 Jan	Bank	26
4 Feb	Share capital	18	28 Feb	Bank	8
4 Feb	Share premium	10			
		34			34

Share capital

			2 Jan	Balance b/d	100
			4 Feb	Appln and allotment	18
					118

Share premium

			4 Feb	Appln and allotment	10

The call and forfeiture can then be entered in the ledger as follows:

Bank

	Balance b/d	29.0			
4 July	Call	17.6			
		46.6			

Call

30 June	Share capital	22.0	4 July	Bank	17.6
			4 July	Forfeited shares	4.4
		22.0			22.0

Share capital

4 July	Forfeited shares	8.0		Balance b/d	118.0
	Balance c/d	132.0	30 June	Call	22.0
		140.0			140.0
				Balance b/d	132.0

Share premium

4 July	Forfeited shares	2.0	Balance b/d		10.0
	Balance c/d	8.0			
		10.0			10.0
			Balance b/d		8.0

Forfeited shares

4 July	Call	4.4	4 July	Share capital	8.0
	Balance c/d	5.6		Share premium	2.0
		10.0			10.0
			Balance b/d		5.6

Finally, the amounts can be entered for the reissue of 4 million shares, thus:

Bank

	Balance b/d	46.6			
18 July	Reissues	3.0			
		49.6			

Share capital

					Balance b/d	132.0
				18 July	Reissues	4.0
						136.0

Share premium

					Balance b/d	8.0
				18 July	Reissues	1.8
						9.8

Forfeited shares

18 July	Reissues	2.8			Balance b/d	5.6
	Balance c/d	2.8				
		5.6				5.6
					Balance b/d	2.8

Reissues

18 July	Share capital	4.0	18 July	Bank	3.0
	Share premium	1.8	18 July	Forfeited shares	2.8
		5.8			5.8

Note

1 The balances can be interpreted thus: the share capital represents the original shares of £100 million plus 36 million shares issued at £1 par value. The forfeited shares account balance of £2.8 million is the remaining 4 million shares not reissued at the 70p application and allotment amounts. The share premium comprises £9 million, being the premium at 25p on the 36 million shares issued, plus the additional premium of £800,000 on the reissue; in the case of the 4 million reissued shares, 75p rather than just the call money of 55p was raised, giving 4 million × 20p = £800,000.

Rights issues

Offering shares for sale to the public is an expensive and potentially risky process. Costs can be saved by offering shares to existing shareholders at below the current market price. This is known as a **rights issue**. Failure to take up their rights to the issue would thus mean that shareholders lose the opportunity of making a gain. As a result, all shareholders can be expected either to take up the issue (providing it is priced sufficiently below the existing market price) or to sell their rights to someone who will. The success of the issue is thus much less risky.

If the full subscription price is payable upon issue, the accounting entries are simple. Recognition must be given to any premium included in the price. Thus, for a company with 15 million shares of £1 which decides to make a one for five rights issue at a price of £1.80 (when the market price is £2.50, say) the entries must reflect the 80p per share premium as shown below:

The journal

	Debit	*Credit*
	£	£
Bank (3 million × £1.8)	5,400,000	
Share capital (3 million × £1)		3,000,000
Share premium (3 million × £0.8)		2,400,000
	5,400,000	5,400,000

Bonus/capitalization issues

A **bonus/capitalization issue** of shares is one where shares are issued to existing shareholders free of charge. Accounting for bonus issues is relatively straightforward. No cash is involved and the issue represents 'converting' capital or revenue reserves into shares and distributing these to existing shareholders. Shares are regarded as a particularly permanent form of capital. The effect of making a bonus issue is to adjust the capital structure portrayed in accounts. The increased permanence of capital that this represents may be taken as an indicator of increased security.

The double entry may make use of a temporary bonus account so that credit amounts can be transferred from reserves to the bonus account and from this to share capital on the issue of the shares. For example, the capital structure of XS plc at 1 May 20X1 may be as follows:

	£000
Share capital 10 million ordinary shares of £1 each	10,000
General reserves	1,800
Share premium	3,000
Shareholders' interests	14,800

It has been decided to make a bonus issue of two ordinary shares for every five existing shares. Since general reserves represent revenue reserves, while share premium is a capital reserve for which the law permits only limited uses, it will probably be more attractive to the company to utilize the share premium first. The ledger entries (in £000) will be as follows:

Share premium

Bonus shares	3,000	Balance b/d	3,000

General reserve

Bonus shares	1,000	Balance b/d	1,800
Balance c/d	800		
	1,800		1,800
		Balance b/d	800

Bonus shares account

Ordinary shares	4,000	Share premium	3,000
		General reserve	1,000
	4,000		4,000

Ordinary share capital

		Balance b/d	10,000
		Bonus shares	4,000
			14,000

Alternatively, the bonus shares account may be omitted and the entries made between the reserve accounts and the share capital account directly.

The balance sheet would indicate a revised capital structure thus:

	£000
Share capital 14 million ordinary shares of £1 each	14,000
General reserves	800
Shareholders' interests	14,800

The same shareholders own the same assets but their ownership is represented by more shares. In theory, they should be in just the same financial position as before the issue.

Purchase and redemption of shares

By contrast to issuing new shares, we now turn to accounting for buying them back. The law identifies two types of buying back shares, **purchase of shares** and **redemption of shares**. Apart from the words that are used to describe the transactions and the change of name in account headings, the accounting procedures are identical for both types. The difference arises from the terms under which the shares are originally issued. Some shares are issued as 'redeemable shares'. Redemption may be during a specifically defined period or merely at the discretion of the company or even the shareholder. Purchase takes place when shares which are not identifiable as 'redeemable' are purchased by the company.

In both cases, important legal restrictions are applicable. A company may only issue redeemable shares provided it has, in issue, some shares that are not redeemable. After any purchase of shares a company must have in issue shares such that at least two shareholders remain owning shares that are not redeemable. Only fully paid shares may be redeemed or purchased and all shares bought back by the company must be cancelled so they are not available for resale. The law does not restrict the classes of shares which may be redeemed, although most examples have tended to deal with preference shares. The illustrations tend to show redemption of preference shares, but purchase or redemption of ordinary shares could equally well be used.

A particular concern embodied in the law is to maintain the called-up capital (and capital reserves). This is intended as a protection for creditors. While shareholders may be entitled, under the Companies Acts, to receive dividends from distributable profits, called-up capital (and capital reserves) cannot be freely distributed. If a company is wound up, creditors must be paid before shareholders receive any capital repayment. The prior claim of the creditors would have been severely undermined if any earlier capital repayments had been made. The law restricts companies from using borrowing to make payments to shareholders beyond any profits made, since this may leave nothing for the creditors. The idea of maintenance of capital, introduced in accounting as a basis for measurement (see Chapter 2), is being utilized here, in restricting dividends to distributable profits, as a legal principle.

The legal considerations relating to the nominal value of shares are separated from those dealing with premiums, so initially this section will address redemption (or purchase) at nominal values first and then introduce the treatment of premiums.

Redemption (or purchase) at nominal value

The legal requirements for maintenance of capital when a redemption is made can be achieved by:

1. Setting aside distributable profits equal to the total nominal value of capital redeemed by transferring that amount to a non-distributable reserve known as '**capital redemption reserve**'. To enable this to be carried out, there must be distributable profits sufficient to redeem the capital repaid and the transfer 'freezes' these profits in a capital form.
2. Issuing new shares (explicitly for the purpose of providing funds for redemption) with a total nominal value not less than that of the shares redeemed. This effectively replaces the capital redeemed by new capital.
3. A combination of new issues and transfers to a capital redemption reserve which, in total, amount to the nominal value of capital redeemed.

Example 28.2 illustrates how these requirements are applied.

Example 28.2

The following is the summarized balance sheet of Jay plc as at 30 June 20X1:

	£000
Sundry assets	280
Bank	160
	440
Preference share capital	80
Ordinary share capital	200
Share premium	20
Unappropriated profit and loss	140
	440

If a company decided to redeem all the preference capital at par (i.e. the nominal value) without any new issue of shares, then the double entry would be as follows.

The journal

	Debit	*Credit*
	£	£
Preference share capital	80,000	
Bank		80,000
Being the repayment of shares		
Unappropriated profit and loss	80,000	
Capital redemption reserve		80,000

The last entry is the transfer of distributable profits to the capital redemption reserve to maintain non-distributable capital. The maintenance of capital can be readily identified by looking at an extract from the balance sheet before and after the redemption as shown below.

	Before		*After*
	£000		£000
Preference share capital	80	Capital redemption reserve	80
Ordinary share capital	200		200
Share premium	20		20
Non-distributable capital	300		300

Now suppose the company had only £60,000 bank and £380,000 sundry assets. It might wish to raise money to contribute to the redemption through the issue of shares. If a rights issue of £50,000 ordinary shares was made, at par, as part of the scheme of redemption the entries would be as follows.

The journal

	Debit	*Credit*
	£	£
Bank	50,000	
Ordinary share capital		50,000
Preference share capital	80,000	
Bank		80,000
Unappropriated profit and loss	30,000	
Capital redemption reserve		30,000

The amount transferred to the capital redemption reserve is the excess of the nominal values of the shares redeemed over the nominal value of the capital issued (i.e. £80, 000 – £50,000 = £30,000).

Again, the maintenance of non-distributable capital can be demonstrated by looking at an extract' from the balance sheet before and after the redemption shown below:

	Before		*After*
	£000		£000
Preference share capital	80	Capital redemption reserve	30
Ordinary share capital	200		250
Share premium	20		20
Non-distributable capital	300		300

Redemption (or purchase) at a premium

Shares are often bought back at a price above the nominal value, the excess representing a premium. Unless the shares were originally issued at a premium, the premium paid must be transferred from distributable profits. Even where the shares were originally issued at a premium, there are limitations on the extent by which the transfer may be reduced. The amount is restricted to the smaller of:

1 the premium on the original issue of the shares;
2 the sum of the balance on the share premium account plus the premium on the new issue used to fund (in part) the redemption.

Example 28.3 illustrates how these rules are applied.

Example 28.3

The following is an extract from the balance sheet of Kay plc as at 31 December 20X0:

	£
Issued share capital	
100,000 ordinary A shares of £1 each fully paid	100,000
20,000 ordinary B shares of £1 each fully paid	20,000
Share premium on ordinary shares	3,000
Revenue reserves	50,000
Shareholders' interests	173,000

The ordinary B shares were originally issued at a premium of 25 per cent. On 1 January 20X1 the company purchased the 20,000 B shares for £29,000, issuing 12,000 A shares at £1.40 to contribute to the funding of the purchase. The relevant entries would be as follows:

Bank

Ordinary A shares	16,800	Ordinary B shares	29,000

Ordinary A shares

		Balance b/d	100,000
		Bank	12,000
			112,000

Share premium

Redemption premium	5,000	Balance b/d	3,000
Balance c/d	2,800	Bank	4,800
	7,800		7,800
		Balance b/d	2,800

Ordinary B shares

Bank	29,000	Balance b/d	20,000
		Redemption premium	9,000
	29,000		29,000

Redemption premium

Ordinary B shares	9,000	Share premium	5,000
		Revenue reserves	4,000
	9,000		9,000

Revenue reserves

Capital redemption reserve	8,000	Balance b/d	50,000
Redemption premium	4,000		
Balance c/d	38,000		
	50,000		50,000
		Balance b/d	38,000

Capital redemption reserve

		Revenue reserves	8,000

Balance sheet extract

	£
Issued share capital	
112,000 ordinary A shares	112,000
Share premium	2,800
Capital redemption reserve	8,000
Revenue reserves	38,000
Shareholders' interests	160,800

Notes

1 The amount transferred from revenue reserves to the capital redemption reserve is the excess of the nominal value of the shares redeemed over the nominal value of the new issue (i.e. £20,000 – £12,000 = £8,000).

2 The amount transferred from the redemption premium account of £5,000 to the share premium account is the maximum permissible amount. This is the lower of:
   a the original premium on the issue of 25 per cent of £20,000 = £5,000; or
   b the sum of the balance on the share premium account of £3,000 plus the premium on the new issue of £4,800 = £7,800.

3 The difference between the two sides of the redemption premium account of £4,000 after the transfer in note 2 of £5,000 must be set against the revenue reserves.

Example 28.4 brings together many of the matters considered in this chapter.

Example 28.4

The following items are extracted from the balance sheet of Weaver (Ropes) plc at 31 December 20X1:

	£
Issued share capital	
250,000 ordinary shares of £1 each fully paid	250,000
75,000 6 per cent redeemable preference shares	75,000
Share premium	5,000
Revenue reserves	70,000
Shareholders' interests	400,000

The preference shares were originally issued at a premium of 14 per cent.

On 1 January 20X2 the company made the following resolutions:

1 To issue 50,000 ordinary shares of £1 each at a premium of 10 per cent, payable 40 per cent on application and the balance on allotment; the issue is to be made to finance in part the redemption of preference shares.
2 To redeem the preference shares at a premium of 20 per cent.
3 To make a bonus issue of one ordinary share for every five ordinary shares.

These actions were duly taken by the company consecutively in the order shown. Applications were received for 54,000 ordinary shares, the application moneys for 4,000 shares being returned.

You are required to present the relevant ledger accounts to record the above transactions and to show how the items appear in Weaver's balance sheet after the transactions have been carried out.

Workings

Application and allotment

Application money = 54,000 @ [40 per cent × (110 per cent × £1)] = £23,760
Refunded = 4,000 @ £0.44 = £1,760
Allotment money = 50,000 @ [60 per cent × (110 per cent × £1)] = £33,000
Share premium per share = 10 per cent × £1 = £0.10
Total share premium = 50,000 × £0.10 = £5,000

Preference share redemption

Redemption payment = £75,000 × 120 per cent = £90,000
Premium on redemption = £90,000 − £75,000 = £15,000

Bonus issue

One-fifth of (250,000 + 50,000) = 60,000 × £1

Application and allotment

Bank	1,760	Bank	23,760
Ordinary shares	50,000	Bank	33,000
Share premium	5,000		
	56,760		56,760

Ordinary shares

		Balance b/d	250,000
		Application and allotment	50,000
		CRR—bonus issue	25,000
		Revenue reserves—bonus	35,000
			360,000

Share premium

Premium on redemption	10,000	Balance b/d	5,000
		Application and allotment	5,000
	10,000		10,000

Preference shares

Bank	90,000	Balance b/d	75,000
		Redemption premium	15,000
	90,000		90,000

Premium on redemption

Preference shares	15,000	Share premium	10,000
		Revenue reserves	5,000
	15,000		15,000

Revenue reserves

Premium on redemption	5,000	Balance b/d	70,000
CRR	25,000		
Ordinary shares—bonus	35,000		
Balance c/d	5,000		
	70,000		70,000
		Balance b/d	5,000

Capital redemption reserve

Ordinary shares—bonus	25,000	Revenue reserves	25,000

Balance sheet extract

	£
Issued ordinary shares	360,000
Revenue reserves	5,000
Shareholders' interests	365,000

Notes

1 The amount transferred from revenue reserves to the capital redemption reserve (CRR) is the excess of the nominal value of the shares redeemed over the nominal value of the new issue (i.e. £75,000 – £50,000 = £25,000).

2 The amount transferred from the premium on redemption account of £10,000 to the share premium account is the lower of:

a the original premium on the issue of 14 per cent of £75,000 = £10,500; or

b the sum of the balance on the share premium account of £5,000, plus the premium on the new issue of £5,000 = £10,000.

3 The difference between the two sides of the premium on redemption account of £5,000 after the transfer in note 2 of £10,000 must be set against the revenue reserves.

4 Since the bonus share issue occurred after the redemption of the preference shares, the capital redemption reserve can be utilized to make this issue. As explained earlier in the chapter, because capital reserves have restricted uses, whereas revenue reserves can be distributed as dividends, it is usual to utilize the maximum possible amount of capital reserves to make a bonus issue. The remainder (i.e. £60,000 − £25,000 = £35,000) will have to be taken from the revenue reserves. Notice that the use of the capital redemption reserve to make a bonus issue does not reduce the non-distributable capital. This was £250,000 + £75,000 + £5,000 = £330,000, and is now £360,000.

Issue and redemption of debentures

Accounting for the issue and redemption of debentures follows the same principles as those for shares with one major difference that makes it considerably easier. There are no legal requirements for the maintenance of capital or restrictions on the treatment of any premium on redemption. Thus, it is not necessary either to make a new issue of shares or debentures, or to transfer an equivalent amount of distributable profits to a capital reserve. Furthermore, any premium on redemption may be set against an existing balance on a share premium account or carried forward and set against any further share premium in the same year. Alternatively, the premium may be charged to the profit and loss account. The same applies to any discount on the issue of debentures.

However, many academics argue that debenture discounts and premiums should be put in the profit and loss account because they represent a financing cost in the form of either a front- or end-loaded interest rate adjustment. In addition, when debentures are not redeemed from a new issue of shares or debentures, some companies voluntarily create a capital redemption reserve either over the life of the debenture or at redemption. Thus, students may encounter examination questions on the redemption of debentures which either allow the freedom of the law or contain specific requirements similar to the redemption of shares.

Summary

Changes in share capital occur when there is a public offer for sale of shares, a rights issue, bonus issue, redemption or purchase by a company of its own shares. When shares are offered for sale to the public, the price usually includes a premium, and is sometimes payable in instalments. These comprise amounts payable on application, allotment of the shares, and any number of later calls. If a shareholder fails to pay a call the shares may be forfeited and later reissued.

A rights issue is an issue of shares to existing shareholders based on the number of shares that they already hold. The price is usually below the current market price but frequently includes a premium. A bonus issue is also an issue of shares to existing shareholders based on the number of shares that they already hold. However, these are free of charge, and represent the conversion of reserves into shares. Companies normally prefer to convert capital reserves into bonus shares before utilizing revenue reserves for this purpose.

Some shares are issued as redeemable, such as redeemable preference shares. A company may also purchase and cancel non-redeemable shares. The law requires that before shares are redeemed or purchased, either (1) a new issue of shares must be made of an equivalent total nominal value; or (2) distributable profits equal to the total nominal value of the shares redeemed or purchased must be transferred to a capital redemption reserve (CRR); or (3) some combination of a new issue and transfer to a CRR equal to the total nominal value of the shares redeemed or purchased. Shares may be redeemed or purchased either at par or at a premium. Any premium on redemption must be transferred from distributable profits, unless the shares were originally issued at a premium. In this case the transfer from distributable profits can be reduced by the lower of: (1) the premium on the original issue; or (2) the sum of the balance on the share premium account plus any premium on a new issue used to fund the redemption or purchase.

Key terms and concepts

Allotment (416)
application (416)
bonus/capitalization issue (421)
calls (416)
capital redemption reserve (422)
forfeited shares (416)
offer for sale (416)
purchase of shares (422)
redemption of shares (422)
reissued shares (416)
rights issue (420)

Review questions

28.1 Describe the procedure relating to an issue of shares to the public where the price includes calls.

28.2 Explain the nature and purpose of: (a) a rights issue, and (b) a bonus issue of shares.

28.3 Describe the legal restrictions on the purchase and redemption of shares, including the reasons for these restrictions.

Exercises

An asterisk after the question number indicates that there is a suggested answer in the Appendix.

28.4 **Level I**

The financial information below was extracted from the balance sheets of two companies as at 30 June 20X0.

	Postgate plc	*Coalux plc*
	£000	£000
Authorized share capital		
£1 ordinary shares	500	400
11 per cent £1 preference shares	250	—
Called-up share capital		
£1 ordinary shares, fully paid	350	400
11 per cent £1 preference shares, fully paid	250	—

Reserves		
Share premium	150	200
Other capital reserves	250	100
Retained earnings	350	300
Loan capital		
9 per cent debenture stock (20X8)	200	—
10 per cent debenture stock (20X6)	—	50
Current liabilities	140	190

Additional information:

1 Both companies revalued their freehold land and buildings with effect from 1 July 20X0. The revaluations were as follows:

	Balance sheet value as at 30 June 20X0	*Balance sheet revaluation*
	£000	£000
Postgate plc	300	500
Coalux plc	150	200

2 The board of directors of Postgate plc had already approved a bonus issue of shares earlier in the year. The bonus issue is to be effected on 1 July 20X0 on the following terms: one bonus share for every ordinary share currently held. The issue is to be funded, one-half from the capital reserves and one-half from the retained earnings.

3 Coalux had approved a rights issue on the following terms: one new ordinary share for every two ordinary shares currently held. The issue price was fixed at £1.50 per share. The issue was fully subscribed and the funds were received on 1 July 20X0.

You are required to show for each of the companies the effects on the balance sheet of items 1 to 3 above. (AEB adapted)

28.5 Level II

The following is the summarized balance sheet of Shares Ltd as at 31 December 20X0:

	£000		£000
Authorized share capital			
500,000 ordinary shares of £1 each	500	*Fixed assets*	695
Issued share capital			
250,000 ordinary shares of £1 each fully paid	250	*Current assets*	865
Revenue reserves			
Unappropriated profit	125		
	375		
11 per cent debenture stock	50		
Current liabilities	1,135		
	1,560		1,560

In order to improve the company's liquidity and consolidate the capital position the following steps were taken:

1 A bonus issue of ordinary shares fully paid was made to the existing shareholders of two shares for every five shares held.

2 The authorized share capital was increased from 500,000 ordinary shares of £1 each to 1,000,000 ordinary shares of £1 each.
3 An issue of 250,000 ordinary shares was made at a premium of 10 per cent, 55p payable on application and 55p payable on allotment.
4 The debenture stock was redeemed in cash at a premium of 5 per cent.

The transactions took place as follows:

1 Jan 20X14	Debenture stock redeemed
	The authorized share capital was increased
	The bonus issue of shares was made
	Applications were received for 400,000 shares.
21 Jan 20X1	The balance of cash due on allotment was received.

All applications for shares were reduced pro rata and the excess moneys received were retained on account of the amounts due on allotment.

You are required to:

a show by journal entries, including cash, the entries necessary to record the above transactions; and
b prepare a balance sheet to show the effect of the above proposal on the liquidity of the company. (ACCA)

28.6 Level II

The authorized and issued share capital of Forward Ltd as at 31 May 20X1 was 150,000 ordinary shares of £1 each, fully paid. On 1 June 20X1, the authorized share capital was increased to £225,000 divided into ordinary shares of £1 each. On the same date 56,000 ordinary shares of £1 each were offered for sale at £1.25 per share payable as follows:

On application	60p
On allotment (including the premium of 25p per share)	40p
On first and final call on 1 September 20X1	25p

The lists were closed on 8 June 20X1 by which date application had been received for 94,000 shares and it was decided to deal with these as follows:

1 To refuse allotment to one applicant for 10,000 shares and return the cash paid in respect of these shares.
2 To reduce proportionately all the other applications and to utilized the surplus received on these applications in part payment of amounts due on allotment.

The amounts payable on allotment were received on 23 June 20X1 with the exception of £50 due from one allottee of 500 shares, and these shares were declared forfeited on 1 August 20X1. The forfeited shares were reissued on 29 September 20X1 as fully paid at £1.15. The first and final call due on 1 September 20X1 was duly paid by the remaining shareholders.

You are required to:

a record the above transactions in the appropriate ledger accounts; and
b show how the balances on such accounts would appear in the company's balance sheet as on 31 October 20X1. (ACCA)

28.7* **Level II**

The summarized balance sheet for Turner plc at 31 May 20X7 was as follows:

	£
Authorized capital	1,000,000
Issued share capital	
800,000 shares of 50p each fully paid	400,000
Revenue reserves	350,000
Shareholders' interests	750,000

On 1 June 20X7, 200,000 shares were offered to the public at 60p, 20p payable on application, 20p on allotment and 20p on call at 31 December 20X7.

Applications were received for 300,000 shares. Those relating to 50,000 shares were returned, the balance of the excess application money being retained to reduce amounts due on allotment. All shares allotted were taken up, but call money on 10,000 shares remained unpaid at 31 January 20X8. These shares were forfeited and reissued as fully paid at 40p per share on 1 February 20X8.

On 29 February 20X8, Turner plc made a one-for-four bonus issue.

You are required to show the ledger accounts to record the above transactions, minimizing any reduction in revenue reserves.

28.8* **Level III**

At 31 July 20X2, the balance sheet of Winder Engineering plc showed the following position:

Issued share capital:	£
80,000 10 per cent redeemable cumulative preference shares of £1 each	80,000
200,000 ordinary £1 shares	200,000
Share premium	20,000
Unappropriated profit and loss	140,000
Shareholders' interests	440,000
Sundry assets	380,000
Cash	60,000
Net assets	440,000

The preference shares were originally issued at a premium of 10 per cent, and are redeemable at a premium of 5 per cent at any time during 20X2. The company decided it would redeem the preference shares as follows:

1 Aug:	40,000 preference shares redeemed for cash.
1 Sep:	25,000 ordinary £1 shares offered for sale at £1.20 per share, 70p on application, the balance on allotment, the issue being made to provide some of the funds for redeeming the remaining preference shares.
15 Sep:	Application lists closed, applications for 30,000 shares having been received. Applications for 5,000 shares were unsuccessful and the cash received in respect of these applications was returned.
20 Sep:	The balance due on allotment was received in full.
29 Sep:	The remaining 40,000 preference shares were redeemed.

Required:

a Prepare the necessary journal entries to record the above transactions.

b Prepare a balance sheet at 30 September 20X2 which incorporates these changes. (Assume that no other transactions took place between 1 August and 30 September 20X2.)

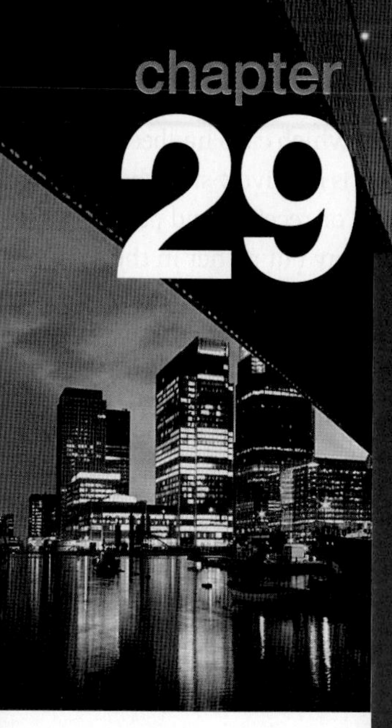

Cash flow statements

Learning objectives

After reading this chapter you should be able to:

1. explain the meaning of the key terms and concepts listed at the end of the chapter;
2. explain the nature and purpose of cash flow statements;
3. explain the advantages and limitations of cash flow statements;
4. explain the relationship between cash flow statements and the profit and loss account and balance sheet;
5. prepare simple cash flow statements for both bodies sole and limited companies;
6. prepare classified cash flow statements using the indirect method for both bodies sole and limited companies in accordance with FRS1 (including notes);
7. explain the nature of the groups of items and subtotals found in classified cash flow statements conforming with FRS1;
8. outline the main differences between the direct and indirect methods of preparing cash flow statements.

The nature and purpose of cash flow statements

In simple terms, the purpose of a **cash flow statement** is to show the reasons for the change in the cash and bank balance over the accounting year. Another common way of expressing this is that the purpose of a cash flow statement is to show the manner in which cash has been generated and used (or where it has gone). It might be thought that this is relatively straightforward, since it could be done in the form of a summarized cash book or receipts and payments account. Unfortunately, however, it is usually not done in this way but rather in the form of changes in the value of the items in the balance sheet between the end of the previous year and the end of the current year.

These changes are classified as either sources or applications of cash funds. Sources essentially relate to receipts and applications to payments. However, in terms of changes in the items in the balance sheet, sources of cash funds comprise the following:

1 The net profit for the year. Any loss for the year is an application of cash funds.
2 Capital introduced and money borrowed during the year in the form of loans received.
3 Proceeds from the sale of fixed assets and investments.
4 Increases in current liabilities and decreases in current assets.

Applications of cash funds comprise the following:

1 Drawings.
2 Any capital or loans repaid during the year.
3 Purchases of fixed assets and investments.
4 Increases in current assets and decreases in current liabilities.

The net profit is a source of cash funds because the amount by which sales exceed purchases and expenses, even though any or all of these may have been on credit, will eventually result in a net cash inflow.

Probably the most confusing aspect of cash flow statements is the changes in current assets and liabilities. Some simplified examples may thus be helpful. An increase in creditors is a source of funds because the money that would otherwise have been used to pay these creditors is available for other purposes. A decrease in debtors is also a source of funds since this results in an inflow of additional money. Similarly, a decrease in stock is a source of funds because the proceeds of sale result in more money being available. Conversely, an increase in stock is an application of funds since money will have been used to pay for it. Similarly, an increase in debtors is an application of funds because allowing debtors additional credit is like giving them a loan. A decrease in creditors is also an application of funds since money will have been paid out to them. Frequently, certain sources of funds have corresponding applications. For example, an increase in stock may be 'financed' by an increase in creditors.

A simple cash flow statement might consist of the above list of sources and applications of cash funds, including a breakdown of the changes in current assets and current liabilities between creditors, debtors and stock. This is illustrated in Example 29.1.

Example 29.1

The following are the balance sheets of A. Cashwood as at 30 September 20X4 and 30 September 20X5:

		30 Sep 20X5		*30 Sep 20X4*
	£	£	£	£
Fixed assets at cost		85,000		97,000
Current assets				
Stock	13,600		10,800	
Debtors	8,400		9,700	
Cash and bank	2,500		3,600	
	24,500		24,100	
Current liabilities				
Creditors	(7,300)		(6,100)	
Net current assets		17,200		18,000
Total assets less current liabilities		102,200		115,000
Long-term liabilities				
Bank loan		(20,000)		(15,000)
Net assets		(82,200)		100,000
Capital				
At start of year		77,700		82,200
Add: Capital introduced		2,800		4,300
Profit for the year		21,600		34,200
		102,100		120,700
Less: Drawings		(19,900)		(20,700)
At end of year		82,200		100,000

You are required to prepare a cash flow statement for the year ended 30 September 20X5.

A. Cashwood
Cash flow statement for the year ended 30 September 20X5

	£	£
Sources of cash funds:		
Profit for the year		34,200
Capital introduced		4,300
Decrease in stock (13,600 – 10,800)		2,800
		41,300
Applications of cash funds		
Drawings	(20,700)	
Repayment of bank loan (20,000 – 15,000)	(5,000)	
Purchase of fixed assets (97,000 – 85,000)	(12,000)	
Increase in debtors (9,700 – 8,400)	(1,300)	
Decrease in creditors (7,300 – 6,100)	(1,200)	
		(40,200)
Increase (decrease) in cash and bank balance		1,100
Cash and bank balance at 1 Oct 20X4		2,500
Cash and bank balance at 30 Sep 20X5		3,600

Advantages and limitations of cash flow statements

The advantages of cash flow statements are often presented in terms of the deficiencies of profit and loss accounts and balance sheets. This should not be interpreted to mean that cash flow statements are an alternative to profit and loss accounts. The profit and loss account and balance sheet have a number of limitations, and cash flow statements provide useful additional information for the following reasons:

1 Most readers and potential readers (e.g. private shareholders) appreciate the meaning and importance of cash and will therefore find cash flow statements easier to understand and more relevant. In contrast, the nature of profit and capital and the contents of the profit and loss account and balance sheet are more difficult to understand.
2 Cash flow statements are more objective in that cash received and paid are observable events. In contrast, the profit and loss account and balance sheet are based on the accruals concept and matching principle, which involve subjective allocations, valuations, etc.
3 Cash flow statements therefore permit more meaningful comparisons of performance over time, and between actual performance and forecasts.
4 Profit is only a symbol or measure of performance. The ultimate success and survival of an enterprise depend on its ability to generate and use cash in the most efficient manner. The cash flow statement provides information that facilitates an evaluation of the efficiency with which cash has been generated and used.
5 Future dividends, the repayment of loans and payments to trade creditors depend primarily on the availability of cash and not profits. Cash flow statements provide information which allows users of company published accounts to make more accurate predictions of future dividends, insolvency, etc.

Few accountants would quarrel with the assertion that cash flow statements provide useful additional information. However, most would be opposed to the idea that they should replace the profit and loss account for the following reasons:

1 A statement which is easier to understand is not necessarily more relevant or useful.
2 The preparation of cash flow statements also involves subjective judgements.
3 The use of cash flow statements in making comparisons and the evaluation of performance can be misleading. The pattern of cash flows over time is often erratic and therefore not indicative of an enterprise's long-term performance.
4 Cash flow statements focus on the financing activities of an enterprise rather than the economic or trading activities. They therefore do not provide meaningful information on either past or future economic performance.

Preparation of cash flow statements of companies

The preparation of cash flow statements of companies involves some additional considerations as follows.

Sources of cash funds include:

1 The profit for the year before taxation and dividends. This is because these two items are shown separately as applications of funds.
2 Capital introduced. This will comprise the amount received from any issues of shares and debentures during the year.

Applications of cash funds include:

1 Corporation tax paid during the year.
2 Instead of drawings, the amounts paid during the year in respect of preference and ordinary share dividends. This will normally comprise the interim dividend plus the final dividend of the previous accounting year.
3 Capital repaid will consist of any shares and debentures redeemed during the year.

The preparation of cash flow statements for both sole traders and companies involves some further complications with regard to the figure for profit (or loss) which is included in the statement. This should reflect the funds generated from a business's operating activities. However, the amount of profit shown in the profit and loss account is after deducting (and adding) certain items which do not involve the movement of cash funds. These consist of:

1 Provisions for depreciation on fixed assets.
2 Profits and losses on the sale of fixed assets.
3 Increases and decreases in provisions for bad debts.

All of these items are purely accounting adjustments which arise from the preparation of the profit and loss account on an accruals matching basis. They do not represent movements of cash funds. It is therefore necessary to adjust the figure of profit shown in the profit and loss account in respect of these items to arrive at the cash funds generated from operations that is entered in the cash flow statement as follows:

Profit per profit and loss account
Add: Provisions for depreciation
Losses on sale of fixed assets
Increase in provision for bad debts
Less: Profits on sale of fixed assets
Decrease in provisions for bad debts
= Cash funds generated from operations

This is illustrated in Example 29.2.

Example 29.2

The following are the balance sheets of C. Flowers Ltd as at 31 March 20X1 and 31 March 20X2:

		31 Mar 20X2		*31 Mar 20X1*
	£	£	£	£
Fixed assets at cost		173,000		165,000
Less: Aggregate depreciation		(46,000)		(52,000)
		127,000		113,000
Current assets				
Stock	48,400		56,700	
Debtors	39,100		36,200	
Less: Provision for bad debts	(1,700)		(1,400)	
	37,400		34,800	
Cash and bank	8,600		17,300	
	94,400		108,800	

Creditors: amounts falling due within one year				
Creditors	(31,400)		(32,800)	
Corporation tax	(15,700)		(18,500)	
Proposed dividends	(26,200)		(29,600)	
	(73,300)		(80,900)	
Net current assets		21,100		27,900
Total assets less current liabilities		148,100		140,900
Creditors: amounts falling due after more than one year				
10 per cent debentures		(52,000)		(20,000)
Net assets		96,100		120,900
Allotted and called-up share capital				
Ordinary shares of £1 each		50,000		60,000
Reserves				
Share premium account	18,000		26,000	
General reserve	6,400		9,600	
Profit and loss account	21,700		25,300	
		46,100		60,900
Shareholders' interests		96,100		120,900

Further information

1 Fixed assets which cost £8,000 and had a written down value of £4,200 were disposed of during the year ended 31 March 20X2 at a price of £3,500. There were no other acquisitions or disposals of fixed assets during the year.
2 The total depreciation on fixed assets for the year was £9,800.
3 The corporation tax outstanding at 31 March 20X1 of £15,700 was paid during the year ended 31 March 20X2.
4 The proposed ordinary dividend at 31 March 20X1 of £26,200 was paid on 1 May 20X1. In addition, an interim ordinary dividend of £8,600 was paid on 1 October 20X1.
5 During the year 10,000 ordinary shares were issued at a price of £1.80 each.

You are required to prepare a cash flow statement for the year ended 31 March 20X2.

This example, like most examination questions, does not contain a profit and loss account. In order to ascertain the profit before tax and dividends, it will therefore be necessary to reconstruct the appropriation section of the profit and loss account. The corporation tax and final dividends must either be given as a note in the question or included under current liabilities on the balance sheet at the end of the current year. Any interim dividends must be given as further information in the question. Transfers to reserves and the retained profit of the current year are found by calculating the difference between the amounts shown on the balance sheet at the end of the current year and the end of the previous year for these items. This is shown below.

Computation of profit before taxation and dividends

	£	£
Increase in balance on profit and loss account— (25,300 – 21,700)		3,600
Transfer to reserve (9,600 – 6,400)		3,200
Ordinary dividends—		
Interim	8,600	
Proposed final	29,600	38,200
Corporation tax		18,500
Profit before taxation and dividends		63,500

C. Flowers Ltd
Cash flow statement for the year ended 31 March 20X2

	£	£
Sources of cash funds		
Profit for the year before tax and dividends	63,500	
Add (Less): Adjustments for items not involving the movement of funds—		
Provision for depreciation	9,800	
Loss on sale of fixed assets (4,200 – 3,500)	700	
Decrease in provision for bad debts (1,700 – 1,400)	(300)	
Cash funds generated from operations		73,700
Issue of shares (10,000 × £1.80)		18,000
Proceeds of sale of fixed assets		3,500
Increase in creditors (32,800 – 31,400)		1,400
Decrease in debtors (39,100 – 36,200)		2,900
		99,500
Applications of cash funds		
Tax paid	(15,700)	
Dividends paid (26,200 + 8,600)	(34,800)	
Repayment of debentures (52,000 – 20,000)	(32,000)	
Increase in stock (56,700 – 48,400)	(8,300)	
		(90,800)
Increase (decrease) in cash and bank balance		8,700
Cash and bank balance at 1 Apr 20X1		8,600
Cash and bank balance at 31 Mar 20X2		17,300

Notes

1 The proceeds from the issue of shares of £18,000 (given in Further information above) should correspond with the increase in ordinary share capital (£60,000 – £50,000) and share premium account (£26,000 – £18,000) shown in the balance sheet (i.e. £10,000 + £8,000). The proceeds from an issue of shares are often not given in the Further information, and thus have to be calculated in terms of the increase in share capital and share premium accounts.

2 The details relating to the acquisition and disposal of fixed assets, and depreciation (given in Further information) should also correspond with the changes in fixed assets and aggregate depreciation shown in the balance sheet as follows:

Fixed assets

20X1			20X2		
1 Apr	Balance b/d	173,000	31 Mar	Bank	3,500
			31 Mar	Provision for depreciation (8,000 – 4,200)	3,800
			31 Mar	Loss on sale	700
			31 Mar	Balance c/d	165,000
		173,000			173,000

Provision for depreciation

20X2			20X1		
31 Mar	Fixed assets (8,000 – 4,200)	3,800	1 Apr	Balance b/d	46,000
			20X2		
31 Mar	Balance c/d	52,000	31 Mar	Depreciation expense	9,800
		55,800			55,800

The reason for understanding how the Further information in respect of issues of shares, fixed assets and depreciation corresponds with changes in the balance sheet is that sometimes not all the information required is given as Further information (e.g. acquisitions of fixed assets, revaluations of assets). The student will then have to ascertain the missing information by examining the changes in the balance sheets. A useful way of doing this is in terms of the ledger accounts.

3 In the preparation of a cash flow statement, investments held as a fixed asset are treated in the same way as other fixed assets. However, investments held as a current asset are treated in the same way as cash and bank, as in the relevant International Accounting Standard. The amount of current asset investments is added to the cash and bank balance and shown on cash flow statements as 'cash and cash equivalents'. **Cash equivalents** have been defined as short-term, highly liquid investments which are readily convertible into known amounts of cash without notice and which were within three months of maturity when acquired, less advances from banks repayable within three months from the date of advance.

4 The dividends used to compute the profit before tax and dividends include the proposed final dividend outstanding at the end of the current accounting year (£29,600) because this will have been deducted in arriving at the retained profit for the year of £3,600. It is often given as a note in examination questions, failing which the amount can be found as a current liability on the balance sheet at the end of the current year. In contrast, the dividends shown as an application of funds include the proposed final dividend at the end of the previous accounting year (£26,200) since this will have been paid during the current year. It is often given as a note in examination questions, failing which the amount can be found as a current liability on the balance sheet at the end of the previous accounting year.

5 The corporation tax used to compute the profit before tax and dividends is the amount outstanding at the end of the current accounting year (£18,500) because this will have been deducted in arriving at the retained profit for the year of £3,600. It is often given as a note in examination questions, failing which the amount can be found as a current

liability on the balance sheet at the end of the current year. In contrast, the corporation tax shown as an application of funds (£15,700) is that outstanding at the end of the previous year since this will have been paid during the current year. It is often given as further information in examination questions, failing which the amount can be found as a current liability on the balance sheet at the end of the previous year.

6 In arriving at the profit before tax and dividends it will also be necessary to add any transfer to reserves to the retained profit for the year. This usually has to be identified from the balance sheets at the end of the previous and current accounting years.

7 Any interim dividend paid would have to be given as a note in the examination question or could be ascertained from the profit and loss account in the unlikely event of its being shown in the question.

8 The current assets might have included prepaid expenses and the current liabilities may have included accrued expenses. These could be dealt with separately in the cash flow statement as sources or applications of cash. However, another acceptable and more expedient treatment is simply to aggregate prepayments with debtors, and accruals with creditors.

Relationship between cash flow statements, profit and loss accounts and balance sheets

Cash flow statement are intended to complement the profit and loss account and balance sheet. The main difference between a cash flow statement and a profit and loss account lies in the observation that profit is not the same as the increase in cash over a given accounting period, but rather is only one source of funds. The relationship between a cash flow statement and a balance sheet is that the former identifies the movements in assets, liabilities and capital which have taken place during the year and the resultant effect on cash funds shown on the latter. It also provides a link between the balance sheet at the beginning of the period, the profit and loss account for the period, and the balance sheet at the end of the period.

Classified cash flow statements—FRS1

In 1991 the Accounting Standards Board (ASB) issued *Financial Reporting Standard 1—Cash Flow Statements* (FRS1). This was revised in 1996.[1] FRS1 defines **cash flow** as 'an increase or decrease in an amount of cash'. **Cash** is defined as 'cash in hand and deposits repayable on demand with any qualifying financial institution, less overdrafts repayable on demand. Deposits are repayable on demand if they can be withdrawn at any time without notice and without penalty or if a maturity or period of notice of not more than 24 hours or one working day has been agreed.'[1]

FRS1 requires the items that are normally contained in a cash flow statement to be classified grouped under seven headings in the following order:

1 **Net cash inflow (or outflow) from operating activities**
This refers to the net increase (or decrease) in cash that results from a company's trading activities. It is discussed in depth in a later section of the chapter.

2 **Returns on investments and servicing of finance**
This refers to receipts arising from the ownership of investments and payments to the providers of finance and non-equity shareholders. Cash inflows comprise interest and

dividends received. Cash outflows comprise interest and dividends paid on preference shares.

3 *Taxation*

This refers to cash received and paid to taxation authorities in respect of a reporting entity's revenue and capital profits. It usually only relates to the corporation tax paid on a company's annual profit. It does not include value added tax (VAT) or property taxes.

4 **Capital expenditure**

This refers to cash flows arising from the acquisition and disposal of fixed assets. The entries in the cash flow statement should distinguish between tangible fixed assets and intangible fixed assets. In each case the receipts from disposal must be shown separately from the payments in respect of acquisitions.

5 *Equity dividends paid*

This refers to the dividends paid on ordinary shares during the year.

6 *Management of liquid resources*

Liquid resources are defined in FRS1 as 'current asset investments held as readily disposable stores of value. A readily disposable investment is one that: (a) is disposable by the reporting entity without curtailing or disrupting its business; and is either: (b) (i) readily convertible into known amounts of cash at or close to its carrying amount, or (b) (ii) traded in an active market.' In short, this refers to cash flows arising from the purchase and sale of current asset investments. Notice the similarity between liquid resources and cash equivalents, and in particular the separate treatment of liquid resources required by FRS1 which is inconsistent with the International Accounting Standard.

7 *Financing*

This refers to cash received and paid to external providers of finance in respect of the principal amounts of finance. The most common external providers of finance are shareholders, loan stock and debenture holders. The term 'principal amounts' refers to the amount borrowed in the case of loans, the essential point being that interest and dividends are not included under this heading, but rather under point 2 above. Cash inflows include the proceeds from issuing shares, loan stock, debentures and other forms of borrowing. Cash outflows include the repayment of loan stock, debentures and other amounts borrowed, and payments to reacquire or redeem the entity's shares.

In addition to presentation, the main differences between the cash flow statement as shown in the earlier sections of this chapter and that required by FRS1 are: (a) the latter necessitates investment income and interest paid to be disclosed under the heading 'returns on investments and servicing of finance'; (b) it also requires a separate disclosure of cash equivalents under the heading 'management of liquid resources'; and (c) the 'net cash inflow from operating activities' is fundamentally different from the 'cash funds generated from operations'. The latter is discussed in depth in a later section of this chapter.

The purpose, uses and advantages of classified cash flow statements

The purpose of cash flow statements is often expressed in a number of different ways. At the start of this chapter it was given in simple terms as being to show the reasons for the change in the cash and bank balance over the accounting year. However, the grouping of items in the classified cash flow statement permits a more precise definition, as follows. The purpose of a classified cash flow statement is to show the effects on cash flows of an entity's operating, investing and financing activities for a period. According to FRS1, the objective of cash flow statements is to provide information that assists in the assessment of liquidity, solvency and financial adaptability. These definitions may be expanded and expressed in slightly different terms to emphasize the potential uses of cash flow statements, as follows:

1 To enable management, investors, creditors and others to see how the various activities of the company have been financed (e.g. which activities have net cash outflows and which have net cash inflows).
2 According to FRS1 'a cash flow statement in conjunction with a profit and loss account and balance sheet provides information on financial position and performance as well as liquidity, solvency, and financial adaptability'.[1] It also 'gives an indication of the relationship between profitability and cash generating ability, and thus of the quality of the profit earned. Historical cash flow information could be useful to check the accuracy of past assessments and indicate the relationship between the entity's activities, and its receipts and payments.'[1]
3 Historical cash flow information may assist users of financial statements in making judgements on the amount, timing and degree of certainty of future cash flows. The cash flow statement may therefore be useful to management, investors, creditors and others in assessing the enterprise's ability to:
   a pay its debts (i.e. loan repayment, trade creditors, etc.) as and when they become due;
   b pay loan interest, dividends, etc.
   c decide whether it will need to raise additional external finance (e.g. issue shares or debentures) in the near future.
4 To explain why an enterprise may have a net profit for the year but nevertheless has less cash at the end of that year (or vice versa), and thus, for example, is only able to pay a small dividend.
5 To allow users to see directly the reasons for the difference between the net profit and its associated cash receipts and payments (i.e. the net cash inflow from operating activities).

When answering examination questions it is often advisable to assume that the function/objective/purpose(s), uses and advantages of cash flow statements all require similar answers but the amount of detail increases with each, respectively. The reader may, therefore, find it useful at this point to refer back to the earlier section of this chapter which deals with the advantages of cash flow statements.

Net cash inflow from operating activities

As the wording suggests, the net cash inflow from operating activities refers to the (net) amount of cash generated from a company's trading activities. According to FRS1, '**cash flows from operating activities** are in general the cash effects of transactions and other events relating to operating or trading activities normally shown in the profit and loss account in arriving at operating profit.'[1]

The net cash inflow from operating activities is sometimes crudely referred to as the cash profit, or more accurately the operating profit computed on a cash basis. In contrast, the 'cash funds generated from operations' shown in the cash flow statements earlier in this chapter refer to the profit computed on an accruals basis as adjusted for certain non-cash items (such as provisions for depreciation and bad debts). It can therefore be argued that including the latter in a cash flow statement (as earlier in this chapter) is theoretically unsound. The complexity of the difference between these two concepts of operating cash flows and operating cash funds is the reason why they have not been discussed until this point. It is also the reason why the cash flow statements have been presented thus far in a theoretically inferior but expedient manner. This will now be remedied.

Under FRS1 the derivation of the net cash inflow from operating activities must be shown in the form of a reconciliation between the operating profit reported in the profit and loss account and the net cash flow from operating activities. This should be given either adjoining the cash flow statement or as a note. It must be compiled using what is known as the indirect method. However, there is another method, known as the direct method, which the ASB does not require but wishes to encourage companies to use. At present this would have to be in addition to the indirect method. Both the direct and indirect methods give the same figure of operating cash flows. Most companies use the indirect method. The reasons are probably because it does not require the disclosure of any new information and if they were to use the direct method this would have to be additional to the indirect method. All the examples and exercises in this book are based on the indirect method.

The **direct method** involves converting all the individual items in the profit and loss account from an accruals basis to a cash basis. It therefore shows the cash received from customers, cash paid to suppliers, and cash paid in wages and for operating expenses. This is all new information not shown elsewhere in the published accounts.

The **indirect method** involves adjusting the operating profit (before tax and dividends) for changes in the working capital and non-cash items such as provisions for depreciation and bad debts, and profits and losses on the disposal of fixed assets. Notice that the operating profit is not the same as the profit before taxation and dividends. The operating profit excludes investment income and is before deducting interest charges.

The indirect method also serves to demonstrate the difference between the net cash inflow from operating activities and the cash funds generated from operations discussed above. The former is simply the latter adjusted for changes in working capital (other than cash).

The requirements of FRS1 with regard to the application of the indirect method of deriving the net cash inflow from operating activities are illustrated in Example 29.3 using the answer to Example 29.2. For the purpose of this illustration it is only necessary to make one change to the question. Let us assume that the net profit before taxation and dividends includes interest received of £5,400 and is after deducting debenture interest paid of £4,700. This means that the operating profit will be the net profit (before tax and dividends) less the interest received, plus the interest paid (i.e. £63,500 – £5,400 + £4,700 = £62,800).

Example 29.3

Notes to the cash flow statement

1 *Reconciliation of operating profit to net cash inflow from operating* activities:

	£
Operating profit	62,800
Depreciation charges	9,800
Loss on sale of tangible fixed assets	700

Provision for bad debts (decrease)	(300)
Increase in creditors	1,400
Decrease in debtors	2,900
Increase in stock	(8,300)
Net cash inflow from operating activities	69,000

Preparation of the classified cash flow statement

The specimen cash flow statement in FRS1 shows only the total of each of the seven groups of items described earlier. Most companies also follow this format. Students may therefore also wish to adopt this approach. However, it necessitates preparing notes to the cash flow statement that show a list of the items under each heading. Thus, given the time constraint in examinations, a quicker and perfectly acceptable alternative adopted in this book is to include the items under each heading within the cash flow statement. This is permissible under FRS1, which states that 'individual categories of inflows and outflows under the standard headings should be disclosed separately either in the cash flow statement or in a note to it'. This is shown below as a continuation of Example 29.3 using the answer to Example 29.2.

Example 29.3 (continued)

C. Flowers Ltd
Cash flow statement for the year ended 31 March 20X2

	£	£
Net cash inflow from operating activities		
(from Note 1 above)		69,000
Returns on investments and servicing of finance:		
Interest received	5,400	
Interest paid	(4,700)	
		700
Taxation		(15,700)
Capital expenditure:		
Receipts from sale of tangible fixed assets	3,500	
Payments to acquire tangible fixed assets	—	
		3,500
		57,500
Equity dividends paid		(34,800)
		22,700
Management of liquid resources		—
Financing		
Issue of ordinary share capital	18,000	
Repayment of debenture loan	(32,000)	
		(14,000)
Increase in cash		8,700

Any receipts from sales of intangible fixed assets and payments to acquire intangible fixed assets must each be shown separately under the heading of capital expenditure.

Similarly, any receipts and payments relating to current asset investments must each be shown separately under the heading of management of liquid resources.

As mentioned above, Note 1—reconciliation of operating profit to net cash inflow from operating activities must be either adjoining the cash flow statement or as a note. That is, it should be shown immediately above or below the cash flow statement. Immediately above is the most common and most practical since it has to be prepared first. It is probably inadvisable to include it in the cash flow statement, even though this appears to be permissible under FRS1, since examiners seem to expect it to be shown separately as in the example in FRS1.

FRS1 also requires two further notes to the cash flow statement. These comprise a reconciliation of net cash flow to movement in net debt and an analysis of changes in net debt. The former must be given either adjoining the cash flow statement or in a note, and the latter should be shown as a note. Net debt is defined in FRS1 as 'the borrowing of the reporting entity less cash and liquid resources. Where cash and liquid resources exceed the borrowings of the entity reference should be made to "net funds" rather than to "net debt"'. Note that debt does not include non-equity/preference shares. According to FRS1 'the objective of the reconciliation of cash flows to the movement in net debt is to provide information that assists in the assessment of liquidity, solvency and financial adaptability'.

An illustration of these two further notes is given below as a continuation of Example 29.3 using the information in Example 29.2.

Example 29.3 (continued)

Notes to the cash flow statement (continued)

2 *Reconciliation of net cash flow to movement in net debt*

		£	£
Increase in cash in the period		8,700	
Cash to repurchase debenture		32,000	
Cash used to increase liquid resources		—	
Change in net debt			40,700
Net debt at 1 April 20X1	(52,000 – 8,600)		(43,400)
Net debt at 31 March 20X2	(20,000 – 17,300)		(2,700)

3 *Analysis of changes in net debt*

	At 1 April 20X1	*Cash flows*	*At 31 Mar 20X2*
	£	£	£
Cash in hand, at bank	8,600	8,700	17,300
Overdrafts	(—)	—	(—)
		8,700	
Debt due within 1 year	(—)	—	(—)
Debt due after 1 year	(52,000)	32,000	(20,000)
Current asset investments	—	—	—
Total	(43,400)	40,700	(2,700)

Notice that at the following are all shown in parentheses—net debt and overdrafts (i.e. credit balances), increase in borrowings, sales of current asset investments and decreases in cash, whereas the following are not shown in parentheses—net funds, cash in hand and current asset investments (i.e. debit balances), repayment of debt, purchases of current asset investments and increases in cash.

Finally, to return to the purpose and uses of classified cash flow statements, the cash flow statement for C. Flowers Ltd in Example 29.3 can be interpreted as showing the following. The cash generated from operating activities of £69,000 has been used to pay corporation tax of £15,700 and dividends of £34,800. There has been no expansion in the business's activities, indeed there has been a slight contraction as shown by the net cash inflow from investing activities of £3,500. The cash generated from operating activities together with the proceeds of issuing additional ordinary shares have been used to repay the debenture loan. In short, this cash flow statement paints a picture of a company well able to cover its financing charges and taxation by cash inflows from operating activities, and which is seeking to reduce its dependence on debt capital by partly replacing it with more permanent ordinary shares. This scenario is often associated with a process of consolidation likely to result in greater financial stability in times of falling profits which frequently occur during an economic recession such as that experienced at the start of this century.

Learning Activity 29.1

There are two basic concepts of funds: cash funds and working capital funds. Cash funds form the basis of cash flow statements, and working capital funds form the basis of funds flow statements or statements of source and application of funds. The purpose of a cash flow statement is to show the reasons for the change in the cash and bank balance over an accounting year.

Summary

The purpose of a cash flow statement is to show the reasons for the change in the cash and bank balance over an accounting year. Another common way of expressing this is that a cash flow statement shows the manner in which cash has been generated and used. The reasons for the change in cash are shown in this statement as either sources or applications of cash funds. The cash flow statement is intended to complement the profit and loss account and balance sheet by providing additional information. It is often regarded as an alternative with its own advantages and limitations. However, the cash flow statement is intended to serve different purposes.

FRS1 requires most companies to include a classified cash flow statement in their annual accounts. The purpose of a classified cash flow statement is to show the effects on cash flows of an entity's operating, investing and financing activities for a given period. The items normally shown in a cash flow statement are classified into seven groups: net cash inflow (or outflow) from operating activities, returns on investments and servicing of finance, taxation, capital expenditure, equity dividends paid, management of liquid resources, and financing. FRS1 requires the net cash inflow (or out-flow) from operating activities to be compiled in a note to the statement using the indirect method. However, there is another method, referred to as the direct method, which the ASB wishes to encourage because it may provide more useful information.

Key terms and concepts

Capital expenditure (442)
cash (441)
cash equivalents (440)
cash flow (441)
cash flow statement (434)
cash flows from operating activities (443)
direct method (444)
indirect method (444)
liquid resources (442)
net cash inflow from operating activities (441)
returns on investments and servicing of finance (441)

References

1. Accounting Standards Board (1996). *Financial Reporting Standard 1—Cash Flow Statements* (ASB).

Review questions

29.1 a Explain the purpose(s) of a cash flow statement.
b Describe the sources and applications of cash funds found in a cash flow statement.

29.2 Describe the advantages and limitations of cash flow statements.

29.3 Explain how cash flow statements differ from: (a) profit and loss accounts; and (b) balance sheets.

29.4 Explain the meaning of each of the following in the context of cash flow statements:
a cash;
b cash equivalents;
c liquid resources.

29.5 List and describe the contents of the seven headings/groups of items found in a cash flow statement prepared in accordance with FRS1.

29.6 Explain the purpose, uses and advantages of classified cash flow statements prepared in accordance with FRS1.

29.7 Explain the difference between the direct and indirect methods of ascertaining the 'net cash inflow from operating activities' shown in a cash flow statement.

Exercises

An asterisk after the question number indicates that there is a suggested answer in the Appendix.

29.8 **Level I**

J. White, a sole trader, has produced the following balance sheets for the years ended 31 March 20X6 and 31 March 20X7.

Balance sheet at 31 March 20X6

	£	£		£	£	£
Capital			*Fixed assets*	*Cost*	*Depn*	*Net*
J. White—Capital			Freehold premises	10,000	–	10,000
account		15,000	Shop fittings	1,000	750	250
Current account	3,000		Motor vehicle	800	400	400
Profit for the year	5,400					
	8,400			11,800	1,150	10,650

Less: Drawings	3,200	5,200	*Current assets*			
Trade creditors		12,000	Stock	11,000		
			Debtors	1,000		
			Cash at bank	9,500		
			Cash in till	50		21,550
		£32,200				£32,200

Balance sheet at 31 March 20X7

Capital			*Fixed assets*	*Cost*	*Depn.*	*Net*
J. White—Capital			Freehold premises	10,000	–	10,000
account		15,000	Shop fittings	1,200	870	330
Current account	5,200		Motor vehicle	800	600	200
Profit for the year	5,800					
	11,000			12,000	1,470	10,530
Less: drawings	4,500	6,500	*Current assets*:			
Trade creditors		8,000	Stock	15,400		
			Debtors	540		
			Cash at bank	3,000		
			Cash in till	30		18,970
		£29,500				£29,500

He is unable to understand why, after he has made a profit for the year ended 31 March 20X7 of £5,800, his bank balance has fallen by £6,500.

You are required to prepare a report explaining how this has occurred. (ACCA)

29.9 Level I

Prepare a cash flow statement in accordance with FRS1 using the information in Question 29.8. There was no investment income or interest paid during the year ended 31 March 20X7.

29.10* Level I

The following are the balance sheets of A. Brooks as at 30 June 20X6 and 30 June 20X7:

		30 June 20X6		*30 June 20X7*
	£	£	£	£
Fixed assets at cost		65,000		72,000
Aggregate depn		(13,000)		(14,500)
		52,000		57,500
Current assets				
Stock	6,700		7,300	
Debtors	5,400		4,100	
Cash and bank	—		900	
	12,100		12,300	
Current liabilities				
Creditors	(4,800)		(6,200)	
Bank overdraft	(1,300)		(—)	
	(6,100)		(6,200)	

Net current assets		6,000		6,100
Total assets less current liabilities		58,000		63,600
Bank loan (5 years)		(15,000)		(10,000)
Net assets		43,000		53,600
Capital				
At start of year		38,500		43,000
Capital introduced		2,700		20,000
Profit for the year		14,100		—
		55,300		63,000
Loss for the year	(—)		(1,800)	
Drawings	(12,300)		(7,600)	
		(12,300)		(9,400)
At end of year		43,000		53,600

There were no disposals of fixed assets during the year.

Brooks cannot understand how there can be a loss for the year 20X6/X7 when there has been an increase in the cash and bank balance. You are required to explain this by preparing a cash flow statement for the year ended 30 June 20X7.

29.11* **Level I**

Prepare a cash flow statement in accordance with FRS1 using the information in Question 29.10. During the year ended 30 June 20X7 there was interest received of £900 and bank interest paid of £1,250.

29.12 **Level II**

The balance sheet of C.F. plc for the year ended 31 December 20X4, together with comparative figures for the previous year, is shown below (all figures in £000s).

		20X4		*20X3*
Fixed assets		270		180
Less: Depreciation		(90)		(56)
		180		124
Current assets:				
Stock	50		42	
Debtors	40		33	
Cash	—		11	
		90		86
Current liabilities:				
Trade and operating creditors	(33)		(24)	
Taxation	(19)		(17)	
Dividend	(28)		(26)	
Bank overdraft	(10)		—	
		(90)		(67)
Net current assets:		—		19
Net assets		180		143
Represented by:				
Ordinary share capital £1 shares		25		20
Share premium		10		8
Profit and loss account		65		55

Shareholders' funds	100	83
15 per cent debentures, repayable 20X8	80	60
Capital employed	180	143

You are informed that:

1 There were no sales of fixed assets during 20X4.
2 The company does not pay interim dividends.
3 New debentures and shares issued in 20X4 were issued on 1 January.

Required:

a Show your calculation of the operating profit of C.F. plc for the year ended 31 December 20X4.

b Prepare a cash flow statement for the year, in accordance with *FRS1 Cash Flow Statements*, including the reconciliation of operating profit to net cash inflow from operating activities.

c State the headings of the other notes which you would be required to include in practice under FRS1.

d Comment on the implications of the information given in the question plus the statements you have prepared, regarding the financial position of the company.

e FRS1 supports the use of the indirect method of arriving at the net cash inflow from operating activities, which is the method you have used to answer part (b) of this question. What is the direct method of arriving at the net cash inflow from operations? State, with reasons, whether you agree with the FRS1 acceptance of the indirect method. (ACCA)

29.13* **Level II**

The directors of J. Kitchens Ltd were pleased when their accountants informed them that the company had made a profit of £24,000 during the year ended 31 December 20X3. However, their pleasure was turned into confusion when the cashier showed them a letter he had received from their banker. This indicated that he had reviewed Kitchens' account and was concerned to note the deterioration in their bank position. During 20X3 a small overdraft of £500 had reached £9,800 and was nearing the limit of their security. The directors would like to see an explanation of this increased overdraft, particularly as they had declared lower dividends than for the previous year. You are given the balance sheets at 31 December 20X2 and 31 December 20X3:

		20X2		*20X3*
	£	£	£	£
Fixed assets				
Leasehold premises—cost	30,000		30,000	
—depn	(6,000)	24,000	(9,000)	21,000
Plant—cost	41,000		48,000	
—depn	(7,000)	34,000	(9,500)	38,500
		58,000		59,500
Current assets				
Stock	14,900		22,500	
Debtors	11,300	26,200	16,400	38,900
		84,200		98,400

Share capital and reserves				
Share capital	20,000		20,000	
Reserves	35,000	55,000	51,000	71,000
Current liabilities				
Creditors	19,700		17,600	
Overdraft	500		9,800	
Dividends payable	9,000	29,200	—	27,400
		£84,200		£98,400

Notes

1 Dividends

	20X2	*20X3*
Interim	3,000	8,000
Final	9,000	—
	£12,000	£8,000

2 During the year, plant costing £10,000 with a net book value of £6,000 was sold for £6,400.

3 The amount included for debtors at 31 December 20X3 is after making a provision for bad debts of £600 (20X2: £400).

You are required to prepare a cash flow statement for the year 20X3 showing why the overdraft has increased.

29.14* **Level II**

Prepare a cash flow statement in accordance with FRS1 using the information in Question 29.13. During the year ended 31 December 20X3 there was bank interest paid of £750.

29.15* **Level II**

The following are the balance sheets of L. Tyler Ltd as at 31 May 20X8 and 31 May 20X9:

	31 May 20X8		*31 May 20X9*	
	£	£	£	£
Fixed assets at cost		143,000		131,000
Aggregate depreciation		(28,000)		(37,000)
		115,000		94,000
Current assets				
Stock	21,600		19,400	
Debtors	11,800		14,200	
Less: provision for bad debts	500		700	
	11,300		13,500	
Investments	3,900		17,100	
Cash and bank	4,600		12,800	
	41,400		62,800	
Current liabilities				
Creditors	(8,400)		(6,700)	
Corporation tax	(5,800)		(7,200)	
Proposed dividends	(19,600)		(21,800)	
	(33,800)		(35,700)	

Net current assets		7,600		27,100
Total assets less current liabilities		122,600		121,100
Long-term liabilities				
8 per cent loan stock		(30,000)		(5,000)
		92,600		116,100
Allotted share capital				
Ordinary shares of 50p each		60,000		70,000
Reserves				
Share premium account	25,000		34,000	
Revenue reserve	4,200		6,900	
Profit and loss account	3,400		5,200	
		32,600		46,100
Shareholders' interests		92,600		116,100

Notes

1 Fixed assets which cost £12,000 and had a book value of £7,500 were sold during the year ended 31 May 20X9 for £8,100. There were no other purchases or sales of fixed assets during that year.

2 The amounts of corporation tax and proposed dividends shown in the balance sheet as outstanding at 31 May 20X8 were paid during the year ended 31 May 20X9. In addition, an interim dividend of £6,400 was paid on 1 January 20X9.

You are required to prepare a cash flow statement for the year ended 31 May 20X9.

29.16* **Level II**

Prepare a cash flow statement in accordance with FRS1 using the information in Question 29.22. During the year ended 31 May 20X9 there was interest received of £1,800 and loan stock interest paid of £1,600.

29.17 **Level II**

The balance sheet of Euston Ltd as at 31 December 20X8, with corresponding amounts, showed the following:

	20X8		*20X7*	
	£000	£000	£000	£000
Freehold property at cost		2,000		2,000
Plant and machinery:				
Cost	3,500		3,000	
Depreciation	1,300		1,000	
		2,200		2,000
		4,200		4,000
Current assets:				
Stock	470		400	
Debtors	800		600	
Prepayments	60		50	
Bank	20		150	
	1,350		1,200	

Current liabilities:				
Creditors	230		200	
Taxation	100		80	
Dividends	50		30	
Accruals	70		90	
	450		400	
Net current assets		900		800
		5,100		4,800
12 per cent debentures		1,000		800
		4,100		4,000
Share capital		2,500		2,500
Retained profit		1,600		1,500
		4,100		4,000

Notes relevant to 20X8

1 An item of plant costing £100,000 with a written down value of £60,000 was sold at a profit of £15,000 during the year. This profit has been included in the profit and loss account for the year.
2 No interim dividend was paid during the year.
3 Tax paid during the year was £80,000.

You are required to prepare a cash flow statement for the year 31 December 20X8.

(JMB adapted)

29.18 Level II

Prepare a cash flow statement in accordance with FRS1 using the information in Question 29.17. During the year ended 31 December 20X8 there was no interest received but there was debenture interest paid of £108,000. None of the debenture interest was accrued at the end of either 20X7 or 20X8.

29.19 Level II

The following are the balance sheets of Waterloo plc for the last two financial years ended on 30 September.

Current liabilities:

	20X8		*20X7*		*Notes*
	£000	£000	£000	£000	
Fixed assets					
Intangible					
Goodwill		200		200	1
Tangible					
Buildings	970		720		2
Plant and machinery	350	1,320	370	1,090	2
		1,520		1,290	
Current assets					
Stocks	420		300		
Trade debtors	220		120		
Balance at bank	—		20		
	640		440		

Creditors, less than one year					
Bank overdraft	120		—		
Trade creditors	190		200		
Proposed dividends	60		45		3
	(370)		(245)		
Net current assets		270		195	
		1,790		1,485	
Creditors, more than one year					
9 per cent debentures		(360)		(400)	
		1,430		1,085	
Capital and reserves:					
Ordinary shares, of 50p each, fully paid		750		500	4
Share premium account	100		350		4
Revaluation reserve	300		—		
Retained profit	280	680	235	585	
		1,430		1,085	

Explanatory notes to the balance sheets:

1 Goodwill arising from the purchase of a business on 1 November 20X6 was valued at £200,000. It is the policy of the company to hold purchased goodwill as a permanent asset in the books of account.

2 The movement during the year to 30 September 20X8 in fixed tangible assets was as follows:

	Buildings		*Plant and machinery*	
	£000	£000	£000	£000
Cost at 1 Oct 20X7	820		600	
Surplus on revaluation	300		—	
Additions	—		100	
Disposals	—		(50)*	
		1,120		650
Provision for depreciation at 1 Oct 20X7	100		230	
Depreciation on disposal	—		(40)*	
Depreciation for year 30 Sep 20X8	50	(150)	110	(300)
		970		350

* The plant and machinery disposed of during the year was sold for £5,000.

3 Apart from the final proposed dividends shown in each balance sheet, interim dividends were paid in each of the years as follows:

20X8	*20X7*
£25,000	£15,000

4 There was a bonus issue during the year to 30 September 20X8 of one new ordinary share for every two held.

Prepare a cash flow statement for the year ended 30 September 20X8, in accordance with FRS1. There was no investment income for the year ended 30 September 20X8 but there was debenture interest paid of £35,000 during the year. (AEB adapted)

29.20 Level II

The summarized balance sheets as at 31 March 20X8 and 20X9 of Higher Ltd are as follows:

	20X9		*20X8*		*Additional information*
	£000	£000	£000	£000	
Fixed assets; at net book value		175		150	1
Current assets	90		80		2
Creditors, less than one year	(70)		(50)		
		20		30	
		195		180	
Creditors, more than one year		(30)		(30)	
		165		150	
Capital and reserves					
Ordinary shares of £1 each		90		80	3
8 per cent redeemable preference shares of 50p each		—		30	3
Share premium account		25		20	3
Capital redemption reserve		15		—	
Profit and loss account		35		20	
		165		150	

Additional information:

1 Fixed assets

	Cost	*Depn*	*Net book value*
	£000	£000	£000
Balance at 31 Mar 20X8	200	50	150
Additions	60	—	60
Disposals	(40)	(25)	(15)
Depreciation for the year to 31 Mar 20X9	—	20	(20)
	220	45	175

Fixed assets disposed of during the year were sold for £22,000.

2 Current assets at 31 March for each of the two years comprise the following:

	20X9	*20X8*
	£000	£000
Stocks	35	27
Debtors	22	28
Bank	24	22
Cash	9	3
	90	80

3 The preference shares were redeemed during the year ended 31 March 20X9. This redemption was funded by a new issue of ordinary shares at a premium.
4 A transfer of £15,000 from the profit and loss account was made to the capital redemption reserve.

Required:

Prepare a cash flow statement for Higher Ltd for the year ended 31 March 20X9, in accordance with FRS1. Assume that there was no investment income, interest paid or dividends paid during the year ended 31 March 20X9. (AEB adapted)

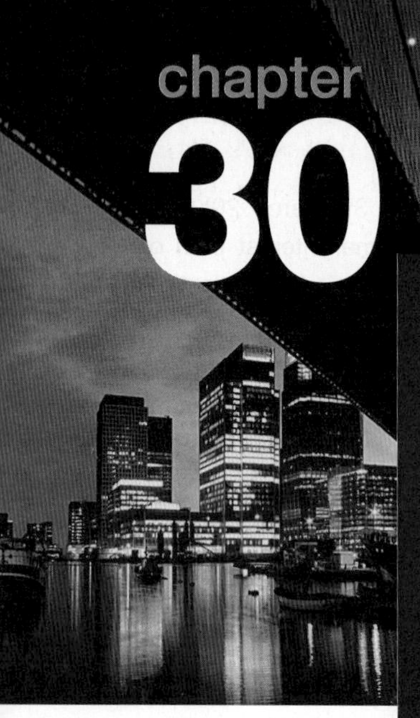

The appraisal of company accounts using ratios

Learning objectives

After reading this chapter you should be able to:

1 explain the meaning of the key terms and concepts listed at the end of the chapter;

2 explain the purposes of ratio analysis;

3 compute various measures of a company's performance, explain what each is intended to measure, and evaluate the results;

4 explain the nature of solvency and liquidity, and discuss the means by which insolvency may be predicted;

5 compute various measures of liquidity and solvency, explain what each is intended to measure, and evaluate the results;

6 compute various ratios used in the appraisal of working capital, explain what each is intended to measure, and evaluate the results;

7 compute various measures of return on investment and risk, explain what each is intended to measure, and evaluate the results;

8 explain the nature of capital gearing, compute the gearing ratio, and describe the effect of gearing on the profit available for distribution as dividends and the earnings per share;

9 discuss the limitations of ratio analysis.

The purposes of ratio analysis

The main function of published company final accounts is to provide information that will enable users of financial statements to evaluate the financial performance and financial position of a company. However, the absolute amount of profit, or assets and liabilities, shown in the accounts is not usually a particularly meaningful criterion for evaluating the performance or financial position of a business. For example, if Company A has a profit of £200,000 and Company B has a profit of £1 million, one cannot conclude that B is more profitable than A. Company B may have used net assets of £10 million to generate this profit whereas Company A may have only used net assets of £0.5 million. Thus, A is said to be more profitable than B because the profit is 40 per cent of the value of its net assets compared with only 10 per cent in the case of B. Similarly, if Company B had a profit of £900,000 last year, one cannot conclude that it is more profitable this year. The value of the net assets last year may only have been £8 million, which gives a return of 11.25 per cent compared with 10 per cent this year.

Indeed, the terms '**profitability**' and '**return**' are taken as referring to the relationship between the profit and the value of the net assets/capital used to generate that profit. Thus, in order to evaluate a company's performance and financial position over time, or in relation to other companies, it is necessary to compute various accounting ratios and percentages. These are primarily intended for the use of external groups of users such as shareholders, and loan and trade creditors, whose only source of accounting information is that contained in published accounts.

It is important to appreciate at the outset that accounting ratios and percentages have a number of limitations. One of these stems from the aggregate nature of information in published accounts. Companies are not required to disclose all the items which enter into the computation of profit or values of assets and liabilities in the balance sheet. As a result, the information needed to compute some ratios may not be available. This necessitates the use of surrogate data in the calculation of some ratios. Furthermore, comparisons of ratios over time and between companies can be misleading when economic conditions change and/or where the companies concerned are operating in substantially different industries. Ratios must therefore always be interpreted in the light of the prevailing economic climate and the particular circumstances of the company or companies concerned. The limitations of ratio analysis will be discussed in the context of each ratio and are summarized at the end of the chapter.

A large number of ratios can be calculated from the information contained in published accounts. These ratios may be grouped under four main headings, each heading reflecting what the ratios are intended to measure: (1) measures of a company's performance; (2) measures of solvency and liquidity; (3) measures of the control of working capital; and (4) measures of return on investment and risk. The most common ratios in each of these four classes are described on the following pages and illustrated using the information in Example 30.1.

Example 30.1

The following is an extract from the published accounts of A. Harry plc, for the year ending 31 January 20X8.

Profit and loss account

	£000
Turnover	5,280
Cost of sales	(3,090)
Gross profit	2,190
Distribution costs	(560)
Administrative expenses	(230)
Interest payable on loan stock	(400)
Profit on ordinary activities before taxation	1,000
Tax on profit on ordinary activities	(250)
Profit on ordinary activities after taxation	750
Proposed dividend on ordinary shares	(400)
Retained profit for the financial year	350

Balance sheet

	£000	£000
Fixed assets at cost		9,470
Aggregate depreciation		(2,860)
		6,610
Current assets		
Stocks	550	
Trade debtors	1,070	
Bank and cash	1,130	
	2,750	
Creditors: amounts falling due within one year		
Trade creditors	(730)	
Proposed dividend	(400)	
Corporation tax	(250)	
	(1,380)	
Net current assets		1,370
Total assets less current liabilities		7,980
Creditors: amounts falling due after more than one year:		
10 per cent loan stock of £100 each		(4,000)
Net assets		3,980
Capital and reserves		
Called-up share capital: 2,000,000 ordinary shares of £1 each		2,000
Profit and loss account		1,980
Shareholders' interests		3,980

Further information

The ordinary shares and loan stock are currently quoted on the International Stock Exchange, London, at £4 and £90, respectively.

Measures of a company's performance

The main function of financial statements is to provide information that will enable users to evaluate the financial performance and financial position of a company. Performance may relate to a number of things, such as productivity, energy conservation and pollution control. From the ordinary shareholders' point of view, financial performance is usually equated with the profit available for distribution as dividends or the earnings per share, as discussed in a later section. However, the term 'financial performance' is normally associated with an entity view of business enterprises. This section therefore examines various measures of a company's performance from the point of view of its being an economic entity separate from the shareholders, and irrespective of the way in which its assets are financed (i.e. the proportion of debt to equity capital).

Return on capital employed (ROCE)

Various accounting ratios are used to measure different aspects of financial performance. Many of these are derived from a single ratio known as the return on capital employed. This is ascertained as follows:

$$\frac{\text{Profit before tax and interest on long-term loans}}{\text{Net capital employed}} \times 100$$

Net capital employed refers to the shareholders' interests + long-term liabilities. Using the data in Example 30.1 this is calculated thus:

$$\frac{£1{,}000{,}000 + £400{,}000}{£3{,}980{,}000 + £4{,}000{,}000} \times 100 = 17.5 \text{ per cent}$$

The logic behind this ratio is perhaps more obvious when it is calculated as the return on assets as follows:

$$\frac{\text{Profit before tax and interest on long-term loans}}{\text{Total assets less current liabilities}} \times 100$$

$$\frac{£1{,}000{,}000 + £400{,}000}{£7{,}980{,}000} \times 100 = 17.5 \text{ per cent}$$

Some authors advocate expressing the return on capital employed in terms of the gross capital employed. This refers to the shareholders' interests + long-term liabilities + current liabilities. A somewhat easier way of calculating this is fixed assets + current assets. Clearly, the return on gross capital employed/total assets will be different from the return on net capital employed/total assets less current liabilities. The latter is more common in practice.

Whatever method is used there is a problem concerning the point in time at which the capital employed should be measured. In the above computation this was taken as being the end of the accounting year, for simplicity. However, this is not really justifiable because the capital employed includes the retained profit for the year and any additional capital raised during the year. The retained profit for the year was not available to generate the profit throughout this year, and it is unlikely that any capital raised during the year provided a significant contribution to the profit for the year. Given the time lags between capital expenditure and assets becoming productive, it may be more appropriate to use the capital employed at the start of the accounting year. Alternatively, if the additional capital is known to have generated profit during the year, the average capital employed for the year would be used. The same considerations apply to the return on equity discussed later.

The return on capital employed is a measure of profitability that is used to indicate how efficiently and effectively a company has utilized its assets during a given accounting period.

It is a common means of evaluating a company's profitability over time, and comparing the profitability of different companies. As a rough guide, the normal target ROCE of many large companies is about 15 per cent.

However, the use of historical cost data in the calculation of this ratio can give a distorted view of the profitability for two reasons. First, during times of rising prices the denominator in the formula comprises a mixture of assets acquired at various points in time when the prevailing levels of prices were different. In times of rising prices, the denominator is also understated because assets are not shown in the balance sheet at their current value. Second, the numerator tends to be overstated, since the historical cost profit is calculated by matching current selling prices with historical costs. Thus, the effect of historical cost accounting in both the denominator and the numerator is to inflate the return on capital and encourage the retention of old assets.

The profit margin and asset turnover ratios

The ROCE can be broken down into two further ratios, as follows:

$$\text{ROCE} = \text{profit margin} \times \text{asset turnover ratio}$$

The **profit margin** is computed thus:

$$\frac{\text{Profit before tax and interest on long-term loans}}{\text{Turnover}} \times 100$$

Using the data in Example 30.1 this will give:

$$\frac{£1{,}000{,}000 + £400{,}000}{£5{,}280{,}000} \times 100 = 26.5 \text{ per cent}$$

The profit margin is often described as a measure of profitability that shows what percentage of sales revenue is profit. Different products have different profit margins. Jewellery and greengrocery, for example, usually have a higher profit margin than electrical goods and clothing. In addition, different sized businesses have different profit margins. Small shops, for example, usually have a higher profit margin than supermarkets. Interfirm comparisons of profit margins should therefore only be made between companies in the same industry and of a comparable size.

The Companies Act requires the disclosure of an analysis of profit and turnover for each class of business. It is therefore possible to calculate the profit margin for each class of business. These could be used in interfirm comparisons of performance. However, this can be misleading because the profit margin constitutes an average for all the products comprising one particular class of business, and few firms sell exactly the same combination of products (i.e. product mix). Time series analysis of profit margins is likely to be more meaningful. Variations in the profit margin over time can be due to a number of factors relating to changes in the product mix, selling prices and unit costs.

The second of the above ratios is referred to as the **asset turnover ratio**, which is calculated as follows:

$$\frac{\text{Turnover}}{\text{Total assets less current liabilities}}$$

Using the data in Example 30.1 this will give:

$$\frac{£5{,}280{,}000}{£7{,}980{,}000} = 0.66$$

This shows the amount of sales revenue that has been generated per £ of capital employed. It is a measure of the level of activity and productivity. Different industries have different asset turnover ratios, primarily because of differences in technology. Labour-intensive industries usually have a high asset turnover ratio, whereas capital-intensive industries tend to have a lower asset turnover ratio. Interfirm comparisons of asset turnover ratios should therefore only be made between companies in the same industry. Time series analysis of asset turnover ratios is likely to be more meaningful. Changes in the asset turnover ratio over time can be due to a number of factors, such as producing at under capacity, labour inefficiency or overstocking.

There is an important relationship between the asset turnover ratio and the profit margin. In order to achieve a satisfactory return on capital employed, a company with a low asset turnover ratio (e.g. capital intensive) will need a high profit margin on its products. Conversely, a company with a high asset turnover ratio (e.g. labour intensive) will only require a low profit margin on its products in order to achieve a satisfactory return on capital employed. The former case of a capital intensive company can be illustrated arithmetically using the asset turnover ratio, profit margin and ROCE for Example 30.1, as follows:

$$0.66 \times 26.5 \text{ per cent} = 17.5 \text{ per cent}$$

The profit margin and asset turnover ratio may be broken down into a number of other ratios in order to pinpoint more precisely the reasons for changes in performance over time. These are as follows:

Profit margin:

$$\frac{\text{Cost of sales}}{\text{Turnover}} \times 100$$

$$\frac{\text{Gross profit}}{\text{Turnover}} \times 100$$

$$\frac{\text{Distribution costs}}{\text{Turnover}} \times 100$$

$$\frac{\text{Administrative expenses}}{\text{Turnover}} \times 100$$

Asset turnover ratio:

$$\frac{\text{Turnover}}{\text{Fixed assets}}$$

$$\frac{\text{Turnover}}{\text{Net current assets}}$$

The last ratio can be further subdivided into a number of other ratios relating to each constituent of net current assets. These are discussed in a later section on the appraisal of working capital.

Measures of solvency and liquidity

The main function of published accounts is to provide information that will enable users to evaluate the performance and financial position of a company. The phrase 'financial position' is normally taken as including whether or not a company will be able to pay its debts as and when they become due. A business that is unable to do so is said to be **insolvent**, and will usually be forced into compulsory liquidation by its creditors. Sometimes profitable businesses face financial crisis, frequently because of overtrading. This broadly means that a company has invested too much in fixed assets and stock but too little in liquid assets and is thus short of cash.

Solvency does not mean that at any point in time a business must have enough money to pay its liabilities. These will fall due at various dates in the future. **Solvency** therefore refers to whether or not liabilities are covered by assets which will be realized as the liabilities fall due. Thus, if the value of current assets is less than the amount of current liabilities a business may be insolvent.

However, even if current assets are equal to or greater than current liabilities this is no guarantee of solvency, since some current assets are less liquid than others. **Liquidity** refers to the ease with which an asset can be turned into cash without loss. Cash in hand and money in a bank current account are the most liquid types of asset, followed by listed investments, trade debtors and stock. Current assets are usually presented in published accounts in what is referred to as a reverse order of liquidity.

Two fairly crude but common ratios used to measure liquidity are explained below.

The working capital/current ratio

This is calculated thus:

$$\frac{\text{Current assets}}{\text{Current liabilities}}$$

Using the data in Example 30.1 this gives:

$$\frac{£2{,}750{,}000}{£1{,}380{,}000} = 2$$

This is a measure of the extent to which current liabilities are covered by current assets. As a generalization, the current ratio should be between 1.5 and 2, although this depends on the type of industry and the prevailing economic climate. A ratio of lower than 1.5 may indicate a poor liquidity position and thus future insolvency. At the other extreme a business can have too much working capital, which normally means that its assets are not being used as profitably as they otherwise might.

The working capital ratio has a serious limitation as a measure of liquidity, which is that some current assets are less liquid than others. In particular, stocks and work in progress are not easily realized without loss in the short term. A better criterion for measuring a company's ability to pay its debts as and when they become due is the liquidity ratio. In this ratio stocks and work in progress are excluded from current assets.

The liquidity/quick ratio or acid test

This is calculated thus:

$$\frac{\text{Current assets} - \text{Stocks and work in progress}}{\text{Current liabilities}}$$

Using the data in Example 30.1 this gives:

$$\frac{£2{,}750{,}000 - £550{,}000}{£1{,}380{,}000} = 1.6$$

Bank overdrafts are frequently excluded from the current liabilities in the calculation of this ratio because, although an overdraft is usually legally repayable at short notice, in practice it is often effectively a long-term liability.

The liquidity ratio indicates whether a company is likely to be able to pay its trade creditors, current taxation, dividends and other current liabilities from its cash at bank, the proceeds of sale of listed investments and the amounts collected from trade debtors, that is, without having to raise additional capital or sell fixed assets. As a generalization, the liquidity ratio should therefore be at least 1. However, this criterion cannot be applied to all types of business. Large retailing companies, for example, often have a liquidity ratio of less than 1. They buy goods on credit, sell them for cash and turn over their stock rapidly. Thus, stock is a relatively liquid asset. It is therefore only necessary for the working capital ratio to be at least 1.

A poor liquidity position usually arises from continual losses, but can be the result of overtrading. At the other extreme a business can have too much liquidity. Where this is not temporary, the excess should be invested in fixed assets (assuming that there are profitable investment opportunities).

The prediction of insolvency

The working capital and liquidity ratios are, at best, crude conventional measures of liquidity. Most users of published accounts are interested in liquidity as an indicator of whether a company will be able to pay its debts, or alternatively whether it is likely to go into liquidation in the near future. There is empirical research which demonstrates that the working capital and liquidity ratios are not particularly good predictors of insolvency. However, certain other ratios have been found to be useful in predicting corporate failure. The two most often cited studies of bankruptcy are by Altman[1] in the US and Taffler[2] in the UK. They each identify a set of five accounting ratios which provide successful predictions of company failure. These are as follows:

Altman	*Taffler*
$\frac{\text{Profit before interest and tax}}{\text{Total assets}}$	$\frac{\text{Profit before interest and tax}}{\text{Opening total assets}}$
$\frac{\text{Working capital}}{\text{Total assets}}$	$\frac{\text{Working capital}}{\text{Net worth}}$
$\frac{\text{Sales}}{\text{Total assets}}$	$\frac{\text{Sales}}{\text{Average stock}}$
$\frac{\text{Retained earnings}}{\text{Total assets}}$	$\frac{\text{Quick assets}}{\text{Total assets}}$
$\frac{\text{Market value of equity}}{\text{Book value of total debt}}$	$\frac{\text{Total liabilities}}{\text{Net capital employed}}$

Both of these studies make use of a statistical technique known as multiple discriminant analysis. This involves taking several ratios together in a multiple regression model. The set of five ratios in Altman's model enabled him correctly to classify as bankrupt or non-bankrupt 95 per cent of the cases in a sample of failed and non-failed US companies. He further claims that these ratios can be used to predict bankruptcy up to two years prior to actual failure. Similarly, Taffler correctly classified all but one company in a sample of UK companies, and asserts that his model exhibits predictive ability for about three years prior to bankruptcy.

However, there are doubts about the validity of the results of studies such as these for a number of reasons. First, the research is not based on a theory which explains why particular ratios should provide successful predictions of insolvency. Second, these studies make use of historical cost data, the deficiencies of which have already been explained. Finally, there are several problems involved in the use of statistical techniques such as discriminant analysis which make the results questionable.

The appraisal of working capital

The phrase working capital has two slightly different meanings. In computational terms it relates to the amount of the net current assets. However, it is also used in a general sense to refer to the current assets and current liabilities. In this section the phrase 'working capital' is intended to be interpreted in the latter sense.

One way of looking at the appraisal of working capital is in terms of the interrelationship between a company's performance and liquidity position. As regards performance, the analysis of working capital is an extension of the asset turnover ratio (or more precisely the ratio of turnover to net current assets) which shows how effective a company's management has been in utilizing the various constituents of working capital. This in turn affects a company's liquidity position.

If there has been a significant change in the working capital and/or liquidity ratios one would want to try to pinpoint the cause(s). In crude terms, the appraisal of working capital reveals whether too much or too little is invested in, for example, trade debtors and stock relative to a company's level of activity (i.e. turnover). In theory there is an optimal level of working capital. However, in practice all that users of published accounts can do is to identify changes in the relative level of current assets such as trade debtors and stock. These are taken as prima facie indicators of the effectiveness of credit control and stock control, respectively.

A number of ratios can be calculated relating to those items that make up the working capital. Each of these must be considered in the light of the particular circumstances of the company, the type of industry and the prevailing economic climate. The most common ratios used in the appraisal of working capital are given below.

The debtors' ratio—average period of credit taken by trade debtors

This is calculated thus:

$$\frac{\text{Trade debtors}}{\text{Turnover}} \times \text{Number of days in a year}$$

Using the data in Example 30.1 this gives:

$$\frac{\pounds 1{,}070{,}000}{\pounds 5{,}280{,}000} \times 365 = 74 \text{ days}$$

Instead of using the debtors at the end of the accounting year in the numerator some authors compute the average trade debtors as follows:

$$\frac{(\text{Debtors at the end of the previous year}) + (\text{Debtors at the end of the current year})}{2}$$

The argument for using this method of computation is that it gives a more representative figure for the 'normal' level of debtors. However, the important point is that the ratio should be computed on a consistent basis, otherwise comparisons will be misleading. Another method of expressing this ratio is referred to as the debtors' turnover ratio. It is calculated by inverting the fraction (and excluding the number of days in a year).

As the title above suggests, this ratio shows the average number of days' credit taken by trade debtors. The most common terms of credit in the UK are that an invoice is due for payment by the end of the calendar month following the calendar month in which the goods are delivered/invoiced. The minimum average period of credit is thus approximately 45 days (i.e. $1\frac{1}{2}$ months). However, many debtors take a longer period than this if they can, since it is obviously beneficial for them to do so. An average period of credit of around 75 days (i.e. $2\frac{1}{2}$ months) is therefore not uncommon.

However, when this ratio is calculated from the information in published accounts it may be nothing like any of these figures. This occurs if a company has both cash and credit sales. Since trade debtors arise because of credit sales, the denominator in the ratio should obviously comprise only the credit sales. However, these are not disclosed separately in published accounts. Consequently, the aggregate of cash and credit sales has to be used in the computation, which results in a lower debtors' collection period than if the denominator comprises only the credit sales. This is therefore clearly not the 'real' average period of credit, and a change in the proportion of cash to credit sales can distort the ratio over time.

The debtors' collection period can also be abnormally high or low because a business's sales are seasonal, such as where these are heavily concentrated either in the summer (e.g. ice cream, soft drinks) or winter, or at Easter or Christmas. This can result in an exceptionally high or low debtors' figure depending on when the accounting year ends, and thus a correspondingly high or low debtors' ratio.

The average period of credit take by trade debtors varies between industries and according to the economic situation. Retailers, for example, usually grant little or no credit whereas wholesalers and manufacturers often allow a considerable period of credit. Comparisons should therefore really only be made between businesses in the same industry and for a particular company over time. Where the period of credit is high compared with other firms (or with the average for the industry), and/or increasing over time, this is normally taken as indicating inadequate credit control procedures.

The creditors' ratio—average period of credit received from trade creditors

The basic principle used in the calculation of the ratio for trade debtors can also be applied to trade creditors in order to ascertain the average period of credit taken by the reporting entity. This is calculated as follows:

$$\frac{\text{Trade creditors}}{\text{Purchases for the year}} \times 365$$

As in the case of debtors, the figure of trade creditors used in the computation of this ratio may be an average of those at the end of the previous year and the end of the current year. Another method of expressing this ratio is referred to as the creditors' turnover ratio. It is calculated by inverting the fraction (and excluding the number of days in a year).

The amount of purchases is not normally disclosed in published accounts. However, if the company is a non-manufacturing business these can be calculated by adjusting the cost of sales figure (given in the profit and loss account) by the change in stock (given in the balance sheet) over the year as follows:

Cost of sales
Add: stock at end of current year
Less: stock at end of previous year
= Purchases

Where the company is a manufacturing business, or the stock at the end of the previous year is not given as a comparative figure, instead of purchases a surrogate has to be used, such as the cost of sales.

Using the data in Example 30.1 this will give:

$$\frac{£730{,}000}{£3{,}090{,}000} \times 365 = 86 \text{ days}$$

It is obviously beneficial to delay paying creditors for as long as possible. However, this may adversely affect the company's credit rating, and creditors may refuse to supply further goods on credit. In addition, where the period of credit is high compared with other firms (or with the average for the industry) and/or increasing over time, this may be an indication of financial weakness.

The stock turnover ratio

This is calculated thus:

$$\frac{\text{Cost of sales}}{\text{Stock of finished goods}}$$

Using the data in Example 30.1 this will give:

$$\frac{£3{,}090{,}000}{£550{,}000} = 5.6$$

As in the calculation of the average period of credit for debtors and creditors, there is an argument for using an average of the stock at the end of the previous year and the current year as the denominator in this ratio. Once again, the important point is that a consistent basis of computation should be used to ensure meaningful comparisons. Another method of expressing this ratio is referred to as the number of days' sales from stock. It is calculated by inverting the fraction and multiplying the answer by 365.

The stock turnover ratio shows the number of times that a business 'turns over'/sells its average/normal level of stock during the accounting year. In very simple terms, a greengrocer who goes to market once a week and sells all of these goods during that week would have a stock turnover ratio of 52 (because there are 52 weeks in a year). Stock turnover ratios vary between industries. Food retailers, for example, have a relatively high stock turnover ratio, whereas jewellery retailers normally have a much lower ratio. Comparisons should therefore really only be made between firms in the same industry and for a particular company over time. Where the stock turnover ratio, is low compared with other firms (or with the average for the industry), and/or decreasing over time, this is normally taken as indicating a lack of adequate stock control.

Measures of return on investment and risk

This group of ratios is primarily intended for the use of shareholders, although a company's management will probably monitor these ratios as a guide to how investors view the company. There are several investment ratios, some of which are published in *The Financial Times*. These include the following:

The dividend yield

This is calculated as:

$$\frac{\text{Annual ordinary dividend}}{\text{Current market value of the ordinary shares}} \times 100$$

For Example 30.1 this will give:

$$\frac{\pounds 400{,}000 \div 2{,}000{,}000}{\pounds 4} \quad \text{or} \quad \frac{\pounds 400{,}000}{2{,}000{,}000 \times \pounds 4} \times 100 = 5 \text{ per cent}$$

The same principle can be used to calculate the dividend yield on preference shares and the interest yield on debentures and loan stock.

The dividend yield is said to measure the ordinary shareholder's annual return on investment, and may be compared with what could be obtained by investing in some other company. However, such comparisons can be misleading for two main reasons. First, companies have different risk characteristics. A comparison of the dividend yields of, for example, a steel company and a bank would be misleading because the former is a riskier investment than the latter. Second, companies have different dividend policies, in that some distribute a greater proportion of their annual profit than others. Put slightly differently, the annual dividend is only part of an investor's total return, in that the investor will also expect to make a capital gain in the form of an increase in the market price of shares. This partly results from companies retaining a proportion of their annual profits.

The dividend yield is often between 2 and 5 per cent, but varies between companies for the reasons outlined above. Some investors regard the dividend yield as important because they are primarily interested in maximizing their annual income (e.g. retired people). However, for other investors the dividend yield may only be of limited importance because they are more interested in capital gains (e.g. for tax reasons) resulting from an increase in the share price. They are therefore often attracted to companies with a low dividend yield but high retained profits.

Dividend cover

This is calculated as:

$$\frac{\text{Profit after corporation tax and preference dividends}}{\text{Annual ordinary dividend}}$$

For Example 30.1 this will give:

$$\frac{\pounds 750{,}000}{\pounds 400{,}000} = 1.875$$

The profit after corporation tax and preference dividends is used in the calculation of this ratio because it represents the profit available for distribution as dividends to ordinary shareholders.

The dividend cover indicates how likely it is that the company will be able to maintain future dividends on ordinary shares at their current level if profits were to fall in future years. It is thus a measure of risk. The amount by which the dividend cover exceeds unity represents what might be called the margin of safety. Thus, a company with a high dividend cover would be more likely to be able to maintain the current level of ordinary dividends than a company with a low dividend cover. The average dividend cover for companies whose shares are listed on the International Stock Exchange, London, is about 2, but clearly this depends on a company's dividend policy.

Earnings per share (EPS)

This is calculated as:

$$\frac{\text{Profit after corporation tax and preference dividends}}{\text{Number of ordinary shares in issue}}$$

For Example 30.1 this will give:

$$\frac{£750{,}000}{2{,}000{,}000} = £0.375$$

The profit after corporation tax and preference dividends is used in the calculation of this ratio because it represents the profit available for distribution as dividends to ordinary shareholders. This is referred to as the earnings. There are complex rules for ascertaining the number of ordinary shares but these are beyond the scope of this book. The rules are applied where the allotted share capital has changed during the year, because, for example, there has been an issue of shares during the year. The calculation involves determining an average number of shares for the year.[3]

EPS is not strictly a measure of return on investment. However, as will be discussed below, it is included in the calculation of another widely used accounting ratio. Furthermore, EPS is generally regarded as an important consideration in investment decisions; it was the subject of one of the first accounting standards (SSAP3) which requires that it be disclosed in published profit and loss accounts for all listed companies.

As explained earlier, the absolute amount of profit (in this context, available for distribution as dividends) is not usually a satisfactory measure of performance because it ignores the amount of net assets/capital which has been used to generate that profit. However, EPS takes this into consideration in the form of the number of ordinary shares and thus provides a useful means of evaluating performance (where performance is defined from the shareholders' point of view as relating to the profit available for distribution as dividends). The trend in EPS over time indicates growth or otherwise in the profit attributable to each ordinary share. Interfirm comparisons of EPS are not advisable.

The price–earnings (P–E) ratio

This is calculated as

$$\frac{\text{Current market price of each ordinary share}}{\text{EPS}}$$

For Example 30.1 this will give:

$$\frac{£4}{£0.375} = 10.67$$

The P–E ratio is often between 10 and 25 but varies considerably between different industries and companies in the same industry. Many authors shy away from explaining the P–E ratio because its meaning is somewhat ambiguous, despite the fact that this is probably the most widely cited accounting ratio. The P–E ratio is a reflection of risk in that it represents the number of years' earnings that investors are prepared to buy at their current level. This is probably better explained in terms of what is essentially a payback period. The P–E ratio shows the number of years it will take to recoup the current price of the shares at the present level of EPS (the share price being recouped in the form of dividends and retained profits). Where an investment is risky, investors will want to get their money back relatively quickly, whereas if an investment is comparatively safe a longer payback period will be acceptable. Thus companies in risky industries such as mining and construction tend to have a low P–E ratio, whereas companies in relatively safe industries such as food manufacturers, and those which are diversified, tend to have a high P–E ratio.

The P–E ratio also varies between companies in the same industry. If investors think that a company's earnings are going to decline, the P–E ratio will tend to be lower than the average for the industry. Conversely, if profits are expected to rise, the P–E ratio will tend to be higher, both of which occur because of decreases and increases in the share price, respectively. The P–E ratio is therefore also a reflection of the expected earnings growth potential of a company. This also means that sometimes industries which one would expect to have a high P–E ratio, since they are relatively safe, in fact have a low P–E ratio because the earnings are expected to decline (and vice versa).

It appears that the P–E ratio is sometimes also used in practice to identify shares which are over- or underpriced. A share is said to be overpriced if its P–E ratio is higher than the norm for the industry or other similar companies, and underpriced if the P–E ratio is lower than the norm for the industry or other similar companies. However, as explained above, this is probably an oversimplification because the intrinsic/real value of a share will depend on the expected future earnings of the particular company.

Another way of looking at the P–E ratio is to invert the formula and express the result as a percentage. This is referred to as the **earnings yield**. For Example 30.1 this will give:

$$\frac{£0.375}{£4} \quad \text{or} \quad \frac{£750{,}000}{2 \text{ million @ } £4} \times 100 = 9.375 \text{ per cent}$$

The earnings yield is not really a yield in the same sense as the dividend yield, since not all of the earnings are distributed as dividends. However, it is often referred to as a measure of return on investment. As in the case of EPS, the earnings yield is a useful means of evaluating performance (where performance is defined from the shareholders' point of view as relating to the profit available for distribution as dividends). The trend in the earnings yield over time indicates how efficiently and effectively a company has utilized the amount of money the shareholders have invested in the company in terms of the current share price. It can also be used to compare the performance of different companies.

Learning Activity 30.1

Obtain two copies of *The Financial Times*, one for a Monday and one for any other day of the week. Turn to the last two pages but one of the section called 'Companies and Markets' headed 'London Share Service'. Look at the last two columns in the Tuesday to Saturday editions headed 'Yield' and 'P/E', which refer to the dividend yield and price–earnings ratio, respectively. Similarly, look at the column in the Monday edition headed 'Div.cov.', which refers to the dividend cover. Examine the values of these three ratios for some large public limited companies in different industries. What do these ratios tell you about those companies?

The return on equity/shareholders' interests (ROE)

This is calculated as:

$$\frac{\text{Profit after corporation tax and preference dividends}}{\text{Shareholders' interests (excluding preference shares)}} \times 100$$

For Example 30.1 this will give:

$$\frac{£750{,}000}{£3{,}980{,}000} \times 100 = 18.8 \text{ per cent}$$

However, some people calculate this ratio using the profit before corporation tax (but after preference dividends) to avoid the distortions that can arise when comparing companies with different tax positions. As in the return on capital employed ratio, it is more appropriate to use the shareholders' interests at the start of the accounting year, or an average, rather than at the end of the year. The latter is unjustifiable and has only been used in this example because it is the only figure available for simplicity.

The ROE is essentially the same as the earnings yield. The difference is that, instead of expressing the earnings as a percentage of the market price/value of the ordinary shares, this is expressed as a percentage of the book value of the ordinary shares in the form of the shareholders' interests. Since the latter is not the 'real' (i.e. market) value of the shareholders' investment this ratio can be said to be inferior to the earnings yield.

However, the ROE, like the earnings yield, is a common measure of return on investment which is used to evaluate profitability (where profitability is defined from the shareholders' point of view as relating to the profit available for distribution as dividends). It is said to indicate how efficiently and effectively a company's management has utilized the shareholders' interests. The ratio may be used to compare the profitability of different companies and/or to examine trends over time.

The gearing ratio

Gearing, or **leverage** as it is called in the US, refers to the relationship between the amount of fixed interest capital (i.e. loan stock, debentures, preference shares, etc.) and the amount of equity capital (i.e. ordinary shares). In discussions of gearing the fixed interest capital is frequently referred to as the debt capital, which is taken to include preference shares. As a broad generalization, where the value of fixed interest capital is less than the value of equity, a company is said to have low gearing. Where the value of debt capital is more than the value of equity, a company is said to have high gearing.

There are two main ways of expressing the gearing ratio. The basis most commonly used in the financial press is to express the debt capital as a fraction (or percentage) of the equity capital thus:

$$\text{Debt/equity ratio} = \frac{\text{Debt capital}}{\text{Equity capital}} (\times 100)$$

However, in accounting it is more common to compute the gearing ratio by expressing the debt capital as a fraction (or percentage) of the total capital thus:

$$\text{Gearing ratio} = \frac{\text{Debt capital}}{\text{Debt capital} + \text{Equity capital}} (\times 100)$$

Using the latter basis, the next issue concerns how the debt and equity capital are to be measured/valued. There are three main methods, as follows:

1 *Using the nominal values* of fixed interest capital and ordinary share capital thus:

$$\frac{\text{Nominal value of debt capital}}{\text{Nominal value of debt capital} + \text{Nominal value of ordinary shares}} \times 100$$

The debt capital refers to the preference shares, loan stock, debentures, bank loans, mortgages and any other long-term borrowing, such as an overdraft for more than one year. An illustration of the calculation of the gearing ratio using this formula is given in Example 30.2. This also highlights the difference between low gearing and high gearing.

Example 30.2

	Company with low gearing	*Company with high gearing*
	£	£
Ordinary shares of £1 each	400,000	100,000
10 per cent preference shares of £1 each	30,000	150,000
10 per cent debentures of £100 each	70,000	250,000
	500,000	500,000
Gearing ratio	20 per cent or 1 : 4	80 per cent or 4 : 1

2 *Including the reserves and retained profits as part of the equity capital* thus:

$$\frac{\text{Nominal value of debt capital}}{\text{Nominal value of debt capital} + \begin{pmatrix}\text{Nominal value of ordinary shares} + \\ \text{Reserves} + \text{Retained profits}\end{pmatrix}} \times 100$$

Returning to the data in Example 30.1 this would be calculated as follows:

$$\frac{£4{,}000{,}000}{£4{,}000{,}000 + (£2{,}000{,}000 + £1{,}980{,}000)} \times 100 = 50 \text{ per cent}$$

This method of expressing the gearing ratio is considered to be superior to the first because reserves and retained profits constitute part of the shareholders' interests and thus the capital which they provide. The logic behind this is perhaps more obvious when the gearing ratio is calculated in terms of the book value of the assets, thus:

$$\frac{\text{Nominal value of debt capital}}{\text{Total assets less current liabilities}} \times 100 = \frac{£4{,}000{,}000}{£7{,}980{,}000} \times 100 = 50 \text{ per cent}$$

This formula highlights that the gearing ratio shows the proportion of the assets which are financed by fixed interest capital.

3 *Using the current market prices* of a company's ordinary shares and debt capital, thus:

$$\frac{\text{Market value of debt capital}}{\text{Market value of debt capital} + \text{Market value of ordinary share capital}} \times 100$$

Using the data in Example 30.1 this would be calculated as follows:

$$\frac{40{,}000 \ @ \ £90 \ (\text{or } £4{,}000{,}000 \times £90/£100)}{(40{,}000 \ @ \ £90) + (2{,}000{,}000 \ @ \ £4)} \times 100 = 31 \text{ per cent}$$

This is generally regarded as being a more theoretically sound method of expressing the gearing ratio because market prices are said to represent the 'real' value of the debt capital and shareholders' interests as distinct from the nominal or book values.

There are several other ways of expressing gearing, which show the relationship between the annual amount of interest on debt capital and the profit for the year. However, these are not used very often.

The gearing ratio is a measure of the 'financial risk' attaching to a company's ordinary shares which arises because of the prior claim that fixed interest capital has on the annual income and assets (in the event of liquidation). This financial risk is additional to the 'operating risk' that is associated with the particular industry or industries in which a company is trading.

Companies are said to engage in gearing because it usually produces substantial benefits for the ordinary shareholders. In crude terms, the money provided by loan creditors is used to generate income in excess of the loan interest. The tax deductibility of interest contributes to this benefit. In technical terms, gearing usually increases the profit available for distribution as dividends to ordinary shareholders and thus the EPS, although it does have an impact on the riskiness of the earnings. These effects are illustrated numerically in Example 30.3. The data are taken from Example 30.2. These two companies are assumed to be identical in all respects except their gearing. Both have a profit after tax (but before interest) of £50,000 and an EPS of 10 pence in year 1. Although this example is clearly unrealistic, it illustrates vividly the impact of gearing.

Example 30.3

	Company with low gearing		*Company with high gearing*	
Year 1				
	£	£	£	£
Profit before interest		50,000		50,000
Preference dividends	3,000		15,000	
Interest	7,000	10,000	25,000	40,000
Distributable profit		40,000		10,000
Earnings per share		10p		10p

Year 2				
Profit before interest		100,000		100,000
Preference dividends	3,000		15,000	
Interest	7,000	10,000	25,000	40,000
Distributable profit		90,000		60,000
Earnings per share		22.5p		60p

Now suppose the profit of both companies doubles in year 2, as shown in Example 30.3. In the case of the company with low gearing, a 100 per cent increase in the profit after tax (but before interest) in year 2 results in a 125 per cent increase (from £40,000 to £90,000) in the profit available for distribution as dividends to ordinary shareholders. By contrast, in the case of the highly geared company, a 100 per cent increase in the profit after tax in year 2 results in a 500 per cent increase (from £10,000 to £60,000) in the distributable profit. Similarly, a 100 per cent increase in the profit after tax results in a 125 per cent increase in the EPS of the low-geared company, compared with a 500 per cent increase for the company with high gearing. This can be summarized in the form of a general rule as follows: any increase in profit (before charging interest) will result in a *proportionately greater* increase in the profit available for distribution (and the EPS) of a highly geared company compared with an equivalent increase for a company with low gearing.

However, gearing is a double-edged sword, in that the same occurs in reverse when there is a decrease in profit, as often happens when there is an economic recession. Imagine that the chronological sequence in Example 30.3 is reversed, giving profit before interest of £100,000 in year 1 and £50,000 in year 2 representing a 50 per cent decrease in the profit after tax (but before interest). This results in a reduction in the distributable profit and EPS of 56 per cent in the case of the low-geared company, compared with 83 per cent for the company with high gearing. This can also be summarized in the form of a general rule as follows: any decrease in the profit (before charging interest) will result in a proportionately greater reduction in the profit available for distribution (and the EPS) of a high-geared company compared with an equivalent decrease for a company with low gearing.

Furthermore, the level of gearing affects a company's break-even point. A company with high gearing will have a larger break-even point than an equivalent company with low gearing. This is because the interest charges of a high-geared company are greater than for an equivalent company with low gearing. In Example 30.3 the break-even point of the high-geared company is £30,000 (i.e. £40,000 – £10,000) higher than that of the low-geared company. This means that a company with high gearing has to earn a greater profit (before interest) before it can declare a dividend compared with an equivalent company that has low gearing. Thus, if the profit after tax of these companies fell to, say, £20,000, the company with low gearing would still be able to declare an ordinary dividend from the current year's trading profit whereas the high-geared company could not.

To sum up, the ordinary shareholders in a high-geared company benefit from gearing when profits are relatively large. However, they run two risks. First, when profits are small the dividends will be less than would be the case with low gearing. Second, if the company goes into liquidation they will not be repaid the value of their shares until after all the fixed interest capital has been repaid. Usually very little or nothing is left for the ordinary shareholders. Thus, the tendency to assume that gearing is advantageous may be a misconception because while it frequently results in a proportionately greater increase in the distributable profit it also makes the ordinary shares riskier. To use an analogy, one should not bet on an outsider in a horse race merely because the winnings would be greater than betting on the favourite. One must weigh up the possible return in relation to the perceived risk.

Learning Activity 30.2

Write to the head office of a large public limited company asking for a copy of their latest annual report and accounts. Using the information contained in this document, compute all the ratios discussed in this chapter for the current and previous year. List any apparent material changes in the value of these ratios, and outline their possible causes. To obtain the maximum benefit from this exercise, choose a company that is known to have had recent financial problems.

The limitations of ratio analysis

Example 30.1 was deliberately kept simple for the purpose of illustration. In particular, it contains no comparative figures for the previous year. Thus, no time series analysis was possible. In addition, in the calculation of some ratios (e.g. EPS, ROE, ROCE) the amount at the end of the accounting year was used when it would have been more appropriate to take the figure at the beginning of the year or an average for the year. Companies are required by law to include comparative figures for the previous year in their published accounts. These would therefore usually be available and should be used where appropriate.

Ratio analysis has a number of limitations. Most of these have already been explained in the context of particular ratios but can be summarized as follows:

1 Comparisons between companies and for a particular company over time may be misleading if different accounting policies are used to calculate profits and value assets.

2 Ratios usually have to be calculated using historical cost data since few companies publish a current cost profit and loss account and balance sheet. These ratios will therefore be distorted because of the effects of inflation and thus comparisons may be misleading.

3 The data needed to compute some ratios are not disclosed in published accounts and thus surrogates have to be used (e.g. the aggregate cash and credit sales in the calculation of the average period of credit taken by trade debtors). This may also mean that comparisons are misleading.

4 The general yardsticks or performance criteria that may be applied to particular ratios (e.g. a liquidity ratio of at least 1) are not appropriate for all types of industry.

5 Changes in a given ratio over time and differences between companies must be considered in the light of the particular circumstances of the reporting entity, the type of industry and the general economic situation. They may also be due to deliberate policy decisions by management such as a build-up of stocks prior to a sales promotion campaign, to rent or own fixed assets, etc.

6 A single ratio may not be very informative by itself, but a number of related ratios taken together should give a general picture of the company's performance or financial position (e.g. in the prediction of insolvency).

Summary

The main purpose of ratio analysis is to enable users of financial statements to evaluate a company's financial performance and financial position over time, and/or in relation to other companies. Ratios may be grouped under four main headings, each reflecting what the ratios are intended to measure, as follows:

1 Measures of a company's performance. These include the return on capital employed, profit margin and asset turnover ratio.
2 Measure of solvency and liquidity. Solvency refers to whether a company is able to pay its debts as they become due. Liquidity refers to the ease with which an asset can be turned into cash without loss. Measures include the current and liquidity ratios.
3 The appraisal of working capital. Measures include the debtors' ratio, creditors' ratio and stock turnover ratio.
4 Measures of return on investment and risk. These include the dividend yield, dividend cover, earnings per share, price–earnings ratio, earnings yield, return on equity and capital gearing ratio.

A single ratio may not be very informative, but a number of related ratios taken together can provide strong indications of a company's performance or financial position, such as in the prediction of insolvency. However, these must be interpreted in the light of the particular circumstances of the company, the type of industry and the current economic climate. General yardsticks are not always appropriate. Furthermore, ratios must be interpreted with caution. The use of historical cost and surrogate data, as well as different accounting policies, can distort comparisons.

Key terms and concepts

Asset turnover ratio (462)
creditors' ratio (467)
debtors' ratio (466)
dividend cover (469)
dividend yield (469)
earnings per share (470)
earnings yield (471)
financial risk (474)
gearing (472)
gearing ratio (472)
insolvent (463)
leverage (472)
liquidity (464)
liquidity ratio (464)
price–earnings (P–E) ratio (470)
profitability (459)
profit margin (462)
return (459)
return on capital employed (461)
return on equity (472)
solvency (464)
stock turnover ratio (468)
working capital (466)
working capital/current ratio (464)

References

1. Altman, E.A. (1968). Financial ratios, discriminant analysis and the prediction of corporate bankruptcy, *Journal of Finance* (September).
2. Taffler, R. J. (1982). Forecasting company failure in the UK using discriminant analysis and financial ratio data, *Journal of the Royal Statistical Society* **145**, Part 3.
3. Accounting Standards Steering Committee (1974). *SSAP3—Earnings per Share* (ICAEW).

Review questions

30.1 Explain what each of the following is intended to measure:

a return on capital employed;

b profit margin;

c asset turnover ratio;

d working capital and liquidity ratios;

e average period of credit taken by debtors;

f stock turnover ratio.

30.2 Examine the empirical evidence relating to the predictive ability of accounting ratios with regard to insolvency.

30.3 Explain what each of the following is intended to measure: (a) dividend yield; (b) dividend cover; (c) earnings per share; (d) price–earnings ratio; and (e) return on equity.

30.4 **a** Explain what is meant by capital gearing/leverage.

b Why might this influence a prospective investor's decision concerning whether or not to buy ordinary shares in a company?

30.5 Explain the limitations of using accounting ratios in time series analysis and interfirm comparisons, giving examples where appropriate.

Exercises

An asterisk after the question number indicates that there is a suggested answer in the Appendix.

30.6 **Level II**

Dale is in business as a sole trader. You are presented with the following summarized information relating to his business for the year to 31 October 20X8:

Trading, profit and loss account for the year to 31 October 20X8

	£000	£000
Sales: cash	200	
credit	600	800
Less: Cost of goods sold—		
opening stock	80	
purchases	530	
	610	
Less: closing stock	70	540
Gross profit		260
Expenses		205
Net profit for the year		55

Balance sheet at 31 October 20X8

	£000	£000
Fixed assets		
Plant and machinery at cost	1,000	
Less: Accumulated depreciation	450	550

Current assets		
Stocks	70	
Trade debtors	120	
Cash	5	
	195	
Less: Current liabilities		
Trade creditors	130	65
		615
Capital		
As at 1 November 20X7		410
Net profit for the year	55	
Less: Drawings	50	5
		415
Loan		200
		615

Required:

a Based on the above information, calculate eight recognized accounting ratios; and

b list what additional information you would need in order to undertake a detailed ratio analysis of Dale's business for the year to 31 October 20X8.

Note that in answering part (a) of the question, each ratio must be distinct and separate. Marks will *not* be awarded for alternative forms of the same ratio. (AAT)

30.7* **Level II**

White and Black are sole traders. Both are wholesalers dealing in a similar range of goods. Summaries of the profit calculations and balance sheets for the same year have been made available to you, as follows:

Profit and loss accounts for the year

	White		*Black*	
	£000	£000	£000	£000
Sales		600		800
Cost of goods sold		450		624
		150		176
Administrative expenses	64		63	
Selling and distribution expenses	28		40	
Depreciation—equipment and vehicles	10		20	
Depreciation—buildings	—	102	5	128
Net profit		48		48

Balance sheets as at end of year

	White		*Black*	
	£000	£000	£000	£000
Buildings		29		47
Equipment and vehicles		62		76
Stock		56		52
Debtors		75		67
Bank balance		8		—
		230		242

Creditors	38		78	
Bank balance	—	38	4	82
Capital		192		160

Required:
Compare the performance and financial position of the two businesses on the basis of the above figures, supporting your comments where appropriate with ratios and noting what further information you would need before reaching firmer conclusions. (ACCA)

30.8* **Level II**

The following is an extract from the published accounts of Blue Light plc for the year ended 31 March 20X8.

Profit and loss account

	£000	£000
Turnover		4,230
Cost of sales		(2,560)
Gross profit		1,670
Distribution costs		(470)
Administrative expenses		(380)
Interest payable on debentures		(240)
Profit on ordinary activities before taxation		580
Tax on profit on ordinary activities		(270)
Profit on ordinary activities after taxation		310
Proposed dividend on ordinary shares		(200)
Retained profit for the financial year		110

Balance sheet

Fixed assets at cost		7,240
Aggregate depreciation		(2,370)
		4,870
Current assets		
Stocks	480	
Trade debtors	270	
Bank and cash	320	
	1,070	
Creditors: amounts falling due within one year		
Trade creditors	(260)	
Proposed dividends	(200)	
Corporation tax	(270)	
	(730)	
Net current assets		340
Total assets less current liabilities		5,210
Creditors: amounts falling due after more than one year:		
8 per cent debentures of £100 each		(3,000)
Net assets		2,210
Capital and reserves		
Called-up share capital: 500,000 ordinary shares of £1 each		500
Profit and loss account		1,710
Shareholders' interests		2,210

Further information
The ordinary shares and debentures are currently quoted on the London Stock Exchange at £5 and £110, respectively.

You are required to calculate the ratios that you would include in a report to a prospective investor relating to measures of performance, liquidity, the appraisal of working capital, and return on investment and risk. Comment briefly on the results and the limitations of your analysis.

30.9* **Level II**

The following is a summary of some of the accounting ratios of two companies in the same industry and of a comparable size for the year ended 30 June 20X5.

	Fish plc	*Chips plc*
Dividend yield	4 per cent	7 per cent
Dividend cover	3.6	2.1
Earnings per share	17p	23p
P–E ratio	14	8
Return on equity	22 per cent	27 per cent
Return on capital employed	18 per cent	15 per cent
Profit margin	20 per cent	25 per cent
Asset turnover ratio	0.9	0.6
Gearing ratio	28 per cent	76 per cent

You are required to write a report to a prospective investor on the comparative return on investment, risk and performance of these two companies.

30.10* **Level II**

B. Beasley Ltd manufactures components for the motor vehicle industry. The following is a summary of some of its accounting ratios as at 30 April 20X3 and 30 April 20X4:

	20X3	*20X4*
Working capital ratio	1.5	1.7
Liquidity ratio	1.1	0.8
Stock turnover	6.3	5.9
Debtors' ratio	52 days	63 days
Creditors' ratio	71 days	78 days

You are required to write a report to one of the company's major shareholders on the change in its liquidity and working capital position over the year ended 30 April 20X4.

30.11 **Level II**

Two retailers show the following accounts for the year to 31 December 20X9.

Balance sheets as at 31 December 20X9

	A. Ltd		*B. Ltd*	
	£000	£000	£000	£000
Fixed assets				
Premises		5,000		8,000
Fixtures		500		1,000
		5,500		9,000

Current assets				
Stock	800		900	
Debtors	50		60	
Bank	330		720	
	1,180		1,680	
Current liabilities	850		980	
		330		700
		5,830		9,700
Long-term loans		800		5,000
		5,030		4,700
Share capital—				
ordinary shares of £1		3,000		2,000
Retained profits		2,030		2,700
		5,030		4,700

Profit and loss accounts for the year ended 31 December 20X9

	£000	£000	£000	£000
Turnover		13,360		16,020
Cost of sales		8,685		10,090
		4,675		5,930
Distribution	2,300		2,870	
Administration	1,375		1,670	
		3,675		4,540
Operating profit		1,000		1,390
Interest		65		400
Net profit		935		990
Dividend		300		400
Retained profit for year		635		590

You are required to:

a compute for each of the two companies:
  i one ratio relevant to an assessment of liquidity;
  ii one ratio relevant to an assessment of gearing;
  iii three ratios relevant to an assessment of profitability and performance.

b summarize briefly the overall strengths and weaknesses of Company A, using each of the ratios you have computed. (JMB)

30.12 Level II

The outline balance sheets of the Nantred Trading Co. Ltd were as shown below:

Balance sheets as at 30 September

	20X5		*20X6*	
	£	£	£	£
Fixed assets (at written down values)				
Premises	40,000		98,000	
Plant and equipment	65,000		162,000	
		105,000		260,000

Current assets				
Stock	31,200		95,300	
Trade debtors	19,700		30,700	
Bank and cash	15,600		26,500	
	66,500		152,500	
Current liabilities				
Trade creditors	23,900		55,800	
Corporation tax	11,400		13,100	
Proposed dividends	17,000		17,000	
	52,300		85,900	
Working capital		14,200		66,600
Net assets employed		119,200		326,600
Financed by				
Ordinary share capital	100,000		200,000	
Reserves	19,200		26,600	
Shareholders' funds		119,200		226,600
7 per cent debentures		—		100,000
		119,200		326,600

The only other information available is that the turnover for the years ended 30 September 20X5 and 20X6 was £202,900 and £490,700, respectively, and that on 30 September 20X4 reserves were £26,100.

Required:

a Calculate, for each of the two years, six suitable ratios to highlight the financial stability, liquidity and profitability of the company.

b Comment on the situation revealed by the figures you have calculated in your answer to (a) above. (ACCA)

30.13 Level II

You are given below, in summarized form, the accounts of Algernon Ltd for 20X6 and 20X7.

Balance sheets

			20X6			20X7
	Cost	*Depn*	*Net*	*Cost*	*Depn*	*Net*
	£	£	£	£	£	£
Plant	10,000	4,000	6,000	11,000	5,000	6,000
Building	50,000	10,000	40,000	90,000	11,000	79,000
			46,000			85,000
Investments at cost			50,000			80,000
Land			43,000			63,000
Stock			55,000			65,000
Debtors			40,000			50,000
Bank			3,000			—
			237,000			343,000

Ordinary shares £1 each	40,000	50,000
Share premium	12,000	14,000
Revaluation reserve	—	20,000
Profit and loss account	25,000	25,000
10 per cent debentures	100,000	150,000
Creditors	40,000	60,000
Proposed dividend	20,000	20,000
Bank	—	4,000
	237,000	343,000

Profit and loss accounts	20X6	20X7
	£	£
Sales	200,000	200,000
Cost of sales	100,000	120,000
	100,000	80,000
Expenses	60,000	60,000
	40,000	20,000
Dividends	20,000	20,000
	20,000	—
Balance b/f	5,000	25,000
Balance c/f	25,000	25,000

a Calculate for Algernon Ltd, for 20X6 and 20X7, the following ratios:
Return on capital employed
Return on owners' equity (return on shareholders' funds)
Debtors' turnover
Creditors' turnover
Current ratio
Quick assets (acid test) ratio
Gross profit percentage
Net profit percentage
Dividend cover
Gearing ratio.

b Using the summarized accounts given, and the ratios you have just prepared, comment on the position, progress and direction of Algernon Ltd. (ACCA)

30.14 Level II

Delta Ltd is an old-established light engineering company. The key performance data for the company between 20X3 and 20X7 are given below.

	20X3	*20X4*	*20X5*	*20X6*	*20X7*
Profit before interest/sales (per cent)	3.6	0.5	0.6	8.1	9.8
Sales/fixed assets (times)	4.6	3.4	3.3	3.5	3.7
Sales/net current assets (times)	2.2	2.5	2.9	3.7	5.1
Cost of sales/stock (times)	1.9	2.0	2.4	2.7	2.9
Debtors/ave. days sales (days)	80	77	75	67	64
Creditors/ave. days sales (days)	58	57	61	64	71
Cost of sales/sales (per cent)	71	73.7	75	71	69.5
Selling and distribution/sales (per cent)	19	18.7	18.5	16	15.6
Administrative/sales (per cent)	6.4	7.1	5.9	4.9	5.1
Current ratio	4.9	2.8	3.3	2.1	1.8

You are required to examine the above data and write a report to the directors of Delta Ltd analysing the performance of the company between 20X3 and 20X7. (JMB)

GENERALLY ACCEPTED ACCOUNTING PRINCIPLES AND PRACTICES

The conceptual framework of accounting

Learning objectives

After reading this chapter you should be able to:

1 explain the meaning of the key terms and concepts listed at the end of the chapter;

2 discuss the qualitative characteristics of financial information contained in the ASB *Statement of Principles for Financial Reporting* (1999);

3 explain the nature, purpose and scope of the conceptual framework of accounting, including the main contents of the ASB *Statement of Principles for Financial Reporting* (1999);

4 describe the conceptual framework and standardization debates and discuss related issues;

5 describe the main types of accounting theories and their implications for a conceptual framework of accounting.

Theoretical review of basic accounting procedures

The foundations of financial accounting were introduced in Chapters 1 and 2 and were extended in Chapter 10 to consider accounting principles, concepts, and policies. Having looked at how these are used in a range of accounting applications, it is now possible to review the accounting processes from a theoretical perspective. It may be helpful, at this stage, to reread the material in Chapter 10 and consider how it has contributed to the various accounting procedures that have been covered in this book.

The major considerations can be briefly restated as follows:

1 The accounting entity is used to determine the boundaries of the organizational unit to be reported upon. The accounting entity is created as an artificial construct, and as such cannot own itself. The external owner's interest is identified as capital in the accounting equation.

2 The life of an accounting entity is divided into accounting periods usually of a year, each seen as a separate entity. Accounts are produced to show the results relating to a particular period. Division into periods is reflected by the emphasis given to periodic reporting.

3 Profit can be defined in terms of the change in capital represented in the balance sheets at the start and end of the period. A parallel approach is transaction based or net production. Here, revenues are recognized in the period when they are realized and the matching principle identifies the costs to be traced to the appropriate period. Critical in this process is the classification of expenditure as either capital or revenue. Costs which are capitalized are carried forward from period to period as balance sheet items. Assets in the balance sheet are carried forward in anticipation of providing benefits to future periods and this may then lead to matching in those periods.

4 Recognition and measurement in financial statements involves the application of two accounting concepts—the accruals concept and the going concern assumption—as well as the selection of a measurement basis, estimation techniques and accounting policies.

5 Any system of accounting for profit has to define either explicitly or implicitly three basic dimensions. These are the unit of measurement, the valuation model and the concept of capital maintenance.

Accounting principles, policies and qualitative characteristics

Chapter 10 provided an outline of the nature of accounting principles in terms of the Accounting Standards Board (ASB) *Statement of Principles for Financial Reporting* (1999).[1] This chapter examines these in more depth, with particular reference to Chapter 3 of the *Statement of Principles for Financial Reporting* which relates to the qualitative characteristics of financial information.

Most of Chapter 10 of this book was devoted to *FRS 18—Accounting Policies* (ASB, 2000),[2] including what it describes as the objectives against which an entity should judge the appropriateness of accounting policies to its particular circumstances, which comprise relevance, reliability, comparability and understandability. This can be restated as follows: the objectives against which an entity should judge the appropriateness of accounting policies to its particular circumstances are the qualitative characteristics of financial information. In other words, FRS18 contains an outline of the qualitative characteristics of financial information as applied in judging the appropriateness of accounting policies. These will now be examined in more detail.

The qualitative characteristics of financial information

According to an earlier draft of the ASB *Statement of Principles for Financial Reporting* published in 1995, 'qualitative characteristics are the characteristics that make the information provided in financial statements useful to users for assessing the financial position, performance and financial adaptability of an enterprise'. The ASB has developed a diagram showing the **qualitative characteristics** of financial information and how these characteristics are related to each other. This is shown in Figure 31.1.

According to the ASB *Statement of Principles for Financial Reporting,*[1] as shown by the diagram (Figure 31.1), there is a threshold quality (of materiality) and four main qualitative characteristics that make financial information useful. These are summarized as follows:

1 Relevance, including predictive value, and confirmatory value.
2 Reliability, including faithful representation, neutral, free from material error, complete, and prudence.
3 Comparability, including consistency and disclosure.
4 Understandability, including users' abilities, and aggregation and classification.

Each of these is explained below.

Threshold quality: materiality

A threshold quality is one that needs to be considered before the other qualities of information. If any information does not pass the test of the threshold quality, it does not need to be considered further. The only threshold quality identified is that of materiality.

Materiality provides guidance as to how a transaction or item of information should be classified in financial statements and/or whether it should be disclosed separately rather than being aggregated with other similar items. This depends on whether the item is of a significant amount, relative to the size of the enterprise. Whether or not a transaction or item is material or significant is generally taken to be a matter of professional judgement. In practice, this is usually regarded as dependent on how large the amount is in relation to an entity's total sales, the value of its assets, or other items of the same type. However, sometimes an item is taken as not being material simply because the absolute amount is small.

A common application of materiality concerns whether an item of expenditure is to be regarded as a fixed asset. Where the amount is not material, the item would be treated as an expense even though it is expected to have a useful life of more than one accounting year and thus normally regarded as a fixed asset (e.g. relatively inexpensive tools and items of office equipment, fixtures and fittings).

Another common application of materiality relates to the separate disclosure of certain items in financial statements. There are numerous references to materiality in the Companies Acts, Statements of Standard Accounting Practice and Financial Reporting Standards which require the separate disclosure of items such as plant hire charges and rents receivable, where the amounts are material.

A related, but slightly different, way of explaining materiality is in terms of the degree of aggregation of data in financial statements. Users are unable to assimilate large amounts of detailed information. This necessitates considerable aggregation of data. Materiality provides guidance on what transactions are to be aggregated by virtue of its specifying which items should be disclosed separately.

FIGURE 31.1 The qualitative characteristics of financial information.

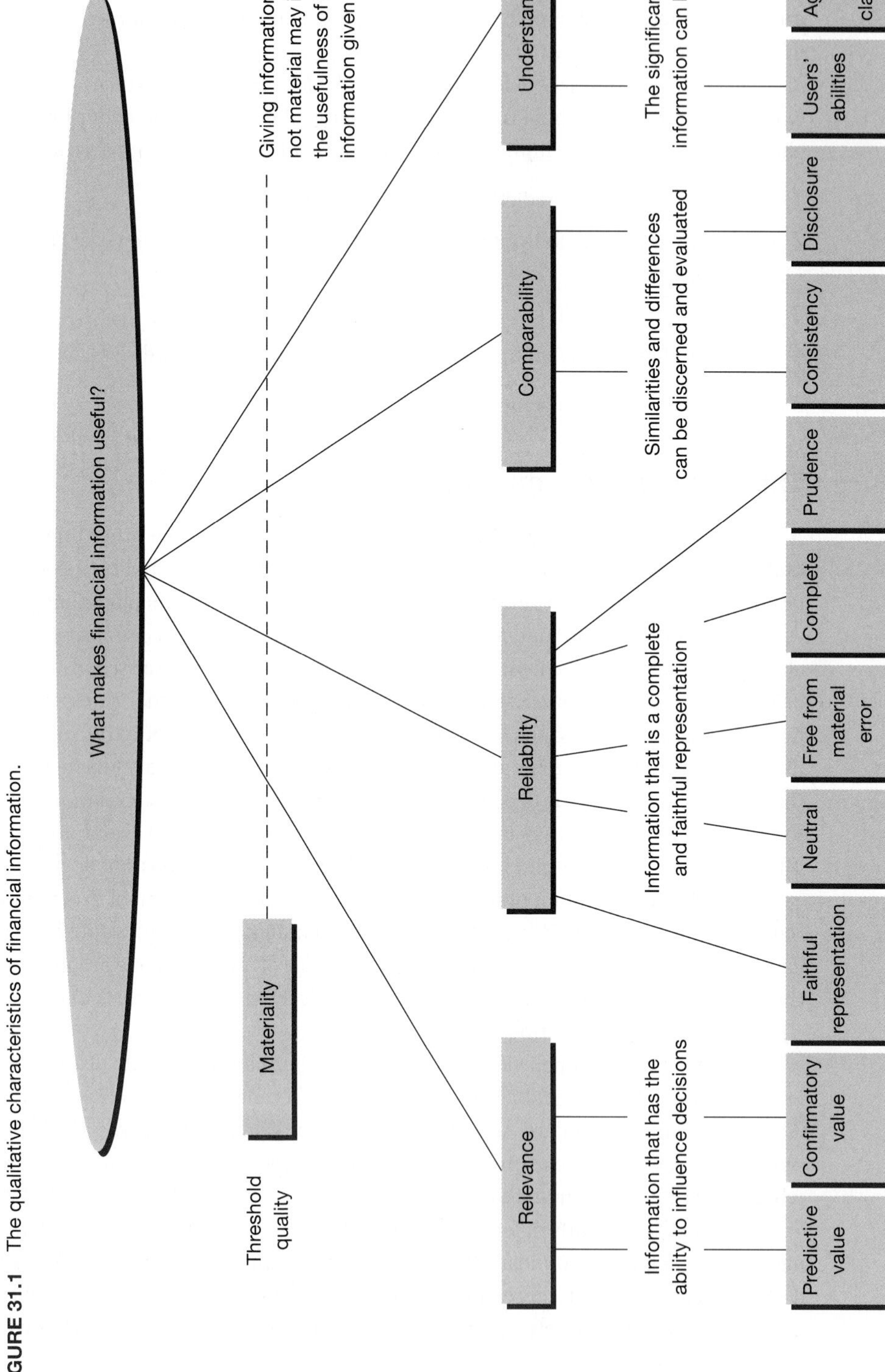

Finally, another interpretation of materiality concerns whether the separate disclosure of certain items is likely to influence decisions made by the users of financial statements. One criterion which can be used to decide whether an item is material is whether or not it may be expected to influence the judgements, decisions or actions of users of financial statements. If this is expected to occur, then the item is said to be material and should be disclosed separately from other similar items.

This interpretation of materiality is contained in the ASB *Statement of Principles for Financial Reporting*[1] which states that 'materiality is the final test of what information should be given in a particular set of financial statements. The materiality test asks whether the resulting information content is of such significance as to require its inclusion in the financial statements. An item of information is material to the financial statements if its misstatement or omission might reasonably be expected to influence the economic decisions of users of those financial statements, including their assessments of management's stewardship.

Whether information is material will depend on the size and nature of the item in question judged in the particular circumstances of the case. The principal factors to be taken into account are set out below. It will usually be a combination of these factors, rather than any one in particular, that will determine materiality.

a The item's size is judged in the context both of the financial statements as a whole and of the other information available to users that would affect their evaluation of the financial statements. This includes, for example, considering how the item affects the evaluation of trends and similar considerations.

b Consideration is given to the item's nature in relation to:

- **i** the transactions or other events giving rise to it;
- **ii** the legality, sensitivity, normality and potential consequences of the event or transaction;
- **iii** the identity of the parties involved; and
- **iv** the particular headings and disclosures that are affected.

If there are two or more similar items, the materiality of the items in aggregate as well as of the items individually needs to be considered.'[1]

There appears to be a contradiction between materiality being a threshold quality, as defined at the start of this section, and its being referred to above as 'the final test'. This inconsistency is further highlighted by its position at the top of the diagram (Figure 31.1), but the explanation in the text of the *Statement of Principles for Financial Reporting* is left until after the other qualitative characteristics.

1 Relevance

According to the ASB *Statement of Principles for Financial Reporting*,[1] information is relevant if it has the ability to influence the economic decisions of users and is provided in time to influence those decisions.

Relevant information has predictive value or confirmatory value. It has **predictive value** if it helps users to evaluate or assess past, present or future events, and it does not need to be in the form of an explicit forecast to have predictive value. Information has **confirmatory value** if it helps users to confirm or correct their past evaluations and assessments. Information may have both predictive value and confirmatory value.[1]

2 Reliability

According to the ASB *Statement of Principles for Financial Reporting,*[1] the 'information provided by financial statements needs to be reliable. Information is reliable if:

- **a** it can be depended upon by users to represent faithfully what it either purports to represent or could reasonably be expected to represent;
- **b** it is free from deliberate or systematic bias (i.e. it is neutral);
- **c** it is free from material error;
- **d** it is complete within the bounds of materiality; and
- **e** in its preparation under conditions of uncertainty, a degree of caution (i.e. prudence) has been applied in exercising judgement and making the necessary estimates.'

To be reliable, information should have the following characteristics.

Faithful representation According to the ASB *Statement of Principles for Financial Reporting,*[1] 'a transaction or other event is faithfully represented in the financial statements if the way in which it is recognised, measured and presented in those statements corresponds closely to the effect of that transaction or event.

Faithful representation involves identifying all the rights and obligations arising from the transaction or event, giving greater weight to those that are likely to have a commercial effect in practice, then accounting for and presenting the transaction or other event in a way that reflects that commercial effect—in other words, in a way that reflects its substance.

The **substance** of a transaction or other event is not always consistent with that suggested by its legal form: although the effects of the legal characteristics of a transaction or other event are themselves a part of its substance and commercial effect, they have to be construed in the context of the transaction as a whole, including any related transactions. For example, an entity may pass legal ownership of an item of property to another party, yet, when the circumstances are looked at as a whole, it may be found that arrangements exist that ensure that the entity continues to have access to the future economic benefits embodied in that item of property. In such circumstances, the accounting needs to reflect this continuing interest.

A group or series of transactions that achieves an overall commercial effect will often need to be viewed as a whole in order to be accounted for in accordance with its substance.'

The classic example of the relevance of substance relates to certain types of lease, such as where a company has contracted to lease a motor vehicle at a given monthly rental for a period of, say, three years, at the end of which it has the option to purchase the vehicle for a nominal/small amount. The legal form of this transaction is a rental agreement. If the legal form were to dictate the accounting entries, the rental payments would appear as an expense in the profit and loss account and the vehicle would not be included in the fixed assets on the balance sheet. This is why such transactions are referred to as a form of **off-balance-sheet finance**. However, the economic substance of this transaction is the purchase of a vehicle payable by instalments, very similar to a hire purchase transaction. Thus, the substance characteristic dictates that the rental payments are not treated as an expense; instead, they are capitalized. This means that the vehicle is recorded as the purchase of a fixed asset and the total rental payments for the three years are shown as a creditor.

Neutrality According to the ASB *Statement of Principles for Financial Reporting,*[1] the information provided by financial statements needs to be neutral—in other words, free from deliberate or systematic bias. Financial information is not neutral if it has been selected or presented in such a way as to influence the making of a decision or judgement in order to achieve a predetermined result or outcome.

Complete and free from material error According to the ASB *Statement of Principles for Financial Reporting*,[1] 'in requiring information provided by financial statements to represent faithfully what it purports to represent and to be neutral, there is an implication that the information is complete and free from error—at least within the bounds of materiality. Information that contains a material error or has been omitted for reasons other than materiality can cause the financial statements to be false or misleading and thus unreliable and deficient in terms of their relevance.

This reference to being complete within the bounds of materiality is important because completeness is relative: financial statements are a highly aggregated portrayal of an entity's financial performance and financial position and therefore cannot show everything.'

Prudence According to the ASB *Statement of Principles for Financial Reporting*,[1] 'uncertainty surrounds many of the events and circumstances that are reported on in the financial statements and it is dealt with in those statements by disclosing the nature and extent of the uncertainty involved and by exercising prudence.

Prudence is the inclusion of a degree of caution in the exercise of the judgements needed in making the estimates required under conditions of uncertainty, such that gains and assets are not overstated and losses and liabilities are not understated. In particular, under such conditions it requires more confirmatory evidence about the existence of, and a greater reliability of measurement for, assets and gains than is required for liabilities and losses.

However, it is not necessary to exercise prudence when there is no uncertainty. Nor is it appropriate to use prudence as a reason for, for example, creating hidden reserves or excessive provisions, deliberately understating assets or gains, or deliberately overstating liabilities or losses, because that would mean that the financial statements are not neutral and, therefore, are not reliable.'

Prudence is deeply embedded in accounting and possibly even in the personality of many accountants. It is one of the main reasons why accountants are often described as conservative, prudent, cautious, pessimistic, and so on. However, the important point is that these references to not overstating gains/income/revenue or assets, and not understating losses/costs/expenses or liabilities essentially refer to not overstating the profit in the profit and loss account and the financial position in the balance sheet. This is achieved by making cautious estimates of items such as the amount of potential bad debts and the depreciation of fixed assets. That is, where the estimate is a range of amounts, prudence dictates that the amount entered in the accounts will be the highest figure of a probable loss or liability, and the lowest figure of a gain or asset.

3 Comparability

According to the ASB *Statement of Principles for Financial Reporting*,[1] 'information in an entity's financial statements gains greatly in usefulness if it can be compared with similar information about the entity for some other period or point in time in order to identify trends in financial performance and financial position. Information about an entity is also much more useful if it can be compared with similar information about other entities in order to evaluate their relative financial performance and financial position.

Information in financial statements therefore needs to be comparable—at least as far as is possible. Furthermore, to help users to make comparisons, such information needs to be prepared and presented in a way that enables users to discern and evaluate similarities in, and differences between, the nature and effects of transactions and other events taking place over time and across different reporting entities. This can usually be achieved through a combination of consistency and disclosure of accounting policies.'

Consistency According to the ASB *Statement of Principles for Financial Reporting*,[1] 'comparability generally implies consistency throughout the reporting entity within each accounting period and from one period to the next. However, consistency is not an end in itself nor should it be allowed to become an impediment to the introduction of improved accounting practices. Consistency can also be useful in enhancing comparability between entities, although it should not be confused with a need for absolute uniformity.'

Disclosure According to the ASB *Statement of Principles for Financial Reporting*,[1] 'in order to determine whether consistency exists or to assist in the making of comparisons despite inconsistencies, users need to be able to identify any differences between:

a the accounting policies adopted by an entity to account for like transactions and other events;

b the accounting policies adopted from period to period by an entity; and

c the accounting policies adopted by different entities.

Disclosure of the accounting policies employed in the preparation of the financial statements, of any changes in those policies and of the effects of such changes therefore enhances the usefulness of financial statements.'

Many academics regard disclosure as a fundamental qualitative characteristic of financial statements. In crude terms, it is argued that if companies use different accounting policies and/or these change over time (i.e. there is a lack of consistency), and/or if companies do not comply with accounting standards, this is not critical; provided there is full disclosure of how the figures are derived, users can make the necessary adjustments in order to achieve comparability.

4 Understandability

Understandability includes **users' abilities** and **aggregation and classification**. According to the ASB *Statement of Principles for Financial Reporting*,[1] 'information provided by financial statements needs to be understandable—in other words, users need to be able to perceive its significance.

Whether financial information is understandable will depend on:

a the way in which the effects of transactions and other events are characterised, aggregated and classified.

b the way in which the information is presented.

c the capabilities of users. Those preparing financial statements are entitled to assume that users have a reasonable knowledge of business and economic activities and accounting and a willingness to study with reasonable diligence the information provided.'[1]

Constraints on the qualitative characteristics

According to the ASB *Statement of Principles for Financial Reporting*,[1] 'on occasion, a conflict will arise between the characteristics of relevance, reliability, comparability and understandability. In such circumstances, a trade-off needs to be found that still enables the objective of financial statements to be met.

Relevance and reliability

Sometimes the information that is the most relevant is not the most reliable and vice versa. Choosing the amount at which to measure an asset or liability will sometimes involve just such a conflict. In such circumstances, it will usually be appropriate to use the information that is the most relevant of whichever information is reliable. Conflict between relevance and reliability can also arise over the timeliness of information. That is because a delay in providing information can make it out-of-date, which will affect its relevance, yet reporting on transactions and other events before all the uncertainties involved are resolved may affect the information's reliability. On the other hand, leaving information out of the financial statements because of reliability concerns may affect the completeness, and therefore reliability, of the information that *is* provided. Although financial information should generally be made available as soon as it is reliable and entities should do all that they reasonably can to speed up the process necessary to make information reliable, financial information should not be provided until it is reliable.

Neutrality and prudence

There can also be tension between two aspects of reliability—neutrality and prudence—because, whilst neutrality involves freedom from deliberate or systematic bias, prudence is a potentially biased concept that seeks to ensure that, under conditions of uncertainty, gains and assets are not overstated and losses and liabilities are not understated. This tension exists only where there is uncertainty, because it is only then that prudence needs to be exercised. When there is uncertainty, the competing demands of neutrality and prudence are reconciled by finding a balance that ensures that the deliberate and systematic understatement of gains and assets and overstatement of losses and liabilities do not occur.

Understandability

It may not always be possible to present a piece of relevant, reliable and comparable information in a way that can be understood by all the users. However, information that is relevant and reliable should not be excluded from the financial statements simply because it is too difficult for some users to understand.'

The conceptual framework of accounting

The nature of a conceptual framework—an analogy

At about this point in their studies students can feel rather confused and frustrated by accounting theory. It is a hurdle that has to be overcome. On the one hand, students frequently have a perception of accounting as being definitive, because much of it is based on the law, and they have been taught a simplified set of rules about double-entry bookkeeping which is very systematic. On the other hand, they frequently think that accountants tend to bend the rules (or 'cook the books'), also known as **creative accounting**. Some of the chapters of this book may reinforce this view because they often suggest that some transactions can be treated in different ways, thus giving possible alternative figures of profit.

It is important to appreciate the difference between 'cooking the books' and the professional judgement involved in decisions between alternative methods of accounting. An analogy may prove useful. Imagine you went to a private consultant because you had backache. In order to maximize his or her fee, the consultant might decide to operate on you. If this was the sole consideration, it would be unethical of the surgeon. Similarly, an accountant who chose a particular form of accounting treatment with the sole intention of reducing the net profit would be acting unethically. However, an ethical physician or accountant is still faced with a number of possible forms of treatment. The physician might prescribe a number of different drugs, but needs to ascertain which is likely to be most appropriate for you. Similarly, the accountant has to choose which accounting treatment of, say, development costs, is the most appropriate in the circumstances.

This analogy can be extended further to illustrate another very important relevant idea. The physician's judgement about your treatment for backache is guided by a body of expert knowledge and research, loosely known as medical science. This includes such disciplines as anatomy and chemistry, which are based on generally accepted theories and concepts similar, in principle, to those discussed in this chapter relating to accounting. Similarly, the accountant's judgement about the most appropriate treatment of certain types of transactions is guided by a body of expert knowledge and research, which is loosely referred to as the theoretical or **conceptual framework of accounting**.

However, unlike medical science, the conceptual framework of accounting is not well developed and thus may contain apparent inconsistencies. Also it is unlikely that a conceptual framework of accounting could be as definitive as, say, medical science in the foreseeable future since accounting theory, like other social sciences, is fundamentally different from natural sciences, such as medical science.

This tension between the need for a set of concepts/principles to guide the practice of accounting, and the awareness that these are unlikely to be conclusive/definitive, has given rise to an extensive debate over the past three decades about the development of a conceptual framework of accounting or what are sometimes called **generally accepted accounting principles (GAAP)**. Note, however, that the abbreviation GAAP is more commonly taken as referring to generally accepted accounting practice, i.e. accounting standards.

The conceptual framework of accounting—a brief history

In order to appreciate fully the sources of authoritative pronouncements about the nature, purpose and scope of a conceptual framework of accounting, it is necessary to start with a brief history of the accountancy profession's attempts to develop a conceptual framework. The earliest comprehensive conceptual framework project started in the mid-1970s in the US by the Financial Accounting Standards Board (FASB), which is the US equivalent of the ASB. This is still the most advanced and comprehensive treatment of the subject in the world. It has also probably been a major influence on subsequent conceptual framework projects by the IASC and ASB discussed below.

In 1989 the International Accounting Standards Committee (IASC), now known as the International Accounting Standards Board, published what might be described as an abbreviated conceptual framework entitled *Framework for the Preparation and Presentation of Financial Statements.*[3]

Then in 1999, the ASB published a *Statement of Principles for Financial Reporting*,[1] which is generally interpreted as being a conceptual framework of accounting. This document closely follows the structure of the IASC framework. Indeed, the ASB stated explicitly that 'it proposes to use wherever possible the IASC text'.

The conceptual framework of accounting—nature, purpose, scope and contents

Probably one of the most concise definitions of a conceptual framework of accounting is contained in the ASC, *Setting Accounting Standards: A Consultative Document*, which is 'a set of broad, internally consistent fundamentals and definitions of key terms'.[4]

Another slightly more informative definition is provided by the FASB in its *Scope and Implications of the Conceptual Framework Project*: 'a constitution, a coherent system of interrelated objectives and fundamentals that can lead to consistent standards and that prescribe the nature, function and limits of financial accounting and financial statements'.[5]

Leaving aside a detailed description of the nature and scope of a conceptual framework for a moment, the FASB definition highlights one of the main purposes of a conceptual framework. That is, to provide standard-setting bodies with a set of internally consistent definitions of accounting principles which can be used as a basis for setting accounting standards that are not contradictory or in conflict with each other. The other main purpose of a conceptual framework, explained earlier using the analogy with medicine, is to provide guidance to accountants in their day-to-day work of choosing appropriate forms of accounting treatments for various transactions and items. These two main purposes and a number of others are contained in an earlier version of the ASB *Statement of Principles for Financial Reporting* issued in 1991, which is reproduced below:

1. Assist the Board in the development of future accounting standards and in its review of existing accounting standards.
2. Assist the Board by providing a basis for reducing the number of alternative accounting treatments permitted by law and accounting standards.
3. Assist preparers of financial statements in applying accounting standards and in dealing with topics that do not form the subject of an accounting standard.
4. Assist auditors in forming an opinion whether financial statements conform with accounting standards.
5. Assist users of financial statements in interpreting the information contained in financial statements prepared in conformity with accounting standards.
6. Provide those who are interested in the work of the Board with information about its approach to the formulation of accounting standards.

The IASC framework[3] has an almost identical list of purposes except that these are expressed in terms of developing international accounting standards and promoting international harmonization.

Returning to the nature and scope of a conceptual framework, various authors and bodies have described this in simple terms as an agreed set of answers to the following sorts of question. For whom are accounts to be prepared? For what purposes do they want to use them? What kind of accounting reports do they want? How far are present accounts suitable for these purposes, and how could we improve accounting practice to make them more suitable?[4]

Probably the most informative way of examining the nature of a conceptual framework in more detail is by reviewing the contents of the frameworks that have been developed to date. The shortest of these is the IASC framework,[3] the scope of which is reproduced below.

Scope
The framework deals with:

1 The objective of financial statements.
2 The qualitative characteristics that determine the usefulness of information in financial statements.
3 The definition, recognition and measurement of the elements from which financial statements are constructed.
4 Concepts of capital and capital maintenance.

The ASB framework is set out in its *Statement of Principles for Financial Reporting* (1999),[1] the contents of which are similar to those of the IASC, but with some significant differences. This is shown below.

Chapter 1	The objective of financial statements
Chapter 2	The reporting entity
Chapter 3	The qualitative characteristics of financial information
Chapter 4	The elements of financial statements
Chapter 5	Recognition in financial statements
Chapter 6	Measurement in financial statements
Chapter 7	Presentation of financial information

The contents of Chapter 1 of the *Statement of Principles for Financial Reporting* have been summarized in Chapter 1 of this book, and the contents of Chapter 3 have been summarized earlier in this chapter. It is beyond the introductory nature of this book to deal with the other chapters of the *Statement of Principles for Financial Reporting* in depth, but these may be compared with the FASB conceptual framework shown in diagrammatic form in Figure 31.2. Notice in particular its hierarchical nature.

Having identified the scope or structure of the conceptual frameworks produced to date, the contents of these may be briefly explained as essentially comprising the following:

1 *The objective of financial reporting*, including the users of financial statements and their information needs.
2 *The attributes or qualitative characteristics* of accounting information that enable financial statements to fulfil their objective, determine what is useful information, and provide criteria for choosing among alternative accounting methods.
3 Definitions of the *elements* of financial statements such as the nature of gains, losses, assets, liabilities and ownership interest. These were defined in Chapter 10.
4 A set of criteria for deciding when the elements are to be *recognized* in financial statements. According to the ASB *Statement of Principles for Financial Reporting*,[1] 'recognised is used ... to mean depicting an item both in words and by a monetary amount in the primary financial statement totals. If a transaction or other event has created a new asset or liability or added to an existing asset or liability, that effect will be recognised if: (a) sufficient *evidence* exists that the new asset or liability has been created or that there has been an addition to an existing asset or liability; and (b) the new asset or liability or the

FIGURE 31.2 The FASB conceptual framework for financial accounting and reporting.

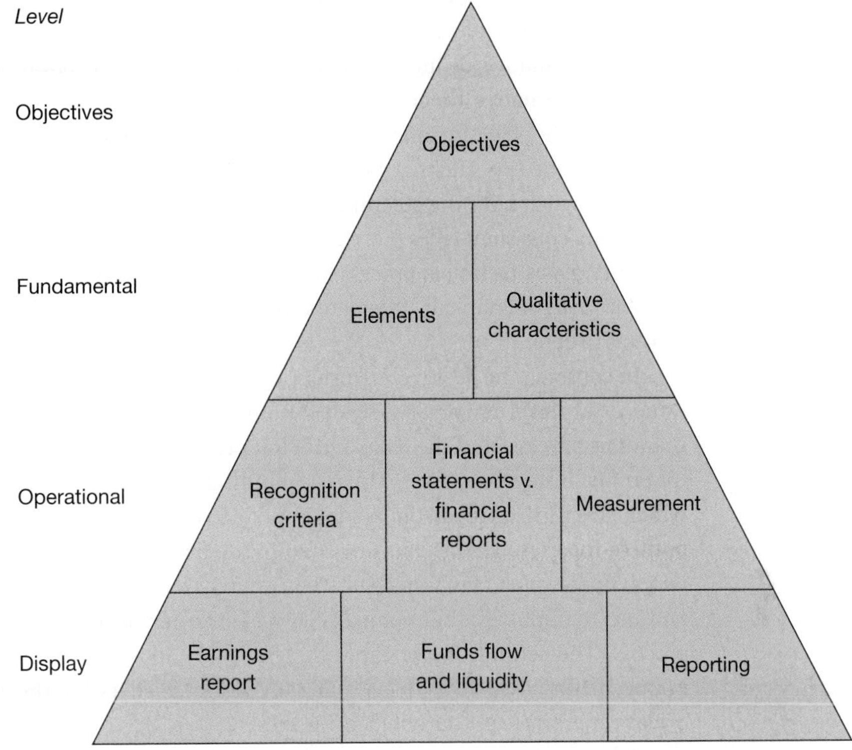

addition to the existing asset or liability can be measured at a monetary amount with sufficient *reliability*.'

5 A set of *measurement* rules for determining the monetary amounts at which the elements of financial statements are to be recognized and carried in the accounts. For example, these might comprise historical cost, replacement cost, net realizable value or present value.

6 Guidelines for the *presentation and disclosure* of the elements in financial statements. These currently take the form of statements of financial performance (i.e. a profit and loss account and a statement of total recognized gains and losses), a balance sheet and cash flow statement. Alternatives include a fund flow statement.[1]

The conceptual framework debate, standardization and choice

Much controversy has surrounded the idea of developing a conceptual framework of accounting, particularly in the UK where the self-regulatory standard setting institutions have limited resources. There are two main related issues. The first is whether the cost of preparing a conceptual framework is justified in terms of its benefits, including whether it is possible to develop a set of consistent fundamentals and whether these will lead to improvements in accounting standard setting. The second issue concerns whether accounting standards just make published accounts more consistent rather than comparable, or alternatively whether more meaningful comparisons would result from allowing companies to choose those accounting policies which are appropriate to their individual circumstances. This has always been an issue in standard setting, but the development of a conceptual framework accentuates the debate because it will presumably lead to greater standardization.

There is a wide variety of schools of thought on the conceptual framework debate, but for the sake of structuring and simplifying the discussion these can be grouped into two extremes comprising the normative/deductive approach and the positive/empiricist approach.

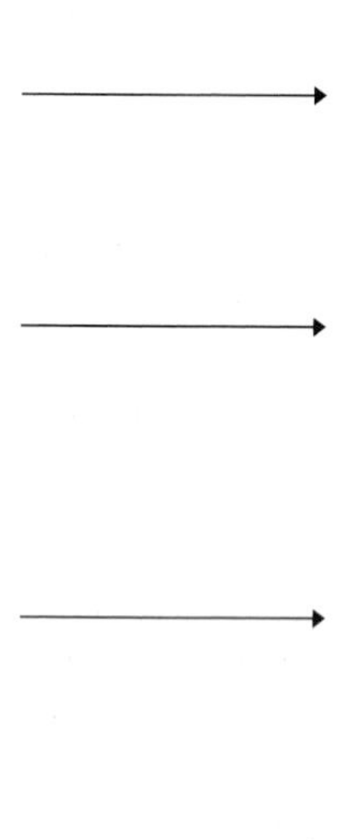

The normative/deductive approach regards a conceptual framework as absolutely essential. **Normative theories** view accounting as a technical process which is capable of measuring the 'true income' of a business given a set of theories which specify how this should be done (e.g. Hicks, 1946). They often use the analogy that financial statements are like maps which have the potential to provide a faithful representation of reality given a set of underlying consistent rules (i.e. a conceptual framework). Similarly, **deductive theories** view accounting as a technical process but advocate a user needs approach based on identifying the objectives of financial statements similar to that taken in all the conceptual framework projects to date.

In contrast, the positive/empiricist approach regards a conceptual framework as at best unnecessary, and at worst positively dysfunctional. **Empirical theories** view accounting as an economic process, and the objective of financial statements as being to facilitate predictions (of profits, insolvency, etc.). Thus, accounting methods should be selected on the basis of which give the best predictions, that is, not according to some conceptual framework. Many **positive theories** view accounting, and particularly standard setting, as a political process which may exploit class interests. They often describe standard setting as quasi-legislation, and use the analogy that company law is determined by parliament, which is a political process. The setting of standards therefore demands consensus and not dictatorial pronouncements based on a conceptual framework which itself is the product of a particular set of class interests (e.g. shareholders' interests).

Advocates of a pragmatic deductive approach appear to have won the debate in the UK. However, it remains to be seen whether the monetary costs of preparing a conceptual framework by the ASB will be justified in terms of the benefits in the form of improvements in standard setting.

Furthermore, the development of a conceptual framework is unlikely to quieten those who argue that accounting standards may promote more consistency of accounting policies between companies but this does not necessarily result in greater comparability. This is the second issue referred to at the start of this section. The reasoning behind the assertion that a conceptual framework of accounting may lead to accounting standards which do not provide comparability between companies is similar to the old argument against accounting standards. There are said to be 'circumstantial variables' or 'differences in circumstances' between companies which necessitate the exercise of managerial discretion in the choice of accounting methods. It is argued that standardization forces companies to use the same accounting policies, but it does not necessarily mean that they are the most appropriate accounting policies for each company and thus comparisons may be misleading. The existence of a conceptual framework is likely to lead to greater standardization and, it is said, more rigidity, a lack of flexibility, and thus less innovation. It is easy to be cynical about innovation when it takes the form of creative accounting, but it must be recognized that standardization taken to the extreme (as uniformity) would probably reduce innovation, which is said to be the case in some countries with uniform national accounting systems specified solely by law.

Summary

All professions need a body of either theological, empirical and/or theoretical knowledge to guide the actions of their practitioners. In accounting this is not as well developed as in some other professions such as medicine, nor is it likely to be in the foreseeable future. The tension between this need for a set of rules to guide practice, and the awareness that these are unlikely to be definitive, has given rise to an extensive debate about the current development of a conceptual framework of accounting, also known as generally accepted accounting principles (GAAP).

The FASB, IASC and ASB have all published conceptual frameworks of accounting. The main purposes of a conceptual framework of accounting are to provide a basis for the development and review of accounting standards, and to assist preparers, users and auditors of financial statements. This takes the form of an internally consistent set of interrelated objectives and fundamentals that prescribe the nature, function and limits of financial statements.

The ASB conceptual framework is contained in its *Statement of Principles for Financial Reporting* (1999).[1] This sets out the objectives of financial statements, the qualitative characteristics of financial information, the elements of financial statements, recognition criteria, measurement rules, and guidelines for the presentation of items in financial statements.

This chapter examined in depth the qualitative characteristics of financial information. Qualitative characteristics are the attributes that make the information provided in financial statements useful to users. According to the ASB *Statement of Principles for Financial Reporting*,[1] the qualitative characteristics of financial information comprise a threshold quality of materiality and four main characteristics that make financial information useful. These comprise relevance, reliability, comparability and understandability. Relevance includes predictive value and confirmatory value. Reliability includes faithful representation, neutrality, free from material error, complete and prudence. Comparability includes consistency and disclosure. Understandability includes users' abilities, and aggregation and classification. There are several constraints on the qualitative characteristics that relate to relevance and reliability, neutrality and prudence, and understandability.

Key terms and concepts

Aggregation and classification (496)
comparability (495)
complete (495)
conceptual framework of accounting (498)
confirmatory value (493)
consistency (496)
creative accounting (498)
deductive theory (502)
disclosure (496)
empirical theory (502)
faithful representation (494)
free from material error (495)
generally accepted accounting principles (GAAP) (498)
materiality (491)
neutrality (494)
normative theory (502)
off-balance-sheet finance (494)
positive theory (502)
predictive value (493)
prudence (495)
qualitative characteristics (491)
relevance (493)
reliability (494)
substance (494)
threshold quality (491)
understandability (496)
users' abilities (496)

References

1. Accounting Standards Board (1999). *Statement of Principles for Financial Reporting* (ASB).
2. Accounting Standards Board (2000). *Financial Reporting Standard 18—Accounting Policies* (ASB).
3. International Accounting Standards Committee (1989). *Framework for the Preparation and Presentation of Financial Statements* (IASC).
4. Accounting Standard Committee (1978). *Setting Accounting Standards: A Consultative Document* (ICAEW).
5. Financial Accounting Standards Board (1976). *Scope and Implications of the Conceptual Framework Project* (FASB).

Review questions

An asterisk after the question number indicates that there is a suggested answer in the Appendix.

31.1 **a** Briefly explain the nature of a qualitative characteristic of financial information.

b Prepare a diagram showing the qualitative characteristics of financial information identified in the ASB *Statement of Principles for Financial Reporting* (1999) and the relationship between each of them.

31.2 Define and explain the qualitative characteristic of relevance, including its predictive value and confirmatory value.

31.3 Define and explain the qualitative characteristic of reliability, including the attributes of faithful representation, substance, neutrality, free from material error, completeness, and prudence.

31.4 Define and explain the qualitative characteristics of comparability and understandability.

31.5 Define and explain the threshold quality of materiality.

31.6 Describe the constraints on the qualitative characteristics of financial information.

31.7 According to the ASB *Statement of Principles for Financial Reporting* (1999) there is a potential 'conflict between the characteristics of relevance and reliability. There can also be tension between two aspects of reliability—neutrality and prudence.' Explain the nature of these conflicts/tensions and how they can be reconciled.

31.8* Describe the purposes of a conceptual framework of accounting.

31.9* Describe the nature and contents of a conceptual framework of accounting.

31.10 'It is unrealistic to expect a conceptual framework of accounting to provide a basis for definitive or even generally accepted accounting standards in the foreseeable future because of inherent conflicts and inconsistencies between, for example, the qualitative characteristics of accounting information as well as the differing information needs and abilities of users.' Discuss.

31.11 'A conceptual framework of accounting is likely to lead to greater standardization, less choice, less innovation and thus reduced comparability because of the existence of fundamental differences between companies in the way they conduct their activities.' Discuss.

chapter 32

International Accounting Standards

Learning objectives

After reading this chapter you should be able to:

1 explain the meaning of the key terms and concepts listed at the end of the chapter;

2 describe the objectives and role of the International Accounting Standards Committee/Board;

3 discuss the current activities of the International Accounting Standards Board in the convergence/harmonization of accounting standards, especially in Europe;

4 describe the main elements of each of the International Accounting Standards that are comparable with the Statements of Standard Accounting Practice and Financial Reporting Standards covered in earlier chapters;

5 explain how each of the above International Accounting Standards differs from its equivalent UK accounting standard;

6 describe how the IASC conceptual framework differs from the ASB Statement of Principles.

Introduction

This chapter examines the role of the International Accounting Standards Committee/Board and the main elements of those International Accounting Standards that are comparable with the SSAPs and FRSs covered in the previous chapters of this book. For reasons that will become apparent on reading the chapter, both UK and International Accounting Standards are currently going through a transitional period aimed at their convergence/harmonization. This means that parts of this edition of the book including this chapter are likely to be superseded quicker than normal. It is most regrettable, but unavoidable, and therefore updates will appear on the web site for the book as soon as they become examinable by the professional accountancy bodies at this level in respect of UK companies.

The International Accounting Standards Committee/Board

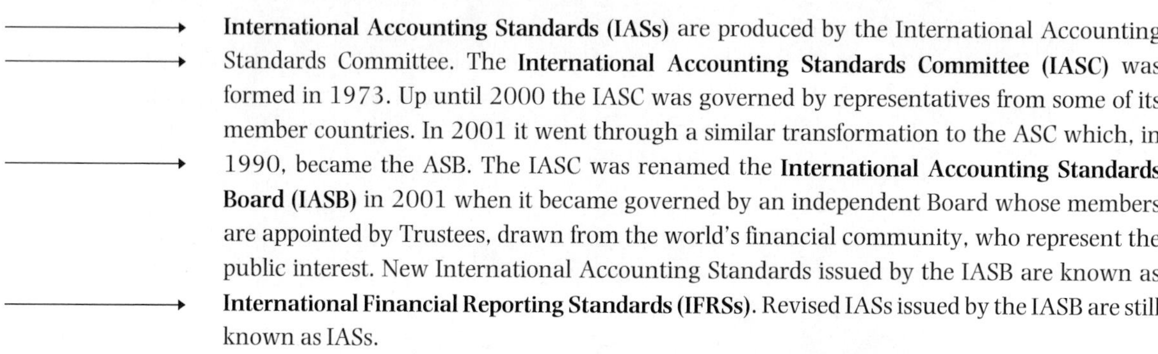

International Accounting Standards (IASs) are produced by the International Accounting Standards Committee. The **International Accounting Standards Committee (IASC)** was formed in 1973. Up until 2000 the IASC was governed by representatives from some of its member countries. In 2001 it went through a similar transformation to the ASC which, in 1990, became the ASB. The IASC was renamed the **International Accounting Standards Board (IASB)** in 2001 when it became governed by an independent Board whose members are appointed by Trustees, drawn from the world's financial community, who represent the public interest. New International Accounting Standards issued by the IASB are known as **International Financial Reporting Standards (IFRSs)**. Revised IASs issued by the IASB are still known as IASs.

The objectives of the IASC as formulated in 1973, and revised in 1982, are as follows:

1. to formulate and publish in the public interest accounting standards to be observed in the presentation of financial statements and to promote their worldwide acceptance and observation; and
2. to work generally for the improvement and harmonization of regulations, accounting standards and procedures relating to the presentation of financial statements.

When the IASC became the IASB in 2001 it revised its constitution, including its objectives. The objectives of the IASB are as follows:

1. to develop, in the public interest, a single set of high quality, understandable and enforceable global accounting standards that require high quality, transparent and comparable information in financial statements and other financial reporting to help participants in the world's capital markets and other users make economic decisions;
2. to promote the use and rigorous application of those standards; and
3. to bring about convergence of national accounting standards and International Accounting Standards to high quality solutions.

The IASB follows much the same procedure as the ASB when it proposes to issue an IAS/IFRS. This starts with the publication of an Exposure Draft that is intended for public comment. The IASB then reviews the comments and may decide to revise the Exposure Draft. Finally a new IAS/IFRS is issued.

Accountancy and standard setting bodies throughout the world are now involved in the work of the IASB, as are various government agencies and stock market regulators.

This includes all the countries of the EU and the US. Because of the UK and US tradition of standard setting, they have probably had the greatest influence, especially given that the working language of the IASC/B is English. Moreover, many IASs are very similar to either UK FRSs and/or their US equivalent, **Statements of Financial Accounting Standards (SFASs)** produced by the **Financial Accounting Standards Board (FASB)**. This is because some were formulated jointly, while others have been either wholly or partly adopted by each of the bodies from each other's standards. However, there are still some very significant differences between IASs and UK and US standards, that are subject to much heated debate.

The first countries to adopt IASs were mostly the developing countries of Africa and Asia, particularly former British colonies, who lack the resources and expertise to develop their own standards from scratch. Many have either adopted IASs en bloc, or adapted them to conform with their own particular economic and legal systems, particularly the capital market.

It is generally acknowledged that up until about 1995 most IASs allowed too many alternative accounting treatments. However, during the late 1990s the IASC engaged on a programme of eliminating many of these alternatives so that the world's major stock market regulators, such as the US Securities and Exchange Commission (SEC), would adopt IASs. Furthermore, in 2000 the EU proposed that as from 2005, all EU listed companies should prepare their consolidated financial statements in accordance with IASs and IFRSs. Since that date the IASB, FASB and ASB have also been engaged on what is known as a 'convergence project' to harmonize international, US and UK accounting standards.

Moreover, the EU seems likely to give up much of its work on formulating accounting practices in favour of extending IASs to all companies in the EU. There is little wonder that in the light of these developments many people have predicted that national accounting standards will probably disappear with the next decade. However, before this happens there are some major differences of opinion between the IASB, EU, USA and the UK that will need to be resolved. Furthermore, national accounting standards may need to be perpetuated because of their application to non-listed companies, for whom IASs could be too onerous and inappropriate to their circumstances.

The IASB clearly has enormous status and authority stemming from the impact of IASs worldwide and its being the focus of the global harmonization of national accounting standards. However, it is easy to overlook that unlike, for example, the Financial Reporting Council in the UK, the IASB really has no power to enforce IASs. Compliance depends on their adoption and enforcement by nation states and their respective stock market regulatory bodies such as the SEC.

International Accounting Standards

The following is a list of the IASs that are equivalent to the UK SSAPs and FRSs covered in the previous chapters of this book.

International Accounting Standards		*Financial Reporting Standards*	
IAS1—	Presentation of financial statements	FRS3—	Reporting financial performance
IAS2—	Inventories	SSAP9—	Stocks and long-term contracts
IAS7—	Cash flow statements	FRS1—	Cash flow statements
IAS8—	Accounting policies, changes in accounting estimates and errors	FRS3—	Reporting financial performance

IAS10— Events after the balance sheet date	SSAP17— Accounting for post balance sheet events
IAS16— Property, plant and equipment	FRS15— Tangible fixed assets
IAS18— Revenue	
IAS35— Discontinuing operations	FRS3— Reporting financial performance
IAS37— Provisions, contingent liabilities and contingent assets	FRS12— Provisions, contingent liabilities and contingent assets
IAS38— Intangible assets	SSAP13— Accounting for research and development
IAS38— Intangible assets	FRS10— Goodwill and intangible assets

The remainder of this chapter explains the main elements of each of the above IASs with particular reference to how they differ from the equivalent SSAP or FRS.

IAS1—Presentation of financial statements[1]

The components of financial statements required by IAS1 consist of an income statement (referred to in the UK as a profit and loss account), balance sheet, statement of changes in equity, and a cash flow statement. There are no prescribed formats for the income statement and balance sheet, but there are lists of the minimum contents and illustrations of formats in the appendix.

The minimum contents of the income statement specified in IAS1 are virtually identical to the main items in the UK Companies Act 1985 prescribed format for the profit and loss account. There is thus little point in reproducing these here.

The minimum contents of the balance sheet specified in IAS1 are also very similar to that required by the UK Companies Act 1985, but the format and terminology are slightly different. In particular, fixed assets are referred to as non-current assets, and long-term liabilities are referred to as non-current liabilities. A specimen balance sheet that complies with the requirements of IAS1 is shown below.

	Euros 000	Euros 000
Assets		
Non-current assets		
Property, plant and equipment	X	
Intangible assets	X	
Financial assets	X	
Investments	X	
		X
Current assets		
Inventories	X	
Trade and other receivables	X	
Cash and cash equivalents	X	
		X
Total assets		X

Equity and liabilities		
Capital and reserves		
Issued share capital	X	
Share premium account	X	
Revaluation reserve	X	
Accumulated profits	X	
		X
Non-current liabilities		
Loan notes		X
Current liabilities		
Trade and other payables	X	
Tax liabilities	X	
		X
Total equity and liabilities		X

The trade and other receivables refer to debtors, and the trade and other payables refer to creditors. The property, plant and equipment is equivalent to the tangible fixed assets shown in the UK format, and is made up of land and buildings, plant and machinery, and fixtures, fittings, tools and equipment. The accumulated profits is equivalent to the balance on the profit and loss account shown in the UK format. The remaining items should be self-explanatory.

At the time of writing, even where EU law allows the adoption of IASs the financial statements of companies must still comply with format prescribed in the EU Fourth Directive. In the case of the UK, this means compliance with the Fourth Schedule to the Companies Act 1985 as described in Chapter 27 of this book. It is unclear whether this will continue to be the case if the EU requires all listed companies to prepare their consolidated financial statements in accordance with IASs as from 2005.

As mentioned above, IAS1 also requires that financial statements include a statement of changes in equity. This is essentially equivalent to a combination of three UK statements that must be given as notes to the accounts: movements on reserves; statement of total recognized gains and losses; and reconciliation of movements in shareholders' funds. A specimen statement of changes in equity that complies with the IAS1 requirements is shown below.

	Share capital	*Share premium*	*Revaluation reserve*	*Accumulated profits*	*Total*
	Euros 000	Euros 000	Euros 000	Euros 000	Euros 000
Balance from previous period	X	X	X	X	X
Changes in accounting policy				(X)	(X)
Restated balance	X	X	X	X	X
Surplus on revaluation of properties			X		X
Deficit on revaluation of investments			(X)		(X)
Net gains and losses not recognized in the income statement			X		X
Net profit for the period				X	X
Dividends				(X)	(X)
Issue of share capital	X	X			X
Balance at end of period	X	X	X	X	X

IAS2—Inventories[2]

The contents of the most recent revision of IAS2 that are examined at the introductory level are almost the same as its UK equivalent, SSAP9. It requires that inventories should be measured at the lower of cost and net realizable value. Cost includes all costs to bring the inventories to their present condition and location. Where specific cost is not appropriate, the benchmark treatment is to use FIFO or weighted average cost. The 1993 version of IAS2 also allowed the use of LIFO. However, this has been eliminated from the latest revision of IAS2 published in 2003.

IAS7—Cash flow statements[3]

There are some very significant differences between IAS7 and its UK equivalent, FRS1. Ironically an earlier version of FRS1 was very similar to IAS7, but this was changed because part of it was difficult to implement. The most fundamental difference is that the IAS7 cash flow statement does not contain the separate heading/classification found in FRS1 relating to the 'management of liquid resources'. This is because IAS7 treats current asset investments as cash and cash equivalents (for a definition of cash equivalents see Chapter 29 of this book). Put another way, FRS1 defines cash flows to include only movements in cash whereas IAS7 defines cash flows as movements in both cash and cash equivalents.

Furthermore, the IAS7 cash flow statement does not use any of the other headings/ classifications found in FRS1, but it does contain essentially the same items. The difference is that in IAS7 these are classified under the headings operating activities, investing activities and financing activities.

Another difference between IAS7 and FRS1 is that IAS7 does not require the separate reconciliation of operating profit to net cash inflow from operating activities found in FRS1. This is built into the IAS7 cash flow statement. IAS7 permits the use of either the direct or indirect method of reporting the cash flows from operating activities. The Appendix to IAS7 contains illustrations of cash flow statements using both of these methods. The illustration using the indirect method is reproduced below to facilitate comparisons with FRS1.

Cash flows from operating activities		
Net profit before taxation, and extraordinary item	X	
Adjustments for:		
Depreciation	X	
Investment income	(X)	
Interest expense	X	
Operating profit before working capital changes	X	
Increase in trade and other receivables	(X)	
Decrease in inventories	X	
Decrease in trade payables	(X)	
Cash generated from operations	X	
Interest paid	(X)	
Income taxes paid	(X)	
Cash flow before extraordinary item	X	
Proceeds from earthquake disaster settlement	X	
Net cash from operating activities		X

Cash flows from investing activities		
Purchase of property, plant and equipment	(X)	
Proceeds from sale of equipment	X	
Interest received	X	
Dividends received	X	
Net cash used in investing activities		(X)
Cash flows from financing activities		
Proceeds from issuance of share capital	X	
Proceeds from long-term borrowings	X	
Dividends paid (could be shown as an operating cash flow)	(X)	
Net cash used in financing activities		(X)
Net increase in cash and cash equivalents		X
Cash and cash equivalents at beginning of period		X
Cash and cash equivalents at end of period		X

A final significant difference between IAS7 and FRS1 is that unlike FRS1, IAS7 does not require a reconciliation of net cash flow to movement in net debt.

IAS8—Accounting policies, changes in accounting estimates and errors[4]

At the introductory level the principles of IAS8 are very similar to FRS3. They both require the separate disclosure on the face of the income statement/profit and loss account of the profit or loss from ordinary activities and the extraordinary items. According to IAS8, extraordinary items are rare, but unlike FRS3, it gives two specific examples, namely the expropriation of assets and an earthquake or other natural disaster. Both standards also require the same treatment of exceptional items, or what IAS8 describes as items of abnormal size, nature or incidence. These are treated as part of the ordinary activities but some will require separate disclosure on the face of the income statement/profit and loss account while others will be shown as a note to the accounts.

IAS8 and FRS3 also both cover changes in accounting policies and the correction of errors. In the case of FRS3 these are dealt with under the heading of prior period adjustments. Both standards require changes in accounting policies and the correction of errors to be treated as prior year adjustments, which includes restating the comparative figures for the prior periods that are affected.

In contrast, changes in accounting estimates should only be included in the financial statements of the current and future accounting periods, and their classification will be unchanged (e.g. depreciation arising from a change in the estimated useful life of a fixed asset).

IAS10—Events after the balance sheet date[5]

IAS10 and SSAP17 are very similar. Like SSAP17, IAS10 states that events occurring after the balance sheet date that provide additional information on conditions existing at the balance sheet date should lead to adjustment of the financial statements. However, disclosure should be made for other events, if necessary for a proper evaluation.

There is, however, one significant difference between IAS10 and SSAP17 that relates to the treatment of proposed dividends. According to IAS10, proposed final dividends on preference and ordinary shares should not be accrued. In contrast, UK financial statements always include proposed dividends in the profit and loss account and balance sheet. However, at the time of writing, *FRED27—Events after the Balance Sheet Date* is proposing to bring the UK into line with IAS10. This will mean that in future proposed dividends would be shown as a note to the accounts. The justification for this is that dividends do not become a liability until they are approved at the annual general meeting.

IAS16—Property, plant and equipment[6]

Most of IAS16 is the same as its UK equivalent, FRS15. There are two minor differences that are relevant at the introductory level and which relate to the provisions of FRS15 covered in Chapter 11 of this book.

Both IAS16 and FRS15 allow companies to revalue their tangible fixed assets from historical cost to current values. However, IAS16 defines current values as 'fair values' which are required to be measured by market values or replacement cost. In contrast, according to FRS15, 'the current value of a tangible fixed asset to the business is the lower of replacement cost and recoverable amount.'

The other difference between IAS16 and FRS15 relates to depreciation and impairment reviews. FRS15 requires that where a fixed asset is not depreciated on the grounds of immateriality, or because the remaining useful life exceeds 50 years, there should be an impairment review of the fixed asset to ensure that the value of the asset has not fallen below its book/carrying value. This impairment review is not required by IAS16.

IAS18—Revenue[7]

There is no UK accounting standard that is equivalent to IAS18, although parts of the ASB *Statement of Principles* discuss revenue recognition. These parts of the *Statement of Principles* are not usually covered at the introductory level, and have thus only been discussed briefly in earlier chapters of this book. A short outline of IAS18 is therefore given below.

IAS18 is concerned with revenue recognition. In particular, it sets out the following rules for determining the accounting year in which sales revenue should be included in the profit and loss account on the sale of goods. This is referred to as when 'performance should be regarded as being achieved'.

'In a transaction involving the sale of goods, performance should be regarded as being achieved when the following conditions have been fulfilled:

a the seller of the goods has transferred to the buyer the significant risks and rewards of ownership, in that all significant acts have been completed and the seller retains no continuing managerial involvement in, or effective control of, the goods transferred to a degree usually associated with ownership; and

b no significant uncertainty exists regarding:
  - **i** the consideration that will be derived from the sale of the goods;
  - **ii** the associated costs incurred or to be incurred in producing or purchasing the goods;
  - **iii** the extent to which the goods may be returned.'

IAS35—Discontinuing operations[8]

IAS35 is equivalent to the part of FRS3 that deals with discontinued operations. The main difference is implied in their use of the terms 'discontinuing' as against 'discontinued'. In FRS3 a discontinued operation is one that is completed either during the accounting year, or before the earlier of three months of the end of the year or the date on which the financial statements are approved. In contrast, IAS35 includes operations that are in the process of being discontinued at the end of the accounting year. Apart from this difference between which operations are to be disclosed, the information that must be given in the financial statements is much the same.

At the time of writing, the IASB and the ASB are in the process of producing a new jointly developed exposure draft on discontinued operations that will bring greater convergence.

IAS37—Provisions, contingent liabilities and contingent assets[9]

IAS37 and its UK equivalent, FRS12, were developed jointly, and thus in the words of FRS12, 'all the requirements of the IAS are included in the FRS and there are no differences of substance between these common requirements'.

IAS38—Intangible assets[10]

Part of IAS38 is very similar to SSAP13 in that they both describe the circumstances relating to the capitalization of development costs in much the same words. However, they differ in principle. SSAP13 states that development expenditure should be written off in the year of expenditure except in defined circumstances when it may be deferred to future periods. In contrast, IAS38 requires that if these defined circumstances apply, development expenditure should be recognized as an asset and amortized. In short, in defined circumstances, SSAP13 gives the option of capitalizing development expenditure whereas IAS38 requires it.

There is also a minor difference between another part of IAS38 and FRS10. Unlike FRS10, IAS38 requires that purchased goodwill should always be amortized. FRS10 contains a 'rebuttable presumption that the useful economic lives of purchased goodwill and intangible assets are limited to periods of 20 years or less. This presumption may be rebutted and a useful economic life regarded as a longer period or indefinite.' In these circumstances positive purchased goodwill may be amortized over a useful economic life of greater than 20 years, or if this is indefinite, should not be amortized. Thus part of IAS38 differs from FRS10 in that it does not allow goodwill to be regarded as having an indefinite useful economic life, and thus must be amortized in all circumstances.

The IASC conceptual framework

There are also some important similarities and differences between the IASC *Framework for the Preparation and Presentation of Financial Statements*[11] and the ASB *Statement of Principles for Financial Reporting.*[12]

The objective of financial statements in the IASC *Framework* makes no explicit reference to the stewardship function. There was considerable pressure to have this included in the ASB *Statement of Principles*. However, the IASC *Framework* acknowledges that financial statements are used for assessing the stewardship or accountability of management but regards this as being included within its reference to economic decisions. This difference in the definition of the objective of financial statements may thus be a hurdle to convergence but is probably not insurmountable.

There are some important similarities between the IASC *Framework* and the ASB *Statement of Principles*. First, they have an identical list of seven users of financial statements and contain a very similar description of their information needs. Second, they both acknowledge the same two underlying assumptions of financial statements, namely going concern and the accruals basis of accounting. Third, they both identify the same four qualitative characteristics of financial information, namely relevance, reliability, comparability and understandability. There is a minor difference in that the IASC regards materiality as an aspect of relevance.

There is, however, said to be a significant difference between the IASC *Framework* and the ASB *Statement of Principles*. The elements of financial statements as set out in the ASB *Statement of Principles* consist of assets, liabilities, ownership interest, gains and losses. In contrast, the elements of financial statements as set out in the IASC *Framework* consist of assets, liabilities, equity, income and expenses. The first three are essentially the same. However, whereas the ASB *Statement of Principles* refers to gains and losses, the IASC *Framework* contains income and expenses.

Some people argue that this reflects a fundamental difference in their approaches to profit measurement. The ASB *Statement of Principles* is said to be based on a balance sheet approach, as outlined in Chapter 2 of this book. In contrast, the IASC *Framework* is said to be based on the assumed primacy of the income statement, or essentially what is described in Chapter 2 of this book as a transaction-based approach in which expenses are matched with income/revenue. This is also reflected in *IAS18—Revenue*. These two approaches to profit measurement are significant differences that may not be easy to resolve if convergence is to be achieved.

Summary

International Accounting Standards (IASs) are prepared by the International Accounting Standards Committee (IASC). In 2001 the IASC went through a substantial restructuring to make it more independent, and was renamed the International Accounting Standards Board (IASB). International Accounting Standards issued by the IASB are to be known as International Financial Reporting Standards (IFRSs).

The objectives of the IASC/B are to develop enforceable global accounting standards, to promote their use worldwide, and to work for the harmonization of financial statements and the convergence of national and international accounting standards.

The first countries to adopt IASs were mostly the developing countries of Africa and Asia. However, during the late 1990s the IASC was engaged on a programme of setting accounting standards that would be acceptable to the world's major stock market regulators such as the SEC. More recently the EU has proposed that as from 2005 all companies whose shares are listed in the EU should/prepare their consolidated financial statements in accordance with IASs and IFRSs. Furthermore, the IASB, FASB and the ASB are currently engaged on a convergence project aimed at harmonizing international, US and UK accounting standards.

There are really only two IASs that are substantially different from the UK accounting standards covered in earlier chapters of this book. One is *IAS1—Presentation of Financial Statements* and the other is *IAS7—Cash Flow Statements*.

IAS1 requires companies to prepare an income statement, which is much the same as the UK profit and loss account, a balance sheet, a statement of changes in equity, and a cash flow statement. The balance sheet is similar to that in the UK Companies Act 1985 but uses different terminology in respect of what it calls non-current assets (i.e. fixed) and non-current liabilities (long term), as well as a few other items. The statement of changes in equity is essentially equivalent to a combination of three statements required by FRS3, namely movements on reserves, statement of total recognized gains and losses, and reconciliation of movements in shareholders' funds.

There are also some very significant differences between *IAS7—Cash Flow Statements* and *FRS1—Cash Flow Statements*. In IAS7 the contents of the cash flow statement are classified into operating activities, investing activities and financing activities. Unlike in FRS1, there is no heading relating to the 'management of liquid resources'. This is because the liquid resources are treated as cash and cash equivalents.

Most of the other IASs only contain minor differences from the FRSs and SSAPs covered in earlier chapters of this book. One of the main reasons for this is that some accounting standards have been developed jointly by the IASC and ASB, notably *IAS37—Provisions, Contingent Liabilities and Contingent Assets* and *FRS12—Provisions, Contingent Liabilities and Contingent Assets*.

Finally, there are some important similarities and differences between the IASC *Framework for the Preparation and Presentation of Financial Statements* and the ASB *Statement of Principles for Financial Reporting*. In particular, some of the elements of financial statements are different. Some people argue that this reflects their two different approaches to profit measurement. The ASB *Statement of Principles* is said to be based on a balance sheet approach whereas the IASC *Framework* is said to be based on an income statement approach.

All of these differences in the conceptual frameworks and accounting standards will need to be resolved if convergence and harmonization is to be achieved.

Key terms and concepts

Financial Accounting Standards Board (FASB) (507)
International Accounting Standard (IAS) (506)
International Accounting Standards Board (IASB) (506)
International Accounting Standards Committee (IASC) (506)
International Financial Reporting Standard (IFRS) (506)
Statement of Financial Accounting Standards (SFAS) (507)

References

1. International Accounting Standards Board (2003). *International Accounting Standard 1—Presentation of Financial Statements* (IASB).
2. International Accounting Standards Board (2003). *International Accounting Standard 2—Inventories* (IASB).
3. International Accounting Standards Committee (1992). *International Accounting Standard 7—Cash Flow Statements* (IASC).
4. International Accounting Standards Board (2003). *International Accounting Standard 8—Accounting Policies, Changes in Accounting Estimates and Errors* (IASB).
5. International Accounting Standards Board (2003). *International Accounting Standard 10—Events after the Balance Sheet Date* (IASB).
6. International Accounting Standards Board (2003). *International Accounting Standard 16—Property, Plant and Equipment* (IASB).

7. International Accounting Standards Committee (1993). *International Accounting Standard 18—Revenue* (IASC).
8. International Accounting Standards Committee (1998). *International Accounting Standard 35—Discontinuing Operations* (IASC).
9. International Accounting Standards Committee (1998). *International Accounting Standard 37—Provisions, Contingent Liabilities and Contingent Assets* (IASC).
10. International Accounting Standards Committee (1998). *International Accounting Standard 38—Intangible Assets* (IASC).
11. International Accounting Standards Committee (1989). *Framework for the Preparation and Presentation of Financial Statements* (IASC).
12. Accounting Standards Board (1999). *Statement of Principles for Financial Reporting* (ASB).

Review questions

32.1 Describe the objectives and role of the International Accounting Standards Committee/Board.

32.2 Discuss the current activities of the International Accounting Standards Board in the convergence/harmonization of accounting standards especially in Europe.

32.3 Explain how the main contents of financial statements required by *IAS1—Presentation of Financial Statements* differ from those in the Fourth Schedule to the Companies Act 1985 and *FRS3—Reporting Financial Performance*.

32.4 Explain how cash flow statements prepared in accordance with *IAS7—Cash Flow Statements* differ from those prepared in accordance with *FRS1—Cash Flow Statements*.

32.5 Explain the main similarities and differences between *IAS8—Accounting Policies, Changes in Accounting Estimates and Errors* and the equivalent parts of *FRS3—Reporting Financial Performance*.

32.6 Explain the main difference(s) between *IAS10—Events after the Balance Sheet Date* and *SSAP17—Accounting for Post Balance Sheet Events*.

32.7 Explain the main difference(s) between *IAS16—Property, Plant and Equipment* and *FRS15—Tangible Fixed Assets*.

32.8 Describe the rules relating to the recognition of revenue set out in *IAS18—Revenue*.

32.9 Explain the main difference(s) between *IAS35—Discontinuing Operations* and the equivalent parts of *FRS3—Reporting Financial Performance*.

32.10 **a** Explain the main difference(s) between *IAS38—Intangible Assets* and the comparable parts of *SSAP13—Accounting for Research and Development*.

b Explain the main difference(s) between *IAS38—Intangible Assets* and the comparable parts of *FRS10—Goodwill and Intangible Assets*.

32.11 Describe the main similarities and differences between the IASC *Framework for the Preparation and Presentation of Financial Statements* and the ASB *Statement of Principles for Financial Reporting*.

An introduction to consolidated accounts

Learning objectives

After reading this chapter you should be able to:

1. explain the meaning of the key terms and concepts listed at the end of the chapter;
2. describe the regulatory requirements of the Companies Acts and FRS2 with regard to consolidated financial statements;
3. explain the nature of goodwill on acquisition and describe the provisions of FRS10 concerning its accounting treatment;
4. prepare consolidated balance sheets, including the entries for goodwill and minority interests;
5. prepare consolidated profit and loss accounts, including the entries for minority interests and simple examples of intragroup sales.

Introduction

Throughout this book there are several exercises containing investments, listed or otherwise. The reader should, therefore, by this point be accustomed to the idea that one company may own shares in another company. Where these shares are held on a long-term basis, they are shown as a fixed asset in the final accounts of the company that owns the shares.

This chapter is also concerned with investments that are held on a long-term basis, but deals with the situation where the holding company owns a relatively large number of shares in another company; more precisely, usually in excess of 50 per cent of the other company's issued ordinary share capital, or even all its shares, both of which are said to constitute control of one company by another. The company that owns the shares is referred to as the parent (or holding) company, and the company whose shares are owned is referred to as a subsidiary of the parent company. When this situation arises these two companies are said to constitute a group. Thus, a group exists when a parent company has one or more subsidiaries. Where the parent company owns all the issued ordinary share capital of a subsidiary it is referred to as a wholly owned subsidiary. If the parent company owns more than 50 per cent but less than 100 per cent of the issued ordinary share capital of a subsidiary it is referred to as a partially owned or partly owned subsidiary.

Where a group exists, the law requires consolidated (also known as group) accounts to be prepared. In simple terms, consolidated accounts are a combination of the final accounts of a parent company with those of its subsidiary (or subsidiaries). Thus, where a group exists, a separate set of financial statements must be prepared for each of the following:

1 the parent company;

2 one for each subsidiary; and

3 consolidated accounts of the parent company and its subsidiary (or subsidiaries).

The latter will be included in the annual report of the parent company, along with its own financial statements.

The regulatory requirements

Consolidated financial statements are governed by the Companies Acts 1985 and 1989[1] as well as *FRS2—Accounting for Subsidiary Undertakings*, issued by the ASB in 1992.[2] Further references to this topic can be found in Chapter 8 of the *Statement of Principles for Financial Reporting* (ASB, 1999).[3]

The Companies Acts and FRS2 define a **group** as 'a parent undertaking and its subsidiary undertakings'. An **undertaking** is defined as 'a body corporate, a partnership or an unincorporated association carrying on a trade or business with or without a view to profit'. In short, a group may include bodies other than limited companies. However, for simplicity, this chapter is confined to undertakings that are limited companies, and where there is only one subsidiary.

The rules relating to whether a group exists (and thus whether consolidated accounts must be prepared) are rather complex in order to avoid companies' circumventing the law. They focus on what constitutes a subsidiary. In the introduction a subsidiary was defined in simple terms as being a company where more than 50 per cent of its issued ordinary share capital is owned by another company. To be more accurate this refers to the company's voting shares. Moreover, this is only meant to be indicative of the main criterion of what constitutes a parent–subsidiary relationship, namely where one company exercises control or dominant influence over another.

Thus, according to the Companies Act, an undertaking is the **parent undertaking** of another undertaking (a **subsidiary undertaking**) if any of the following apply.

a It holds a majority of the voting rights in the undertaking.

b It is a member of the undertaking and has the right to appoint or remove directors holding a majority of the voting rights at meetings of the board on all, or substantially all, matters.

c It has the right to exercise a dominant influence over the undertaking:
- **i** by virtue of provisions contained in the undertaking's memorandum or articles; or
- **ii** by virtue of a control contract.

d It is a member of the undertaking and controls alone, pursuant to an agreement with other shareholders or members, a majority of the voting rights in the undertaking.

e It has a participating interest in the undertaking and:
- **i** it actually exercises a dominant influence over the undertaking; or
- **ii** it and the undertaking are managed on a unified basis.

Dominant influence is defined in FRS2 as 'influence that can be exercised to achieve the operating and financial policies desired by the holder of the influence, notwithstanding the rights or influence of any other party'.

Control is defined in FRS2 as 'the ability of an undertaking to direct the financial and operating policies of another undertaking with a view to gaining economic benefits from its activities'.

A **participating interest** essentially refers to where the holding company owns 20 per cent or more of the shares in another undertaking on a long-term basis in order to exercise control or influence.

The Companies Act and FRS2 require parent undertakings to provide financial information about the economic activities of their groups by preparing **consolidated financial statements**. These are defined in FRS2 as 'the financial statements of a group prepared by consolidation'. The latter is defined in FRS2 as 'the process of adjusting and combining financial information from the individual financial statements of a parent undertaking and its subsidiary undertaking to prepare consolidated financial statements that present financial information for the group as a single economic entity'.

There is one final key term that needs to be explained at this point. As mentioned earlier, some subsidiaries may be only partially owned by a parent company. This means that a minority of its shares are owned by other organizations and/or individuals who also have a financial interest in the entity. These are thus referred to as minority interests. The **minority interest** in a subsidiary undertaking is defined in the Companies Act as 'the interest in a subsidiary undertaking included in the consolidation that is attributable to the shares held by or on behalf of persons other than the parent undertaking and its subsidiary undertakings'. This minority interest has to be accounted for in consolidated financial statements, for reasons that will become apparent later.

Goodwill on acquisition

When one company buys another company (by purchasing its shares), the price paid is usually greater than the value of its net assets. The excess of the purchase price over the value of its net assets relates to the cost of goodwill. In other words, when a parent company acquires a subsidiary this usually gives rise to what is referred to as goodwill on acquisition, or more accurately, **purchased goodwill**. This is defined in *FRS10—Goodwill and Intangible Assets* (ASB, 1997)[4] as 'the difference between the cost of an acquired entity and the aggregate of the fair values of that entity's identifiable assets and liabilities'. The purchased goodwill is calculated in precisely the manner explicit in its definition. This has to be reflected in the consolidated balance sheet as shown in the next section.

There are complex rules in another FRS about what constitutes the 'fair values' of an acquired entity's identifiable assets and liabilities. These are too advanced for an introductory textbook, and it is sufficient at this stage to point out that book values are not usually 'fair values'. However, for the sake of simplicity, this chapter assumes that the book values are 'fair values'.

Goodwill was dealt with in detail in Chapter 25 on changes in partnerships. Students following a syllabus that does not include changes in partnerships, but does include goodwill, are advised to read the two sections entitled 'the nature of goodwill' and 'the recognition of goodwill in accounts' at this point, if they have not already done so. The most relevant aspect of the latter is that FRS10 requires goodwill to be amortized.

The consolidated balance sheet

As explained earlier, the balance sheet of the parent company will normally contain only one entry relating to its subsidiary: the cost of the investment in its subsidiary. That is, the price paid to acquire the shares of the subsidiary. This is shown under the heading of fixed asset investments. It does not change as a result of consolidation. The consolidated balance sheet is part of a separate set of consolidated financial statements.

The main objective of consolidated balance sheets is to provide information about the group's financial position to the ordinary shareholders of the parent company. The consolidated balance sheet is prepared by aggregating on a line-by-line basis all the assets and liabilities of the parent company with those of its subsidiary. The result is a balance sheet containing the assets and liabilities of the two entities as if they were owned by a 'single economic entity'. A simple illustration is given in Example 33.1.

Example 33.1

The following are the balance sheets of Parent plc and Subsidiary Ltd as at 31 December 20X5:

	Parent plc	*Subsidiary Ltd*
	£million	£million
Fixed assets:		
Tangible	3,400	600
Investment in Subsidiary Ltd	900	—
	4,300	600
Net current assets	400	200
	4,700	800
Allotted ordinary share capital	3,000	500
Reserves	1,700	300
	4,700	800

Parent plc purchased all the ordinary shares of Subsidiary Ltd on the 31 December 20X5. The assets and liabilities of Subsidiary Ltd are shown in its accounts at what are agreed to be fair values under FRS10.

You are required to prepare a consolidated balance sheet as at 31 December 20X5.

Workings

Purchased goodwill = £(900m – 800m) = £100m

Parent Group
Consolidated balance sheet as at 31 December 20X5

	£million
Fixed assets:	
Intangible assets—goodwill	100
Tangible assets £(3,400 + 600)	4,000
	4,100
Net current assets £(400 + 200)	600
	4,700
Allotted ordinary share capital	3,000
Reserves	1,700
	4,700

Notice that only the assets and liabilities of each entity are aggregated. The share capital and reserved are not; those of the subsidiary do not appear on the consolidated balance sheet. Many authors explain the reason for this as being because the consolidation process simply replaces the investment in the subsidiary shown in the parent company's balance sheet with the net assets of the subsidiary (and any goodwill). This is true in an accounting sense, but students should remember that the balance sheet of the parent company does not change as a result of consolidation.

A more meaningful way of explaining the exclusion of the subsidiary's capital and reserves perhaps lies in the nature and function of consolidated accounts. The consolidated balance sheet is meant to relate to 'a single economic entity'. The net assets of that entity belong to the ordinary shareholders of the parent company. Thus, only their equity interests are shown on the balance sheet. As 'a single economic entity' the subsidiary, its shares and its shareholder(s) simply do not exist. Thus, the share capital and reserves of the subsidiary do not appear in the consolidated balance sheet.

There is, however, a much more important legal reason why the reserves of the subsidiary do not appear in the consolidated balance sheet. This is because they arose prior to its acquisition by the parent company, which is why they are referred to as pre-acquisition reserves.

The rest of this chapter focuses on post-acquisition revenue reserves/retained profits. However, before moving on it is important to appreciate that the above discussion relating to the treatment of pre-acquisition reserves applies to all reserves—both revenue and capital. That is, any retained profits, share premium account and/or revaluation reserve in the accounts of the subsidiary which arose prior to acquisition must not be included in the consolidated balance sheet.

This brings us to the next important point in consolidated balance sheets. Whereas preacquisition reserves of a subsidiary are not included in a consolidated balance sheet, post-acquisition reserves are included. This is because they are generated after acquisition, are represented by an increase in the net assets of the subsidiary, and belong to the ordinary shareholders of the parent company. In other terms, post-acquisition reserves constitute an increase in the value of the parent company's investment in its subsidiary. This is illustrated in Example 33.2, which is a continuation of Example 33.1.

Example 33.2

During the year ended 31 December 20X6, Parent plc made a profit of £750 million, and Subsidiary Ltd made a profit of £250 million. This has resulted in an equivalent increase in their net current assets and reserves as shown below in their balance sheets as at 31 December 20X6.

	Parent plc £million	*Subsidiary Ltd* £million
Fixed assets:		
Tangible	3,400	600
Investment in Subsidiary Ltd	900	—
	4,300	600
Net current assets	1,150	450
	5,450	1,050
Allotted ordinary share capital	3,000	500
Reserves	2,450	550
	5,450	1,050

Goodwill on acquisition is to be amortized over 20 years using the straight line method.

You are required to prepare a consolidated balance sheet as at 31 December 20X6.

Workings

Amortization of goodwill = 5 per cent × £100m = £5m

Reserves = £(2,450m + [550m – 300m] – 5m) = £2,695m

Parent Group
Consolidated balance sheet as at 31 December 20X6

	£million
Fixed assets:	
Intangible assets – goodwill £(100 – 5)	95
Tangible assets £(3,400 + 600)	4,000
	4,095
Net current assets £(1,150 + 450)	1,600
	5,695
Allotted ordinary share capital	3,000
Reserves	2,695
	5,695

Minority interest

So far in this section it has been assumed that the subsidiary is wholly owned. As has already been mentioned, a subsidiary may be partially owned by its parent company, in which case there will be a minority interest, as defined earlier. What needs to be explained at this stage is why minority interests appear in consolidated balance sheets. The reason is essentially that one of the basic underlying principles of consolidation is that consolidated financial statements are prepared on the basis that the parent and subsidiary are 'a single economic entity'. That is, all the assets and liabilities of the parent and subsidiary are aggregated without regard to the proportion of the subsidiary's voting shares that are owned by the parent. However, it must be recognized that a proportion of these net assets is owned/financed by the other (minority) shareholders. This is achieved by entering the value of the minority interest on the consolidated balance sheet as a part of the group's capital. This is illustrated in Examples 33.3 and 33.4. The latter is a continuation of the former.

Example 33.3

The following are the balance sheets of Holding plc and Subsidy Ltd as at 30 June 20X5:

	Holding plc £million	*Subsidy Ltd* £million
Fixed assets:		
Tangible	3,760	600
Investment in Subsidy Ltd	540	—
	4,300	600
Net current assets	400	200
	4,700	800
Allotted ordinary share capital	3,000	500
Reserves	1,700	300
	4,700	800

Holding plc purchased 60 per cent of the ordinary shares of Subsidy Ltd on 30 June 20X5 at a price of £540million. The assets and liabilities of Subsidy Ltd are shown in its accounts at what are agreed to be fair values under FRS10.

You are required to prepare a consolidated balance sheet as at 30 June 20X5.

Workings

Purchased goodwill = £540m – (60 per cent × £800m) = £60m

Minority interest = 40 per cent × £800m = £320m

Holding Group

Consolidated balance sheet as at 30 June 20X5

	£million
Fixed assets:	
Intangible assets—goodwill	60
Tangible assets £(3,760 + 600)	4,360
	4,420
Net current assets £(400 + 200)	600
	5,020
Allotted ordinary share capital	3,000
Reserves	1,700
Minority interest	320
	5,020

Example 33.4

During the year ended 30 June 20X6, Holding plc made a profit of £750 million, and Subsidy Ltd made a profit of £250 million. This has resulted in an equivalent increase in their net current assets and reserves as shown below in their balance sheets as at 30 June 20X6.

	Holding plc £million	*Subsidy Ltd* £million
Fixed assets:		
Tangible	3,760	600
Investment in Subsidy Ltd	540	—
	4,300	600
Net current assets	1,150	450
	5,450	1,050
Allotted ordinary share capital	3,000	500
Reserves	2,450	550
	5,450	1,050

Goodwill on acquisition is to be amortized over 20 years using the straight line method.

You are required to prepare a consolidated balance sheet as at 30 June 20X6.

Workings

Amortization of goodwill = 5 per cent × £60m = £3m

Reserves = £(2,450m + 60 per cent[550m – 300m] – 3m) = £2,597m

Minority interest = 40 per cent × £1,050m = £420m

Holding Group

Consolidated balance sheet as at 30 June 20X6

	£million
Fixed assets:	
Intangible assets—goodwill £(60 – 3)	57
Tangible assets £(3,760 + 600)	4,360
	4,417
Net current assets £(1,150 + 450)	1,600
	6,017
Allotted ordinary share capital	3,000
Reserves	2,597
Minority interest	420
	6,017

The consolidated profit and loss account

The profit and loss account of a parent company will normally contain only one entry relating to its subsidiary—the dividends received from the subsidiary. This is referred to in published accounts as 'income from shares in group undertakings'. It does not change as a result of consolidation. The consolidated profit and loss account is part of a separate set of consolidated financial statements.

The main objective of consolidated profit and loss accounts is to provide information about the group's financial performance to the ordinary shareholders of the parent company. The principles of preparing a consolidated profit and loss account are much the same as those relating to the consolidated balance sheet. That is, most of the items in the parent company's profit and loss account are aggregated on a line-by-line basis with those in the subsidiary company's profit and loss account.

However, there are complications arising from what are referred to as intragroup transactions and items. These take two main forms, intragroup sales and the dividends paid to the parent company by its subsidiary. Since the consolidated profit and loss account is intended to reflect the trading activities of the group as 'a single economic entity', these must be eliminated. In arithmetic terms, they cancel each other out. This is illustrated in Example 33.5.

Example 33.5

The following are the profit and loss accounts of Parent plc and Subsidiary Ltd for the year ended 31 December 20X6:

	Parent plc	*Subsidiary Ltd*
	£million	£million
Turnover	10,050	3,300
Cost of sales	(6,700)	(2,200)
Gross profit	3,350	1,100
Distribution costs	(550)	(275)
Administrative expenses	(350)	(125)
Dividends from Subsidiary Ltd	150	—
Profit on ordinary activities before taxation	2,600	700
Tax on profit on ordinary activities	(1,200)	(300)
Profit on ordinary activities after taxation	1,400	400
Dividends	(650)	(150)
Retained profit for the financial year	750	250

Parent plc acquired all the ordinary shares of Subsidiary Ltd on the 31 December 20X5. During the year Parent plc sold goods for £50 million, to Subsidiary Ltd who has sold them all to third parties during the year.

You are required to prepare a consolidated profit and loss account for the year ended 31 December 20X6.

Parent Group
Consolidated profit and loss account for the year ended 31 December 20X6

	£million
Turnover £(10,050 – 50 + 3,300)	13,300
Cost of sales £(6,700 + 2,200 – 50)	(8,850)
Gross profit	4,450
Distribution costs £(550 + 275)	(825)
Administrative expenses £(350 + 125)	(475)
Profit on ordinary activities before taxation	3,150
Tax on profit on ordinary activities £(1,200 + 300)	(1,500)
Profit on ordinary activities after taxation	1,650
Dividends	(650)
Retained profit for the financial year	1,000

Notice that the retained profit in the consolidated profit and loss account equals the retained profit of the parent company plus that of the subsidiary (where it is wholly owned).

Any amortization of goodwill on acquisition would also have to be entered in the consolidated profit and loss account. Using the data in Example 33.2, this will reduce the profit and retained profit by £5million. The Parent Group consolidated balance sheet will be as shown in Example 33.2 if the data given at the start of Example 33.2 is amended by changing the references to profit to read retained profit. The figure for reserves on this consolidated balance sheet would be computed as follows:

	£million
Balance at 31 Dec 20X5 (given on the consolidated balance sheet in Example 33.1)	1,700
Retained profit for the financial year £(1,000 – 5)	995
Balance at 31 Dec 20X6	2,695

Minority interest

As already discussed, a subsidiary may be only partially owned by its parent company, in which case there will be a minority interest, as defined earlier. The minority interest will not only be reflected in the consolidated balance sheet, but also appear in the consolidated profit and loss account. The reason is essentially that one of the basic underlying principles of consolidation is that consolidated financial statements are prepared on the basis that the parent and subsidiary are 'a single economic entity'. That is, the revenue and costs of the parent and subsidiary are aggregated without regard to the proportion of the subsidiary's voting shares that are owned by the parent. However, it must be recognized that a proportion of the profit (or loss) of the subsidiary belongs to the other (minority) shareholders. This is achieved by deducting the amount of the minority interest from the profit on ordinary activities after taxation in the consolidated profit and loss account. This is illustrated in Example 33.6.

Example 33.6

The following are the profit and loss accounts of Holding plc and Subsidy Ltd for the year ended 30 June 20X6:

	Holding plc	*Subsidy Ltd*
	£million	£million
Turnover	10,050	3,300
Cost of sales	(6,700)	(2,200)
Gross profit	3,350	1,100
Distribution costs	(550)	(275)
Administrative expenses	(290)	(125)
Dividends from Subsidy Ltd	90	—
Profit on ordinary activities before taxation	2,600	700
Tax on profit on ordinary activities	(1,200)	(300)
Profit on ordinary activities after taxation	1,400	400
Dividends	(650)	(150)
Retained profit for the financial year	750	250

Holding plc acquired 60 per cent of the ordinary shares of Subsidy Ltd on 30 June 20X5.

You are required to prepare a consolidated profit and loss account for the year ended 30 June 20X6.

Workings

Minority interest = 40 per cent × £400m = £160m

Holding Group

Consolidated profit and loss account for the year ended 30 June 20X6

	£million
Turnover £(10,050 + 3,300)	13,350
Cost of sales £(6,700 + 2,200)	(8,900)
Gross profit	4,450
Distribution costs £(550 + 275)	(825)
Administrative expenses £(290 + 125)	(415)
Profit on ordinary activities before taxation	3,210
Tax on profit on ordinary activities £(1,200 + 300)	(1,500)
Profit on ordinary activities after taxation	1,710
Minority interest	(160)
Profit for the financial year	1,550
Dividends	(650)
Retained profit for the financial year	900

Notice that the retained profit in the consolidated profit and loss account equals the retained profit of the parent/holding company plus its share of the retained profit of the subsidiary. That is, in the above example £750m + (60 per cent × £250m) = £900m.

Any amortization of goodwill on acquisition would also have to be entered in the consolidated profit and loss account. Using the data in Example 33.4, this will reduce the profit and retained profit by £3million. The Holding Group consolidated balance sheet will be as shown in Example 33.4 if the data given at the start of Example 33.4 is amended by changing the references to profit to read retained profit. The figure for reserves on this consolidated balance sheet would be computed as follows:

	£million
Balance at 30 June 20X5 (given on the consolidated balance sheet in Example 33.3)	1,700
Retained profit for the financial year £(900 – 3)	897
Balance at 30 June 20X6	2,597

The figure for minority interest on this consolidated balance sheet would be computed as follows:

	£million
Balance at 30 June 20X5 (given on the consolidated balance sheet in Example 33.3)	320
Minority interest in consolidated profit and loss account	160
	480
Dividends paid to minority shareholders £(150 – 90) or (40% × £150)	(60)
Balance at 30 June 20X6	420

This increase in the minority interest on the consolidated balance sheet of £160m – £60m = £100m is their share of the profit after tax (but before dividends) less the dividends paid to them from their share of the profit. Those students who conceptualize the preparation of the consolidated profit and loss account as an arithmetic combination of the profit and loss accounts of the parent and subsidiary may have observed that £100m was in a sense 'lost' in the process. It has now 'reappeared' as the increase in minority interest in the consolidated balance sheet.

Learning Activity 33.1

Visit the website of a large listed/quoted public limited company that has a subsidiary whose shares are also listed, and find their latest annual report and accounts. Examine the contents of the profit and loss account, balance sheet and notes to the accounts, paying particular attention to the items relating to goodwill and minority interests.

Summary

The Companies Acts 1985 and 1989 as well as FRS2 require the preparation of consolidated accounts where a group exists. A group is defined as a parent undertaking and its subsidiary undertakings. There are detailed legal regulations regarding when a parent–subsidiary relationship exists. The main criteria include: where the parent undertaking holds a majority of the voting rights in the subsidiary undertaking; or has the right to exercise a dominant influence and thus control; or has a participating interest and actually exercises a dominant influence or manages the two entities on a unified basis. Dominant influence and control refer to the influence that a parent undertaking has over the operating and financial policies of the subsidiary undertaking.

Consolidated financial statements are defined in FRS2 as the financial statements of a group prepared by consolidation. The latter is described in FRS2 as the process of adjusting and combining financial information from the individual financial statements of a parent undertaking and its subsidiary undertaking to prepare consolidated financial statements that present financial information for the group as a single economic entity.

Consolidated financial statements include a consolidated profit and loss account and a consolidated balance sheet. These are prepared by aggregating on a line-by-line basis most of the items in the parent undertaking's financial statements with those in the subsidiary undertaking's financial statements while at the same time eliminating certain intragroup items, referred to above as adjustments.

The process of consolidation usually gives rise to goodwill on acquisition. This must be accounted for in accordance with FRS10, which refers to it as purchased goodwill.

Where a subsidiary is only partially owned by the parent undertaking, the process of consolidation also gives rise to minority interests in both the consolidated profit and loss account and the consolidated balance sheet. A minority interest is defined in the Companies Act as the interest in a subsidiary undertaking included in the consolidation that is attributable to the shares held by or on behalf of persons other than the parent undertaking and its subsidiary undertakings.

The minority interest is shown in the consolidated profit and loss account as a deduction from the profit on ordinary activities after taxation, and computed as their share of this amount in the subsidiary's profit and loss account. The minority interest is also usually shown in the consolidated balance sheet as part of the group's capital, and is computed as their share of the subsidiary's net assets.

Key terms and concepts

Consolidated financial statements (519)
control (519)
dominant influence (519)
group (518)
minority interest (519)
parent undertaking (519)
participating interest (519)
purchased goodwill (520)
subsidiary undertaking (519)
undertaking (518)

References

1. Companies Acts 1985 and 1989.
2. Accounting Standards Board (1992). *Financial Reporting Standard 2—Accounting for Subsidiary Undertakings* (ASB).
3. Accounting Standards Board (1999). *Statement of Principles for Financial Reporting* (ASB).
4. Accounting Standards Board (1997). *Financial Reporting Standard 10—Goodwill and Intangible Assets* (ASB).

Review questions

33.1 Define each of the following in accordance with the Companies Acts 1985 and 1989 and *FRS2—Accounting for Subsidiary Undertakings* (ASB, 1992):

a a group;
b an undertaking;
c consolidated financial statements;
d consolidation.

33.2 Describe fully the provisions of the Companies Acts 1985 and 1989 with regard to what constitutes a parent undertaking and a subsidiary undertaking.

33.3 **a** Explain the nature of goodwill arising on the acquisition of a subsidiary undertaking and how it is measured.
b Describe the requirements of *FRS10—Goodwill and Intangible Assets* (ASB, 1997) with regard to the accounting treatment of purchased goodwill.

33.4 **a** Explain the objective(s) of consolidated financial statements.
b Describe in general terms the principles of consolidation.

33.5 Parhold plc has bought for cash of £12 million all the voting shares of Subsid plc, whose net assets have been valued at £10 million. Describe how this transaction would affect:

a the balance sheet of Parhold plc; and
b the balance sheet of Parhold Group, given that Subsid plc is the only subsidiary.

You need only describe the effects on these balance sheets on the date of acquisition of Subsid's shares.

33.6 Given the circumstances in Question 33.5 above, describe how this relationship between Parhold plc and Subsid plc would affect the following at the end of the first accounting year after acquisition:

a the financial statements of Subsid plc;
b the financial statements of Parhold plc; and
c the consolidated financial statements of Parhold Group.

33.7 **a** Define a minority interest in accordance with the Companies Acts 1985 and 1989.
b Explain why minority interests arise in consolidated financial statements in the context of the principles of consolidation.
c Describe the effects of a minority interest on the consolidated financial statements.

Exercises

An asterisk after the question number indicates that there is a suggested answer in the Appendix.

33.8* **Level II**

At 1 January 20X0 H Ltd acquired 80 per cent of the share capital of S for £160,000. At that date the share capital of S consisted of 100, 000 ordinary shares of £1 each and its reserves totalled £40,000. Goodwill on acquisition of subsidiaries is amortized on the straight line basis over five years.

In the consolidated balance sheet of H and its subsidiary S at 31 December 20X3 the amount appearing for goodwill should be:

a £16,000;
b £19,200;
c £28,800; or
d £4,000? (ACCA)

33.9* **Level II**

At 1 January 20X0 H Ltd acquired 60 per cent of the share capital of S for £180,000. At that date the share capital of S consisted of 200,000 shares of 50p each. The reserves of H and S are stated below:

	At 1 Jan 20X0	*At 31 Dec 20X2*
	£	£
H	280,000	340,000
S	50,000	180,000

In the consolidated balance sheet of H and its subsidiary S at 31 December 20X2, what amount should appear for the minority interest in S?

a £92,000;
b £280,000;
c £152,000;
d £112,000. (ACCA)

33.10* **Level II**

H Ltd acquired 75 per cent of the share capital of S for £280,000 on 1 January 20X0. Goodwill arising on consolidation has been fully amortized. Details of the share capital and reserves of S are as follows:

	At 1 January 20X0	*At 31 December 20X6*
	£	£
Share capital	200,000	200,000
Profit and loss account reserve	120,000	180,000

At 31 December 20X6 the profit and loss account reserve of H amounted to £480,000.

What figure should appear in the consolidated balance sheet of H and S for the profit and loss account reserve at 31 December 20X6?

a £530,000;
b £525,000;
c £485,000;
d £575,000. (ACCA)

33.11* **Level II**

The following are the balance sheets of Gold plc and Silver plc as at 1 January 20X1:

	Gold plc	*Silver plc*
	£000	£000
Fixed assets:		
Tangible	13,600	2,500
Investment in Silver plc	3,600	—
	17,200	2,500
Net current assets	1,600	700
	18,800	3,200
Called-up ordinary share capital	5,000	1,000
Share premium	4,000	800
Revaluation reserve	3,000	200
Profit and loss account	6,800	1,200
	18,800	3,200

Gold plc purchased all the ordinary shares of Silver plc on 1 January 20X1. The assets and liabilities of Silver plc are shown in its accounts at what are agreed to be fair values under FRS10.

You are required to prepare a consolidated balance sheet as at 1 January 20X1.

33.12* **Level II**

(This is a continuation of Exercise 33.11.)

The following are the profit and loss accounts and balance sheets of Gold plc and Silver plc for the year ended 31 December 20X1:

Profit and loss accounts	*Gold plc*	*Silver plc*
	£000	£000
Turnover	20,100	6,600
Cost of sales	(13,400)	(4,400)
Gross profit	6,700	2,200
Distribution costs	(1,100)	(550)
Administrative expenses	(700)	(250)
Dividends from Silver plc	300	—
Profit on ordinary activities before taxation	5,200	1,400
Tax on profit on ordinary activities	(2,400)	(600)
Profit on ordinary activities after taxation	2,800	800
Dividends	(1,300)	(300)
Retained profit for the financial year	1,500	500

Balance sheets	*Gold plc*	*Silver plc*
	£000	£000
Fixed assets:		
Tangible	13,600	2,500
Investment in Silver plc	3,600	—
	17,200	2,500
Net current assets	3,100	1,200
	20,300	3,700

Called-up ordinary share capital	5,000	1,000
Share premium	4,000	800
Revaluation reserve	3,000	200
Profit and loss account	8,300	1,700
	20,300	3,700

You are required to prepare a consolidated profit and loss account for the year and a consolidated balance sheet as at 31 December 20X1. Ignore the amortization of goodwill.

33.13 Level II

The following are the balance sheets of Wood plc and Stone plc as at 1 May 20X8:

	Wood plc	*Stone plc*
	£000	£000
Fixed assets:		
Tangible	10,000	3,000
Investment in Stone plc	4,800	—
	14,800	3,000
Net current assets	3,500	2,000
	18,300	5,000
Called-up ordinary share capital	6,000	1,500
Share premium	4,500	750
Revaluation reserve	2,500	650
Profit and loss account	5,300	2,100
	18,300	5,000

Wood plc purchased 80 per cent of the ordinary shares of Stone plc on 1 May 20X8 at a price of £4,800,000. The assets and liabilities of Stone plc are shown in its accounts at what are agreed to be fair values under FRS10.

You are required to prepare a consolidated balance sheet as at 1 May 20X8.

33.14 Level II

(This is a continuation of Exercise 33.13.)
The following are the profit and loss accounts and balance sheets of Wood plc and Stone plc for the year ended 30 April 20X9:

Profit and loss accounts	*Wood plc*	*Stone plc*
	£000	£000
Turnover	15,680	3,400
Cost of sales	(9,840)	(2,300)
Gross profit	5,840	1,100
Distribution costs	(725)	(225)
Administrative expenses	(875)	(275)
Dividends from Stone plc	160	—
Profit on ordinary activities before taxation	4,400	600
Tax on profit on ordinary activities	(1,800)	(150)
Profit on ordinary activities after taxation	2,600	450
Dividends	(1,500)	(200)
Retained profit for the financial year	1,100	250

Balance sheets	*Wood plc*	*Stone plc*
	£000	£000
Fixed assets:		
Tangible	10,000	3,000
Investment in Stone plc	4,800	—
	14,800	3,000
Net current assets	4,600	2,250
	19,400	5,250
Called-up ordinary share capital	6,000	1,500
Share premium	4,500	750
Revaluation reserve	2,500	650
Profit and loss account	6,400	2,350
	19,400	5,250

You are required to prepare a consolidated profit and loss account for the year and a consolidated balance sheet as at 30 April 20X9. Ignore the amortization of goodwill.

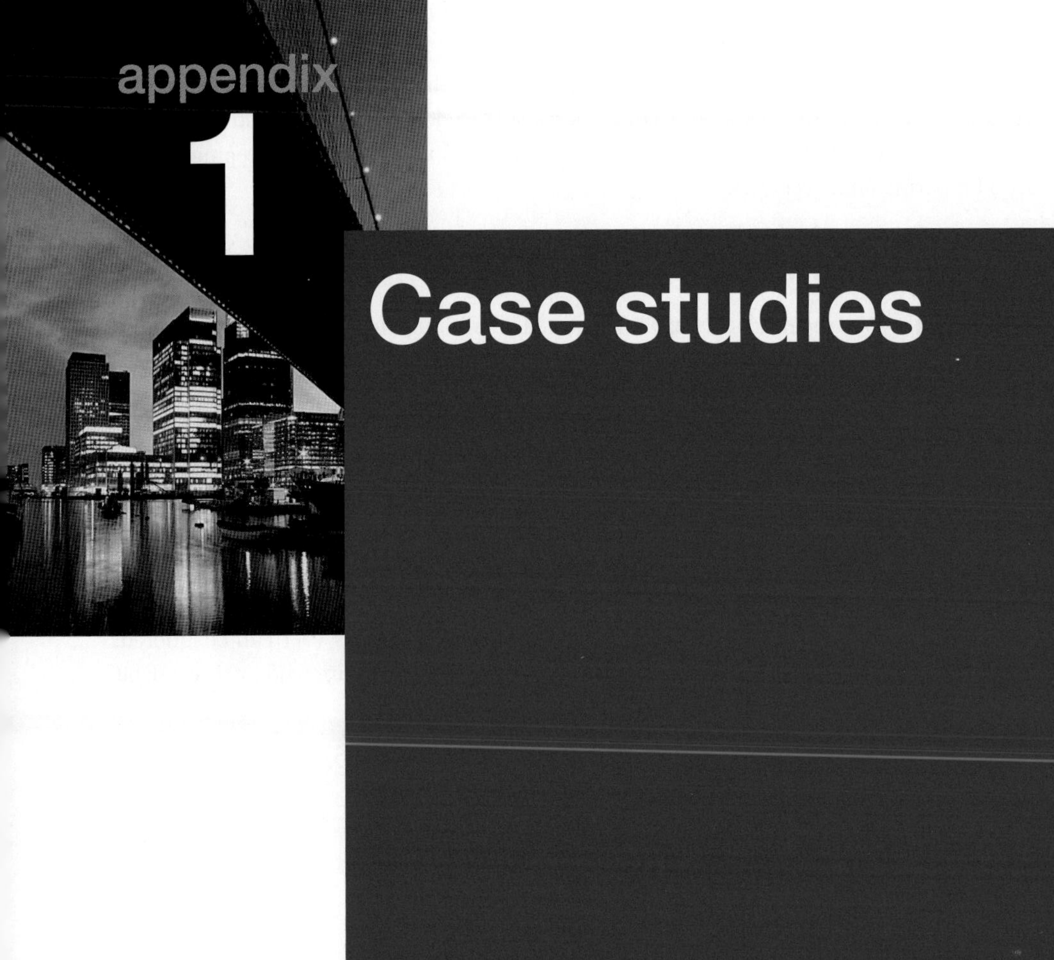

Case studies

Case Study 1

The following case study shows how to track entries from the book of original entries right through to the preparation of final accounts for a sole trader. Details and instructions are given on how to complete the relevant sections for Part 2 Double-entry bookkeeping and for Part 3 Preparing final accounts.

Trading details and supporting documentation

Mr O'Donnell, a sole trader has owned and operated an antique furniture store for a number of years. He specializes in the purchase and sale of antique furniture from different countries and deals with a small number of reputable suppliers and reliable customers.

You have been employed by Mr O'Donnell as a qualified accountant to maintain his accounts and prepare his financial statements. Following discussions with Mr O'Donnell, from which he believes he has supplied you with all the necessary details, and after obtaining a copy of all relevant documentation, you have established an opening trial balance at the start of the financial year 1 October 2003. Furthermore you identify all his business transactions for the year ended 30 September 2004. You also ascertain that VAT of 25 per cent applies to the sale, purchase and return of goods. In all other respects VAT can be ignored. VAT and PAYE/PRSI returns are submitted on an annual basis and are paid by direct debit every December.

O'Donnell's Opening Trial Balance as at 1 October 2003

Account title	Debit €	Credit €
Fixed assets		
Delivery vans (2)	26,000	
Accumulated depreciation on delivery vans		11,500
Fittings	12,000	
Accumulated depreciation on fittings		2,000
Current assets		
Stock	44,000	
Trade debtors (Murphy €7,000; Foley €7,000)	14,000	
Cash at bank		1,750
Petty cash	130	
Current liabilities		
Trade creditors (Cronin €11,000; Broderick €4,000)		15,000
VAT		1,000
PAYE/PRSI		100
Owner's equity		
Capital		67,150
Drawings		
Selling & distribution expenses		
Motor/delivery expenses	600	
Administration expenses		
Postage, stationery and telephone		130
Light & heat		100
Rent	2,000	
	98,730	98,730

The transactions which occurred during the year to 30 September 2004 are listed below:

October:

2	Sold goods on credit to Murphy for €5,000. Invoice no. 580.
6	Purchases goods on credit from Cronin for €3,750.
11	Paid €7 for stationery from petty cash.
23	Received and lodged to bank all money outstanding from Foley (no discount allowed).

November:

4	Returned €1,250 worth of goods purchased from Cronin.
11	Sold goods on credit to Foley for €5,000. Invoice no. 581.
19	Paid cheques no. 23985, €45, for electricity and no. 23986, €175, for petty cash.
24	Purchased goods on credit from Broderick for €1,250.

December:

1	Murphy returned goods in the amount of €1,000 and credit note 14 was issued to him.
12	Received and lodged cheque in amount of €3,000 from Murphy and allowed him a discount of €100.
19	Paid cheque no. 23987 in amount of €2,000 to Cronin and received €200 discount.
24	Withdrew €2,500 for personal use.
27	Paid VAT and PAYE/PRSI outstanding from previous year by direct debit.
30	Paid motor insurance, €1,200 by cheque no. 23988 to cover the following six months.
31	Paid from petty cash: €7 postage; €11 motor repairs; €50 advertising.

January:

7	Sold goods on credit to Foley for €400, invoice no. 582, and to Doolan for €4,000, invoice no. 583.
8	Lodged cash sales of €1,250.
9	Purchased goods on credit for €1,500 from Broderick.
22	Foley returned goods in the amount of €1,000 so credit note 15 was issued to him.
23	Sent cheque no. 23989 for €100 to Foley to cover the cost of returning goods.
30	Paid €6,000 by cheque no. 23990, being rent due for 12 months from 1 of February 2004.

February:

1	Received and lodged all money due from Foley after allowing him discount of €400.
7	Sold goods to Doolan for €3,000, invoice no. 584; paid cheque no. 23991 worth €73 for motor expenses.
17	Purchased goods from Cronin on credit, €7,200.
22	Returned goods to Cronin to the value of €3,000.
30	Paid from petty cash: €12 postage; €20 stationery; €20 petrol.

March:

3	Sold goods on credit to Doyle to the value of €5,000 invoice no. 585.
7	Sold goods on credit to O'Haire, €11,000, invoice no. 586.

11 Paid cheque no. 23992 worth €2,700 to Getaway Travel for a family holiday.
12 Withdrew €3,000 from bank for use on holiday.

April:

7 Returned to find that Doyle in financial difficulties and his accountant has temporarily suspended all payment. However, you decided to take no action yet.
8 Paid cheque no. 23993, to Cronin to the amount of €3,200 and received a discount of €200.
9 Paid motor tax, €133 by cheque no. 23994.
10 Paid cheque no. 23995 to the value of €400 to cover repairs to delivery van.
17 Sold goods on credit to Brennan for €7,000, invoice no. 587.
19 Purchased goods on credit from Cronin, €3,000.
25 Paid Cronin €5,000 (cheque no. 23996) and received a discount of €200.
31 Paid from petty cash: advertising €22; postage €12; petrol €44.

May:

7 Sold goods to Kelly on credit for €4,000, invoice no 588.
10 Received €400 unexpectedly from Doyle's accountants, lodged money immediately.
17 Kelly returned damaged goods in the amount of €2,000. Credit note 16 was issued to him.
22 Purchased goods from Sabura on credit worth €2,000.
23 Received and lodged cheques from Brennan in full settlement after allowing for a discount of €100.
31 Paid from petty cash: stationery €5; motor expenses €81; postage €12.

June:

2 Sold goods on credit to O'Haire worth €5,000, invoice no. 589.
3 Purchased goods on credit from Broderick to the value of €3,000.
9 Purchased goods from Cronin on credit worth €1,750.
17 Lodged cash sales worth €400.
22 Paid Broderick the full amount due less discount €350 (Cheque no. 23997).
29 Withdrew €2,000 for personal use. O'Donnell also received letter from bank dated 28 June stating that his bank account was seriously overdrawn and that if money was not lodged soon to reduce it serious action would have to be taken.

July:

2 Sold goods on credit to O'Haire for €7,000, invoice no. 590.
3 Paid cheque no 23998 to the amount of €300 to petty cash.
11 O'Haire returned goods of €1,000. Credit note 17 was issued.
14 O'Haire settled account in full, less agreed discount of €450. Proceeds lodged.
19 Sold goods on credit to Doolan for €11,000, invoice no. 591.
25 Withdrew €3,000 for personal use.
30 Paid motor insurance of €1,200 by cheque no. 23999 to cover following three months.

August:

3 Purchased goods on credit from Cronin for €9,000.
7 Returned goods worth €2,000 to Cronin. Credit note N274 received.

11 Cash sales of €500 lodged.
20 Paid telephone bill of €432 by cheque no. 24000.
20 Sold goods to O'Haire on credit for €500, invoice no. 592.
21 Sold goods on credit to Doolan worth €4,000, invoice no. 593.
26 Paid Cronin €10,000 on account, cheque no. 24001. Discount received €100.
29 Received and lodged €12,000 from Doolan. Discount allowed €500.
30 Doolan returned goods in the amount of €100. Credit note 18 issued.

September:
1 Purchased goods on credit from Slatery worth €5,000.
3 Sold goods on credit to O'Haire for €3,000, invoice no. 594.
6 Received and lodged balance due from O'Haire, less an agreed discount of €100.
7 Paid electricity bill of €298 by cheque no. 24002.
9 Sold goods to Murphy on credit worth €2,000, invoice no. 595 and to Doolan for €3,000, invoice no. 596.
13 Lodged cash sales worth €490.
16 Sold goods to O'Sullivan on credit for €3,000, invoice no. 597.
19 Received and lodged €2,500 from O'Sullivan. Discount allowed €200.
20 Received and lodged €1,000 from Murphy. Discount allowed €50.
21 Paid Cronin by cheque no. 24003 to the amount of €4,000. Discount received €200.
22 Paid Slatery €2,500 by cheque no. 24004. Discount received €100. Cash sales €2,450 lodged by Credit Transfer.
23 Paid Sergi, a temporary employee, to the amount of €1,300 by cheque no. 24005.
24 Withdrew €7,000 for personal use.
30 Paid from petty cash: stationery €42; postage €35; petrol €88; deliver expenses €94.
31 Received and lodged €3,500 from J. Cunningham to whom you sold a delivery van.

Mr O'Donnell's bank, First Time Bank, have supplied you with the following Bank Statement:

Account Number: 809234
Customer: O'Donnell's Furniture, New Street, Ballydune, Cork.
Statement No 9

Date 2003/2004	Details	Debit €	Credit €	Balance dr = overdrawn
1 Oct	Balance			1,750 cr
23 Oct	Lodgement		7,000	5,250 cr
22 Nov	Cheque no 23985	45		5,205 cr
25 Nov	Cheque no 23986	175		5,030 cr
12 Dec	Lodgement		3,000	8,030 cr
23 Dec	Cheque no 23987	2,000		6,030 cr
24 Dec	Withdrawal	2,500		3,530 cr
27 Dec	Direct debit 7422986	1,000		2,530 cr
27 Dec	Direct debit 7422987	100		2,430 cr
31 Dec	Cheque no 23988	1,200		1,230 cr
31 Dec	Interest and charges	90		1,140 cr
8 Jan	Lodgement		1250	2,390 cr
26 Jan	Cheque no 23989	100		2,290 cr
1 Feb	Lodgement		4,000	6,290 cr
6 Feb	Cheque no 23990	6,000		290 cr

Date 2003/2004	Details	Debit €	Credit €	Balance dr = overdrawn
12 Mar	Withdrawal	3,000		2,710 dr
20 Mar	Cheque no 23992	2,700		5,410 dr
21 Mar	Cheque no 23991	73		5,483 dr
12 Apr	Cheque no 23994	133		5,616 dr
15 Apr	Cheque no 23995	400		6,016 dr
28 Apr	Cheque no 23996	5,000		11,016 dr
10 May	Lodgement		400	10,616 dr
23 May	Lodgement		6,900	3,716 dr
17 June	Lodgement		400	3,316 dr
17 June	Cheque no 23993	3,200		6,516 dr
28 June	Cheque no 23997	9,400		15,916 dr
29 June	Withdrawal	2,000		17,916 dr
30 June	Interest and charges	1,185		19,101 dr
3 July	Cheque no 23998	300		19,401 dr
14 July	Lodgement		21,550	2,149 cr
25 July	Withdrawal	3,000		851 dr
11 Aug	Lodgement		500	351 dr
25 Aug	Cheque no 24000	432		783 dr
26 Aug	Lodgement		12,000	11,217 cr
30 Aug	Cheque no 24001	100		1,217 cr
6 Sep	Lodgement		3,400	4,617 cr
13 Sep	Lodgement		490	5,107 cr
19 Sep	Lodgement		2,500	7,607 cr
20 Sep	Lodgement		1,000	8,607 cr
23 Sep	Cheque no 24004	2,500		6,107 cr
24 Sep	Cheque no 24005	1,300		4,807 cr
24 Sep	Withdrawal	7,000		2,193 dr
30 Sep	Lodgement		3,500	1,307 cr

Required:

Firstly, prepare the books of original entry, i.e. journals (sales, sales returns, purchases and purchases returns), cheque payments book, cash receipts book and petty cash book. This requires that you make one entry in these books for each transaction listed above.

Next, you must complete the debtors and creditors ledgers. To do this you extract the relevant information from the books of original entry, which you have just completed. Include the opening balances for individual debtors and creditors shown in the trial balance at 1 October 2003. You should also extract debtors and creditors schedules. These will be used later to check control a/c balances.

The next stage is writing up the nominal ledger. Remember to enter the opening balances for the individual relevant accounts shown in the trial balance at 1 October 2003. You complete this stage by preparing a bank reconciliation statement at 30 September 2004.

At this point you may extract a preliminary trial balance by extracting balances from the nominal ledger accounts you have just completed. Remember to enter the individual opening balances for the relevant accounts shown in the trial balance at 1 October 2003.

Note: Case Study 2: Preparing final accounts is a continuation from this point.

By Sandra Brosnan

To check your answers please see the Online Learning Centre for this textbook, which can be found at **www.mcgraw-hill.co.uk/textbooks/thomas**.

Case Study 2

Using the preliminary trial balance you extracted in Case Study 1: Double-entry book-keeping, and taking account of the following post trial balance adjustments, you are required to prepare the trading, profit and loss account and balance sheet for O'Donnell for the year ended 30 September 2004.

Post trial balance adjustments:

1. Closing stock is valued at €35,000.
2. On 30 September 2004 Mr O'Donnell decided to dispose of one of his vans. This had been acquired in 2001 at a cost of €10,000 and had been depreciated at a rate of 25 per cent per annum on cost. Sale proceeds amounted to €3,500 and this was lodged by Mr O'Donnell into his account in First Time Bank on 30 September. No other entry relating to this transaction has been made in the books.
3. Mr O'Donnell's depreciation policy is as follows: Depreciation is to be charged on delivery vans at 25 per cent on cost and on fittings at 10 per cent using the reducing balance method. Depreciation is not to be charged in the year of disposal.
4. Light and heat worth €120 and telephone worth €215 are outstanding at the year end.
5. You have decided to charge Mr O'Donnell €2,000 for your accounting services.
6. There is PAYE/PRSI of €256 outstanding in respect of Sergi which must be forwarded to the tax authorities.
7. The rent payment made on 30 January was in respect of the subsequent 12 months. The motor insurance payment made on 30 July related to the subsequent three months.
8. After discussing matters with Mr O'Donnell, you decide that there is little likelihood of any further payments from Doyle and that the remaining balance should be written off as a bad debt.
9. In the light of the experience with Doyle, you have advised Mr O'Donnell that it would be prudent to create a provision for doubtful debts. He has agreed that a provision equal to 6 per cent of closing debtors should be established.

Note: A cashflow statement may also be requested here.

By Sandra Brosnan

To check your answer please see the Online Learning Centre for this textbook, which can be found at **www.mcgraw-hill.co.uk/textbooks/thomas**.

Case Study 3

This case study tests your understanding of the incomplete records topic. In order to fully answer the questions in the case study, it is necessary to draw upon earlier topics including accruals and prepayments, depreciation, doubtful debts, and the purpose of financial statements.

Wendy set up the printing shop business on 2 January 20X4. She is new to running a business, and so has only been able to maintain some basic records, including those of her cash transactions. Wendy has hired you for an agreed fee of £1,000 to prepare her end of year financial accounts and to explain some accounting principles which are puzzling her. The agreed fee will be paid after you have completed the accountancy work. She has provided you with the following letter which contains information about her business activities during the year.

Dear Accounting Expert 31 December 20X4

Thank you very much for agreeing to act as my accountant and also for agreeing to deal with some rather puzzling points which, I have to confess, have been making my brain hurt! I started the printing shop business with just £2,000 in cash, which I deposited in the business bank account on 2 January of this year. All cash transactions have gone through the business bank account. I was fortunate in obtaining a loan of £28,000, from the Sunnydale Bank, on 2 January. I immediately used the loan to purchase some essential desktop printing equipment for £20,000 in cash. I used the remainder of the loan to purchase a van, to be used for delivering printing orders to clients, for £8,000 in cash. I also purchased on 2 January a stock of paper on good credit terms for £30,000. An experienced businesswoman friend of mine has explained that I need to depreciate both my printing equipment and the van. I do not understand this point at all, as I paid for both of the items in cash—surely that is the only cost that matters, as I have paid for both the assets in full? Anyway, my friend tells me that it is standard practice in my line of business to depreciate the printing equipment evenly over its six-year life, and to depreciate the van at 25 per cent on the reducing balance basis. I am told that the printing equipment has a scrap value of £2,000. I am not clear as to what all of this advice on depreciation means, but I am sure that you will be able to explain it and work it all out for me.

During the year, I have paid an assistant a salary of £10,000, but I still owe her £1,000 for the overtime which she kindly agreed to work for me in December 20X4. I have also drawn £25,000 in cash for myself out of the business bank account over the year. I obtained premises to rent at the start of the year, and paid rent of £12,000 in advance in cash on 2 January to cover me up to the end of June 20X5. There have been several van expenses which have arisen during the year and have been paid in cash. Petrol expenses amounted to £1,500. Also, there were van repairs which totalled £500 and additional payments for tax and insurance which came to £1,000. Electricity expenses paid in cash during the year amounted to £1,000. This figure for electricity included the last bill for £300 for three months: it covered the months of November and December 20X4 as well as the month of January 20X5. Business rates of £9,600 were paid in cash in advance on 1 April 20X4, and covered the 12 months up to 31 March 20X5. The council kindly agreed not to charge me rates for the first three months of 20X4.

At the end of the year, I was advised by friends to carry out a comprehensive stocktake for the business. This revealed that I had a stock of paper worth £40,000. I also found that I had spent £60,000 in cash on purchases of paper during the year, and also owed creditors £50,000 for purchases of paper during the year. I have received cash from sales of printing work of £120,000 during 20X4. I also discovered that I had debtors who owed me £40,000 for printing work, which I had carried out for them during the year. I also appear to have a problem debtor. The bank has informed me that a cheque from one debtor, Shark Enterprises, which owes me £4,000, has 'bounced' many times and so unfortunately I am not likely to obtain any money from that firm now or in the future. The bank manager has also suggested that I should make a provision of 10 per cent of the remaining debtors in order to allow for possible problems with people who do not settle their debts in future. I am not clear as to how this might be done, but hope that this suggestion makes sense to you when you put all this business information together.

During the year, as you may want to know, I took a modest amount of paper for my own use out of the business. This paper was worth £1,000. Also, I was able to pay the total interest of £3,000 which was due on the loan in cash, and was able to repay £2,000 of the loan to the Sunnydale Bank.

I hope that you can make sense of all the information that I have provided for you above. I understand that you can prepare some accounts for me, although I am not really sure if it is necessary to do this. If I can aim just to end up with a cash surplus at the end of the year, then is that not sufficient to show everyone that the business is doing well?

Best wishes

Yours sincerely

Wendy

Required:

1 Draw up a profit and loss account for Wendy's Printing Shop for the year ended 31 December 20X4 and a balance sheet as at that date. Include in your workings both the depreciation policies suggested by Wendy's friend and the treatment of bad and doubtful debts suggested by her bank manager.

2 Explain to Wendy the purpose and importance of depreciating fixed assets.

3 Explain to Wendy the purpose and importance of making a provision for doubtful debts.

4 Compare the cash position of Wendy's business at the end of the year with the performance shown by the profit and loss account. Explain the difference between the two, and how a profit and loss statement and a balance sheet can be useful to Wendy.

By Robert Jupe

To check your answers please see the Online Learning Centre for this textbook, which can be found at **www.mcgraw-hill.co.uk/textbooks/thomas**.

Case Study 4

Mr O'Donnell, originally a sole trader had owned and operated an antique furniture store in Cork for a number of years. He specialized in the purchase and sale of antique furniture from different countries and dealt with a small number of reputable suppliers and reliable customers. However, due to growing demand and growing opportunities Mr O'Donnell decided two years ago to register as a private limited company named Antique Furniture Supplies Ltd to facilitate expansion into a growing international market and secured a number of interested investors to provide the necessary capital. Antique Furniture Supplies Ltd filed all the necessary documentation (memorandum of association and articles of association) with the Registrar of Companies in accordance with the Companies Act 1963. Antique Furniture Supplies Ltd maintained all of its existing customer base and suppliers but has also attracted a number of large customers that have enabled the company to be quite successful.

You have been employed by Antique Furniture Supplies Ltd, as a qualified accountant, to maintain its company accounts and prepare the necessary financial statements. Following discussions with Antique Furniture Supplies Ltd, and after obtaining a copy of all relevant documentation, you have established an opening trial balance at the start of the financial year 1 October 2003. Furthermore you identify all his business transactions for the year

Antique Furniture Supplies Ltd's opening trial balance as at 1 October 2003

Account title	Debit €	Credit €
Fixed assets		
Delivery vans	42,000	
Accumulated depreciation on delivery vans		11,500
Fittings	16,000	
Accumulated depreciation on fittings		2,000
Premises	200,000	
Accumulated depreciation		40,000
Current assets		
Stock	54,000	
Trade debtors (Murphy €12,000; Foley €12,000)	24,000	
Cash at bank	35,550	
Petty cash	130	
Current liabilities		
Trade creditors (Cronin €11,000; Broderick €4000)		15,000
VAT		2,400
Corporation tax		10,000
Financed by:		
Ordinary share capital (200,000 €1 shares)		200,000
Share premium	20,000	
Profit & loss a/c 1 October 2003		53,150
10 per cent long-term loan		60,000
Selling & distribution expenses		
Motor/delivery expenses	600	
Administration expenses		
Postage, stationery and telephone		130
Light & heat		100
Rent	2,000	
	394,280	394,280

ended 30 September 2004. You also ascertain that VAT of 25 per cent applies to the sale, purchase and return of goods. In all other respects VAT can be ignored. VAT returns are submitted on an annual basis and are paid by direct debit every December.

The transactions which occurred during the year to 30 September 2004 are listed below:

October:

2	Sold goods on credit to Murphy for €5,000.
5	Sold goods on credit to Hulgerstein for €20,000.
6	Purchased goods on credit from Cronin for €53,750.
11	Paid €70 for stationery from petty cash.
23	Received and lodged to bank all money outstanding from Foley (no discount allowed).
30	Paid employee wages of €8,000 by direct debit.

November:

4	Returned €10,250 worth of goods purchased from Cronin.
11	Sold goods on credit to Foley for €5,000.
12	Sold goods on credit to Williams for €15,000.
19	Paid cheques no 23985 for light and heat (€1,450) and no 23986 for petty cash €600.
24	Purchased goods on credit from Broderick for €21,250.
30	Paid employee wages of €8,000 by direct debit.

December:

1	Murphy returned goods in the amount of €1,000 and credit note 14 was issued to him.
2	Received and lodged €19,000 from Hulgerstein after allowing him a 5 per cent discount.
12	Received and lodged cheque in amount of €13,000 from Murphy and allowed him a discount of €650.
19	Paid cheque no 23987 in amount of €42,000 to Cronin and received €1,500 discount.
24	Received €13,000 from Williams and allowed him a discount of €750.
27	Paid VAT outstanding from previous year by direct debit.
30	Paid motor insurance, €2,400 by cheque no 23988 to cover the following six months.
30	Paid employee wages of €8,000 by direct debit.
31	Paid from petty cash: €27 postage; €350 stationery.

January:

7	Sold goods on credit to Foley for €4,000 and to Doolan for €4,000.
8	Lodged cash sales of €24,500.
9	Purchased goods on credit for €31,500 from Broderick.
22	Foley returned goods in the amount of €1,000 so credit note 15 was issued to him.
26	Murphy lodged amount outstanding on his account.
30	Paid €8,000 by cheque no 23989, being rent due for 12 months from 1 February 2004.
30	Paid employee wages of €8,000 by direct debit.

February:

1 Received and lodged all money due from Foley after allowing him discount of €400.
7 Sold goods to Doolan for €3,000; paid cheque no 23990 worth €5,300 for motor expenses.
10 Sold goods on credit for €20,000 to Williams.
17 Purchased goods from Cronin on credit, €37,500.
22 Returned goods to Cronin to the value of €3,000.
28 Paid from petty cash: €80 postage; €200 stationery.
28 Paid employee wages of €8,000 by direct debit.

March:

3 Sold goods on credit to Doyle to the value of €8,000.
7 Sold goods on credit to O'Haire, €11,000.
8 Paid €36,750 to Broderick for goods previously purchased (cheque no 23991).
10 Purchased goods on credit for €21,000 from Broderick.
11 Paid cheque no 23992, to Cronin to the amount of €33,200 and received a discount of €2,000.
16 Paid for light and heat to the amount of €4,350 with cheque no 23993.
25 Williams lodged €18,000 into bank account.
26 Paid €3,500 for advertising with cheque no 23994.
30 Paid employee wages of €8,000 by direct debit.
30 Received a letter from Doyle's accountant to state that Doyle is in financial difficulty and probably will not be able to settle his debt.

April:

7 Paid motor tax, €1,000 by cheque no 23995.
8 Paid cheque no 23996 to the value of €900 to cover repairs to delivery van.
17 Sold goods on credit to Brennan for €17,000.
19 Purchased goods on credit from Cronin, €13,000.
20 Sold goods worth €25,000 to Hulgerstein on credit.
25 Paid Cronin €15,000 (cheque no 23997) and received a discount of €800.
28 Sold a further €50,000 worth of goods on credit to Williams.
30 Received a letter from your bank stating that the company has overdrawn beyond its agreed credit limits and that if the overdraft was not reduced serious action will have to be taken.
30 Paid employee wages of €8,000 by direct debit.
30 Paid from petty cash €12 for postage.

May:

7 Sold goods to Kelly on credit for €4,000.
12 Received €1,000 unexpectedly from Doyle's accountants, lodged money immediately.
17 Kelly returned damaged goods in the amount of €2,000.
19 Hulgerstein paid €20,000 on his account and was allowed a discount of €500.
22 Purchased goods from Sabura on credit worth €2,000.
23 Received and lodged cheques from Brennan in full settlement after allowing for a discount of €100.
30 Paid employee wages of €8,000 by direct debit.
31 Paid from petty cash: stationery €50; postage €12.

June:

2 Sold goods on credit to O'Haire worth €25,000.
3 Purchased goods on credit from Broderick to the value of €13,000.
9 Purchased goods from Cronin on credit worth €15,750.
17 Lodged cash sales worth €14,000.
20 Credit sale of €10,000 to Hulgerstein.
22 Paid Broderick €53,650 due less discount €350 (cheque no 23998).
29 Paid motor and delivery expenses of €3,500 (cheque no 23999)
30 Williams settled his account (no discount allowed).
30 Paid employee wages of €8,000 by direct debit.

July:

2 Sold goods on credit to O'Haire for €17,000.
3 Paid cheque no 24000 to the amount of €300 to petty cash.
13 O'Haire returned goods of €1,000.
14 O'Haire settled account in full, less agreed discount of €450. Proceeds lodged.
19 Sold goods on credit to Doolan for €11,000.
24 Hulgerstein settled his account (discount allowed of €450).
30 Paid employee wages of €8,000 by direct debit.
31 Paid motor insurance of €2,400 by cheque no 24001 to cover following three months.

August:

3 Purchased goods on credit from Cronin for €19,000.
7 Returned goods worth €6,000 to Cronin.
10 Sold goods on credit to Baralux Ltd to the amount of €50,000.
11 Cash sales of €6,000 lodged.
20 Paid telephone bill of €4,500 by cheque no 24002.
20 Sold goods to O'Haire on credit for €5,000.
21 Sold goods on credit to Doolan worth €4,000.
26 Paid Cronin €26,000 on account, cheque no 24003. Discount received €250.
29 Received and lodged €12,000 from Doolan. Discount allowed €500.
30 Doolan returned goods in the amount of €100.
30 Paid employee wages of €8,000 by direct debit.

September:

1 Purchased goods on credit from Slatery worth €20,000.
3 Sold goods on credit to O'Haire for €6,000.
6 Received and lodged balance due from O'Haire, less an agreed discount of €100.
7 Paid light and heat worth €2,528 by cheque no 24004.
9 Sold goods to Murphy on credit worth €6,000, and to Doolan for €3,000.
13 Lodged cash sales worth €4,900.
14 Baralux Ltd paid €35,000 on its account. Discount allowed €1,000.
16 Sold goods to O'Sullivan on credit for €3,000.
19 Received and lodged €2,500 from O'Sullivan. Discount allowed €200.
20 Received and lodged €4,000 from Murphy. Discount allowed €100.
21 Paid Cronin by cheque no 24005 to the amount of €9,000.
22 Paid Slatery €2,500 by cheque no 24006. Discount received €100. Cash sales €2,450 lodged by credit transfer.

23 Purchased goods on credit from Slatery for €26,000.
30 Paid from petty cash: stationery €42; Postage €35.
30 Received and lodged €5,500 from J. Cunningham to whom you sold a delivery van.
30 Paid employee wages of €8,000 by direct debit.

Antique Furniture Supplies Ltd's bank, First Time Bank, have supplied you with the following bank statement:

Account Number: 659289
Customer: Antique Furniture Supplies Ltd, Link Road, Ballydune, Cork.
Statement No 11

Date 2003/2004	Details	Debit €	Credit €	Balance dr = overdrawn
1 Oct	Balance			35,550 cr
23 Oct	Lodgement		12,000	47,550 cr
30 Oct	Direct debit 7422984	8,000		39,550 cr
19 Nov	Cheque no 23985	1,450		38,100 cr
19 Nov	Cheque no 23986	600		37,500 cr
30 Nov	Direct debit 7422985	8,000		29,500 cr
2 Dec	Lodegement		19,000	48,500 cr
12 Dec	Lodgement		13,000	61,500 cr
19 Dec	Cheque no 23987	42,000		19,500 cr
24 Dec	Lodgement		13,000	32,500 cr
27 Dec	Direct debit 7422986	2,400		30,100 cr
30 Dec	Cheque no 23988	2,400		27,700 cr
30 Dec	Direct debit 7422987	8,000		19,700 cr
31 Dec	Interest and charges	1,900		17,800 cr
8 Jan	Lodgement		24,500	42,300 cr
27 Jan	Lodgement		2,350	44,650 cr
30 Jan	Cheque no 23989	8,000		36,650 cr
30 Jan	Direct debit 7422988	8,000		28,650 cr
1 Feb	Lodgement		7,600	36,250 cr
8 Feb	Cheque no 23990	5,300		30,950 cr
28 Feb	Direct debit 7422989	8,000		22,950 cr
15 Mar	Cheque no 23992	33,200		10,250 dr
21 Mar	Cheque no 23991	36,750		47,000 dr
25 Mar	Lodgement	18,000		29,000 dr
28 Mar	Cheque no 23,994	3,500		32,500 dr
30 Mar	Direct debit 7422990	8,000		40,500 dr
15 Apr	Cheque no 23995	1,000		41,500 dr
16 Apr	Cheque no 23996	900		42,400 dr
28 Apr	Cheque no 23997	15,000		57,400 dr
30 Apr	Direct debit 7422991	8,000		65,400 dr
12 May	Lodgement		1,000	64,400 dr
20 May	Lodgement		20,000	44,400 dr
23 May	Lodgement		16,900	27,500 dr
30 May	Direct debit 7422992	8,000		35,500 dr
17 June	Lodgement		14,000	21,500 dr
17 June	Cheque no 23993	4,530		26,030 dr
28 June	Cheque no 23998	53,650		79,680 dr
29 June	Cheque no 23999	3,500		83,180 dr
30 June	Lodgement		53,250	29,930 dr

Date 2003/2004	Details	Debit €	Credit €	Balance dr = overdrawn
30 June	Interest and charges	1,185		31,115 dr
30 June	Direct debit 7422993	8,000		39,115 dr
3 July	Cheque no 24000	300		39,415 dr
14 July	Lodgement		51,550	12,135 cr
25 July	Lodgement		9,550	21,685 cr
30 July	Direct debit 7422994	8,000		13,685 cr
3 Aug	Cheque no 24001	2,400		11,285 cr
11 Aug	Lodgement		6,000	17,285 cr
25 Aug	Cheque no 24002	4,500		12,785 cr
29 Aug	Lodgement		12,000	24,785 cr
30 Aug	Cheque no 24003	26,000		1,215 dr
30 Aug	Direct debit 7422995	8,000		9,215 dr
6 Sep	Lodgement		10,900	1,685 cr
13 Sep	Lodgement		4,900	6,585 cr
15 Sep	Lodgement		35,000	41,585 cr
20 Sep	Lodgement		2,500	44,085 cr
21 Sep	Lodgement		4,000	48,085 cr
23 Sep	Cheque no 24004	2,528		45,557 cr
24 Sep	Cheque no 24005	9,000		36,557 cr
24 Sep	Lodgement		2,450	39,007 cr
24 Sep	Cheque no 24006	2,500		36,507 cr
30 Sep	Lodgement		5,500	42,007 cr
30 Sep	Direct debit	8,000		34,007 cr

Required:
Firstly, prepare the books of original entry, i.e. journals (sales, sales returns, purchases and purchases returns), cheque payments book, cash receipts book and petty cash book. This requires that you make one entry in these books for each transaction listed above.

Next, you must complete the debtors and creditors ledgers. To do this you extract the relevant information from the books of original entry, which you have just completed. Include the opening balances for individual debtors and creditors shown in the trial balance at 1 October 2003. You should also extract debtors and creditors schedules. These will be used later to check control a/c balances.

The next stage is writing up the nominal ledger. Remember to enter the opening balances for the individual relevant accounts shown in the trial balance at 1 October 2003. You complete this stage by preparing a bank reconciliation statement at 30 September 2004.

At this point you may extract a preliminary trial balance by extracting balances from the nominal ledger accounts you have just completed. Remember to enter the individual opening balances for the relevant accounts shown in the trial balance at 1 October 2003.

Using the preliminary trial balance you extracted above, and taking account of the following post trial balance adjustments, you are required to prepare the trading, profit and loss account for Antique Furniture Supplies Ltd for the year ended 30 September 2004 and a balance sheet at that date. Also, comment on Antique Furniture Supplies Ltd's cashflow position throughout the year and suggest ways to improve its working capital cycle.

Post trial balance adjustments:

1. Closing stock is valued at €35,000.
2. On the 30 September 2004 Antique Furniture Supplies Ltd decided to dispose of one of its vans. This had been acquired in 2001 at a cost of €12,000 and had been depreciated at a rate of 20 per cent per annum on cost. Sale proceeds amounted to €5,500 and this was lodged by Mr O'Donnell into his account in First Time Bank on 30 September. No other entry relating to this transaction has been made in the books.
3. Antique Furniture Supplies Ltd depreciation policy is as follows: depreciation is to be charged on both delivery vans and premises at 20 per cent on cost and on Fittings at 10 per cent using the reducing balance method. Depreciation is not to be charged in the year of disposal.
4. Light and heat worth €175 and telephone worth €265 are outstanding at the year end along with wages of €2,000.
5. You have decided to charge Antique Furniture Supplies Ltd €12,000 for your accounting services.
6. The rent payment made on 30 January was in respect of the subsequent 12 months. The motor insurance payment made on July 30 related to the subsequent 3 months.
7. After discussing matters with Antique Furniture Supplies Ltd, you decide that there is little likelihood of any further payments from Doyle and that the remaining balance should be written off as a bad debt.
8. In the light of the experience with Doyle, you have advised Antique Furniture Supplies Ltd that it would be prudent to create a provision for doubtful debts. It is agreed that a provision equal to 5 per cent of closing debtors should be established.
9. Corporation tax for this accounting period is €10,000 and has not been paid.
10. Interest on the long-term loan is outstanding at the year end.
11. It is proposed that a final dividend of 5 per cent ordinary share capital should be paid.

Note: A cashflow statement may also be requested here.

By Sandra Brosnan

To check your answer please see the Online Learning Centre for this textbook, which can be found at **www.mcgraw-hill.co.uk/textbooks/thomas**.

Solutions to exercises

Contents

Preface to Appendix

This appendix contains suggested answers to those exercises with an asterisk after the question number. These comprise most of the numerical exercises that were written by the author, and some of those of the examining bodies. All the short written review questions are designed so that they can be answered directly from the relevant section of the chapter. There is thus little point in reprinting these sections as suggested solutions. However, the Appendix includes suggested answers to the other review questions designed by the author, where they are sufficiently demanding to constitute a possible examination question.

This appendix is intended to enable the student to monitor the progress of his or her learning. It will be most effective if you first attempt each question without referring to the answer. When you have finished, or done as much as you are able, then check your answer against the suggested solution. Students are also strongly advised to record the time it takes them to answer each question. Most questions carry around 20 to 25 marks, which means that the time allowed to answer them in a 3-hour examination is about 36 to 45 minutes. If you take considerably longer than this, attempt the question again at a later date (e.g. for revision) to see whether you can answer it more quickly. When you can answer most of the questions in the allocated time, you should be sufficiently prepared for the examination!

1 The nature and objectives of financial accounting

1.5 a There are three sources of rules and regulations that govern the content and format of company final accounts as follows:

1. The Companies Acts (the most recent being the 1985 Act as modified by the 1989 Act) with which all companies are required to comply.
2. The International Stock Exchange, London Admission of Securities to Listing (commonly known as the Yellow Book) regulations with which all companies whose shares are listed on the London Stock Exchange are expected to comply.
3. Statements of Standard Accounting Practice (SSAP) issued by the Accounting Standards Committee (ASC), and Financial Reporting Standards (FRS) issued by the Accounting Standards Board (ASB) with which most (but not all) companies are expected to comply.

b The institutional framework by which the accountancy profession has influenced the content and format of company final accounts during the last two decades primarily comprises the Accounting Standards Committee (ASC) and the Accounting Standards Board (ASB). From 1975 to 1990 the ASC issued accounting standards known as Statements of Standard Accounting Practice (SSAP). The ASB was formed in 1990, and since then has issued accounting standards known as Financial Reporting Standards.

The ASB is a subsidiary of the Financial Reporting Council (FRC) which has overall responsibility for standard setting in the UK. The FRC has another subsidiary, the Financial Reporting Review Panel (FRRP), which investigates complaints about any company's final accounts that do not comply with the Companies Acts and/or accounting standards.

The ASB also has a committee, the Urgent Issues Task Force (UITF), which publishes Abstracts. These are intended to clarify the accounting treatment that should be adopted where an accounting standard or Companies Act provision exists, but the interpretation is ambiguous.

2 The accounting equation and its components

2.7 *J. Frank*
Balance sheet as at 1 January 20X9

Assets	£	*Liabilities*	£
Land & buildings	7,500	Mortgage	4,000
Fixtures	560	*Capital*	5,800
Bank	1,740		
	9,800		9,800

J. Frank
Balance sheet as at 31 December 20X9

Assets	£	*Liabilities*	£
Land & buildings	7,500	Mortgage	5,000
Fixtures	560	Sundry creditors	800
Delivery van	650	*Capital*	5,450
Sundry debtors	470		
Stock	940		
Bank	1,050		
Cash	80		
	11,250		11,250

Note
In both of the above balance sheets the capital is the difference between the two sides after entering all the assets and liabilities.

J. Frank
Statement of profit or loss for the year ended 31 December 20X9

	£
Capital at 31 Dec	5,450
Less: Capital at 1 Jan	5,800
Apparent loss	(350)
Add: Drawings	500
Net profit for the year	150

3 Basic documentation and books of account

3.5 i The sales day book is used to record the sale on credit of those goods bought specifically for resale. It is written up from copies of the sales invoices and debit notes retained by the seller.

ii The sales returns day book is used to record goods sold on credit that are returned by customers. It is written up from copies of the credit notes retained by the seller.

iii The purchases day book is used to record the purchase on credit of goods intended for resale. It is written up from the purchase invoices and debit notes received from suppliers.

iv The purchases day book is used to record goods purchased on credit that are returned to suppliers. It is written up from the credit notes received from suppliers.

v The cash book is used to record cheques received and cash paid into the bank and payments by cheque. It is written up from the bank paying-in book and cheque book stubs.

vi The petty cash book is used to record cash received and cash paid. It is written up from receipts and petty cash vouchers.

vii The journal is used to record transactions and items not appropriate to any of the other books of prime entry such as the purchase and sale of fixed assets on credit, correction of errors, etc. It is written up from copies of the invoices.

viii The bills receivable book is used to record bills of exchange received by the business. It is written up from copies of the bills of exchange receivable.

ix The bills payable book is used to record bills of exchange given to creditors as a means of payment. It is written up from copies of the bill of exchange payable.

4 The general ledger

4.1

Cash

Date	Details	Amount	Date	Details	Amount
20X6			20X6		
1 Oct	Capital	5,000	1 Oct	Rent	200
6 Oct	S. Ring	3,500	2 Oct	Purchases	970
12 Oct	Sales	1,810	4 Oct	Fixtures & fittings	1,250
24 Oct	Sales	1,320	9 Oct	Motor vehicles	2,650
			15 Oct	Wages	150
			18 Oct	Purchases	630
			19 Oct	Drawings	350
			21 Oct	Motor expenses	25
			22 Oct	Printing	65
			25 Oct	Motor expenses	45
			27 Oct	Wages	250
			28 Oct	Stationery	35
			30 Oct	Rates	400
			31 Oct	Drawings	175
			31 Oct	Balance c/d	4,435
		11,630			11,630
1 Nov	Balance b/d	4,435			

Capital

Date	Details	Amount	Date	Details	Amount
			1 Oct	Cash	5,000

Loan—S. Ring

Date	Details	Amount	Date	Details	Amount
			6 Oct	Cash	3,500

Sales

Date	Details	Amount	Date	Details	Amount
			12 Oct	Cash	1,810
			24 Oct	Cash	1,320

Rent & rates

Date	Details	Amount	Date	Details	Amount
1 Oct	Cash	200			
30 Oct	Cash	400			

Purchases

Date	Details	Amount	Date	Details	Amount
2 Oct	Cash	970			
18 Oct	Cash	630			

Fixtures & fittings

Date	Details	Amount	Date	Details	Amount
4 Oct	Cash	1,250			

Motor vehicles

Date	Details	Amount	Date	Details	Amount
9 Oct	Cash	2,650			

Wages

Date	Details	Amount	Date	Details	Amount
15 Oct	Cash	150			
27 Oct	Cash	250			

Drawings

Date	Details	Amount	Date	Details	Amount
19 Oct	Cash	350			
31 Oct	Cash	175			

Motor expenses

Date	Details	Amount	Date	Details	Amount
21 Oct	Cash	25			
25 Oct	Cash	45			

Printing & stationery

Date	Details	Amount	Date	Details	Amount
22 Oct	Cash	65			
28 Oct	Cash	35			

4.2

Bank

Date	Details	Amount	Date	Details	Amount
20X8			20X8		
1 Mar	Capital	10,000	1 Mar	Leasehold premises	5,000
18 Mar	Sales	540	2 Mar	Office equipment	1,400
28 Mar	G. Lion	280	6 Mar	Postage	35
			9 Mar	Purchases	420
			13 Mar	Drawings	250
			20 Mar	Telephone	120
			24 Mar	Light & heat	65
			26 Mar	E. Lamb	230
			30 Mar	Light & heat	85
			31 Mar	Bank charges	45
			31 Mar	Balance c/d	3,170
		10,820			10,820
1 Apr	Balance b/d	3,170			

Capital

Date	Details	Amount	Date	Details	Amount
			1 Mar	Bank	10,000

Sales

Date	Details	Amount	Date	Details	Amount
			11 Mar	G. Lion	880
			18 Mar	Bank	540

G. Lion

Date	Details	Amount	Date	Details	Amount
11 Mar	Sales	880	22 Mar	Sales returns	310
			28 Mar	Bank	280

Sales returns

Date	Details	Amount	Date	Details	Amount
22 Mar	G. Lion	310			

Leasehold premises

Date	Details	Amount	Date	Details	Amount
1 Mar	Bank	5,000			

Office equipment

Date	Details	Amount	Date	Details	Amount
2 Mar	Bank	1,400			

Postage & telephone

Date	Details	Amount	Date	Details	Amount
6 Mar	Bank	35			
20 Mar	Bank	120			

Purchases

Date	Details	Amount	Date	Details	Amount
4 Mar	E. Lamb	630			
9 Mar	Bank	420			

E. Lamb

Date	Details	Amount	Date	Details	Amount
16 Mar	Purchases returns	180	4 Mar	Purchases	630
26 Mar	Bank	230			

Purchases returns

Date	Details	Amount	Date	Details	Amount
			16 Mar	E. Lamb	180

	Drawings
13 Mar Bank	250

	Light & heat
24 Mar Bank	65
30 Mar Bank	85

	Bank charges
31 Mar Bank	45

5 The balancing of accounts and the trial balance

5.3 ***S. Baker***

Trial balance as at 31 January 20X0

	Debit	*Credit*
	£	£
Cash	875	
Capital		1,000
Loan—London Bank		500
Sales		600
Rent	100	
Fixtures & fittings	300	
Purchases	400	
Carriage inwards	25	
Stationery	50	
Wages	200	
Drawings	150	
	2,100	2,100

5.4 ***H. George***

Trial balance as at 31 October 20X6

	Debit	*Credit*
	£	£
Cash	4,435	
Capital		5,000
Loan—S. Ring		3,500
Sales		3,130
Rent & rates	600	
Purchases	1,600	
Fixtures & fittings	1,250	
Motor vehicles	2,650	
Wages	400	
Drawings	525	
Motor expenses	70	
Printing & stationery	100	
	11,630	11,630

5.5 ***L. Johnson***

Trial balance as at 31 March 20X8

	Debit	*Credit*
	£	£
Bank	3,170	
Capital		10,000
Sales		1,420
G. Lion	290	
Sales returns	310	
Leasehold premises	5,000	
Office equipment	1,400	
Postage & telephone	155	
Purchases	1,050	
E. Lamb		220
Purchases returns		180
Drawings	250	
Light & heat	150	
Bank charges	45	
	11,820	11,820

5.7 ***C. Rick***

Trial balance as at 31 May 20X3

	Debit	*Credit*
	£	£
Bank	2,368	
Purchases	12,389	
Sales		18,922
Wages & salaries	3,862	
Rent & rates	504	
Insurance	78	
Motor expenses	664	
Printing & stationery	216	
Light & heat	166	
General expenses	314	
Premises	10,000	
Motor vehicles	3,800	
Fixtures & fittings	1,350	
Debtors	3,896	
Creditors		1,731
Cash	482	
Drawings	1,200	
Capital		12,636
Bank loan		8,000
	41,289	41,289

5.8 ***R. Keith***

Trial balance as at 30 June 20X2

	Debit	*Credit*
	£	£
Capital		39,980
Drawings	14,760	
Loan—Bromsgrove Bank		20,000
Leasehold premises	52,500	
Motor vehicles	13,650	
Investments	4,980	
Trade debtors	2,630	
Trade creditors		1,910
Cash	460	
Bank overdraft		3,620
Sales		81,640
Purchases	49,870	
Returns outwards		960
Returns inwards	840	
Carriage	390	
Wages & salaries	5,610	
Rent & rates	1,420	
Light & heat	710	
Telephone & postage	540	
Printing & stationery	230	
Bank interest	140	
Interest received		620
	148,730	148,730

5.9

- **a** Debit wages account with £250
- **b** Credit sales account with £100
- **c** Credit creditors account with £9 (i.e. £198—£189)
- **d** Change the amount shown in the trial balance in respect of drawings to £300
- **e** Debit the bank account with £172 (i.e. £86 × 2)

6 Day books and the journal

6.4 ***Purchases day book***

Date	Name of creditor	Amount
20X7		£
1 Aug	Desks Ltd	750
3 Aug	Chairs Ltd	350
18 Aug	Cabinets Ltd	720
		1,820

Purchases returns day book

Date	Name of creditor	Amount
20X7		£
10 Aug	Desks Ltd	225
21 Aug	Chairs Ltd	140
		365

Sales day book

Date	Name of creditor	Amount
20X7		£
6 Aug	British Cars Ltd	630
13 Aug	London Beds Ltd	680
23 Aug	English Carpets Ltd	1,170
		2,480

Sales returns day book

Date	Name of creditor	Amount
20X7		£
16 Aug	British Cars Ltd	270
25 Aug	London Beds Ltd	85
		355

The ledger

Purchases

20X7					
31 Aug	Per PDB	1,820			

Purchases returns

			20X7		
			31 Aug	Per PRDB	365

Desks Ltd

10 Aug	Returns	225	1 Aug	Purchases	750
31 Aug	Balance c/d	525			
		750			750
			1 Sep	Balance b/d	525

Chairs Ltd

21 Aug	Returns	140	3 Aug	Purchases	350
31 Aug	Balance c/d	210			
		350			350
			1 Sep	Balance b/d	210

Cabinets Ltd

			18 Aug	Purchases	720

Sales

			31 Aug	Per SDB	2,480

Sales returns

31 Aug	Per SRDB	355			

British Cars

6 Aug	Sales	630	16 Aug	Returns	270
			31 Aug	Balance c/d	360
		630			630
1 Sep	Balance b/d	360			

London Beds

13 Aug	Sales	680	25 Aug	Returns	85
			31 Aug	Balance c/d	595
		680			680
1 Sep	Balance b/d	595			

English Carpets

23 Aug	Sales	1,170			

6.5 ***The journal***

Date	Details/account		Debit	Credit
20X5			£	£
20 Apr	Plant & machinery	Dr	5,300	
	To Black Ltd			5,300
	Being purchase of machine on credit			
23 Apr	White Ltd	Dr	3,600	
	To Motor vehicles			3,600
	Being sale of delivery vehicle on credit			
26 Apr	Fixtures & fittings	Dr	480	
	To Grey Ltd			480
	Being purchase of shop fittings on credit			
28 Apr	Yellow Ltd	Dr	270	
	To Office equipment			270
	Being sale of typewriter on credit			

The ledger

Plant & machinery

20X5					
20 Apr	Black Ltd	5,300			

Black Ltd

			20X5		
			20 Apr	Plant & machinery	5,300

White Ltd

23 Apr	Motor vehicles	3,600			

Motor vehicles

			23 Apr	White Ltd	3,600

Fixtures & fittings

26 Apr	Grey Ltd	480			

Grey Ltd

			26 Apr	Fixtures & fittings	480

Yellow Ltd

28 Apr	Office equipment	270			

Office equipment

			28 Apr	Yellow Ltd	270

6.6 *The journal*

Date	Details/account		Debit	Credit
20X8			£	£
1 Aug	Premises	Dr	55,000	
	Plant & machinery	Dr	23,000	
	Stock	Dr	14,600	
	Trade debtors	Dr	6,300	
	To Trade creditors			2,900
	To Capital			96,000
			98,900	98,900
	Being assets and liabilities introduced into business by owner from takeover of L. House			

The ledger

Premises

Date	Details	£	Date	Details	£
20X8					
1 Aug	Capital	55,000			

Plant & machinery

Date	Details	£	Date	Details	£
1 Aug	Capital	23,000			

Stock

Date	Details	£	Date	Details	£
1 Aug	Capital	14,600			

Trade debtors

Date	Details	£	Date	Details	£
1 Aug	Capital	6,300			

Trade creditors

Date	Details	£	Date	Details	£
20X8					
			1 Aug	Capital	2,900

Capital

Date	Details	£	Date	Details	£
			1 Aug	Assets & liabilities	96,000

Note

1 The trade debtors and creditors would be entered in their individual personal accounts.

7 The cash book

7.5 *The cash book*

Date	Details	Memo discount received	Bank	Cash	Date	Details	Memo discount received	Bank	Cash
20X7		£	£	£	20X7		£	£	£
1 Sep	Balance b/d		1,950	860	4 Sep	Purchases			230
3 Sep	Sales		470		6 Sep	Light & heat		510	
9 Sep	Sales		380		10 Sep	Wages		250	
12 Sep	Sales			290	15 Sep	Travelling expenses			40
22 Sep	Cash		350		16 Sep	Rates		410	
24 Sep	Capital		500		19 Sep	Drawings			150
26 Sep	B. Jones—loan		1,000		20 Sep	Purchases		320	
27 Sep	Purchases returns			170	21 Sep	Postage & telephone			30
29 Sep	Bank			180	22 Sep	Bank			350
30 Sep	British Cars	10	350		25 Sep	Vehicles		2,500	
30 Sep	London Beds	15	580		28 Sep	Motor expenses			280
30 Sep	English Carpets		1,100		29 Sep	Cash		180	
					30 Sep	Desks Ltd	25	500	
					30 Sep	Chairs Ltd	20	190	
					30 Sep	Cabinets Ltd		500	
					30 Sep	Balance c/d		1,320	420
		25	6,680	1,500			45	6,680	1,500
1 Oct	Balance c/d		1,320	420					

7.6 ***The ledger***

Capital

			20X7		
			1 Sep	Balance b/d	2,810
			24 Sep	Bank	500
					3,310

Loan—B. Jones

			26 Sep	Bank	1,000

Sales

			31 Aug	Per SDB	2,480
			3 Sep	Bank	470
			9 Sep	Bank	380
			12 Sep	Cash	290
					3,620

Sales returns

20X7					
31 Aug	Per SRDB	355			

British Cars

1 Sep	Balance b/d	360	30 Sep	Bank	350
			30 Sep	Discount allowed	10
		360			360

London Beds

1 Sep	Balance b/d	595	30 Sep	Bank	580
			30 Sep	Discount allowed	15
		595			595

Discount allowed

30 Sep	Total per Cash Book	25			

English Carpets

23 Aug	Sales	1,170	30 Sep	Bank	1,100
			30 Sep	Balance c/d	70
		1,170			1,170
1 Oct	Balance b/d	70			

Purchases

31 Aug	Per PDB	1,820			
4 Sep	Cash	230			
20 Sep	Bank	320			
		2,370			

Purchases returns

			31 Aug	Per PRDB	365
			27 Sep	Cash	170
					535

Desks Ltd

30 Sep	Bank	500	1 Sep	Balance b/d	525
30 Sep	Discount received	25			
		525			525

Chairs Ltd

30 Sep	Bank	190	1 Sep	Balance b/d	210
30 Sep	Discount received	20			
		210			210

Discount received

			30 Sep	Total per Cash Book	45

Cabinets Ltd

30 Sep	Bank	500	18 Aug	Purchases	720
30 Sep	Balance c/d	220			
		720			720
			1 Oct	Balance b/d	220

Light & heat

6 Sep	Bank	510			

Wages

10 Sep	Bank	250			

Travelling expenses

15 Sep	Cash	40			

Rates

16 Sep	Bank	410			

Drawings

19 Sep	Cash	150			

Postage & telephone

21 Sep	Cash	30			

Motor vehicles

25 Sep	Bank	2,500			

Motor expenses

28 Sep	Cash	280			

B. Player
Trial balance as at 30 September 20X7

	Debit £	*Credit* £
Cash	420	
Bank	1,320	
Capital		3,310
Loan—B. Jones		1,000
Sales		3,620
Sales returns	355	
Discount allowed	25	
English Carpets	70	
Purchases	2,370	
Purchases returns		535
Discount received		45
Cabinets Ltd		220
Light & heat	510	
Wages	250	
Travelling expenses	40	
Rates	410	
Drawings	150	
Postage & telephone	30	
Motor vehicles	2,500	
Motor expenses	280	
	8,730	8,730

Note

1 Discount taken by debtors such as English Carpets which is not allowed is usually simply not entered in the discount allowed column of the cash book since the business whose books we are preparing has disallowed the discount.

8 The petty cash book

8.3 *Petty cash book*

Debit amount	Date	Details	Credit amount	Purchases	Wages	Motor expenses	Travelling expenses	Printing & stationery	Postage & telephone	Misc.
£	20X2	£	£	£	£	£	£	£	£	
400	1 Feb	Balance b/d								
	1 Feb	Purchases	31	31						
	3 Feb	Wages	28		28					
	6 Feb	Petrol	9			9				
	8 Feb	Bus fares	3				3			
	11 Feb	Pens & pencils	8					8		
	12 Feb	Casual labour	25		25					
	14 Feb	Repairs	17			17				
	16 Feb	Paper	15					15		
	19 Feb	Purchases	22	22						
	20 Feb	Train fares	12				12			
	21 Feb	Repairs to premises	35							35
	22 Feb	Postage	6						6	
	23 Feb	Drawings	20							20
	24 Feb	Taxi fares	7				7			
	25 Feb	Envelopes	4					4		
	26 Feb	Purchases	18	18						
	27 Feb	Wages	30		30					
	28 Feb	Petrol	14			14				
304	28 Feb	Bank	304	71	83	40	22	27	6	55
	28 Feb	Balance c/d	400							
704			704							
400	1 Mar	Balance b/d								

The ledger

Purchases

20X2
28 Feb Per PCB 71

Wages

28 Feb Per PCB 83

Motor expenses

28 Feb Per PCB 40

Travelling expenses

28 Feb Per PCB 22

Printing & stationery

28 Feb Per PCB 27

Postage & telephone

28 Feb Per PCB 6

Repairs to premises

21 Feb Cash 35

Drawings

23 Feb Cash 20

Bank

20X2
28 Feb Cash 304

9 The final accounts of sole traders

9.4 ***R. Woods***
Trading and profit & loss accounts
for the year ended 30 September 20X6

	£	£
Sales		18,922
Less: Cost of sales		
Stock at 1 Oct 20X5	2,368	
Add: purchases	12,389	
	14,757	
Less: stock at 30 Sep 20X6	2,946	
		11,811
Gross profit		7,111
Less: Expenditure		
Salaries & wages	3,862	
Rent & rates	504	
Insurance	78	
Motor expenses	664	
Printing & stationery	216	
Light & heat	166	
General expenses	314	
		5,804
Net profit for year		1,307

R. Woods
Balance sheet as at 30 September 20X6

	£	£
Fixed assets		
Premises		5,000
Motor vehicles		1,800
Fixtures & fittings		350
		7,150
Current assets		
Stock	2,946	
Debtors	3,896	
Bank	482	
	7,324	
Less: Current liabilities		
Creditors	1,731	
Net current assets		5,593
Net assets		12,743
Capital		
Balance at 1 Oct 20X5		12,636
Add: profit for the year		1,307
		13,943
Less: drawings		1,200
Balance at 30 Sep 20X6		12,743

9.5 ***Joytoys***
Trading and profit and loss accounts for the year ended 31 December 20X3

	£	£	£
Sales			167,000
Less: returns inwards			1,000
Net sales			166,000
Less: Cost of sales			
Stock at 1 Jan 20X3		12,000	
Add: purchases	108,000		
Less: returns outwards	4,000	104,000	
		116,000	
Less: stock at 31 Dec 20X3		19,500	
			96,500
Gross profit			69,500
Add: discount received			3,000
			72,500
Less: Expenditure			
Rent, rates & insurance		15,000	
Discount allowed		1,600	
Bank interest		400	
Wages & salaries		13,000	
Light & heat		9,000	
			39,000
Net profit for the year			33,500

Joytoys
Balance sheet as at 31 December 20X3

	£	£
Fixed assets		
Plant & machinery		70,000
Office furniture & fittings		24,000
		94,000
Current assets		
Stock	19,500	
Debtors	22,500	
Bank	500	
	42,500	
Less: Current liabilities		
Creditors	16,000	
Net current assets		26,500
Total assets less current liabilities		120,500
Less: Long-term liabilities		
Bank loan		22,000
Net assets		98,500
Capital		
Balance at 1 Jan 20X3		75,000
Add: profit for the year		33,500
		108,500
Less: drawings		10,000
Balance at 31 Dec 20X3		98,500

9.6 ***A. Evans***
Trading and profit & loss accounts for the year ended 30 June 20X2

	£	£	£
Sales			81,640
Less: returns inwards			840
Net sales			80,800
Less: Cost of sales			
Stock at 1 July 20X1		5,610	
Add: purchases	49,870		
Less: returns outwards	960	48,910	
		54,520	
Less: stock at 30 June 20X2		4,920	
			49,600
Gross profit			31,200
Add: interest received			620
			31,820
Less: Expenditure			
Carriage outwards		390	
Rent & rates		1,420	
Light & heat		710	
Telephone & postage		540	
Printing & stationery		230	
Bank interest		140	
			3,430
Net profit for the year			28,390

A. Evans
Balance sheet as at 30 June 20X2

	£	£	£
Fixed assets			
Leasehold premises			52,500
Motor vehicles			13,650
			66,150
Current assets			
Stock		4,920	
Debtors		2,630	
Investments		4,980	
Cash		460	
		12,990	
Less: Current liabilities			
Creditors	1,910		
Bank overdraft	3,620	5,530	
Net current assets			7,460
Total assets less current liabilities			73,610
Less: Long-term liabilities			
Loan—Solihull Bank			20,000
Net assets			53,610

Capital

Balance at 1 July 20X1	39,980
Add: profit for the year	28,390
	68,370
Less: drawings	14,760
Balance at 30 June 20X2	53,610

Note

1 The student should state that she or he is assuming that the investments are intended to be held for less than one year from the date of the balance sheet and are thus a current asset. Alternatively, it may be assumed that the investments are to be held for more than one accounting year and are therefore a fixed asset.

10 Accounting principles, concepts and policies

10.6 According to FRS18, 'the objectives against which an entity should judge the appropriateness of accounting policies to its particular circumstances are:

a relevance;
b reliability;
c comparability; and
d understandability' (ASB, 2000).

These are described below.

Relevance

Relevance is explained in FRS18 as follows: 'Financial information is relevant if it has the ability to influence the economic decisions of users and is provided in time to influence those decisions. Relevant information possesses either predictive or confirmatory value or both' (ASB, 2000).

Reliability

Reliability is explained in FRS18 as follows: 'Financial information is reliable if:

a it can be depended upon by users to represent faithfully what it either purports to represent or could reasonably be expected to represent, and therefore reflects the substance of the transactions and other events that have taken place;
b it is free from deliberate or systematic bias (i.e. it is neutral);
c it is free from material error;
d it is complete within the bounds of materiality; and
e under conditions of uncertainty, it has been prudently prepared (i.e. a degree of caution has been applied in exercising judgement and making the necessary estimates).

Appropriate accounting policies will result in financial information being presented that is reliable. They will present transactions and other events in a way that reflects their substance. A transaction or other event is faithfully represented in financial statements if the way in which it is recognised, measured and presented in those statements corresponds closely to the effect of that transaction or event.

Often there is uncertainty, either about the existence of assets, liabilities, gains, losses and changes to shareholders' funds, or about the amount at which they should be measured. Prudence requires that accounting policies take account of such uncertainty in recognising and measuring those assets, liabilities, gains, losses and changes to shareholders' funds. In conditions of uncertainty, appropriate accounting policies will require more confirmatory evidence about the existence of an asset or gain than about the existence of a liability or loss, and a greater reliability of measurement for assets and gains than for liabilities and losses' (ASB, 2000).

Comparability

Comparability is explained in FRS18 as follows: 'Information in an entity's financial statements gains greatly in usefulness if it can be compared with similar information about the entity for some other period or point in time, and with similar information about other entities. Such comparability can usually be achieved through a combination of consistency and disclosure' (ASB, 2000).

Understandability

Understandability is explained in FRS18 as follows: 'Information provided by financial statements needs to be capable of being understood by users having a reasonable knowledge of business and economic activities and accounting and a willingness to study with reasonable diligence the information provided' (ASB, 2000).

11 Depreciation and fixed assets

11.14 ***Workings***

Cost of machines purchased on 1 October 20X0 should include all transportation and installation expenditure:

£3,100 + £130 + £590 + £180 = £4,000
Cost per machine = £4,000 ÷ 2 = £2,000

Disposal

Aggregate depreciation from the date brought into use (1 April 20X1) until the date of disposal (31 March 20X9) = 10% × £2,000 × 8 years = £1,600
Book value at 31 March 20X9 = £2,000 − £1,600 = £400
Proceeds of sale = £800 − £100 = £700
Profit on sale = £700 − £400 = £300

b *Provision for depreciation* for year ended 30 September 20X9:

Machine owned all year: 10% × £2,000 = £200
Machine sold: 10% × £2,000 × 6 months = £100
Machine acquired—depreciation from the date brought into use (1 July 20X9) to the end of the accounting year:
10% × £2,800 × 3 months = £70
Total depreciation expense for year:
£200 + £100 + £70 = £370

a ***The journal***

			Debit	*Credit*
20X9			£	£
31 Mar	Machinery disposals	Dr	2,000	
	Machinery account			2,000
	Being the transfer of the cost of the machine sold to the disposals account			

Date	Particulars		Dr	Cr
31 Mar	Depreciation expense	Dr	100	
	Provision for depreciation			100
	Being depreciation for the current year on the machine sold			
31 Mar	Provision for depreciation	Dr	1,600	
	Machinery disposals			1,600
	Being the aggregate depreciation on the disposal			
31 Mar	H. Johnson/bank	Dr	800	
	Machinery disposals			800
	Being proceeds of sale of machinery sold			
31 Mar	Machinery disposals	Dr	100	
	Wages			100
	Being the labour cost of dismantling the machine sold			
31 Mar	Machinery disposals	Dr	300	
	Profit and loss account			300
	Being profit on sale of machine			
1 May	Machinery account	Dr	2,800	
	R. Adams/bank			2,800
	Being purchase of new machine			

Notes

1 It is likely that in practice the entries relating to depreciation and the profit on sale would be done at the end of the accounting year. However, examination questions like this often expect students to do them on the date of disposal.

2 Although not required by the question, students may find it useful to start by constructing the machinery disposals account in rough form as follows:

Machinery disposals

Machinery—cost	2,000	Provision for depreciation —aggregate depreciation	1,600
Wages—dismantling costs	100	H. Johnson—proceeds of sale	800
P & L—profit on sale	300		
	2,400		2,400

11.16 ***Workings***

Plant

Cost at 31 December 20X6 = 96,920 + 33,080 − 40,000 = £90,000

Depreciation for 20X6 = 10% × 90,000 = £9,000

Disposal:

Aggregate depreciation = 10% × 40,000 × 6 years = £24,000

Book value at disposal = 40,000 − 24,000 = £16,000

Loss on sale = 16,000 − 15,000 = £1,000

Vehicles

Disposal 1:

Aggregate depreciation—

20X3 = 25% × 3,200 = 800

20X4 = 25% × (3,200 − 800) = 600

20X5 = 25% × (3,200 − [800 + 600] = 450

Total = 800 + 600 + 450 = £1,850

Book value at disposal = 3,200 − 1,850 = £1,350

Loss on sale = 1,350 − 1,300 = £50

Disposal 2:

Aggregate depreciation—

20X4 = 25% × 4,800 = 1,200

20X5 = 25% × (4,800 − 1,200) = 900

Total = 1,200 + 900 = £2,100

Book value at disposal = 4,800 − 2,100 = £2,700

Profit on sale = 2,960 − 2,700 = £260

Remainder

Cost at 31 December 20X6 = 25,060 + 4,750 − 3,200 − 4,800 = £21,810

Aggregate depreciation at 31 December 20X6 = 14,560 − 1,850 − 2,100 = £10,610

Depreciation for 20X6 = 25% × (21,810 − 10,610) = £2,800

a ***The ledger***

Plant

20X6			20X6		
1 Jan	Balance b/d	96,920	31 Dec	Bank	15,000
31 Dec	Bank	33,080	31 Dec	Provision for dep'n	24,000
			31 Dec	P & L—loss	1,000
			31 Dec	Balance c/d	90,000
		130,000			130,000
20X7					
1 Jan	Balance b/d	90,000			

Provision for depreciation on plant

20X6			20X6		
31 Dec	Plant	24,000	1 Jan	Balance b/d	50,120
31 Dec	Balance c/d	35,120	31 Dec	P & L	9,000
		59,120			59,120
			20X7		
			1 Jan	Balance b/d	35,120

Vehicles

20X6			20X6		
1 Jan	Balance b/d	25,060	31 Dec	Bank—Vehicle	1,300
31 Dec	Bank	4,750	31 Dec	Provision for dep'n	1,850
			31 Dec	P & L—loss	50
			31 Dec	Bank—Vehicle	2,960
31 Dec	P & L—Profit	260	31 Dec	Provision for dep'n	2,100
			31 Dec	Balance c/d	21,810
		30,070			30,070
20X7					
1 Jan	Balance b/d	21,810			

Provision for depreciation on vehicles

20X6			20X6		
31 Dec	Vehicles	1,850	1 Jan	Balance b/d	14,560
31 Dec	Vehicles	2,100	31 Dec	P & L	2,800
31 Dec	Balance c/d	13,410			
		17,360			17,360
			20X7		
			1 Jan	Balance b/d	13,410

Profit & loss account

Dep'n on plant	9,000	Profit on sale vehicle	260
Dep'n on vehicles	2,800		
Loss on sale plant	1,000		
Loss on sale vehicle	50		

b *The journal*

			Debit	Credit
20X6		£	£	
31 Dec	Profit & loss account	Dr	9,000	
	Provision for dep'n—plant			9,000
	Being depreciation on plant for 20X6			
31 Dec	Profit & loss account	Dr	2,800	
	Provision for dep'n—vehicles			2,800
	Being depreciation on vehicles for 20X6			

Alternative method—disposals account

Plant

20X6		20X6		
1 Jan	Balance b/d 96,920	31 Dec	Disposals	40,000
31 Dec	Bank 33,080	31 Dec	Balance c/d	90,000
	130,000			130,000
20X7				
1 Jan	Balance b/d 90,000			

Plant disposals

20X6		20X6		
31 Dec	Plant 40,000	31 Dec	Bank	15,000
		31 Dec	Provision for dep'n	24,000
		31 Dec	P & L—loss	1,000
	40,000			40,000

Vehicles

20X6		20X6		
1 Jan	Balance b/d 25,060	31 Dec	Disposal 1	3,200
31 Dec	Bank 4,750	31 Dec	Disposal 2	4,800
		31 Dec	Balance c/d	21,810
	29,810			29,810
20X7				
1 Jan	Balance b/d 21,810			

Vehicle disposals

20X6		20X6		
31 Dec	Vehicles 1 3,200	31 Dec	Bank—Vehicle	11,300
31 Dec	Vehicles 2 4,800	31 Dec	Provision for dep'n	1,850
		31 Dec	P & L—loss	50
		31 Dec	Bank—Vehicle	2,960
31 Dec	P & L—profit 260	31 Dec	Provision for dep'n	2,100
	8,260			8,260

11.18 a The criteria that must be met under *SSAP13—Accounting for Research and Development* if development expenditure is to be capitalized are as follows:

a there is a clearly defined project; and

b the related expenditure is separately identifiable; and

c the outcome of such a project has been assessed with reasonable certainty as to:

i its technical feasibility, and

ii its ultimate commercial viability; and

d the aggregate of the deferred development costs, any further development costs, and related production, selling and administration costs is reasonably expected to be exceeded by related future sales or other revenues, and

e adequate resources exist, or are reasonably expected to be available, to enable the project to be completed and to provide any consequential increase in working capital.

b *Workings*

Development expenditure

Project	Balance at 30.9.X7 £000	Expenditure in current year to be written off £000	Expenditure in previous years to be written off £000	Amortization in current year £000	Capitalized in current year £000	Balance at 30.9.X8 £000
A	600			200		400
B	2,400			440		1,960
C	3,600				400	4,000
D	1,200	300	1,200			
E					800	800
F					400	400
	7,800	300	1,200	640	1,600	7,560

Amortization: A = £1m × 0.2 = £200k; B = £2,400k × 0.2 × $\frac{11}{12}$ = £440k

Current year's R&D expenditure = £(1,800k + 300k) = £2,100k

Charge to P&L = £(2,100k + 1,200k + 640k) = £3,940k

Profit & loss account

Included in the cost of sales will be research & development of £3,940,000.

Balance sheet

Disclosed separately under the heading of intangible assets, where material, will be development costs of £7,560,000.

c *Notes to the accounts*

Accounting policies

Research expenditure is written off in the year in which it is incurred. Development expenditure meeting the criteria in SSAP13 is capitalized and amortized on a straight line basis over 5 years beginning when sales revenue is first generated.

Research & development

The charge to the profit and loss account is made up as follows:

	£000	£000
Research & development		
Current year's expenditure		2,100
Past year's expenditure written off	1,200	
Amortization of deferred expenditure		
from previous years	640	1,840
		3,940

The development expenditure shown in the balance sheet is made up as follows:

	£000	£000
Deferred development expenditure		
Balance at 30 Sep 20X7		7,800
Written off during the year	(1,200)	
Amortization	(640)	(1,840)
		5,960
Expenditure capitalized in year		1,600
Balance at 30 Sep 20X8		7,560

12 Bad debts and provisions for bad debts

12.5 ***Workings***

	£
Debtors at 31 July 20X1	15,680
Less: bad debts (410 + 270)	680
Revised debtors at 31 July 20X1	15,000
Provision for bad debts = 4% × £15,000 = £600	

The ledger

A. Wall

20X1		20X1	
31 July Balance b/d	410	31 July Bad debts	410

B. Wood

31 July Balance b/d	270	31 July Bad debts	270

Bad debts

31 July A. Wall	410	31 July Profit & loss	680
31 July B. Wood	270		
	680		680

Provision for bad debts

		31 July Profit & loss	600

Profit & loss account

Bad debts	680
Provision for bad debts	600

12.6 ***Workings***

	£
Debtors at 30 Apr 20X5	19,500
Less: bad debts (620 + 880)	1,500
Revised debtors at 30 Apr 20X5	18,000
Provision for bad debts at 30 Apr 20X5	
(3% × 18,000)	540
Less: provision for bad debts at 30 Apr 20X4	750
Reduction in provision for bad debts	210

The ledger

A. Winters

20X5		20X5	
30 Apr Balance b/d	620	30 Apr Bad debts	620

D. Spring

30 Apr Balance b/d	880	30 Apr Bad debts	880

Bad debts

30 Apr A. Winters	620	30 Apr Profit & loss	1,500
30 Apr D. Spring	880		
	1,500		1,500

Provisions for bad debts

20X5		20X4	
30 Apr Profit & loss	210	30 Apr Balance b/d	750
30 Apr Balance c/d	540		
	750		750
		20X5	
		1 May Balance b/d	540

Profit & loss account

Bad debts	1,500	Provision for bad debts	210

12.11 ***Workings***

	£	£	£
Provision for bad debts			
Specific provision (320 – 70)			250
General provision—			
Debtors at 31 Dec 20X7		12,610	
Less: bad debts (210 + [260 – 110])	360		
specific provision	250	610	
Revised debtors at 31 Dec 20X7		12,000	
Provision at 31 Dec 20X7			
(5% × 12,000)			600
Total provision for bad debts at 31 Dec 20X7			850
Less: provision for bad debts at 31 Dec 20X6			1,260
Reduction in provision for bad debts			410

Provision for depreciation

Date of purchase or sale	Details	Depreciation on disposal £	Depreciation for year ended 31 Dec 20X7 £
	Depreciation on disposal		
1 July 20X5	For year ending 31.12.X5—25% × 8,000 × $\frac{6}{12}$	1,000	
	For year ending 31.12.X6—25% × (8,000 − 1,000)	1,750	
31 Mar 20X7	For year ending 31.12.X7— 25% × (8,000 − [1,000 + 1,750]) × $\frac{3}{12}$	328	328
		3,078	
	Book value at 31.3.X7: 8,000 − 3,078 = £4,922		
	Loss on sale: 4,922 − 4,000 = £922		
	Depreciation on acquisition		
31 Mar 20X7	25% × (4,000 + 1,000) × $\frac{9}{12}$		938
	Depreciation on remainder		
	Cost = 30,000 − 8,000 = £22,000		
	Aggregate depreciation: 12,500 − (1,000 + 1,750) = £9,750		
	WDV = 22,000 − 9,750 = £12,250		
	Depreciation = 25% × 12,250		3,063
			4,329

a ***The ledger***

A. Bee

20X7			20X7		
1 Jan	Balance b/d	320	30 Apr	Bank	70
			30 Apr	Balance c/d	250
		320			320
1 May	Balance b/d	250			

J. Kay

1 Jan	Balance b/d	210	15 June	Bad debts	210

C. Dee

1 Jan	Balance b/d	180	3 Aug	Bank	180

F. Gee

1 Jan	Balance b/d	260	7 Oct	Bank	110
			7 Oct	Bad debts	150
		260			260

Bad debts

15 June	J. Kay	210	31 Dec	Profit & loss	360
7 Oct	F. Gee	150			
		360			360

Provision for bad debts

31 Dec	Profit & loss	410	1 Jan	Balance b/d	1,260
31 Dec	Balance c/d	850			
		1,260			1,260
			20X8		
			1 Jan	Balance b/d	850

Plant & machinery

1 Jan	Balance b/d	30,000	31 Mar	Part exchange	4,000
31 Mar	Bank	1,000	31 Dec	Provision for depreciation	3,078
31 Mar	Part exchange	4,000	31 Dec	Profit & loss—loss on sale	922
			31 Dec	Balance c/d	27,000
		35,000			35,000
20X8					
1 Jan	Balance b/d	27,000			

Provision for depreciation

31 Dec	Plant & machinery	3,078	1 Jan	Balance b/d	12,500
31 Dec	Balance c/d	13,751	31 Dec	Profit & loss	4,329
		16,829			16,829
			20X8		
			1 Jan	Balance b/d	13,751

Profit & loss account

Bad debts	360	Provision for bad debts	410
Provision for depreciation	4,329		
Loss on sale of plant	922		

b Provisions for bad debts and depreciation are both provisions. A provision is the setting aside of income to meet a known or highly probable future liability or loss, the amount and/or timing of which cannot be ascertained exactly, and thus an estimate has to be made. Provisions for bad debts and depreciation are both intended to provide for a future loss. A provision for bad debts provides for the loss which occurs when debtors fail to pay their debts. Depreciation is the loss in value of a fixed asset, and a provision for depreciation is intended to provide for the loss when fixed assets are sold at a price below their cost.

13 Accruals and prepayments

13.2 ***The ledger***

Rent

		£			£
20X2			20X2		
1 Jan	Prepayment b/d	300	31 Dec	Profit & loss	3,730
29 Jan	Bank	930	31 Dec	Prepayment c/d	320
2 May	Bank	930			
30 July	Bank	930			
5 Nov	Bank	960			
		4,050			4,050
20X3					
1 Jan	Prepayment b/d	320			

Light & heat

		£			£
20X2			20X2		
6 Mar	Bank	420	1 Jan	Accrual b/d	140
4 June	Bank	360	31 Dec	Profit & loss	1,450
3 Sep	Bank	270			
7 Dec	Bank	390			
31 Dec	Accrual c/d	150			
		1,590			1,590
			20X3		
			1 Jan	Accrual b/d	150

Workings

Rent prepaid at 1 Jan 20X2 = $\frac{1}{3} \times 900 =$ £300

Rent prepaid at 31 Dec 20X2 = $\frac{1}{3} \times 960 =$ £320

Light & heat accrued at 1 Jan 20X2 = $\frac{1}{3} \times 420 =$ £140

Light & heat accrued at 31 Dec 20X2 = $\frac{1}{3} \times 450 =$ £150

13.5 The entries in a rent receivable account are on the opposite side to those in a rent payable account. The credit to the profit and loss account is the difference between the two sides of the ledger account after entering all the prepayments (or accruals).

The derivation of the purchases on credit will be unfamiliar to students at this point in their studies. It is discussed in depth in Chapter 19. However, the principle is very similar to expense accounts containing accruals. A total creditors' (control) account is used in place of the individual personal accounts of the creditors. The creditors at the start and end of the year are entered on the same sides as accruals in an expense account, as are the payments. The credit purchases for the year is then the difference between the two sides of the creditors' account.

The ledger

Rents receivable

		£			£
20X5			20X4		
31 May	P & L	4,004	1 June	Prepayment b/d	463
31 May	Prepayment c/d	517	20X5		
			31 May	Bank	4,058
		4,521			4,521
			1 June	Prepayment b/d	517

Rent & rates payable

		£			£
20X4			20X4		
1 June	Prepayment b/d	1,246	1 June	Accrual b/d	315
20X5			20X5		
31 May	Bank—rent	7,491	31 May	P & L	10,100
31 May	Bank—rates	2,805	31 May	Prepayment c/d	1,509
31 May	Accrual c/d	382			
		11,924			11,924
1 June	Prepayment b/d	1,509	1 June	Accrual b/d	382

Total creditors

		£			£
20X5			20X4		
31 May	Bank	75,181	1 June	Balance b/d	5,258
31 May	Discount rec'd	1,043	20X5		
31 May	Balance c/d	4,720	31 May	P & L—purchases	75,686
		80,944			80,944
			1 June	Balance b/d	4,720

14 The preparation of final accounts from the trial balance

14.1 ***Workings***

Rent prepaid = $\frac{3}{6} \times \frac{6}{12} \times$ £6,400 = £1,600

Rates prepaid = $\frac{3}{12} \times$ £1,488 = £372

Rent and rates prepaid = £(1,600 + 372) = £1,972

Provision for doubtful debts:

At 31 December 20X9 = 5% × £(72,300 − 1,420) = £3,544

Reduction in provision = £(3,702 − 3,544) = £158

Depreciation on car = 20% × £7,200 = £1,440

C. Jones

Extended trial balance as at 31 December 20X9

	Trial balance		Adjustments		Profit & loss a/c		Balance sheet	
	Dr £	Cr £	Dr £	Cr £	Dr £	Cr £	Dr £	Cr £
Capital		45,214	9,502					35,712
Drawings	9,502			9,502				
Purchases	389,072				389,072			
Sales		527,350				527,350		
Wages & salaries	33,440		3,012	3,012	36,452			3,012
Rent & rates	9,860		1,972	1,972	7,888		1,972	
Light & heat	4,142				4,142			
Bad debts	1,884		1,420		3,304			

	Trial balance		Adjustments		Profit & loss a/c		Balance sheet	
	Dr	Cr	Dr	Cr	Dr	Cr	Dr	Cr
	£	£	£	£	£	£	£	£
Provision doubtful debts		3,702	158			158		3,544
Debtors	72,300			1,420			70,880	
Creditors		34,308						34,308
Bank	2,816						2,816	
Cash	334						334	
Stock	82,124		99,356	82,124	82,124	99,356	99,356	
Motor car—cost	7,200						7,200	
Motor car—depreciation		2,100		1,440	1,440			3,540
Profit					102,442			102,442
	612,674	612,674			626,864	626,864	182,558	182,558

C. Jones
Trading and profit & loss accounts
for the year ended 31 December 20X9

	£	£
Sales		527,350
Less: cost of sales		
Stock at 1 Jan 20X9	82,124	
Add: purchases	389,072	
	471,196	
Less: stock at 31 Dec 20X9	99,356	371,840
Gross profit		155,510
Add: reduction in provision for doubtful debts		158
		155,668
Less: Expenditure		
Wages & salaries	36,452	
Rent & rates	7,888	
Light & heat	4,142	
Bad debts	3,304	
Provision for depreciation	1,440	
		53,226
Net profit		102,442

C. Jones
Balance sheet as at 31 December 20X9

	£	£	£
Fixed assets			
Motor car at cost			7,200
Less: provision for depreciation			3,540
			3,660
Current assets			
Stock		99,356	
Debtors	70,880		
Less: provision for doubtful debts	3,544	67,336	
Prepayments		1,972	
Bank		2,816	
Cash		334	
		171,814	
Less: Current liabilities			
Creditors	34,308		
Accruals	3,012	37,320	
Net current assets			134,494
Net assets			138,154

Capital	
Balance at 1 Jan 20X9	45,214
Add: net profit for the year	102,442
	147,656
Less: drawings	9,502
Balance at 31 Dec 20X9	138,154

14.2 ***J. Clark***
Trading and profit & loss accounts
for the year ended 31 March 20X6

	£	£	£
Sales (58,640 – 400)			58,240
Less: Returns inwards			3,260
Net sales			54,980
Less: Cost of sales—			
Opening stock		4,670	
Add: Purchases (34,260 – 350)	33,910		
Less: Returns outwards	2,140		
	31,770		
Add: Carriage inwards	730	32,500	
		37,170	
Less: Closing stock (3,690 + 300)		3,990	33,180
Gross profit			21,800
Add: Discount received			1,970
Investment income			460
			24,230
Less: Expenditure			
Carriage outward		420	
Discount allowed		1,480	
Depreciation on plant (25% × [11,350 – 4,150])		1,800	
Depreciation on vehicles		1,986	
Loss on sale of vehicle		264	
Interest payable		1,000	
Wages		7,180	
Rent & rates (4,300 – 210)		4,090	
Provision for bad debts ([10% × (8,070 – 370 – 400)] – 530)		200	
Bad debts		370	
Light & heat (2,640 + 130)		2,770	
Stationery (450 – 230)		220	21,780
Net profit			2,450

J. Clark
Balance sheet as at 31 March 20X6

	£ Cost	£ Aggreg depn	£ WDV
Fixed assets			
Freehold premises	32,000	—	32,000
Plant & machinery (4,150 + 1,800)	11,350	5,950	5,400
Motor vehicles (13,290 – 1,000)	12,290	4,498	7,792
	55,640	10,448	45,192
Goodwill			5,000
			50,192
Current assets			
Stationery stock		230	
Stock (3,690 + 300)		3,990	
Trade debtors (8,070 – 370 – 400)	7,300		
Less: Provision for bad debts	730	6,570	
Sundry debtor		458	
Prepayments		210	
Quoted investments		6,470	
Bank & cash		2,850	
		20,778	
Less: Current liabilities			
Creditors	4,340		
Accruals	130	4,470	
Net current assets			16,308
Total assets less current liabilities			66,500
Less: Long-term liabilities			
Mortgage on premises			10,000
Net assets			56,500
Capital			
Balance at 1 April 20X5			60,000
Add: Net profit for year			2,450
			62,450
Less: Drawings (5,600 + 350)			5,950
Balance at 31 March 20X6			56,500

Workings: Depreciation on vehicles

	Previous years £	*This year* £
Disposal		
20X3/X4 20% × £1,000 × $\frac{3}{12}$	50	
20X4/X5 20% × (£1,000 – £50)	190	
	240	
20X5/X6		
20% × [£1,000 – (£50 + £190)] × $\frac{3}{12}$	38	38
	278	

Book value at sale = £1,000 – £278 = £722
Loss on sale = £722 – £458 = £264

Depreciation on remaining		
20% × [(£13,290 – £1,000) – (£2,790 – £240)]		1,948
		1,986

Aggregate depreciation at 31 March 20X6
£2,790 + £1,986 – £278 = £4,498

Note

1 It is assumed that the quoted investments are to be held for less than one accounting year.

15 Manufacturing accounts and the valuation of stock

15.11 ***Upton Upholstery***
Manufacturing, trading and profit & loss accounts for the year ended 30 April 20X4

	£		£
Direct materials			
Stock at 1 May 20X3	4,000	*Cost of completed production* c/d	114,900
Add: purchases	84,000		
carriage inwards	1,200		
	89,200		
Less: stock at 30 Apr 20X4	5,400		
	83,800		
Direct wages (19,900 + 600)	20,500		
Prime costs	104,300		
Factory overheads			
Depreciation: machinery (28,000 ÷ 7)	4,000		
Light & heat (3,000 × $\frac{4}{5}$)	2,400		
Rent & rates (6,600 – [$\frac{1}{3}$ × 600]) × $\frac{3}{4}$	4,800		
Manufacturing costs	115,500		
Add: WIP at 1 May 20X3	16,400		
	131,900		
Less: WIP at 30 Apr 20X4	17,000		
	114,900		114,900
Finished goods		Sales	140,000
Stock at 1 May 20X3	9,000		
Add: cost of completed production b/d	114,900		
	123,900		
Less: stock at 30 Apr 20X4	8,000		
Cost of sales	115,900		
Gross profit c/d	24,100		
	140,000		140,000
Selling & distribution costs:		*Gross profit* b/d	24,100
Carriage outwards	700		
Sales commission	1,400		
Provision for doubtful debts	1,000		
Administrative costs:			
Depreciation: equipment 25% × (2,000 – 800)	300		
Light & heat (3,000 × $\frac{1}{5}$)	600		
Rent & rates (6,600 – [$\frac{1}{3}$ × 600]) × $\frac{1}{4}$	1,600		
Office wages (5,200 + 100)	5,300		
	10,900		
Net profit	13,200		
	24,100		24,100

Upton Upholstery
Balance sheet as at 30 April 20X4

	£	£	£
Fixed assets	*Cost*	*Aggreg. depn*	*WDV*
Factory machinery (5,000 + 4,000)	28,000	9,000	19,000
Office equipment (800 + 300)	2,000	1,100	900
	30,000	10,100	19,900
Current assets			
Stocks (5,400 + 17,000 + 8,000)		30,400	
Trade debtors	15,000		
Less: provision for bad debts	1,000	14,000	
Prepaid rent		200	
Cash & bank		2,300	
		46,900	
Less: Current liabilities			
Trade creditors	16,000		
Accrued costs (600 + 100)	700	16,700	
Net current assets			30,200
Total assets less current liabilities			50,100
Less: long-term liabilities			
Bank loan			11,000
Net assets			39,100
Capital			
Balance at 1 May 20X3			35,000
Add: profit for the year			13,200
			48,200
Less: drawings			9,100
Balance at 30 April 20X4			39,100

Note

1 The manufacturing, trading and profit & loss accounts have been shown in account form for the purpose of emphasizing that these are accounts in the ledger. However, students are advised to use vertical form in answering other questions in this chapter.

15.12 *Manufacturing account for the year ended 31 December 20X9*

	£	£
Raw materials:		
Stock at 1 Jan 20X9		2,453
Add: purchases (47,693 – 2,093)	45,600	
Less: returns outward	4,921	
		40,679
		43,132
Less: stock at 31 Dec 20X9		3,987
		39,145
Direct wages (23,649 – 549)		23,100
Direct expenses:		
Carriage inwards	683	
Royalties	7,500	8,183
Prime cost		70,428
Factory overheads:		
Supervisors' wages	5,617	
Electricity—factory	2,334	
Depreciation on plant	13,400	
Rent and rates—factory	3,600	
Insurance on plant	1,750	
Repairs to plant	917	27,618
Factory costs		98,046
Add: WIP at 1 Jan 20X9		1,617
		99,663
Less: WIP at 31 Dec 20X9		2,700
		96,963
Less: proceeds from the sale of scrap		199
Factory cost of completed production		96,764

Trading and profit & loss account for the year ended 31 December 20X9

	£	£
Sales		145,433
Less: cost of sales:		
Stock of finished goods at 1 Jan 20X9	3,968	
Add: factory cost of production	96,764	
Purchases of finished goods	367	
	101,099	
Less: stock of finished goods at 31 Dec 20X9	5,666	
Cost of sales		95,433
Gross profit		50,000
Add: discount received		2,310
		52,310
Selling and distribution overheads:		
Carriage outwards	487	
Salaries and commission	8,600	
Bad debts	726	
Discount allowed	1,515	
Depreciation—vehicles	3,700	
Delivery expenses	593	
Advertising	625	
	16,246	
Administrative overheads:		
Salaries	10,889	
Light and heat	998	
Depreciation—fixtures & furniture	1,900	
Rent and rates	1,200	
Postage and telephone	714	
Printing and stationery	363	
	16,064	
Financial charges:		
Loan interest	3,000	
Bank charges	100	
	3,100	
		35,410
Net profit		16,900

Notes

1 The carriage inwards could have been added to the cost of purchases of raw materials.

2 The proceeds from the sale of scrap metal could have been deducted from the cost of raw materials.

15.18 a *Cost of sales*

FIFO

Quantity	Purchases Price £	Value £	Quantity	Cost of sales Price £	Value £	Quantity	Stock Price £	Value £
1,200	1.00	1,200				1,200	1.00	1,200
1,000	1.05	1,050				2,200		2,250
			800	1.00	800	400	1.00	400
						1,000	1.05	1,050
						1,400		1,450
600	1.10	660				2,000		2,110
			400	1.00	400			
			200	1.05	210	800	1.05	840
			600		610	600	1.10	660
						1,400		1,500
900	1.20	1,080				2,300		2,580
			800	1.05	840			
			300	1.10	330	300	1.10	330
			1,100		1,170	900	1.20	1,080
						1,200		1,410
800	1.25	1,000				2,000		2,410
			300	1.10	330			
			900	1.20	1,080			
			100	1.25	125	700	1.25	875
			1,300		1,535			
700	1.30	910				1,400		1,785
			400	1.25	500	300	1.25	375
						700	1.30	910
5,200		5,900	4,200		4,615	1,000		1,285

LIFO

Quantity	Purchases Price £	Value £	Quantity	Cost of sales Price £	Value £	Quantity	Stock Price £	Value £
1,200	1.00	1,200				1,200	1.00	1,200
1,000	1.05	1,050				2,200		2,250
			800	1.05	840	200	1.05	210
						1,200	1.00	1,200
						1,400		1,410
600	1.10	660				2,000		2,070
			600	1.10	660	1,400		1,410
900	1.20	1,080				2,300		2,490
			900	1.20	1,080			
			200	1.05	210			
			1,100		1,290	1,200	1.00	1,200
800	1.25	1,000				2,000		2,200
			800	1.25	1,000			
			500	1.00	500	700	1.00	700
			1,300		1,500			
700	1.30	910				1,400		1,610
			400	1.30	520	300	1.30	390
						700	1.00	700
5,200		5,900	4,200		4,810	1,000		1,090

Weighted average

	£
Purchases	5,900
Less: stock 1,000 @ (5,900 ÷ 5,200)	1,135
Cost of sales	4,765

b *Workings*

Sales	*Quantity* Units	*Price* £	*Value* £
	800	1.70	1,360
	600	1.90	1,140
	1,100	2.00	2,200
	1,300	2.00	2,600
	400	2.05	820
	4,200		8,120

Bank

Capital	6,000	Purchases	5,900
Sales	8,120	Expenses (1,740 − 570)	1,170
		Balance c/d	7,050
	14,120		14,120
Balance b/d	7,050		

	FIFO £	*LIFO* £	*WA* £
Profit & loss account			
Sales	8,120	8,120	8,120
Less: cost of sales	4,615	4,810	4,765
Gross profit	3,505	3,310	3,355
Less: expenses	1,740	1,740	1,740
Net profit	1,765	1,570	1,615
Balance sheet			
Stock	1,285	1,090	1,135
Bank	7,050	7,050	7,050
Total assets	8,335	8,140	8,185
Less: accrued expenses	570	570	570
Net assets	7,765	7,570	7,615
Capital at start of period	6,000	6,000	6,000
Add: profit for year	1,765	1,570	1,615
Capital at end of period	7,765	7,570	7,615

16 The bank reconciliation statement

16.4 *The ledger*

Cash book

Balance b/d	2,880	Bank charges	105
Dividends	189	Refer to drawer	54
		Error (£141 × 2)	282
		Balance c/d	2,628
	3,069		3,069

Grow Ltd

Bank reconciliation statement at 31 March 20X9

	£	£
Balance per cash book		2,628
Add: Cheques not yet presented (642 + 1,200)		1,842
		4,470
Less: Amounts not yet credited	1,904	
Cheque debited in error by bank	216	
		2,120
Balance per bank statement		2,350

16.5 a *Mrs Lake*

Bank reconciliation statement as at 30 April 20X8

	£	£
Balance per bank account		1,310.40
Add: Error cheque no. 236130 (£87.77—£77.87)	9.90	
Receipts not entered in bank account	21.47	
Cheques not yet presented (£30 + £52.27)	82.27	113.64
		1,424.04
Less: Payments not entered in bank account (£12.80 + £32.52)	45.32	
Amounts not yet credited	192.80	238.12
		1,185.92
Less: Undetected error		19.47
Balance per bank statement		1,166.45

b The undetected error would require further investigation. The amount is the same as cheque number 427519 on 10 April. This cheque number is different from the sequence of the others, which suggests that it may have been debited to Mrs Lake's account in error.

Note

1 Students should have realized that cheques numbered 236126 and 236127 shown on the bank statement are in the cash book for March and were unpresented at 31 March (Reconciliation at 31 March 20X8: £1,053.29 − £15.21 − £210.70 = £827.38). No entries are required in the bank reconciliation at 30 April 20X8 since these are on the bank statement for April.

17 Control accounts

17.2 *The ledger*

Sales ledger control

20X6			20X7		
1 July	Balance b/d	40,000	30 June	Returns inwards	15,750
20X7					
30 June	Sales	386,829	30 June	Discount allowed	5,443
			30 June	Bad debts	3,400
			30 June	Bank	230,040
			30 June	Balance c/d	172,196
		426,829			426,829
1 July	Balance b/d	172,196			

Purchases ledger control

20X7			20X6		
30 June	Returns outwards	8,660	1 July	Balance b/d	31,200
			20X7		
30 June	Discount received	3,187	30 June	Purchases	222,954
30 June	Bank	108,999			
30 June	Balance c/d	133,308			
		254,154			254,154
			1 July	Balance b/d	133,308

17.4 ***The ledger***

Debtors' control account

20X1			20X1		
1 Jan	Balance b/d	4,200	1 Jan	Balance b/d	300
31 Jan	Sales	23,000	31 Jan	Returns inward	750
31 Jan	Dishonoured cheques	1,850	31 Jan	Bank	16,250
			31 Jan	Discount allow.	525
31 Jan	Bad debts recovered	230	31 Jan	Bad debts	670
			31 Jan	Bills receivable	5,300
31 Jan	Interest on overdue accts	120	31 Jan	Creditors contra	930
			31 Jan	Allowances	340
31 Jan	Balance c/d	240	31 Jan	Balance c/d	4,575
		29,640			29,640
1 Feb	Balance b/d	4,575	1 Feb	Balance b/d	240

Creditors' control account

1 Jan	Balance b/d	250	1 Jan	Balance b/d	6,150
31 Jan	Returns outward	450	31 Jan	Purchases	21,500
			31 Jan	Balance c/d	420
31 Jan	Bank	19,800			
31 Jan	Discount rec'd	325			
31 Jan	Bills payable	4,500			
31 Jan	Debtors contra	930			
31 Jan	Allowances rec'd	280			
31 Jan	Balance c/d	1,535			
		28,070			28,070
1 Feb	Balance b/d	420	1 Feb	Balance b/d	1,535

Notes

1 The following items do not appear in control accounts: carriage inwards, carriage outwards; provision for bad debts; cash received from bills receivable; cash paid on bills payable.

2 The debit balance on the debtors' control account is calculated by subtracting the total of the credit side from the debit side. The credit balance on the creditors' control account is calculated in a similar way.

3 The credit balances on the debtors' control account are probably the result of debtors overpaying, possibly in instances where they have been sent a credit note for goods and also paid for them. Similarly, the debit balances on the creditors' control account may be due to this business overpaying some of its creditors.

4 Although credit balances on the debtors' control account and debit balances on the creditors' control account are frequently encountered in examinations, in practice each control account can only throw up one balance which would naturally be the difference between the two sides of the control account. This balance should then agree with the difference between the total of the debit and credit balances of the personal accounts in the personal ledger.

5 Sometimes goods are bought from a business to whom goods were also sold. In these circumstances the amounts owed may be set off against each other and a cheque paid/received for the difference. The amount set off is referred to as a personal ledger contra and in the above example is £930.

6 It is assumed that the actual money received that relates to debts that were previously written off as bad (£230) is included in cheques received from debtors. Thus, the item 'bad debts recovered' is treated as an instruction to reverse the entry by which they were originally written off.

17.5 a ***The ledger***

Debtors' control

Balance b/d	14,364	Bank	118,258
Sales	138,208	Discount allowed	3,692
Bad debts recovered	84	Returns inwards	1,966
Cash	132	Bills receivable	6,486
Interest on overdue accts	20	Bad debts	1,186
		Creditors ledger	606
		Balance c/d	20,614
	152,808		152,808
Balance b/d	20,614		

b *Debtors' ledger control account*

	£
Original balance	20,614
Add: Sales day book undercast	1,000
	21,614
Less: Discount allowed omitted	50
Amended balance	21,564
Debtors' ledger	
Original balances	20,914
Add: Amount of cheque transposed (£4,300 – £3,400)	900
	21,814
Less: Returns posted incorrectly (£125 × 2)	250
Amended balance	21,564

17.6 a ***The ledger***

Debtors' control

	£		£
Balance b/d	17,220	Bank	45,280
Sales	98,730	Returns inwards	18,520
		Bills receivable	29,160
		Discount allowed	6,940
		Bad debts	4,920
		Transfer to creditors	2,850
		Balance c/d	8,280
	115,950		115,950
Balance b/d	8,280		

Creditors' control

Bank	38,020	Balance b/d	20,490
Returns outwards	16,010	Purchases	85,860
Bills payable	21,390	Cash	2,430
Discount received	7,680		
Transfer to debtors	2,850		
Balance c/d	22,830		
	108,780		108,780
		Balance b/d	22,830

b *Creditors' ledger*

	£
Original balances	20,700
Add: cheque posted wrongly (£3,400 – £340)	3,060
	23,760
Less: returns outward error (£180 × 2)	360
Amended balance	23,400
Creditor ledger control:	
Original balance	22,830
Add: discount received (£210 – £120)	90
	22,920
Less: purchases day book overcast	500
Amended balance	22,420

Undetected error = £23,400 – £22,420 = £980

18 Errors and suspense accounts

18.4 *The Journal*

		Debit £	Credit £
1 Light & heat	Dr	32	
Suspense			32
Being correction of posting error			
2 Suspense	Dr	28	
Wages			28
Being correction of arithmetic error			
3 Rent	Dr	720	
Suspense			720
Being correction of transposed figures			
4 Motor vehicles	Dr	3,000	
Purchases			3,000
Being correction of error of principle			
5 A Watson	Dr	80	
A. Watt			80
Being correction of an error of commission			
6 Sales	Dr	100	
Loose tools			100
Being correction of error of principle			
7 Postage & telephone	Dr	17	
Carriage outwards			17
Being correction of error of commission			
8 Bank charges	Dr	41	
Cash book			41
Being correction of error of omission			
9 Stationery	Dr	9	
Sales			9
Being correction of a compensating error			
10 J. Bloggs/Debtors' control	Dr	108	
Sales			108
Being correction of error of prime entry			
11 Suspense	Dr	124	
Trial balance			124
Being correction of extraction error			

The ledger

Suspense

Difference per trial balance	600	Light & heat	32
Wages	28	Rent	720
Extraction error	124		
	752		752

18.8 a *The journal*

20X9			Debit £	Credit £
March 31	Cash book	Dr	10,000	
	Suspense account			10,000
	Being correction of undercast on debit side of cash book			
	Freehold premises:	Dr	5,000	
	Suspense account			5,000
	Being correction of purchase of building in cash book not posted to ledger			
	Suspense account	Dr	900	
	Purchases			900
	Being correction of purchases of £100 entered in PDB summary as £1,000			
	Carriage	Dr	405	
	Suspense account			405
	Being correction of transport charge of £450 entered in PDB summary as £45			
	Rent receivable	Dr	45	
	Suspense account			45
	Being correction of rent received of £45 posted twice to the ledger			
	Debtors' control	Dr	100	
	Suspense account			100
	Being correction of undercast on debit side of debtors' control account			

Notes

1 Item 3 relates to errors in a PDB summary which is used to post the nominal ledger. It is assumed that the creditors' personal ledger is posted from the PDB and not the summary, and thus the individual creditors' personal account and control account are correct.
2 Item 5 assumes that the debtors' control account is part of the double entry in the ledger and thus the balance is included in the balance sheet.
3 Items 6 to 9 do not necessitate entries in the suspense account but will require journal entries for their correction.
4 Check that the balance on the suspense account has been eliminated as follows:

Suspense

Per trial balance	14,650	Cash book	10,000
Purchases	900	Freehold premises	5,000
		Carriage	405
		Rent receivable	45
		Debtors' control	100
	15,550		15,550

b ***Workings***

For examination purposes these are probably best done by simple horizontal calculations. However, the ledger accounts are shown below to aid the student's understanding of the double entry involved.

Bank account

Correction of undercast	10,000	Balance b/d	1,230
		Bank charges	3,250
		Balance c/d	5,520
	10,000		10,000
Balance b/d	5,520		

Freehold premises

Balance b/d	60,000
Correction of posting error	5,000
	65,000

Debtors' control

Balance b/d	37,140
Correction of undercast	100
	37,240

Provision for depreciation on vehicles

Balance b/d	11,935
P & L a/c	500
	12,435

Stock

Balance b/d	75,410
Undervaluation	1,250
	76,660

Creditors' control

Balance b/d	41,360
Purchases	2,110
	43,470

Profit & loss account

Carriage	405	Balance b/d	33,500
Rent receivable	45	Purchases	900
Bank charges	3,250	Stock	1,250
Depreciation on vehicles	500		
Purchases	2,110		
Revised profit	29,340		
	35,650		35,650

Miscup
Balance sheet as at 31 March 20X9

	£	£	£
Fixed assets	*Cost*	*Agg. dep'n*	*WDV*
Freehold premises	65,000	—	65,000
Motor vehicles	25,000	12,435	12,565
Fixtures and fittings	1,500	750	750
	91,500	13,185	78,315
Current assets			
Stock		76,660	
Debtors		37,240	
Bank		5,520	
Cash		75	
		119,495	
Less: Current liabilities			
Trade creditors and accrued charges		43,470	
Net current assets			76,025
Net assets			154,340

Capital	125,000
Add: profit for the year	29,340
	154,340

19 Single entry and incomplete records

19.2 ***Workings for plant***

	£	£
Cost at 30 June 20X4		50,000
Add: additions		20,000
		70,000
Less: disposals		10,000
Cost at 30 June 20X5		60,000
Aggregate depreciation		
Depreciation at 30 June 20X4 (£50,00 – £31,000)		19,000
Add: depreciation for the year		
on addition (10% × £20,000 × 3 mths)	500	
on disposal (10% × £10,000 × 3 mths)	250	
on rest (10% × [£50,000 – £10,000])	4,000	
		4,750
		23,750
Less: aggregate depreciation on disposal 10% × £10,000 × 2 years 9 mths		2,750
Depreciation at 30 June 20X5		21,000

Round Music
Balance sheet as at 30 June 20X5

	£	£	£
Fixed assets:			
Plant at cost			60,000
Less: aggregate depreciation			21,000
			39,000
Current assets:			
Stock (8,630 – 1,120)		7,510	
Debtors	6,120		
Less: provision for doubtful debts	310	5,810	
Prepayments		80	
		13,400	
Less: current liabilities			
Creditors	3,480		
Accruals	130		
Bank overdraft	1,430	5,040	
Net current assets:			8,360
Total assets less current liabilities			47,360
Less: long-term loan			7,000
Capital at 30 June 20X5			40,360

Round Music
Statement of profit for the year ended 30 June 20X5

	£
Capital at 30 June 20X5	40,360
Less: capital at 30 June 20X4	42,770
	(2,410)
Add: drawings (18,500 + 750)	19,250
	16,840
Less: capital introduced	5,000
Profit for the year	11,840

19.4 ***Workings***

Credit purchases = £(5,720 + 33,360 − 5,220) = £33,860
Total purchases = £(33,860 + 1,120 + 4,500) = £39,480
Credit sales = (5,840 + 31,860 − 6,540) = £31,160
Cash sales = £(18,920 + 4,000 + 1,120 + 980 + 170) = £25,190
Total sales = £(25,190 + 31,160) = £56,350
Telephone = £(120 + 280 − 140) = £260
Light & heat = £(370 + 290 − 60) = £600
Motor expenses = £(1,810 + 980) = £2,790
Depreciation on fixtures and fittings = 20% × £5,800 = £1,160
Accumulated depreciation on fixtures and fittings = (£10,000 − £5,800) + £1,160 = £5,360

A. Fox
Trading and profit & loss accounts for the year ended 31 July 20X9

	£	£
Sales		56,350
Less: cost of sales		
Stock at 1 Aug 20X8	3,300	
Add: purchases (39,480 − 530)	38,950	
	42,250	
Less: stock at 31 July 20X9	3,920	
		38,330
Gross profit		18,020
Less: expenditure		
Wages	5,640	
Telephone (120 + 280 − 140)	260	
Light & heat (370 + 290 − 60)	600	
Motor expenses (1,810 + 980)	2,790	
Printing	560	
Cleaning	170	
Depreciation (20% × 5,800)	1,160	
		11,180
Net profit		6,840

A. Fox
Balance sheet as at 31 July 20X9

	£	£	£
Fixed assets	*Cost*	*Agg. depn*	*WDV*
Freehold land & buildings	35,000	—	35,000
Fixtures & fittings	10,000	5,360	4,640
	45,000	5,360	39,640
Current assets:			
Stock		3,920	
Debtors		5,840	
Prepayments		140	
Bank		8,260	
		18,160	
Less: current liabilities			
Creditors	5,720		
Accruals	290	6,010	
Net current assets:			12,150
Net assets:			51,790
Capital:			
Balance at 1 Aug 20X8			48,480
Add: capital introduced			1,000
Profit for year			6,840
			56,320
Less: drawings (4,000 + 530)			4,530
Balance at 31 July 20X9			51,790

20 The final accounts of clubs

20.8 a ***Elite Bowling & Social Club***
Statement of affairs as at 31 October 20X7

	£	£	£
Fixed assets	*Cost*	*Agg. depn*	*WDV*
Furniture, fixtures & fittings	440	44	396
Mower	120	100	20
	560	144	416
Current assets:			
Subscriptions in arrear		30	
Bar stock		209	
Bank—deposit account		585	
—current account		263	
Cash		10	
		1,097	
Less: current liabilities			
Bar creditors	186		
Accrued rent & rates	12		
Accrued light & heat	9	207	
Net current assets:			890
General fund at 31 Oct 20X7			1,306

Workings

1 *Net bar purchases*

Creditors' control

20X8			20X7		
31 Oct	R&P	1,885	31 Oct	Balance b/d	186
31 Oct	Balance c/d	248	20X8		
			31 Oct	Net purchases	1,947
		2,133			2,133

2 *Subscriptions*

Subscriptions

20X7			20X8		
31 Oct	Subs in arrear b/d	30	31 Oct	R&P (30 + 574 + 44)	648
20X8			31 Oct	Subs in arrear c/d	50
31 Oct	Subs for year	624			
31 Oct	Subs in advance c/d	44			
		698			698

3 *Fixed assets*

Cost of furniture, fixtures & fittings = £(440 + 460) = £900
Depreciation on furniture, fixtures & fittings = 10% × £900 = £90
Accumulated depreciation on furniture, fixtures & fittings = (£440 − £396) + £90 = £134
Profit on disposal of mower = £40 − £20 = £20
Cost of new mower = £120 + £40 = £160

Elite Bowling & Social Club
Bar trading account for the year ended 31 October 20X8

	£	£
Bar takings		2,285
Less: cost of sales		
Bar stock at 1 Nov 20X7	209	
Add: purchases	1,947	
	2,156	
Less: bar stock at 31 Oct 20X8	178	
		1,978
Gross profit		307

b ***Elite Bowling & Social Club***
Income & expenditure account
for the year ended 31 October 20X8

	£	£
Income		
Subscriptions		624
Profit on bar		307
Spectators' entrance fees		54
Deposit account interest		26
Catering receipts	120	
Less: catering purchases	80	
	40	
Stewards' bonus (40% × £40)	16	
Profit on catering		24
Profit on disposal of mower		20
		1,055
Less: expenditure		
Wages	306	
Rent & rates (184 − 12 + 26)	198	
Light & heat (143 − 9 + 11)	145	
General expenses	132	
Depreciation on furniture	90	
		871
Excess of income over expenditure		184

c ***Elite Bowling & Social Club***
Balance sheet as at 31 October 20X8

	£	£	£
Fixed assets	*Cost*	*Agg. depn*	*WDV*
Furniture, fixtures & fittings	900	134	766
Mower	160	—	160
	1,060	134	926
Current assets:			
Subs in arrear		50	
Bar stock		178	
Bank—deposit account		497	
—current account		176	
Cash		8	
		909	
Less: current liabilities			
Subs in advance	44		
Bar creditors	248		
Accrued rent & rates	26		
Accrued light & heat	11		
Stewards' bonus	16	345	
Net current assets:			564
Net assets:			1,490
General fund			
Balance at 31 Oct 20X7			1,306
Add: excess of income over expenditure			184
Balance at 31 Oct 20X8			1,490

Notes

1. If it had been known that the wages were paid to bar staff, these would have been put in the bar trading account.
2. All the items relating to the catering, could also have been put in the bar trading account.

20.9 *Assumption*

In order to answer this question it is necessary to make an assumption about the cost of the defence bonds. The £1,500 given in the question is their face value. They could have been purchased at any price. However, the most reasonable assumption is that they were purchased at their face value of £1,500.

Workings

1 *Accumulated/General fund*
Statement of affairs at 30 June 20X7

	£	£	£
Fixed assets	*Cost*	*Agg. depn*	*WDV*
Freehold building	6,000	—	6,000
Billiard tables (see workings 3)	1,200	500	700
	7,200	500	6,700
Prize fund investments			1,500
			8,200
Current assets:			
Subs in arrear		20	
Bar stock		150	
Bank		390	
		560	
Less: current liabilities			
Accrued interest on mortgage (5% × £4,000)		200	
Net current assets:			360
Total assets less current liabilities			8,560
Less: long-term liabilities			
5% mortgage			4,000
Net assets:			4,560
Accumulated fund (balancing figure)			2,585
Life members' fund (see workings 2)			400
Prize fund (see workings 4)			1,575
			4,560

Note

The ACCA suggested answer has another treatment for the prize fund. The prize fund and prize fund investment accounts are ignored, and the interest is removed from the bank balance. This is essentially a short-cut method for the purpose of calculating the accumulated fund.

2 *Subscriptions*

Subscriptions

		£			£
20X7			20X8		
30 June	Subs in arrear b/d	20	30 June	Bank	340
20X8			30 June	Subs in arrear c/d	10
30 June	Subs for year	330			
		350			350

Life members' fund

		£			£
20X8			20X7		
30 June	Accum. fund (3 @ £16)	48	30 June	Balance b/d (25 @ £16)	400
30 June	Balance c/d (25 + 5 − 3) @ £16	432	20X8		
			30 June	Bank	80
		480			480

3 *Fixed assets*: billiard tables
Aggregate depreciation at 30 June 20X7 =
5 years × (£1,200 ÷ 12) = £500
Depreciation for year = (£1,200 + £300) ÷ 12 = £125
Aggregate depreciation at 30 June 20X8 = £500 + £125 = £625

4 *Prize fund*

Prize fund

20X8		20X7		
30 June Bank—prizes	75	30 June Balance b/d		
30 June Balance c/d	1,575		(1,500 + 75)	1,575
		20X8		
		30 June Bank—income		75
	1,650			1,650

There are no entries in the prize fund investment account.

Bar trading account
For the year ended 30 June 20X8

	£	£
Bar receipts		4,590
Less: cost of sales		
Stock at 1 July 20X7	150	
Add: purchases	3,680	
	3,830	
Less: stock at 30 June 20X8	180	
	3,650	
Stewards' wages & expenses	400	4,050
Gross profit on bar		540

Income & expenditure account
For the year ended 30 June 20X8

	£	£	£
Income			
Annual subscriptions			330
Profit on bar			540
Sundry lettings			180
Receipts for billiards		275	
Less: repairs to tables	50		
depreciation of tables	125	175	
Surplus from billiards			100
			1,150
Less: expenditure			
Rates		140	
Light & heat		72	
Cleaning & laundry		138	
Sundry expenses		80	
Mortgage interest (5% × £4,000)		200	630
Excess of income over expenditure			520

Balance sheet as at 30 June 20X8

	£	£	£
Fixed assets	*Cost*	*Agg. depn*	*WDV*
Freehold building	6,000	—	6,000
Billiard tables	1,500	625	875
	7,500	625	6,875
Prize fund investments			1,500
			8,375
Current assets:			
Subs in arrear		10	
Bar stock		180	
Bank		95	
		285	
Less: current liabilities		—	
Net current assets:			285
Net assets:			8,660

Accumulated fund		
Balance at 1 July 20X7		2,585
Add: excess of income over expenditure		520
transfer from life members' fund		48
gifts from members		3,500
Balance at 30 June 20X8		6,653
Life members' fund		
Balance at 1 July 20X7	400	
Add: subscriptions received	80	
	480	
Less: transfer to accumulated fund	48	
Balance at 30 June 20X8		432
Prize fund		
Balance at 1 July 20X7	1,575	
Less: prizes awarded for previous year	75	
	1,500	
Add: income	75	
Balance at 30 June 20X8		1,575
		8,660

Notes

1 The ACCA suggested answer has another treatment for the prize fund investment account. The £75 included in the bank balance at 30 June 20X8 relating to the income from the defence bonds is added to the prize fund investment account and removed from the bank balance as shown on the balance sheet. This highlights that is an asset of the prize fund even though it is held in a general bank account, and is probably a better method for the purpose of presenting an informative balance sheet. The method adopted by the author above reflects the balances on the relevant ledger accounts.

2 Notice that the gifts from members are not included in the income & expenditure account because the amount is so large and presumably non-recurring.

3 The mortgage is computed as follows:

$(5\% \times 2 \text{ years}) \times m = £4{,}400 - m$

$\frac{10m}{100} = £4{,}400 - m$

$\frac{110m}{100} = £4{,}400$

$m = £4{,}000$

21 Value added tax, columnar books of prime entry and the payroll

21.4 ***The journal***

		Debit	Credit
		£	£
Wages & salaries	Dr.	7,820	
Bank/cash			5,170
Inland Revenue			2,650
		7,820	7,820

Being record of payroll for w/e 24 Jan 20X9

Workings
Net wages = £6,800 – (£950 + £680) = £5,170
Inland Revenue = £950 + £680 – £1,020 = £2,650

21.8 a i *Purchases day book*

Date		*Total*	*Repair materials*	*Tools and equipment*	*Appliances for resale*
20X5		£	£	£	£
Jan	Dee & Co.	337.74		337.74	
	AB Supplies	528.20	528.20		
Feb	Simpson	141.34	141.34		
	Cotton Ltd	427.40			427.40
	Dee & Co	146.82	146.82		
Mar	AB Supplies	643.43	643.43		
	Simpson	95.60	95.60		
		2,320.53	1,555.39	337.74	427.40

ii *Sales day book*

Date		*Total*	*Repair work*	*Appliance sales*
20X5		£	£	£
Jan	D. Hopkins	362.80	362.80	
	P. Bolton	417.10	417.10	
Feb	G. Leivers	55.00		55.00
	M. Whitehead	151.72	151.72	
	N. John Ltd	49.14		49.14
	A. Linnekar	12.53		12.53
Mar	E. Horton	462.21	462.21	
	S. Ward	431.08	431.08	
	W. Scothern	319.12	319.12	
	N. Annable	85.41	85.41	
		2,346.11	2,229.44	116.67

b *Cash book (debit side)*

Date	*Item*	*Discount allowed*	*Total*	*Debtors*	*Repair work*	*Appliance sales*	*Sundries*
20X5	£	£	£	£	£	£	
Jan	Capital		250.00				250.00
	Loan		2,000.00				2,000.00
	Repairs		69.44		69.44		
Feb	D. Hopkins	5.80	357.00	357.00			
	Repairs		256.86		256.86		
Mar	P. Bolton		417.10	417.10			
	G. Leivers		55.00	55.00			
	A. Linnekar		12.53	12.53			
	S. Ward	5.08	426.00	426.00			
	Repairs		182.90		182.90		
	Appliances		112.81			112.81	
		10.88	4,139.64	1,267.63	509.20	112.81	2,250.00
						Capital	250.00
						Loan	2,000.00
							2,250.00

Cash book (credit side)

Date	*Item*	*Discount received*	*Total*	*Creditors*	*Repair materials and bank*	*Drawings*	*Expenses*
20X5		£	£	£	£	£	£
Jan	Repair materials		195.29		195.29		
	Rent		400.00				400.00
	Rates		150.00				150.00
	Stationery		32.70				32.70
	Car expenses		92.26				92.26
	Drawings		160.00			160.00	
Feb	Repair materials		161.03		161.03		
	Sundries		51.54				51.54
	Car expenses		81.42				81.42
	Drawings		160.00			160.00	
Mar	Dee & Co.	7.74	330.00	330.00			
	AB Supplies		528.20	528.20			
	Simpson	3.34	138.00	138.00			
	Cotton Ltd		130.00	130.00			
	Dee & Co.	6.82	140.00	140.00			
	Repair materials		22.06		22.06		
	Sundries		24.61				24.61
	Car expenses		104.52				104.52
	Drawings		160.00			160.00	
	Bank		500.00			500.00	
		17.90	3,561.63	1,266.20	378.38	980.00	937.05
	Balance c/d		578.01				
			4,139.64				

Drawings	480.00	
Bank	500.00	
	980.00	
Rent		400.00
Rates		150.00
Stationery		32.70
Car expenses		278.20
Sundries		76.15
		937.05

c

Creditors' ledger control

20X5		£	20X5		£
Mar	Cash paid	1,266.20	Mar	Purchases	2,320.53
	Discount received	17.90			
	Balance c/d	1,036.43			
		2,320.53			2,320.53
			Apr	Balance b/d	1,036.43

Debtors' ledger control

20X5		£	20X5		£
Mar	Sales	2,346.11	Mar	Cash received	1,267.63
				Discount allowed	10.88
				Balance c/d	1,067.60
		2,346.11			2,346.11
Apr	Balance b/d	1,067.60			

d

Sales

		Repair	*Appliances*			*Repairs*	*Appliances*
20X5		£	£	20X5		£	£
Mar	Trading account	2,738.64	229.48	Mar	Debtors ledger control	2,229.44	116.67
					Cash received	509.20	112.81
		2,738.64	229.48			2,738.64	229.48

Cost of sales

		Repairs	*Appliances*			*Repairs*	*Appliances*
20X5		£	£	20X5		£	£
Mar	Creditors' ledger control	1,555.39	427.40	Mar	Stock c/d	691.02	320.58
	Cash paid	378.38			Trading a/c	1,242.75	106.82
		1,933.77	427.40			1,933.77	427.40

e ***M. Faraday***
Trading and profit and loss account for the quarter ended 31 March 20X5

	Repairs	*Appliances*	*Total*
	£	£	£
Sales	2,738.64	229.48	2,968.12
Cost of sales	1,242.75	106.82	1,349.57
Gross profit	1,495.89	122.66	1,618.55
f *Add*: Discount received			17.90
			1,636.45
Less: expenditure			
Discount allowed		10.88	
Rent (400.00 – 200.00 prepaid)		200.00	
Rates		150.00	
Stationery		32.70	
Car expenses		278.20	
Sundry expenses		76.15	
Heating and lighting		265.00	
Loan interest (10% × £2,000 × $\frac{3}{12}$)		50.00	
Depreciation:			
Car (700.00 – 600.00)		100.00	
Tools and equipment (337.74 – 300.00)		37.74	
			1,200.67
Net profit			435.78

g ***M. Faraday***
Balance sheet as at 31 March 20X5

	Cost	*Depn*	*Net*
	£	£	£
Fixed assets			
Tools and equipment	337.74	37.74	300.00
Car	700.00	100.00	600.00
	1,037.74	137.74	900.00
Current assets			
Stocks: repair materials	691.02		
appliances	320.58		
		1,011.60	
Debtors		1,067.60	
Prepayments		200.00	
Bank		500.00	
Cash		578.01	
		3,357.21	
Less current liabilities			
Creditors	1,036.43		
Accruals (£50 interest plus £265 heating)	315.00		
		1,351.43	
Net current assets			2,005.78
Total assets less current liabilities			2,905.78
Less: long-term liabilities			
10% loan			2,000.00
Net assets			905.78

	£
Capital: opening (700 + 250)	950.00
Add: net profit for quarter	435.78
	1,385.78
Less: drawings	480.00
Capital: closing	905.78

21.9 *Purchases day book*

Date	*Name of creditor*	*Total*	*VAT*	*Purchases*	*Motor expenses*	*Misc.*
20X7		£	£	£	£	£
3 Dec	English Coal	470	70	400		
4 Dec	Solihull Garage	282	42		240	
7 Dec	Scottish Coal	376	56	320		
13 Dec	Solihull Garage	423	63		360	
15 Dec	Solihull Garage	4,700	700			4,000
16 Dec	English Telecom	658	98			560
		6,909	1,029	720	600	4,560

Sales day book

Date	*Name of debtor*	*Total*	*VAT*	*Sales*	*Misc.*
20X7		£	£	£	£
6 Dec	Black	705	105	600	
12 Dec	White	940	140	800	
17 Dec	Solihull Garage	2,350	350		2,000
		3,995	595	1,400	2,000

Cash book (debit side)

Date	*Details*	*Total*	*VAT*	*Debtors*	*Disc. allow.*	*Sales*	*Misc.*
20X7		£	£	£	£	£	£
1 Dec	Balance b/d	5,000					5,000
10 Dec	Sales	611	91			520	
18 Dec	Sales	752	112			640	
23 Dec	Motor vehicle	3,525	525				3,000
28 Dec	Black	680		680	25		
29 Dec	White	905		905	35		
		11,473	728	1,585	60	1,160	8,000
20X8							
1 Jan	Balance b/d	7,727					

Cash book (credit side)

Date	*Details*	*Total*	*VAT*	*Creditors*	*Disc. rec'd*	*Purchases*	*Stationery*	*Misc.*
20X7		£	£	£	£	£	£	£
5 Dec	Stationery	282	42				240	
8 Dec	Wages	350						350
11 Dec	Purchases	846	126			720		
14 Dec	Purchases	564	84			480		
19 Dec	Motor expenses	720						720
20 Dec	Stationery	188	28				160	
30 Dec	English Coal	450		450	20			
31 Dec	Scottish Coal	346		346	30			
		3,746	280	796	50	1,200	400	1,070
31 Dec	Balance c/d	7,727						
		11,473						

The ledger

Sales

		£	20X7		£
			31 Dec	Total per SDB	1,400
			31 Dec	Total per CB	1,160
					2,560

Black

20X7					
6 Dec	Sales + VAT	705	28 Dec	Bank	680
			28 Dec	Discount allowed	25
		705			705

White

12 Dec	Sales + VAT	940	29 Dec	Bank	905
			29 Dec	Discount allowed	35
		940			940

Purchases

31 Dec	Total per PDB	720
31 Dec	Total per CB	1,200
		1,920

English Coal

30 Dec	Bank	450	3 Dec	Purchases + VAT	470
30 Dec	Discount received	20			
		470			470

Scottish Coal

31 Dec	Bank	346	7 Dec	Purchases + VAT	376
31 Dec	Discount received	30			
		376			376

Motor expenses

19 Dec	Bank	720
31 Dec	Total per PDB	600
		1,320

Motor vehicles

15 Dec	Solihull Garage	4,000	17 Dec	Solihull Garage	2,000
			23 Dec	Bank	3,000

Solihull Garage

17 Dec	Vehicles + VAT	2,350	4 Dec	Motor expenses + VAT	282
31 Dec	Balance c/d	3,055	13 Dec	Motor expenses + VAT	423
			15 Dec	Vehicles + VAT	4,700
		5,405			5,405
			1 Jan	Balance b/d	3,055

Telephone & postage

16 Dec	English Telecom	560

English Telecom

16 Dec	Telephone + VAT	658

Printing & stationery

31 Dec	Total per CB	400

Wages

8 Dec	Bank	350

Discount allowed

31 Dec	Total per CB	60

Discount received

31 Dec	Total per CB	50

VAT

31 Dec	Total per PDB	1,029	31 Dec	Total per SDB	595
31 Dec	Total per CB	280	31 Dec	Total per CB	728
31 Dec	Balance c/d	14			
		1,323			1,323
			1 Jan	Balance b/d	14

22 The role of computers in accounting

22.4 If the 'look and feel' of software resembles that of traditional bookkeeping this is likely to have several advantages for the staff who are using it. Many of them will have had training in bookkeeping, or will have previous experience of bookkeeping using paper records. If they find that the headings and terminology are familiar, they will feel comfortable with the software, which should mean that they will have fewer problems learning how to use it. This should reduce the costs of training staff, and make it easier to recruit clerks to look after the entering of data and other routine activities on the system.

Staff will also be less likely to make mistakes, particularly if they have responsibility for activities such as entering corrections via journals or setting up new account codes on the ledgers, since they should find that all the nomenclature is clear and unambiguous.

If the software presents its output and reports in the format used for conventional financial reports, these will be readily understood by a wide range of people. As far as they are concerned, the fact that a computer system has been used in the preparation of the report will be irrelevant.

Finally, the ability of external auditors to check the accounts should be improved, since the entries adhere to all the normal conventions, and the auditors will know exactly where to look for the entries that they expect to find.

An example of a function that might present accounting information in a new and different way is in order tracking. In a conventional accounting system, the information about any particular order will be fairly limited and difficult to get at. The individual events in the life of the order (the order receipt, despatch, invoice, payment, etc.) will be recorded as a series of separate entries in books or on forms.

The computerized system, in contrast, can link all these events together and present them in a combined report on the screen. It can also tap into records held as part of the stock control or manufacturing systems in the company, enabling an accounts clerk to find out whether the goods ordered have left the warehouse or are still being manufactured. The computer software should also be better at presenting more complex situations, such as those where orders have been part-filled or substitutions have been made.

Thus, by focusing on the progress of the order over time (which is the way the customer sees it) rather than the entries in the accounting books (which represent the way accountants see things) the clerk should be able to respond quickly to enquiries from customers and thereby encourage them to feel that the company is efficient and concerned about their well-being.

23 Accounting for changing price levels

23.9 a *Workings*

HCA sales = (50 × 4) @ F5 = F1,000

CPPA sales = $F1,000 \times \frac{105}{102.5} = F1,024$

CPPA cost of sales = $F500 \times \frac{105}{100} = F525$

CPPA loss from holding monetary assets—cash of F1,000:

$\frac{105 - 102.5}{102.5} \times F1,000 = F24$

Sally Johnson
Profit & loss account for the week ended...

	HCA	RCA	CPPA
	F	F	F
Sales	1,000	1,000	1,024
Less: cost of sales	500	650	525
Operating profit	500	350	499
Less: loss from holding monetary assets	—	—	24
Net profit	500	350	475

Sally Johnson
Balance sheet as at ....

	HCA	RCA	CPPA
	F	F	F
Assets			
Cash	1,000	1,000	1,000
Capital			
Introduced	500	500	500
Capital maintenance reserve	—	150	25
Net profit	500	350	475
	1,000	1,000	1,000

b The HCA profit of F500 may be useful if Sally returns home after a week's holiday and thus does not intend to replace the melons or make further purchases in francs (although this ignores the effect of inflation on the exchange rate). Generally, HCA is of limited usefulness where the replacement cost of assets or inflation is rising.

However, the question implies that Sally intends to replace the melons. Since the cost has risen by F150, she needs to provide for the increased replacement cost, which means that her profit on a RCA basis is only F350. RCA is useful because it takes into account the increased replacement cost of the goods sold.

The purchasing power of Sally's capital of F500 has reduced by 5% of F500 = F25, which means that her profit on a CPPA basis is only F475. CPPA is useful because it takes into account the reduction in the purchasing power of a currency. It is also said to make accounts more comparable over time since they are computed on a uniform basis.

In this case, because the replacement cost of melons is greater than the historical cost and the inflation adjusted cost, it may be argued that RCA is more useful than either HCA or CPPA.

24 The final accounts of partnerships

24.7 *Workings*

Interest on loan:

Hammond—5% × £20,000 × $\frac{3}{12}$ = £250

Interest on capital:

Clayton—(8% × £90,000) + (8% × £10,000 × $\frac{8}{12}$) = £7,733

Hammond—8% × £60,000 = £4,800

Interest on drawings:

Clayton—

4% × £3,000 × $\frac{9}{12}$ = £ 90

4% × £5,000 × $\frac{4}{12}$ = £ 67

£ 157

Hammond—

4% × £2,000 × $\frac{9}{12}$ = £ 60

4% × £1,000 × $\frac{4}{12}$ = £ 13

£ 73

Clayton and Hammond
Profit & loss appropriation account 30 June 20X6

	£	£		£	£
Interest on loan			Net profit b/d		67,500
Hammond		250	Interest on drawings:		
Salaries:			Clayton	157	
Clayton	17,000		Hammond	73	230
Hammond	13,000	30,000			
Interest on capital:					
Clayton	7,733				
Hammond	4,800	12,533			
Shares of residual profit:					
Clayton	12,474				
Hammond	12,473	24,947			
		67,730			67,730

Current account

	Clayton	Hammond		Clayton	Hammond
	£	£		£	£
Drawings	8,000	3,000	Balance b/d	16,850	9,470
Interest on drawings	157	73	Interest on loan	—	250
Balance c/d	45,900	36,920	Salaries	17,000	13,000
			Interest on capital	7,733	4,800
			Shares of residual profit	12,474	12,473
	54,057	39,993		54,057	39,993
			Balance b/d	45,900	36,920

Capital

	Clayton	Hammond		Clayton	Hammond
			Balance b/d	90,000	60,000
			Bank	10,000	—
				100,000	60,000

Loan-Hammond

	Bank	20,000

24.10 *Workings*

Interest on loan:

Peace—5% × £2,000 × $\frac{3}{12}$ = £25

Interest on capital:

Peace—

10% × (£10,000 – £1,000 – £2,000) = £700

10% × £1,000 × $\frac{9}{12}$ = £ 75

£775

Quiet—10% × £5,000 = £500

Interest on drawings:

Peace—8% × £2,200 × $\frac{8}{12}$ = £117

Quiet—8% × £1,800 × $\frac{4}{12}$ = £48

Peace & Quiet
Trading and profit and loss accounts
for the year ended 31 December 20X8

	£	£
Sales		69,830
Less: cost of sales		
Stock at 1 Jan 20X8	6,630	
Add: purchases	45,620	
	52,250	
Less: stock at 31 Dec 20X8	5,970	
		46,280
Gross profit		23,550
Less: expenditure		
Shop assistants' salaries	5,320	
Light & heat (1,850 + 60)	1,910	
Stationery (320 – 50)	270	
Bank interest and charges	45	
Depreciation on equipment 10% × (8,500 – 1,200)	730	
		8,275
Net profit		15,275

Profit & loss appropriation account 31 December 20X8

	£	£	£
Net profit			15,275
Add: Interest on drawings—			
Peace		117	
Quiet		48	165
			15,440
Less: Interest on loan—Peace			25
Interest on capital—			
Peace	775		
Quiet	500	1,275	
Salaries—			
Peace	6,200		
Quiet	4,800	11,000	
			12,300
			3,140
Shares of residual profit—			
Peace			1,570
Quiet			1,570
			3,140

Current accounts

	Peace	Quiet		Peace	Quiet
Drawings	2,200	1,800	Balance	1,280	3,640
Interest on drawings	117	48	Interest on loan loan	25	—
Balance c/d	7,533	8,662	Interest on capital	775	500
			Salaries	6,200	4,800
			Shares of residual profit	1,570	1,570
	9,850	10,510		9,850	10,510
			Balance b/d	7,533	8,662

Capital accounts

	Peace	Quiet		Peace	Quiet
Loan account	2,000		Balance b/d	10,000	5,000
Balance c/d	8,000	5,000			
	10,000	5,000		10,000	5,000
			Balance b/d	8,000	5,000

Peace & Quiet
Balance sheet as at 31 December 20X8

	£	£	£
Fixed assets	*Cost*	*Agg. depn*	*WDV*
Leasehold shop	18,000	—	18,000
Equipment (1,200 + 730)	8,500	1,930	6,570
	26,500	1,930	24,570

Current assets:			
Stock		5,970	
Stationery		50	
Debtors		1,210	
Bank		3,815	
		11,045	
Less: current liabilities			
Creditors	4,360		
Accrued expenses	60	4,420	
Net current assets:			6,625
Net assets:			31,195
Capital	*Peace*	*Quiet*	
Capital accounts	8,000	5,000	13,000
Current accounts	7,533	8,662	16,195
	15,533	13,662	29,195
Loan—Peace			2,000
			31,195

24.11 ***Workings***

Interest on loan:
Peter—5% × £12,000 = £600
Interest on capital:
Peter—10% × £100,000 = £10,000
Paul—10% × £80,000 = £8,000
Interest on drawings:
Peter—5% × £6,000 × $\frac{4}{12}$ = £100
Paul—5% × £8,000 × $\frac{9}{12}$ = £300

Peter & Paul
Trading and profit & loss accounts
for the year ended 30 June 20X8

	£	£
Sales (56,332 – 200)		56,132
Less: cost of sales		
Stock at 1 July 20X7	6,734	
Add: purchases	19,868	
	26,602	
Less: stock at 30 June 20X8 (8,264 + 160)	8,424	
		18,178
Gross profit		37,954
Add: decrease in provision for bad debts (216–180)		36
		37,990
Less: expenditure		
Light & heat (3,428 – 58 + 82)	3,452	
Warehouses wages (23,500 – 6,000 – 8,000)	9,500	
Rates (5,169 – 34)	5,135	
Postage & telephone	4,257	
Printing & stationery	2,134	
Selling expenses	1,098	
Bad debts	240	
Depreciation—plant & machinery (10% × 77,000)	7,700	
Depreciation—vehicles (20% × 36,500)	7,300	
Depreciation—loose tools (1,253 – 927)	326	
		41,142
Net loss		3,152

Profit & loss appropriation account 30 June 20X8

	£	£
Net loss for year		3,152
Add: Interest on loan—Peter		600
Interest on capital—		
Peter	10,000	
Paul	8,000	18,000
Salaries—		
Peter	20,000	
Paul	18,000	38,000
		59,752
Less: Interest on drawings—		
Peter	100	
Paul	300	400
		59,352
Shares of residual loss—		
Peter		29,676
Paul		29,676
		59,352

The ledger

Current accounts

	Peter	*Paul*		*Peter*	*Paul*
Balance b/d	804	—	Balance b/d	—	21,080
Drawings	6,000	8,000	Interest on loan	600	—
Interest on drawings	100	300	Interest on capital	10,000	8,000
Shares of residual loss	29,676	29,676	Salaries	20,000	18,000
Balance c/d	—	9,104	Balance c/d	5,980	—
	36,580	47,080		36,580	47,080
Balance b/d	5,980	—	Balance b/d	—	9,104

Peter & Paul
Balance sheet as at 30 June 20X5

	£	£	£
Fixed assets	*Cost or valuation*	*Agg. depn*	*WDV*
Freehold premises	115,000	—	115,000
Plant & machinery (22,800 + 7,700)	77,000	30,500	46,500
Motor vehicles (12,480 + 7,300)	36,500	19,780	16,720
Loose tools	1,253	326	927
	229,753	50,606	179,147
Current assets			
Stock (8,264 + 160)		8,424	
Debtors (4,478 – 200 – 240)	4,038		
Less: provision for bad debts	180	3,858	
Prepayments		34	
Bank		7,697	
		20,013	
Less: current liabilities			
Creditors	3,954		
Accruals	82	4,036	
Net current assets			15,977
Net assets			195,124
Capital	*Peter*	*Paul*	
Capital accounts	100,000	80,000	180,000
Current accounts	(5,980)	9,104	3,124
	94,020	89,104	183,124
Loan—Peter			12,000
			195,124

24.12 ***Workings—vehicles***

	Depreciation on sale	*Depreciation this year*
	£	£
Depreciation on disposal:		
20X7—10% × £2,400 × $\frac{9}{12}$	180	
20X8—10% × £2,400	240	
20X9—10% × £2,400 × $\frac{10}{12}$	200	200
Aggregate depreciation	620	
Book value = £2,400 − £620 = £1,780		
Profit on sale = £1,900 − £1,780 = £120		
Depreciation on remainder:		
10% × (£30,000 − £2,400)		2,760
		2,960

Aggregate depreciation at 31 December 20X9:
£18,000 + £2,960 − £620 = £20,340

Simon, Wilson & Dillon
Trading and profit & loss accounts
for the year ended 31 December 20X9

	£	£	£
Sales			130,000
Less: returns			400
			129,600
Less: cost of sales			
Stock at 1 Jan 20X9		34,900	
Add: purchases	64,000		
Less: returns	600	63,400	
		98,300	
Less: stock at 31 Dec 20X9		31,000	67,300
Gross profit			62,300
Add: investment income (800 + 320)			1,120
profit on sale of vehicle			120
			63,540
Less: expenditure			
Salesmen's salaries		19,480	
Rates (12,100 − 160)		11,940	
Motor expenses (2,800 + 240)		3,040	
Mortgage interest (8% × 40,000)		3,200	
Printing and stationery (1,100 − 170)		930	
Bad debts		2,000	
Provision for bad debts— ([2% × (28,000 − 2,000)] − 400)		120	
Provision for depreciation on—			
Vehicles		2,960	
Tools (1,200 − 960)		240	
Bank charges		130	44,040
Net profit c/d			19,500

Profit & loss appropriation account 31 December 20X9

	£	£	£
Net profit b/d			19,500
Less: salaries—			
Simon	15,000		
Dillon	10,000		
		25,000	
Interest on capital—			
Simon (10% × 35,000)	3,500		
Wilson (10% × 25,000)	2,500		
Dillon (10% × 10,000)	1,000		
		7,000	
			32,000
			(12,500)
Shares of residual loss—			
Simon			5,000
Wilson			5,000
Dillon			2,500
			12,500

The ledger

Current account

	S	W	D		S	W	D
Balance b/d	—	—	1,800	Balance b/d	5,600	4,800	—
Shares of residual loss	5,000	5,000	2,500	Salaries	15,000	—	10,000
				Interest	3,500	2,500	1,000
Balance c/d	19,100	2,300	6,700				
	24,100	7,300	11,000		24,100	7,300	11,000
				Balance b/d	19,100	2,300	6,700

Simon, Wilson & Dillon
Balance sheet as at 31 December 20X9

	£ *Cost*	£ *Agg. depn*	£ *WDV*
Fixed assets			
Freehold land & buildings (65,000 + 5,000)	70,000	—	70,000
Delivery vehicles (30,000 − 2,400)	27,600	20,340	7,260
Loose tools	1,200	240	960
	98,800	20,580	78,220
Good will			11,000
Unquoted investments			6,720
			95,940
Current assets			
Stocks (31,000 + 170)		31,170	
Prepayments		160	
Debtors (28,000 − 2,000)	26,000		
Less: provision for bad debts	520	25,480	
Sundry debtor		1,900	
Income accrued		320	
Bank (10,100 − 130)		9,970	
		69,000	
Less: current liabilities			
Creditors	25,000		
Accruals (240 + 1,600)	1,840	26,840	
Net current assets			42,160
Total assets less current liabilities			138,100
Less: long-term liabilities			
8% mortgage on premises			40,000
Net assets			98,100
Capital accounts—			
Simon			35,000
Wilson			25,000
Dillon			10,000
			70,000

Current accounts

Simon	19,100	
Wilson	2,300	
Dillon	6,700	28,100
		98,100

Notes

1 It is assumed that the unquoted investments are intended to be kept for more than one accounting year.
2 The capital and current accounts could have been presented in the balance sheet in columnar form.

25 Changes in partnerships

25.7 ***Workings***

Shares of goodwill	£
Brown $\frac{1}{2} \times £90,000$	45,000
Jones $\frac{1}{2} \times £90,000$	45,000
	90,000
Jones $\frac{3}{5} \times £90,000$	54,000
Smith $\frac{2}{5} \times £90,000$	36,000
	90,000

The ledger

Revaluation account

Stock		4,000	Premises	35,000
Provision for bad debts		3,000	Fixtures	8,000
Profit—				
Brown	18,000			
Jones	18,000	36,000		
		43,000		43,000

Capital

	Brown	Jones	Smith		Brown	Jones	Smith
Goodwill	—	54,000	36,000	Balance b/d	110,000	87,000	—
Cash	173,000	—	—	Cash	—	—	100,000
Balance c/d	—	96,000	64,000	Profit on revaluation	18,000	18,000	—
				Goodwill	45,000	45,000	—
	173,000	150,000	100,000		173,000	150,000	100,000
				Balance b/d	—	96,000	64,000

25.8 ***Workings***

Valuation of goodwill:	£
Net asset value before revaluation (£30,100 – £2,500)	27,600
Less: loss on revaluation (see below)	600
Net asset value after revaluation	27,000
Estimated profit for 20X9	48,750
Less: partners' salaries (3 @ £15,000)	45,000
Earnings/super profit	3,750

$$\text{P–E ratio} = \frac{\text{price}}{\text{earnings}}$$

∴ Price = earnings × P–E ratio
Capitalized value of estimated super profits = £3,750 × 8 = £30,000
Goodwill = £30,000 – £27,000 = £3,000

The ledger

Vehicles

Balance b/d	7,000	Prov. for depn.	1,800
Revaluation	1,500	Balance c/d	6,700
	8,500		8,500
Balance b/d	6,700		

Stock

Balance b/d	9,200	Revaluation	1,200
		Balance c/d	8,000
	9,200		9,200
Balance b/d	8,000		

Provision for bad debts

		Revaluation	900

Revaluation account

Stock	1,200	Vehicles		1,500
Provision for bad debts	900	Loss on revaluation—		
		Capital B	200	
		Capital P	200	
		Capital N	200	
				600
	2,100			2,100

Capital

	B	P	N	L		B	P	N	L
Revaluation	200	200	200	—	Balance b/d	10,000	8,000	5,000	—
Loan account	—	—	5,800	—	Bank	—	—	—	6,000
Balance c/d	10,800	8,800	—	6,000	Goodwill	1,000	1,000	1,000	—
	11,000	9,000	6,000	6,000		11,000	9,000	6,000	6,000
					Balance b/d	10,800	8,800	—	6,000

Goodwill

Capital—Blackburn	1,000		
Capital—Percy	1,000		
Capital—Nelson	1,000		
	3,000		

Current account—Nelson

Loan account	1,400	Balance b/d	1,400

Loan—Nelson

		Capital account	5,800
		Current account	1,400
			7,200

26 The nature of limited companies and their capital

26.5

Ordinary/equity shares	*Preference shares*	*Loan stock/debentures*
1 Owners of the company who are normally entitled to vote at general meetings of the company's shareholders (e.g. to elect directors)	1 No voting rights	1 No voting rights
2 Receive a dividend the rate of which is decided annually by the company's directors. It varies each year depending on the profit and is an appropriation of profit	2 Receive a fixed rate of dividend each year which constitutes an appropriation of profit. Have priority over ordinary dividends	2 Receive a fixed rate interest which constitutes a charge against income in computing the profit. Have priority over preference dividends
3 Last to be repaid the value of their shares in the event of the company going into liquidation	3 Repaid before the ordinary shareholder in the event of liquidation	3 Repaid before the ordinary and preference shareholders in the event of liquidation
4 Non-repayable except on the liquidation of the company	4 All but one particular type are non-repayable except on liquidation	4 Normally repayable after a fixed period of time
5 Rights in Articles of Association	5 Rights in Articles of Association	5 Rights specified in the terms of issue
6 Dividends non-deductible for tax purposes	6 Dividends non-deductible for tax purposes	6 Interest deductible for tax purposes

27 The final accounts of limited companies

27.19 *D. Cooper Ltd*

Profit & loss account for the year ended 30 September 20X9

	£	£
Sales		135,250
Less: Cost of sales		
Stock at 1 Oct 20X8	9,400	
Add: purchases	49,700	
	59,100	
Less: stock at 30 Sep 20X9	13,480	
		45,620
Gross profit		89,630
Add: Investment income		650
		90,280
Less: Expenditure		
Directors' salaries	22,000	
Rates (4,650 – [$\frac{3}{6}$ × 2,300])	3,500	
Light and heat	3,830	
Plant hire	6,600	
Interest on debentures (10% × 24,000)	2,400	
Preliminary expenses	1,270	
Provision for bad debts [(10% × 11,200) – 910]	210	
Audit fees	1,750	
Bad debts	700	
Depreciation on plant (15% × 80,000)	12,000	
Depreciation on tools (9,100 – 7,800)	1,300	
		55,560
Profit on ordinary activities before taxation		34,720
Less: tax on profit on ordinary activities		6,370
Profit on ordinary activities after taxation		28,350
Less: Dividends—		
preference (7% × 25,000)	1,750	
ordinary (3,250 + 13,000)	16,250	18,000
Retained profit for the financial year		10,350
Less: transfer to reserve		2,500
		7,850

D. Cooper Ltd

Balance sheet as at 30 September 20X9

	£	£	£
Fixed assets	*Cost or valuation*	*Agg. depn*	*WDV*
Leasehold premises	140,000	—	140,000
Plant and machinery	80,000	25,100	54,900
Loose tools	13,000	5,200	7,800
	233,000	30,300	202,700
Goodwill			20,000
			222,700
Current assets			
Stocks		13,480	
Debtors	11,200		
Less: provision for bad debts	1,120	10,080	
Prepayments		1,150	
Listed investments		8,000	
		32,710	
Less: creditors: amounts falling due within one year			
Bank overdraft	7,800		
Creditors	8,300		
Corporation tax	6,370		
Debenture interest (2,400 – 1,200)	1,200		
Preference dividends	1,750		
Ordinary dividends	13,000	38,420	

Net current liabilities		(5,710)
Total assets less current liabilities		216,990
Less: creditors: amounts falling due after more than one year		
10% debentures		24,000
Net assets		192,990
Authorized, allotted and called-up share capital		
100,000 ordinary shares of £1 each		100,000
50,000 7% preference shares of 50p each		25,000
		125,000
Reserves		
Share premium account	35,000	
Revaluation reserve	9,860	
Revenue reserve (10,200 + 2,500)	12,700	
Profit and loss account (2,580 + 7,850)	10,430	
		67,990
Shareholders' interests		192,990

Notes

1. Preliminary expenses could have been written off against the balance on the share premium account instead of being charged to the profit and loss account.
2. It is assumed that listed investments will be held for less than one accounting year.
3. Aggregate depreciation on plant and machinery = £80,000 − £66,900 + £12,000 = £25,100.
4. Aggregate depreciation on loose tools = £13,000 − £7,800 = £5,200.

27.20 *L. Johnson Ltd*

Profit & loss account for the year ended 31 December 20X8

	£	£	£
Turnover			130,846
Less: returns inwards			1,629
Net sales			129,217
Less: cost of sales—			
Stock at 1 Jan 20X8		9,436	
Add: purchases	78,493		
Less: returns outwards	1,834	76,659	
		86,095	
Less: stock at 31 Dec 20X8		12,456	73,639
Gross profit			55,578
Add: Other income			
Reduction in provision for bad debts (860 − [5% × 11,600])			280
Discount received			396
Dividends received			310
			56,564
Less: Expenditure			
Wages and salaries		5,948	
Bad debts		656	
Discount allowed		492	
Directors' emoluments		13,000	
Rates (596 − 100)		496	
Light and heat (1,028 + 220)		1,248	
Audit fee		764	
Depreciation on:			
Vehicles (25% × 29,400)	7,350		
Plant (20% × 32,950)	6,590		
Development costs (10% × 6,600)	660	14,600	
Debenture interest (10% × 30,000)		3,000	40,204
Profit on ordinary activities before taxation			16,360
Less: tax on profit on ordinary activities			2,544
Profit on ordinary activities after taxation			13,816
Less: dividends—			
Preference shares (5% × 50,000)		2,500	
Ordinary shares (6.25p × 80,000)		5,000	7,500
Retained profit for the financial year			6,316
Less: transfer to revenue reserve			4,000
			2,316

L. Johnson Ltd

Balance sheet as at 31 December 20X8

	£	£	£
Fixed assets	*Cost or valuation*	*Agg. depn*	*WDV*
Freehold buildings	137,000	—	137,000
Motor vehicles	35,000	12,950	22,050
Plant & machinery	40,000	13,640	26,360
Development costs	10,000	4,060	5,940
	222,000	30,650	191,350
Goodwill			10,000
			201,350
Current assets			
Stock		12,456	
Debtors	11,600		
Less: provision for bad debts	580	11,020	
Prepayments		100	
Listed investments		4,873	
		28,449	
Less: creditors: amounts falling due within one year			
Bank overdraft	3,643		
Creditors	8,450		
Accruals	220		
Debenture interest	3,000		
Corporation tax	2,544		
Preference dividend (2,500 − 1,250)	1,250		
Ordinary dividend	5,000	24,107	
Net current assets			4,342
Total assets less current liabilities			205,692
Less: creditors: amounts falling due after more than one year			
10% debentures			30,000
Net assets			175,692
Authorized capital			
200,000 ordinary shares of £1 each			200,000
90,000 5% preference shares of £1 each			90,000
			290,000
Allotted and called-up share capital			
80,000 ordinary shares of £1 each			80,000
50,000 5% preference shares of £1 each			50,000
			130,000
Reserves			
Share premium account (5,600 − 250)		5,350	
Revaluation reserve		13,500	
Capital redemption reserve		9,000	
Revenue reserve (8,400 + 4,000)		12,400	
Profit & loss account (3,126 + 2,316)		5,442	45,692
Shareholders' interests			175,692

Notes

1. It is assumed that the listed investments are to be held for less than one accounting year.
2. Aggregate depreciation on:
   Motor vehicles = £35,000 – £29,400 + £7,350 = £12,950
   Plant & machinery = £40,000 – £32,950 + £6,590 = £13,640
   Development costs = £10,000 – £6,600 + £660 = £4,060

27.21 *Oakwood Ltd*

Profit & loss account for the year ended 30 June 20X5

	£	£	£
Sales (120,640 – 1,000)			119,640
Less: returns inwards			230
Net sales			119,410
Less: cost of sales			
Stock at 1 July 20X4		8,760	
Add: purchases	81,230		
Less: returns outwards	640		
	80,590		
Add: carriage inwards	310	80,900	
		89,660	
Less: stock at 30 June 20X5 (11,680 + 500)		12,180	77,480
Gross profit			41,930
Add: other income			
Discount received		440	
Interest received		410	
Provision for bad debts ([5% × (10,400 – 1,000)] – 730)		260	1,110
			43,040
Less: expenditure			
Administrative salaries		6,370	
Bad debts		740	
Discount allowed		290	
Audit fee		390	
Directors' remuneration		14,100	
Rates (600 – 150)		450	
Light & heat (940 + 270)		1,210	
Postage & telephone		870	
Consumable tools		300	
Debenture interest (10% × 20,000)		2,000	
Depreciation on—			
Development costs (25% × 5,400)		1,350	
Vehicles (10% × 18,700)		1,870	
Plant (20% × [31,900 – 300])		6,320	
			36,260
Profit on ordinary activities before taxation			6,780
Less: tax on profit on ordinary activities			1,080
Profit on ordinary activities after taxation			5,700
Add: retained profit of previous years			7,700
			13,400
Less: Dividends—			
Preference (5% × 60,000)		3,000	
Ordinary (2,000 × [3.2p × 125,000])		6,000	9,000
Undistributed profits			4,400
Less: transfer to reserve			3,000
Retained profit at end of financial year			1,400

Oakwood Ltd

Balance sheet as at 30 June 20X5

	£	£	£
Fixed assets	*Cost*	*Agg. depn*	*WDV*
Freehold buildings	165,000	—	165,000
Development costs	12,000	7,950	4,050
Delivery vehicles	28,000	11,170	16,830
Plant & machinery (34,000 – 300)	33,700	8,420	25,280
	238,700	27,540	211,160
Goodwill			8,000
			219,160
Current assets			
Stock (11,680 + 500)		12,180	
Debtors (10,400 – 1,000)	9,400		
Less: provision for bad debts	470	8,930	
Prepayments		150	
Listed investments		3,250	
		24,510	
Less: creditors: amounts falling due within one year			
Bank overdraft	2,630		
Creditors	7,890		
Accruals	270		
Corporation tax	1,080		
Debenture interest	2,000		
Preference dividends (3,000 – 1,500)	1,500		
Proposed ordinary dividend	4,000	19,370	
Net current assets			5,140
Total assets less current liabilities			224,300
Less: creditors: amounts falling due after more than one year			
10% debentures			20,000
Net assets			204,300
Share capital		*Authorized*	*Called-up*
Ordinary shares of £1 each		150,000	125,000
5% preference shares of £1 each		70,000	60,000
		220,000	185,000
Reserves			
Share premium account (9,000 – 200)		8,800	
Revenue reserve (6,100 – 3,000)		9,100	
Profit & loss account		1,400	19,300
Shareholders' interests			204,300

Notes

1. It is assumed that the investments are to be held for less than one accounting year.
2. Aggregate depreciation on:
   Development costs = £12,000 – £5,400 + £1,350 = £7,950
   Delivery vehicles = £28,000 – £18,700 + £1,870 = £11,170
   Plant & machinery = £34,000 – £31,900 + £6,320 = £8,420

27.25 a i *Topaz Ltd*

Profit & loss account for the year ended 31 December 20X6

	£000	£000
Turnover:		
Continuing operations		68,000
Discontinued operations		13,000
		81,000
Cost of sales (41 + 8)m		(49,000)
Gross profit		32,000
Net operating expenses (6 + 1 + 4 +2)m		(13,000)

Operating profit		
Continuing operations (68 – 41 – 6 – 4)m	17,000	
Discontinued operations (13 – 8 – 1 – 2)m	2,000	
		19,000
Profit on disposal of discontinued operations		2,500
Reorganization costs of continuing operations		(1,800)
Profit on ordinary activities before interest		19,700
Interest payable		(1,000)
Profit on ordinary activities before taxation		18,700
Tax on profit on ordinary activities		(4,800)
Profit on ordinary activities after taxation		13,900
Dividends (2 + 4)m		(6,000)
Retained profit for the financial year		7,900

Notes

1 *Analysis of cost of sales and net operating expenses*

	Continuing	*Discontinued*
	£000	£000
Cost of sales	41,000	8,000
Net operating expenses:		
Distribution costs	6,000	1,000
Administrative expenses	4,000	2,000
	10,000	3,000

2 *Distribution costs* for continuing operations include a bad debt of £1.9m that is regarded as an exceptional item under FRS3.

ii *Statement of total recognized gains and losses*

	£000
Profit for the financial year	13,900
Unrealized surplus on revaluation of properties	4,000
Total gains (and losses) relating to the year and recognized since last annual report	17,900

b The reasons why the changes to the profit and loss account introduced by FRS3 improve the quality of information available to users of financial statements are because they facilitate more meaningful comparisons over time, with other companies and/or forecasts. They also facilitate more accurate predictions of future profits, cash flows, dividends, etc. This is achieved because FRS3 requires an analysis of turnover and operating profit between continuing operations, acquisitions and discontinued operations. It also demands the disclosure of various exceptional items, extraordinary items and prior period adjustments. For example, exceptional items include profits or losses on the disposal of discontinued operations. This is a classic example of an item that users would need to exclude in making predictions of future profits based on the current year's results because it is of a non-recurring nature.

28 Changes in share capital

28.7 ***Workings***

Application and allotment

Application money = 300k @ £0.20 = £60k

Refunded = 50k @ £0.20 = £10k

Allotment money = (200k @ £0.20) – (50k @ £0.20) = £30k

Share premium per share = £0.60 – £0.50 = £0.10

Total share premium = 200k @ £0.10 = £20k

Nominal value of application and allotment = 200k @ (£0.20 + £0.20 – £0.10) = £60k

Call

Nominal value of call = 200k @ £0.20 = £40k

Call money received = 190k @ £0.20 = £38k

Forfeiture

Called up value of forfeited shares excluding the share premium = 10k @ £0.50 = £5k

Premium included in the amount called up relating to forfeited shares = 10k @ £0.10 = £1k

Amount in call account relating to arrears on forfeited shares = 10k @ £0.20 = £2k

Reissue

Reissue money received = 10k @ £0.40 = £4k

Nominal value of shares reissued = 10k @ £0.50 = £5k

Bonus issue

(800k + 200k) ÷ 4 = 250k @ £0.50 = £125k

The ledger

Cash

			£
Application	60,000	Application—refund	10,000
Allotment	30,000	Balance c/d	122,000
Call	38,000		
Reissue	4,000		
	132,000		132,000
Balance b/d	122,000		

Application and allotment

Cash—refund	10,000	Cash—application	60,000
Share capital	60,000	Cash—allotment	30,000
Share premium	20,000		
	90,000		90,000

Share capital

Forfeited shares	5,000	Balance b/d	400,000
Balance c/d	625,000	Appl. & allot.	60,000
		Call	40,000
		Reissue	5,000
		Bonus issue	125,000
	630,000		630,000
		Balance b/d	625,000

Share premium

Forfeited shares	1,000	Appl. & allot.	20,000
Share capital—bonus issue	22,000	Reissue	3,000
	23,000		23,000

Call

Share capital	40,000	Cash	38,000
		Forfeited shares	2,000
	40,000		40,000

Forfeited shares

Call	2,000	Share capital	5,000
Reissue	4,000	Share premium	1,000
	6,000		6,000

Shares reissued

Share capital	5,000	Cash	4,000
Share premium	3,000	Forfeited shares	4,000
	8,000		8,000

Revenue reserves

Share capital—bonus issue (125,000 – 22,000)	103,000	Balance b/d	350,000
Balance c/d	247,000		
	350,000		350,000
		Balance b/d	247,000

Check: Balance sheet

	£
Share capital	625,000
Revenue reserves	247,000
	872,000
Sundry assets	750,000
Cash	122,000
	872,000

28.8 a *The journal*

			Debit £	Credit £
20X2				
1 Aug	Preference shares	Dr	40,000	
	Share premium	Dr	2,000	
	Cash			42,000
			42,000	42,000
	Being redemption of 40,000 preference shares			
1 Aug	Profit & loss account	Dr	40,000	
	Capital redemption reserve			40,000
	Being transfer of distributable profits to capital reserve due to redemption of shares			
15 Sep	Cash	Dr	21,000	
	Application & allotment			21,000
	Being application money on issue of ordinary shares			
15 Sep	Application & allotment	Dr	3,500	
	Cash			3,500
	Being refund of application money for 5,000 shares			
20 Sep	Cash	Dr	12,500	
	Application & allotment			12,500
	Being balance of allotment money received			
20 Sep	Application & allotment	Dr	30,000	
	Ordinary share capital			25,000
	Share premium			5,000
			30,000	30,000
	Being allotment of 25,000 ordinary shares			
29 Sep	Preference shares	Dr	40,000	
	Share premium	Dr	2,000	
	Cash			42,000
			42,000	42,000
	Being redemption of remaining preference shares			
29 Sep	Profit & loss account	Dr	15,000	
	Capital redemption reserve			15,000
	Being transfer of distributable profits to capital reserve due to redemption of shares			

b *Winder Engineering plc*
Balance sheet as at 30 September 20X2

	£	£
Sundry assets		380,000
Cash (60 – 42 + 21 – 3.5 + 12.5 – 42)k		6,000
		386,000
Issued share capital		
225,000 ordinary shares of £1 each		225,000
Reserves		
Share premium (20 – 2 + 5 –2)k	21,000	
Capital redemption reserve (40 + 15)k	55,000	
Profit & loss (140 – 40 – 15)k	85,000	161,000
Shareholders' interests		386,000

29 Cash flow statements

29.10 *A Brooks*

Cash flow statement for the year ended 30 June 20X7

	£	£
Sources of cash funds		
Capital introduced		20,000
Decrease in debtors (5,400 – 4,100)		1,300
Increase in creditors (6,200 – 4,800)		1,400
		22,700
Applications of cash funds		
Net loss for the year	(1,800)	
Less: provision for depreciation (14,500 – 13,000)	1,500	
Cash funds applied in operations	(300)	
Drawings	(7,600)	
Repayment of bank loan (15,000 – 10,000)	(5,000)	
Purchase of fixed assets (72,000 – 65,000)	(7,000)	
Increase in stock (7,300 – 6,700)	(600)	
		(20,500)
Increase in cash and bank balance		2,200
Bank balance at 30 June 20X6 (overdraft)		(1,300)
Cash & bank balance at 30 June 20X7		900

29.11 *A Brooks*

Notes to the cash flow statement

1 *Reconciliation of operating loss to net cash inflow from operating activities*

	£
Operating loss (1,800 + 900 – 1,250)	(1,450)
Depreciation charges	1,500
Increase in stock (7,300 – 6,700)	(600)
Decrease in debtors (5,400 – 4,100)	1,300
Increase in creditors (6,200 – 4,800)	1,400
Net cash inflow from operating activities	2,150

A. Brooks
Cash flow statement for the year ended 30 June 20X7

	£	£
Net cash inflow from operating activities		2,150
Returns on investments and servicing of finance		
Interest received	900	
Interest paid	(1,250)	(350)
Taxation		—

		£
Capital expenditure		
Payments to acquired tangible fixed assets (72,000 – 65,000)		(7,000)
		(5,200)
Equity dividends paid		—
		(5,200)
Management of liquid resources		—
Financing		
Capital introduced	20,000	
Drawings	(7,600)	
Repayment of bank loan (15,000 – 10,000)	(5,000)	7,400
Increase in cash		2,200

Notes to the cash flow statement (continued)

2 *Reconciliation of net cash flow to movement in net debt*

	£
Increase in cash in period	2,200
Cash to repay bank loan	5,000
Change in net debt	7,200
Net debt at 1 July 20X6 (15,000 + 1,300)	(16,300)
Net debt at 30 June 20X7 (10,000 – 900)	(9,100)

3 *Analysis of changes in net debt*

	At 1 July 20X6	*Cash flows*	*At 30 June 20X7*
	£	£	£
Cash in hand, at bank	—	900	900
Overdrafts	(1,300)	1,300	—
		2,200	
Debt due after 1 year	(15,000)	5,000	(10,000)
Total	(16,300)	7,200	(9,100)

29.13 Workings

Provision for depreciation plant

20X3			20X3		
31 Dec	Plant—depn on disposal (10,000 – 6,000)	4,000	1 Jan	Balance b/d	7,000
31 Dec	Balance c/d	9,500	31 Dec	Profit & loss	6,500
		13,500			13,500

The charge to the profit & loss account in respect of depreciation on plant for the year of £6,500 is the difference between the two sides of the above account.

Plant

20X3			20X3		
1 Jan	Balance b/d	41,000	31 Dec	Bank—disposal	6,400
31 Dec	Profit & loss—profit on sale	400	31 Dec	Depn on disposal (10,000 – 6,000)	4,000
31 Dec	Bank—acquisitions	17,000	31 Dec	Balance c/d	48,000
		58,400			58,400

The cost of plant acquired of £17,000 is the difference between the two sides of the above account.

J. Kitchens Ltd

Cash flow statement for the year ended 31 December 20X3

	£	£
Sources of cash funds		
Profit for the year	24,000	
Add (less): Adjustments for items not involving the movement of funds—		
Depreciation on plant (workings above)	6,500	
Depreciation on premises (9,000 – 6,000)	3,000	
Profit on sale of plant (6,400 – 6,000)	(400)	
Increase in provision for bad debts (600 – 400)	200	
Cash funds generated from operations		33,300
Proceeds of sale of plant		6,400
		39,700
Applications of cash funds		
Dividends paid (9,000 + 8,000)	(17,000)	
Purchases of plant (workings above)	(17,000)	
Increase in stock (22,500 – 14,900)	(7,600)	
Increase in debtors (16,400 + 600) – (11,300 – 400)	(5,300)	
Decrease in creditors (19,700 – 17,600)	(2,100)	
		(49,000)
Decrease in cash & cash equivalents		(9,300)
Cash & cash equivalents at 31 Dec 20X2		(500)
Cash & cash equivalents at 31 Dec 20X3		(9,800)

29.14 Workings

See answer to Question 29.13.

J. Kitchens Ltd

Notes to the cash flow statement

1 *Reconciliation of operating profit to net cash inflow from operating activities*

	£	£
Operating profit (24,000 + 750)		24,750
Depreciation charges—		
Plant (see workings)	6,500	
Premises (9,000 + 6,000)	3,000	9,500
Profit on sale of tangible fixed assets (6,400 – 6,000)		(400)
Provision for bad debts (600 – 400)		200
Increase in stock (22,500 – 14,900)		(7,600)
Increase in debtors (16,400 + 600) – (11,300 + 400)		(5,300)
Decrease in creditors (19,700 – 17,600)		(2,100)
Net cash inflow from operating activities		19,050

J. Kitchens Ltd

Cash flow statement for the year ended 31 December 20X3

	£	£
Net cash inflow from operating activities		19,050
Returns on investments and servicing of finance		
Interest paid		(750)
Taxation		—
Capital expenditure		
Payments to acquire tangible fixed assets (see workings)	(17,000)	
Receipts from sales of tangible fixed assets	6,400	(10,600)
		7,700
Equity dividends paid (9,000 + 8,000)		(17,000)
		(9,300)
Management of liquid resources		—
Financing		—
Decrease in cash		(9,300)

Notes to the cash flow statement (continued)

2 *Reconciliation of net cash flow to movement in net debt*

	£
Decrease in cash in the period	(9,300)
Change in net debt	(9,300)
Net debt at 1 Jan 20X3	(500)
Net debt at 31 Dec 20X3	(9,800)

3 *Analysis of changes in net debt*

	At 1 Jan 20X3 £	Cash flow £	At 31 Dec 20X3 £
Overdrafts	(500)	(9,300)	(9,800)

29.15 *Workings*

Provision for depreciation

20X9			20X8		
31 May	Fixed assets— depn. on disposal (12,000 – 7,500)	4,500	31 May	Balance b/d	28,000
			20X9		
			31 May	Profit & loss	13,500
31 May	Balance c/d	37,000			
		41,500			41,500

The charge to the profit & loss account in respect of depreciation for the year of £13,500 is the difference between the two sides of the above account.

Computation of profit before taxation and dividends

	£	£
Increase in balance on P & L account (5,200 – 3,400)		1,800
Transfer to reserve (6,900 – 4,200)		2,700
Ordinary dividends—		
Interim	6,400	
Proposed final	21,800	
		28,200
Corporation tax		7,200
		39,900

L. Tyler Ltd
Cash flow statement for the year ended 31 May 20X9

	£	£
Sources of cash funds		
Profit for the year before tax & dividends	39,900	
Add (less): Adjustments for items not involving the movement of funds—		
Provision for depreciation (see workings)	13,500	
Profit on sale of fixed assets (8,100 – 7,500)	(600)	
Increase in provision for bad debts (700 – 500)	200	
Cash funds generated from operations		53,000
Issue of shares (70,000 – 60,000) + (34,000 – 25,000)		19,000
Proceeds of sale of fixed assets		8,100
Decrease in stock (21,600 – 19,400)		2,200
		82,300
Applications of cash funds		
Tax paid	(5,800)	
Dividends paid (19,600 + 6,400)	(26,000)	
Repayment of loan stock (30,000 – 5,000)	(25,000)	
Increase in debtors (14,200 – 11,800)	(2,400)	
Decrease in creditors (8,400 – 6,700)	(1,700)	
		(60,900)
Increase in cash & cash equivalents		21,400
Cash & cash equivalents at 31 May 20X8 (3,900 + 4,600)		8,500
Cash & cash equivalents at 31 May 20X9 (17,100 + 12,800)		29,900

29.16 *Workings*

See answer to Question 29.15.

L. Tyler Ltd
Notes to the cash flow statement

1 *Reconciliation of operating profit to net cash inflow from operating activities*

	£
Operating profit (39,900 + 1,600 – 1,800)	39,700
Depreciation charges (see workings)	13,500
Profit on sale of tangible fixed assets (8,100 – 7,500)	(600)
Provision for bad debts (700 – 500)	200
Decrease in stock (21,600 – 19,400)	2,200
Increase in debtors (14,200 – 11,800)	(2,400)
Decrease in creditors (8,400 – 6,700)	(1,700)
Net cash inflow from operating activities	50,900

L. Tyler Ltd
Cash flow statement for the year ended 31 May 20X9

	£	£
Net cash inflow from operating activities		50,900
Returns on investments and servicing of finance		
Interest received	1,800	
Interest paid	(1,600)	200
Taxation		(5,800)
Capital expenditure		
Receipts from sales of tangible fixed assets		8,100
		53,400
Equity dividends paid (19,600 + 6,400)		(26,000)
		27,400
Management of liquid resources		
Purchase of investments (17,100 – 3,900)		(13,200)
Financing		
Issuing of ordinary share capital (70,000 – 60,000) + (34,000 – 25,000)	19,000	
Repayment of loan stock (30,000 – 5,000)	(25,000)	(6,000)
Increase in cash		8,200

Notes to the cash flow statement (continued)

2 *Reconciliation of net cash flow to movement in net debt*

	£
Increase in cash in the period	8,200
Cash to repay loan stock	25,000
Cash used to increase liquid resources (17,100 – 3,900)	13,200
Change in net debt	46,400
Net debt at 1 June 20X8 (30,000 – [3,900 + 4,600])	(21,500)
Net funds at 31 May 20X9 (5,000 – [17,100 + 12,800])	24,900

3 *Analysis of changes in net debt*

	At 1 June 20X8 £	Cash flows £	At 31 May 20X9 £
Cash in hand, at bank	4,600	8,200	12,800
Debt due after 1 year	(30,000)	25,000	(5,000)
Current asset investments	3,900	13,200	17,100
Total	(21,500)	46,400	24,900

30 The appraisal of company accounts using ratios

30.7 When answering questions such as this with apparently open-ended requirements that do not specify which ratios to calculate, it is very important to consider the data carefully in order to decide what ratios should be computed. First, note that these are sole traders not companies. Second, a related point, as in the case of companies where no share price is given, it is not possible to compute the return on investment ratios. Third, there are no long-term liabilities and thus no gearing ratio. Fourth, search the requirements carefully for key words and phrases such as in this question, performance and financial position. The latter is often taken to include solvency, liquidity and the appraisal of working capital. Fifth, the number of ratios you are expected to compute may be influenced by the marks/time allocated to the question.

The ACCA suggested answer contains references to the following accounting ratios (all money values are in 000s):

	White	*Black*
Return on capital employed	$\frac{£48}{£192} \times 100 = 25\%$	$\frac{£48}{£160} \times 100 = 30\%$
Gross profit to sales	$\frac{£150}{£600} \times 100 = 25\%$	$\frac{£176}{£800} \times 100 = 22\%$
Net profit to sales	$\frac{£48}{£600} \times 100 = 8\%$	$\frac{£48}{£800} \times 100 = 6\%$
Turnover of capital employed	$\frac{£600}{£192} = 3.125$	$\frac{£800}{£160} = 5$
Stock turnover	$\frac{£450}{£56} = 8$	$\frac{£624}{£52} = 12$
Debtors' collection period	$\frac{£75}{£600} \times 52 = 6.5$ weeks	$\frac{£67}{£800} \times 52 = 4.4$ weeks
Creditors' period of credit	$\frac{£38}{£450} \times 52 = 4.4$ weeks	$\frac{£78}{£624} \times 52 = 6.5$ weeks
Liquidity ratio	$\frac{£75 + £8}{£38} = 2.2$	$\frac{£67}{£78 + £4} = 0.82$

Comparison of ratios

1 Black has a higher ROCE than White, which shows that it is more profitable.
2 Black has a lower GP and NP to sales (profit margin) than White, which suggests either higher unit costs and/or lower selling prices.
3 Black has a higher turnover of capital employed (asset turnover) than White. The lower profit margin and higher asset turnover ratio may be the result of selling large quantities at a lower price. This strategy appears to be resulting in a higher ROCE.
4 Black has a higher stock turnover ratio and longer period of credit from creditors than White, and a lower debtors' collection period. This suggests that Black is more effective and efficient at controlling its working capital.
5 Black has a considerably lower liquidity ratio than White, which shows that it is stretching itself financially and may encounter liquidity problems.

Overall impressions

Black's performance is superior to White's. It is more profitable, and has a higher level of activity and better control of working capital. However, Black appears to have a weak liquidity position. This may be the result of overtrading.

Further information needed

1 Do either of Black or White work in their businesses? If one does and the other does not the profit is not strictly comparable without a notional salary for the one who does work in the business.
2 There is a difference in accounting policy for the depreciation of buildings. Black has a charge of £5,000 whereas White has no depreciation. This distorts comparisons. Are there any other differences in accounting policies?
3 Are there differences between the two businesses in the ages of their fixed assets such as equipment and vehicles? These will also make comparisons misleading.
4 What differences are there between the two businesses with regard to their trading policies? For example, Black's lower margin (and presumably selling prices) may be offset by higher selling and distribution expenses.

30.8

Return on capital employed =

$$\frac{£580{,}000 + £240{,}000}{£5{,}210{,}000} \times 100 = 15.74\%$$

$$\text{Profit margin} = \frac{£580{,}000 + £240{,}000}{£4{,}230{,}000} = 19.39\%$$

$$\text{Asset turnover} = \frac{£4{,}230{,}000}{£5{,}210{,}000} = 0.81$$

$$\text{Working capital ratio} = \frac{£1{,}070{,}000}{£730{,}000} = 1.47$$

$$\text{Liquidity ratio} = \frac{£1{,}070{,}000 - £480{,}000}{£730{,}000} = 0.81$$

$$\text{Stock turnover ratio} = \frac{£2{,}560{,}000}{£480{,}000} = 5.33$$

$$\text{Debtors' collection period} = \frac{£270{,}000}{£4{,}230{,}000} \times 365 = 23 \text{ days}$$

$$\text{Creditors' period} = \frac{£260{,}000}{£2{,}560{,}000} \times 365 = 37 \text{ days}$$

$$\text{Dividend yield} = \frac{£200{,}000}{£500{,}000 \times £5} \times 100 = 8\%$$

$$\text{Dividend cover} = \frac{£310{,}000}{£200{,}000} = 1.55$$

$$\text{Earnings per share} = \frac{£310{,}000}{£500{,}000} = £0.62$$

$$\text{Price–earnings ratio} = \frac{£5}{£0.62} = 8.07$$

$$\text{Return on equity} = \frac{£310{,}000}{£2{,}210{,}000} \times 100 = 14.03\%$$

$$\text{Gearing ratio} = \frac{£3{,}000{,}000}{£3{,}000{,}000 + £2{,}210{,}000} = 0.58$$

Gearing ratio (market values) =

$$\frac{30{,}000 \times £110}{(30{,}000 \times £110) + (500{,}000 \times £5)} = 0.57$$

Comments on ratios

1 The return on capital employed and return on equity are reasonable, indicating satisfactory profitability.
2 The asset turnover ratio appears low (but may be because the company is capital intensive).
3 The working capital ratio is a little low and the liquidity ratio is weak indicating a poor liquidity position and possible insolvency.
4 The debtors' and creditors' ratios are very low. See limitations below.
5 The dividend yield is high, which means an above average return on investment.
6 The dividend cover is somewhat low and the gearing ratio is rather high. These make the ordinary shares a risky investment.
7 The P–E ratio, profit margin and stock turnover ratio are probably about normal.

Limitations include:

1 The lack of comparative figures for previous years and other companies means generalizations about the results can only be tentative.
2 It is not possible to make judgements about the acceptability of these ratios without knowing the type of industry and the current economic climate.
3 The ratios may be distorted since they are calculated using historical cost data.
4 The calculation of some ratios necessitates the use of surrogate data which may give misleading results. For example, the debtors' (and creditors') collection period appears to be extremely low, which may be because the turnover (cost of sales) includes cash sales (purchases).

30.9 The following are points that should be included in a report.

Comparison of ratios

1 The dividend yield of Chips plc is relatively high.
2 The dividend cover of Fish plc is relatively high.
3 The EPS are not really comparable.
4 The P–E ratio of Fish plc is higher; earnings growth may be expected. The P–E ratio of Chips plc is lower; little growth in earnings may be expected.
5 The ROCE suggests that Fish plc has made more profitable use of its assets.
6 The profit margin indicates that Chips plc has higher selling prices and/or lower unit costs.
7 The asset turnover suggests that both companies are capital intensive but Fish plc has a higher level of activity.
8 The gearing of Chips plc is high, suggesting greater financial risk.
9 The high gearing ratio of Chips plc has probably resulted in a larger return on equity.

Overall impressions

Fish plc may be a better investment because it has a lower financial risk (i.e. low gearing and high dividend cover), is more profitable (i.e. greater ROCE), and has a higher level of activity (i.e. asset turnover). Also, although Fish plc has a lower dividend yield, it probably offers growth in earnings (and thus dividends) resulting from retained profits (as shown by the high dividend cover and P–E ratio). It appears to be pursuing a policy of low selling prices, high turnover and expansion by internal financing from retained profits.

In contrast, Chips plc provides a higher dividend yield but with greater risk.

30.10 The following are points that should be included in a report.

Comparison of ratios

1 The working capital ratio has improved but the liquidity ratio has worsened. This suggests a possible build-up of stocks.
2 The stock turnover has slowed, which also points to either an increase in stocks and/or a decrease in sales.
3 The debtors' ratio shows that debtors are being allowed to take a considerably longer period of credit.
4 The creditors' ratio shows that this company is taking longer to pay its debts.

Overall impressions

There is deterioration in liquidity and control of working capital. It appears that there is overstocking, poor stock control and a relaxation of credit control procedures.

31 The conceptual framework of accounting

31.8 According to the Accounting Standards Board (ASB), *Statement of Principles for Financial Reporting* (1991), the purposes of a conceptual framework of accounting are to:

1 assist the Board in the development of future accounting standards and in its review of existing accounting standards;
2 assist the Board by providing a basis for reducing the number of alternative accounting treatments permitted by law and accounting standards;
3 assist preparers of financial statements in applying accounting standards and in dealing with topics that do not form the subject of an accounting standard;
4 assist auditors in forming an opinion whether financial statements conform with accounting standards;
5 assist users of financial statements in interpreting the information contained in financial statements prepared in conformity with accounting standards; and
6 provide those who are interested in the work of the Board with information about its approach to the formulation of accounting standards.

31.9 Various authors and bodies have described the nature and contents of a conceptual framework of accounting in simple terms as an agreed set of answers to the following sorts of question: For whom are accounts to be prepared? For what purposes do they want to use them? What kind of accounting reports do they want? How far are present accounts suitable for these purposes, and how could we improve accounting practice to make them more suitable? (ASC, 1978).

Probably one of the most concise definitions of a conceptual framework of accounting is contained in the Accounting Standards Committee, *Setting Accounting Standards: A Consultative Document* (1978), as follows:
'a set of broad, internally consistent fundamentals and definitions of key terms' (ASC, 1978).

Another slightly more informative definition is provided by the Financial Accounting Standards Board in its *Scope and Implications of the Conceptual Framework Project*

(1976), as follows:

'a constitution, a coherent system of interrelated objectives and fundamentals that can lead to consistent standards and that prescribe the nature, function and limits of financial accounting and financial statements' (FASB, 1976).

The contents of a conceptual framework of accounting are set out in the Accounting Standards Board, *Statement of Principles for Financial Reporting* (1999) as follows:

1 *The objective of financial reporting* including the users of financial statements and their information needs.
2 *The attributes or qualitative characteristics* of accounting information that enable financial statements to fulfil their objective, determine what is useful information, and provide criteria for choosing among alternative accounting methods.
3 Definitions of the *elements* of financial statements such as the nature of gains, losses, assets, liabilities and ownership interest.
4 A set of criteria for deciding when the elements are to be *recognized* in financial statements.
5 A set of *measurement* rules for determining the monetary amounts at which the elements of financial statements are to be recognized and carried in the accounts.
6 Guidelines for the *presentation and disclosure* of the elements in financial statements.

33 An introduction to consolidated accounts

33.8

	£
Cost of shares in S	160,000
Less: 80% of the share capital and reserves (80% × £[100k + 40k])	112,000
Goodwill	48,000
Less: goodwill already amortized ($\frac{3}{5}$ × £48k)	28,800
Goodwill at 31 December 20X3	19,200

33.9 Minority interest = 40% × £(100k + 180k) = £112,000

33.10

	£
H's reserves	480,000
S's post-acquisition reserves (75% × £[180k + 120k])	45,000
	525,000
Less: amortization of goodwill £(280k – 75%[200k + 120k])	40,000
Profit and loss account reserve at 31 December 2,000	485,000

33.11 *Workings*
Purchased goodwill = £(3,600k – 3,200k) = £400k

Gold Group
Consolidated balance sheet as at 1 January 20X1

	£000
Fixed assets:	
Intangible assets—goodwill	400
Tangible assets £(13,600k + 2,500k)	16,100
	16,500
Net current assets £(1,600k + 700k)	2,300
	18,800
Called-up ordinary share capital	5,000
Share premium	4,000
Revaluation reserve	3,000
Profit & loss account	6,800
	18,800

33.12 *Gold Group*

Consolidated profit and loss account for the year ended 31 December 20X1

	£000
Turnover £(20,100k + 6,600k)	26,700
Cost of sales £(13,400k + 4,400k)	(17,800)
Gross profit	8,900
Distribution costs £(1,100k + 550k)	(1,650)
Administrative expenses £(700k + 250k)	(950)
Profit on ordinary activities before taxation	6,300
Tax on profit on ordinary activities £(2,400k + 600k)	(3,000)
Profit on ordinary activities after taxation	3,300
Dividends	(1,300)
Retained profit for the financial year	2,000

Gold Group
Consolidated balance sheet as at 31 December 20X1

	£000
Fixed assets:	
Intangible assets—goodwill	400
Tangible assets £(13,600k + 2,500k)	16,100
	16,500
Net current assets £(3,100k + 1,200k)	4,300
	20,800
Called-up ordinary share capital	5,000
Share premium	4,000
Revaluation reserve	3,000
Profit & loss account £(6,800k + 2,000k)	8,800
	20,800

Index